UNITED STATES ARMY IN THE WORLD WAR
1917-1919

REPORTS OF
COMMANDER-IN-CHIEF, A. E. F.,
STAFF SECTIONS AND SERVICES

HISTORICAL DIVISION
DEPARTMENT OF THE ARMY
WASHINGTON, D.C., 1948

For sale by the Superintendent of Documents, U. S. Government Printing Office
Washington 25, D. C. — Price $2.50

DISTRIBUTION:
   GSUSA (1): SSUSA (1): Adm Sv(1): Tech Sv(1):
      AFF(1): A(1): FC(1): Sch(3) except
      C&GSC(20),NWC(10),USMA(5),
      ICAF(5), 7, 17(5), 14,16,19(2): ROTC(1):
      State AG(1): Sr Army Instr NG(1):
      Spec Distribution.
   For explanation of distribution formula, see SR 310-90-1

CONTENTS

PREFACE

Final reports presented in this and the following three volumes give in resume the operations of those offices of American Expeditionary Forces Headquarters charged with the management of the entire complicated military machine in France.

General Pershing's Preliminary and Final Reports head the volumes, followed in sequence by those of his Chief of Staff and Chiefs of the several Staff Sections at General Headquarters, A. E. F. In turn, these reports are supplemented by those of the arms of service, Artillery, Tank Corps, Chemical Warfare Service, and the like.

G-3, GHQ, AEF: 1123: Report

Preliminary Report of the Commander-in-Chief

[Editorial Note.---This document is found in two forms, one cabled to the War
Department on November 20, 1918, the other a corrected copy printed at CHAUMONT
on January 16, 1919. The two versions have been compared, and no material variation in meaning is discovered; the changes are merely improvements in accuracy,
completeness and clarity of expression. The text here presented is that of the
corrected copy.]

GENERAL HEADQUARTERS, A. E. F.,

Chaumont, November 19, 1918.
[Corrected January 16, 1919.]

To the Secretary of War:

My Dear Mr. Secretary:

In response to your request, I have the honor to submit this brief summary of the
organization and operations of the American Expeditionary Forces from May 26, 1917, until
the signing of the Armistice November 11, 1918.

Pursuant to your instructions, immediately upon receiving my orders, I selected a
small staff and proceeded to Eurpoe in order to become familiar with conditions at the
earliest possible moment.

The warmth of our reception in England and France was only equalled by the readiness
of the Commanders-in-Chief of the veteran armies of the Allies and their staffs to place
their experience at our disposal. In consultation with them the most effective means of
cooperation of effort were considered. With French and British armies at their maximum
strength, and all efforts to dislodge the enemy from his firmly entrenched positions in
Belgium and France having failed, it was necessary to plan for an American force adequate
to turn the scale in favor of the Allies. Taking account of the strength of the Central
Powers at that time, the immensity of the problem which confronted us could hardly be
overestimated. The first requisite being an organization that could give intelligent
direction to effort, the formation of a general staff occupied my early attention.

GENERAL STAFF

A well organized general staff through which the Commander exercises his functions
is essential to a successful modern army. However capable our divisions, our battalions
and our companies as such, success would be impossible without thoroughly coordinated endeavor. A general staff broadly organized and trained for war had not hitherto existed
in our army. Under the Commander-in-Chief, this staff must carry out the policy, and
direct the details of administration, supply, preparation and operations of the army as a
whole, with all special branches and bureaus subject to its control. As models to aid us

we had the veteran French General Staff and the experience of the British, who had similarly formed an organization to meet the demands of a great army. By selecting from each
the features best adapted to our basic organization, and fortified by our own early experience in the war, the development of our great general staff system was completed.

The General Staff is naturally divided into five groups, each with its chief, who is
an assistant to the Chief of the General Staff. G-1 (General Staff-1) is in charge of
organization and equipment of troops, replacements, tonnage, priority of overseas shipments, the auxiliary welfare associations and cognate subjects; G-2 has censorship, enemy
intelligence, gathering and disseminating information, preparation of maps and all similar
subjects; G-3 is charged with all strategic studies and plans, movement of troops and the
supervision of combat operations; G-4 coordinates important questions of supply, construction, transport arrangements for combat, and the operations of the Services of Supply, and
of hospitalization and the evacuation of the sick and wounded; G-5 supervises the various
schools and has general direction and coordination of education and training.

The first Chief of Staff was Colonel (now Major General) James G. Harbord, who was
succeeded in May, 1918, by Major General James W. McAndrew, To these officers to the
Deputy Chief of Staff, and to the Assistant Chiefs of Staff, who as heads of sections
aided them, great credit is due for the results obtained, not only in perfecting the general
staff organization, but in applying correct principles to the multiplicity of problems that
have arisen.

ORGANIZATION AND TRAINING

After a thorough consideration of allied organizations, it was decided that our combat divisions should consist of two infantry brigades of two regiments each, an artillery
brigade of three regiments, a machine gun battalion, an engineer regiment, a trench mortar
battery, a signal battalion, and headquarters, trains and military police; that our infantry regiments were to consist of approximately 3,700 men organized as follows: a headquarters company, a supply company, a machine gun company, and three battalions with four
companies, each of 250 men, to a battalion. These with medical and other units made a
total of over 28,000 men, or practically double the size of a French or German division.
Each corps would normally consist of six divisions, four combat and one depot and one replacement division, and also two regiments of cavalry, and each army of from three to five
corps. With four divisions fully trained, a corps could take over an American sector,
with two divisions in line and two in reserve, with the depot and replacement divisions
prepared to fill the gaps in the ranks.

Our purpose was to prepare an integral American force which should be able to take
the offensive in every respect. Accordingly the development of a self-reliant infantry by
thorough drill in the use of the rifle and in the tactics of open warfare was always upper-
most. The plan of training after arrival in France allowed a division one month for acclimatization and instruction in small units from battalions down, a second month in quiet
trench sectors by battalions, and a third month after it came out of the trenches, when it
should be trained as a complete division in war of movement.

Very early a system of schools was outlined and started, having the advantage of instruction by officers direct from the front. At the great school center at Langres, one
of the first to be organized was the staff school, where the principles of general staff
work as laid down in our own organization were taught to carefully selected officers. Men
in the ranks who had shown qualities of leadership were sent to the school of candidates
for commissions. A school of the line taught younger officers the principles of leadership, tactics and the use of the different weapons. In the Artillery School at Saumur
young officers were taught the fundamental principles of modern artillery, while at
Issoudun an immense plant was built for training cadets in aviation. These and other
schools with their well-considered curriculums for training in every branch of our organ-

izations were coordinated in a manner best to develop an efficient army out of willing and industrious young men, many of whom had not before known even the rudiments of military technique. Both Marshal Haig and General Pétain placed officers and men at our disposal for instructional purposes, and we are deeply indebted for the opportunities given to profit by their veteran experience.

AMERICAN ZONE

The eventual place the American Army should take on the western front was to a large extent influenced by the vital questions of communication and supplies. The northern ports of France were crowded by the British Army's shipping and supplies, while the southern ports, though otherwise at our service, had not adequate port facilities for our purposes, and these we should have to build. The already overtaxed railway system behind the active front in northern France would not be available for us as lines of supply, and those leading from the southern ports to northeastern France would be unequal to our needs without much new construction. Practically all warehouses, supply depots and regulating stations must be provided by fresh construction. While France offered us such material as she had to spare after a drain of three years of war, yet there were enormous quantities of material to be brought across the Atlantic.

With such a problem any temporization or lack of definiteness in making plans might cause failure even with victory within our grasp. Moreover, broad plans commensurate with our national purpose and resources would bring conviction of our power to every soldier in the front line, to the nations associated with us in the war, and to the enemy. The tonnage for material for necessary construction and for the supply of an army of three and perhaps four million men would require a mammoth program of shipbuilding at home, and miles of dock construction in France, with a correspondingly large project for additional railways and for storage depots.

All these considerations led to the inevitable conclusion that, if we were to handle and supply the great forces deemed essential to win the war, we must utilize the southern ports of France, Bordeaux, La Pallice, St-Nazaire, and Brest, and the comparatively unused railway systems leading therefrom to the northeast. Generally speaking, then, this would contemplate the use of our forces against the enemy somewhere in that direction, but the great depots of supply must be centrally located, prefereably in the area included by Tours, Bourges and Châteauroux, so that our armies could be supplied with equal facility wherever they might be serving on the western front.

GROWTH OF THE SERVICES OF SUPPLY

To build up such a system there were talented men in the Regular Army, but more experts were necessary than the Army could furnish. Thanks to the patriotic spirit of our people at home, there came from civil life men trained for every sort of work involved in building and managing an organization that was to handle and transport such an army and keep it supplied. With such assistance the construction and general development of our plans have kept pace with the growth of the forces, and the Services of Supply is now able to discharge from ships and move 45,000 tons daily, besides transporting troops and material necessary in the conduct of active operations.

As to organization, all the administrative and supply services, except the Adjutant General's, Inspector General's and Judge Advocate General's Departments, which remain at General Headquarters, have been transferred to the Headquarters of the Services of Supply at Tours, under a Commanding General responsible to the Commander-in-Chief for supply of the armies. The Chief Quartermaster, Chief Surgeon, Chief Signal Officer, Chief of Ordnance, Chief of Air Service, Chief of Chemical Warfare Service and the General Purchasing Agent, in all that pertains to questions of procurement of supply, the Provost Marshal General in the maintenance of order in general, and the Director General of Transportation in all that affects such matters, and the Chief Engineer in all matters of administration and supply, are subordinate to the Commanding General of the Services of Supply, who assisted by a staff especially organized for the purpose, is charged with the administrative coordination of all these services.

The Transportation Department under the Services of Supply directs the operation and maintenance of railways, the operation of terminals, the unloading of ships and transportation of material to warehouses or to the front. Its functions make necessary the most intimate relationship between our organization and that of the French, with the practical result that our transportation department has been able to improve materially the operation of railways generally. Constantly laboring under a shortage of rolling stock the Transportation Department has nevertheless been able by efficient management to meet every emergency.

The Engineer Corps is charged with all construction, including light and standard-gauge railways and roads. It has planned and constructed the many projects required, the most important of which are the new wharves at Bordeaux and Nantes, and the immense storage depots at La Pallice, Montoir and Gievres, besides innumerable hospitals and barracks in various ports of France. These projects have all been carried on by phases, keeping pace with our needs. The Forestry Service under the Engineers Corps has cut the greater part of the timber and railway ties required.

To meet the shortage of supplies from America due to lack of shipping, the representatives of the different supply departments were constantly in search of available material and supplies in Europe. In order to coordinate these purchases and to prevent competition between our departments, a general purchasing agency was created early in our experience to coordinate our purchases and, if possible, induce our Allies to apply the principle among the Allied Armies. While there was no authority for the general use of appropriations, this was met by grouping the purchasing representatives of the different departments under one control, charged with the duty of consolidating requisitions and purchases. Our efforts to extend the principle have been signally successful, and all purchases for the Allied Armies are now on an equitable and cooperative basis. Indeed, it may be said that the work of this Bureau has been thoroughly efficient and businesslike.

ARTILLERY, AIRPLANES AND TANKS

Our entry into the war found us with few of the auxiliaries necessary for its conduct in the modern sense. Among our most important deficiencies in material were artillery, aviation and tanks. In order to meet our requirements as rapidly as possible, we accepted the offer of the French Government to provide us with the necessary artillery equipment of 75's, 155-mm. Howitzers and 155 G. P. F. guns from their own factories for 30 divisions. The wisdom of this course is fully demonstrated by the fact that, although we soon began the manufacture of these classes of guns at home, there were no guns of the calibers mentioned manufactured in America on our front at the date the Armistice was signed. The only guns of these types produced at home thus far received in France are 109 75-mm. guns.

In aviation we were in the same situation, and here again the French government came to our aid until our own aviation program should be under way. We obtained from the French the necessary planes for training our personnel, and they have provided us with a total of 2,676 pursuit, observation and bombing planes. The first airplane received from home arrived in May, and altogether we have received 1,379 planes. The first American squadron completely equipped by American production, including airplanes, crossed the German lines on August 7, 1918. As to tanks we were also compelled to rely upon the French. Here, however, we were less fortunate, for the reason that the French production could barely meet the requirements of their own armies.

It should be fully realized that the French government has always taken a most liberal attitude, and has been most anxious to give us every possible assistance in meeting our deficiencies in these as well as in other respects. Our dependence upon France for artillery, aviation and tanks was, of course, due to the fact that our industries had not been exclusively devoted to military production. All credit is due our own manufacturers for their efforts to meet our requirements, as at the time the armistice was signed we were able to look forward to the early supply of practically all our necessities from our own factories.

WELFARE OF THE TROOPS

The welfare of the troops touches my responsibility as Commander-in-Chief to the mothers and fathers and kindred of the men who came to France in the impressionable period of youth. They could not have the privilege accorded European soldiers during their periods of leave of visiting their families and renewing their home ties. Fully realizing that the standard of conduct that should be established for them must have a permanent influence on their lives and on the character of their future citizenship, the Red Cross, the Young Men's Christian Association, the Knights of Columbus, the Salvation Army, and the Jewish Welfare Board, as auxiliaries in this work, were encouraged in every possible way. The fact that our soldiers, in a land of different customs and language, have borne themselves in a manner in keeping with the cause for which they fought, is due not only to the efforts in their behalf, but much more to their high ideals, their discipline and their innate sense of self-respect. It should be recorded, however, that the members of these welfare societies have been untiring in their desire to be of real service to our officers and men. The patriotic devotion of these representative men and women has given a new significance to the Golden Rule, and we owe to them a debt of gratitude that can never be repaid.

COMBAT OPERATIONS

During our periods of training in the trenches some, of our divisions had engaged the enemy in local combats the most important of which was Seicheprey by the 26th Division on April 20, in the Toul sector but none had participated in action as a unit. The 1st Division, which had passed through the preliminary stages of training, had gone to the trenches for its first period of instruction at the end of October, and by March 21, when the German offensive in Picardy began, we had four divisions with experience in the trenches, all of which were equal to any demands of battle action. The crisis which this offensive developed was such that our occupation of an American sector had to be postponed.

On March 28 I placed at the disposal of Marshal Foch, who had been agreed upon as Commander-in-Chief of the Allied Armies, all of our forces, to be used as he might decide. At his request the 1st Division was transferred from the Toul sector to a position in reserve at Chaumont-en-Vexin. As German superiority in numbers required prompt action, an agreement was reached at the Abbeville Conference of the Allied Premiers and Commanders and myself on May 2 by which British shipping was to transport ten American divisions to the British Army area, where they were to be trained and equipped, and additional British shipping was to be provided for as many divisions as possible for use elsewhere.

On April 26, the 1st Division had gone into the line in the Montdidier Salient on the Picardy battle front. Tactics had been suddenly revolutionized to those of open warfare, and our men confident of the results of their training were eager for the test. On the morning of May 28 this division attacked the commanding German position in its front, taking with splendid dash the town of Cantigny and all other objectives which were organized, and held steadfastly against vicious counterattacks and galling artillery fire. Although local, this brilliant action had an electrical effect, as it demonstrated our fighting qualities under extreme battle conditions, and also that the enemy's troops were not altogether invincible.

The Germans' Aisne offensive, which began on May 27, had advanced rapidly toward the River Marne and Paris, and the Allies faced a crisis equally as grave as that of the Picardy offensive in March. Again every available man was placed at Marshal Foch's disposal, and the 3d Division, which had just come from its preliminary training area, was hurried to the Marne. Its motorized machine gun battalion preceded the other units, and successfully held the bridgehead at the Marne opposite Château-Thierry. The 2d Division, in reserve near Montdidier, was sent by motor trucks and other available transport to check the progress of the enemy toward Paris. The division attacked and retook the town and railroad station at Bouresches and sturdily held its ground against the enemy's best Guard division. In the battle of Belleau Wood which followed, our men proved their superiority, and gained a strong tactical position with far greater loss to the enemy than to ourselves. On July 1, before the 2d Division was relieved, it captured the village of Vaux with most splendid precision.

Meanwhile, our II Corps, under Major General George W. Read, had been organized for the command of our divisions with the British which were held back in training areas or assigned to second line defenses. Five of the ten divisions were withdrawn from the British area in June, three to relieve divisions in Lorraine and the Vosges, and two to the Paris area to join the group of American divisions which stood between the city and any further advance of the enemy in that direction.

The great June-July troop movement from the States was well under way, and, although these troops were to be given some preliminary training before being put into action, their very presence warranted the use of all the older divisions in the confidence that we did not lack reserves. Elements of the 42d Division were in the line east of Reims against the German offensive of July 15, and held their ground unflinchingly. On the right flank of this offensive four companies of the 28th Division were in position in face of the advancing waves of the German infantry. The 3d Division was holding the south bank , of the Marne from a point 1 1/2 kilometers east of Mezy to Chierry, which is just east of Château-Thierry, where a large force of German infantry sought to force a passage under support of powerful artillery concentrations and under cover of smoke screens. A single regiment of the 3d Division wrote one of the most brilliant pages in our military annals on this occasion. It prevented the crossing at certain points on its front, while, on either flank, the Germans who had gained a footing pressed forward. Our men firing in three directions met the German attacks with counterattacks at critical points, and succeeded in throwing two German divisions into complete confusion, capturing six hundred prisoners.

The great force of the German Château-Thierry offensive established the deep Marne Salient, but the enemy was taking risks and the vulnerability of this pocket to attack might be turned to his disadvantage. Seizing the opportunity to support my conviction, every division with any sort of training was made available for use in a counteroffensive. The place of honor in the thrust toward Soissons on July 18 wws given to our 1st and 2d Divisions, in company with chosen French divisions. Without the usual brief warning of a preliminary bombardment, the massed French and American artillery, firing by the map, laid down its rolling barrage at dawn wile the infantry began its charge. The tactical handling of our troops under these trying conditions was excellent throughout the action. The enemy brought up large numbers of reserves and made a stubborn defense both with machine guns and artillery, but through five days' fighting the 1st Division continued to advance until it had gained the heights above Soissons and captured the village of Berzy-le-Sec. The 2d Division took Beaurepaire Farm and Vierzy in a very rapid advance, and reached a position in front of Tigny at the end of its second day. These two divisions captured 7,000 prisoners and over 100 pieces of artillery.

On July 18, the I Corps, commandered by Major General Hunter Liggett, consisting of the American 26th Division and the French 167th Division, held a sector just northwest of Château-Thierry. During the first stages of the attack on Soissons starting on July 18, the 26th Division acted as a pivot, resting its right on Hill 204 just west of Château-Thierry, until the battle line to the northwest had been straightened out. On July 20, this had been accomplished and the I Corps then became the marching flank of a much larger pivotal movement which rested its left flank on the hills southwest of Soissons. At the time of the above attack the 3d Division just east of Château-Thierry was crossing the Marne in pursuit of the retreating enemy. The attack of the I Corps was continued on July 21 and the enemy withdrew past the Château-Thierry---Soissons Road. The 3d Division continuing its progress took the heights of Mont-St-Pere and the villages of Charteves and Jaulgonne in the face of both machine-gun and artillery fire.

On the 24th, after the Germans had fallen back from Trugny and Epieds, our 42d Divisions, which had been brought over from the Champagne, relieved the 26th Division, and, fighting its way through the Foret de Fere, overwhelmed the nests of machine guns in its path. By the 27th it had reached the Ourcq, whence the 3d and 4th Divisions were already advancing, while the French divisions with which we were cooperating were moving forward at other points.

The 3d Division had made its advance into Roncheres Wood on the 29th, and was relieved for rest by a brigade of the 32d Division. The 42d and 32d Divisions undertook the task of conquering the heights beyond Cierges, the 42d capturing Sergy and the 32d capturing Hill 230, both American divisions joining in the rapid pursuit of the enemy to the Vesle, and thus the operation of reducing the salient was finished.

On August 3, the 42d Division was relieved by the 4th Division at Chery-Chartreuve, and on August 9 the 32d Division was relieved by the 28th Division. The 4th Division in turn was relieved on August 12 by the 77th Division. The I Corps operated in this region until August 13 when it was transferred to the vicinity of Toul. The III Corps, in which the 28th, 32d and 77th Divisions served at various times, Major General Robert L. Bullard commanding, took part in the offensive on the Vesle from August 5 until September 9, on which date the command passed to the French, and corps headquarters was transferred to the region of Verdun.

BATTLE OF ST-MIHIEL

With the reduction of the Marne Salient we could look forward to the concentration of our divisions in our own zone. In veiw of the forthcoming operation against the St-Mihiel Salient, which had long been planned as our first ofensive action on a large scale, the First Army was organized on August 10 under my personal command. While American units had held different divisional and corps sectors all along the western front, there had not been up to this time, for obvious reasons, a distinct American sector; but in view of the important part the American forces were now to play, it was necessary to take over a permanent portion of the line. Accordingly on August 30 the line beginning at Port-sur-Seille, east of the Moselle and extending to the west through St-Mihiel, thence north to a point opposite Verdun, was placed under my command. The American sector was afterward extended across the Meuse to the western edge of the Argonne Forest, and included the French II Colonial Corps which held the point of the salient, and the French XVII Corps which occupied the heights above Verdun.

The preparation for a complicated operation against the formidable defenses in front of us included the assembling of divisions, and of corps and army artillery, transport, aircraft, tanks, ambulances, the location of hospitals, and the moulding together of all the elements of a great modern army, with its own railheads, supplied directly by our own Services of Supply. The concentration for this operation, which was to be a surprise, involved the movement mostly at night of approximately 600,000 troops, and required for its success the most careful attention to every detail.

The French were generous in giving us assistance in corps and army artillery, with its personnel, and we were confident from the start of our superiority over the enemy in guns of all calibers. Our heavy guns were able to reach Metz and to interfere seriously with German rail movements. The French independent air force was placed under my command, which, together with the British bombing squadrons and our own air forces, gave us the largest assembly of aviation that had ever been engaged in one operation on the western front.

From Les Eparges around the nose of the salient of St-Mihiel to the Moselle River the line was roughly forty miles long and situated on commanding ground, greatly strengtened by artificial defenses. Our I Corps (82d, 90th, 5th and 2d Divisions), under command of Major General Hunter Liggett, resting its right on Pont-a-Mousson, with its left joining our IV Corps (the 89th, 42d and 1st Divisions), under Major General Joseph T. Dickman, in line to Xivray, were to swing in toward Vigneulles, on the pivot of the Moselle River, for the initial assault. From Xivray to Mouilly the French II Colonial Corps was in line in the center, and our V Corps, under command of Major General George H. Cameron, with the American 26th and 4th Divisions and the French 15th Colonial Division at the western base of the salient, were to attack three difficult hills, Les Eparges, Combres and Amaranthe. Our I Corps had in reserve the 78th Division, our IV Corps the 3d Division, and our First Army the 35th and 91st Divisions, with the 80th and 33d Divisions available. It should be understood that our corps organizations are very elastic, and that we have at no time had permanent assignments of divisions to corps.

After four hours' artillery preparation the seven American divisions in the front line advanced at 5 a. m., on September 12, assisted by a limited number of tanks, manned partly by Americans and partly by the French. These divisions, accompanied by groups of wire cutters and others armed with bangalore torpedoes, went through the successive bands of barbed wire that protected the enemy's front line and support trenches in irresistible waves on schedule time, breaking down all defense of an enemy demoralized by the great volume of our artillery fire and our sudden appearance out of the fog.

Our I Corps took Thiaucourt, while our IV Corps curved back to the southwest through Nonsard. The French II Colonial Corps made the slight advance required of it on very difficult ground, and the V Corps took its three ridges and repulsed a counterattack. A rapid march brought reserve regiments of a division of the V Corps into Vigneulles in the early morning, where it linked up with patrols of our IV Corps, closing the salient and forming a new line west of Thiaucourt to Vigneulles and beyond Fresnes-en-Woëvre. At the cost of only 7,000 casualties, mostly light, we had taken 13,751 prisoners and 443 guns, a great quantity of matériel, released the inhabitants of many villages from enemy domination and established our lines in a position to threaten Metz. The signal success of the new American Army in its first offensive was of prime importance. The Allies found they had a formidable army to aid them, and the enemy learned finally that he had one to reckon with.

MEUSE-ARGONNE OFFENSIVE---FIRST PHASE

On the day after we had taken the St-Mihiel Salient, much of our corps and army artillery which had operated at St. Mihiel, and our divisions in reserve at other points, were already on the move toward the area back of the line between the Meuse River and the western edge of the forest of Argonne. With the exception of St-Mihiel, the old German front line from Switzerland to the east of Reims was still intact. In the general attack planned all along the line, the operation assigned the American Army as the hinge of this Allied offensive was directed toward the important railroad communications of the German Armies through Mezieres and Sedan. The enemy must hold fast to this part of his lines or the withdrawal of his forces with four years' accumulation of plants and material would be dangerously imperiled.

The German Army had as yet shown no demoralization, and, while the mass of its troops had suffered in morale, its first-class divisions and notably its machine-gun defense were exhibiting remarkable tactical efficiency as well as courage. The German General Staff was fully aware of the consequences of a success on the Meuse-Argonne line. Certain that he would do everything in his power to oppose us, the action was planned with as much secrecy as possible, and was undertaken with the determination to use all our division in forcing a decision. We expected to draw the best German divisions to our front and consume them, while the enemy was held under grave apprehension lest our attack should break his line, which it was our firm purpose to do.

Our right flank was protected by the Meuse, while our left embraced the Argonne Forest, whose ravines, hills and elaborate defenses screened by dense thickets had been generally considered impregnable. Our order of battle from right to left was the III Corps from the Meuse to Malancourt, with the 33d, 80th and 4th Divisions in line and the 3d Division as corps reserve; the V Corps from Malancourt to Vavquois, with the 79th, 37th and 91st Divisions in line and the 32d Division in corps reserve; and the I Corps, from Vauqouis to Vienne-le-Château, with the 35th, 28th and 77th Divisions in line and the 92d Division in corps reserve. The Army reserve consisted of the 1st, 29th and 82d Divisions.

On the night of September 25 our troops quietly took the place of the French who thinly held the line in this sector, which had long been inactive. In the attack which began on the 26th we drove through the barbed wire entanglements and the sea of shell craters across "No Man's Land," mastering all the first line defenses. Continuing on the 27th and 28th, against machine guns and artillery of an incrasing number of enemy reserve divisions, we penetrated to a depth of from three to seven miles and took the village of Montfaucon and its commanding hill, and Exermont, Gercourt-et-Drillancourt, Cuisy, Septsarges, Malancourt, Ivoiry, Epinonville, Charpentry, Very and other villages. We had taken 10,000 prisoners; we had gained our point of forcing the battle into the open, and were prepared for the enemy's reaction which was bound to come, as he had good roads and ample railroad facilities for bringing up his artillery and reserves.

In the chill rain of dark nights our engineers had to build new roads across spongy, shell-torn areas, repair broken roads beyond "No Man's Land," and build bridges. Our gunners, with no thought of sleep, put their shoulders to wheels and drag-ropes to bring their guns through the mire in support of the infantry now under the increasing fire of the enemy's artillery. Our attack had taken the enemy by surprise, but, quickly recovering himself, he began fierce counterattacks in strong force, supported by heavy bombardments with large quantities of gas. From September 28 until October 4 we maintained the offensive against patches of woods defended by snipers and continuous lines of machine guns and pushed forward our guns and transport, seizing strategical points in preparation for further attacks.

OTHER UNITS WITH ALLIES

Other divisions attached to the Allied Armies were doing their part. It was the fortune of our II Corps, composed of the 27th and 30th Divisions, which had remained with the British, to have a place of honor, in cooperation with the Australian Corps, on September 29 and October 1, in the assault upon the Hindenburg Line, where the St-Quentin Canal passes through a tunnel under a ridge. The 30th Division speedily broke through the main line of defense for all its objectives, while the 27th Division pushed on impetuously through the main line until some of its elements reached Guoy. In the midst of the maze of trenches and shell craters, and under cross fire from machine guns, the other elements fought desperately against odds. In this and in later actions, from October 6 to October 19, our II Corps captured over 6,000 prisoners and advanced over 13 miles. The spirit and aggressiveness of these divisions have been highly praised by the British Army Commander under whom they served.

On October 2 - 9 our 2d and 36th Divisions were sent to assist the French in an important attack against the old German positions before Reims. The 2d Division conquered the complicated defense works on their front against a persistent defense worthy of the grimmest period of trench warfare, and attacked the strongly held wooded hill of Blanc-Mont, which they captured in a second assult, sweeping over it with consummate dash and skill. This division then repulsed strong counterattacks before the village and cemetery of St-Etienne, and took the town, forcing the Germans to fall back from before Reims and yield positions they had held since September 1914. On October 9 the 36th Division relieved the 2d Division, and, in its first experience under fire, withstood very severe artillery bombardment, and rapidly took up the pursuit of the enemy now retiring behind the Aisne.

MEUSE-ARGONNE OFFENSIVE---SECOND PHASE

The Allied progress elsewhere cheered the efforts of our men in this crucial contest as the German command threw in more and more first class troops to stop our advance. We made steady headway in the almost impenetrable and strongly held Argonne Forest, for despite his reinforcements, it was our Army that was doing the driving. Our aircraft was increasing in skilll and numbers and forcing the issue, and our infantry and artillery were improving rapidly with each new experience. The replacements fresh from home were put into exhausted divisions with little time for training, but they had the advantage of serving beside men who knew their business and who had almost become veterans overnight. The enemy had taken every advantage of the terrain, which especially favored the defense, by a prodigal use of machine guns manned by highly trained veterans and by using his artillery at short ranges. In the face of such strong frontal positions we should have been unable to accomplish any progress according to previously accepted standards, but I had every confidence in our aggressive tactics and the courage of our troops.

On October 4 the attack was renewed all along our front. The III Corps tilting to the left followed the Brieulles-Cunel Road; our V Corps took Gesnes, while along the irregular valley of the Aire River and in the wooded hills of the Argonne that border the river, used by the enemy with all his art and weapons of defense, the I Corps advanced for over two miles. This sort of fighting continued against an enemy striving to hold every foot of ground and whose very strong counterattacks challenged us at every point. On the 7th the I Corps captured Châtel-Chénery and continued along the river to Cornay. On the east of the Meuse sector, one of the two divisions cooperating with the French captured Consenvoye and the Haumont Woods. On the 9th, the I Corps, in its progress up the Aire, took Fléville, and the V Corps advanced in the rolling open country north of Gesnes. The III Corps, which had continuous fighting against odds, was working its way through Brieulles and Cunel. On the 10th, we had cleared the Argonne Forest of the enemy. The 1st Division, operating successively under the I Corps and under the V Corps between October 4 and October 11 drove a salient into the enemy's territory extending from the Apremont-Epinonville Road to the north of the Cote de Maldah, over a distance of 7 kilometers, against the most powerful opposition, Positions embraced in this area were of vital importance to the continuation of the general advance. Their capture entailed some of the hardest fighting of the campaign.

It was now necessary to constitute a Second Army, and on October 10 the immediate command of the First Army was turned over to Lieutenant General Hunter Liggett. The command of the Second Army, whose divisions occupied a sector in the woëvre, was given to Lieutenant General Robert L. Bullard, who had been commander of the 1st Division and then of the III Corps. Major General Dickman was transferred to the command of the I Corps, while the V Corps was placed under Major General Charles P. Summerall, who had recently commanded the 1st Division. Major General John L. Hines, who had gone rapidly up from regimental to division commander, was assigned to the III Corps. These officers hand been in France from the early days of the Expedition and had learned their lesson in the school of pratical warfare.

Our constant pressure against the enemy brought day by day more prisoners, mostly survivors from machine-gun nests captured in fighting at close quarters. On October 18, there was very fierce fighting in the Caures Woods, east of the Meuse, and in the Ormont Wood. On the 14th the I Corps took St-Juvin, and the V Corps, by hand to hand encounters, entered the formidable Kriemhilde Line, where the enemy had hoped to check us indefinitely. Later the V Corps penetrated further the Kriemhilde Line, and the I Corps took Champigneulles and the important town of Grand-Pre. Our dogged offensive was wearing down the enemy, who continued desperately to throw his best troops against us, thus weakening his line in front of our Allies and making their advance less difficult.

DIVISIONS IN BELGIUM

Meanwhile, we were not only able to continue the battle, but our 37th and 91st Divisions were hastily withdrawn from our front and dispatched to help the French Army in Belgium. Detraining in the neighborhood of Ypres, these divisions advanced by rapid stabes to the fighting line and were assigned to adjacent French corps. On October 31, in continuation of the Flanders offensive, they attacked and methodically broke down all enemy resistance. On November 3, the 37th Division had completed its mission in driving the enemy across the Scheldt River and firmly established itself along the east bank included in the division zone of action. By a clever flanking movement, troops of the 91st Division captured Spitaals Bosschen, a difficult wood extending across the central part of the division sector reached the Scheldt and penetrated into the town of Audenarde. These divisions received high commendation from their corps commanders for their dash and energy.

MEUSE-ARGONNE OFFENSIVE---LAST PHASE

On October 23, the III and V Corps pushed northward to the level of Bantheville. From this time until November 1 no attempt was made to advance. Every effort was concentrated on the preparation for the great attack which was soon to be made. Evidence of loss of morale by the enemy gave our men more confidence and more fortitude in enduring the fatigue of incessant effort and the hardships from inclement weather.

With comparatively well-rested divisions the final advance in the Meuse-Argonne front was begun on November 1. Our increased artillery force acquitted itself magnificently in support of the advance, and the enemy broke before the determined infantry, which by its persistent fighting of the past weeks and the dash of its attack had overcome his will to resist. The III Corps took Aincreville, Doulcon, and Andevanne, and the V Corps took Landres-et-St-Georges and pressed through successive lines of resistance to Bayonville, Chennery and to the north of the Bois de Barricourt. On the 2d, the I Corps joined in the movement, which now became an impetuous onslaught that could not be strayed.

On the 3d, advance troops were hurried forward in pursuit, some by motor trucks, while the artillery pressed along the country roads close behind. The I Corps reached Authe and Chatillon-sur-bar, the V Corps, Fosse and Nouart, and the III Corps, Halles penetrating the enemy's lines to a depth of twelve miles. Our large caliber guns had advanced and were skillfully brought into position to fire upon the important railroad lines at Montmédy, Longuyon and Conflans. Our III Corps crossed the Meuse on the 5th, and the other corps, in full confidence that the day was theirs, eagerly cleared the way of machine guns as they swept northward, maintaining complete coordination throughout. On the 6th, a division of the I Corps reached a point on the Meuse opposite Sedan, twenty-five miles from our line of departure. The strategical goal which was our highest hope was gained. We had cut the enemy's main line of communications, and nothing but surrender or an armistice could save his army from complete disaster.

On the night of November 10, the V Corps forced a crossing of the Meuse against heavy enemy resistance between Mouzon and Pouilly, and advanced to the Inor-Mouzon Road with two battalions holding the high ground northwest of Inor. Early on the morning of the 11th, a detachment of the V Corps crossed the Meuse at Stenay and occupied that town in conjunction with elements of the III Corps. Bridges were at once constructed at Pouilly and Stenay. These divisions were heavily engaged up to the moment of the Armistice.

In all, forty-four enemy divisions had been used against us in the Meuse-Argonne battle. Between September 26 and November 6 we took 16,059 prisoners and 468 guns on this front. Our divisions engaged were the 1st, 2d, 3d, 4th, 5th, 26th, 28th, 29th, 32d, 33d, 35th, 37th, 42d, 77th, 78th, 79th, 80th, 81st, 82d, 89th, 90th and 91st. Many of our divisions remained in line for a length of time that required nerves of steel, while others were sent in again after only a few days of rest. The 1st, 5th, 32d, 42d, 77th, 79th and 80th Divisions were in the line twice. Although some of the divisions were fighting their first battle, they soon became equal to the best.

OPERATIONS EAST OF THE MEUSE

On the three days preceding November 10, the III Corps and the II Colonial and French XVII Corps fought a difficult struggle through the Meuse Hills south of Stenay and forced the enemy into the plain. Meanwhile my plans for further use of the American Forces contemplated an advance between the Meuse and the Moselle in the direction of Longwy by the First Army, while at the same time the Second Army should assume the offensive toward the rich iron fields of Briey. These operations were to be followed by and offensive toward Chateau-Salins east of the Moselle, thus isolating Metz. Accordingly, attacks on the American front had been ordered, and that of the Second Army was in progress on the morning of November 11 when instructions were received that hostilities should cease at 11 o' clock a. m.

At this moment, the line of the American sector from right to left began at Port-sur-Seille, thence across the Moselle to Vandieres and through the Woëvre to Bezonvaux in the foothills of the Meuse, thence along the foothills and through the northern edge of the Woëvre forests to the Meuse beyond Stenay, thence along the west bank, crossing the river kilometer northwest of Inor, thence along the eastern edge of the Bois de Hache, west to northern edge of Autreville, thence northwest of Mouline-Mouzon Road, along that road to Bellefontaine Ferme, thence northwest crossing the Meuse; from there along the west bank of the Meuse to a point near Sedan where we connected with the French.

RELATIONS WITH THE ALLIES

Cooperation among the allies has at all times been most cordial. A far greater effort has been put forth by the Allied Armies and Staffs to assist us than could have been expected. The French Government and Army have always stood ready to furnish us with supplies, equipment and transportation and to aid us in every way. In the towns and hamlets wherever our troops have been stationed or billeted, the French people have everywhere received them more as relatives and intimate friends than as soldiers of a foreign army. For these things, words are quite inadequate to express our gratitude. There can be no doubt that the relations growing out of our associations here assure a permanent friendship between the two peoples. Although we have not been so intimately associated with people of Great Britain, yet their troops and ours when thrown together have always warmly fraternized. The reception of those of our forces who have passed through England and of those who have been stationed there has always been enthusiastic. Altogether, it has been deeply impressed upon us that the ties of language and blood bring the British and ourselves together completely and inseparably.

STRENGTH

There are in Europe altogether, including a regiment and some sanitary units with the Italian Army and the organizations at Archangel, also including those en route from the States, approximately 2,053,347 men, less our losses. Of this total there are in France 1,338,169 combatant troops. Forty divisions have arrived, of which the infantry personnel of 10 have been used as replacements, leaving 30 divisions now in France, organized into three armies of three corps each.

The losses of the American Army up to November 18 are: Killed and died of wounds, 36,154; died of disease, 14,811; deaths unclassified, 2,204; wounded, 179,625; prisoners 2,163; missing 11,660. We have captured altogether about 44,000 prisoners and 1,400 guns, howitzers and trench mortars.

COMMENDATION

The duties of the General Staff, as well as those of the Army and corps staffs, have been very ably performed. Especially is this true when we consider the new and difficult problems with which they have been confronted. This body of officers, both as individuals and as an organization, have, I believe, no superiors in professional ability, in efficiency, or in loyalty.

Nothing that we have in France better reflects the efficiency and devotion to duty of Americans in general than the Services of Supply, whose personnel is thoroughly imbued with a patriotic desire to do its full duty. They have at all times fully appreciated their responsibility to the rest of the Army, and the results produced have been most gratifying.

Our Medical Corps is especially entitled to praise for the general effectiveness of its work both in hospitals and at the front. Embracing men of high professional attainments, and splendid women devoted to their calling and untiring in their efforts, this Department has made a new record for medical and sanitary proficiency.

The Quartermaster Department has had a difficult and varied task, but it has more than met all demands that have been made upon it. Its management and its personnel have been exceptionally efficient and deserve every possible commendation.

As to the more technical services, the able personnel of the Ordnance Department in France has splendidly fulfilled its functions both in procurement and in forwarding the immense quantities of ordnance required. The officers and men and the young women of the Signal Corps have performed their duties with a large conception of the problem and with a devoted and patriotic spirit to which the perfection of our communication daily testifies. While the Engineer Corps has been referred to in another part of this report it should be further stated that their work has required large vision and high professional skill, and great credit is due their personnel for the high efficiency that they have constantly maintained.

Our aviators have no equals in daring or in fighting ability, and have left a record of courageous deeds that will ever remain a brilliant page in the annals of our army. While the Tank Corps has had limited opportunity its personnel has responded gallantly on every possible occasion and has shown courage of the highest order.

The Adjutant General's Department has been directed with a systematic thoroughness and excellence that surpasses any previous work of its kind. The Inspector General's Department has risen to the highest standards and throughout has ably assisted commanders in the enforcement of discipline. The able personnel of the Judge Advocate General's Department has solved with judgment and wisdom the multitude of difficult legal problems many of them involving questions of great international importance.

It would be impossible in this brief preliminary report to do justice to the personnel of all the different branches of this organization, which I shall cover in detail in a later report.

The Navy in European waters has at all times most cordially aided the Army, and it is most gratifying to report that there has never before been such perfect cooperation between these two branches of the service.

As to Americans in Europe not in the military services, it is the greatest pleasure to say that, both in official and in private life, they are intensely patriotic and loyal, and have been invariably sympathetic and helpful to the Army.

Finally, I pay the supreme tribute to our officers and soldiers of the line. When I think of their heroism, their patience under hardship, their unflinching spirit of offensive action, I am filled with emotion which I am unable to express. Their deeds are immortal and they have earned the eternal gratitude of our country.

I am, Mr. Secretary,

Very respectfully,

JOHN J. PERSHING,
General, Commander-in-Chief,
American Expeditionary Forces.

AWC Lib: Report

Final Report of General John J. Pershing

GENERAL HEADQUARTERS, A. E. F.,

Paris, September 1, 1919.

To the SECRETARY OF WAR.

SIR: I have the honor to submit herewith my final report as Commander-in-Chief of the American Expeditionary Forces in Europe.

PART I

[Extract]

PERIOD OF ORGANIZATION

1. I assumed the duties of this office on May 26, 1917, and, accompanied by a small staff, departed for Europe on board the S. S. *Baltic* May 28. We arrived at London on June 9 and, after spending some days in consulation with the British authorities, reached Paris on June 13.

2. Following the rather earnest appeals of the Allies for American troops, it was decided to send to France, at once, 1 complete division and 9 newly organized regiments of engineers. The division was formed of regular regiments, necessary transfers of officers and men were made, and recruits were assigned to increase these units to the required strength.

The offer by the Navy Department of one regiment of Marines to be reorganized as infantry was accepted by the Secretary of War, and it became temporarily a part of the 1st Division.

Prior to our entrance into the war, the regiments of our small Army were very much scattered, and we had no organized units, even approximating a division, that could be sent overseas prepared to take the field. To meet the new conditions of warfare an entirely new organization was adopted in which our infantry divisions were to consist of 4 regiments of infantry of about treble their original size, 3 regiments of artillery, 14 machine gun companies, 1 engineer regiment, 1 signal battalion, 1 troop of cavalry and other auxiliary units, making a total strength of about 28,000 men.

MILITARY SITUATION

3. In order that the reasons for many important decisions reached in the early history of the American Expeditionary Forces may be more clearly understood and the true value of the American effort more fully appreciated, it is desirable to have in mind the main events leading up to the time of our entry into the war.

1914

4. Although the German drive of 1914 had failed in its immediate purpose, yet her armies had made very important gains. German forces were in complete possession of Belgium and occupied rich industrial regions of northern France, embracing one-fourteenth of her population and about three-fourths of her coal and iron. The German Armies held a strongly fortified line 468 miles in length, stretching from the Swiss border to Nieuport on the English Channel; her troops were within 48 miles of Paris and the initiative remained in German hands.

In the east, the rapidity of the Russian mobilization forced Germany, even before the Battle of the Marne, to send troops to that frontier, but the close of 1914 found the Russian Armies ejected from East Prussia and driven back on Warsaw.

The entry of Turkey into the war, because of the moral effect upon the Moslem world and the immediate constant threat created against Allied communications with the Far East, led to an effort by the Allies in the direction of the Dardanelles.

1915

5. Italy joined the Allies in May and gave their cause new strength, but the effect was more or less offset when Bulgaria entered on the side of the Central Powers.

The threatening situation on the Russian front and in the Balkans was still such that Germany was compelled to exert an immediate offensive effort in those directions and to maintain only a defensive attitude on the western front. German arms achieved a striking series of successes in the vicinity of the Mazurian Lakes and in Galicia, capturing Warsaw, Brest-Litovsk, and Vilna. The Central Powers overran Serbia and Montenegro. Meanwhile, the Italian Armies forced Austria to use approximately one-half of her strength against them.

In the west, the French and British launched offensives which cost the German Armies considerable loss; but the objectives were limited and the effect was local.

The Dardanelles Expedition, having failed in its mission, was withdrawn in January, 1916. In Mesopotamia the Allies operations had not been successful. Although the British fleet had established its superiority on the sea, yet the German submarine blockade had developed into a serious menace to Allied shipping.

1916

6. Germany no doubt believed that her advantage on the eastern front at the close of 1915 again warranted an offensive in the west, and her attack against Verdun was ac-

cordingly launched in the spring of 1916. But Russia was not yet beaten and early in June, aided at the same time by the threat of an Italian offensive in the west, she began the great drive in Galicia that proved so disastrous to Austria.

Roumania, having entered on the side of the Allies, undertook a promising offensive against Austria. The British and French Armies attacked along the Somme. Germany quickly returned to the defensive in the west, and in September initiated a campaign in the east which, before the close of 1916, proved unfortunate for Russia as well as Roumania.

SPRING OF 1917

7. Retaining on the eastern front the forces considered sufficient for the final conquest of Russia, Germany prepared to aid Austria in an offensive against Italy. Meanwhile, the Russian revolution was well under way and, by the midsummer of 1917, the final collapse of that government was almost certain.

The relatively low strength of the German forces on the western front led the Allies with much confidence to attempt a decision on this front; but the losses were very heavy and the effort signally failed. The failure caused a serious reaction especially on French morale, both in the Army and throughout the country, and attempts to carry out extensive or combined operations were indefinitely suspended.

In the five months ending June 30, German submarines had accomplished the destruction of more than three and one-quarter million tons of Allied shipping. During three years Germany had seen practically all her offensives except Verdun crowned with success. Her battle lines were held on foreign soil and she had withstood every Allied attack since the Marne. The German General Staff could now foresee the complete elimination of Russia, the possibility of defeating Italy before the end of the year and, finally, the campaign of 1918 against the French and British on the western front which might terminate the war.

It can not be said that German hopes of final victory were extravagant, either as viewed at that time or as viewed in the light of history. Financial problems of the Allies were difficult, supplies were becoming exhausted and their Armies had suffered tremendous losses. Discouragement existed not only among the civil population but throughout the Armies as well. Such was the Allies morale that, although their superiority on the western front during the last half of 1916 and during 1917 amounted to 20 per cent, only local attacks could be undertaken and their effect proved wholly insufficient against the German defense. Allied resources in man power at home were low and there was little prospect of materially increasing their armed strength, even in the face of the probability of having practically the whole military strength of the Central Powers against them in the spring of 1918.

8. This was the state of affairs that existed when we entered the war. While our action gave the Allies much encouragement yet this was temporary, and a review of conditions made it apparent that America must make a supreme material effort as soon as possible. After duly considering the tonnage possibilities I cabled the following to Washington on July 6, 1917:

Plans should contemplate sending over at least 1,000,000 men by next May.

ORGANIZATION PROJECTS

9. A general organization project, covering as far as possible the personnel of all combat, staff, and administrative units, was forwarded to Washington on July 11. This was prepared by the Operations Section of my staff and adopted in joint conference with the War Department Committee then in France. It embodied my conclusions on the military organization and effort required of America after a careful study of French and British experience. In forwarding this project I stated:

It is evident that a force of about 1,000,000 is the smallest unit which in modern war will be a complete, well-balanced, and independent fighting organization. However, it must be equally clear that the adoption of this size force as a basis of study should not be construed as representing the maximum force which should be sent to or which will be needed in France. It is taken as the force which may be expected to reach France in time for an offensive in 1918, and as a unit and basis of organization. Plans for the future should be based, especially in reference to the manufacture of artillery, aviation, and other material, on three times this force---i. e., at least 3,000,000 men.

* * * * * *

With a few minor changes, this project remained our guide until the end.

10. While this general organization project provided certain Services of Supply troops, which were an integral part of the larger combat units, it did not include the great body of troops and services required to maintain an army overseas. To disembark 2,000,000 men, move them to their training areas, shelter them, handle and store the quantities of supplies and equipment they required called for an extraordinary and immediate effort in construction. To provide the organization for this purpose, a project for engineer services of the rear, including railways, was cabled to Washington August 5, 1917, followed on September 18, 1917, by a complete service of the rear project, which listed item by item the troops considered necessary for the Services of Supply. Particular attention is invited to the charts herewith, which show the extent to which this project had developed by November 11, 1918, and the varied units required, many of which did not exist in our Army prior to this war.

11. In order that the War Department might have a clear-cut program to follow in the shipment of personnel and material to insure the gradual building up of a force at all times balanced and symmetrical, a comprehensive statement was prepared covering the order in which the troops and services enumerated in these two projects should arrive. This schedule of priority of shipments, forwarded to the War Department on October 7, divided the initial force called for by the two projects into six phases corresponding to combatant corps of six divisions each.

The importance of the three documents, the general organization project, the service of the rear project, and the schedule of priority of shipments should be emphasized, because they formed the basic plan for providing an army in France together with its material for combat, construction, and supply.

AMERICAN FRONT AND LINE OF COMMUNICATIONS

12. Before developing plans for a line of communications it was necessary to decide upon the probable sector of the front for the eventual employment of a distinctive American force. Our mission was offensive and it was essential to make plans for striking the enemy where a definite military decision could be gained. While the Allied Armies had endeavored to maintain the offensive, the British, in order to guard the Channel ports, were committed to operations in Flanders and the French to the portion of the front protecting Paris. Both lacked troops to operate elsewhere on a large scale.

To the east the great fortified district east of Verdun and around Metz menaced central France, protected the most exposed portion of the German line of Communications, that between Metz and Sedan, and covered the Briey iron region, from which the enemy obtained the greater part of the iron required for munitions and material. The coal fields east of Metz were also covered by these same defenses. A deep advance east of Metz, or the capture of the Briey region, by threatening the invasion of rich German territory in the Moselle Valley and the Saar Basin, thus curtailing her supply of coal or iron, would have a decisive effect in forcing a withdrawal of German troops from northern France. The military and economic situation of the enemy, therefore, indicated Lorraine as the field promising the most fruitful results for the employment of our armies.

13. The complexity of trench life had enormously increased the tonnage of supplies required by troops. Not only was it a question of providing food but enormous quantities of munitions and material were needed. Upon the railroads of France fell the burden of meeting the heavy demands of the three and one-half million Allied combatants then engaged.

The British were crowding the Channel ports and the French were exploiting the manufacturing center of Paris, so that the railroads of northern France were already much overtaxed. Even though the Channel ports might be used to a limited extent for shipments through England, the railroads leading eastward would have to cross British and French zones of operation, thus making the introduction of a line of communications based on ports and railways in that region quite impracticable. If the American Army was to have an independent and flexible system it could not use the lines behind the British-Belgium front nor those in rear of the French front covering Paris.

The problem confronting the American Expeditionary Forces was then to superimpose its rail communications on those of France where there would be the least possible disturbance to the arteries of supply of the two great Allied armies already in the field. This would require the utmost use of those lines of the existing French railroad system that could bear and added burden. Double-track railroad lines from the ports of the Loire and the Gironde Rivers unite at Bourges, running thence via Nevers, Dijon, and Neufchateau, with lines radiating therefrom toward the right wing of the Allied front. It was estimated that these with the collateral lines available, after considerable improvement, could handle and additional 50,000 tons per day, required for an army of 2,000,000 men. The lines selected, therefore, were those leading from the comparatively unused south-Atlantic ports of France to the northeast where it was believed the American Armies could be employed to the best advantage.

14. In the location of our main depots of supply, while it was important that they should be easily accessible, yet they must also be at a safe distance, as we were to meet an agressive enemy capable of taking the offensive in any one of several directions. The area embracing Tours, Orleans, Montargis, Nevers, and Chateauroux was chosen, as it was centrally located with regard to all points on the arc of the western front.

The ports of St-Nazaire, La Pallice, and Bassens were designated for permanent use, while Nantes, Bordeaux, and Pauillac were for emergency use. Several smaller ports, such as St-Malo, Sables-d'Olonne, and Bayonne, were available chiefly for the importation of coal from England. From time to time, certain trans-Atlantic ships were sent to Le Havre and Cherbourg. In anticipation of a large increase in amount of tonnage that might be required later, arrangements were made during the German offensive of 1918 to utilize the ports of Marseilles and Toulon as well as other smaller ports on the Mediterranean.

For all practical purposes the American Expeditionary Forces were based on the American Continent. Three thousand miles of ocean to cross with the growing submarine menace confronting us, the quantity of ship tonnage that would be available then unknown and a line of communications by land 400 miles long from French ports to our probable front presented difficulties that seemed almost insurmountable as compared with those of our Allies.

15. For purposes of local administration our line of communications in France was subdivided into districts or sections. The territory corresponding to and immediately surrounding the principal ports was, respectively, called base sections, with an intermediate section embracing the region of the great storage depots and an advance section extending to the zone of operations, within which the billeting and training areas for our earlier divisions were located.

16. In providing for the storage and distribution of reserve supplies an allowance of 45 days in the base sections was planned, with 30 days in the intermediate section and 15 days in the advance section. After the safety of our sea transport was practically assured, this was reduced to a total of 45 days, distributed proportionately. When the Armistice was signed all projects for construction had been completed and supplies were on hand to meet the needs of 2,000,000 men, while further plans for necessary construction and for the supply of an additional 2,000,000 were well under way.

GENERAL STAFF

17. The organization of the General Staff and supply services was one of the first matters to engage my attention. Our situation in this regard was wholly unlike that of our Allies. The French Army was at home and in close touch with its civil government and war department agencies. While the British were organized on an overseas basis, they were within easy reach of their base of supplies in England. Their problems of supply and replacement were simple as compared with ours. Their training could be carried out at home with the experience of the front at hand, while our troops must be sent as ships were provided and their training resumed in France where discontinued in the States. Our available tonnage was inadequate to meet all the initial demands, so that priority of material for combat and construction, as well as for supplies that could not be purchased in Europe, must be estsblished by those whose perspective included all the services and who were familiar with general plans. For the proper direction and coordination of the details of administration, intelligence, operations, supply, and training, a General Staff was an indispensable part of the Army.

The functions of the General Staff at my headquarters were finally allotted to the five sections, each under an Assistant Chief of Staff, as follows: To the First, or Administrative Section---ocean tonnage, priority of overseas shipments, replacement of men and animals, organization and types of equipment for troops, billeting, prisoners of war, military police, leaves and leave areas, welfare work and amusements; to the Second, or Intelligence Section---information regarding the enemy, including espionage and counterespionage, maps and censorship; to the Third, or Operations Section---strategic studies and plans and employment of combat troops; to the Fourth Section---coordination of supply services, including Construction, Transportation, and Medical Departments, and control of regulating stations for supply; to the Fifth, or Training Section---tactical training, schools, preparation of tactical manuals, and athletics. This same system was applied in the lower echelons of the command down to include divisions, except that in corps and divisions the Fourth Section was merged with the First and the Fifth Section with the Third.

18. As the American Expeditionary Forces grew, it was considered avisable that, in matters of procurement, transportation, and supply, the chiefs of the several supply services, who had hitherto been under the General Staff at my headquarters, should be placed directly under the supervision of the commanding general, Services of Supply. At General Headquarters, a Deputy Chief of Staff to assist the Chief of Staff was provided, and the heads of the five General Staff sections became Assistant Chiefs of Staff.

The General Staff at my headquarters thereafter concerned itself with the broader phase of control. Under my general supervision and pursuant to clearly determined policies, the Assistant Chiefs of Staff, coordinated by the Chief of Staff, issued instructions and gave general direction to the great combat units and to the Services of Supply, keeping always in close touch with the manner and promptness of their fulfillment. Thus a system of direct responsibility was put into operation which contemplated secrecy in preparation, prompt decision in emergency, and coordinate action in execution.

19. With the growth of our forces the demand for staff officers rapidly increased, but the available number of officers trained for staff duty was very limited. To meet this deficiency, a General Staff college was organized at Langres on November 28, 1917,

for the instruction of such officers as could be spared. An intensive course of study
of three months was prescribed embracing the details of our staff organization and administration and our system of supply, and teaching the combined employment of all arms and
services in combat. Officers were carefully chosen for their suitability and, considering
the short time available, graduates from this school returned well equipped for staff
duties and with a loyal spirit of common service much accentuated. The Staff College
carried to completion four courses of three months each, graduating 537 stsff officers.

TRAINING

20. Soon after our arrival in Europe careful study was made of the methods followed
by our Allies in training combat troops. Both the French and British maintained continuously a great system of schools and training centers, which provided for both the-
oretical and practical instruction of inexperienced officers and noncommissioned officers.
These centers were required not only to train new troops, but to prepare officers and
soldiers for advancement by giving them a short course in the duties of their new grades.
These school systems made it possible to spread rapidly a knowledge of the latest methods
developed by experience and at the same time counteract false notions.

21. A similar scheme was adopted in August, 1917, for our Armies in which the importance of teaching throughout our forces a sound fighting doctrine of our own was
emphasized. It provided for troop training in all units up to include divisions. Corps
centers of instruction for noncommissioned officers and unit commanders of all arms were
established. These centers also provided special training for the instructors needed at
corps schools. Base training centers for replacement troops and special classes of
soldiers, such as cooks and mechanics, were designated. The army and corps schools were
retained under the direct supervision of the Training Section, General Staff. The schools
mentioned graduated 21,330 noncommissioned officers and 13,916 officers.

Particular care was taken to search the ranks for the most promising soldiers, in
order to develop leaders for the command of platoons and companies. There were graduated
from these candidate schools in France 10,976 soldiers. It was planned to have 22,000
infantrymen under instruction by January 1, 1919, graduating 5,000 to 6,000 each month.
In addition, there were to be graduated monthly 800 artillerymen, 400 engineers, and
200 signalmen, making a total of about 7,000 soldiers each month. Prior to November 14,
1918, 12,732 soldiers were commissioned as officers.

It must not be thought that such a system is ideal, but it represents a compromise
between the demand for efficiency and the imperative and immediate necessity for trained
replacement officer.

22. Every advantage was taken of the experience of our Allies in training officers.
It was early recommended to the War Department that French and British officers be asked
for to assist in the instruction of troops in the United States. Pending the organization
and development of our own schools, a large number of our officers were sent to centers
of instruction of the Allied armies. The training of our earlier divisions was begun in
close association with the French divisions, under conditions set forth in the following
paragraph on divisional training:

Trench warfare naturally gives prominence to the defensive as opposed to
the offensive. To guard against this, the basis of instruction should be
essentially the offensive both in spirit and in practice. The defensive is
accepted only to prepare for future offensive.

For training our artillery units, special localities such as Valdahon, Coëtquidan,
Meucon, and Souge, had to be sought, and the instruction was usually carried on in conjunction with French artillery followed up later, as far as possible, with field practice
in cooperation with our own infantry.

23. The long period of trench warfare had so impressed itself upon the French and
British that they had almost entirely dispensed with training for open warfare. It was

to avoid this result in our Army and to encourage the offensive spirit that the following was published in October, 1917:

1. . . . (a) The above methods to be employed must remain or become distinctly our own.

(b) All instruction must contemplate the assumption of a vigorous offensive. This purpose will be emphasized in every phase of training until it becomes a settle habit of thought.

(c) The general principles governing combat remain unchanged in their essence. This war has developed special features which involve special phases of training, but the fundamental ideas enunciated in our Drill Regulations, Small Arms Firing Manual, Field Service Regulations, and other service manuals remain the guide for both officers and soldiers and constitute the standard by which their efficiency is to be measured, except as modified in detail by instructions from these headquarters.

(d) The rifle and the bayonet are the principal weapons of the infantry soldier. He will be trained to a high degree of skill as a marksman, both on the target range and in field firing. An aggressive spirit must be developed until the soldier feels himself, as a bayonet fighter, invincible in battle.

(e) All officers and soldiers should realize that at no time in our history has discipline been so important; therefore, discipline of the highest order must be exacted at all times. The standards for the American Army will be those of West Point. The rigid attention, upright bearing, attention to detail, uncomplaining obedience to instructions required of the cadet will be required of every officer and soldier of our armies in France. . . .

Recommendations were cabled to Washington emphasizing the importance of target practice and musketry training, and recommending that instruction in open warfare be made the mission of troops in the United States, while the training in trench warfare so far as necessary be conducted in France. Succeeding divisions, whether serving temporarily with the British or French, were trained as thus indicated. The assistance of the French units was limited to demonstrations, and, in the beginning, French instructors taught the use of French arms and assisted in the preparation of elementary trench warfare problems.

Assuming that divisions would arrive with their basic training completed in the United States, one month was allotted for the instruction of small units from battalions down, a second month of experience in quiet sectors by battalions, and a third month for field practice in open warfare tactics by division, including artillery. Unfortunately many divisions did not receive the requisite amount of systematic training before leaving the States and complete preparation of such units for battle was thus often seriously delayed.

24. The system of training profoundly influenced the combat efficiency of our troops by its determined insistence upon an offensive doctrine and upon training in warfare of movement. Instruction which had hitherto been haphazard, varying with the ideas and conceptions of inexperienced commanding officers and indifferent instructors, was brought under a system based on correct principles. Approved and systematic methods were maintained and enforced largely by the continual presence of members of the Training Section with the troops both during the training period and in campaign.

INTELLIGENCE

25. Before our entry into the war, European experience had shown that military operations can be carried out successfully and without unnecessary loss only in the light of complete and reliable information of the enemy. Warfare with battle lines

separated by short distances only, made possible the early acquirement of information, such as that obtained through airplane photography, observation from balloons and planes, sensitive instruments for detecting gun positions and raids to secure prisoners and documents. All such information, together with that from Allied sources, including military, political, and economical, was collected, classified, and rapidly distributed where needed.

26. From careful studies of the systems and actual participation by our officers in methods in use at various Allied headquarters, and Intelligence Service was evolved in our forces which operated successfully from its first organization in August, 1917.

With us the simpler methods, such as observation from the air and ground and the exploitation of prisoners and documents, have proved more effective than the less direct means. Every unit from the battalion up had an intelligence detachment, but only in divisions and larger organizations did the intelligence agencies embrace all available means and sources, including radio interception stations and sound and flash-ranging detachments.

27. The subjects studied by the Intelligence Section embraced the location of the enemy's front line, his order of battle, the history and fighting value of his divisions, his manpower, his combat activities, circulation and movement, his defensive organizations supply, construction and material, air service, radio service, strategy and tactics, and what he probably knew of our intentions. The political and economic conditions within the enemies' countries were also of extreme importance.

28. To disseminate conclusions, daily publications were necessary, such as a Secret Summary of Intelligence containing information of the broadest scope, which concerned only General Headquarters; and a Summary of Information, distributed down to include the divisions, giving information affecting the western front. A Press Review and a Summary of Air Intelligence were also published.

Maps showing graphically the disposition and movement of enemy troops in our front were the best means for distributing information to our troops. At the base printing plant and at General Headquarters base maps wer prepared while mobile printing plants, mounted on trucks, accompanied corps and army headquarters. Combat troops were thus supplied with excellent maps distributed, just before and during an attack, down to include company and platoon commanders. Between July 1 and November 11, 1918, over 5,000,000 maps were used.

29. The secret service, espionage and counterespionage was organized in close co-operation with the French and British. To prevent indiscretions in the letters of officers and soldiers, as well as in articles written for the press, the Censorship Division was created. The Base Censor examined individual letters when the writer so desired, censored all mail written in foreign languages, of which there were over 50 used, and frequently checked up letters of entire organizations.

30. The policy of press censorship adopted aimed to accomplish three broad results:

To prevent the enemy from obtaining important information of our forces;

To give to the people of the United States the maximum information consistent with the limitations imposed by the first object;

To cause to be presented to the American people the facts as they were known at the time.

There were with our forces 36 regularly accredited correspondents, while visiting correspondents reached a total of 411.

SUMMER OF 1917 TO SPRING OF 1918

31. In order to hinder the enemy's conquest of Russia and, if possible, prevent a German attack on Italy or in the near east, the Allies sought to maintain the offensive on the western front as far as their diminished strength and morale would permit. On June 7, 1917, the British took Messines, while a succession of operations known as the

Third Battle of Ypres began on July 31 and terminated with the capture of the Passchendaele Ridge November 6-10. The British attack at Cambrai is of special interest, since it was here that American troops (11th Engineers) first participated in active fighting.

The French successfully attacked on a limited front near Verdun, capturing Mort Homme on August 20 and advancing their lines to La Forge Brook. In another offensive, begun on October 23, they gained considerable ground on Chemin-des-Dames Ridge. These French attacks were characterized by most careful preparation to insure success in order to improve the morale of their troops.

32. Notwithstanding these Allied attacks on the western front, the immense gains by the German armies in the east, culminating at Riga on September 3, precipitated the collapse of Russia. The following month, the Austrians with German assistance surprised the Italians and broke through the lines at Caporetto, driving the Italian armies back to the Piave River, inflicting a loss of 300,000 men, 600,000 rifles, 3,000 guns, and enormous stores. This serious crisis compelled the withdrawal of 10 French and British divisions from the western front to Italy. The German situation on all other theaters was so favorable that as early as November they began the movement of divisions toward the western front. If needed, her divisions could be withdrawn from the Italian front before the French and British dared recall their divisions.

33. At first the Allies could hardly hope for a large American Army. Marshal Joffre during his visit to America had made special request that a combat division be sent at once to Europe as visual evidence of our purpose to participate actively in the war, and also asked for engineer regiments and other special service units.

The arrival of the First Division and the parade of certain of its elements in Paris on July 4 caused great enthusiasm and for the time being French morale was stimulated. Still Allied apprehension was deep-seated and material assistance was imperative. The following extract is quoted from the cabled summary of an Allied conference held on July 26 with the French and Italian Commanders in Chief and the British and French Chiefs of Staff:

> General conclusions reached were necessity for adoption of purely defensive attitude on all secondary fronts and withdrawing surplus troops for duty on western front. By thus strengthening western front believed Allies could hold until American forces arrive in numbers sufficient to gain ascendency.

The conference urged the immediate study of the tonnage situation with a view to accelerating the arrival of American troops. With the approach of winter, depression among the Allies over the Russian collapse and the Italian crisis was intensified by the conviction that the Germans would undertake a decisive offensive in the spring.

A review of the situation showed that with Russia out of the war the Central Powers would be able to release a large number of divisions for service elsewhere, and that during the spring and summer of 1918, without interfering with the status quo at Salonika, they could concentrate on the western front a *force* much stronger than that of the Allies. In view of this, it was represented to the War Department in December as of the utmost importance that the Allied preparations be expedited.

34. On December 31, 1917, there were 176,665 American troops in France and but one division had appeared on the front. Disappointment at the delay of the American effort soon began to develop. French and British authorities suggested the more rapid entry of our troops into the line and urged the amalgamation of our troops with their own, even insisting upon the curtailment of training to conform to the strict minimum of trench requirements they considered necessary.

My conclusion was that, although the morale of the German people and of the armies was better than it had been for two years, only an untoward combination of circumstances could give the enemy a decisive victory before American support as recommended could be made effective, provided the Allies secured unity of action. However, a situation might arise which would necessitate the temporary use of all American troops in the units of our Allies for the defensive, but nothing in the situation justified the relinquishment of our firm purpose to form our own Army under our own flag.

While the Germans were practicing for open warfare and concentrating their most aggressive personnel in shock divisions, the training of the Allies was still limited to trench warfare. As our troops were being trained for open warfare, there was every reason why we could not allow them to be scattered among our Allies, even by divisions, much less as replacements, except by pressure of sheer necessity. Any sort of permanent amalgamation would irrevocably commit America's fortunes to the hands of the Allies. Moreover it was obvious that the lack of homogeneity would render these mixed divisions difficult to maneuver and almost certain to break up under stress of defeat, with the consequent mutual recrimination. Again there was no doubt that the realization by the German people that independent American divisions, corps, or armies were in the field with determined purpose would be a severe blow to German morale and prestige.

It was also certain that an early appearance of the larger American units on the front would be most beneficial to the morale of the Allies themselves. Accordingly, the 1st Division, on January 19, 1918, took over a sector north of Toul; the 26th Division went to the Soissons front early in February; the 42d Division entered the line near Luneville, February 21, and the 2d Division near Verdun, March 18. Meanwhile, the I Army Corps Headquarters, Maj. Gen. Hunter Liggett, commanding, was organized at Neufchâteau on January 20, and the plan to create an independent American sector on the Lorraine front was taking shape.

This was the situation when the Great German offensive was launched on March 21, 1918.

PART II

OPERATIONS

EXPEDITING SHIPMENT OF TROOPS

1. The War Department planned as early as July, 1917, to send to France by June 15, 1918, 21 divisions of the then strength of 20,000 men each, together with auxiliary and replacement troops, and those needed for the line of communications, amounting to over 200,000, making a total of some 650,000 men. Beginning with October, 6 divisions were to be sent during that quarter, 7 during the first quarter of 1918, and 8 the second quarter. While these numbers fell short of my recommendation of July 6, 1917, which contemplated at least 1,000,000 men by May, 1918, it should be borne in mind that the main factor in the problem was the amount of shipping to become available for military purposes, in which must be included tonnage required to supply the Allies with steel, coal, and food.

2. On December 2, 1917, an estimate of the situation was cabled to the War Department with the following recommendation:

> Paragraph 3. In view of these conditions, it is of the utmost importance to the Allied cause that we move swiftly. The minimum number of troops we should plan to have in France by the end of June is 4 Army corps of 24 divisions in addition to troops for service of the rear. Have impressed the present urgency upon Gen. Bliss and other American members of the conference. Gens. Robertson, Foch, and Bliss agree with me that this is the minimum that should be aimed at. This figure is given as the lowest we should think of and is placed no higher because the limit of available transportation would not seem to warrant it.

> Paragraph 4. A study of transportation facilities shows sufficient American tonnage to bring over this number of troops, but to do so there

must be a reduction in the tonnage allotted to other than Army needs. It is estimated that the shipping needed will have to be rapidly increased up to 2,000,000 tons by May, in addition to the amount already allotted. The use of shipping for commercial purposes must be curtailed as much as possible. The Allies are very weak and we must come to their relief this year, 1918. The year after may be too late. It is very doubtful if they can hold on until 1919 unless we give them a lot of support this year. It is therefore strongly recommended that a complete readjustment of transportation be made and that the needs of the War Department as set forth a above be regarded as immediate. Further details of these requirements will be sent later.

and again on December 20, 1917:

Understood here that a shipping program based on tonnage in sight prepared in War College Division in September contemplated that entire First Corps with its corps troops and some 32,000 auxiliaries were to have been shipped by end of November, and that an additional program for December, January, and February contemplates that the shipment of the Second Corps with its corps troops and other Auxiliaries should be practically completed by the end of February. Should such a program be carried out as per schedule and should shipments continue at corresponding rate, it would not succeed in placing even three complete corps, with proper proportion of Army troops and auxiliaries, in France by the end of May. The actual facts are that shipments are not even keeping up to that schedule. It is now the middle of December and the First Corps is still incomplete by over two entire divisions* and many corps troops. It can not be too emphatically declared that we should be prepared to take the field with at least four corps by June 30. In view of past performances with tonnage heretofore available such a project is impossible of fulfillment, but only by most strenuous attempts to attain such a result will we be in a position to take a proper part in operations in 1918. In view of fact that as the number of our troops here increases a correspondingly greater amount of tonnage must be provided for their supply, and also in view of the slow rate of shipment with tonnage now available, it is of the most urgent importance that more tonnage should be obtained at once as already recommended in my cables and by Gen. Bliss.

3. During January, 1918, discussions were held with the British authorities that resulted in an agreement, which became know as the six-division plan and which provided for the transportation of six entire divisions in British tonnage, without interference with our own shipping program. High commanders, staff, infantry, and auxiliary troops were to be given experience with British divisions, beginning with battalions, the artillery to be trained under American direction, using French materiel. It was agreed that when sufficiently trained these battalions were to be re-formed into regiments and that when the artillery was fully trained all of the units comprising each division were to be united for service under their own officers. It was planned that the period of training with the British should cover about 10 weeks. To supervise the administration and training of these divisions the II Corps staff was organized February 20, 1918.

In the latter part of January, joint note No. 12, presented by the Military Representatives with the Supreme War Council, was approved by the Council. This note concluded that France would be safe during 1918 only under certain conditions, namely:

---

*The 1st, 42d, 2d, and 26th Divisions had arrived; but not the Replacement and the Depot Division.

(a) That the strength of the British and Frrnch troops in France are continously kept up to their present total strength and that they receive the expected reinforcements of not less than two American divisions per month.

THE GERMAN OFFENSIVES OF 1918 AND RELATED ALLIED AGREEMENTS

4. The first German offensives of 1918, beginning March 21, overran all resistance during the initial period of the attack. Within eight days the enemy had completely crossed the old Somme battlefield and had swept everything before him to a depth of some 56 kilometers. For a few days the loss of the railroad center of Amiens appeared imminent. The offensive made such inroads upon French and British reserves that defeat stared them in the face unless the new American troops should prove more immediately available than even the most optimistic had dared to hope. On March 27 Military Representatives with the Supreme War Council prepared their joint note No. 18. This note repeated the previously quoted statement from joint note No. 12, and continued:

The battle which is developing at the present moment in France, and which can extend to the other theaters of operations, may very quickly place the Allied Armies in a serious situation from the point of view of effectives, and the Military Representatives are from this moment of opinion that the above-detailed condition (see (a) par. 3) can no longer be maintained, and they consider as a general proposition that the new situation requires new decisions.

The Military Representatives are of opinion that it is highly desirable that the American Government should assist the Allied Armies as soon as possible by permitting in principle the temporary service of American units in Allied Army corps and divisions. Such reinforcements must, however, be obtained from other units than those American divisions which are now operating with the French, and the units so temporarily employed must eventually be returned to the American Army.

The Military Representatives are of the opinion that from the present time, in execution of the foregoing, and until otherwise directed by the Supreme War Council, only American infantry and machine-gun units, organized as that Government may decide, be brought to France, and that all agreements or conventions hitherto made in conflict with this decision be modified accordingly.

The Secretary of War, who was in France at this time, Gen. Bliss, the American Military Representative with the Supreme War Council, and I at once conferred on the terms of this note, with the result that the Secretary recommended to the President that joint note No. 18 be approved in the following sense:

The purpose of the American Government is to render the fullest co-operation and aid, and therefore the recommendation of the Military Representatives with regard to the preferential transportation of American infantry and machine-gun units in the present emergency is approved. Such units, when transported, will be under the direction of the Commander-in-Chief of the American Expeditionary Forces, and will be assigned for training and use by him in his discretion. He will use these and all other military forces of the United States under his command in such manner as to render the greatest military assistance, keeping in mind always the determination of this Government to have its various military forces collected, as speedily as their training and the military situation permit, into an independent American Army, acting in concert with the armies of Great Britain and France, and all arrangements made by him for their temporary training and service will be made with that end in view.

While Note No. 18 was general in its terms, the priority of shipments of infantry more especially pertained to those divisions that were to be trained in the British area, as that Government was to provide the additional shipping according to the six-division plan agreed upon even before the beginning of the March 21 offensive.

On April 2 the War Department cabled that preferential transportation would be given to American infantry and machine-gun units during the existing emergency. Preliminary arrangements were made for training and early employment with the French of such infantry units as might be sent over by our own transportation. As for the British agreement, the six-division plan was to be modified to give priority to the infantry of those divisions. However, all the Allies were now urging the indefinite continuation of priority for the shipment of infantry and its complete incorporation in their units, which fact was cabled to the War Department on April 3, with the specific recommendation that the total immediate priority of infantry be limited to four divisions, plus 45,500 replacements, and that the necessity for future priority be determined later.

5. The Secretary of War and I held a conference with British authorities on April 7, during which it developed that the British had erroneously assumed that the preferential shipment of infantry was to be continuous. It was agreed at this meeting that 60,000 infantry and machine-gun troops, with certain auxiliary units to be brought over by British tonnage during April, should go to the British area as part of the six-division plan, but that there should be a further agreement as to subsequent troops to be brought over by the British. Consequently, a readjustment of the priority schedule was undertaken on the basis of postponing shipment of all noncombatant troops to the utmost possible to meet present situation, and at the same time not make it impossible to build up our own Army.

6. The battle line in the vicinity of Amiens had hardly stabilized when, on April 9, the Germans made another successful attack against the British lines on a front of some 40 kilometers in the vicinity of Armentieres and along the Lys River. As a result of its being included in a salient formed by the German advance, Passchendaele Ridge, the capture of which had cost so dearly in 1917, was evacuated by the British on April 17.

The losses had been heavy and the British were unable to replace them entirely. They were, therefore, making extraordinary efforts to increase the shipping available for our troops. On April 21, I went to London to clear up certain questions concerning the rate of shipment and to reach the further agreement provided for in the April 7 Conference. The result of this London Agreement was cabled to Washington April 24, as follows:

(a) That only the infantry, machine guns, engineers, and signal troops of American divisions and the headquarters of divisions and brigades be sent over in British and American shipping during May for training and service with the British Army in France up to six divisions and that any shipping in excess of that required for these troops be utilized to transport troops necessary to make these divisions complete. The training and service of these troops will be carried out in accordance with plans already agreed upon between Sir Douglas Haig and Gen. Pershing, with a view at an early date of building up American divisions.

(b) That the American personnel of the artillery of these divisions and such corps troops as may be required to build up American corps organizations follow immediately thereafter, and that American artillery personnel be trained with French matériel and join its proper divisions as soon as thoroughly trained.

(c) If, when the program outlined in paragraphs (a) and (b) is completed, the military situation makes advisable the further shipment of infantry, etc., of American divisions, then all the British and American shipping available for transport of troops shall be used for that purpose under such arrangement as will insure immediate aid to the Allies, and at the same time provide at the earliest moment for bringing over American artillery and other necessary units to complete the organization of American divisions and corps. Provided that the combatant troops mentioned in (a) and (b) be followed by such Service of the Rear and other troops as may be considered necessary by the American Commander-in-Chief.

(d) That it is contemplated American divisions and corps when trained and organized shall be utilized under the American Commander-in-Chief in an American group.

(e) That the American Commander-in-Chief shall allot American troops to the French or British for training or train them with American units at his discretion, with the understanding that troops already transported by British shipping or included in the six divisions mentioned in paragraph (a) are to be trained with the British Army, details as to rations, equipment, and transport to be determined by special agreement.

7. At a meeting of the Supreme War Council held at Abbeville May 1 and 2, the entire question of the amalgamation of Americans with the French and British was reopened. An urgent appeal came from both French and Italian representatives for American replacements or units to serve with their armies. After prolonged discussion regarding this question and that of priority generally the following agreement was reached, committing the Council to an independent American Army and providing for the immediate shipment of certain troops:

It is the opinion of the Supreme War Council that, in order to carry the war to a successful conclusion, an American Army should be formed as early as possible under its own commander and under its own flag. In order to meet the present emergency it is agreed that American troops should be brought to France as rapidly as Allied transportation facilities will permit, and that, as far as consistent with the necessity of building up an American Army, preference will be given to infantry and machine-gun units for training and service with French and British Armies; with the understanding that such infantry and machine-gun units are to be withdrawn and united with its own artillery and auxiliary troops into divisions and corps at the direction of the American Commander-in-Chief after consultation with the Commander-in-Chief of the Allied Armies in France.

Subparagraph A. It is also agreed that during the month of May preference should be given to the transportation of infantry and machine-gun units of six divisions and that any excess tonnage shall be devoted to bringing over such other troops as may be determined by the American Commander-in-Chief.

Subparagraph B. It is further agreed that this program shall be condition that the British Government shall furnish transportation for a minimum of 130,000 men in May and 150,000 men in June, with the understanding that the first six divisions of infantry shall go to the British for training and service, and that troops sent over in June shall be allocated for training and service as the American Commander-in-Chief may determine.

Subparagraph C. It is also further agreed that if the British Government shall transport an excess of 150,000 men in June that such excess shall be infantry and machine-gun units, and that early in June there shall be a new review of the situation to determine further action.

The gravity of the situation had brought the Allies to a full realization of the necessity of providing all possible tonnage for the transportation of American troops. Although their views were accepted to the extent of giving a considerable priority to infantry and machine gunners, the priority agreed upon as to this class of troops was not as extensive as some of them deemed necessary, and the Abbeville Conference was adjourned with the understanding that the question of further priority would be discussed at a conference to be held about the end of May.

8. The next offensive of the enemy was made between the Oise and Berry-au-Bac against the French instead of against the British, as was generally expected, and it came as a complete surprise. The initial Aisne attack, covering a front of 35 kilometers, met with remarkable success, as the German Armies advanced no less than 50 kilometer in four days. On reaching the Marne that river was used as a defensive flank and the German advance was directed toward Paris. During the first days of June something akin to a panic seized the city and it was estimated that 1,000,000 people left during the spring of 1918.

The further conference which had been agreed upon at Abbeville was held at Versailles on June 1 and 2. The opinion of our Allies as to the existing situation and the urgency of their insistence upon further priority for infantry and machine gunners are shown by the following message prepared by the Prime Ministers of Great Britain, France, and Italy, and agreed to by Gen. Foch:

The Prime Ministers of France, Italy, and Great Britain, now meeting at Versailles, desire to send the following message to the President of the United States:

We desire to express our warmest thanks to President Wilson for the remarkable promptness with which American aid, in excess of what at one time seemed practicable, has been rendered to the Allies during the past month to meet a great emergency. The crisis, however, still continues. Gen. Foch has presented to us a statement of the utmost gravity, which points out that the numerical superiority of the enemy in France, where 162 Allied divisions now oppose 200 German divisions, is very heavy, and that, as there is no possibility of the British and French increasing the number of their divisions (on the contrary, they are put to extreme straits to keep them up) there is a great danger of the war being lost unless the numerical inferiority of the Allies can be remedied as rapidly as possible by the advent of American troops. He, therefore, urges with the utmost insistence that the maximum possible number of infantry and machine gunners, in which respect the shortage of men on the side of the Allies is most marked, should continue to be shipped from America in the months of June and July to avert the immediate danger of an Allied defeat in the present campaign owing to the Allied reserves being exhausted before those of the enemy. In addition to this, and looking to the future, he represents that it is impossible to foresee ultimate victory in the war unless America is able to provide such an Army as will enable the Allies ultimately to establish numerical superiority. He places the total American force required for this at no less than 100 divisions, and urges the continuous raising of fresh American levies, which, in his opinion, should not be less than 300,000 a month, with a view to establishing a total American force of 100 divisions at as early a date as this can possibly be done.

We are satisfied that Gen. Foch, who is conducting the present campaign with consummate ability, and on whose military judgment we continue to place the most absolute reliance, is not overestimating the needs of the case, and we feel confident that the Government of the United States will do everything that can be done, both to meet the needs of the immediate situation and to proceed with the continuous raising of fresh levies, calculated to provide, as soon as possible, the numerical superiority which the Commander-in-Chief of the Allied Armies regards as essential to ultimate victory.

A separate telegram contains the arrangements which Gen. Foch, Gen. Pershing, and Lord Milner have agreed to recommend to the United States Government with regard to the dispatch of American troops for the months of June and July.

CLEMENCEAU,
D. LLOYD GEORGE,
ORLANDO.

Such extensive priority had already been given to the transport of American infantry and machine gunners that the troops of those categories which had received even partial training in the United States were practically exhausted. Moreover, the strain on our Services of Supply made it essential that early relief be afforded by increasing its personnel. At the same time, the corresponding services of our Allies had in certain departments been equally over-taxed and their responsible heads were urgent in their representations that their needs must be relieved by bringing over American specialists. The final agreement was cable to the War Department on June 5, as follows:

The following agreement has been concluded between Gen Foch, Lord Milner, and myself with references to the transportation of American troops in the months of June and July:

The following recommendations are made on the assumption that at least 250,000 men can be transported in each of the months of June and July by the employment of combined British and American tonnage. We recommend:

(a) For the month of June: (1) Absolute priority shall be given to the transportation of 170,000 combatant troops (viz, six divisions without artillery, ammunition trains, or supply trains, amounting to 126,000 men and 44,000 replacements for combat troops): (2) 25,400 men for the service of the railways, of which 13,400 have been asked for by the French Minister of Transportation; (3) the balance to be troops of categories to be determined by the Commander-in-Chief, American Expeditionary Forces.

(b) For the month of July: (1) Absolute priority for the shipment of 140,000 combatant troops of the nature defined above (four divisions minus artillery et cetera amounting to 84,000 men, plus 56,000 replacement); (2) the balance of the 250,000 to consist of troops to be disignated by the Commander-in-Chief, American Expeditionary Forces.

(c) It is agreed that if the available tonnage in either month allows of the transportation of a larger number of men than 250,000, the excess tonnage will be employed in the transportation of combat troops as defined above.

(d) We recognize that the combatant troops to be dispatched in July may have to include troops which have had insufficient training, but we consider the present emergency is such as to justify a temporary and exceptional departure by the United States from sound principles of training, especially as a similar course is being followed by France and Great Britain.

FOCH.
MILNER.
PERSHING.

9. The various proposals during these conferences regarding priority of shipment, often very insistent, raised questions that were not only most difficult but most delicate. On the other hand, there was a critical situation which must be met by immediate action, while, on the other hand, any priority accorded a particular arm necessarily postponed the formation of a distinctive American fighting force and the means to supply it. Such a force was, in my opinion, absolutely necessary to win the war. A few of the Allied representatives became convinced that the American Services of Supply should not be neglected but should be developed in the common interest. The success of our divisions during May and June demonstrated fully that it was not necessary to draft Americans under foreign flags in order to utilize American manhood most effectively.

ALLIED COMMANDER-IN-CHIEF

10. When, on March 21, 1918, the German Army on the western front began its series of offensives, it was by far the most formidable force the world had ever seen. In fighting men and guns it had a great superiority, but this was of less importance than advantage in morale, in experience, in training for mobile warfare, and in unity of command. Ever since the collapse of the Russian Armies and the crisis on the Italian front in the fall of 1917, German Armies were being assembled and trained for the great campaign which was to end the war before America's effort could be brought to bear. Germany's best troops, her most successful generals, and all the experience gained in three years of war were mobilized for the supreme effort.

The first blow fell on the right of the British Armies, including the junction of the British and French forces. Only the prompt cooperation of the French and British general headquarters stemmed the tide. The reason for this objective was obvious and strikingly illustrated the necessity for having someone with sufficient authority over all the Allied Armies to meet such an emergency. The lack of complete cooperation among the Allies on the western front had been appreciated and the question of preparation to meet a crisis had already received attention by the Supreme War Council. A plan had been adopted by which each of the Allies would furnish a certain number of divisions for a general reserve to be under the direction of the military representatives of the Supreme War Council of which Gen. Foch was then the senior member. But when the time came to meet the German offensive in March these reserves were not found available and the plan failed.

This situation resulted in a conference for the immediate consideration of the question of having an Allied Commander-in-Chief. After much discussion during which my view favoring such action was clearly stated, an agreement was reached and Gen. Foch was selected. His appointment as such was made April 3 and was approved for the United States by the President on April 16. The terms of the agreement under which Gen. Foch exercised his authority were as follows:

BEAUVAIS, April 3, 1918.

Gen. Foch is charged by the British, French, and American Governments with the coordination of the action of the Allied Armies on the western front; to this end there is conferred on him all the powers necessary for its effective realization. To the same end, the British, French, and American Governments confide in Gen. Foch the strategic direction of military operations.

The Commander-in-Chief of the British, French, and American Armies will exercise to the fullest extent the tactical direction of their armies. Each Commander-in-Chief will have the right to appeal to his Government if in his opinion his Army is placed in danger by the instructions received from Gen. Foch.

G. CLEMENCEAU
PETAIN
F. FOCH
LLOYD GEORGE
D. HAIG, F. M.
HENRY WILSON,
 General.
TASKER H. BLISS,
General and Chief of Staff.
JOHN J. PERSHING,
General, U. S. A.

EMPLOYMENT OF AMERICAN DIVISIONS FROM MARCH TO SEPTEMBER, 1918

11. The grave crisis precipitated by the first German offensive caused me to make a hurried visit to Gen. Foch's headquarters at BOMBON, during which all our combatant forces were placed at his disposal. The acceptance of this offer meant the dispersion of our troops along the Allied front and a consequent delay in building up a distinctive American force in LORRAINE, but the serious situation of the Allies demanded this divergence from our plans.

On March 21, approximately 300,000 American troops had reached France. Four combat divisions, equivalent in strength to eight French or British divisions, were available--- the 1st and 2d then in line, and the 26th and 42d just withdrawn from line after one month's trench warfare training. The last two divisions at once began taking over quiet sectors to release divisions for the battle; the 26th relieved the 1st Division, which was sent to northwest of PARIS in reserve; the 42d relieved two French divisions from quiet sectors. In addition to these troops, one regiment of the 93d Division was with the French in the ARGONNE, the 41st Depot Division was in the Services of Supply, and three divisions (3d, 32d, and 5th) were arriving.

12. On April 25 the 1st Division relieved two French divisions on the front near MONTDIDIER and on May 28 captured the important observation stations on the heights of CANTIGNY with splendid dash. French artillery, aviation, tanks, and flame throwers aided in the attack, but most of this French assistance was withdrawn before the completion of the operation in order to meet the enemy's new offensive launched May 27 toward CHATEAU-THIERRY. The enemy reaction against our troops at Cantigny was extremely violent, and apparently he was determined at all costs to counteract the most excellent effect the American success had produced. For three days his guns of all calibers were concentrated on our new position and counterattack succeeded counterattack. The desperate efforts of the Germans gave the fighting at Cantigny a seeming tactical importance entirely out of porportion to the numbers involved.

13. Of the three divisions arriving in France when the first German offensive began, the 32d, intended for replacements, had been temporarily employed in the Services of Supply to meet a shortage of personnel, but the critical situation caused it to be re-assembled and by May 21 it was entering the line in the Vosges. At this time the 5th Division, though still incomplete, was also ordered into the line in the same region. The 3d Division was assembling in its training area and the III Corps staff had just been organized to administer these three divisions. In addition to the eight divisions already mentioned, the 28th and 77th had arrived in the British area, and the 4th, 27th, 30th, 33d, 35th, and 82d were arriving there. Following the agreements as to British shipping, our troops came so rapidly that by the end of May we had a force of 600,000 in France.

The third German offensive on May 27, against the French on the Aisne, soon developed a desperate situation for the Allies. The 2d Division, then in reserve northwest of Paris and preparing to relieve the 1st Division, was hastily diverted to the vicinity of Meaux on May 31, and, early on the morning of June 1, was deployed across the Chateau-Thierry---Paris road near Montreuil-aux-Lions in a gap in the French line, where it stopped the German advance on Paris. At the same time the partially trained 3d Division was placed at French disposal to hold the crossings of the Marne, and its motorized machine-gun battalion succeeded in reaching Chateau-Thierry in time to assist in successfully defending that river crossing.

The enemy having been halted, the 2d Division commenced a series of vigorous attacks on June 4, which resulted in the capture of Belleau Woods after very severe fighting. The village of Bouresches was taken soon after, and on July 1 Vaux was captured. In these operations the 2d Division met with most desperate resistance by Germany's best troops.

14. To meet the March offensive, the French had extended their front from the Oise to Amiens, about 60 kilometers, and during the German drive along the Lys had also sent reinforcements to assist the British. The French lines had been further lengthened about 45 kilometers as a result of the Marne pocket made by the Aisne offensive. This increased frontage and the heavy fighting had reduced French reserves to an extremely low point.

Our II Corps, under Maj. Gen. George W. Read, had been organized for the command of the 10 divisions with the British, which were held back in training areas or assigned to second-line defenses. After consultation with Field Marshal Haig on June 3, 5 American divisions were relieved from the British area to support the French. The 77th and 82d Divisions were moved south to release the 42d and 26th for employment on a more active portion of the front; the 35th Division entered the line in the Vosges, and the 4th and 28th Divisions were moved to the region of Meaux and Chateau-Thierry as reserves.

On June 9 the Germans attacked the Montdidier-Noyon front in an effort to widen the Marne pocket and bring their lines nearer to Paris, but were stubbornly held by the French with comparatively little loss of ground. In veiw of the unexpected results of the three preceding attacks by the enemy, this successful defense proved beneficial to the Allied morale, particularly as it was believed that the German losses were unusually heavy.

15. On July 15, the date of the last German offensive, the 1st, 2d, 3d, and 26th Divisions were on the Chateau-Thierry front with the 4th and 28th in support, some small units of the last two divisions gaining front-line experience with our troops or with the French; the 42d Division was in support of the French east of Reims; and four colored regiments were with the French in the Argonne. On the Alsace-Lorraine front we had five divisions in line with the French. Five were with the British Army, three having elements in the line. In our training areas four divisions were assembled and four were in the process of arrival.

The Marne Salient was inherently weak and offered an opportunity for a counteroffensive that was obvious. If successful, such an operation would afford immediate relief to the Allied defense, would remove the threat against Paris, and free the Paris-Nancy Railroad. But, more important than all else, it would restore the morale of the Allies and remove the profound depression and fear then existing. Up to this time our units had been put in here and there at critical points as emergency troops to stop the terrific German advance. In every trail, whether on the defensive or offensive, they had proved themselves equal to any troops in Europe. As early as June 23 and again on July 10 at Bombon, I had very strongly urged that our best divisions be concentrated under American command, if possible, for use as a striking force against the Marne Salient. Although the prevailing view among the Allies was that American units were suitable only for the defensive, and that at all events they could be used to better advantage under Allied command, the suggestion was accepted in principle, and my estimate of their offensive fighting qualities was soon put to the test.

The enemy had encouraged his soldiers to believe that the July 15 attack would conclude the war with a German peace. Although he made elaborate plans for the operation, he failed to conceal fully his intentions, and the front of attack was suspected at least one week ahead. On the Champagne front the actual hour for the assualt was known and the enemy was checked with heavy losses. The 42d Division entered the line near Somme-Py immediately,

and five of its infantry battalions and all its artillery became engaged. Southwest of
Reims and along the Marne to the east of Chateau-Thierry the Germans were at first somewhat successful, a penetration of 8 kilometers beyond the river being effected against the
French immediately to the right of our 3d Division. The following quotation from the report
of the commanding general 3d Division gives the result of the fighting on his front:

> Although the rush of the German troops overwhelmed some of the front-line
> positions, causing the infantry and machine-gun companies to suffer, in some
> cases a 50 per cent loss, no German soldier crossed the road from Fossoy to
> Crezancy, except as a prisoner of war, and by noon of the following day
> (July 16) there were no Germans in the foreground of the 3d Division sector
> except the dead.

On this occasion a single regiment of the 3d Division wrote one of the most brilliant
pages in our military annals. It prevented the crossing at certain points on its front,
while on either flank the Germans who had gained a footing pressed forward. Our men,
firing in three directions, met the German attacks with counterattacks at critical points
and succeeded in throwing two German divisions into complete confusion, capturing 600
prisoners.

16. The Selection by the Germans of the Champagne sector and the eastern and southern
faces of the Marne pocket on which to make their offensive was fortunate for the Allies,
as it favored the launching of the counterattack already planned. There were now over
1,200,000 American troops in France, which provided a considerable force of reserves.
Every American division with any sort of training was made available for use in a counteroffensive.

Gen. Petain's initial plan for the counterattack involved the entire western face of
Marne salient. The American 1st and 2d Divisions, with the French Moroccan 1st Division
between them, were employed as the spearhead of the main attack, driving directly eastward, through the most sensitive portion of the German lines, to the heights south of
Soissons. The advance began on July 18, without the usual brief warning of a preliminary
bombardment, and these three divisions at a single bound broke through the enemy's infantry defenses and overran his artillery, cutting or interrupting the German communications
leading into the salient. A general withdrawal from the Marne was immediately begun by
the enemy, who still fought stubbornly to prevent disaster.

The 1st Division, throughout 4 days of constant fighting, advanced 11 kilometers,
capturing Berzy-le-Sec and the heights above Soissons and taking some 3,500 prisoners
and 68 field guns from the 7 German divisions employed against it. It was relieved by a
British division. The 2d Division advanced 8 kilometers in the first 26 hours, and by
the end of the second day was facing Tigny, having captured 3,000 prisoners and 66 field
guns. It was relieved the night of the 19th by a French division. The result of this
counteroffensive was of decisive importance. Due to the magnificent dash and power displayed on the field of Soissons by our 1st and 2d Divisions the tide of war was definitely
turned in favor of the Allies.

Other American divisions participated in the Marne counteroffensive. A little to
the south of the 2d Division, the 4th was in line with the French and was engaged until
July 22. The American I Corps, Maj. Gen. Hunter Liggett commanding, with the 26th Division
and a French division, acted as a pivot of the movement toward Soissons, capturing Torcy
on the 18th and reaching the Chateau-Thierry---Soissons Road on the 21st. At the same time
the 3d Division crossed the Marne and took the heights of Mont-St-Pere and the villages
of Charteves and Jaulgonne.

In the I Corps, the 42d Division relieved the 26th on July 25 and extended its front
on the 26th, relieving the French division. From this time until August 2 it fought its
way through the Forest de Fere and across the Ourcq, advancing toward the Vesle until relieved by the 4th Division on August 3. Early in this period elements of the 28th Division
participated in the advance.

Farther to the east the 3d Division forced the enemy back to Poncheres Wood, where it was relieved on July 30 by the 32d Division from the Vosges front. The 32d, after relieving the 3d and some elements of the 28th on the line of the Ourcq River, advanced abreast of the 42d toward the Vesle. On August 3 it passed under control of our III Corps, Maj. Gen. Robert L. Bullard commanding, which made its first appearance in battle at this time, while the 4th Division took up the task of the 42d Division and advanced with the 32d to the Vesle River, where, on August 6, the operation for the reduction of the Marne Salient terminated.

In the hard fighting from July 18 to August 6 the Germans were not only halted in their advance but were driven back from the Marne to the Vesle and committed wholly to the defensive. The force of American arms had been brought to bear in time to enable the last offensive of the enemy to be crushed.

17. The I and III Corps now held a continuous front 11 kilometers along the Vesle. On August 12 the 77th Division relieved the 4th Division on the I Corps front, and the following day the 28th relieved the 32d Division in the III Corps, while from August 6 to August 19 the 6th Infantry Brigade of the 3d Division held a sector on the river line. The transfer of the I Corps to the Woëvre was ordered at this time, and the control of its front was turned over to the III Corps.

On August 18, Gen. Pétain began an offensive between Reims and the Oise. Our III Corps participated in this operation, crossing the Vesle on September 4 with the 28th and 77th Divisions and overcoming stubborn opposition on the plateau south of the Aisne, which was reached by the 77th on September 6. The 28th was withdrawn from the line on September 7. Two days later the III Corps was transferred to the region of Verdun, the 77th Division remaining in line on the Aisne River until September 17.

The 32d Division, upon its relief from the battle on the Vesle, joined a French Corps north of Soissons and attacked from August 29 to 31, capturing Juvigny after some particularly desperate fighting and reaching the Chauny-Soissons Road.

18. On the British front, two regiments of the 33d Division participated in an attack on Hamel July 4, and again on August 9 as an incident of the Allied offensive against the Amiens Salient. One of these regiments took Gressaire Wood and Chipilly Ridge, capturing 700 prisoners and considerable matériel.

ASSEMBLING THE FIRST AMERICAN ARMY

19. In conference with Gen. Pétain at Chantilly on May 19 it had been agreed that the American Army would soon take complete charge of the sector of the Woëvre. The 26th Division was already in line in the Woëvre north of Toul and was to be followed by other American divisions as they became available, with the understanding that the sector was to pass to our control when four divisions were in the line. But demands of the battle then going on farther west required the presence of our troops, and the agreement had no immediate result. Due to the presence of a number of our divisions northeast of Paris, the organization of an American corps sector in the Château-Thierry region was taken up with Gen. Pétain, and on July 4 the I Corps assumed tactical control of a sector in that region. This was an important step, but it was by no means satisfactory, as only one American division at the moment was operating under the control of the I Corps, while we had at this time eight American divisions in the front line serving in French corps.

20. The counteroffensives against the Marne Salient in July and against the Amiens Salient in August had gained such an advantage that it was apparent that the emergency, which justified the dispersion of our divisions, had passed. The moment was propitious for assembling our divisions. Scattered as they were along the Allied front, their supply had become very difficult. From every point of view the immediate organization of an idependent American force was indicated. The formation of the Army in the Château-Thierry Region and its early transfer to the sector of the Woëvre, which was to extend from Nomeny, east of the Moselle, to north of St-Mihiel, was therefore decided upon by Marshal Foch

and myself on August 9, and the details were arranged with Gen. Pétain later on the same day.

ST-MIHIEL OPERATION

21. At Bombon on July 24 there was a conference of all the Commanders-in-Chief for the purpose of considering Allied operations. Each presented proposals for the employment of the armies under his command and these formed the basis of future cooperation of the Allies. It was emphatically determined that the Allied attitude should be to maintain the offensive. As the first operation of the American Army, the reduction of the salient of St-Mihiel was to be undertaken as soon as the necessary troops.and material could be made available. On account of the swampy nature of the country it was especially important that the movement be undertaken and finished before the fall rains should begin, which was usually about the middle of September.

Arrangements were concluded for successive belief of American divisions and the organization of the American First Army under my personal command was announced on August 10, with La Ferte-sous-Jouarre as headquarters. This Army nominally assumed control of a portion of the Vesle front, although at the same time directions were given for its secret concentration in the St-Mihiel Sector.

22. The force of American soldiers in France at that moment was sufficient to carry out this offensive, but they were dispersed along the front from Switzerland to the Channel. The three Army Corps headquarters to participate in the St-Mihiel attack were the I, IV, and V. The I was on the Vesle, the IV at Toul, and the V not yet completely organized. To assemble combat divisions and service troops and undertake a major operation, within the short period available and with staffs so recently organized, was an extremely difficult task. Our deficiencies in artillery, aviation, and special troops, caused by the shipment of an undue proportion of infantry and machine guns during the summer, were largely met by the French.

23. The reduction of the St-Mihiel salient was important, as it would prevent the enemy from interrupting traffic on the Paris-Nancy Railroad by artillery fire and would free the railroad leading north through St-Mihiel to Verdun. It would also provide us with an advantageous base of departure for an attack against the Metz-Sedan railroad system which was vital to the German armies west of Verdun, and against the Briey Iron Basin which was necessary for the production of German armament and munitions.

The general plan was to make simultaneous attacks against the flanks of the salient. The ultimate objective was tentatively fixed as the general line Marieulles (east of the Moselle)---heights south of Gorze---Mars-la-Tour---Etain. The operation contemplated the use on the western face of 3 or 4 American divisions, supported by the attack of 6 divisions of the French Second Army on their left, while 7 American divisions would attack on the southern face, and 3 French divisions would press the enemy at the tip of the salient. As the part to be taken by the French Second Army would be closely related to the attack of the American First Army, Gen. Pétain placed all the French troops involved under my personal command.

By August 30, the concentration of the scattered divisions, corps, and army troops, of the quantities of supplies and munitions required, and the necessary construction of light railways and roads, were well under way.

24. In accordance with the previous general consideration of operations at Bombon on July 24, an allied offensive extending practically along the entire active front was eventually to be carried out. After the reduction of the St-Mihiel sector the Americans were to cooperate in the concerted effort of the Allied armies. It was the sense of the conference of July 24, that the extent to which the different operations already planned might carry us could not be then foreseen, especially if the results expected were achieved before the season was far advanced. It seemed reasonable at that time to look forward to a combined offensive for the autumn, which would give no respite to the enemy and

would increase our advantage for the inauguration of succeeding operations extending into 1919.

On August 30, a further discussion with Marshal Foch was held at my headqusrter at Ligny-en-Barrois. In view of the new successes of the French and British near Amiens and the continued favorable results toward the Chemin-des-Dames on the French front, it was now believed that the limited allied offensive, which was to prepare for the campaign of 1919, might be carried further before the end of the year. At this meeting it was proposed by Marshal Foch that the general operations as far as the American Army was concerned should be carried out in detail by:

(a) An attack between the Meuseaand the Argonne by the French Second Army, reinforced by from four to six American divisions.

(b) A French-American attack, extending from the Argonne west to the Souain Road, to be executed on the right by an American Army astride the Aisne and on the left by the French Fourth Army.

To carry out these attacks the 10 to 11 American divisions suggested for the St-Mihiel operation and the 4 to 6 for the French Second Army, would leave 8 to 10 divisions for an American Army on the Aisne. It was proposed that the St-Mihiel operation should be initiated on September 10 and the other two on September 15 and 20, respectively.

25. The plan suggested for the American participation in these operations was not acceptable to me because it would require the immediate separation of the recently formed American First Army into several groups, mainly to assist French armies. This was directly contrary to the principle of forming a distinct American Army, for which my contention had been insistent. An enormous amount of preparation had already been made inconstruction of roads, railroads, regulating stations, and other installations looking to the use and supply of our Armies on a particular front. The inherent disinclination of our troops to serve under Allied commanders would have grown and American morale would have suffered. My position was stated quite clearly that the strategical employment of the First Army as a unit would be undertaken where desired, but its disruption to carry out these proposals would not be entertained.

A further conference at Marshal Foch's Headquarters was held on September 2, at which Gen. Pétain was present. After discussion the question of employing the American Army as a unit was conceded. The essentials of the strategical decision previously arrived at provided that the advantageous situation of the Allies should be exploited to the utmost by vigorously continuing the general battle and extending it eastward to the Meuse. All the Allied Armies were to be employed in a converging action. The British Armies, supported by the left of the French Armies, were to pursue the attack in the direction of Cambrai; the center of the French Armies, west of Reims, would continue the actions, already begun, to drive the enemy beyond the Aisne; and the American Army, supported by the right of the French Armies, would direct its attack on Sedan and Méziéres.

It should be recorded that although this general offensive was fully outlined at the conference no one present expressed the opinion that the final victory could be won in 1918. In fact, it was believed by the French High Command that the Meuse-Argonne attack could not be pushed much beyond Montfaucon before the arrival of winter would force a cessation of operations.

26. The choice between the two sectors, that east of the Aisne including the Argonne Forest, or the Champagne sector, was left to me. In my opinion, no other Allied troops had the morale or the offensive spirit to overcome successfully the difficulties to be metin the Meuse-Argonne sector and our plans and installations had been prepared for an expansion of operations in that direction. So the Meuse-Argonne front was chosen. The entire sector of 150 kilometers of front, extending from Port-sur-Seille, east of the Moselle, west to include the Argonne Forest, was accordingly placed under my command, including all French divisions then in that zone. The American First Army was to proceed with the St-Mihiel operation, after which the operation between the Meuse and the western edge of the Argonne Forest was to be prepared and launched not later then September 25.

As a result of these decisions, the depth of the St-Mihiel operation was limited to the line Vigneulles---Thiaucourt---Régnieville. The number of divisions to be used was reduced and the time shortened. 18 to 19 divisions were to be in the front line. There were 4 French and 15 American divisions available, 6 of which would be in reserve, while the two flank divisions of the front line were not to advance. Furthermore, two army corps headquarters, with their corps troops, practically all the Army artillery and aviation, and the 1st, 2d, and 4th Divisions, the first two destined to take a leading part in the St-Mihiel attack, were all due to be withdrawn and started for the Meuse-Argonne by the fourth day of the battle.

27. The salient had been held by the Germans since September, 1914. It covered the most sensitive section of the enemy's position on the western front; namely, the Méziéres ---Sedan---Metz Railroad and the Briey Iron Basin; it threatened the entire region between Verdun and Nancy, and interrupted the main rail line from Paris to the east. Its primary strength lay in the natural defensive features of the terrain itself. The western face of the salient extended along the rugged, heavily wooded eastern heights of the Meuse; the southern face followed the heights of the Meuse for 8 kilometers to the east and then crossed the plain of the Woëvre, including within the German lines the detached heights of Loupmont and Montsec which dominated the plain and afforded the enemy unusual facilities for observation. The enemy had reinforced the positions by every artificial means during a period of four years.

28. On the night of September 11, the troops of the First Army were deployed in position. On the southern face of the salient was the I Corps, Maj. Gen. Liggett commanding, with the 82d, 90th, 5th, and 2d Divisions in line, extending from the Moselle westward. On its left was the IV Corps, Maj. Gen. Joseph T. Dickman commanding, with the 89th, 42d, and 1st Divisions, the left of this corps being opposite Montsec. These two army corps were to deliver the principal attack, the line pivoting on the center division of the I Corps. The 1st Division on the left of the IV Corps was charged with the double mission of covering its own flank while advancing some 20 kilometers due north toward the heart of the salient, where it was to make contact with the troops of the V Corps. On the western face of the salient lay the V Corps, Maj. Gen. George H. Cameron commanding, with the 26th Division, French 15th Colonial Division, and the 4th Division in line, from Mouilly west to Les Éparges and north to Watronville. Of these three divisions, the 26th alone was to make a deep advance directed southeast toward vigneulles. The French division was to make a short progression to the edge of the heights in order to cover the left of the 26th. The 4th Division was not to advance. In the center, between our IV and V Army Corps, was the French II Colonial Corps, Maj. Gen. E. J. Blondlat commanding, covering a front of 40 kilometers with 3 small French divisions. These troops were to follow up the retirement of the enemy from the tip of the salient.

The French independent air force was at my disposal which, together with the British bombing squadrons and our own air forces, gave us the largest assembly of aviation that had ever been engaged in one operation. Our heavy guns were able to reach Metz and to interfere seriously with German rail movements.

At dawn on September 12, after four hours of violent artillery fire of preparation, and accompanied by small tanks, the infantry of the I and IV Corps advanced. The infantry of the V Corps commenced its advance at 8 a. m. The operation was carried out with entire precision. Just after daylight on September 13, elements of the 1st and 26th Divisions made a junction near Hattonchâtel and Vigneulles, 18 kilometers northeast of St-Mihiel. The rapidity with which our divisions advanced overwhelmed the enemy and all objectives were reached by the afternoon of September 13. The enemy had apparently started to withdraw some of his troops from the tip of the salient on the eve of our attack, but had been unable to carry it through. We captured nearly 16,000 prisoners, 443 guns, and large stores of material and supplies. The energy and swiftness with which the operation was carried out enabled us to smother opposition to such an extent that we suffered less than 7,000 casualties during the actual period of the advance.

During the next two days the right of our line west of the Moselle River was advanced beyond the objectives laid down in the original orders. This completed the operation for the time being and the line was stablized to be held by the smallest practicable force.

29. The material results of the victory achieved were very important. An American Army was an accomplished fact, and the enemy had felt its power. No form of propaganda could overcome the depressing effect on the morale of the enemy of this demonstration of our ability to organize a large American force and drive it successfully through his defenses. It gave our troops implicit confidence in their superiority and raised their morale to the highest pitch. For the first time wire entanglements ceased to be regarded as impassable barriers and open-warfare training, which had been so urgently insisted upon, proved to be the correct doctrine. Our divisions concluded the attack with such small losses and in such high spirits that without the usual rest they were immediately available for employment in heavy fighting in a new theater of operations. The strength of the First Army in this battle totaled approximately 500,000 men, of whom about 70,000 were French.

MEUSE-ARGONNE OPERATION

30. The definite decision for the Meuse-Argonne phase of the great allied convergent attack was agreed to in my conference with Marshal Foch and Gen. Pétain on September 2. It was planned to use all available forces of the First Army, including such divisions and troops as we might be able to withdraw from the St-Mihiel front. The Army was to break through the enemy's successive fortified zones to include the Kriemhilde-Stellung, or Hindenburg Line, on the front Brieulles---Romagne-sous-Montfaucon---Grandpré, and thereafter, by developing pressure toward Méziéres, was to insure the fall of the Hindenburg Line along the Aisne River in front of the French Fourth Army, which was to attack to the west of the Argonne Forest. A penetration of some 12 to 15 kilometers was required to reach the Hindenburg Line on our front, and the enemy's defenses were virtually continuous throughout that depth.

The Meuse-Argonne front had been practically stabilized in September, 1914, and, except for minor fluctuations during the German attacks on Verdun in 1916 and the French counteroffensive in August, 1917, remained unchanged until the American advance in 1918. The net result of the four years' struggle on this ground was a German defensive system of unusual depth and strength and a wide zone of utter devastation, itself a serious obstacle to offensive operations.

31. The strategical importance of this portion of the line was second to none on the western front. All supplies and evacuations of the German armies in northern France were dependent upon two great railway systems---one in the north, passing through Liege, while the other in the south, with lines coming from Luxemburg, Thionville, and Metz, had as its vital section the line Carignan---Sedan---Mezieres. No other important lines were available to the enemy, as the mountainous masses of the Ardennes made the construction of east and west lines through that region impracticable. The Carignan--Sedan--- Méziéres line was essential to the Germans for the rapid strategical movement of troops. Should this southern system be cut by the Allies before the enemy could withdraw his forces through the narrow neck between Méziéres and the Dutch frontier, the ruin of his armies in France and Belgium would be complete.

From the Meuse-Argonne front the perpendicular distance to the Carignan---Méziéres Railroad was 50 kilometers. This region formed the pivot of German operations in northern France, and the vital necessity of covering the great railroad line into Sedan resulted in the convergence on the Meuse-Argonne front of the successive German defensive positions. The effect of this convergence can be best understood by reference to Plate No. 3. It will be seen, for example, that the distance between "No Man's Land" and the third German withdrawal position in the vicinity of the Meuse River was approximately 18 kilometers; the distance between the corresponding points near the tip of the great salient of the western front was about 65 kilometers, and in the vicinity of Cambrai was over 30 kilometers. The effect of penetration of 18 kilometers by the American Army would be equivalent to an advance of 65 kilometers farther west; furthermore, such an advance on our front was far more dangerous to the enemy than an advance elsewhere. The vital importance of this portion of this position was fully appreciated by the enemy, who had suffered tremendous losses in 1916 in attempting to improve it by the reduction of Verdun. As a consequence it had been elaborately fortified, and consisted of practically a continous series of positions 20 kilometers or more in depth.

In addition to the artifical defenses, the enemy was greatly aided by the natural features of the terrain. East of the Meuse the dominating heights not only protected his left but gave him positions from which powerful arillery could deliver an oblique fire on the western bank. Batteries located in the elaborately fortified Argonne forest covered his right flank, and could cross their fire with that of the guns on the east bank of the Meuse. Midway between the Meuse and the forest, the heights of Montfaucon offered perfect observation and formed a strong natural position which had been heavily fortified. The east and west ridges abutting on the Meuse and Aire River valleys afforded the enemy excellent machine-gun positions for the desperate defense which the importance of the position would require him to make. North of Montfaucon densely wooded and rugged heights constituted natural features favorable to defensive fighting.

32. When the First Army became engaged in the simultaneous preparation for two major operations, and interval of 14 days separated the initiation of the two attacks. During this short period the movement of the immense number of troops and the amount of supplies involved in the Meuse-Argonne battle, over the few roads available, and confined entirely to the hours of darkness, was one of the most delicate and difficult problems of the war. The concentration included 15 divisions, of which 7 were involved in the pending St-Mihiel drive, 3 were in sector in the Vosges, 3 in the neighborhood of Soissons, 1 in a training area, and 1 near Bar-le-Duc. Practically all the artillery, aviation, and other auxiliaries to be employed in the new operations were committed to the St-Mihiel attack and therefore could not be moved until its success was assured. The concentration of all units not to be used at St-Mihiel was commenced immediately, and on September 13, the second day of St-Mihiel, reserve divisions and army artillery units were withdrawn and placed in motion toward the Argonne front.

That part of the American sector from Fresnes-en-Woëvre, southeast of Verdun, to the western edge of the Argonne Forest, while nominally under my control, did not actively become a part of my command until September 22, on which date my headquarters were established at Souilly, southwest of Verdun. Of French troops, in addition to the French II Colonial Corps composed of 3 divisions, there was also the French XVII Corps of 3 divisions holding the front north and east of Verdun.

33. At the moment of the opening of the Meuse-Argonne battle, the enemy had 10 divisions in line and 10 in reserve on the front between Fresnes-en-Woëvre and the Argonne Forest, inclusive. He had undoubtedly expected a continuation of our advance toward Metz. Successful ruses were carried out between the Meuse River and Luneville to deceive him as to our intentions, and French troops were maintained as a screen along our front until the night before the battle, so that the actual attack was a tactical surprise.

34. The operations in the Meuse-Argonne battle really form a continuous whole, but they extended over such a long period of continuous fighting that they will here be considered in three phases, the first from September 26 to October 3, the second from October 4 to 31, and the third from November 1 to 11.

MEUSE-ARGONNE, FIRST PHASE

35. On the night of September 25, the 9 divisions to lead in the attack were deployed between the Meuse River and the western edge of the Argonne Forest. On the right was the III Corps, Maj. Gen. Bullard commanding, with the 33d, 80th, and 4th Divisions in line;

- 41 -

next came the V Corps, Maj. Gen. Cameron commanding, with the 79th, 37th, and 91st Divisions; on the left was the I Corps, Maj. Gen. Liggett commanding, with the 35th, 28th, and 77th Divisions. Each corps had 1 division in reserve and the Army held 3 divisions as a general reserve. About 2,700 guns, 189 small tanks, 142 manned by Americans, and 821 airplanes, 604 manned by Americans, were concentrated to support the attacks of the infantry. We thus has a superiority in guns and aviation, and the enemy had no tanks.

The axis of the attack was the line Montfaucon---Romagne---Buzancy, the purpose being to make the deepest penetration in the center, which with the French Fourth Army advancing west of the Argonne, would force the enemy to evacuate that forest without our having to deliver a heavy attack in that difficult region.

36. Following three hours of violent artillery fire of preparation, the infantry advanced at 5:30 a. m. on September 26, accompanied by tanks. During the first two days of the attack, before the enemy was able to bring up his reserves, our troops made steady progress through the network of defenses. Montfaucon was held tenaciously by the enemy and was not captured until noon of the second day.

By the evening of the 28th a maximum advance of 11 kilometers had been achieved and we had captured Baulny, Epinonville, Septsarges, and Dannevoux. The right had made a splendid advance into the woods south of Brieulles-sur-Meuse, but the extreme left was meeting strong resistance in the Argonne. The attack continued without interruption, meeting six new divisions which the enemy threw into first line before September 29. He developed a powerful machine-gun defense supported by heavy artillery fire, and made frequent counterattacks with fresh troops, particularly on the front of the 28th and 35th Divisions. These divisions had taken Varennes, Cheppy, Baulny, snd Charpentry, and the line was within 2 kilometers of Apremont. We were no longer engaged in a maneuver for the pinching out of a salient, but were necessarily committed, generally speaking, to a direct frontal attack against strong, hostile positions fully manned by a determined enemy.

37. By nightfall of the 29th the First Army line was approximately Bois de la Cote Lemont---Nantillois---Apremont---southwest across the Argonne. Many divisions, especially those in the center that were subjected to cross-fire of artillery, had suffered heavily. The severe fighting, the nature of the terrain over which they attacked, and the fog and darkness sorely tried even our best divisions. On the night of the 29th the 37th and 79th Divisions were relieved by the 32d and 3d Divisions, respectively, and on the following night the 1st Division relieved the 35th.

38. The critical problem during the first few days of the battle was the restoration of communications over "No Man's Land." There were but four roads available across this deep zone, and the violent artillery fire of the previous period of the war had virtually destroyed them. The spongy soil and the lack of material increased the difficulty. But the splendid work of our engineers and pioneers soon made possible the movement of the troops, artillery, and supplies most needed. By the afternoon of the 27th all the divisional artillery, except a few batteries of heavy guns, had effected a passage and was supporting the infantry action.

MEUSE-ARGONNE, SECOND PHASE

39. At 5:30 a. m. on October 4 the general attack was renewed. The enemy divisions on the front from Fresnes-en-Woëvre to the Argonne had increased from 10 in the first line to 16, and included some of his best divisions. The fighting was desperate, and only small advances were realized, except by the 1st Division on the right of the I Corps. By evening of October 5 the line was approximately Bois de la Cote Lemont---Bois du Fays ---Gesnes---Hill 240---Fléville---Chehery---southwest through the Argonne.

It was especially desirable to drive the enemy from his commanding positions on the heights east of the Meuse, but it was even more important that we should force him to use his troops there and weaken his tenacious hold on positions in our immediate front. The further stabilization of the new St-Mihiel line permitted the withdrawal of certain divisions for the extension of the Meuse-Argonne operation to the east bank of the Meuse River.

40. On the 7th the I Corps, with the 82d Division added, launched a strong attack northwest toward Cornay to draw attention from the movement east of the Meuse and at the same time outflank the German position in the Argonne. The following day the French XVII Corps, Maj. Gen. Claudel commanding, initiated its attack east of the Meuse against the exact point on which the German Armies must pivot in order to withdraw from northern France. The troops encountered elaborate fortifications and stubborn resistance, but by nightfall had realized an advance of 6 kilometers to a line well within the Bois de Consenvoye, and including the villages of Beaumont and Haumont. Continous fighting was maintained along our entire battle front, with especial success on the extreme left, where the capture of the greater part of the Argonne Forest was completed. The enemy contested every foot of ground on our front in order to make more rapid retirements farther west and withdraw his forces from northern France before the interruption of his railroad communications through Sedan.

41. We were confronted at this time by an insufficiency of replacements to build up exhausted divisions. Early in October, combat units required some 90,000 replacements, a and not more than 45,000 would be available before November 1 to fill the existing and prospective vacancies. We still had two divisions with the British and two with the French. A review of the situation, American and Allied, especially as to our own resources in men for the next two months, convinced me that the attack of the First Army and of the Allied Armies further west should be pushed to the limit. But if the First Army was to continue its aggressive tactics our divisions then with the French must be recalled, and replacements must be obtained by breaking up newly arrived divisions.

In discussing the withdrawal of our divisions from the French with Marshal Foch and Gen. Pétain, on October 10, the former expressed his appreciation of the fact that the First Army was striking the pivot of the German withdrawal, and also held the view that the Allied attack should continue. Gen. Petain agreed that the American divisions with the French were essential to us if we were to maintain our battle against the German pivot. The French were, however, straining every nerve to keep up their attacks and, before those divisions with the French had been released, it became necessary for us to send the 37th and 91st Divisions from the First Army to assist the French Sixth Army in Flanders.

42. At this time the First Army was holding a front of more than 120 kilometers; its strength exceeded 1,000,000 men; it was engaged in the most desperated battle of our history, and the burden of command was too heavy for a single commander and staff. Therefore, on October 12, that portion of our front extending from Port-sur-Seille, east of the Moselle, to Fresnes-en-Woevre, southeast of Verdun, was transferred to the newly constituted Second Army with Lieut. Gen. Robert L. Bullard in command, under whom it began preparations for the extension of operations to the east in the direction of Briey and Metz. On October 16, the command of the First Army was transferred to Lieut. Gen. Hunter Liggett, and my advance headquarters was established at Ligny-en-Barrois, from which the command of the group of American Armies was exercised.

43. Local attacks of the First Army were continued in order particularly to adjust positions preparatory to a renewed general assualt. The 1st and 5th Divisions were relieved by the 42d and 80th Divisions, which were now fresh. An attack along the whole front was made on October 14. The resistance encountered was stubborn, but the stronghold on Cote Dame Marie was captured and the Hindenburg Line was broken. Cunel and Romagne-sous-Montfaucon were taken and the line advanced 2 kilometers north of Sommerance. A maximum advance of 17 kilometers had been made since September 26 and the enemy had been been forced to throw into the fight a total of 15 reserve divisions.

During the remainder of the month, important local operations were carried out, which involved desperate fighting. The I Corps, Maj. Gen. Dickman commanding advanced through Grandpre; the V Corps, Maj. Gen. Charles P. Summerall commanding, captured the Bois de Bantheville; the III Corps, Maj. Gen. John L. Hines commanding, completed the occupation of Cunel Heights; and the French XVII Corps drove the enemy from the main ridge south of La Grande Montagne. Particularly heavy fighting occurred east of the Meuse on October 18, and in the further penetration of the Kriemhilde-Stellung on October 23 the 26th Division entering the battle at this time relieved the French 18th Division.

44. Summarizing the material results which had been attained by the First Army by the end of October, we had met an increasing number of Germany's best divisions, rising from 20 in line and reserve on September 26, to 31 on October 31; the enemy's elaborately prepared positions, including the Hindenburg line, in our front had been broken; the almost impassable Argonne Forest was in our hands; an advance of 21 kilometers had been effected; 18,600 prisoners, 370 cannon, 1,000 machine guns, and a mass of material captured; and the great railway artery through Carignan to Sedan was now seriously threatened.

The demands of incessant battle which had been maintained day by day for more than a month had compelled our divisions to fight to the limit of their capacity. Combat troops were held in line and pushed to the attack until deemed incapable of further effort because of casualties or exhaustion; artillery once engaged was seldom withdrawn and many batteries fought until practically all the animals were casualties and the guns were towed out of line by motor trucks. The American soldier had shown unrivaled fortitude in this continuous fighting during most inclement weather and under many disadvantages of position. Through experience, the Army had developed into a powerful and smooth-running machine, and there was a supreme confidence in our ability to carry through the task successfully.

While the high pressure of these dogged attacks was a great strain on our troops, it was calamitous to the enemy. His divisions had been thrown into confusion by our furious assaults, and his morale had been reduced until his will to resist had well-nigh reached the breaking point. Once a German division was engaged in the fight, it became practially impossible to effect its relief. The enemy was forced to meet the constantly recurring crises by breaking up tactical organizations and sending hurried detachments to widely separated portions of the field.

Every member of the American Expeditionary Forces, from the front line to the base ports, was straining every nerve. Magnificient efforts were exerted by the entire Services of Supply to meet the enormous demands made on it. Obstacles which seemed insurmountable were overcome daily in expediting the movements of replacements, ammunition and supplies to the front, and of sick and wounded to the rear. It was this spirit of determination animating every American soldier that made it impossible for the enemy to maintain the struggle until 1919.

MEUSE-ARGONNE, THIRD PHASE

45. The detailed plans for the operations of the Allied Armies on the western front changed from time to time during the course of this great battle, but the mission of the American First Army to cut the great Carignan---Sedan---Mézières Railroad remained unchanged. Marshal Foch coordinated the operations along the entire front, continuing persistently and unceasingly the attacks by all Allied Armies; the Belgian Army, with a French Army and two American divisions, advancing eastward; the British Armies and two American divisions, with the French First Army on their right, toward the region north of Givet; the American First Army and French Fourth Army, toward Sedan and Mézières.

46. On the 21st my instructions were issued to the First Army to prepare thoroughly for a general attack on October 28, that would be decisive if possible. In order that the attack of the First Army and that of the French Fourth Army on its left should be simultaneous, our attack was delayed until November 1. The immediate purpose of the First Army was to take Buzancy and the heights of Barricourt, to turn the forest north of Grandpré, and to establish contact with the French Fourth Army near Boult-aux-Bois. The Army was directed to carry the heights of Barricourt by nightfall of the first day and then to exploit this success by advsncing its left to Boult-aux-Bois in preparation for the drive toward Sedan. By strenuous effort all available artillery had been moved well forward to the heights previously occupied by the enemy, from which it could fully cover and support the initial advance of the infantry.

On this occasion and for the first time the Army prepared for its attack under normal conditions. We held the front of attack and were not under the necessity of taking over a new front, with its manifold installations snd services. Our own personnel handled the communications, dumps, telegraph lines, and water service; our divisions were either on the line or close in rear; the French artillery, aviation, and technical troops which had previously made up our deficiencies had been largely replaced by our own organizations; and our army, corps, and divisional staffs were by actual experience second to none.

47. On the morning of November 1, three army corps were in line between the Meuse River and the Bois de Bourgogne. On the right the III Corps had the 5th and 90th Divisions; the V Corps occupied the center of the line, with the 89th and 2d Divisions, and was to be the wedge of the attack on the first day; and on the left the I Corps deployed the 88th, 77th and 78th Divisions.

Preceded by two hours of violent artillery preparation the infantry advanced closely followed by accompanying guns. The artillery acquitted itself magnificently, the barrages being so well coordinated and so dense that the enemy was overwhelmed and quickly submerged by the rapid onslaught of the infantry. By nightfall the V Corps, in the center, had realized an advance of almost 9 kilometers, to the Bois de la Folie, and had completed the capture of the heights of Barricourt, while the III Corps, on the right, had captured Aincreville and Andevanne. Our troops had broken through the enemy's last defense, captured his artillery positions, and had precipitated a retreat of the German forces about to be isolated in the forest north of Grandpré. On the 2d and 3d we advanced rapidly against heavy fighting on the fronts of the right and center corps; to the left the troops of the I Corps hurried forward in pursuit, some by motor trucks, while the artillery pressed along the country roads close behind. Our heavy artillery was skillfully brought into position to fire upon the Carignan-Sedan Railroad and the junctions at Longuyon and Conflans. By the evening of the 4th, our troops had reached La Neuville, opposite Stenay, and had swept through the great Forêt de Dieulet, reaching the outskirts of Beaumont, while on the left we were 8 kilometers north of Boult-aux-Bois.

The following day the advance continued toward Sedan with increasing swiftness. The III Corps, turning eastward, crossed the Meuse in a brilliant operation by the 5th Division, driving the enemy from the heights of Dun-sur-Meuse and forcing a general withdrawal from the strong positions he had so long held on the hills north of Verdun.

By the 7th the right of the III Corps had exploited its river crossing to a distance of 10 kilometers east of the Meuse, completely ejecting the enemy from the wooded heights and driving him out into the swamp plain of the Woëvre; the V and I Corps had reached the line of the Meuse River along their respective fronts and the left of the latter corps held the heights dominating Sedan, the strategical goal of the Meuse-Argonne operation, 41 kilometers from our point of departure on November 1. We had cut the enemy's main line of communications. Recognizing that nothing but a cessation of hostilities could save his armies from complete disaster, he appealed for an immediate armistice on November 6.

48. Meanwhile general plans had been prepared for the further employment of American forces in an advance between the Meuse and the Moselle, to be directed toward Longwy by by the First Army, while the Second Army was to assume the offensive toward the Briey Iron Basin. Orders directing the preparatory local operations involved in this enterprise were issued on November 5.

Between the 7th and 10th of November the III Corps continued its advance eastward to Rémoiville, while the French XVII Corps, on its right, with the American 79th, 26th and 81st Divisions, and 2 French divisions, drove the enemy from his final foothold on the heights east of the Meuse. At 9 p. m. on November 9 appropriate orders were sent to the First and Second Armies in accordance with the following telegram from Marshal Foch to the Commander of each of the Allied Armies:

The enemy, disorganized by our repeated attacks, retreats along the entire front.

It is important to coordinate and expedite our movements.

I appeal to the energy and the initiative of the Commanders-in-Chief and of their Armies to make decisive the results obtained.

In consequence of the foregoing instructions, our Second Army pressed the enemy along its entire front. On the night of the 10th/11th and the morning of the 11th the V Corps, in the First Army, forced a crossing of the Meuse east of Beaumont and gained the commanding heights within the reentrant of the river, thus completing our control of the Meuse River line. At 6 a. m. on the 11th notification was received from Marshal Foch's Headquarters that the Armistice had been signed and that hostilities would cease at 11 a. m. Preparatory measures had already been taken to insure the prompt transmission to the troops of the announcement of an Armistice. However, the advance east of Beaumont on the morning of the 11th had been so rapid and communication across the river was so difficult that there was some fighting on isolated portions of that front after 11 a. m.

49. Between September 26 and November 11, 22 American and 4 French divisions, on the front extending from southeast of Verdun to the Argonne Forest, had engaged and decisively beaten 47 different German divisions, representing 25 perccent of the enemy's entire Divisional strength on the western front. Of these enemy divisions 20 had been drawn from the French front and 1 from the British front. Of the 22 American divisions 12 had, at different times during this period, been engaged on fronts other than our own. The First Army suffered a loss of about 117,000 in killed and wounded. It captured 26,000 prisoners, 847 cannon, 3,000 machine guns, and large quantities of material.

The dispositions which the enemy made to meet the Meuse-Argonne offensive, both immediately before the opening of the attack and during the battle, demonstrated the importance which he ascribed to this section of the front and the extreme measures he was forced to take in its defense. From the moment the American offensive began until the Armistice, his defense was desperate and the flow of his divisions to our front was continous. * * *

OPERATIONS OF THE SECOND ARMY

50. Under the instructions issued by me on November 5, for operations by the Second Army in the direction of the Briey Iron Basin, the advance was undertaken along the entire front of the Army and continued during the last three days of hostilities. In the face of the stiff resistance offered by the enemy, and with the limited number of troops at the disposal of the Second Army, the gains realized reflected great credit on the divisions concerned. On November 6 Marshal Foch requested that 6 American divisions be held in readiness to assist in an attack which the French were preparing to launch in the direction of Chateau-Salins. The plan was agreed to, but with the provision that our troops should be employed under the direction of the Commanding General, Second Army.

This combined attack was to be launched on November 14, and was to consist of 20 French divisions under Gen. Mangin and the 6 American division under Gen. Bullard. Of the divisions designated for this operation the 3rd, 4th, 29th, and 36th were in Army reserve and were starting their march eastward on the morning of November 11, while the 28th and 35th were being withdrawn from line on the Second Army front.

AMERICAN ACTIVITIES ON OTHER FRONTS

51. During the first phase of the Meuse-Argonne battle, American divisions were participating in important attacks on other portions of the front. The II Army Corps, Maj. Gen. Read commanding, with the 27th and 30th Divisions on the British front, was assigned the task, in cooperation with the Australian Corps, of breaking the Hindenburg Line at Le Cateau, where the St-Quentin Canal passes through a tunnel under a ridge. In this attack, carried out on September 29 and October 1, the 30th Division speedily broke through the main line of defense and captured all of its objectives, while the 27th progressed

until some of its elements reached Gouy. In this and later actions from October 6 to 19, our II Corps captured over 6,000 prisoners and advanced about 24 kilometers.

52. On October 2-9, our 2d and 36th Divisions assisted the French Fourth Army in its advance between Reims and the Argonne. The 2d Divisions completed its advance on this front by the assault of the wooded heights of Mont Blanc, the key point of the German position, which was captured with consummate dash and skill. The division here repulsed violent counterattacks, and then carried our lines into the village of St-Etienne, thus forcing the Germans to fall back before Reims and yield positions which they had held since September, 1914. On October 10 the 36th Division relieved the 2d, exploiting the latter's success, and in two days advanced, with the French, a distance of 21 kilometers, the enemy retiring behind the Aisne River.

53. In the middle of October, while we were heavily engaged in the Meuse-Argonne, Marshal Foch requested that 2 American divisions be sent immediately to assist the French Sixth Army in Belguim, where slow progress was being made. The 37th and 91st Divisions, the latter being accompanied by the artillery of the 28th Division, were hurriedly dispatched to the Belgian front. On October 30, in continuation of the Flanders offensive, these divisions entered the line and attacked. By November 3 the 37th Division had completed its mission by rapidly driving the enemy across the Scheldt River and had firmly established. itself on the east bank, while the 91st Division, in a spirited advance, captured Spitaals Bosschen, reached the Schedlt, and entered Audenarde.

AMERICAN TROOPS IN ITALY

54. The Italian Government early made request for American troops, but the critical situation on the western front made it necessary to concentrate our efforts there. When the Secretary of War was in Italy during April, 1918, he was urged to send American troops to Italy to show America's interest in the Italian situation and to strengthen Italian morale. Similarly a request was made by the Italian Prime Minister at the Abbeville conference. It was finally decided to send one regiment to Italy with the necessary hospital and auxiliary services, and the 332d Infantry was selected, reaching the Italian front in July, 1918. These troops participated in action against the Austrians in the fall of 1918 at the crossing of the Piave River and in the final pursuit of the Austrian Army.

AMERICAN TROOPS IN RUSSIA

55. It was the opinion of the Supreme War Council that Allied troops should be sent to cooperate with the Russians, either at Murmansk or Archangel, against the Bolshevist forces, and the British Government, through its Ambassador at Washington, urged American participation in this undertaking. On July 23, 1918, the War Department directed the dispatch of three battalions of infantry and three companies of engineers to join the Allied expedition. In compliance with these instructions the 339th Infantry, the 1st Battalion, 310th Engineers, 337th Field Hospital Company, and 337th Ambulance Company were sent through England, whence they sailed on August 26.

The mission of these troops was limited to guarding the ports and as much of the surrounding country as might develop threatening conditions. The Allied force operated under British command, through whose orders the small American contingent was spread over a front of about 450 miles. From September, 1918, to May, 1919, a series of minor engagements with the Bolshevist forces occurred, in which 82 Americans were killed and 7 died of wounds.

In April, 1919, two companies of American railroad troops were added to our contingent. The withdrawal of the American force commenced in the latter part of May, 1919, and on August 25 there was left only a small detachment of Graves' Registration troops.

56. In accordance with the terms of the Armistice, the Allies were to occupy all German territory west of the Rhine, with bridgeheads of 30 kilometer radius at Cologne, Coblenz, and Mayence. The zone assigned the American command was the bridgehead of Coblenz and the district of Treves. This territory was to be occupied by an American Army, with its reserves held between the Moselle---Meuse Rivers and the Luxemburg frontier.

The instructions of Marshal Foch, issued on November 16, contemplated that 2 French infantry divisions and 1 French cavalry division would be added to the American forces that occupied the Coblenz bridgehead, and that 1 American division would be added to the French force occupying the Mayence bridgehead. As this arrangement presented possibilities of misunderstanding due to difference of views regarding the government of occupied territory, it was represented to the Marshal that each nation should be given a well defined territory of occupation, employing within such territory only the troops of the commander responsible for the particular zone. On December 9, Marshal Foch accepted the principle of preserving the entity of command and troops, but reduced the American bridgehead by adding a portion of the eastern half to the French command at Mayence.

57. Various reasons made it undesirable to employ either the First or Second Army as the Army of Occupation. Plans had been made before the Armistice to organize a Third Army and, on November 14, this Army, with Maj. Gen. Joseph T. Dickman as commander, was designated as the Army of Occupation. The III and IV Army Corps staffs and troops, less artillery, the 1st, 2d, 3d, 4th, 32d, and 42d Divisions, and the 66th Field Artillery Brigade were assigned to the Third Army. This force was later increased by the addition of the VII Corps, Maj. Gen. William M. Wright commanding, with the 5th, 89th, and 90th Divisions.

The advance toward German territory began on November 17 at 5 a. m., six days after signing the Armistice. All of the Allied forces from the North Sea to the Swiss border moved simultaneously in the wake of the retreating German armies. Upon arrival at the frontier, a halt was made until December 1, when the leading elements of all Allied Armies crossed the line into Germany. The Third Army Headquarters were established at Coblenz and an Advance General Headquarters located at Treves. Steps were immediately taken to organize the bridghead for defense, and dispositions were made to meet a possible renewal of hostilities.

The advance to the Rhine required long arduous marches, through cold and inclement weather, with no opportunity for troops to rest, refit, and refresh themselves after their participation in the final battle. The Army of Occupation bore itself splendidly and exhibited a fine state of discipline both during the advance and throughout the period of occupation.

58. The zone of march of our troops into Germany and the line of communications of the Third Army after reaching the Rhine lay through Luxemburg. After the passage of the Third Army, the occupation of Luxemburg, for the purpose of guarding our line of communications, was intrusted to the 5th and 33d Divisions of the Second Army. The city of Luxemburg, garrisoned by French troops and designated as the headquarters of the Allied Commander-in-Chief, was excluded from our control.

Upon entering the Duchy of Luxemburg in the advance, a policy of noninterference in the affairs of the Grand Duchy was announced. Therefore, when the French commander in the city of Luxemburg was given charge of all troops in the Duchy, insofar as concerned the administration of the Grand Duchy of Luxemburg, my instructions were that our troops would not be subject to his control. Later, at my request, and in order to avoid possible friction, Marshal Foch placed the entire Duchy in the American Zone.

RETURN OF TROOPS TO THE UNITED STATES

59. On the day the Armistice was signed, the problem of the return of our troops to the United States was taken up with the War Department and, on November 15, a policy recommended of sending home certain auxiliaries so that we could begin to utilize all avail-

able shipping without delay. On December 21 the War Department announced by cable that it had been decided to begin immediately the return of our forces and continue as rapidly as transportation would permit. To carry this out, a schedule for the constant flow of troops to the ports was established, having in mind our international obligations pending the signing of the Treaty of Peace.

60. While more intimately related to the functions of the Services of Supply than to Operations, it is logical to introduce here a brief recital of the organizations created for the return of our troops to America. Prior to the Armistice but 15,000 men had been returned home. Although the existing organization was built for the efficient and rapid handling of the incoming forces, the embarkation of this small number presented no difficulties. But the Armistice suddenly and completely reversed the problem of the Services of Supply at the ports and the handling of troops. It became necessary immediately to reorganize the machinery of the ports, to construct large embarkation camps, and to create an extensive service for embarking the homeward-bound troops.

Brest, St-Nazaire, and Bordeaux became the principal embarkation ports, Marseilles and Le Havre being added later to utilize Italian and French liners. The construction of the embarkation camp during unseasonable winter weather was the most trying problem. These, with the billeting facilities available, gave accommodation for 55,000 at Brest, 44,000 at St-Nazaire, and 130,000 at Bordeaux. Unfortunately, the largest ships had to be handled at Brest, where the least shelter was available.

To maintain a suitable reservoir of men for Brest and St-Nazaire, an Embarkation Center was organized around Le Mans, which eventually accommodated 230,000 men. Here the troops and their records were prepared for the return voyage and immediate demobilization. As the troops arrived at the base ports, the embarkation service was charged with feeding, reclothing, and equipping the hundreds of thousands who passed through, which required the maintenance of a form of hotel service on a scale not hitherto attempted.

61. On November 16 all combat troops, except 30 divisions and a minimum of corps and army troops, were released for return to the United States. It was early evident that only limited use would be made of the American divisions, and that the retention of 30 divisions was not necessary. Marshal Foch considered it indispensable to maintain under arms a total, including Italians, of 120 to 140 divisions, and he proposed that we maintain 30 divisions in France until February 1, 25 of which should be held in the Zone of the Armies, and that on March 1 we should have 20 divisions in the Zone of the Armies and 5 ready to embark. The plan for March 1 was satisfactory, but the restrictions as to the divisions that should be in France on February 1 could not be accepted, as it would seriously interfere with the flow of troops homeward.

In a communication dated December 24 the Marshal set forth the minimum forces to be furnished by the several Allies, requesting the American Army to furnish 22 to 25 divisions one infantry. In the same note he estimated the force to be maintained after the signing of the preliminaries of peace at about 32 divisions, of which the American Army was to furnish 6.

In reply it was pointed out that our problem of repatriation of troops and their demobilization was quite different from that of France or Great Britain. On account of our long line of communications in France and the time consumed by the ocean voyage and travel in the United States, even with the maximum employment of our then available transportation, at least a year must elapse before we could complete our demobilization. Therefore, it was proposed by me that the number of American combat divisions to be maintained in the Zone of the Armies should be reduced on April 1 to 15 divisions and on May 1 to 10 divisions, and that in the unexpected event that the preliminaries of peace should not be signed by May 1 we would continue to maintain 10 divisions in the zone of the Armies until the date of signature.

The Allied Commander-in-Chief later revised his estimate, and, on January 24, stated to the Supreme War Council that the German demobilization would permit the reduction of the Allied forces to 100 divisions, of which the Americans were requested to furnish 15. In reply, it was again pointed out that our problem was entirely one of transportation, and that such a promise was unnecessary inasmuch as it would probably be the summer of 1919 before we could reduce our forces below the number asked. We were, therefore, able to keep our available ships filled, and by May 19 all combat divisions, except 5 still in the Army of Occupation, were under orders to proceed to ports of embarkation. This provided sufficient troops to utilize all troop transports to include July 15.

62. The President had informed me that it would be necessary for us to have at least one regiment in occupied Germany, and left the details to be discussed by me with Marshal Foch. My cable of July 1 summarizes the agreement reached:

By direction of President, I have discussed with Marshal Foch question of forces to be left on the Rhine. Following agreed upon: The 4th and 5th Divisions will be sent to base ports immediately, the 2d Division will commence moving to base ports on July 15, and the 3d Division on August 15. Date of relief of First Division will be decided later. Agreement contemplates that after compliance by Germany with military conditions to be completed within first three months after German ratification of treaty, American force will be reduced to one regiment of Infantry and certain auxiliaries. Request President be informed of agreement.

As a result of a later conference with Marshal Foch, the 3d Division was released on August 3 and the 1st Division on August 15.

PART III

SUPPLY, COORDINATION, MUNITIONS, AND ADMINISTRATION
THE SERVICES OF SUPPLY

1. In February, 1918, the Line of Communications was reorganized under the name of the Services of Supply. At that time all staff services and departments, except The Adjutant General's, the Inspector General's, and the Judge Advocate General's Departments, were grouped for supply purposes under one coordinating head, the Commanding General, Services of Supply, with a General Staff paralleling, so far as necessary, the General Staff at General Headquarters.

The principal functions of the Services of Supply were the procurement, storage, and transportation of supplies. These activities were controlled in a general way by the Commanding General, Services of Supply, the maximum degree of independence being permitted to the several services. This great organization was charged with immense projects in connection with roads, docks, railroads, and buildings; the transportation of men, animals, and supplies by sea, rail, and inland waterways; the operation of telegraph and telephone systems; the control and transportation of replacements; the hospitalization necessary for an army of 2,000,000 men; the reclassification of numerous officers and men; the establishment of leave areas and of welfare and entertainment projects; the liquidation of our affairs in France; and the final embarkation of our troops for home.

The growth of the permanent port personnel, the location near the base ports of certain units for training, and other considerations led to the appointment of a territorial commander for the section around each port who, while acting as the representative of the Commanding General, Services of Supply, was given the local authority of a district commander. For similar reasons, an intermediate section commander and an advance section commander were appointed. Eventually there were nine base sections, including one in England, one in Italy, and one comprising Rotterdam and Antwerp, also one intermediate and one advance section.

The increasing participation of the American Expeditionary Forces in active operations necessitated the enlargement of the responsibilities and authority of the Commanding General, Services of Supply. In August, 1918, he was charged with complete responsibility for all supply matters in the Services of Supply, and was authorized to correspond by cable directly with the War Department on all matters of supply not involving questions of policy.

In the following discussion of the Services of Supply the subjects of coordination of supply at the front, ocean tonnage, and replacements are included for convenience, though they were largely or entirely under the direct control of General Staff sections at my headquarters.

COORDINATION OF SUPPLY AT THE FRONT

2. Our successful participation in the war required that all the different services immediately concerned with the supply of combat troops should work together as a well-regulated machine. In other words, there must be no duplication of effort, but each must perform its functions without interference with any other service. The Fourth Section of the General Staff was created to control impartially all these services, and, under broad lines of policy, to determine questions of transportation and supply in France and coordinate our supply services with those of the Allies.

This section did not work out technical details but was charged with having a general knowledge of existing conditions as to supply, its transportation, and of construction affecting our operations or the efficiency of our forces. It frequently happened that several of the supply departments desired the same site for the location of installations, so that all plans for such facilities had to be decided in accordance with the best interests of the whole.

3. In front of the advance depots, railroad lines and shipments to troops had to be carefully controlled, because mobility demanded that combat units should not be burdened with a single day's stores above the authorized standard reserve. Furthermore, accumulations at the front were exposed to the danger of destruction or capture and might indicate our intentions. Each combat division required the equivalent of 25 French railway carloads of supplies for its daily consumption to be delivered at a point within reach of motor or horsedrawn transportation. The regular and prompt receipt of supplies by combatant troops is of first importance in its effect upon the morale of both officers and men. The officer whose mind is preoccupied by the question of food, clothing, or ammunition, is not free to devote his energy to training his men or to fighting the enemy. It is necessary that paper work be reduced to an absolute minimum and that the delivery of supplies to organizations be placed on an automatic basis as far as possible.

4. The principle of flexibility had to be borne in mind in planning our supply system in order that our forces should be supplied, no matter what their number, or where they might be called upon to enter the line. This high degree of elasticity and adaptability was assured and maintained through the medium of the regulating station. It was the connecting link between the armies and the services in the rear, and regulated the railroad transportation which tied them together. The regulating officer at each such station was a member of the Fourth Section of my General Staff, acting under instructions from his chief of section.

Upon the regulating officer fell the responsibility that a steady flow of supply was maintained. He must meet emergency shipments of ammunition or engineering material, sudden transfers of troops by rail, the hastening forward of replacements, or the unexpected evacuation of wounded. All the supply services naturally clamored to have their shipments rushed through. The regulating officer, acting under special or secret instructions, must declare priorities in the supply of things the Army needed most. Always informed of the conditions at the front, of the status of supplies, and of military plans and intentions, nothing could be shipped to the regulating station or in front of the advance depots except on his orders. The chiefs of supply services fulfilled their responsibilities when they delivered to the regulating officer the supplies called for by him, and he met his obligation when these supplies were delivered at the proper railheads at the time they were needed. The evacuation of the wounded was effected over the same railroad lines as those carrying supplies to the front, therefore, this control had also to be centralized in the regulating officer.

The convenient location of the regulating stations was of prime importance. They had to be close enough to all points in their zones to permit trains leaving after dusk or during the night to arrive at their destinations by dawn. They must also be far enough to the rear to be reasonably safe from capture. Only two regulating stations were actually constructed by us in France, Is-sur-Tille and Liffol-le-Grand, as the existing French facilities were sufficient to meet our requirements beyond the reach of those stations.

As far as the regulating officer was concerned, supplies were divided into four main classes. The first class constituted food, forage and fuel, needed and consumed every day; the second, uniforms, shoes, blankets and horse shoes, which wear out with reasonable regularity; the third, articles of equipment which require replacement at irregular intervals, such as rolling kitchens, rifles, and escort wagons; the fourth class covered articles, the flow of which depended upon tactical operations, such as ammunition and construction material. Articles in the first class were placed on an automatic basis, but formal requisition was eliminated as far as possible for all classes.

5. In order to meet many of the immediate needs of troops coming out of the line and to relieve to some extent the great strain on the railheads during active fighting, a system of army depots was organized. These depots were supplied by bulk shipments from the advance depots through the regulating stations during relatively quiet periods. They were under the control of the chiefs of the supply services of the armies and required practically no construction work, the supplies being stored in open places protected only by dunnage and camouflaged tarpaulins.

6. * * * The Services of Supply can be likened to a great reservoir divided into three main parts---the base depots, the intermediate depots, and the advance depots. The management of this reservoir is in charge of the Commanding General, Services of Supply, who administers it with a free hand, controlled only by general policies outlined to him from time to time. Each of the supply and techinical services functions independently in its own respective sphere; each has its share of storage space in the base depots, in the intermediate depots, and in the advance depots. Then comes the distribution system, and here the control passes to the chief of the Fourth Section of the General Staff, who exercises his powers through the regulating stations.

PURCHASING AGENCY

7. The consideration of requirements in food and material led to the adoption of an automatic supply system, but, with the exception of foodstuffs, there was an actual shortage, especially in the early part of the war, of many things, such as equipment pertaining to land transportation and equipment and material for combat. The lack of ocean tonage to carry construction material and animals at the beginning was serious. Although an increasing amount of shipping became available as the war progressed, at no time was there nage to sufficient for our requirements. The tonnage from the States reached about seven and one-half million tons to December 31, 1918, which was a little less than one-half of the total amount obtained.

The supply situation made it imperative that we utilize European resources as far as possible for the purchase of material and supplies. If our Services of Supply departments had entered the market of Europe as purchasers without regulation or coordination, they would have been thrown into competition with each other, as well as with buyers from the Allied armies and the civil populations. Such a system would have created an unnatural elevation of prices, and would have actually obstructed the procurement of supplies. To meet this problem from the standpont of economical business mnnagement, directions were given in August, 1917, for the creation of a General Purchasing Board to coordinate and control our purchases both among our own services and among the Allies as well. The supervision and direction of this agency was placed in the hands of an experienced business man, and every supply department in the American Expeditionary Forces was represented on the board. Agents were stationed in Switzerland, Spain, and Holland, besides the Allied countries. The character of supplies included practically the entire category of necessities, although the bulk of our purchases consisted of raw materials for construction, ordnance, air equipment and animals. A total of about 10,000,000 tons was purchased abroad by this agency to December 31, 1918, most of which was obtained in France.

The functions of the Purchasing Agency were gradually extended until they included a wide field of activities. In addition to the coordination of purchases, the supply resources of our Allies were reconnoitered and intimate touch was secured with foreign agencies; a Statistical Bureau was created which classified and analyzed our requirements; quarterly forecasts of supplies were issued; civilian manual labor was procured and organized; a Technical Board undertook the coordination, development, and utilization of the electric power facilities in France; a Bureau of Reciprocal Supplies viséed the claims of foreign governments for raw materials from the United States; and a general printing plant was established. Some of these activities were later transferred to other services as the latter became ready to undertake their control.

The principles upon which the usefulness of this agency depended were extended to our Allies, and in the summer of 1918 the General Purchasing Agent became a member of the Interallied Board of Supplies. This Board undertook, with signal success, to coordinate the supply of the Allied armies in all those classes of material necessities that were in common use in all the armies. The possibility of immense savings was fully demonstrated, but the principles had not be comeof general application before the Armistice.

OCEAN TONNAGE

8. Following a study of tonnage requirements, an officer was sent to Washington in December, 1917, with a general statement of the shipping situation in France as understood by the Allied Maritime Council. In March, 1918, tonnage requirements for transport and maintenance of 900,000 men in France by June 30 were adopted as a basis upon which to calculate supply requisitions and the allocation of tonnage.

In April the Allied Maritime Transport Council showed that requirements for 1918 greatly exceeded the available tonnage. Further revisions of the schedule were required by the Abbeville Agreement in May, under which American infantry and machine-gun units were to be transported in British shipping, and by the Versailles Agreement in June.

In July, a serious crisis developed as the allotment for August made the American Expeditionary Forces by the Shipping Control Committee was only 575,000 dead-weight tons, afterwards increased to 700,000, whereas 803,000 tons (not including animals) were actually needed. It was strongly urged by me that more shipping be diverted from trades and that a larger percentage of new shipping be placed in transport service.

9. Early in 1918, a scheme had been proposed which would provide priority for essential supplies only, based upon monthly available tonnage in sight. Although it was the understanding that calls for shipping should be based upon our actual needs, much irregularity was found in tonnage allotments, as shown by the following cables sent September 14, 1918.

The following variations from cable orders are noticeable:
Q. M. supplies cabled for, for August delivery, 182,287 short tons.
Q. M. supplies actually received during August, 231,850 short tons.
T. D. supplies (rolling stock, etc.) called for, for August delivery, 113,482 short tons.
T. D. supplies actually received during August, 67,521 short tons.

You must prepare to ship supplies we request, instead of shipping excessive amounts of supplies of which we have a due proportion.

An increase in the allotment of tonnage must be made, even for September. It is imperative. I can not too strongly urge that the allotment be reconsidered in the light of the above showing of our deficiencies. . . .

At the present time our ability to supply and maneuver our forces depends largely on motor transportation . . . We are able to carry out present plans due to fact that we have been able to borrow temporarily large numbers of trucks and ambulances from the French . . . The shortage of ambulances to move our wounded is critical . . . We have reached the point where we can no longer improvise or borrow. The most important plans and operations depend upon certainty that the home Government will deliver at French ports material and equipment cabled for. It is urged that foregoing be given most serious consideration and that tonnage allotted for supply of Army in France be sufficient to deliver material and equipment, properly proportioned in kinds and amount, to meet the needs of our troops . . .

The following is a brief summary of the tonnage asked for and the amount actually received in France during the critical period from July to October, 1918:

Month	Cabled for by American Expeditionary Forces	Received in France from United States	Shortage
July-----------------------------	480,891*	438,047	42,844
August----------------------------	700,527	511,261	189,266
September-------------------------	869,438	539,018	330,420
October---------------------------	1,022,135	623,689	398,446
Total--------------------	3,072,991	2,112,015	960,976

*Tons of 2,000 pounds.

REPLACEMENTS OF PERSONNEL

10. Under the original organization project there were to be two divisions in each corps of six divisions which were to be used as reservoirs of replacements. One half of the artillery and other auxiliaries of these two divisions were to be utilized as corps and army troops. They were to supply the first demands for replacements from their original strength, after which a minimum of 3,000 men per month for each army corps in France was to be forwarded to them from the United States. It was estimated that this would give a sufficient reservoir of personnel to maintain the fighting strength of combat units, provided the sick and wounded were promptly returned to their own units upon recovery.

The 32d and 41st Divisions were the first to be designated as replacement and depot divisions of the I Army Corps, but the situation soon became such that the 32d Division had to be employed as a combat division. For the same reason all succeeding divisions had to be trained for combat, until June 27, when the need for replacements made it necessary to designate the 83d as a depot division.

11. By the middle of August we faced a serious shortage of replacements. Divisions had arrived in France below strength, and each division diverted from replacement to combat duty increased the number of divisions to be supplied and at the same time decreased the supply.

On August 16 the War Department was cabled, as follows:

Attention is especially invited to the very great shortage in arrivals of replacements heretofore requested. Situation with reference to replacements is now very acute. Until sufficient replacements are available in France to keep our proven divisions at full strength, replacements should by all means be sent in preference to new divisions.

At this time it became necessary to transfer 2,000 men from each of three combat divisions (the 7th, 36th, and 81st) to the First Army, in preparation for the St-Mihiel offensive.

By the time the Meuse-Argonne offensive was initiated the replacement situation had become still more acute. The infantry and machine-gun units of the 84th and 86th Divisions, then in the vicinity of Bordeaux, were utilized as replacements, leaving only a cadre of two officers and twenty-five men for each company. To provide immediate replacements during the progress of the battles new replacement organizations were formed in the Zone of Operations; at first, as battalions, and later, as regional replacement depots.

12. On October 3, a cable was sent the War Department, reading as follows:

Over 50,000 of the replacements requested for the months of July, August, and September have not yet arrived. Due to extreme seriousness of the replacement situation, it is necessary to utilize personnel of the 84th and 86th Divisions for replacement purposes. Combat divisions are short over 80,000 men. Vitally important that all replacements due, including 55,000 requested for October, be shipped early in October. If necessary, some divisions in United States should be stripped of trained men and such men shipped as replacements at once.

Altogether seven divisions had to be skeletonized, leaving only one man per company and one officer per regiment to care for the records. As a further measure to meet the situation, the authorized strength of divisions was reduced in October by 4,000 men, thus lowering the strength of each infantry company to approximately 174 men. The 30 combat divisions in France at that time needed 103,513 infantry and machine-gun replacements, and only 66,490 were available.

Attention of the War Department was invited on November 2 to the fact that a total of 140,000 replacements would be due by the end of November, and the cable closed by saying:

To send over entire divisions, which must be broken up on their arrival in France so we may obtain replacements that have not been sent as called for, is a wasteful method, and one that makes for inefficiency; but as replacements are not otherwise available, there is no other course open to us. New and only partially trained divisions can not take the place of older divisions that have had battle experience. The latter must be kept up numerically to the point of efficiency . . . .

13. The shortage of animals was a serious problem throughout the war. In July, 1917, the French agreed to furnish our forces with 7,000 animals a month, and accordingly the War Department was requested to discontinue shipments. On August 24, however, the French advised us that it would be impossible to furnish the number of animals originally stated, and Washington was again asked to supply animals, but none could be sent over until November, and then only a limited number.

Early in 1918, after personal intervention and much delay, the French Government made requisition on the country, and we were able to obtain 50,000 animals. After many difficulties, the Purchasing Board was successful in obtaining permission, in the summer of 1918, to export animals from Spain, but practically no animals were received until after the Armistice.

Every effort was made to reduce animal requirements---by increased motorization of artillery and by requiring mounted officers and men to walk---but in spite of all these efforts, the situation as to animals grew steadily worse. The shortage by November exceeded 106,000, or almost one-half of all our needs. To relieve the crisis in this regard, during the Meuse-Argonne battle, Marshal Foch requisitioned 13,000 animals from the French Armies and placed them at my disposal.

RECLASSIFICATION OF PERSONNEL

14. An important development in the Services of Supply was the reclassification system for officers and men. This involved not only the physical reclassification of those partially fit for duty, but also the reclassification of officers according to fitness for special duties. A number of officers were found unfit for combat duty, and many in noncombatant positions were found unsuited to the duties on which employed. An effort was made to reassign these officers to the advantage of themselves and the Army. A total of 1,101 officers were reclassified in addition to the disabled, and 270 were sent before efficiency boards for elimination. 962 wounded or otherwise disabled officers were reclassified, their services being utilized to release officers on duty with the Services of Supply who were able to serve with combat units.

CONSTRUCTION BY ENGINEER CORPS

15. Among the most notable achievements of the American Expeditionary Forces was the large program of construction carried out by our engineer troops in the Services of Supply and elsewhere. The chief projects were port facilities including docks, railroads, warehouses, hospitals, barracks, and stables. These were planned to provide ultimately for an army of 4,000,000 men, the construction being carried on conincident with the growth of the American Expeditionary Forces.

The port plans contemplated 160 new berths, including the necessary facilities for discharge of cargo, approximately one-half of which were completed at the time of the Armistice. Construction of new standard-gauge railroad track amounted to 1,002 miles, consisting mainly of cut-offs, double tracking at congested points, and yards at ports depots. Road construction and repair continued until our troops were withdrawn from the several areas, employing at times upward of 10,000 men, and often using 90,000 tons of stone per week.

Storage requirements necessitated large supply depots at the ports and in the inter-mediate and advance sections. Over 2,000,000 square feet of covered storage was secured from the French, but it was necessary to construct approximately 20,000,000 square feet additional. The base hospital centers at Mars and Mesves, each with 4,000-bed convales-cent camps, are typical of the large scale upon which hospital accommodations were provided. The hospital city at Mars, of 700 buildings, covered a ground space of 33 acres and in-cluded the usual road, water, sewerage, and lighting facilities of a municipality.

16. Advantages of economy and increased mobility caused the adoption of the system of billeting troops. Billeting areas were chosen near the base ports, along the line of com-munications, and in the advanced zone, as strategical requirements dictated. The system was not altogether satisfactory, but with the number of troops to be accommodated no other plan was practicable. Demountable barracks were used for shelter to supplement lack of billets, 16,000 barracks of this type being erected, particularly at base ports where large camps were necessary. Stables at remount stations were built for 43,000 animals. Other construction included refrigerating plants, such as the one at Giévres with a capac-ity of 6,500 tons of meat and 500 tons of ice per day; and mechancial bakeries like that at Is-sur-Tille with capacity of 800,000 pounds of bread per day. If the buildings con-structed were consolidated, with the width of a standard barrack, they would reach from St-Nazaire across France to the Elbe River in Germany, a distance of 730 miles.

In connection with construction work, the Engineer Corps engaged in extensive forestry operations, producing 200,000,000 feet of lumber, 4,000,000 railroad ties, 300,000 cords of fuel wood, 35,000 pieces of piling, and large quantities of miscellaneous products.

TRANSPORTATION CORPS

17. The Transportation Corps as a separate organization was new to our Army. Its exact relation to the supply departments was conceived to be that of a system acting as a common carrier operating its own ship and rail terminals. The equipment and operation of port terminals stands out as a most remarkable achievement. The amount of tonnage handled at all French ports grew slowly, reaching about 17,000 tons daily at the end of July, 1918. An emergency then developed as a result of the critical military situation, and the capacity of our terminals was so efficiently increased that, by November 11, 45,000 tons were being handled daily.

The French railroads, both in management and material, had dangerously deteriorated during the war. As our system was superimposed upon that of the French it was necessary to provide them with additional personnel and much materiel. Experienced American rail-road men brought into our organization, in various practical capacities, the best talent in the country, who, in addition to the management of our own transportation, materially aided the French. The relation of our Transportation Corps to the French railroads and to our own supply departments presented many difficulties, but these were eventually over-come and a high state of efficiency established.

18. It was early decided, as expedient for our purposes, to use American rolling stock on the French railroads, and approximately 20,000 cars and 1,500 standard-gauge locomotives were brought from the United States and assembled by our railroad troops. We assisted the French by repairing with our own personnel 57,385 French cars and 1,947 French locomotives. The lack of rolling stock for Allied use was at all times a serious handicap, so that the number of cars and locomotives built and repaired by us was no small part of our contri-bution to the Allied cause.

19.   The Quartermaster Corps was able to provide a larger tonnage of supplies from the States than any of the great supply departments. The operations of this corps were so large and the activities so numerous that they can best be understood by a study of the report of the Commanding General, Services of Supply.

The Quartermaster Corps in France was called upon to meet conditions never before presented, and it was found advisable to give it relief. Transportation problems by sea transport and by rail were handled by separate corps organized for that purpose, and already described. Motor transport was also placed under an organization of its own. The usual routine supplies furnished by this department reached enormous proportions. Except for the delay early in 1918 in obtaining clothing and the inferior quality of some that was furnished, and an occasional shortage in forage, no army was ever better provided for. Special services created under the Quartermaster Corps included a Remount Service, which received, cared for, and supplied animals to troops; a Veterinary Service, working in conjunction with the remount organization; an Effects Section and Baggage Service; and a Salvage Service for the recovery and preparation for reissue of every possible article of personal equipment. Due to the activities of the Salvage Service, an estimated saving of $85,000,000 was realized, tonnage and raw material were conserved, and what in former wars represented a distinct liability was turned into a valuable asset.

The Graves' Registration Service, also under the Quartermaster Corps, was charged with the acquisition and care of cemeteries, the identification and reburial of our dead, and the correspondence with relatives of the deceased. Central cemeteries were organized on the American battle fields, the largest being at Romagne-sous-Montfaucon and at Thiaucourt in the Woevre. All territory over which our troops fought was examined by this service, and, generally speaking, the remains of our dead were assembled in American cemeteries and the graves marked with a cross or six-pointed star and photographed. A few bodies were buried where they fell or in neighboring French or British cemeteries. Whereever the soldier was buried, his identification tag, giving his name and Army serial number, was fastened to the marker. A careful record was kept of the location of each grave.

SIGNAL CORPS

20.   The Signal Corps supplied, installed, and operated the general service of telephone and telegraphic communications throughout the Zone of the Armies, and from there to the rear areas. At the front it handled radio, press, and intercept stations; provided a raido network in the Zone of Advance; and also managed the meteorological, pigeon, and general photographic services. Our communication system included a cable across the English Channel, the erection of 4,000 kilometers of telephone and telegraph lines on our own poles, and the successful operation of a system with 215,500 kilometers of lines.

MOTOR TRANSPORT CORPS

21.   The quantity and importance of gasoline-engine transportation in this war necessitated the creation of a new service known as the Motor Transport Corps. It was responsible for setting up motor vehicles received from America, their distribution, repair, and maintenance. Within the zone of the Services of Supply, the Motor Transport Corps controlled the use of motor vehicles, and it gave technical supervision to their operation in the Zone of the Armies. It was responsible for the training and instruction of chauffeurs and other technical personnel. Due to the shortage of shipments from America, a large number of trucks, automobiles, and spare parts had to be purchased in France.

22. A Renting, Requisition, and Claims Service was organized in March, 1918, to procure billeting areas, supervise the quartering of troops with an organization of some and town majors, and to have charge of the renting, leasing, and requisitioning of all lands and buildings required by the American Expeditionary Forces. Under the provisions of an act of Congress, approved in April, 1918, the Claims Department was charged with the investigation, assessment, and settlement of all claims of inhabitants of France or any other European country not an enemy or ally of an enemy for injuries to persons or damages to property occasioned by our forces. The procedure followed was in accordance with the law and practice of the country in question. The efficient administration of this service had an excellent effect upon the people of the European countries concerned.

23. The various activities of the Services of Supply which, at its height on November 11, 1918, reached a numerical strength in personnel of 668,312, including 23,772 civilian employees, can best be summed up by quoting the telegram sent by me to Maj. Gen. James G. Harbord, the Commanding General, Services of Supply, upon my relinquishing personal command of the First Army:

> I want the S. O. S. to know how much the First Army appreciated the prompt response made to every demand for men, equipment, supplies, and transportation necessary to carry out the recent operations. Hearty congratulations. The S. O. S. shares the success with it.

MUNITIONS

ORDNANCE

24. Our entry into the war found us with few of the auxiliaries necessary for its conduct in the modern sense. The task of the Ordnance Department in supplying artillery was especially difficult. In order to meet our requirements as rapidly as possible, we accepted the offer of the French Government to supply us with the artillery equipment of 75's, 155-mm. howitzers, and 155 G. P. F. guns from their own factories for 30 divisions. The wisdom of this course was fully demonstrated by the fact that, although we soon began the manufacture of these classes of guns at home, there were no guns of American manufacture of the calibers mentioned on our front at the date of the Armistice. The only guns of these types produced at home which reached France before the cessation of hostilities were one hundred and nine 75-mm. guns. In addition, twenty-four 8-inch howitzers from the United States reached our front and were in use when the Armistice was signed. Eight 14-inch naval guns of American manufacture were set up on railroad mounts, and most of theses were successfully employed on the Meuse-Argonne front under the efficient direction of Admiral Plunkett of the Navy.

AVIATION

25. In aviation we were entirely dependent upon our Allies, and here again the French Government came to our aid until our own program could be set under way. From time to time we obtained from the Frech such planes for training personnel as they could provide. Without going into a complete discussion of aviation materiel, it will be sufficient to state that it was with great difficulty that we obtained equipment even for training. As for up-to-date combat planes, the development at home was slow, and we had to rely upon the French who provided us with a total of 2,676 pursuit, observation, and bombing machines.

The first aeroplanes received from home arrived in May, and altogether we received 1,379 planes of the De Haviland type. The first American squadron completely equipped by American production, including aeroplanes, crossed the German lines on August 7, 1918. As to our aviators, many of whom trained with our Allies, it can be said that they had no superiors in daring and in fighting ability. During the battles of St-Mihiel and Meuse-Argonne our aviators excelled all others. They have left a record of courageous deeds that will ever remain a brilliant page in the annals of our Army.

TANKS

26. In the matter of tanks, we were compelled to rely upon both the French and the English. Here, however, we were less fortunate for the reason that our Allies barely had sufficient tanks to meet their own requirements. While our Tank Corps had limited opportunity, its fine personnel responded gallantly on every possible occasion and showed courage of the highest order. We had one battalion of heavy tanks engaged on the English front. On our own front we had only the light tanks, and the number available to participate in the last great assault of November 1 was reduced to 16 as a result of the previous hard fighting in the Meuse-Argonne.

CHEMICAL WARFARE SERVICE

27. The Chemical Warfare Service represented another entirely new departure in this war. It included many specialists from civil life. With personnel of a high order, it developed rapidly into one of our most efficient auxiliary services. While the early employment of gas was in the form of clouds launched from special projectors, its use later on in the war was virtually by means of gas shells fired by the light artillery. One of the most important duties of the Chemical Warfare Service was to insure the equipment of our troops with a safe and comfortable mask, and the instruction of the personnel in the use of this protector. Whether or not gas will be employed in future wars is a matter of conjecture, but the effect is so deadly to the unprepared that we can never afford to neglect the question.

ADMINISTRATION

MEDICAL AND SANITARY CONDITIONS

28. The general health of our armies under conditions strange and adverse in many ways to our American experience and mode of life was marvelously good. The proportionate number of men incapacitated from other causes than battle casualties and injuries was low. Of all deaths in the American Expeditionary Forces (to September 1, 1919) totaling 81,141, there were killed in action, 35,556; died of wounds received in battle, 15,130; other wounds and injuries, 5,669; and died of disease, 24,786. Therefore, but little over two-sevenths the total loss of life in the American Expeditionary Forces was caused by disease.

Our armies suffered from the communicable diseases that usually affect troops. Only two diseases have caused temporarily excessive sick rates, epidemic diarrhea and influenza, and of these influenza only, due to the fatal complicating pneumonia, caused a serious rise in the death rate. Both prevailed in the armies of our Allies and enemies and in the civilian population of Europe.

Venereal disease has been with us always, but the control was successful to a degree never before attained in our armies, or in any other army. It has been truly remarkable when the environment in which our men lived is appreciated. The incidence of venereal disease varied between 30 and 60 per thousand per annum, averaging under 40. Up to September , 1919, all troops sent home were free from venereal disease. The low percentage was due largely to the fine character of men composing our armies.

29. Hospitalization represented one of the largest and most difficult of the medical problems in the American Expeditionary Forces. That the needs were always met and that there was always a surplus of several thousand beds, were the results of great effort and the use of all possible expedients to make the utmost of resources available. The maximum number of patients in hospital on any one day was 193,026, on November 12, 1918.

Evacuation of the sick and wounded was another difficult problem, especially during the battle periods. The total number of men evacuated in the Zone of the Armies was 214,467, of whom 11,281 were sent in hospital trains to base ports. The number of sick and wounded sent to the United States up to November 11, 1918, was 14,000.

Since the Armistice, 103,028 patients have been sent to the United States.

30. The Army and the Medical Department were fortunate in obtaining the services of leading physicians, surgeons, and specialists in all branches of medicine from all parts of the United States, who brought the most skillful talent of the world to the relief of our sick and wounded. The Army Nurse Corps deserves more than passing comment. These women, working tirelessly and devotedly, shared the burden of the day to the fullest extent with the men, many of them submitting to all the dangers of the battle front.

RECORDS, PERSONNEL, AND MAIL SERVICE

31. New problems confronted the Adjutant General's Department in France. Our great distance from home necessitated records, data, and executive machinery to represent the War Department as well as our forces in France. Unusually close attention was paid to individual records. Never before have accuracy and completeness of reports been so strictly insisted upon. Expedients had to be adopted whereby the above requirements could be met without increasing the record and correspondence work of combat units. The organization had to be elastic to meet the demands of any force maintained in Europe.

A Statistical Division was organized to collect data regarding the special qualifications of all officers and to keep an up-to-date record of the location, duties, health, and status of every officer and soldier, nurse, field clerk, and civilian employee, as well as the location and strength of organizations. The Central Records Office at Bourges received reports from the battle front, evacuation and base hospitals, convalescent-leave areas, reclassification camps, and base ports, and prepared for transmission to the War Department reports of individual casualties. Each of the 299,599 casualties was considered as an individual case. A thorough investigation of the men classed as missing in action reduced the number from 14,000 at the signing of the Armistice to 22 on August 31, 1919.

32. In addition to printing and distributing all orders from General Headquarters, the Adjutant General's Department had charge of the delivery and collection of official mail and finally of all mail. The Motor Dispatch Service operated 20 courier routes, over 2,300 miles of road, for the quick dispatch and delivery of official communications. After July 1, 1918, the Military Postal Express Service was organized to handle all mail, official and personal, and operated 169 fixed and mobile post offices and a railway post-office service.

While every effort was exerted to maintain a satisfactory mail service, frequent transfers of individuals, especially during the hurried skeletonizing of certain combat divisions, numerous errors in addresses, hasty handling and readdressing of mail by regimental and company clerks in the Zone of Operations, and other conditions incident to the continuous movement of troops in battle, made the distribution of mail an exceedingly difficult problem.

33.   The Inspector General's Department, acting as an independent agency not responsible for the matters under its observation, made inspections and special investigations
for the purpose of keeping commanders informed of local conditions.   The inspectors worked
unceasingly to determine the manner in which orders were being carried out, in an effort
to perfect discipline and team play.

The earnest belief of every member of the Expeditionary Forces in the justice of our
cause was productive of a form of self-imposed discipline among our soldiers which must be
regarded as an unusual development of this war, a fact which materially aided us to organize and employ in an incredibly short space of time the extraordinary fighting machine developed in France.

Our troops generally were strongly imbued with an offensive spirit essential to success.
The veteran divisions had acquired not only this spirit, but the other elements of fine
discipline.   In highly trained divisions, commanders of all grades operate according to a
definite system calculated to concentrate their efforts where the enemy is weakest.   Straggling is practically eliminated; the infantry, skillful in fire action and the employment
of cover, gains with a minimum of casualties; the battalion, with all of its accompanying
weapons, works smoothly as a team in which the parts automatically assist each other; the
artillery gives the infantry close and continuous support; and unforeseen situations are
met by prompt and energetic action.

This war has only confirmed the lessons of the past.   The less experienced divisions,
while aggressive, were lacking in the ready skill of habit.   They were capable of powerful
blows, but their blows were apt to be awkward---teamwork was often not well understood.
Flexible and resourceful divisions can not be created by a few maneuvers or by a few
months' association of their elements.   On the other hand, without the keen intelligence,
the endurance, the willingness, and enthusiasm displayed in the training area, as well as
on the battle field, the successful results we obtained so quickly would have been utterly
impossible.

MILITARY JUSTICE

34.   The commanders of armies, corps, divisions, separate brigades, and certain territorial districts, were empowered to appoint general courts-martial.   Each of these commanders had on his staff an officer of the Judge Advocate General's Department, whose duty
it was to render legal advice and to assist in the prompt trial and just punishment of
those guilty of serious infractions of discipline.

Prior to the signing of the Armistice, serious breaches of discipline were rare, considering the number of troops.   This was due to the high sense of duty of the soldiers and
their appreciation of the seriousness of the situation.   In the period of relaxation following the cessation of hostilities, infractions of discipline were naturally more numerous,
but not even then was the number of trials as great in proportion to the strength of the
force as is usual in our service.

35.   It was early realized that many of the peace-time methods of punishment were not
the best for existing conditions.   In the early part of 1918, it was decided that the
award of dishonorable discharge of soldiers convicted of an offense involving moral turpitude, would not be contemplated, except in the most serious cases.   To remove these
soldiers temporarily from their organizations, division commanders were authorized to form
provisional temporary detachments to which such soldiers could be attached.   These detachments were retained with their battalions so that offenders would not escape the
dangers and hardships to which their comrades were subjected.   Wherever their battalion
was engaged, whether in front-line trenches or in back areas, these men were required to

perform hard labor. Only in emergency were they permitted to engage in combat. Soldiers in these disciplinary battalions were made to understand that if they acquitted themselves well, they would be restored to full duty with their organizations.

All officers exercising disciplinary powers were imbued with the purpose of these instructions and carried them into effect. So that nearly all men convicted of military offenses in combat divisions remained with their organizations and continued to perform their duty as soldiers. Many redeemed themselves by rendering valiant service in action and were released from the further operation of their sentences.

36. To have the necessary deterrent effect upon the whole unit, courts-martial for serious offenses usually imposed sentences considerably heavier than would have been awarded in peace times. Except where the offender earned remission at the front, these sentences stood during hostilities. At the signing of the Armistice, steps were at once taken to reduce outstanding sentences to the standards of peace time.

PROVOST MARSHAL GENERAL'S DEPARTMENT

37. On July 20, 1917, a Provost Marshal General was appointed with station in Paris, and later the department was organized as an administrative service with the Provost Marshal General functioning under the First Section, General Staff. The department was developed into four main sections---the Military Police Corps which served with divisions, corps, and armies and in the sections of the Services of Supply; the Prisoner of War Escort Companies; the Criminal Investigation Department; and the Circulation Department. It was not until 1918 that the last-mentioned department became well trained and efficient. On October 15, 1918, the strength of the Corps was increased to 1 per cent of the strength of the American Expeditionary Forces, and provost marshals for armies, corps, aand divisions were provided.

The military police of the American Expeditionary Forces developed into one of the most striking bodies of men in Europe. Wherever the American soldier went, there our military police were on duty. They controlled traffic in the battle zone, in all villages occupied by American troops, and in many cities through which our traffic flowed; they maintained order, so far as the American soldiers were concerned, throughout France and in portions of England, Italy, Belgium, and occupied Germany. Their smart appearance and military bearing and the intelligent manner in which they discharged their duties left an excellent impression of the typical American on all with whom they came in contact.

PART IV

MISCELLANEOUS SUBJECTS

PRISONERS OF WAR

1. All prisoners taken by the American troops were kept at least 30 kilometers behind our lines under guard by the Provost Marshal General's Department, except wounded or sick prisoners who were immediately sent to hospitals for treatment. Arrangements were made with the French and British that prisoners taken by our units operating with them should be sent to American enclosures. The Provost Marshal General was instructed to follow the principles of The Hague and the Geneva conventions in the treatment of prisoners, although these were not recognized by the United States as binding in the present war. Prisoners were organized into labor companies, and were employed on work which had no distinct bearing on military operations. The officer prisoners of war were accorded the same treatment as received by American officers confined in Germany. A Prisoner of War Information Bureau was established in the Central Records Office. Under a mutual understanding with the German Government, payments were made to prisoners in the form of credits, and,

subject to censorship, they were allowed to send and receive letters and packages. Religious meetings were held by prisoner chaplains, assisted by our Army chaplains and welfare workers.

2. From June, 1918, to the end of March, 1919, a total of 48,280 enemy prisoners were handled by the Provost Marshal General's Department, of whom 93 died and 73 escaped and were not recaptured. At the request of the French Government, 516 prisoners, natives of Alsace-Lorraine, were released after examination by a French commission. In accordance with the provisions of the Geneva Convention, 59 medical officers and 1,783 men of the Sanitary Personnel, including 333 members of the German Red Cross, were repatriated. On April 9, 1919, we commenced to repatriate enemy prisoners who were permanently unfit for futher military duty and those who could not perform useful labor.

3. Through the Berlin Red Cross and the International Red Cross at Geneva, an American Red Cross committee at Berne received lists of all American prisoners taken by the German troops, to each of whom, when located, was sent a package containing food, tobacco, clean underclothing and toilet articles, and thereafter two packages a week. By a system of return post cards, it was determined that 85 per cent of these packages were received.

As soon as the Armistice was signed the Germans released large numbers of Allied prisoners who immediately started toward the Allied lines. Four American regional replacement departments were established, to which all returning Americans were sent until proper records could be made. Those in good physical condition were sent to their commands, while the others were sent to hospitals or to leave areas for a rest.

An Allied commission was formed in Berlin early in December 1918, for the repatriation of Allied prisoners, with representatives from each of the American, British, French, and Italian Armies. American prisoners were evacuated through Switzerland in fully equipped trains, including hospital cars, provided by the Swiss Government and paid for by our Government. These were met by American trains at the Swiss border. It was planned to withdraw all our prisoners by this route, but a number had already been withdrawn through the northern ports and taken to England in British ships.

The Allied Commission obtained a statement of moneys paid Americans while in German prisons; investigated complaints concerning tratment of Americans; obtained possession of effects of prisoners who had died in captivity, or which had been left behind by those repatriated; and also located the graves of the American dead.

4. On November 11, 1918, there were 248 American officers and 3,302 men in the hands of the Germans, all of whom were evacuated by February 5, 1919. None of our prisoners was condemned to death, although 1 officer and 20 men died in captivity.

5. An Inter-Allied agreement on January 13, 1919, created a commission for the control of Russian prisoners in Germany. The British and American representatives, aided by small unarmed detachments, were charged with the administration of the Russian prison camps, and succeeded in discharging their duties despite the civil disorders in Germany.

Early in January, 1919, the Red Cross outlined a plan to send a commission to assist in caring for and feeding Russian prisoners, and an American officer was detailed to assist and accompany this commission. The Red Cross being financially unable to furnish the necessary food, arrangements were finally made with the French Government to furnish funds for its purchase from our Army stores, without any responsibility being assumed by the Army, as was desired by the Allied Food Commission. Such supplies as could be spared by the Army were sold to the French, and American officers were detailed to assist in their distribution. On April 10, 1919, the Supreme Allied War Council decided to give the German Government complete freedom in repatriating Russian prisoners of war, stipulating only that none should be repatriated by force, and that all who left must be provided with sufficient food for the journey.

6. To insure law and order, it was necessary that an American civil administration be created in the occupied territory. Different policies were adopted toward Luxemburg and occupied Germany, the former being a disarmed neutral and the latter occupied enemy territory. In both regions we issued proclamations defining our attitude toward the inhabitants.

In accordance with the precedent of our Government under similar circumstances, the local civil government remained in full possession of its former power and retained jurisdiction over all civil matters. The organization of our civil administration in occupied territory provided for the control of civil affairs by the Officer in Charge of Civil Affairs in Occupied Territory, under whom army, corps, and division commanders detailed suitable officers in local charge of civil matters. In the Grand Duchy of Luxemburg, civil affairs were regulated by a corresponding representative with an office in the city of Luxemburg.

7. The principle of requisitioning supplies was exercised extensively throughout the area, always under central control and without abuse of the privilege. Under a board of appraisal payment was made for all property requisitioned, the money being obtained from the German Government under the terms of the Armistice. Food and forage were not requisitioned, and during most of the period of occupation our officers and men were not allowed to purchase any German food and were forbidden to eat in the restaurants and cafes.

In Luxemburg, billeting arrangements and payment therefore were provided for by an agreement with the Government of Luxemburg.

Under instructions from the State Department, the interests of American citizens found in occupied Germany were referred to the American Embassy in Paris; in Luxemburg to the American Legation at The Hague.

8. We insisted upon the Germans maintaining all public utilities. After being inspected, measures were taken to assure priority of fuel supply in case of coal shortage due to strikes in the Ruhr and Saar districts or other causes. One of our chief problems was the maintenance and repair of roads and highways, and this at first necessitated the employment of soldier labor. As soon as possible a satisfactory system of road preservation and improvement was inaugurated, utilizing German civil labor.

To control and supervise the movement of funds and securities, all banks and banking houses were required to submit monthly reports. Trade and blockade regulations were controlled through the American Section of the Inter-Allied Economic Committee.

9. The Civil Administration issued instructions relative to courts. Army, corps, and divisional commanders were authorized to convene military commissions and appoint superior provost courts for their respective districts; and commanding officers of each city, town or canton, appointed an inferior provost court. All of these courts were for the trial of offenses against the laws of war or the Military Government. Our legal machinery was simple, and successful results in maintaining law and order were due to uniform and strict enforcement of such few regulations as proved necessary.

Strict censorship was maintained over postal, telephone, and telegraphic communications. Passes and circulation were first handled by the Department of Civil Affairs, but on January 24, 1919, the Third Army took charge of those matters.

In connection with the reconstruction work in France and Belgium, the Department of Civil Affairs prepared a record of all recovered stolen property and measures were taken to protect it against deterioration or unauthorized removal.

10. The fraternization problem was sharply raised by the sudden transition from the rigors of war conditions in France to the comforts of undisturbed German cities and homes, but a realization by our troops of their position in enemy territory and of their duty to maintain the dignity of their own country reduced infractions of rules on the subject to a minimum.

11. The first Armistice agreement provided for supervision by a Permanent International Armistice Commission to function under the authority of the Commander-in-Chief of the Allied Armies. The United States, Great Britain, Belgium, France, Italy and Germany were represented on the Permanent International Armistice Commission. The chairmen of this commission and of the five main committees were French. These committees were organized to care specifically for the work in connection with material, transportation, prisoners of war, *entretien*, and restitution. The United States was represented on each of these main committees.

12. The Germans unsuccessfully attempted to enter the Permanent International Armistice Commission on the basis of negotiation. Many adjustments were made because of the difficulties under which the German authorities were working, but, in general, they were held strictly to the spirit of the terms of the Armistice agreement. Time of delivery was often extended, but penalties were imposed for failure to comply with the conditions. All aeroplanes were not obtained until a penalty was imposed of 20 horses for each undelivered plane. Evacuation of occupied territory, and repatriation of civilian inhabitants and of prisoners of war, were begun immediately and carried out promptly.

13. In the distribution among the Allied Armies of ordnance and aeroplanes surrendered by the enemy, the Belgian Army received one-tenth, American Army two-tenths, British Army three-tenths, and French Army four-tenths. Our share was 720 field guns, 534 heavy guns, 589 trench mortars, 10,356 machine guns and 340 aeroplanes. Railway rolling stock was divided according to the needs of the railway systems serving the different armies.

14. The question of expense of maintenance of the armies of occupation caused considerable discussion among the Allies and protests from the Germans. This was due to the diversity of opinion as to the items properly chargeable to the expense of an army of occupation. My policy was that, pending final settlement by the Peace Conference, Germany would be liable for all expenses of the American Army of Occupation; that any payments made by Germany for this purpose were to be considered as partial payments on account of the whole sum, and not as a liquidation of any specific expenses. Money was deposited in Coblenz banks to the credit of the United States, in amounts notified as necessary, to cover all expenditures made in the occupied area. The total expense as calculated by the different Allied Armies, before any of our troops were withdrawn, was based on the effective strength as shown by their Tables of Organization, and appears as follows:

Armies	Officers	Men	Horses	Cost per Month in Francs
French	11,570	35,500	116,100	175,948,815.00
Belgian	1,834	39,430	11,600	30,195,142.60
British	12,000	240,000	70,000	127,935,000.00
United States	12,358	275,617	58,755	269,068,184.10
Total	------	------	------	------------

UNITED STATES LIQUIDATION COMMISSION

15. In February, 1919, upon my recommendation, the Secretary of War appointed the United States Liquidation Commission, War Department, which had charge of the liquidation of our affairs in France, the sale of our property and installations and the settlement of claims exclusive of those arising out of torts, which were handled by the Renting, Requisition and Claims Service. While not under my supervision, the Liquidation Commission played

such an important part in the closing chapter of our activities that some mention of it should be made in this report. With the dissolution of the American Expeditionary Forces we were confronted with the problem of disposing of large port and other installations and immense quantities of transportation, materiel supplies, and equipment. Much of this was of an immovable nature and the shipping situation forbade the transfer to the United States of most of the movable effects. There was little or no demand for many of the articles to be disposed of, and the expense of maintaining a force of caretakers until the market improved would have been prohibitive. The successful negotiations of the Commission led to the liquidation of our affairs with France by the payment of a lump sum to the United States by the French Government.

RELATIONS WITH THE ALLIES

16. Our troops arrived in Europe after France and Great Britain had been fighting desperately for nearly three years, and their reception was remarkable in its cordiality. The resources of our Allies in men and material had been taxed to the limit, but they always stood ready to furnish us with needed supplies, equipment and transportation when at all available. We were given valuable assistance and cooperation in our training program by both the French and British armies and, when the shortage of labor personnel in our forces became acute, the French Government rendered material assistance in the solution of this problem.

It was our good fortune to have a year in France to organize and train our forces. When our troops entered the battle the veteran soldiers of France and England gave them moral and physical support. The artillery of our Allies often supported the advance of American troops; British and French tanks frequently cooperated with our infantry; and their aviators fought in the air to assist the American soldier.

Throughout France our troops have been intimately associated with the French people, particularly the French peasant, and the relations growing out of these associations assure a permanent friendship between the two peoples. The small force of Americans serving in Italy was accorded a warm welcome and established with the Italian people the most friendly relations. The hospitable reception of those of our forces who passed through England has impressed upon us how closely common language and blood have brought together the British and ourselves.

The cooperation of our soldiers with the French, British, Belgians and Italians was decisive in bringing the war to a successful conclusion, and will have an equally decisive effect in welding together the bonds of sympathy and good will among the peoples of these nations and ourselves.

WELFARE WORK

ALLIED FOOD COMMISSION

17. At the request of the Allied Food Commission a selected personnel of 320 officers and 464 men was placed at the disposal of the Commission. There was no other American personnel in Europe or elsewhere available for this necessary work. Our officers were sent to various countries in charge of food distribution, and were everywhere received with the utmost friendliness. These officers and men, by their executive and administrative ability and their energetic resourcefulness, were in a large measure responsible for the manner in which these food supplies were delivered to the various peoples in central Europe during a period of civil unrest or complete disorder. By their disinterested conduct of this charitable work, they won for the American Army the admiration of the populations whom they served.

SOCIETIES

18. In their respective spheres of activity the Red Cross and Y. M. C. A. undertook the burden of supplying the needs of the entire American Expeditionary Forces. Their efforts were in many respects limited by a lack of tonnage. But shortage in tonnage, transportation, or personnel meant inability to carry out completely their appointed tasks; whereas with the smaller societies it meant inability to expand. In order to avoid duplication of effort, it was directed in August, 1917, that the Red Cross confine its activities to relief work, and the Y. M. C. A. to amusement and recreation. The Knights of Columbus and the Salvation Army were later given official recognition. The Y. W. C. A., Jewish Welfare Board, and American Library Association conducted their activities through one of the established societies.

19. The American Red Cross maintained within our zones a system of Line of Communication Canteens, which furnished refreshments and relief to troops in transit and became a valuable feature of the Red Cross work. The statistical work of the searcher attached to statistical sections and to hospitals obtained much information for relatives. This society also aided in locating American prisoners to whom it sent food from Switzerland.

20. To avoid depleting our personnel, the Y. M. C. A. agreed to operate our canteens and was at first allotted 208 ship-tons per 25,000 men per month to bring supplies from the United States, but the requirements of other services later made it necessary to reduce this allotment to 100 tons. This materially reduced the valuable service the Y. M. C. A. might have rendered in this work. The termination of hostilities made it possible to relieve the society of this responsibility.

21. The need of greatly expanded welfare work after hostilities, such as athletics and education was at once recognized, and the cooperation of the welfare societies in all these activities was of inestimable value. Immediately after the Armistice steps were taken to provide diversion and entertainment for our troops. Entertainment officers were appointed in all units, and the Y. M. C. A. Entertainment Department furnished professionals and acted as a training and booking agency for soldier talent. Approximately 650 soldier shows were developed, which entertained hundreds of thousands of soldiers, who will remember this as one of the pleasant and unique enterprises of the American Expeditionary Forces.

The athletic program in the spring of 1919 culminated in the Inter-Allied games in June, held in the concrete stadium erected by our Engineers near Paris, the necessary funds being contributed by the Y. M. C. A. In number of participants and quality of entry, these games probably surpassed any of the past Olympic contests.

LEAVES AND LEAVE AREAS

22. A leave system announced in general orders provided for a leave of seven days every four months, but it was necessary to suspend the privilege during active operations. In the leave areas free board and lodging at first-class hotels were provided for soldiers, and the Y. M. C. A. furnished recreational and amusement facilities. A number of new areas were opened by the Services of Supply immediately after the Armistice, improved transportation accommodations were eventually secured, and arrangements were made whereby men could visit England, Belgium, and Italy.

It was my desire that every man in the American Expeditionary Forces should be given an opportunity to visit Paris before returning to the United States, but the crowded condition of the city during the Peace Conference, transportation difficulties, and other reasons, made it necessary to limit the number of such leaves.

RELIGIOUS WORK

23. Religious work in our Army before the war was carried on by chaplains, one to each regiment. To meet the greatly increased size of regiments, legislation was recommended by me to provide not less than one chaplain for each 1,200 men. Although such act was passed in June, 1918, there was a continuous shortage of chaplains with the fighting units and in the hospitals and camps in the rear areas. This was largely met through the ready cooperation of the Welfare Societies who sent ministers and priests where most needed. Religious workers in the Y. M. C. A. and Knights of Columbus and Red Cross also aided in the work, the Red Cross sending chaplains to the States with units in many instances.

The religious work was directed and coordinated by a Board of Chaplains at general headquarters, of which Bishop Charles H. Brent was the head. With great devotion to duty this work was maintained despite a lack of transportation and other facilities. Chaplains, as never before, became the moral and spiritual leaders of their organizations, and established a high standard of active usefulness in religious work that made for patriotism, discipline and unselfish devotion to duty.

EDUCATIONAL WORK

24. Prior to the Armistice, educational work was conducted through the organization of voluntary classes under the Y. M. C. A., the popular subjects studied being French language, French history, and the causes of the war. After the Armistice, measures were taken for a systematic organization of nonmilitary educational training.

The formal school work began January 2, with post schools. Then divisional educational centers gave the equivalent of high school instruction and specialized on vocational training. The American Expeditionary Forces University at Beaune carried on undergraduate and graduate work for the technical professions, while postgraduate work was provided by the entrance of our officers and soldiers into French and British universities. Special schools were organized to meet demands, such as the Practical Agricultural School at Allery and the Art Training Center at Paris, for painting, sculpture, architecture, and interior decoration, advanced students being entered in the best ateliers of Paris. Active instruction was carried on in the base hospitals and convalescent camps.

An important branch of the educational work was the field institute of short courses and educational extension lectures, organized to meet conditions due to the rapid repatriation of our soldiers and the constant movement of troops. At least half of our forces were reached by this means with brief intensive courses in business, trades, engineering, agriculture, occupational guidance, and in citizenship.

25. On April 15 all educational work came under the complete control of the Training Section of the General Staff. The advantage of this change in management was at once apparent in the better coordination of the work of an excellent body of educators. The total attendance in the organized school system of the American Expeditionary Forces was 020,000, of which number 181,475 attended post schools, 27,250 educational centers, 8,528 the American Expeditionary Forces University at Beaune, 367 Art Training Centers, 4,144 Mechanical Trade Schools, 6,300 French universities and 1,956 British universities. The attendance upon the institute short courses totaled 690,000 more, and at the extension lectures 750,000, giving a grand total of attendance at all educational formations of 1,670,020.

The educational work in the American Expeditionary Forces was of undoubted value, not only in improving morale, but in concrete benefit to the individual officer and soldier. It demonstrated satisfactorily that a combined military and educational program can be carried out in the Army with little detriment to pure military training and with decided advantage to the individual.

26. The Stars and Stripes was a weekly newspaper conceived with the idea of increasing the morale of American troops by providing a common means of voicing the thought of the entire American Expeditionary Forces. Edited and managed by enlisted men who declined promotion, preferring to remain in the ranks in order better to interpret the spirit of the Army, it was a great unifying force and materially aided in the development of an esprit de corps. It lent loyal and enthusiastic support to Army athletics and to the educational program. In leading the men of our Army to laugh at their hardships, it was a distinct force for good and helped to create a healthy viewpoint. The campaign it conducted for the benefit of French orphans resulted in a fund of 2,250,000 francs.

APPRECIATION

27. In this brief summary of the achievements of the American Expeditionary Forces it would be impossible to cite in detail the splendid ability, loyalty, and efficiency that characterized the service of both combatant and non-combatant individuals and organizations. The most striking quality of both officers and men was the resourceful energy and common sense employed, under all circumstances, in handling their problems.

The highest praise is due the commanders of armies, corps, and divisions, and their subordinate leaders, who labored loyally and ably toward the accomplishment of their task, suppressing personal opinions and ambitions in the pursuit of the common aim; and to their staffs, who developed, with battle experience, into splendid teams without superiors in any army.

To my Chiefs of Staff, Maj. Gen. James G. Harbord, who was later placed in command of the Services of Supply, and Maj. Gen. James W. McAndrew, I am deeply indebted for highly efficient services in a post of great responsibility.

The important work of the staff at General Headquarters in organization and administration was characterized by exceptional ability and a fine spirit of cooperation. No. chief ever had a more loyal and efficient body of assistants.

The officers and men of the Services of Supply fully realized the importance of their duties, and the operations of that vast business system were conducted in a manner which won for them the praise of all. They deserve their full share in the victory.

The American civilians in Europe, both in official and private life, were decidedly patriotic and loyal, and invariably lent encouragement and helpfulness to the armies abroad.

The various societies, especially their women, including those of the theatrical profession, and our Army nurses, played a most important part in brightening the lives of our troops and in giving aid and comfort to our sick and wounded.

The Navy in European waters, under command of Admiral Sims, at all times cordially aided the Army. To our sister service we owe the safe arrival of our armies and their supplies. It is most gratifying to record that there has never been such perfect understanding between these two branches of the service.

Our armies were conscious of the support and cooperation of all branches of the Government. Behind them stood the entire American people, whose ardent patriotism and sympathy inspired our troops with a deep sense of obligation, of loyalty, and of devotion to the country's cause never equaled in our history.

Finally, the memory of the unflinching fortitude and heroism of the soldiers of the line fills me with greatest admiration. To them I again pay the supreme tribute. Their devotion, their valor and their sacrifices will live forever in the hearts of their grateful countrymen.

In closing this report, Mr. Secretary, I desire to record my deep appreciation of the unqualified support accorded me throughout the war by the President and yourself. My task was simplified by your confidence and wise counsel. I am, Mr. Secretary,

Very respectfully,

JOHN J. PERSHING,
General, Commander-in-Chief,
American Expeditionary Forces.

C-in-C Rept. File: Fldr. 16: Report

Relations with Allied Governments and Armies

GENERAL HEADQUARTERS, A. E. F.,

Chaumont, Haute-Marne, June 30, 1919.

[Extract]

Opening Relations: In order to appreciate porperly the relationships that grew up between the United States and the Allied armies and governments it is essential to understand the military situation as it existed when the United States entered the war.

This situation has been presented in detail in the report of the operations section (G-3), but in brief it may be said that it so happened that the United States entered the war at a moment when the morale of France was at a particularly low ebb. The reason for this may be indicated in a very few words. France had attempted with insufficient military means to defeat the German army decisively on French soil by a series of vigorously conducted attacks. The results had been poor. A comparatively slight amount of ground had been gained; the German army had demonstrated its ability to maintain a safe defensive in its chosen positions, while the French army had been called on to face such heavy casualties that discontent and discouragement that arose in the ranks of the army seized public opinion also, plunging the nation into a state of profound discouragement.

When the United States declared war, on April 6, 1917, France immediately despatched a special mission to America, composed of Marshal Joffre and M. Viviani. England also sent us General Bridges, one of her ablest officers, and Lord Balfour, a distinguished statesman. It is hardly necessary to recall how warmly they were received nor how generously they were treated. They came to tell us that what the Allies needed was materiel, supplies, and gold; but chiefly men.

We offered them freely not only all that we had but all we could hope to have, and it may be truly said that never did a nation engaging its resources and the lives of its citizens do less bargaining or show more complete response than we did on that occasion. The effect of this on the representatives of France was a fact of quite an exceptional nature, and Marshal Joffre may be singled out as the man who to this day would, in all probability, with that simplicity and honesty which are his, state with due emphasis what the mode of his reception in America did for the morale of France through her representatives.

We were totally unprepared for war and our army was inexperienced in the conduct of joint operations in conjunction with the armies of Allied powers. Practically our sole participation in such operations up until our war with Germany had been the minor one of the China Expedition of 1900.

Viewpoint of the Allies: The Allied armies and governments appreciated our military weakness and unpreparedness as well as our potential strength. The object of their military missions to the United States was to assist us in developing our military resources and to place at our disposal their ability and experience, so that our great potential strength might be transformed at the earliest possible moment into actual strength for the Allied cause. From their point of view this could be done in the shortest possible time by the utilization of our man power as a reservoir from which they might draw in order to keep their depleted major units at full strength. This idea persisted in the minds of the Allies, so that its effects continued to be evidenced up to the fall of 1918.

They presented the idea that they possessed seasoned, smooth working divisions, which had become depleted through serious losses, and urged upon us the acceptance of the idea that these divisions could absorb a large percentage of comparatively raw recruits and still be able to function creditably. In brief, both British and French tried to persuade us that the quickest way to employ effectively our untrained man power would be to incorporate our soldiers as individuals or in small units into existing French and British divisions. Their divisions were depleted, due to the fact that they had used their man power to such an extent in the development of the engines and agencies necessary for stabilized warfare that they had been obliged to reduce the proportion of infantry in their divisions. So critical was their situation that in the spring of 1917 they found themselves unable to furnish replacements for even the small proportion of infantry that still remained. The thought of an almost inexhaustible reservoir from which, without expense to themselves, they could draw men to keep up their depleted units, was naturally most appealing. Such was the foreign idea and the principle that underlay their dealings with the American High Command and the American Government.

The American Viewpoint: From the American viewpoint no greater mistake could have been made than to abandon the idea of creating an independent American army, into which all American forces would be assembled as soon as they were ready to operate. Only the thought of an American army under its own commander and its own flag would have drawn from the American people the wholehearted support which provided our forces with the men and the materials necessary to an Allied victory. Only under such conditions would the American soldier display the valor and endure the hardships necessary to enable the United States to do its part in securing that victory.

For the purposes of training, and later to meet the exigencies of the military situation, small American units were placed under foreign command. These American soldiers always adapted themselves to their new environment with the same broad spirit of helpfulness and unselfishness that has actuated all of their service in Europe. They displayed at all times the greatest heroism and the greatest desire to do their best. Individualistic as our men are, and accustomed as they are to the national American habit of freedom of action and thought, it was not always easy for them to accept the rigid and conventional methods of the old world. It would have been comprehensible and excusable if friction had occurred while they were serving temporarily under foreign command. But their relations with the foreign troops among which they were serving, and with the foreign commanders under whom they served, were generally amicable and better than could have been foreseen. Their desire to play teamwork, to do their duty as loyal soldiers, and, above all, to win the war, inspired them to submerge all personal considerations and national prejudices. Instead of separating themselves mentally from our Allies they fitted themselves into the spirit and aims of the nation with which they happened to be serving.

Nevertheless, evidence was not absent that only this desire to play the game and the assurance of ultimately forming part of a wholly American force under American command permitted the temporary employment of them under foreign command.

I believe that it is not too much to say that the Allied cause would have been lost had we neglected the influence of national phychology and despised the pride of a people in the accomplishments of its soldiers by accepting any proposal to employ our man power in such a way that the results of their heroic efforts would have served to enhance the glory of any flag but their own.

Upon my arrival, therefore, I was presented with the problems of organizing the American forces with the end in view that they should be employed as an American army. It was a foregone conclusion that with a thorough understanding of the Allied viewpoint as to the utilization of our forces I would encounter difficulties in my relationships with the Allies. It was early seen that to bring about satisfactory relationships between the various armies and our own that I should have to create certain mechancial agencies for dealing with them. I therefore adopted the means of commissions and liaison officers as a method of intercommunication. This was in accordance with the principles used by the Allied armies.

Agencies created: The necessity for my headquarters being in intimate touch with each of the headquarters of our Allies was immediately apparent.

Missions: As soon as I arrived in Paris the French Ministry of War detailed a group of liaison officers for services at my headquarters. Later on, when moving to Chaumont, liaison with the French Ministry of War was maintained through the military mission which Marshal (then general) Pétain established in Chaumont.

The same principle employed in dealing with the French was adopted for treating with other countries. Naturally these means were developed from time to time so that eventually I was kept in touch with the various headquarters of our Allies both by foreign missions at my headquarters and by American missions at Allied headquarters. By this double system of liaison the proper American and foreign viewpoints were exchanged, interpreted and understood.

Allied missions were established at American G. H. Q., as follows:

	Dating from
French Ministry of War	June 14, 1917
French G. Q. G. and Ministry of War combined	Sept. 1, 1917
Interallied Headquarters (Marshal Foch) was represented by the same agency as soon as established	
British Military Mission	Sept. 1, 1917
Belgian Military Mission	March 10, 1918
Italian Military Mission	July 6, 1918

On our side, we were represented at Allied Headquarters as shown below:

Mission to	Dating from
Liaison Officer at French G. Q. G. (Marshal Petain)	June 25, 1917
Military Mission at French Gl Q. G. (" ")	Dec. 17, 1917
" " " Allied G. Q. G. (Marshal Foch)	Apr. 17, 1918
Liaison Officer at British G. H. Q. (Marshal Haig)	July 12, 1917
Military Mission at British G. H. Q. (Marshal Haig)	Jan. 8, 1918
Liaison Officer at Belgian Hq. (In addition to duties at British G. H. Q.)	Dec. 8, 1917
Separate Liaison Officer at Belgian G. H. Q.	Feb. 2, 1918
Military Mission at Belgian Hq.	Mar. 11, 1918
Military Mission to Italy	Feb. 18, 1918

All of the above missions remained on duty until the spring of 1919, when, as their services were no longer needed, they began to be withdrawn gradually, finally disappearing either with the closing of my own headquarters or of the Allied Headquarters to which they were assigned.

It is with pleasure that I record the splendid attitude of helpfulness that characterized the work of the Allied Missions at my headquarters. They evinced at all times a sincere desire to be of assistance to me, as well as to perform their functions for the headquarters which they represented. Their unfailing courtesy and their readiness to do everything possible to maintain the relations between our Allies and ourselves upon the most cordial and mutually helpful status was greatly appreciated by all at my headquarters.

Equally deserving of praise are the American Missions at Allied Headquarters. In fact the manner in which all of the missions, both Allied and American, performed their different duties, is entitled to high praise. Only by their courtesy, tact, and painstaking efforts were the channels of communications kept upon a plane of such usefulness as to be invaluable to the American Expeditionary Forces.

Liaison Officers: In addition to the military missions I established a liaison service with the object of facilitating the business of Americans dealing with French and British. This service was composed of officers who were familiar with the French language and customs and thereby enabled to assist American officers whose duties required them to treat with our Allies. On the other hand, I authorized the French Government to detail selected French officers and interpreters with the American combat forces, divisions, corps and armies, and at certain designated headquarters in the S. O. S.

Not only were there foreign officers with the combat forces, but I accepted the offers of both French and British Governments to utilize the services of trained instructors at our various schools. These officers were most efficient in the performance of their duties, rendering us valuable aid, especially in the formative period.

Due to the sector in which our troops were to be employed, the location of our training areas, and other installations, we were associated more closely with the French than with the British. The difference in language, therefore, made it desirable to authorize a large number of English speaking French officers at first. But as our divisions progressed in their training and as our forces became more and more amalgamated the necessity for liaison officers gradually grew less. Their services were consequently dispensed with, but on account of the difference of laws and customs to which our soldiers were habituated and those existing in the country where we were operating I found it necessary to continue to employ a certain number of such officers and soldiers as liaison agents al long as the A. E. F. remained in Europe. As these officers and soldiers were put to considerable personal expense in living away from their own organizations, whereby they had to subsist and shelter themselves as individuals or in small groups, I arranged to pay them a small sum for their services so that those who had no large personal income could afford to engage upon this duty. * * *

Relationships during Organization Period: It is only possible to mention a few of the manifold problems that confronted the headquarters of the American Expeditionary Forces upon its arrival in Europe. Chief among them was to get in touch with the existing military situation, which was but imperfectly understood in America, and to formulate intelligent and conservative recommendations as to the military effort required of the United States.

The outbreak of the war found us without any military organization higher than the regiment and without an adequate staff. Consequently, I had been charged with studying the question of organization and of submitting to the War Department an organization project. But before this could be done it was first essential to create a suitable staff.

Staff Organization: After a careful study of both British and French staff systems, it was decided to mould ours more closely along the lines of the French, retaining some of our own methods, and some of the British.

With a staff formed, I was enabled to proceed with my work. Upon arrival in Europe both the British War Office and the French Ministry of War placed all possible facilities at my disposal. During the first months in France staff officers from my headquarters were constantly conferring with British and French staffs for the purpose of obtaining information and advice.

Cooperation of the Allies: In order to base our organization upon sound principles I caused my staff to learn the experience of the Allies upon such matters as average losses to be expected in men and animals, average amounts of ammunition to be consumed, average sickness under conditions of field service, average number of replacements required, and subjects of similar importance. All of this secret information was unreservedly placed at our disposal and we were freely advised upon the value of different types of armament and equipment and the different methods of training. * * *

It is proper that I should express here my grateful appreciation of the great assistance rendered the American army during its formative period by the Allied commanders and their staffs. The frank and open hearted manner in which data of all kinds, including the most secret documents, was placed in our possession, showed an international confidence which has probably never been surpassed in history. On my part, I was careful never to ask for secret data until I had need of it, and always to preserve all such data inviolate.

Joffre: Not the least assistance was that rendered us by Marshal Joffre. It was with great pleasure that I learned on June 16, 1917 * * * that Marshal Joffre had been disignated by the French Ministry of War to assist the American High Command, with instructions to give us the benefit of his advice in preparing ourselves for the great efforts that we would be called upon to make. Marshal Joffre insisted that his mission be carried out in accordance with the wishes of the American High Command, and from our earliest arrival we have looked upon him as our great friend and advisor.

General Organization Project: After the most careful study and consideration of the advice given us by the Allied Governments my staff evolved the general organization project, the services of the rear project, and the priority schedule of shipments, which three documents formed the broad plan which was to be the basis of all of our future effort in France, and of our effort at home in preparing for war in France. In the light of past events, and viewing the projects in retrospection, it is a matter of pride that in July 1917, this conception of our needs later proved to be very correct. The details of the organization embodied in each of the above documents are treated in the discussion upon organization, which forms a separate part of the main report.

Ports; R. R.'s: Chief among the matters to be taken up with the French were the ports to be used, the lines of communication to be turned over to the Americans, and the sites that were to be transferred to us for our necessary installations. Before leaving Washington, certain features as to the location of the American forces and the ports to be used had been discussed, but no decision, other than that our forces were to be employed in closer association with the French than with the British, had been reached. I therefore had my staff treat these important questions and on July 1, 1917, I cabled * * * the outline of a complete plan covering the ports of debarkation, the use of railroad lines, the location of depots and hospitals, training areas, and zones of operation. These plans required the most careful consideration, inasmuch as we were preparing to care for an eventual army of three, and perhaps four million men. Our plans for the services of supply necessitated dock construction in France, with a correspondingly large project for additional railroads and supply depots. Everything had to be considered from the viewpoint of the eventual employment of our forces. Circumstances forced us to utilize the southwestern ports of France, namely, Bordeaux, La Pallice, St-Nazaire and Brest, and the comparatively unused railroad systems leading therefrom to the northeast. Generally speaking, then, this contemplated the use of our forces against the enemy somewhere in that direction, but it was decided to establish the great depots of supply in a central location in the area included by Tours, Bourges and Chateauroux, so that our armies could be supplied with equal facility wherever they might be serving on the western front.

When our Allies finally grasped the far reaching plans that we had adopted and saw by our determination that we were sincere in our conclusions that millions of Americans must be brought to France, there was substituted among the Allies a certain confidence instead of the uncertainty which had been expressed at the Quai d'Orsay conference of May 4 as to the military effort to be expected from America.

Tonnage: On July 26, 1917 I held a conference with the French and Italian Commanders-in-Chief and the British and French Chiefs of Staff, at which it was decided that the necessity existed for adopting a purely defensive on all secondary fronts and withdrawing surplus troops for duty on the western front. By thus strengthening the western front our Allies expressed the belief that they could hold until the American forces should arrive in numbers sufficient to gain the ascendancy. The Allies at this conference urged the immediate study of the tonnage situation, with a view to accelerating the arrival of American troops. They stated that they had little reliance on further military assistance on a large scale from Russia.

Training Areas: Among the matters treated not the least important was the selection of the training areas. A strategical study that had been made by my staff convinced me that the eventual American sector should be in Lorraine, and all plans were made with such a sector in view. Later on this plan was realized, despite difficulties and obstacles which at times appeared almost insuperable. No full appreciation of the events which transpired in 1918 can be gained unless it is borne in mind that in the development of our forces and in our relations with the British and French my one underlying idea was always that the American Expeditionary Forces were to be a separate and distinct component of the combined Allied forces, and that our national identity was to be preserved. This policy was in accordance both with the President's basic instructions and with sound military judgment.

Training Areas: The selection of a sector was the determining factor in the location of training areas for the divisions. Committees, both of Marshal Foch's staffs and from Marshal Petain's headquarters, in consultation with the operations sections of my headquarters, studied the question both in its relation to the French Ministry of War and to the zone of the Armies, with the result that it was decided to locate the training areas near Neufchateau. I was anxious that the camps should be in the zone of the Armies in order that the instruction of the divisions should be given in the atmosphere of war.

It was not possible, however, to train the artillery brigades in the same areas with the infantry, as there was no available ground for artillery firing. The French consequently placed at our disposal their training camp for field artillery at Le Valdahon and on at Coetquidan. In addition, other camps were established at Meucon, Souge, La Courtine, and at Mailly * * *

Equipment and Material: The question of equipment received serious attention and study. Especially lacking were we in field artillery. Our small supply of this arm was one of the greatest handicaps of the United States. Negotiations were at once opened with the French to obtain matériel until such time as the United States could manufacture its own. They agreed to furnish us the 75-mm. and 155-mm. material, but could not furnish long range artillery. We adopted, therefore, these two types of gun and the wisdom of this action is shown by the fact that when the Armistice went into effect on November 11 not a single American made gun of these types had reached the front.

Besides the question of artillery, matters affecting the transportation of the Army, questions of organization, and training, were discussed at length with the French, and satisfactory conclusions reached, * * *

It is seen that the early months in France were taken up with the all important general organization plans, questions of supply and installations. In every way, we were assisted by the Allies to build up our machinery to care for the anticipated arrivals of American forces, and the important questions just mentioned were settled amicably and harmoniously. Full details of all of these matters are given in separate reports of the staff sections and services.

The Supreme War Council: The treatment of so many questions between the various governments demonstrated the necessity of a central body wherein such discussions might be heard, and where each government would be kept in touch with the needs of the other Allies.

The Allies had of course held conferences frequently, but finally, in November 1917, it was decided to establish a supreme war council, a permanent body which should sit at Versailles and whose purpose should be to deliberate upon the military situation, the mutual needs of the Allies, and to make suitable recommendations to the respective governments. Its principal object was to secure cooperation among the Allies. Upon its organization the President designated General Tasker H. Bliss to represent the United States.
* * *

American Troops with French: With the arrival of American troops, however, the subject of discussion between the Allies and myself dealt more and more upon the training and employment of our forces.

1st Division Arrives: The military situation of the Allies in the spring of 1917 was such that both France and Great Britain urged that the United States dispatch at least some troops to France without delay. (See report on Operations.) Though it was certain to the minds of all commanders that these troops could not be actually employed for some months, the 1st Division was sent to France in June 1917, to be a visible sign of our participation in the war, and to encourage the peoples of our Allies.

The first ships arrived at St-Nazaire June 26, 1917, and were greeted with an enthusiasm approaching frenzy. The advent of American troops in Europe produced a profound impression upon the people of both Great Britain and France, and the heartening effect which was hoped for by the Allied States was more than realized. The French people especially, always so impressionable, were thrilled with the thought that America had emerged from her distant isolation and had come forward to fight shoulder to shoulder with the armies of Europe. Of course they did not stop to think that the throwing over of a division in this manner was of no immediate value. To them, our advent meant salvation, and for the moment lifted them out of the depression into which they had, for the time being, fallen.

The 1st Division went immediately into a training area to prepare for its tour at the front, and its eventual employment in battle. At the requests of the French Government, however, one battalion was sent to Paris on July 14, 1917, to participate in the parade of the National Fete Day, so as to furnish ocular proof to the people of France that America had made good her promise. The troops were greeted with an enthusiasm that challenges description.

During the autumn the 26th, 42d and 2d Divisions arrived and were all likewise placed in training.

American General Plan of Training: From our own experience a general plan of training was adopted for our divisions. Briefly, it consisted in allowing a division one month after its arrival for acclimatization and for instruction in small units from battalions down, a second month in a quiet sector by battalions, regiments and brigades, respectively, and a third month in a training area for divisional instruction in war of movement. * * *

The military situation in the fall of 1917 and in March 1918, prevented the realization of this program in its entirety, but as strict an adherence to it was maintained throughout as events permitted.

French Depression Over Our Efforts: The military reverses of Russia and Italy in the fall of 1917, following the ineffectual efforts of the French and British in this year, caused great depression among the Allies toward the end of the year. Nor did America's presence offset this depression. Superficially, it appeared to them at this time that the American war effort would prove disappointing. We had few troops in Europe, and had found it difficult to rush over these few divisions. Our factories, of course, were working hard, and our War Department was creating and building the framework of an army, but the French were not in sufficient touch with our processes, and once more gave way to a feeling of disappointment gradually deepening into considerable depression in the winter of 1917-

1918. This depression was intensified by the thought that Germany, with Russia out of the way, would presumably change from the defensive to the offensive on the western front.

Political Manoeuvres for our use of American Troops: Both British and French then became impatient at the apparent slowness of America's active participation in the fight. The severe fighting and their losses had greatly depleted their forces and they began overtures to use Americans as replacements for their ranks.

The military and political powers both judged that French and British divisions should be maintained at full strength and that, as the manpower of their respective countries was practically exhausted, American troops should be used to make good the deficit. Aside from this idea, they felt that it would be impossible for America to form an idependent army in time to play an effective part in the war. They consequently spared no efforts to use our troops as replacements for their divisions.

I held a different view. America could not afford to sacrifice her national identity, but more important still, it was my judgment that the creation of an independent American army was the only method of gaining victory. Such employment of our forces as desired by the French and British could be entertained only for limited periods of training or to avert a catastrophe.

At the end of 1917, it appeared to me that no conditions existed which would warrant any such use of American forces, and I determined to pursue the plan of training that we had agreed upon, and of employing our troops eventually in Lorraine.

French Demands: The French were the first to initiate requests for our troops. On December 23, 1917, I had a conference with Marshal Petain, at which he made definite proposals for the use of American troops. * * *

He desired in brief, to accelerate the instructions of American units in France, and requested our earliest collaboration. The essence of his proposals was the incorporation of our regimental units in French divisions. This was in effect a continuation of the proposals begun before my headquarters left America.

I could not accede to any proposition involving the impossibility of creating an American army at the earliest moment, but I accepted, in general, the underlying principles of General Pétain's proposals for hastening the appearance of our troops at the front, with reservations as to the length of time that the divisional elements should remain brigaded, and I agreed to hasten the training of the divisions so as to be prepared for the expected German offensive in the spring.

My attitude was not accepted as final, however, by the French, for Clémenceau cabled the French Ambassador at Washington that this conference developed differences of opinion between General Petain and myself as to the wisdom of attaching regiments to French divisions, and instructed him to urge the Secretary of War to accept the French viewpoint and to command it to me. This was not done by the Secretary of War, who left the matter entirely to my discretion. I thereupon wrote M. Clémenceau, inviting his cooperation in settling such questions in France, and pointing out the likelihood of wrong impressions being created in Washington of serious disagreements between General Pétain and me when such was not the case. * * * I thought it best to settle such questions harmoniously with the French military authorities.

The subject of using our troops in French divisions was again brought up by General Rageneau, Chief of the French Mission at Headquarters A. E. F., at a conference held in Chaumont, January 7. * * * He emphasized the need of haste in training our troops and urged the incorporation of regiments with French divisions, not only for the period before entering the trenches but for actual employment in the front line.

Of course such a scheme would have rendered the American Command superfluous. The motive behind General Pétain's plan for training our troops was to increase French divisions for the front line. I could make no such concessions. I was willing and anxious to brigade the divisional elements with French and British units for training in trench warfare, as it was desirable to accustom gradually our troops to life at the front, but it was unthinkable to permit the French or British to keep their divisions at full strength by incorporating in them American regiments.

As General Rageneau was insistent, I indicated the possibility of employing some battalions with the British, a contingency that he seemed not to have contemplated. I also printed out that we were the best judges of our own training and that it progressed more rapidly and more satisfactorily without French tutelage than with it. Our methods were different and the difference in language was a bar to perfect understanding.

The American view of the proper method of training prevailed, of course, and the first 3 months of 1918 saw the American 1st Division holding a sector of its own east of St-Mihiel, and the 2d, 26th, and 42d brigaded with French divisions for short period of hardening in trench warfare preparatory to taking over divisional sectors. These latter were much scattered, the 26th near Soissons, the 2d south of Verdun, and the 42d near Luneville, but the presence of American troops in the line during the first months of 1918, when public confidence was at a low ebb did much to allay the growing anxiety of the Allies, for it was felt that our military effort was finally a reality.

American Sector: While, however, I was much gratified to be able to assist the Allies with all my resources, the delay in securing an American sector along the front caused me no little anxiety. It was extremely difficult to supply the American forces, scattered as they were, however desirable it might be from the French point of view to have our units incorporated in their divisions. And again, it became increasingly evident that our divisions could not attain their maximum efficiency and development until administered as a unit under exclusive American control. The question of an American sector as consequently a pressing necessity in order that we might have homogeneous training and in order not to fritter our forces away.

The immediate establishment of an exclusive American sector under American command was not welcomed at this time by the French, due no doubt to their anxiety regarding the expected German offensive. Also, the establishment of our sector would mean a renunciation upon their part of all efforts to incorporate our forces in their own and in British divisions.

I indicated my wishes to the French on February 6, 1918, that I had tentatively decided to adopt as an American sector the present front of the 1st Division extending the lines to the left, and that I desired it to become purely American on June 1, at which time I would have 4 trained conbatant divisions, together with the proper proportion of army and corps troops. These questions were being studied by the French Command when the Germans launched their offensive on March 21 with such disastrous effects upon the Allies as to upset all of my plans and defer their execution.

Relations with the British: It was at this point in our development that our relations with the British, which had begun in January, assumed greater importance, rising to an equality with our dealings with the French. As a matter of fact, the crisis caused by the German offensive necessitated the pooling of Allied interests. Before treating of this new phase of our relationship with the Allies, I will briefly review the relations with the British during the first quarter of 1918. * * *

On Dec. 25 I was informed that England as well as France was urging the President to permit the amalgamation of our forces with hers by regiments, battalions or companies. I replied by cable * * *

* * * * * *

A few days later I held a joint conference on this subject with Field Marshal Haig and General Petain at which a full and frank discussion took place, and America's viewpoint presented to both of our Allies.

The British in January 1918, through Sir William Robertson, * * * presented a request for 150 battalions of infantry to serve with British divisions, and offered to provide the necessary transportation for these reinforcements by diverting shipping from commercial use. The proposed arrangement was in no way to interfere with our own program for shipping our troops.

The question of manpower was important and our own shipping program so far behind that I did not think the opportunity should be lost of accepting the British offer to provide sea transportation for such extra men as we could furnish for temporary service with their army.

Accordingly a conference was held at Versailles on January 30, 1918, between the British representatives and myself to arrive at a mutually satisfactory arrangement. I presented the objections of the American Government to having our troops serve under a foreign flag, and among other things pointed out that additional manpower could be provided by other means than amalgamation. I therefore proposed that the British Government utilize the available sea transportation in question for bringing over the personnel of complete American divisions instead of simply infantry battalions. The British accepted my modifications and agreed to bring over six complete divisions, of which the infantry was to undergo a course of training in British divisions for ten weeks, at the end of which it was to be withdrawn to join its artillery, which meanwhile had been trained under American direction in French material.

The German offensive caused, however, a modification of this six division agreement before it went into effect.

The offensive made such inroads upon the reserves of the French and British that defeat stared them in the face unless the new American army should prove more numerous and more immediately available than even the most optimistic had dared to hope.

Both French and British turned at once to America for assistance. I realized the gravity of the situation and considered the German offensive so formidable that I temporarily abandoned my own plans and did my utmost to offset the new and incalculable elements that had entered the situation by immediately placing all of our forces at Marshal Foch's disposal.

At this time the Secretary of War was in Europe, and a meeting of the supreme war council was held at Versailles March 27, 1918, to consider what measures might be taken to meet the crisis. At this conference the military representatives of the Allied Governments requested the American Government to assist the Allied armies as soon as possible by permitting in principle the temporary service of American units in Allied army corps and divisions. They urged also that only American infantry and machine-gun units be brought to France and that all agreements or conventions hitherto made in conflict with this decision be modified accordingly. This played into the British hand, as originally they opposed my project of bringing over complete divisions. It seemed as if everything conspired to prevent us from forming an American army.

The foregoing resolutions of the Supreme War Council were considered by the Secretary of War, General Bliss and by me. We realized that the proposed changes in the order of shipment of American troops to France would necessarily postpone the organization and training of complete American divisions as parts of an independent American army. It was our opinion that this ought to be conceded only in view of the then critical situation and continue only so long as that situation demanded it. We felt that the question of replacements would continue to embarrass the British and French Governments and we must anticipate efforts on their part to satisfy that need by retaining American units assigned to them. We determined that we should keep in mind the formation of an American army, but at the same time we did not wish to seem to sacrifice joint efficiency at a critical moment, to that object.

Upon the presentation of these recommendations to Washington the President cabled his approval of the joint note of the Supreme War Council, * * *

* * * * * *

The War Department then informed me on April 2 * * * that preferential transportation would be given to American infantry and machine-gun units during the present emergency. I immediately completed preliminary arrangements for training and early employment with the French of such units of infantry as should be sent over by our own transportation. The British were to receive under the new arrangement the infantry and machine-gun units of the first six divisions which they should bring under their own transportation. It was never the intention to allow our units to replace losses of British or French organizations and the War Department was requested to hold in readiness our artillery and to have it follow the infantry in order that our divisional organizations might be completed at the earliest possible moment when the opportunity should present itself. I insisted that the Allies fully comprehend that any aid we gave in this manner must be considered temporary only and in order to meet the existing emergency. Any other general policy would have been disastrous to us. In a discussion of this subject of the employment of our infantry with the British, with the military representatives of the Supreme War Council, it became known that the French representative wanted the same concession made to his government and the Italian representative asked whether his government might expect the same assistance by our infantry units. It was necessary for me to stand firm in this matter and to have the Allies thoroughly understand that our infantry was to be returned as soon as practicable so as to form our own divisions.

More specifically on April 3, 1918, I recommended to the War Department that we should not look further into the future of giving priority to the infantry beyond four divisions, two of which should go to the British in accordance with our agreement. The War Department adopted my suggestion.

In the interval, on April 3, I was informed that the British through their ambassador in Washington were negotiating for the continuation of exclusive infantry shipments up to July, at the rate of 120,000 men per month divided equally between British and American controlled tonnage. The President agreed that all possible measures should be taken to insure the maximum use of troop tonnage. The creation of such a preponderance of infantry would delay the formation of an American army until the spring of 1919, and would prevent our exercising anything more than a purely fictitious control over these officers and soldiers for many months after July 1, 1918.

The entire matter was brought to a head at a conference on April 7 between the Secretary of War, myself and a representative of the British War Office. In the course of the discussion it developed that the British interpreted the Versailles Note 18 as abrogating the previous six division agreement and opening the way for brigading our infantry with their forces and the French in numbers limited only by the capacity of their ships. We contended, on the contrary, that the original six division agreement was merely modified, so as to give priority to the infantry movement.

* * * * * *

On April 11 I sent a new priority schedule to the War Department to cover the months of April, May and June, based on a capacity of 120,000 men per month. Its fundamental principle was to postpone shipment of all noncombatant troops to the utmost possible in order to meet the existing situation and at the same time not make it impossible to build up our own army.

As was to be expected, therefore, this schedule bore the marks of a compromise. In deference to the recommendations of the Versailles Conference, the shipment of 78,000 S. O. S. troops, all tank personnel and a large amount of air personnel was postponed. Provision was made for the shipment on British tonnage during April and May of the infantry and machine guns, or what came to be known as the A units, of six divisions of the II Corps, with the addition in June of the A units of one division of the III Corps, 24,000 replacements and 18,000 S. O. S. troops; during the same time there would arrive at the American ports two complete divisions (a priority of two months being given to the infantry of one) all the B units of the II Corps divisions, 20,000 replacements and the balance of S. O. S. troops.

This schedule was at first approved * * * but afterwards was canceled * * * for reasons indicated, although not explicitly stated in No. 1184-R. This latter cable under date of April 26, transmitted a note from our government addressed to the British Ambassador dated April 19, stating the intentions of the United States to continue throughout the months of April, May, June and July to supply for transportation in both its own owned and controlled tonnage and in that made available by Great Britain, infantry and machine gun personnel.

This was, however, limited as follows:

It being understood that this program, to the extent that it is a departure from the plan to transport and assemble in Europe complete American divisions is is made in view of the exigency of the present military situation and in order to bring into useful cooperation at the earliest possible moment the largest possible number of American personnel in the military arm most needed by our Allies. It being also understood that this statement is not to be regarded as a commitment from which the government of the United States is not free to depart when the exigency no longer requires it; and also that the preferential transportation of infantry and machine gun units here set forth as a policy and principle is not to be regarded as so exclusive as to prevent the Government of the United States from including in the troops carried by its own tonnage from time to time relatively small numbers of personnel of other arms as may be deemed wise by the United States.

The above note was first brought to my attention at a conference with the British Secretary of State for War, held in London beginning April 21. Under the last previous agreement the priority of shipment of infantry had been limited to the troops transported on British tonnage during April At this London Conference a new agreement was reached (961-S) which again embodied mutual concessions. In favor of the British it provided that during May, American shipping as well as British would be primarily devoted to the transportation of troops for training and service with the British Army in France, up to six divisions. On the other side, this preferential shipment was extended beyond infantry and machine guns to include divisional engineers and signal troops and it was further provided that the artillery and corps troops for these divisions should immediately follow, together with much service of the rear and other troops as may be considered necessary by the American Commander-in-Chief.

The London Agreement was simply a modification of our original six-division agreement with the British, to conform with the recommendations of the Versailles Note 18.

A new situation arose, however. Although the original project had been approved by the French, they took exception to the new terms which assured the shipment of infantry to the British during May on both American and British tonnage without any guarantee that the program would be continued for the benefit of the French in June and July. As a result of their representations, a conference was held at Abbeville on May 2 at which the whole subject was reopened. The proceedings are reported in Cables 1042-S and 1064-S. An agreement was reached essentially as follows: * * *

1st: The British guaranteed to transport 130,000 troops in May, the first to be infantry and machine-gun units of six divisions for service with the British.

2d: The British guaranteed to transport 150,000 troops in June, the first to be infantry and machine-gun units of six divisions to be allocated for training and service as might be determined by the American Commander-in-Chief.

3d: All American tonnage and all excess British tonnage during both months to be used as might be determined by the American Commander-in-Chief, with the limitation in the following paragraph.

4th: All British tonnage in excess of 150,000 troops in June, to transport infantry and machine-gun units only - (In return for this Mr. Lloyd George agreed informally to use British shipping to complete these divisions in July.)

The agreement also contained the following significant declaration:

It is the opinion of the Supreme War Council that, in order to bring the war to a successful conclusion, an American army should be formed as early as possible under its own commander and under its own flag.

A further readjustment of the priority schedule was required by the Abbeville Agreement and I cabled the new program to Washington on May 12 * * *

No sooner has the text of the Abbeville Agreement reached the United States with its terms so evidently favorable to the building up of a balanced homogeneous American force, than the British and French Ambassadors in Washington renewed their perssure upon our government for an exclusive infantry program. I was accordingly informed by Cable No. 1297-R, dated May 11, as follows:

It has been suggested to the President that General Foch may reopen this subject with you and the President hopes that you will approach any such interview as sympathetically as possible, particularly if the situation as to replacements which has been presented to him is as critical as it seems.

In the meantime I had been confidentially informed by the Chief of Staff that there was left at this time in the United States, excluding three divisions at ports of embarkation, 263,852 infantrymen of sufficient training for overseas service, and that unless the acceptance of untrained infantrymen was desired that there was a practical limit to the extent to which the infantry and machine-gun program could be carried. I knew from the above cable that the Allies were certain to urge an extension of the Abbeville Agreement and I therefore caused studies to be undertaken to provide me with the necessary data for the approaching conference. These studies enabled me to cable to the War Department a forecast of the position that I had decided to take * * * May 25. In this cable I stated:

Preliminary studies show that it is essential that large amount of available tonnage for July and August be devoted to bringing over indispensable service of supply troops and combat units necessary to care for our troops and to complete divisions, elements of which will have embarked prior to June 30. A reference to priority schedule will show original scheme which is now far behind. Detailed study of subject now being made and will be cabled within few days.

The War Department replied on May 28:

Reference 1 A your 1186, all supply and other troops on priority schedule can be shipped in a short time as soon as it is decided to slow up on shipment of divisions. March.

A study prepared by the Asst. Chief of Staff, 3d Section, dated May 26, showed that on June 30 there would be a shortage of approximately 380,000 troops necessary to the formation of a selfsustaining American army in France. The most important deficiencies were the B units of the IV Corps, 55,000; S. O. S. troops, 143,000; and replacements for July alone 40,000. With reference to this latter item it was stated:

The only way to avoid bringing over at least 40,000 replacements is to break up divisions. Certainly our Allies cannot ask this of us. The figure 40,000 must very probably be increased.

In view of the fact that by the end of June we should have embarked from the United States a total of 860,000 men, it was evident to me that the shipping during July and August should be used to balance our forces and to put into effect the declaration of the Abbeville Agreement looking to the formation as early as possible of an American army under its own commander and under its own flag.

Versailles Conference: * * * On June 2 a conference was held at Versailles attended by representative of France, Great Britain and the United States, at which the question of shipments for June as well as July was considered. The discussion centered about the desire of both British and French to continue in July the preferential shipment of 170,000 infantry and machine-gun units, but as I had been informed by the Chief of Staff, General March, that the number of such troops available at home was limited, I insisted on the imperative necessity of building up my service of supply and especially the transportation facilities essential to the maintenance of an American army.

At this conference the Abbeville Agreement was substantially changed to our advantage by including among the divisional units to be given priority, the train headquarters and military police, engineer trains and sanitary trains. On the other hand I was committed to the transportation of the infantry of four divisions in July on shipping which it was hoped to allot to other needs.

I then cabled the War Department * * * a detailed program of shipments in accordance with the Versailles Agreement. The space left to my discretion was allocated so as to complete by the end of July the six divisions whose infantry and machine guns were to be shipped in June and the four divisions whose infantry and machine guns were to be shipped in July, with the exception of the artillery of the latter. This brings us to the end of the shipment program as laid down for June and July.

An Allied Commander-in-Chief: While the events just described were in process of negotiation, it became increasingly evident that the efforts of the Allies would be better coordinated and more effective under an Allied Commander-in-Chief. This idea had been suggested many times before, but for various reasons, political and otherwise, it had never became a *fait accompli*.

The threatened German offensive in March demonstrated the need for immediate decision in the matter. Naturally the choice of such a commander lay between the British and French. An American was out of the question owing to our relatively small force and to our having no immediate defensive object in France. The British felt that they must defend the channel ports at all cost, whereas the French considered the defense of Paris as of paramount importance. Each side saw the necessity for a supreme commander, but national sentiment and public opinion had acted as a bar heretofore. British opinion feared that a French commander might sacrifice the channel ports to the defense of Paris. From the American viewpoint a supreme commander was most desirable inasmuch as our perspective of the war from across the ocean had shown us how much effort was wasted by lack of coordination among the Allies.

Finally, however, the choice of a coordinator fell upon Marshal (then General) Foch. The Convention of Doullens on March 26 gave Marshal Foch certain consulting and coordinating powers but without specific power to issue orders to enforce coordination. This led to friction and resulted in the Convention of Beauvais on April 3, in which specific powers were given to General Foch to issue orders to carry out his plans.

Neither the Convention of Doullens nor that of Beauvais gave any powers in respect to the Italian front. The Supreme War Council in session at Abbeville May 2 and 3 vested in General Foch over the Italian front the powers of the Doullens Convention, namely, consulting and coordinating powers. But the Italian Government refused to give him any power of command on the Italian front until there should be Allied Armies operating in Italy in the same sense as in France.

America was at all times willing to accept a supreme command. On April 5, I received a letter from Mr. Clémenceau in which he said:

Mr. Lloyd George informs me that he accepts my proposition to bestow upon General Foch the title of Commander-in-Chief of the Allied Armies in France. I hasten to ask if you agree to this proposition, subject, naturally, to the approval of the American Government.

I replied as follows:

In reply to your letter repeated to me this morning by telephone, I hasten to express my full and complete agreement with your view and that of Mr. Lloyd George as to conferring on General Foch the title of Commander-in-Chief of the Allied Armies in France. This is subject to confirmation of my Government, which I have no doubt will be immediate.

On April 16, I received a cable from Washington stating that the President has given his approval for the United States. * * *

American aid tendered Allies March-July: In order to clear up the perspective of the reader, it is well to give a brief résumé of the aid rendered the Allies during the critical months of March to July, when the representatives of the Allied Governments were in constant conferences. The relationship between the other Allies and ourselves referred during this period almost exclusively to the use of our forces. It is proper to point out the part played by America due to the increased arrivals. On March 18, two days before the German offensive began, there were in France 296,819 officer and men, of which 167,672 were combatant troops represented by four combat divisions, one replacement and one depot division and one regiment of infantry - colored troops - serving with the French.

On May 11, I cabled to the War Department. * * * the status of the American Expeditionary Forces. * * * We had increased our troops to a grand total of 488,224. Of this total 11,410 were actually serving with the British and 12,234 with the French. In addition, 34,334 were in training areas back of British and 8,199 in training with French forces.

The French had had turned over to them four Negro regiments of the 3d Division, approximately 5,500 motor mechanics, 6 machine shop truck units and 80 sections of the U. S. Ambulance Service.

In addition to the assistance being given to the French and British Armies in the form of infantry and special troops, our troops on May 11 were actually holding 35 miles of the front lines. The significance of this fact can be better appreciated when it is realized that this is more than the front held by the British Army during the first year of the war.

Then too, our divisions began to participate actively in the operations starting with the Marne offensive of the Germans, May 27. The details of the operations at Château-Thierry and Soissons will be found in the operations section report. Suffice to say that their actual fighting stopped the German advance in May, drove him back in June, and at the counterattack of July 18, broke his defense, causing the evacuation of the Marne Salient. America was represented on other fronts besides the western. Italy had made requests for troops, and the Russia situation seemed to make it expedient to send a small force to Archangel.

Troops in Italy: In April when the Secretary of War was in Italy he was urged by everybody to send American troops to Italy, so as to show America's interest in the Italian situation and to strengthen the Italian morale.

The subject was considered by me and at a conference with Mr. Orlando, I offered to send not more than one regiment to begin with, with a prospect of gradually increasing it to a division. The Italians desired a large force, and in July urged the President to send more troops. The President, however, outlined to the Italian Government the policy of the United States which briefly was to build up our Army on the western front and that to dispatch large bodies of troops elsewhere would be inconsistent with the general purpose expressed. Consequently a single regiment of the 83d Division was dispatched to Italy in the summer of 1918, where it remained until the Armistice. * * *

Troops in Russia:

The Murmansk Expedition: It was the opinion of the Supreme War Council that an Allied expedition should be sent to cooperate with the Russians either at Murmansk or Archangel. It was also their desire for active intervention via Vladivostok.

The President, however, disapproved of the latter project, but expressed himself as heartily in sympathy with any practical military efforts which could be made from either of the other two places. * * *

The War Department cabled the Supreme War Council, General Bliss, June 15, that Lord Milner had made an urgent request upon the President for the dispatch of an American force to the ports of Murmansk and Archangel, consisting of three battalions of infantry and machine guns, two batteries of field artillery, three companies of engineers, and the necessary administrative and medical service, aggregating more than 4,000 men. On July 23, General Bliss was informed by cable * * * that the President approved of three battalions of infantry to be contributed by the United States provided Marshal Foch could spare them. These battalions were to come from my forces. He also authorized three companies of engineers, provided I could spare them. He disapproved furnishing any artillery.

In accordance, therefore, with instructions of my government, I ordered the following forces to Russia, to form part of the Allied Expeditionary Forces: 1 regiment of infantry, 1 battalion of engineers, 1 ambulance company and 1 field hospital. They sailed from Castle, England, August 26, 2918.

Necessity for an American Sector: * * * It has been seen that even as late as July in this counteroffensive on the Marne our troops were engaged as single divisions under French corps commanders. The continuance of the German offensive, it should be stated, from March to July created a situation that interferred most seriously with the plans of the American High Command. The emergency conditions had to be met by emergency measures and with great reluctance the plans which had been long delayed, for the creation of an independent American sector and for the formation of an American Army, had been sacrificed to the necessity of reinforcing the Allied lines at all costs. Our troops had been put in at all points of the line with no consideration whatever for our own military interests. This represented a very real sacrifice to the Allied cause; the sacrifice was made without hesitation but we felt repaid inasmuch as the help rendered to the Allies was largely responsible for their restored morale, and for the change in the situation from that of a desperate defense to a confident offence.

But the question of supplying our Army, scattered as they were along the Allied front, had reached a critical stage and I again made representations to the Allied Commander-in-Chief of the immediate necessity for establishing an American Army and for creating an American sector.

After the third German offensive I had an interview with General Pétain at Chantilly on May 19 upon this question and we agreed substantially that as soon as the circumstances permitted, the American Army would take complete charge of the sector of the Woëvre. At that time the nucleus of the sector mentioned was occupied by the 26th Division. It was the plan that as other American divisions became available each of them would be sent to take its place on the right and left of this sector, and that when four American divisions were in the line and two in reserve the sector would be definitely turned over to the American Army and would function with the American Army's resources as an American sector. It was further agreed upon that if the fluctuations of the battle which was then in progress should make it necessary to take American divisions in the American sector for employment elsewhere after such sector had been definitely established, that the French High Command would replace the American divisions with French divisions which would be placed under the American Command.

General Pétain then gave orders for the General commanding the Group of Armies of the East to make a complete study of the sector in question to determine the limits of the sector and the necessary communications, establishments, local services, etc., that should be turned over to the Americans. Nothing further, however, was done owing to the employment of our divisions as described above.

On July 14, I again sought an interview with Marshal Foch to whom I outlined my reasons for the desirability of the early assembly of the American forces. I expressed my willingness insofar as concerned the immediate future to assemble these troops wherever necessary, as around Château-Thierry for example, but I insisted that it was necessary to look farther into the future and consider the early establishment of a permanent American sector within which our forces might be developed and expanded as they arrived. I indicated the region Toul-Nancy as the logical American sector. Marshal Foch agreed that America had the right to have her Army organized as such and that the American Army must be an accomplished fact. He stated moreover that the cause of the Allies would be better served by an American Army under its own chief than by an American Army with its units dispersed. He stated that he would like to have our forces assembled into a temporary sector in the vicinity of Château-Thierry, but notwithstanding his statement, an impression was gained that he was not favorable to the idea of establishing an American sector with any degree of permanency before October 1. We discussed the plans for the 1919 campaign and while we were in accord as to the efforts that should be made and to the necessity for coordinated attacks by every available Allied division, whether it be American, French or British, I could not agree *in toto* with the principle of the employment of the forces. His idea was that a frontal attack would be made simultaneously by the three Allies, and that the effort should be continuous, the American attacking between Reims and the Argonne. This was not the sector that I desired for our forces. I favored Lorraine. I believe that a powerful attack should be made between Baccarat and Nancy which would so threaten the vital region of the German line as to make certain the withdrawal of masses of hostile troops from northern France. It seemed to me that an attack in Lorraine as well as in northern France was essential. Moreover the Lorraine front was better suited for an American sector than the Champagne or any other part of the front, for the following reasons:

(a) The location of our forces, depots and line of communications was in better relation to the front, St-Mihiel---St-Die.

(b) It had been understood from the beginning that Lorraine was the portion of the front which we were to occupy and our development had all been made to that end. A change at this time would have delayed matters and rendered necessary the duplication of much work and material peculiar to our needs. With an American sector in Lorraine we had the possibility of extending our front into the Vosges where we could place the new divisions which must continue to arrive. This would give me control over our new units to an extent which would be impracticable were our sector elsewhere.

On July 21, I again had an interview with Marshal Foch and General Pétain relative to the formation of the American Army and the American sector. I also informed Marshal Foch at this time that I would myself take command of this First Army and I offered to place myself, in all that concerned operations, under the command of the General Commander-in-Chief of the French Armies of the North and Northeast. Marshal Foch accepted my offer and we agreed that the First Army should be formed in the region north of the Marne around the nucleus already in this locality where the American I Corps was.

I pressed the point for a calm sector to be given, at the earliest possible moment, to the American Army, and on July 22 Marshal Foch informed me that he had decided that the sector extending from Nomeny to the north of St-Mihiel would be placed progressively under American command according as units which might be sent there were available.

The situation therefore at the end of July was that the American First Army should be temporarily constituted in the Château-Thierry sector but that eventually the American Army should take over the Toul-Nancy sector. Accordingly orders were issued and the staff of the American First Army was sent to La Ferte-sous-Jouarre where it began to function on August 10.

At the interview, July 24, the question of the reduction of the St-Mihiel Salient was also discussed, and Marshal Foch agreed that he would entrust this operation to the American Army but no date was settled upon inasmuch as the battles along the Aisne and Somme were then in full progress, and it could not be immediately foreseen how the military situation would develop.

The Allied High Command were rather reluctant to assemble our forces while the counter-offensive was in progress but in my judgement the creation of an army had been sufficiently deferred and any further delay, I believed, would irremediably effect the future success of American Armies. I, of course, appreciated the difficulty of bringing our widely scattered groups together during the battle but the time had arrived for firm adherence to this principle.

Throughout the whole period of operations of 1918, French interests and French views were dominant in the conduct of operations. In this respect it might be fairly said that our military policy was merely the confirmation of the national policy and that the constant efforts of our High Command to meet the views of the French High Command was the logical continuation of the attitude displayed by our sentiments and our people toward France at the moment when we entered the war. One of the specific incidents, in this respect, was the ready support given the appointment of Marshal Foch as the Generalissimo of the Allied Armies.

The French war plans which we accepted were directly dominated by a somewhat narrow conception of the French national interests, as previously indicated. It is clear that the French conception of the operations was largely territorial in scope, aiming at reconquest of portions of French soil. If heavy fighting and subsequent destruction was to take place, it was best from the French view that this should happen in districts where the damage would be least felt.

The American High Command was confirmed in the belief that the best way to serve the Allied cause was by the formation of American Armies to be employed as tactical troops along sections of the front of the greatest strategic importance. The creation, therefore, of our American First Army was the beginning of our independent action.

After my interview on July 24, I caused a study to be made to ascertain the number of divisions that would be necessary to carry out the St-Mihiel operation which had been ordered by the Commander-in-Chief of the Allied Armies. On August 8, I decided that in view of the different situation in the region of the Marne and of the number of divisions that would be required for the St-Mihiel operation that it was advisable to abandon the project of forming the First Army in the region of the Marne. I accordingly sought an interview with the Allied Commander-in-Chief for the purpose of making the necessary arrangements. This interview was held at Sarcus on August 9. I indicated to Marshal Foch that the situation on the Vesle appeared to be stabilizing and presented my views as to the desirability of carrying out the St-Mihiel offensive. I requested him to reduce the American forces in the Marne region to the lowest possible limit and to bring at least three American divisions from the British front, and finally organize the First Army in the Toul region. The Allied

Commander-in-Chief agreed and together we discussed the outline of the projected operation. That same evening I had an interview with General Pétain at his headquarters. He and I went over the conditions of the projected operation and we finally settled upon the details of the organization of the First Army in the Toul region. General Pétain further agreed to the reduction of the divisions to be left in the Marne region to three.

Further American Effort: On June 23, 1918, I held a conference with Marshal Foch at my residence, Val des Ecoliers, near Chaumont, regarding the American effort. It was concluded, after a full consideration of the deficiencies of the Allies in manpower, and on account of new indications of probable substantial increases of German forces from the eastern front, that our part in the Allied effort should be enlarged.

I placed before the War Department the joint recommendations of Marshal Foch and me, that to win the victory in 1919 we should have in France 80 divisions by April and 100 in July. M. Clémenceau, who was present at the conference, gave assurance that every possible efvort would be made by the French Government to supplement deficiencies in our supplies and equipment, including munitions and aviation. No definite hope was held out to the Allies that America would be able to make this stupendous effort, as so many questions had to be considered, shipping, material, and the industrial output of the United States. On July 3, in private conversation with M. Clémenceau and Mr. Lloyd George, the latter affirmed Great Britian's intention of providing all the shipping possible, showing that they fully appreciated the situation. * * *

The War Department considered the 80-division program as the maximum effort that we should make. Consequently, I again set forth fully my views * * * urging the 100-division program by July 1919.

On September 26, 1918, the War Department cabled me * * * that the 80-divisions in France program was the official program and directed that I give instructions that rate of shipments and requirements be worked out to correspond therewith. And so the matter rested when the Armistice occurred.

* * * * * *

GENERAL HEADQUARTERS, A. E. F.,

Chaumont, Haute-Marne, June 30, 1919.

GENERAL STAFF
at
GENERAL HEADQUARTERS

[Extract]

Upon its arrival in France June 13, 1917, the Headquarters, A. E. F., consisted of:

G. S. officers and other officers. 59
Clerks 56
Soldiers for Hq. Guard and Orderlies 67
Interpreters 4

186

The outbreak of the war had found the army without any military organization higher than a regiment, and without an adequate staff, and besides the various arms of the service were not balanced to meet the needs of the Europe war. It was therefore necessary to change the peace time organization of our army to meet the conditions of its employment in a very specialized warfare.

But before this problem could be approached, it was first essential to organize the nucleus of a suitable general staff. It is true that the United States army possessed a small general staff prior to the war, but the adherence of the army to the bureau system made its general staff nominal only, and distinctly different from the general staff system as practiced in European armies. The C-in-C determined, however, to employ the general staff system of organization, and to install general staff control as practiced alike by our Allies and by our enemies. At this time the only general staff that existed in the A. E. F. was at General Headquarters, with the exception of the small general staff of the one division that had arrived. Studies were begun at once to determine the proper staff organization but while its development was in progress, General Headquarters began to grow rapidly due to the necessity for officers to handle the many problems arising. * * *

In speaking therefore of the period preceding the final decision of the staff question, it will be necessary to include the entire officer personnel at headquarters, in order to narrate the growth of the general staff.

After a preliminary study, a tentative staff organization was adopted, comprising three sections: Administrative, Intelligence and Operations, and the officers who had accompanied the C-in-C and who were available for general staff duty were assigned accordingly. * * * Offices were installed in two small buildings at 29 and 31 Rue Constantine, Paris (near the Invalides), and in these modest rooms was begun the huge task of organizing the army to fight in France.

In the same building with the staff had been installed the technical services or departments, but the rapid growth of the headquarters personnel soon made it desirable to move the services to the Hotel Ste-Anne, No. 10, Rue Ste-Anne.

The chief problem that occupied the attention of the staff was the adoption of a suitable project for organizing the army and for transporting the troops across seas. Inasmuch as the army had no organization of any scope, it was not a question of regulating an existing organization but of making a new one. * * *

In addition, the complex problems of training required careful study, and it was now evident that a separate staff section should be created for this work, rather than overburden the operations section whose immediate attention was being given to the general organization project. Fundamentally, of course, the training of troops and their employment in battle are closely related, and in other armies, the subject of training is dealt with by a committee or subsection of the operations section of the general staff. At first, this principle was followed by us, but it was apparent that the task of training our projected army in France was so immense that it was early determined to create a separate training section. This was done by taking from the operations section its training committee and enlarging it.

Likewise, a new section was needed to coordinate the work of the various services which roughly correspond to our supply departments. It was known that the French General Staff organization provided for such a section, and even our short experience had demonstrated its necessity and desirability. The C-in-C therefore added a coordination section to the general staff at general headquarters. These changes were ordered by a G. H. Q. memorandum on August 11, 1917.

Thus, the general staff had been divided into five sections * * * and neither the number of sections nor the general class of duties assigned to each was ever again changed. It might be said that thus far the general staff had never been organized. In reality, it had been a natural growth rather than a careful organization.

Hardly, however, had the staff commenced its work when it became evident that the few officers available for general staff duty were entirely inadequate for the work that would be required of them. The C-in-C therefore began urging the war department to send to France additional officers suitable for general staff duty.

* * * * * *

Unfortunately, since the number of such officers in our army was limited the War Department found itself unable to spare many of them from the duty they were performing in the United States. Without, however, desisting from making appeals to the War Department, yet the paucity of available staff officers both at home and abroad made it soon evident that a new source of supply for general staff officers would have to be instituted before extensive training or operations could be begun. With the approval of the War Department, the training committee of the operations section was caused to begin the organization of a general staff college. * * *

Meanwhile, the C-in-C had been urging the War Department to authorize him to appoint qualified officers as acting general staff officers so as to relieve the situation. On October 27, 1917, such authorization was received * * * and thereafter, in assigning duty, no distinction was made between the officers so appointed and those regularly appointed general staff officers according to law.

It was regrettable indeed that our general staff prior to the war was so small, for the lack of enough fully trained staff officers was felt throughout the entire stay of the A. E. F. in France. Had it been otherwise, the personnel employed on general staff duty in France could have been materially reduced.

Meanwhile the General Headquarters of the A. E. F. was rapidly growing in size, and it was evident that additional space must be provided for it. Inasmuch as training areas for our troops had already been determined upon in the general vicinity of the upper MARNE, and this location of billeting areas would also determine the part of the front upon which our troops would most naturally be employed, it seemed desirable to locate General Headquarters in that vicinity. Vittel, a summer resort, and CHAUMONT-en-BASSIGNY were discussed. It was determined to move to CHAUMONT, where General Headquarters was established in the former barrack of a French infantry regiment. The move was made Saturday, September 1, 1917.

Since June 13, General Headquarters had grown until upon that date it consisted of:

Officers 74
Clerks 122
Soldiers 1146

The continued expansion of the headquarters personnel made it desirable to decide upon a maximum that should conform to a definite organization. By December 1917 it was possible to make such a study. In consequence, General Headquarters tables of organization were drawn up, which provided for:

Officers	547
Field Clerks	229
Interpreters	22
Soldiers	3471
Total	4271

and included the General Headquarters organization for general staff, administrative departments and supply department. * * *

These proposed tables of organization were accepted on December 22, 1917, and forwarded to the War Department for approval. After being slightly modified, they were approved by cablegram received 743 paragraph 5 * * * Slight modifications were made by later cablegrams received, 1030 paragraph 2-A sent 1246 paragraph 7, and received 1551 paragraph 3 * * *

Until this time the official title of general headquarters had been "Headquarters American Expeditionary Forces," but shortly afterwards in pursuance of authority contained in War Department cablegram (No. 636 R) the name was changed to read "General Headquarters, American Expeditionary Forces," with the abbreviation "G. H. Q., A. E. F." (See G. O. 11, Jan. 17, 1918, A. E. F.).

Meanwhile the experience which had enabled the testing of the good and bad features of the preliminary staff organization in operation, demonstrated the necessity of its revision so as to meet our own peculiar needs.

A careful detailed study of staff organization was ordered to be made in which British and French staff organizations were considered in relation to American laws and experiences.

The British and French staff organizations differed materially from each other, nevertheless, both the British and French armies would have been glad to have us exactly copy their organization, for that would have greatly facilitated their future dealings with us.

France had adopted the system of general staff control in 1911 and Great Britain had adopted a general staff system in 1909, which was a compromise between the system of general staff control and the bureau system. Both armies had met the needs which the war had developed by the piece-meal addition of new agencies. In the sense of being perfect in themselves neither British nor French staff officers regarded their own organizations as models. We had our own laws to consider, particularly those which organize our supply departments and designate their duties. Even had it been deemed desirable to copy exactly either of these staff systems our laws did not permit of our doing so. Further, it was known that both systems were the growth of necessity and were modified by legal and political considerations that did not apply to our forces.

As a result of these studies the staff organization given in G. O. 31, 1918 was decided upon * * *

During the time that this study on staff organization was being made it was determined to remove all the supply departments from general headquarters to the headquarters of the service of supply. This determination was based upon the following considerations.

(a) It is a well known fact that a commander or an executive can deal effectively with but a limited number of responsible subordinates. This number is variously placed by different writers. However, it is the object of all organizations to so divide responsibility that the number of responsible subordinates with whom an executive must deal directly shall be reduced to a workable number. Under the bureau system of staff organization, with the large number of departments required by modern conditions, the number of heads of departments is too great for an executive to deal directly with all of them and to do so efficiently. From this it results that they must be so grouped that their action will be coordinated, but that the executive will be required to deal directly only with the representatives of the groups. By authorizing heads of general staff sections to issue orders pertaining to routine matters in the name of the C-in-C and to present for consideration matters of policy which, after being decided, became routine matters, the C-in-C could reduce the number of persons with whom he must deal directly and continuously to a workable number. The presence at general headquarters of the chiefs of all these important departments of the service made it inevitable that he would deal directly with them, so that unless they were physically absent the benefit desired would not be obtained. A mere paper division of duties and responsibilities would not suffice.

(b) For the performance of their duty in matters pertaining to supply they would be more conveniently located near the center of the activities of their departments at the headquarters of the service of supply. (Until now called line of communications.)

(c) It was evident that the small town of CHAUMONT would not be able to afford billets and office space for all the persons who would eventually be required to conduct the official business of the whole Headquarters, which by this time had grown until it numbered:

134 officers

302 clerks and

1414 soldiers

It was accordingly decided to move all the supply departments to TOURS, the headquarters of the services of supply. This move took place, beginning February 16, 1918.

The removal of the supply departments to the headquarters of the service of supply made so much of the tables of organization as pertained to them inapplicable but so much as pertained to the general staff and to the administrative departments (Inspector General's Department, Adjutant General's Department and Judge Advocate) remained in force.

This organization of the general staff sections at General Headquarters were thereafter found to be adequate, except for a separate historical section which was later instituted by Par. III, G. O. 29, 1919 * * *

G. O. 31, 1918 referred to above, operated therefore to separate the general staff, the administrative staff (Inspector General's Department, Adjutant General's Department, Judge Advocate) and the personal staff of the C-in-C into one group and the technical staff of the supply departments into another.

The general staff, including the personal staff of the C-in-C and the headquarters guard, clerks and orderlies now numbered 128 officers, of whom 47 were regularly appointed general staff officers or acting general staff officers; 55 field clerks, 620 orderlies. This personnel was increased in June 1918 by the addition of 34 officers of whom 11 were general staff officers, or acting general staff officers (cablegram received 1551 Paragraph 3).

All of the officers employed in general staff sections particularly at General Headquarters or at Army Headquarters, did not need to be general staff officers. Many were employed in a clerical or technical capacity that could have been filled by field clerks or sergeants of sufficient military or technical experience, but in our army men of the required qualifications could be found only in the commissioned grades.

Growth of General Staff throughout A. E. F: When G. O. 31, 1918 went into effect on February 16, 1918, all of the general staff officers on duty in the A. E. F. pertained to General Headquarters, with the exception of those who belonged to the six combat divisions which had then arrived in France. Thereafter, however, the general staff on duty with tactical units grew rapidly in size, contemporaneous with the increasing strength of our army in Europe.

The staff college at LANGRES was giving good results since only officers who gave promise of general staff qualifications were admitted and as the basis of the course was to prepare students for the particular duty they would be called upon to perform in France. Again, to give further training in general staff duty, the graduates of the staff college, together with regular officers whose records indicated previous preparation for general staff work, were attached to the staffs of foreign corps or divisions, or later to the staffs of our own divisions for a tour of duty. In this manner they became experienced in the particular work for which they were destined before they were actually detailed for general staff duty.

In some instances, this resulted in making the staffs of divisions and corps cumbersome. When a division or corps general staff officer had one or two prospective general staff officers assigned to him to be instructed fully and carefully in the details of the work they would later be called upon to perform themselves, he instructed them by requiring them to do the actual work under his supervision. When they were taken away he felt the need of an assistant and had one detailed. A belief, consequently, grew up among many officers that large staffs were a necessity, whereas, as a matter of fact a much less number would have sufficed had there been available on adequate number of trained general staff officers and trained clerks.

Every effort was made to keep appointments of acting general staff officers to the smallest practicable number, and to be assured that an officer was qualified for general staff duty before he was so appointed in orders. To this end, the following instructions were issued on August 10, 1918:

August 18, 1918.

From: Chief of Staff

Subject: General Staff Officers

1. For your information, and to guide you in making recommendations, the following rules to govern eligibility for appointment of general staff officers are furnished you.

(a) Former general staff officers and those shown on the army register as graduates of army school of line, army staff college and army war college, to be eligible on their record.

(b) Others, to have satisfactorily performed general staff duty for at least two months before appointment, or to possess specific special qualifications to be shown in the recommendation.

(c) Special care to be exercised in the selection of any officer not of the regular establishment for such appointment.

(d) No appointment to be made except to fill a specific vacancy under tables of organization, and within the command of an officer recommending the appointment.

(e) Twenty-five general staff officers are allowed to the S. O. S.

LeROY ELTINGE,
Deputy Chief of Staff.

The principles enunciated in this order had been followed previously in passing upon recommendations for appointment of acting general staff officers, but had not been published.

It is to be remembered that all members of general staff sections were not general staff officers, for in many instances such officers perform duties that do not require a great amount of previous military knowledge, as for example the collection and tabulation of topographical, industrial, economic and political data concerning our own and enemy countries and the keeping of such data up to date. Such positions required technical rather than military experience and ability. Whenever practicable, officers from civil life were employed on these duties. When, however, the duty was such that had a regular officer been employed thereon he would *ipse facto* have been appointed a general staff officer, then the officer from civil life was so appointed.

Many officers regarded it as a distinction to wear the insignia of a general staff officer and large numbers of applications for appointment as an acting general staff officer were received, based on the desire for the honor of the position or a claim that it would facilitate the officer's dealings with foreign officers if he appeared to them to be recognized by our army as performing duty of the class to which a regularly appointed general staff officer was assigned. Such applications were refused.

Many, even of our senior officers, seemed unable to understand the difference between a staff officer and a general staff officer. Sometimes the head of a particular arm or service would urge that particular officers of his arm or service be placed upon particular sections of the general staff to represent the interests of his arm or service. The C-in-C always held to the principle that any officer doing staff duty was a staff officer but that a general staff officer could be employed only in a position where he was by the nature of his duties required to view the service as a whole and to exercise a coordinating influence in the successful joint employment of all arms and services. A man who is unable to disassociate himself from the narrow special interests of a particular arm or service is unfit to be a general staff officer. The presence on the general staff of men with this narrow viewpoint was not tolerated.

To give general staff officers a proper perspective and to prevent the growth of inflexible bureaucratic ideas, the principle was early decided upon of having frequent exchanges made between officers on general staff duty and those on duty with combat troops. Thus officers would not become one-sided in their experience and the staff would be closely in touch with front line conditions. * * *

The C-in-C believed this principle to be sound and most important.

The rapid growth, however, of our army and the lack of qualified general staff officers operated to prevent as complete an application of this principle as was desired. Nevertheless, general staff officers were never permitted to get out of touch with troops. They were constantly sent into the field to gain positive information concerning actual conditions, and to observe how existing orders were being executed. In this way, these officers kept their respective commanders in touch with existing circumstances and were able to submit consturctibe criticism regarding any deficiencies in equipment, supply, organization, armament, training or discipline. This principle was so fully carried out that whenever large numbers of our troops were engaged in combat, general staff officers from general headquarters, as well as all subordinate headquarters, were actually in the front line observing events. They were thus enabled not only to give first hand information but also to make recommendations which resulted in constant improvement in the value of our troops.

In this connection, it may be of interest to note that the chief of the operations section (G-3) was wounded while in the front line trenches making an inspection.

While no statistics were kept, it may be estimated that an average of one-third of all general staff officers were at all times away from their desks inspecting the actual employment of combat troops; directing the training of units not yet fully instructed, supervising arrangements for supply, conducting negotiations with Allied staffs to secure information or to complete arrangements for the harmonious joint employment of troops or facilities. In this way, these officers were called upon for great physical as well as mental activity.

The number of officers in the A. E. F. on November 11, 1918, who were performing duties to which tables of organization allot a general staff officer was 390. This figure includes the acting general staff officers, the regular general staff officers, and officers who thought performing the duties of a general staff officer had never been appointed to either of the above classes. The number of acting general staff officers appointed up to March 1919 was 296, of whom 77 were not regular army officers. * * *

For comparison, it may be here stated that the German "Great" General Staff is believed to have consisted of 900 officers during the latter part of the war. Prior to the
war, the French General Staff contained approximately 800 officers. During the last month
of the war, the French army had 2661 officers and the British armies in France about 3,400
officers performing general staff duty. The British army has no regular appointment as
general staff officer, all members of general staff sections being ex-officio general
staff officers for the time being.

EXCHANGE OF GENERAL STAFF OFFICERS
between
United States and France

It was early recognized by both the War Department and general headquarters that close
relations must be established between the general staff in the United States and that of
the American Expeditionary Forces. Numerous cablegrams were exchanged upon this subject
* * *

In September, 1917, the War Department decided to send the commanding generals of 15
divisions, accompanied by their chiefs of staff, to France for a short tour of observation,
to enable them to become familiar with the situation before the arrival of their respective
divisions.

In October 1917, the War Department decided to send a few general staff officers to
France for general staff instruction with a view to their later returning to the United
States for duty.

By December 1917, it had been decided, upon recommendation of the C-in-C to send a
portion of the general staff of each division to France in advance of its division.

In March 1918, a definite plan was instituted by the War Department for a rotation of
general staff officers between the War Department and the American Expeditionary Forces.

At about this time decisions were taken which resulted in the sudden expansion of the
American Expeditionary Forces and greatly increased participation of these forces in active
operations. As a result of this it became impossible to fully carry out the plan for rotation of general staff officers. The plan was, nevertheless, and excellent one. In future operations outside the continental limits of the United States a similar plan should
be accepted at the very start and adequate preparations to put it into effect should be
made as part of the original plan for the expedition.

The general staff at the War Department issues a daily summary of important papers in
the day's work. This was not furnished general headquarters by courier till the fall of
1918. It would have done a great deal toward effecting the coordination of the work of
the general staff at the War Department as well as that at general headquarters had this
summary been furnished from the beginning, and had a similar summary been made at general
headquarters and furnished to the War Department. Such a summary might well have been
made at general headquarters for the orientation of the general staff as well, though this
did not become apparent until an advance general headquarters was established, because the
same purpose had been served by the daily meeting of all heads of general staff sections,
held in the office of the chief of staff.

Conclusion: The work of the general staff of the American Expeditionary Forces is
entitled to the highest praise. Their work was marked by ability, loyalty and painstaking
effort and it is not too much to say that the success of the American Expeditionary Forces
was attained only through the work which they so ably performed.

After the Armistice had been signed, there was time available in which to consider
calmly the lessons in staff organization that could be learned from our experiences in
Europe. A board was convened for this purpose and selected for its members particularly
able staff officers of diversified experience. The final conclusions of this board, which

were approved by the C-in-C are given below to show the final opinion upon the most desirable staff organization for a large expeditionary force.

ASSISTANT CHIEF OF STAFF, G-1, GHQ, AEF

C-in-C: Fldr. 55:   Report

Final Report of Assistant Chief of Staff, G-1

1st Section, General Staff   GENERAL HEADQUARTERS, A. E. F.

Chaumont, Haute-Marne, April 22, 1919.

INTRODUCTION

[Extract]

[The first paragraphs discuss the content and arrangement of the body of the report.]

* * * * * *

In the organization and operation of the 1st Section, General Staff, and in its larger work of supervising and coordinating many of the important functions of the American Expeditionary Forces, it has been the constant effort to study, develop, and apply sound principles of General Staff administration.

In any discussion of the duties of a General Staff or of its Sections, the difference should constantly be borne in mind between General Staff functions, which are those of supervision, coordinating, and directing and the strictly administrative functions of the Army, which are performed by the several administrative, supply, and technical services, such as the Quartermaster Corps, the Engineer Corps, the Adjutant General, and others.

It is the duty of the chief of a staff section to be thoroughly familiar with the policies and orders of the Commander-in-Chief and of the Chief of Staff, and, within the limits of his own authority, to see that such policies and orders are properly carried out. He must also study and recommend policies affecting his own activities, interpret and apply existing policies and orders to the multitude of new conditions constantly arising, and see that they are properly adjusted to the constantly changing requirements of the military situation. He must issue such additional orders and instructions, in the name of the Commander-in-Chief, as will most promptly and effectively carry out approved policies. When an entirely new situation arises, or one of unusual importance or complexity, it is his duty to confer with or submit recommendations to the Chief of Staff and always to keep the Chief of Staff informed as to current matters of unusual interest and importance.

But in carrying outtthis well defined plan of action he must place upon the proper official the full responsibility for definite results. He must be alert to avoid unnecessary direction of detail or undue interference with the sound discretion of the officer upon whom responsibility for results has been placed. Any other course tends to destroy real lines of responsibility and to transform the General Staff into a great bureau, overloaded with detail, and wholly unable to concentrate upon its own proper and important duties. The Chief of Section has behind him all the authority of the Commander-in-Chief; and if this authority is exercised promptly and wisely, there will be no necessity for any departure from sound principles of General Staff administration.

Applying these principles to the organization of the First Section itself, it was found that its duties naturally grouped themselves into several large subdivisions, the number and nature of which necessarily varied with the status of the military situation. Experienced and competent officers were selected as chief of these divisions, each of whom was held responsible for the prompt and accurate dispatch of all business referred to him. They, in turn, gathered around them officers who were specially qualified for the duties which they were called upon to perform, each officer making a special study of one or more related subjects. In this way there was always a competent officer, familiar to the last detail with each particular subject and each group of subjects.

After thorough study of a particular subject, a course of action was recommended by the Chief of Division; which, in turn, was submitted to the Chief of Section for approval or disapproval. This subdivision of work into Divisions, together with a Deputy Chief of Section who was thoroughly familiar with all its work, and an Executive Secretary, constituted the organization of the First Section of the General Staff of the A. E. F. It will be found described in detail in Chapter II.

AVERY D. ANDREWS,
Brig. Gen., G. S.
A. C. of S., G-1.

CHAPTER I

CHRONOLOGICAL REVIEW OF IMPORTANT ACTIVITIES OF G-1

A. UNDER G. O. No. 8, 1917

Establishment of the Administrative Section: G. O. No. 8, A. E. F., July 5, 1917, in its original form announced the first division of the General Staff into sections and the distribution among them of general staff duties. By it were created the Operations, Intelligence, and Administrative Sections and the latter (the predecessor of G-1) assigned the following functions:

Policy relating to staff organization.
Policy relating to coordination of staff relations and duties.
Policy relating to replacement of losses.
Policy relating to police and discipline.
Policy relating to ammunition.
Policy relating to supplies.
Policy relating to evacuation of sick and wounded.
Policy relating to connection between field forces and the line of
    communications.
Policy relating to camps.
Policy relating to billets.
Policy relating to liaison not pertaining exclusively to Operations and
    Intelligence.

Shortly after the publication of G. O. No. 8 the Administrative Section was organized with the following personnel:

Maj. James A. Logan, Jr., Q. M. C., Chief of Section.
Maj. Frank R. McCoy, G. S., Assistant.

On July 28, Lieutenant Colonel W. D. Connor, C. E. was assigned to duty in the Section.

Although formally announced by order of July 5, 1917, the General Staff scheme was at this time in a formative state, and during the month of July the three sections gradually evolved into five. This organization proved permanent, and on August 14, was embodied in a corrected copy of G. O. No. 8, which was published under its original date. The five sections then announced were Administrative, Intelligence, Operations, Training, and Coordination. The Administrative Section was assigned the following functions:

1. General matters of administrative policy.
2. Administrative staff organization.
3. Replacements.
4. Evacuation of sick and wounded.
5. Ratio of combat troops to Line of Communication troops.
6. Supplies.
7. Possibilities of production and transportation in connection with
    contemplated operations.
8. Operations of railways in France.
9. Priority of supply shipments, and locality of purchase.
10. General weighing and balancing of demands and requirements in men and
    materials from the standpoint of Operations Section.
11. Recommends decisions on general policy on above mentioned matters.

12. Preparation of cablegrams and letters stating matters of administrative policy.

13. Liaison with technical and administrative services on questions of policy.

14. Details of organization and equipment of Line of Communication and Transportation Department troops and services.

These were explained by the Chief of Staff in a letter of August 14, as follows:

The Administration Section is charged in general with the discussion and deter-determination of policies. Its work will cover policy as related to Staff Organization, priority of shipments to France, replacement of losses, police and discipline, ammunition and other supplies, evacuation of sick and wounded, line of communications, camps and billets, liaison and organization not pertaining exclusively to Operations and Intelligence.

Following the amendment and republication of G. O. No. 8, the Section comprised the following personnel:

Major James A. Logan, Jr., Q. M. C., Chief of Section.
Major Frank R. McCoy, G. S., Assistant.
Major Campbell King, A. G. D., Assistant.
Mr. C. S. Forbes, Civilian Clerk.

Replacement System: The General Organization Project was approved by the Commander-in-Chief on July 11, and transmitted to Washington. It provided for corps of six divisions, four combat divisions, one replacement and school division, and one base and training division, so creating two echelons of replacement machinery. It was stated that during operations a minimum of 3000 men per month for each corps in France would have to be forwarded from the United States and be used as replacements. It was also recommended that a seventh or home division be provided for in order to train officers and higher commanders before forwarding them to France. This entire scheme was approved by Washington on September 26, 1917, except the seventh or home division, the place of which, it was stated, had been filled by replacement battalions.

Division of Work between Red Cross and Y. M. C. A.: While the supervision of Red Cross and Y. M. C. A. activities had not been expressly assigned to the Administrative section a decision concerning the division of functions between them, which was adhered to throughout the war, was made at this time and deserves mention. Section II, G. O. No. 26, A. E. F., August 18, 1917, laid down the broad rule that the Red Cross would provide for relief work and the Y. M. C. A. for the amusement and recreation of the troops by means of its usual program of social, educational, physical, and religious activities.

Animal Situation: The first difficulties with respect to the supply of animals, which were to recur at frequent intervals and with uniform seriousness throughout the history of the A. E. F., arose during the latter part of August. Early in July the French had promised to furnish the A. E. F. with 7,000 animals per month, beginning September 1. However, on August 24 they advised that the best they could do was to turn over 4,000 animals immediately with the understanding that they would be replaced by November 1, and a cable was immediately dispatched to Washington requesting that all troops be accompanied by their authorized allowance of animals. On September 15 the total requirements had reached 11,470 while only 6,123 were on hand, producing a shortage of 5,347.

Transfer of G. H. Q. to Chaumont: On September 1 the Administrative Section was moved with A. E. F. Headquarters from Paris to Chaumont.   At that time the personnel consisted of Major Logan, Chief of the Section, Major King, Mr. Forbes, and three clerks.

Y. M. C. A. Canteens: Shortly after the move to Chaumont an important policy was announced in connection with the Y. M. C. A. On August 10 the Commander-in-Chief had asked them whether they would assume the operation of canteens throughout the A. E. F., and so avoid depleting the personnel of combat organizations for this purpose. Mr. E. C. Carter, Chief of the Y. M. C. A., immediately agreed to undertake this work and the arrangement was made effective by the publication of Section III, G. O. No. 33, A. E. F., September 6, 1917, which provided that these activities should follow the general lines of post exchanges and that no such exchanges should be maintained in commands where the Y. M. C. A. was operating.

Service of the Rear Project: The first important piece of organization work done by the Section was the preparation of the Service of the Rear Project which fell to it under items 5 and 14 of G. O. No. 8, as revised. The General Organization Project stated that recommendations as to Line of Communications troops would be forwarded later. That project had provided for rearward services constituting 20% of the forward services in strength, or one-sixth of the whole, but when the Service of the Rear Project came to be prepared it was found to be necessary to make the rearward services 33 1/3% of the forward, or 25% of the whole. This 25% included divisional trains, hospital units and similar non-combatant personnel forming parts of combat divisions. This plan was forwarded to Washington on September 18, 1917, was subsequently approved, and from that time on furnished the basis for the development and expansion of what later came to be known as the S. O. S. [Services of Supply.]

Creation of Tonnage Division: By September 18, the work of the Section in connection with supply and tonnage matters had developed to a point justifying the separate organization of a Tonnage Division within the Section and this was done on that date. The duties of the division were as follows:

(a) To balance and coordinate all requisitions submitted by the several supply services for transmission to the United States, and maintain records of all these calls of automatic or exceptional supplies in order to control the priority of shipments.

(b) To supervise and maintain a record of supplies requisitioned from European sources through the agency of the General Purchasing Board.

(c) To maintain a record of the operation of base ports of the tonnage of supplies received, discharged and evacuated from the custody of the Army Transport Service (A. T. S.).

(d) To supervise the operation of transports as to turnaround, detention in French ports, and maintain a balance between the tonnage available for shipping and the tonnage of supplies requisitioned.

Until the transfer to Tours of the detailed administration of tonnage matters under G. O. No. 130, A. E. F., August 6, 1918, this was one of the most important divisions of the Section.

Welfare Societies: On October 4 a cable was despatched to the War Department reporting that the work of the Red Cross and Y. M. C. A. was being well coordinated and satisfactorily covering the field and recommending that the applications of other societies to come to France be disapproved. The Department replied that the Knights of Columbus had already been authorized to work with our troops and the Salvation Army was at that time working independently of any of the others and was shortly thereafter recognized in A. E. F. orders, so that by the fall of 1917 four welfare organizations were officially attached to the A.E.F. Red Cross Commissions:

Red Cross Commissions: As early as July there had been cable correspondence between the Commander-in-Chief and the War Department concerning the advisability of commissioning Red Cross officers. Although at first opposed, he finally expressed the opinion that some sort of militarization was desirable, and accordingly G. O. No. 82, W. D., 1917, provided for Red Cross commissions with assimilated rank but without military authority, obligation, pay, or allowances. The first Red Cross commissions, limited in number, were recommended by the Commander-in-Chief on October 9, 1917, and subsequently a large number were granted. Supplies for American Prisoners of War: On September 28 the War Department raised the question of extra food for American prisoners that might be captured by the enemy and directed that recommendations on the subject be submitted. The War Department was advised in reply that the Red Cross was arranging to ship to Berne sufficient food for 5,000 prisoners for six months and that the American Legation at that point was making arrangements to send it to prisoners as needed. On November 12 a letter was received from the Quartermaster General advising that the Secretary of War had authorized the Chief Quartermaster to furnish supplies to the Red Cross for this purpose and on January 3, 1918, the latter advised that they would undertake to handle them. The result was a system of supply, including food, clothing, and toilet articles, which was administered from Berne, Switzerland, and reached more than 85% of the American prisoners in Germany.

Change of Duties under Memorandum No. 129: During the latter part of November there was a redistribution of staff functions between the Administrative and Coordination Sections which was published in Memorandum No. 129, A. E. F., November 19, 1917. The following matters were assigned to the Administrative Section, those [underscored] being in addition to the duties prescribed by G. O. No. 8, corrected:

> *Strength reports.*
> *Disposal of captured men and material.*
> *Replacement of losses in men and animals.*
> Ratio of combat troops to L. of C. troops.
> *Remount Service.*
> *Provost Marshal questions.*
> *Billets and Billeting.*
> *Order of Battle.*
> Priority of shipment and locality of purchase.
> *Ocean tonnage and requisitions on War Department.*
> *Red Cross, Y. M. C. A., and other similar agencies.*
> *General Purchasing Board, War Risk Bureau, Auditors, and*
>   *Field Ambulance Service.*
> Details of organization and equipment of Line of Communications and
>   Transportation Department troops and services.
> The following subjects were eliminated:
> General matters of administrative policy.
> Administrative staff organization.
> Evacuation of sick and wounded.
> Supplies.
> Possibilities of production and transportation in connection with
>   contemplated operations.
> Operations of railways in France.
> General weighing and balancing of requirements in men and materials
>   from standpoint of Operations Section.
> Recommend decisions on general policy in connection with above mentioned
>   matters.
> Preparation of cablegrams and letters stating matters of administrative
>   policy.
> Liaison with technical and administration services on questions of policy.

While General matters of administrative policy was omitted from the express enumeration of the Section's functions, the practice of referring to it, as the Administrative Section, all staff questions not expressly delegated elsewhere, particularly those concerning administration, continued and grew throughout the history of the A. E. F., so that its duties at all times included many subjects of a miscellaneous character and more or less importance for which no written authority existed.

As a result of this change of the jurisdiction of the Section a reorganization became necessary and was announced on December 1, 1917, as follows:

Chief of Section: - Lt. Col. James A. Logan, Jr., Q. M. C.

Asst. Chief of Section: - Lt. Col. Alvin B. Barber, Engrs.

Personnel Division

Capt. Adelno Gibson, C. A. C.

Lt. Albert M. Skinner, Inf.

(Strength Reports, Replacements and Losses of Men and Animals, Ratio of Combatant Troops to Line of Communications Troops, Remount Service, Order of Battle.)

Organization and Equipment Division

Maj. Charles H. Grant, Ord. Dept.

(Details of Organization, Equipment, Line of Communications, and Transportation Departments, Troops, and Services.)

Police and Billeting Division

Maj. George L. Hamilton, Q. M. C.

(Provost Marshal questions, Billets and Billeting.)

Tonnage Division

Maj. George L. Hamilton, Q. M. C.

Lt. Earl H. Cotton, Cav.

Lt. Hamilton B. Downe, Cav.

(Priority of Shipment and locality of Purchase, Ocean Tonnage and Requisitions of War Dept. and General Purchasing Board.)

Auxiliary Services Division

Capt. C. Stewart Forbes, Inf.

(Red Cross, Y. M. C. A., and other similar agencies. War Risk Bureau, Auditors, and Field Ambulances Services.)

On December 4, 1917, in response to an inquiry from the Secretary of the General Staff, concerning the qualifications requisite for duty in the Administrative Section, which was occasioned by the inauguration of personnel qualification records throughout the A. E. F., the following statement was submitted:

In general, the qualifications requisite for the proper carrying out of the duties assigned to the Administrative Section, G. S., are sound judgment, breadth of vision, common sense, business ability, and familiarity with military organizations.

In particular, those charged with "Strength Reports, Replacements and Losses of Men and Animals, Ratio of Combatant Troops to Line of Communications Troops, Remount Service" should be familiar with use of graphics in curves or other forms to illustrate facts in engineering or concerning personnel; familiar with mechanical drawing or statistical work; experienced in managing large aggregation of men.

Those charged with "Details of Organization, Equipment, Line of Communications and Transportation Departments, Troops and Services" should be familiar with army organization, regulations, laws and orders, methods of supply, and relation with transportation facilities. Reserve officers who have had previous National Guard service together with experience in business, manufacturing, or in transportation companies would be of use in this section.

Those charged with "Provost Marshal questions, billets and billeting" should be familiar with French, French manners and customs. Knowledge of German helpful, a good organizer.

Those charged with "Priority of Shipment and locality of purchases, ocean tonnage and requisitions of War Department and General Purchasing Board" should be experienced as purchasing agents and providing supplies for large corporations. Familiar with ocean shipping conditions; familiar with army methods to determine whether requisitions are in accordance with regulations.

Those charged with "Red Cross, Y. M. C. A., and other similar Agencies, War Risk Bureau, Auditors, and Field Ambulance Service" should be familiar with business principles, accounting, familiar with ambulance service conditions in France.

Expansion of the Tonnage Division: On December 14, 1917, Lt. Col. Bruce Palmer, Aviation Section Signal Corps, was made chief of the Tonnage Division and the period of that division's greatest activity commenced shortly thereafter. Daily reports of the port situation were inaugurated on Director General of Transportation forms 8, 9, 10, and 11, and wall charts were kept showing the daily discharge and evacuation at ports, for the information of the Administrative and Coordination Sections. A little later the practice of having the requisitions of the supply services on the War Department submitted through the Administrative Section was instituted and they were recorded, checked, and coordinated in the Tonnage Division. Still later the classification of supplies into automatic and exceptional was inaugurated, as well as the submission with the requisitions of tonnage tables, showing dead weight and ship tons required. At the same time Capt. W. B. Ryan, Engrs., was attached to the Tonnage Division as a shipping expert to study the shipping program and port operations.

Tables of Organization for the Section:

[This paragraph gives the details of the tables of organization for the section.]

* * * * * *

All of the G. H. Q. tables were at that time submitted to Washington for approval, which was received on February 7, 1918.

Leaves: The question of developing a policy respecting leaves was broached as early as August, and in October the draft of a general order was submitted to the Chief of Staff. This led to a conference with the French and the principles there agreed upon were embodied in G. O. No. 6, A. E. F., Jan. 8, 1918. Briefly stated this provided for:

(a) A leave of seven days, time of travel not included, to be granted to officers and soldiers every four months.

(b) Leave centers to be chosen by the American authorities in concurrence with the French.

(c) The development of leave areas progressively in accordance with the needs of the A. E. F., subject to the approval of the French.

(d) The organization of special trains for men on leave.

(e) Discipline to be maintained by military police on trains, particular emphasis being placed on the fact that the men should not carry arms.

(f) The same principles to apply to units in the interior as the units in the line.

(g) Leaves of twenty-four hours not to be granted in the armies, as they were not given to the French, although they could be granted in the interior.

Reduction in Divisional Allowance of Animals: The great shortage of animals which existed as early as September, 1917, and has already been referred to, continued so that by January it was necessary to reduce the divisional allowance and so partially solve the problem of supply. In August. 1917, the allowance had been fixed at 8,777 and on January 14, 1918, Tables of Organization Series A reduced it to 6,617, but this number did not include the animals required by the 6-inch Howitzer Regiment and the Trench Mortar Battery, which were shown in the tables as motorized. The allowance of animals for them until they were motorized increased by 1,660, the total of 6,617 given above, making an aggregate of 8,277 animals as the authorized allowance for a division. This reduction of 500 animals was effected by dismounting certain officers and men, substituting bicycles for horses, and motorizing certain units. As will be seen later this was only the first step in this direction and the same expedient had to be resorted to in even greater degree at two later periods.

Replacement System: As stated in the explanation of the replacement system, one division in each corps was to be a replacement and school division and one a base and training division. The fifth division to arrive in France was the 41st, whose first elements landed on December 11, 1917, and last on February 6, 1918. The original intention was to use it as the replacement division for the I Corps, but later it was decided to use it as a base division instead. Its headquarters were established at St-Aignan-des-Noyers (Loir-et-Cher), and on January 15 it was designated by G. O. No. 9, A. E. F., 1918, as the "Base and Training Division, I Corps." Later, on March 5, this was changed to "Depot Division" by telegram to the Commanding General, Service of the Rear. On account of its geographical location the division was placed under the command of the Commanding General, Service of the Rear, but, pending the promulgation of formal orders concerning the procedure to be followed in effecting replacements, they were not permitted to be forwarded except on authority from the Administrative Section.

On February 4 the other echelon of the replacement system was provided by announcing the 32d Division, the sixth to arrive, as the replacement division of the I Corps.

Animal Priority Schedules: As already explained, one of the methods adopted to alleviate the shortage of animals was reduction in the divisional allowances. Another method which was early resorted to and used throughout hostilities was the issuance of priority schedules indicating the sequence in which the authorized allowance of animals was to be issued to the units of the A. E. F. In this way the divisions engaged in active operations were assured a sufficient supply of animals to maintain their mobility. The schedules were issued by G-3 after consultation with G-1, the latter notifying the Remount Service. The first priority schedule was issued on January 18, 1918, and established the following sequence:

1st Division
26th Division
42d Division
2d Division

Thenceforward priority schedules were constantly in effect, being changed from time to time as the military situation demanded.

Treatment of Prisoners of War: Instructions on this subject were received from the War Department under date of January 19, 1918, wherein it was stated that, while neither the Geneva nor Hague conventions were considered as binding in this war, inasmuch as some of the belligerents were not signatories, their principles would be followed and this rule has been consistently observed.

Billeting Areas: When the A. E. F. first began to arrive in France, areas within which to billet troops were assigned by the French and the process of administering them carried out through the existing French machinery. The first area thus assigned was the Gondrecourt Area which was turned over in June, 1917, and others followed as the need for them arose.

As the number of American areas increased it became necessary more and more to provide independent American machinery for administrering them. This was accomplished gradually and and finally the right to billet and quarter troops under the law of 1877 was conferred by the French Government upon the A. E. F. On January 31, 1918, complete instructions were published in G. O. No. 18, A. E. F., 1918, and have been in effect in substantially that form since that date.

B. UNDER G. O. NO. 31, 1918

Reorganization under G. O. No. 31: On February 8, 1918, the so-called Hagood Board met at G. H. Q. and remained in session for approximately one month, receiving written and oral statements concerning the proposed reorganization of the General Staff and changes in the administration of supply, and visiting many important centers. Both written and oral statements were presented by the Chief of the Administrative Section.

The first series of recommendations of the Board were submitted personally to the Commander-in-Chief on February 14, 1918, were approved by him, and were immediately carried into effect by G. O. No. 31, A. E. F., February 16, 1918. Other important recommendations were submitted later, and a revised edition of G. O. No. 31, was published early in March, but under the original date of February 14. Under this order the designation of the Administrative Section, General Staff, was changed to 1st Section (G-1), General Staff, and the designation of the Chief from Chief of Administrative Section to Assistant Chief of Staff, G-1. At the same time the following functions were assigned to G-1, those [underscored] being in addition to those assigned by G. O. No. 8, and Memorandum No. 129.

Supervises:

Ocean tonnage and requisitions on War Department.
Priority of overseas shipments (Troop shipments in consultation
  with G-3).
Disposal of captured men and material.
Replacements of losses in men and animals.
Organization and equipment of troops (in consultation with G-3):
Ratio of combat troops to S. O. S. troops.
Billets and Billeting.
Provost Marshal Service.
Red Cross, Y. M. C. A., War Risk Bureau, Auditors, and other similar
  agencies.
Remount Service.

Prepares:

Strength reports *and graphics.*
Order of battle.

The following subjects were eliminated:
Locality of purchase.
General Purchasing Board.
Field Ambulance Service.

G. O. No. 31, in addition to reorganizing the General Headquarters of the A. E. F., made sweeping changes in the Service of the Rear Project. The Line of Communications was reorganized and expanded into the Service of the Rear (later corrected to the Services of Supply), with headquarters at Tours. Under it were grouped all of the supply and technical services, the administration of which was thereby centralized under the Commanding General, S. O. S. As one of the supply services, the Service of Utilities was created, and under it were placed the Transportation Department, the Department of Construction and Forestry, the Department of Light Railways and Roads, and the Department of Motor Transportation.

The four last-mentioned departments were created by G. O. No. 8, S. O. R., March 12, 1918.

At this time the Service of the Rear Project totalled 337,773 and constituted 34% of the A. E. F. The excess over 25%, the proportion called for by the General Organization Project, was due to the fact that the rearward services were being built up in advance so as to be able to supply combat troops that were to come later.

Expansion of Organization and Equipment Division: In view of the assignment to G-1, under G. O. No. 31, of the subject of organization and equipment of troops, a request was addressed to the Chief of Staff on February 20 asking that the personnel which had formerly handled the subject in G-3 be assigned to G-1 and that at the same time all records pertaining to the subject be transferred. This was done, and on February 23 the Organization and Equipment Division was enlarged and reorganized with Lt. Col. W. D. Smith, F. A., as chief. The duties assigned to that division included preparation of tables of organization, preparation of cables to the War Department concerning changes in approved tables of organization, the organization of the S. O. S., and the determination of the type and quantity of equipment for organizations.

Coincidentally with the enlargement of the Organization and Equipment Division, it was decided that, based on a thorough study of conditions at the front, both among American troops and those of the Allies, requirements as to the equipment of combat troops should be prescribed in the form of equipment manuals, each manual showing the equipment that should be furnished by each supply department, and serving both as a basis of requisition on the one hand and supply on the other. The Division was so organized that a number of its officers could be on duty at the front at all times and a special effort was made to send as many as possible during offensives. All decisions concerning equipment were based upon the knowledge of members of the Division gained in this way.

Horses from France: On January 29, in a letter to the French Under Secretary of State, the question of securing animals in France was reopened and the suggestion was made that there was a large number which could be made available for military purposes. After a discussion of details the French acceded to the suggestion and on February 22 a cable was sent to Washington stating that we have been assured 50,000 animals at the rate of 10,000 a month and that this figure might later be increased to 100,000 or perhaps 150,000. It was accordingly recommended that the conversion of ships into animal transports be discontinued and animal shipments continued only at the rate of 2,000 heavy draft horses per month.

Tonnage Allotment: By the first of March the shortage of available shipping made necessary the adoption of some system which would compel the supply services to eliminate from their requisitions all but their essential requirements. In order to accomplish this end, on March 5, 1918, a scheme of tonnage allotment was recommended to the War Department for adoption. It provided for (a) advise from the War Department on the 15th of each month of the amount of dead weight tonnage and ship tonnage that would be available for supplies during the succeeding month, (b) an apportionment of this amount among the supply services after having deducted 10% as a margin of safety and the amount necessary to provide for initial and automatic Quartermaster supplies, and (c) designation by the respective services of the supplies theretofore requisitioned by them which should be shipped on their allotment of tonnage or advice that the allotment should be turned over to their representatives in the United States for use as they saw fit. The first allotments under this scheme, those for April, were cabled to the War Department on March 26, 1918.

Order of Battle: Memorandum 129, of November 19, 1917, had assigned to the Administrative Section the keeping of the Order of Battle. From that time until March 15, 1918, it was issued at various intervals as necessity required and on the latter date the regular semi-monthly issue was begun. At the same time, a fixed form modeled on the British Order of Battle was adopted and, with minor changes, was adhered to throughout hostilities.

American Library Association: This society had entered the field in February, not seeking, however, to conduct its work independently, but rather through the channels afforded by the organizations already functioning. It sought official approval of its work, a mono- poly in its special field, and a small tonnage allotment. On the recommendation of these headquarters their proposal was approved by Washington and they were given a monthly allot- ment of 50 ship tons. By May, the work of this society was well under way and was pro- ducing good results.

Cessation of Animal Shipments: As previously stated the shipment of animals from the United States was reduced to 2,000 heavy draft horses per month of February 22. On March 21 a further cable was sent stating that, on account of the tonnage situation and the shortage of forage in France, all animal shipments should be discontinued and the French and British sources relied on exclusively. As will appear later the supply from these sources proved wholly inadequate and eventually shipment from the United States had to be resumed.

Replacement System: The system of replacements, established as already described by the designation of the 32d and 41st Divisions as the replacement and depot divisions respectively of the I Corps. was formally promulgated by G. O. No. 46, A. E. F., March 26, 1918. How- ever, in less than two weeks the military situation became so serious as a result of the great German drive, which had commenced on March 21, that the 32d Division was ordered in- to the line for training as a combat division, and it was announced on April 10 that it had temporarily ceased to function as a replacement division and that the 41st would serve both depot and replacement purposes. Thereafter it was necessary to train all new divi- sions for the line until the arrival of the 83d which was designated as the 2d Depot Divi- sion on June 27. Meanwhile the 41st functioned as both replacement and depot division for the entire A. E. F., which at the time of the designation of the 2d Depot Division included nine divisions in line, seven others complete and in training, and six in process of ar- rival.

Disposition of Hospital Evacués: From the outset it was the announced official policy of the A. E. F. to return hospital évacués, fit for combat duty, to their original organiza- tions, as such a course was recognized as contributing largely to the maintenance of mo- rale and esprit and the encouragement of divisional pride. This policy was first offi- cially promulgated in Section XI, G. O. No. 46, A. E. F., March 26, 1918, and was frequently reiterated in orders, letters, and telegrams so that it might be constantly impressed on all concerned. It was generally carried out, and instances in which men were not returned to their proper organizations will be found to have been due to loss of soldiers' records, mistakes made at hospitals, regulating stations, or replacement organizations, or military exigencies.

Departure from Priority Schedule: Following a meeting of the Supreme War Council during the latter part of March an agreement was made with the British by which infantry and machine gun troops were to be brought to France in large numbers in British shipping, and the troop transports previously in use were to continue according to the original program. This necessitated an extensive revision of the priority schedule which was cabled to Washington on April 11 after having been prepared jointly by G-3 and G-1. About a month later, on May 2, the policy of expediting the movement of infantry and machine-gun units was continued by the Abbeville Agreement, and the priority schedule revised accordingly for May and June. Similarly on June 3 a further agreement required a further revision covering the June and July priorities. Both the May and June revisions were prepared jointly by G-3 and G-1 as had been the April revision.

Port Situation: On April 2, at the direction of the Commander-in-Chief, the Commanding General, S. O. S. convened a Board by S. O. 20, Hq. S. O. S., 1918, for the purpose of considering and reporting on the dock and port situation at that date and further port development to be undertaken. The report of the Board was submitted to G-1 and recommended the provisions of facilities, exclusive of the port of Marseille, for a daily discharge of 50,000 tons per day, entailing the construction projects of American Bassens, Montoir, and

Talmont docks. On two important subjects a disagreement developed in the Board and as a result both majority and minority reports were submitted. The majority took the view that in order to reach the necessary figure of 50,000 tons per day the Talmont project was necessary, while the minority maintained that it was unnecessary and that effort should be concentrated on the other projects. The majority also reported that the docks at Bassens were not suited to the heavy gantry cranes that had been obtained from the United States and recommended that they be disposed of to the French and light cranes obtained from England. The erection and use of the gantries was later authorized.

Young Women's Christian Association: The question of the status of this society in the A. E. F. had first been raised in January, 1918. Their activities were for the benefit of women connected with the A. E. F., including women associated with other welfare societies, and French women munition workers, and they desired independent recognition. The A. E. F. welcomed their work but insisted that they should conduct it, so far as official relations with the A. E. F. were concerned, through the medium of one of the societies already recognized. The question was the subject of correspondence until April when it was definitely settled as stated, by an exchange of cables with the War Department.

Replacement System: The transfer of the 32d Division from replacement duty to the line on April 10, leaving the 41st Division as the only replacement unit, has already been referred to. On April 12 authority was received from the War Department to organize such provisional replacement units as might be necessary from time to time. In accordance with this authority the Commanding General of the III Corps was directed on May 15 to organize within his corps a corps replacement battalion for the purpose of handling efficiently the forwarding of replacements to units of the corps and the return of men evacuated from hospital. Similar organizations were authorized in the II Corps on May 30 and in the I and IV Corps on June 11. Official provision was subsequently made for these battalions in G. O. No. 111, A. E. F., July 8, 1918, which directed that one would be organized in each corps to function until the designation of a corps replacement division. Following the publication of this order corps replacement battalions were established in the V, VI, and VII Corps and all such battalions continued in existence until absorbed by the regional replacement depots.

Jewish Welfare Board: Early in May this society had been recognized in the United States as an agency for welfare work in the camps. During the same month the question of its activities in the A. E. F. was considered and on the 25th approval of the proposal was given subject to the qualification that its work must be conducted through the medium of the Y. M. C. A. Subsequently numerous applications were received for the recognition of other agencies, including for example, the Massachusetts Soldiers and Sailors Information Bureau and the American Soldiers and Sailors Club. To these the uniform reply was made that such enterprises could be conducted in the A. E. F. only as a part of or under the auspices of one of the established agencies. Later, this policy was confirmed and applied by the President of the United States, in correspondence with representatives of the Masonic Fraternity and others.

Equipment Manuals: The first of the Series A Equipment Manuals, covering the infantry division, were ready for distribution during the latter part of May, 1918. Series A, No. 1, covering the infantry regiment, appeared first and was followed by numbers 2 to 14 which completed the infantry division. No. 15, a summary of all the equipment of an infantry division appeared on August 24 and completed Series A. French Horse Requisition

French Horse Requisition: On March 21 the supply of animals from the United States had been countermanded in reliance on the undertaking of the French to supply us. On May 31 the French advised that, due to recent military developments on the Western Front, they had issued orders suspending the purchase of any further animals for the American forces. The Chief of Staff was immediately notified that 103,000 animals in all would be required by July 1 to meet the accelerated troop movement due to the Abbeville Agreement. The Commander-in-Chief took the matter up personally with the Chief of the Commission for

Franco-American War Affairs, and the outcome was an agreement by the French to a system of enforced requisition throughout France beginning on June 20 and ending on August 1.

On June 25, just after the commencement of the requisition, there was a shortage in the A. E. F. of more than 25,000 animals. The requisition was expected to yield a total of 160,000 animals, half of which would go to the French and half to the A. E. F. It did not progress as favorably as anticipated, and in an effort to assure the supply of 80,000 to the A. E. F. as promised, the French first diverted two-thirds of those requisitioned and later all; and before the requisition was complete promised to make up any deficit which should exist from French remount depots.

The final number netted by the requisition was 74,070, and in addition 3,450 were delivered from French remount depots and other sources, making a grand total of 77,520. Thus the promise of 80,000 was substantially kept. Shortly after the completion of the requisition and on September 4, Marshal Foch directed that 13,000 animals be placed at the disposal of the A. E. F. in connection with preparations for the Argonne offensive. This was done, about 8,000 being received in September and over 4,000 in October, and went far towards relieving the immediate situation and permitting the full force of the American arms to be felt.

Other Aspects of Remount Problem: On June 4 a second effort was made to alleviate the animal shortage by reducing the divisional allowance of animals. This was done after protracted consultation between G-3, G-1, the Commanding Generals of the 1st and 42d Divisions, and the Chief Surgeon and was finally put into effect by G. O. No. 92, A. E. F., 1918, on the date named. The amount of saving effected by this order was 831 animals, but this included 332 items marked X which were to be issued when available, making a net reduction under the order of 499.

During the latter part of June negotiations were conducted with the British authorities concerning the possibility of obtaining more animals from Great Britain, but the best that could be accomplished in this direction was a promise on their part to equip the divisions trained with them, which in the aggregate amounted to about 18,000 animals.

On June 30 a cable was sent to Washington recommending that 8,000 heavy draft animals be shipped every month. Early in July contracts were let in Spain for 17,000 animals 5,000 to be delivered in July, 6,000 in August, and 6,000 in September. There was hope of obtaining more, but although reports received the middle of the month indicated that 35,000 might be secured, the Spanish Government passed a law prohibiting the exportation of animals on July 22 when less than 6,000 had been received.

On July 16 a cable was despatched to Washington recommending the shipment of animals at the rate of 25,000 per month. The War Department replied that this would mean the division of 100,000 tons of ship tonnage per month and that not more than 11,000 animals could be shipped before September 1. They suggested that meanwhile the shipment of motor transportation should be expedited. To this reply was made that motorization would be expedited but that animals also were essential and that to avoid diverting essential cargo tonnage certain vessels should immediately be converted into horse transports. No animals were received in France from the united States in August. 1,839 were received in September and 2,570 in October.

Prisoners of War: At the end of May the question was taken up with the French of delivering into American custody prisoners of War captured by American troops serving with the French. On June 3 Marshal Foch agreed to this proposal and at about the same time the matter was also taken up with the British and the same arrangement made.

Beginning in January the question of retaining prisoners of war in France or sending them to the United States had been discussed with the War Department and on February 20 the Department had advised that prisoners would be kept in France and guarded by our own troops unless the number should become so great as to make this course impracticable. The question was raised again in May and on June 5 the Department directed that prisoners be sent to the United States, but when it was pointed out that the A. E. F. had been compelled to borrow prisoners from the French and British for labor purposes and to meet this need had just completed arrangements to have turned over to it all prisoners captured by American troops serving with the French or British, the instructions were withdrawn and permission was given to keep prisoners in France, a course that was adhered to throughout.

Change in Chief of Tonnage Division: On June 5, 1918, Lt. Col. Palmer, thereto Chief of the Tonnage Division, was designated Deputy A. C. of S., G-1. At the same time Mr. L. H. Shearman of the United States Shipping Board, who was the representative at G. H. Q. of the Allied Maritime Transport Council, was made Chief of the Tonnage Division, succeeding Lt. Col. Palmer. Shortly thereafter a joint daily report by the Tonnage and Personnel Divisions was inaugurated, showing the progress of troop arrivals and tonnage discharged at ports.

The 80-Division Program: On June 19 a cable was sent to Washington outlining a program of troop shipments to be completed in May, 1919, and designed to bring the A. E. F. to a strength of 66 divisions with a proportionate number of corps, army, S. O. S., and replacement troops. On June 23 Marshal Foch came to Chaumont for a conference with the Commander-in-Chief on this subject and following this conference a cable was sent to Washington on June 25 proposing an army in France of 46 divisions in October, 1918, 64 in January, 1919, 80 in April 1919, and 100 in July, 1919. The five Assistant Chiefs of Staff were immediately directed to study this program and a little later they were advised that the Commander-in-Chief desired these studies to relate to a force of 80 combat divisions. The monthly priorities which had been determined on the basis of the 66-division program ran to the early part of September. All subsequent monthly programs were based on what was known as the 80-division program, which was understood here to mean 80 combat divisions, or, with one depot division to each 5 combat, 96 divisions in all, with necessary corps, army, and S. O. S. troops.

Individual Equipment: In June G-1 undertook the task of making a study of the individual equipment to be brought to France by all officers and soldiers. There was great need for standardization in this matter as numerous lists of necessary equipment, more or less conflicting, had been published in the United States, and the tonnage problem had reached a point which made necessary the limitation of troop baggage to the minimum. Accordingly on June 25 a cable was sent to Washington enumerating in detail the individual equipment which was necessary for service in France and recommending that baggage be so limited.

Chemical Warfare Service: During the latter part of June the Organization and Equipment Division completed its work on the reorganization of the Gas Service, which had so expanded in size and importance under the conditions of modern warfare as to necessitate an enlarged organization and a personnel of its own. This was approved by the War Department on June 25 with a change of name to Chemical Warfare Service, and on June 28 the new corps was created by G. O. No. 105, A. E. E., 1918.

Prisoners of War: The handling and treatment of prisoners of war had during the early months been governed by a set of "Orders and Instructions" which were promulgated informally and served as a tentative guide. Later, work was commenced on a general order and, after conference with G-2, the Adjutant General, and the Judge Advocate, G. O. No. 106, A. E. F., July 11, 1918, was published. At the same time detailed regulations and instructions were issued for use with the order as provided in Section VIII. After the publication of these two documents a revision of both of them was considered and a large amount of work was put on the matter in conjunction with G-2, G-4, and the Provost Marshal General, with the result that in September these were put in final form, but they were not published pending the outcome of the diplomatic negotiations then proceeding at Berne, which were not concluded until the day of the Armistice.

Purchase of Quartermaster Tobacco by Y. M. C. A.: On July 1 the Acting Quartermaster General recommended (with subsequent approval of the Secretary of War) that the Y. M. C. A. be permitted to buy tobacco, cigars, and cigarettes from the Quartermaster and resell at Quartermaster retail prices. An arrangement was immediately made between the Quartermaster Department and the Y. M. C. A. whereby, in return for the release of equivalent tonnage, the former would furnish the latter with 15 short tons per month of these articles for each 25,000 men in France, to be sold at current quartermaster prices. The arrangement was approved by G-1 and took effect towards the end of July.

Establishment of Statistical Division (G-1): On March 25 the Commander-in-Chief had asked the Chief of Staff in Washington to send a force of trained statisticians to France to establish a bureau of military statistics at G. H. Q. similar to that existing at Washington. A unit was selected from the Statistics Branch of the General Staff, Washington, and sent to France in charge of Lt. Col. L. P. Ayres, then Chief Statistical Officer of the War Department, and arrived at G. H. Q., on July 6, 1918.

It was immediately incorporated in G-1 and became the Statistical Division of the Section, with Lt. Col. Ayres as Chief.

It was soon found that so much of the work of this division related to questions of supply that it was necessary to transfer a part of it to Tours and that was done on August 11. Since that date the Statistical Divisions at both headquarters have issued secret weekly reports in graphic form for the use of the Commander-in-Chief and the Commanding General, S. O. S., and their respective Staffs, dealing with the most important phases of shipping, supply, constuction, transportation, and personnel. Subsequently daily reports were also inaugurated.

Military Police Corps: On July 8 the Military Police Corps, the second new corps to be created in the A. E. F., was established by Section XI, G. O. No. 111, A. E. F., in accordance with the plan of organization prepared by the Organization and Equipment Division of G-1. It superseded divisional military police companies, theretofore the only authorized police units, and furnished the necessary personnel and organization to meet the novel situation existing in the A. E. F. The new corps was approved by the War Department on October 7 and was subsequently reorganized by Sec. I, G. O. No. 180, A. E. F., October 15, 1918, to provide for a Provost Marshal General's Department and Military Police companies of 6 officers and 200 enlisted men instead of 5 officers and 125 enlisted men as originally.

Abolition of the Service of Utilities: The Services of Supply as announced by G. O. No. 31 were reorganized early in July by the publication of G. O. No. 114, A. E. F., July 11, 1918. That order abolished the Service of Utilities and made the Transportation Service and the Motor Transport Corps independent services functioning directly under the Commanding General, S. O. S. On the next day the Division of Military Engineering and Engineer Supplies, the Division of Construction and Forestry, and the Division of Light Railways and Roads (the last two of which had formerly been under the Service of Utilities) were announced by G. O. No. 29, S. O. S., July 12, 1918, as subdivisions of the office of the Chief Engineer Officer.

Motor Transport Corps: It will be noted that the department charged with motor transportation under G. O. No. 31 was called Motor Transport Service, while under G. O. No. 114 it was called Motor Transport Corps. The immensity of the task of procuring, maintaining, repairing, replacing, and technically supervising the motor transportation of the A. E. F. required the creation of a separate corps charged exclusively with these functions. Tables of organization were prepared by this Section in June and approved by the War Department on June 24 and in G. O. No. 114 the new corps was announced as the successor of the Motor Transport Service.

Transportation Corps: A similar development which also went hand in hand with the abolition of the Service of Utilities was the establishment of the Transportation Corps. This was part of the move to make railroad and ocean transportation an independent organization in France and to provide it with an adequate personnel of its own. The proposed organization was approved by the War Department on June 25, 1918, and on September 7 the new corps was created by G. O. No. 42, S. O. S., 1918. At the same time all regiments, battalions, companies, and detachments of transportation specialists, most of which had formerly been in the Corps of Engineers, were transferred into it.

Change in Policy respecting Ocean Tonnage: In July a serious crisis developed in the ocean tonnage situation. The allotment made to the A. E. F. for August by the Shipping Control Committee was 575,000 dead weight tons. This was so far below the actual needs of the

A. E. F. that an urgent cable was immediately forwarded to Washington pointing out the vital necessity of assigning more tonnage to the A. E. F. and making certain proposals as to the source of the tonnage to be assigned. The cable is quoted herewith in its entirety [Cable 1487; Pershing to War Dept., July 19, 1918]:

Paragraph 1. A. Expected tonnage as reported in your 1712 entirely inadequate to supply even the 30 divisions that will be in France by September. Since the successful outcome of this war is dependent on maintaining an uninterrupted flow of men and supplies from America to France, I urge the revision of the estimates to conform to the figures of my 1342 which were on the extremely low basis of 30 pounds per man per day plus construction materials. This will involve shipments of thousands of short tons of cargo as follows: July 690, August 803, September 903, October 1,021, November 1,131, December 1,220. Horses will be in addition to these figures. Our records indicate that by careful economy our operations can be maintained on the basis of tonnage thus computed, but they cannot be maintained on the basis suggested in your 1712.

B. While I realize that this would involve the closest economy in the United States, it would appear to be possible since only about one quarters of the tonnage so far built for the Shipping Board has been assigned to direct Army use, while less than half the Dutch, Swedish and other ships recently taken over are in Army service, and the new estimates of your 1712 appear to contemplate the assignment to the Army of less than half the new steel tonnage estimated to be completed before the close of the current year.

C. It is my very best judgment that the satisfactory out come of the War is absolutely dependent on the United States increasing its forces to at least 80 divisions by May or by July next year at the latest. In order therefore to enable the continuation of shipment of the maximum number of troops and supplies, including horses, I request and recommend in detail:

First. That at least 500,000 D. W. tons of vessels now employed in other trades be withdrawn and placed in Army Service. The fact that out of 530,000 D. W. tons of Dutch vessels requisitioned only 244,000 tons have been assigned to Army transport; that no part of the tonnage secured under the Japanese agreement has been so assigned; that 200,000 tons is being secured by the Swedish agreement, of which 100,000 tons has been assigned to the Army or Allied Service, leads me to conclusion that not less than 500,000 D. W. tons of vessels can be diverted to meet this most pressing need.

Second. That the equivalent of all new steel cargo tonnage be assigned to Army as fast as completed.

Third. That as far as possible, all new wooden and composite ships, be so employed that an equivalent amount of steel tonnage may be released for Army service.

D. The tonnages mentioned can be unloaded promptly and handled through ports here without delay, and every energy is being devoted to increasing our capacity to handle cargoes. Please advise as early as practicable as to possibility of securing necessary shipping to carry out our program. The importance of making the necessary allotments suggested is imperative.

PERSHING.

When the August tonnage allotments and priority schedules were cabled to WASHINGTON on July 26 the policy was adopted of requesting what was essential to the functioning of the A. E. F., irrespective of the amount of space assigned to the A. E. F. by the Shipping Control Committee. As a result of the prior cable (quoted above) the August allotment was increased to 700,000 tons and a supplemental priority cable was sent to cover the additional allowance.

Thereafter requests for monthly tonnage allotments were based on the essential needs of the A. E. F. and not space available, and as a result of this policy the War Department advised on October 18, 1918, that thenceforward they would meet our allotments as far as possible. G. O. No. 130, A. E. F., 1918: On August 6, Sec. I, G. O. No. 130 was published.

Paragraphs (a), (b), and (c) of this order transferred to the Commanding General, S. O. S., and his subordinates all of the detailed work theretofore done in the Tonnage Division of G-1 in connection with requisitions, allotments, and priorities. The purpose of this change was to centralize the control of all questions of supply and expedite cable communication between the supply service and WASHINGTON. Incident to this transfer of duties. Mr. Shearman was relieved as head of the Tonnage Division for return to the United States and Maj. W. B. Ryan, Engrs., succeeded him. At the same time four junior officers were transferred to the Tonnage Division, G-1, S. O. S., and certain of the charts and graphics theretofore kept were discontinued.

G. O. No. 130 also had the effect of transferring to the C. G., S. O. S. all matters pertaining to the organization and equipment of S. O. S. troops and at the same time, in order to assist in the inauguration of the work, one officer was transferred from G-1, G. H. Q., to G-1, S. O. S. Thereafter the organization of all new corps and services in the S. O. S. was announced in S. O. S. orders.

Welfare Personnel: Early in August the requests of the Y. M. C. A. for authority to bring over additional personnel, based upon the requests of local commanders, reached such a point that a letter was written to the First Army and the independent corps directing that no such requests be made except through these headquarters. This action was prompted by the seriousness of the tonnage situation and the consequent necessity of keeping the numbers of non-combatant personnel at a minimum. A little earlier the Y. M. C. A. had submitted a statement of its personnel requirements and urged the importance of expediting the granting of passports and facilitating the departure of 1,500 men then ready to sail from the United States. Further similar requests were received up to the end of September and finally on October 7 a cable was sent to the War Department urging that all available facilities be afforded to bring over Y. M. C. A. personnel, to which it was replied that every effort was being made to minimize delay.

Medical Representatives with G-1: On August 14 the Chief of Staff advised that the Medical Corps had asked for fuller representation on the General Staff and that the Commander-in-Chief desired this request to be complied with. Accordingly, Lt. Col. A. P. Plark, M. C., who had been on duty with G-1 for some little time, was made an Acting General Staff officer and all divisions of the Section were advised that he should be consulted on:

(a) All affairs of the Red Cross that have any possible connection with the Medical Department.

(b) All tables of organization of medical units or which should show medical personnel attached.

(c) Changes in type of equipment or clothing or ration so far as they may affect health or where, in the case of equipment, it is for the Medical Corps.

(d) Miscellaneous questions affecting the Medical Department.

Reorganization of Personnel Division: On August 14, Lt. Col. Gibson, who had been Chief of the Personnel Division since its establishment in November, 1917, was relieved and succeeded by Col. G. T. Bowman, G. S. The division was thereupon reorganized into three departments, the first in charge of replacement of losses of personnel, the second in charge of priority of troop shipments from overseas, statistics of troop arrivals, and organization and designation of units formed in the A. E. F., and the third in charge of strength of the A. E. F., graphics of personnel, and the order of battle. The division continued in this form during the period of great activity that extended from this to the Armistice.

On the same date that Colonel Bowman became chief of the Personnel Division the first complete regular weekly issue of graphics of personnel was made and these have been continued since that date in practically the same form.

Change of Assistant Chief of Staff, G-1: Sec. I, G. O. No. 137, A. E. F., August 21, 1918, detailed Col. Avery D. Andrews, Engineers (later Brigadier General), as an Acting General Staff officer and announced him as Asst. Chief of Staff, G-1, in the stead of Colonel James A. Logan, G. S., relieved.

Shortage of Replacements: As a result of the fact that divisions had arrived under strength and the fact that replacements had not been furnished in the amounts requested, the A. E. F. faced a serious replacement shortage by the middle of August. Urgent requests were sent to Washington for large numbers of this class of personnel and emphasis was placed on the importance of giving them priority over new divisions. During the latter half of August, in preparation for the St-Mihiel operation, it was necessary to transfer 6,000 men form outside divisions to the First Army.

Early in September 55,000 replacements were requested for October in addition to all those still due on prior requests and the War Department was urged to ship nothing but replacements during that month, inasmuch as the use of all replacements then in base divisions would leave a shortage of 60,000 in combat divisions and allow for no replacement reserve whatsoever. A few days later 68,000 replacements were asked for in November in addition to all previously requested and on September 14, the War Department was advised that due to the shortage then existing it was necessary to send men to front line divisions five or six days after arrival in France. On September 18, 106,000 replacements were requested for December, including eight lieutenants per thousand.

Change in Replacement System: The original replacement system as embodied in the General Organization Project is described in Section A of this chapter. The impossibility of adhering to it for more than a few weeks on account of the German offensive of March 21 is referred to in Section B. On August 26 a cable was sent to the War Department recommending an important change in the system in the light of experience gained since the recommendation. It was pointed out that due to the critical situation theretofore existing, five divisions out of six had been used for combat and all replacements handled through one base division, without the intermediate echelon of a replacement division as originally contemplated. It was stated that the original project might profitably be modified by omitting replacement divisions entirely and continuing one base depot division in each group of six. Recommendations to this effect were made and were subsequently approved, so that a one-echelon replacement system superseded the original two-echelon system.

Skeletonizing Divisions: When the Meuse-Argonne operation was opened on September 26 the replacement situation was most unfavorable. In order to meet the heavy losses which were certain to occur, prompt measures were necessary to make adequate replacements available. On October 2 it was recommended to the Chief of Staff that the entire personnel of both the 84th and 86th Divisions, which were then in process of arriving, be used at one for replacements. This was approved, subject to the retention of a cadre in each division, rifle companies to consist of 25 men and at least 2 officers, in order that the identity of the division might be preserved and subsequent reconstitution made possible. The following day the Commanding General, S. O. S., was ordered to forward 25,000 replacements, chiefly from these divisions. In order to equip them properly they were all forwarded through the 1st and 2d Depot Divisions. The necessity for speed was so great that special arrangements were made to handle them at those points, with the result that the 18 trains carrying them were not delayed more than one hour apiece on the average and all arrived at St-Dizier, the First Army regulating station, between October 9 and 12.

On October 3 the War Department was advised of the breaking of these divisions and was urged to ship all replacements due early in October including those requested for that month. At that time combat divisions were short over 80,000 men.

The shortage continued and by the middle of October it was recommended and approved by the Chief of Staff that the enlisted personnel of the 34th and 38th Divisions, then beginning to arrive, be used as replacements. This process was carried out as the units landed in the same way as in the case of the 84th and 86th Divisions. At the same time three regiments of white pioneer infantry, the 4th, 55th, and 57th, which had been scheduled to form part of the 96th, 99th, and 100th Divisions, respectively, were broken in a similar fashion and the personnel, which was untrained, passed through the 2d Depot Division. A few days later authority was secured to break the 31st Division, which had been designated on September 20, as a depot division and was then arriving, and this was carried out, enough personnel only being retained to care for the records.

Finally on October 28, in view of the continued need, it was recommended that the 4th Depot Division (85th) and 6th Depot Division (40th), which had been moved to forward areas to act as regional replacement units, be further skeletonized for replacement purposes, that the 3d Depot Division (76th) and the 5th Depot Division (39th) be abolished as depot divisions and used as replacements, except the personnel necessary to care for the records, and that the same course be followed with the already skeletonized 34th, 38th, 84th, and 86th Divisions. These recommendations were approved and instructions issued on October 29.

On November 2 the following was sent to the War Department concerning the replacement situation: [Cable 1861; Pershing to War Dept., Nov. 2, 1918.]

Paragraph 1. Reference P 1746, A 2040, P 1812, and A 2088. It is evident that necessary preparations were not made to meet our replacement needs. It was reported to you that 50,000 of replacements requested had not arrived up to the end of September. In addition, 55,000 replacements were on priority for October. During October 33,000 replacements and casuals have been received. As a result we are short over 72,000 replacements which were requested and for which priority was given. Priority for November provides for 68,000 replacements. This makes a total of 140,000 replacements due by the end of November and conditions imperatively demand that they be shipped early in that month. Four combat divisions and three depot divisions have been skeletonized and four depot divisions have been reduced to training cadres in order to obtain replacements absolutely necessary for divisions in the line. It is again recommended that, if necessary, divisions in the United States be stripped of trained or even partially trained men and that they be shipped immediately. To send over entire divisions which must be broken up on their arrival in France so we may obtain replacements that have not been sent as called for is a wasteful method and one that makes for inefficiency, but as replacements are not otherwise available there is no other course open to us. New and only partially trained divisions cannot take the place of older divisions that have had battle experience. The latter must be kept up numerically to the point of efficiency. Cannot this matter be given the consideration its importance deserves?

PERSHING.

Policy in Taking Prisoners; During August claims were made by the German press that in recent battles certain Americans refused to give quarter after resistance had ceased and offers of surrender been made. On August 22 a confidential letter was sent to the commanding generals of all corps and divisions inviting attention to these reports, stating that the evident purpose was to increase the German power of resistance, and impressing upon them the policy of the United States to accept offers of surrender in the absence of treachery and give the prisoners food, shelter, and protection in accordance with International Law.

Army Service Corps: The last of the new corps to be created in the A. E. F. was the Army Service Corps. Its purpose was to relieve combat troops of service behind the lines and the original intention was to include in it all enlisted men of the Provost Marshal General's Department, the Post Office, the War Risk Bureau, and labor organizations. After an exchange of cables with the War Department the recommendation was changed to provide for the transfer into the new corps of stevedore regiments, the Graves Registration Service, administrative companies, and fire truck and hose companies and in compliance with this recommendation the Army Service Corps was authorized to consist of 4,000 officers and 100,000 men. It was announced in G. O. No. 38, S. O. S., August 22, 1918.

Red Cross Representatives with Divisions: Beginning in April the Red Cross had attached to many divisions permanent representatives whose chief duties were to handle supplies and conduct home communication work. This service was subsequently regularized by G. O. No. 139, A. E. F., August 24, 1918, which authorized the Red Cross to attach to each division one field director (captain), one assistant to the field director (1st lieutenant), one officer in charge of casualty service (lieutenant), and one officer in charge of home service (captain); and to each army one field director (major). In addition Red Cross personnel was authorized to be attached to separate camps, hospitals, and the various zones of the armies and sections of the S. O. S.

Temporary Transfer of Supervision of Remounts: On August 24, the subject of replacement of losses in animals and supervision of the Remount Service was transferred to G-4 by G. O. No. 139, A. E. F., 1918. This was done on the theory that the problem was one of supply, rather than replacement, and should therefore rest with the section charged with supply generally. The transfer was never made, and after a short interval the order of transfer was revoked.

Personnel for Statistical Division: On September 2, 1918, the Assistant Chief of Staff, G-1, addressed a memorandum to the Chief of Staff stating that he planned to made the Statistical Division an office for the receiving and recording of statistics sent from Washington and other sources and for collecting and publishing statistics for the A. E. F., and that additional trained personnel would be necessary for this purpose. Two additional officers were immediately requested from Washington by courier cablegram. Before this was delivered in Washington, however, a cable was received at these headquarters directing that Lt. Col. Ayres be returned to the United States. Strong representations were made to the War Department of the great importance of the Statistical Division and the need for Lt. Col. Ayers here, but he was nevertheless required to return and on September 24 he was relieved and succeeded by 1st Lt. R. B. Feagin as Chief of the Division.

Overseas Tonnage: A peculiarly acute tonnage crisis arose early in September and on the 13th three urgent cables were despatched to Washington emphasizing the imperative need for additional ocean tonnage and referring particularly to the vital necessity for animal and motor transportation. Washington replied that every effort was being made to ship the supplies requested. Nevertheless the shortage of shipping continued and at no time until the close of hostilities on November 11 was the tonnage of supplies received from the United States adequate to the needs of the A. E. F. The extent of the shortage is indicated by the following figures:

	Tons cabled for by A. E. F.	Tons received in France from U. S.
August	700,527	511,261
September	869,438	530,018
October	1,022,135	623,689

Animals from the United States: On September 14 a cable was sent to Washington by the Com-Commanding General, S. O. S., requesting shipments at the rate of 31,700 per month, to which the reply was received that this was impossible except by diverting essential tonnage. During September only three horse transports arrived and at the end of the month another cable was sent emphasizing the vital importance of increasing the rate of shipment. At that time there were 139,500 animals with combat organizations while the requirements were for a total of 245,700, or 106,200 more than were available.

Troop Shipment Program: On September 23 the Secretary of War, who was at that time in the A. E. F., invited the attention of the War Department to the fact that the 80-division program (which had been adopted in the A. E. F. after the conference between the Commander-in-Chief and Marshal Foch on June 23 and which had been used as the basis for computing the monthly programs submitted to Washington since that date) was far in excess of what it had been understood to be in Washington. The War Department replied that that program as understood here was impracticable of execution. In reply to this it was strongly recommended that the program be approved, especially with respect to the priorities for which it provided, and the January program which was cabled shortly thereafter was computed on this basis. That, however, was the last monthly priority cablegram sent, as the Armistice intervened on November 11 and all requests for troop shipments overseas were cancelled except those covering a limited number of special personnel.

Supervision of Welfare Activities: On September 18 the Commander-in-Chief directed the attention of G-1 to the enlarged scope that had been taken on by welfare activities and the importance of coordination and control. The first step was to secure additional personnel and repeated efforts were made to do so, first from Blois and, having failed there, from the 84th and 86th Divisions, which had recently been skeletonized to make replacements. At first, only one officer with suitable qualifications could be obtained, but later more were secured and on October 21, Lt. Col. H. S. Grier, G. S., reported for duty and was made chief of the Miscellaneous Division, which was charged with that subject.

  Meanwhile, efforts were being made to secure from the United States a man of high standing with suitable training and ability to be commissioned and sent to France for the purpose of being assigned to duty in G-1 and stationed in Paris as a supervisor and co-ordinator of welfare activities. However, the Secretary of War replied stating that Mr. Raymond B. Fosdick, Chairman of the War Department Commission on Training Camp Activities, was shortly coming over for the same general purpose.

Enemy Sanitary Personnel: Late in September it was learned that there was some sanitary personnel among the prisoners of war at the Central Prisoner of War Enclosure and the question of their technical status and the treatment to which they were entitled was immediately referred to the Judge Advocate. The latter's opinion was forwarded to the Provost Marshal General on October 2 with the following instructions:

  (a) To take immediate steps to select and separate from the enemy prisoners of war those who fall within the classes entitled to preferential treatment under the Geneva Convention.

  (b) To forward a report of all such prisoners to G. H. Q., stating with respect to each prisoner whether his services were indispensable in connection with care of the enemy sick and wounded.

  (c) To accord to all such prisoners the preferential treatment to which they were entitled, until such time as necessary arrangements for their repatriation could be made.

  (d) To keep accurate accounts of the compensation to which they may be entitled for services performed.

  (e) To instruct all officers in his command having custody of prisoners of war prior to their delivery to Central Prisoner of War Enclosure to take all reasonable precautions to distinguish from among other prisoners those who should be classed as sanitary personnel, and to accord to them the treatment to which they were entitled.

  At about the same time an inquiry was sent by G-1 to the Commission then sitting at Berne as to what organizations had been notified to Germany as authorized relief societies under the Geneva Convention. In reply it was learned that the following had been named:

American Red Cross.

Young Men's Christian Association.

National Catholic War Council (with the Knights of Columbus operating
    under it).

Jewish Welfare Board.

Salvation Army.

Sale of Condemned Animals to the French: Prior to October 1, 1918, condemned animals had been sold for butchery purposes. The French, however, in the belief that many of the animals so sold were suitable for agricultural uses, entered into an agreement on October 5 under the terms of which they agreed to take over all condemned animals at the flat rate of 450 francs each. The procedure specifying this agreement was published in Bulletin No. 84, A. E. F., October 28, 1918, and Sec. I, Bul. No. 92, A. E. F., November 13, 1918.

Proposed Revision of G. O.'s No. 31, 44, and 105: Early in October, 1918, the Chief of Staff referred to G-1 for study a proposed general order reorganizing the General Staff and the system of supply and transportation in the then recently created Zone of the Armies. G-1 recommended that the proposed order be divided and published as two separate orders, one dealing with the subject matter of G. O. No. 31 and the other with the supply and transportation system. Referring to the first, a number of changes in the language describing the functions of G-1 were proposed for the purpose of making the order entirely consistent with the existing situation. In addition it was recommended that the Personnel Bureau, proposed in the order as a separate organization reporting directly to the Chief of Staff, be incorporated in one of the General Staff Sections and it was pointed out that on principle the Section selected for this purpose should be G-1, inasmuch as it already was charged with the organization and replacement of all enlisted personnel and the replacement of commissioned personnel, so far as handled by the replacement system. It was also recommended that the Statistics Bureau, General Staff, be not separated from G-1 where it had been functioning successfully as the Statistical Division since the arrival of Lt. Col. Ayres and the statistics unit from Washington on July 6.

Reorganization of Bands: On March 3, 1918, a cablegram had been sent to Washington emphasizing the importance of excellent military bands in the A. E. F. and recommending an increase in the size of all authorized bands, the commissioning of band leaders, the organization of a drum and bugle corps in each regiment of infantry, and the procurement in France of the necessary instruments. These recommendations were approved on May 31, 1918, but due to the pressure of operations during the summer and early fall nothing was done for several months. On October 21 the new band organization was announced in G. O. No. 183, A. E. F. 1918, and at the same time the Chief Quartermaster was authorized to purchase the necessary instruments.

Proposed Reorganization of Administration: On October 15, 1918, G-1 received from the Chief of Staff certain "Notes on the General Administration of the A. E. F." which were marked "For consideration by General Staff, J. H. P." Briefly stated these notes proposed either the assignment of the Commanding General, S. O. S., to duty at G. H. Q. as the Head "Head of Administration," together with such chiefs of services as he should select, or, if that was not practicable, the transfer from G-1 and G-4, G. H. Q., to the Commanding General, S. O. S., of all duties other than those relating to questions of policy, and the appointment of a Deputy Commanding General, S. O. S., at G. H. Q. It was pointed out that the Commanding General, S. o. S., would then really control all administrative matters throughout the A. E. F.

The Assistant Chief of Staff, G-1, submitted his comments to the Chief of Staff on October 24. He pointed out that this proposal constituted a complete reversal of the conclusions of the Hagood Board which had been carried into effect in G. O. No. 31; that the extension of the authority of the Commanding General, S. O. S., beyond the regulating stations where it then stopped had not been justified, but on the contrary was in direct opposition to a new organization project then under consideration; that the vesting in the Commanding General, S. O. S., of the administration, supervision, and control of the entire A. E. F. as well as the duty of coordination between the front and rear, in addition to his already enormous duties and responsibilities would seriously complicate a problem of organization that was then presenting difficulties; that the wisdom of such further centralization of power had not been shown; that by G. O. No. 31 and G. O. No. 130 all duties other than matters of policy and subjects inseparably related thereto had already been transferred to Tours; and that the entire proposal was antagonistic to the system of General Staff control which was fundamental to the organization of the A. E. F.

Abolition of Corps Replacement Battalions: The origin and purpose of Corps Replacement Battalions has already been described. During the operations of the summer and early fall of 1918 they proved to be impracticable. The corps had become so flexible an organization and the movement of divisions between corps so frequent that the replacement battalions often received personnel intended for a division no longer in the corps. Furthermore the battalions were too small to fulfill their purpose and were not sufficiently mobile to follow the corps in its rapid movements.

Another difficulty had also developed. The divisional and evacuation hospitals necessarily sent to the rear the large number of slight casualties which were occuring in October, so greatly delaying the return to their units of men who should have been back in the line in a few days and encumbering transportation facilities.

To obviate all of these difficulties it was recommended to the Chief of Staff on October 21, 1918, that the 4th Depot Division (85th) and the 6th Depot Division (40th) be transferred to the Advance Section for the purpose of constituting regional replacement depots which would afford suitable facilities for receiving, equipping, and forwarding to the divisions the large number of officers and men evacuated from hospitals, men absent without leave, casuals, and stragglers of all kinds, as well as replacements. The recommendation was approved and on October 24 instructions were given under which the 4th Depot Division established a Regional Replacement Depot at Chaudenay, near Toul, and the 6th Depot Division established Regional Replacement Depots at Revigny, a short distance north of St-Dizier, Chelles, near Paris, and Saleux, near Amiens.

Joint Committee of Welfare Societies: At the time efforts were being made to secure from the War Department authority to commission and bring over an officer for the special purpose of supervising the activities of the welfare societies, a letter from the President of the United States to the Secretary of War, commenting upon a letter from Mr. Fosdick to the Secretary of War concerning the organization in the United States of a joint committee of all agencies participating in the United War Work campaign, then in progress, was transmitted to this Section. Steps were immediately taken to create a similar committee in the A. E. F. for the purpose of coordinating effort and considering matters of mutual interest. The first meeting was held on October 23 and as a result of that and subsequent conferences the organization was made permanent and was officially announced in Bul. No. 96, A. E. F., November 30, 1918.

Y. M. C. A. Work for German Prisoners of War: On October 24, when the number of German prisoners of war in the hands of the A. E. F. had grown to considerable size, the Y. M. C. advised that they were ready, with the permission of G-1, to undertake certain activities for their benefit. After consultation with G-2, permission was given to furnish German newspapers, circulating libraries of German books, musical instruments, athletic material, occasional moving pictures and German speaking secretaries, subject to the qualification that athletic material and moving pictures should not be furnished to the prejudice of similar service to our own troops and that the German newspapers should be subject to censorship.

Animals from Spain: In spite of the law that had been passed in Spain in October prohibiting the exportation of animals, the American diplomatic service succeeded on November 7 in obtaining a permit to buy 35,000 animals in that country and to bring 15,000 more through from Portugal. However, difficulties in connection with transportation made the procurement of these animals very slow and only 10,797 had been obtained before the cancellation of the arrangement following the Armistice. About 2,500 animals were obtained in England at this time and negotiations were also in progress in Italy but no contracts were made in the latter country.

C. THE ARMISTICE

The Armistice: The cessation of hostilities on November 11 brought substantially to an end certain of the activities of G-1. This was true of organization and equipment, ocean tonnage, and priority of overseas troop shipment. On the other hand other subjects immediately increased in importance and volume, as for example, military police activities, leaves, and the work of welfare societies, while other entirely new matters came into existence, such as the repatriation of American prisoners of war and the return of troops to the United States. As a result the work of the section for several months following the Armistice was as large in Volume and as important in character as during operations.

War Trophies: Prior to the Armistice the section had recieved a number of requests from combat organizations for permission to ship to the United States captured war trophies for presentation to municipalities or organizations of a semi-public character. These requests increased in number after the cessation of hostilities and commenced also to be received from various sources in the United States. On November 19, 1918, the War Department directed that all questions relating to trophies should be referred to it and thenceforward that was done.

Establishment of Separate Remounts Division: Prior to November 25 the subject of animal replacements and supervision of the Remount Service and the subject of billets and billeting had been in charge of one division of G-1 known as the Remounts and Billets Division. By that date remount work had increased so in importance that the Remounts Division was constituted separately from the Billets Division, with Colonel M. C. Bristol, Q. M. C., in charge. Colonel Bristol was Chief Remount Officer in the United States until the middle of October, when he came to France at the request of G-1 to take charge of the remount work in the General Staff.

Movement of Animals to Third Army: Following the Armistice great difficulty developed in the movement of remounts to the Third Army in its area in the occupied territory. Although the supply of animals was by this time abundant it was impossible to secure rail transportation because of the advance to the Rhine. the repatriation of prisoners, and the return of the civil population to northern France, Finally the situation was relieved by arranging for an overland convoy of 500 animals per day from Lux (the remount depot near Is-sur-Tille) to Longuyon, where they are taken over by the Third Army.

Material Delivered Pursuant to the Armistice: When material began to be received from the Germans under the Armistice it was at first reported to G-1 because of its analogy to captured material, but it soon became apparent that the questions involved were largely those of technical examination, transportation, and storage and on December 4 the entire matter was therefore turned over to G-4 at the direction of the Chief of Staff.

Repatriation of Prisoners of War: Immediately upon the signing of the Armistice, large numbers of Allied prisoners, including many Americans, who had been held in the German lines lines were precipitously and unsystematically released and permitted to proceed in a disorganized mass to the Allied lines, without food, adequate clothing, or transportation. On November 15 instructions were received from Marshal Foch for the establishment of barriers to receive these prisoners and send them to sorting stations. The Americans received in the American and Allied lines were sent to the regional replacement depots at Chaudenay (Toul), Revigny (north of St-Dizier) Chelles (near Paris) and Saleux (near Amiens), where complete reports and records were made. Those in good physical condition were handled in the same manner as personnel evacuated from hospitals, while those not in good physical condition were sent to hospitals or to leave areas for rest and recuperation.

On November 25 word was received of 1,000 wounded Allied soldiers, including 157 Americans, in a hospital at Treves and in need of medical attention and food. Permission was immediately secured from the German High Command to send suitable medical and Red Cross personnel and supplies ahead of the Allied lines to care for these persons and the matter turned over to G-4 to be carried out in conjunction with the Red Cross.

Several plans were proposed for the repatriation of the principal body of American prisoners who were in the prison camp at Rastatt. On November 26 a plan was perfected and approved for moving them by train through Switzerland and into France via Bellegrade. The details were handled by the military attache at Berne, who was given full authority, and the entire movement was completed without difficulty early in December.

A number of plans were also considered for evacuating the isolated groups of Americans scattered through northern Germany. Due to the lack of rail transportation and the fact that large numbers of British were being evacuated by sea via the northern ports, arrangements were made with England to move via this route such of our prisoners as were in that territory and that was done, arrangements for their care in England being made by the Commanding General, Base Section Number 3.

There remained only the work of searching for isolated cases scattered through Germany. On December 5 two officers of this Section proceeded into Alsace on this mission and three days later in company with a medical officer from G-4 crossed the Rhine and went to the prison camp at Rastatt. After conferring there with a representative of the German War Office charged with repatriation and a Swiss army officer who at the request of G-1 had been sent into southern Germany by the Red Cross on the same mission, they recommended the establishment of a medical base at the west end of the Rhine bridge at Seltz, equipped to search through southern Germany and remove and care for all isolated Americans who should be found. This recommendation was approved and the work successfully carried out under the direction of the Swiss officer referred to. Isolated cases in northern Germany were found and cared for by General Harries, who reached Berlin on December 8.

Repatriated Americans, both officers and men, were in most cases without funds. In order to meet this situation G-4 was asked to make payments to them in substantial amount on account, subject to final adjustment, and this was done.

School for Care of Animals: The care of animals in the A. E. F. had always been a matter of difficulty because of the inexperience of a large number of the men of the A. E. F. in the use and care of horses. On November 16, G-1 recommended the opening of schools for instruction in this subject. The proposal was approved by the Commander-in-Chief and the matter turned over to G-5 as it was considered to partake of the character of training.

Supply of Animals: On the date of the Armistice the A. E. F. was short more than 63,000 animals. In view of the cessation of operations it was possible to reduce requirements and cancel this shortage by changes in the numbers authorized to be issued to various organizations, and during the last of November and first of December such changes were announced and the importation of animals from Spain, Great Britain, and the United States was discontinued.

Y. M. C. A. Representatives with Divisions: In July the Y. M. C. A. had sought authority to attach a stated amount of personnel to divisions so that they might move whenever the division moved. No action was taken at that time. During the fall when the personnel of the K. of C. was increasing it became difficult to distribute it among the American divisions, particularly in the case of divisions serving outside of the American zone where the French were very exacting in the matter of circulation. To remedy this G-1 proposed an arrangement by which a definite number of representatives of each society should be authorized attached to each division and secured the concurrence of the societies mentioned and of G-2, but when the matter came to G-3 on November 25 it was disapproved by them and and their views were upheld by the Chief of Staff.

Statistics of Troop Departures: Prior to the Armistice the subject of troop departures was not sufficiently important to justify keeping a special record at these headquarters. However, with the cessation of operations and the adoption of a program of troop movement westward it became necessary to inaugurate a system for keeping accurate account of the returning personnel. This was done by the personnel Division of G-1, and the record was kept in this section until February 15 when it was transferred to G-1, S. O. S., where the entire westbound movement was controlled and it was therefore more convenient to keep the figures.

Care of Animals: As already stated the care of animals in the A. E. F. had not been entirely satisfactory. During an inspection made early in December it was discovered that much of the trouble was due to the evacuation of infected animals from remount depots and veterinary hospitals in the Advance Section to the Intermediate Section. Instructions were immediately issued, December 4, prohibiting the shipment of diseased animals except when unavoidable and enforcing a strict segregation of such animals.

About a month later another inspection revealed the fact that some divisions were without necessary veterinary medicines. Instructions were immediately issued for their supply and also for the construction of dipping vats for mange, which eventually greatly improved the situation.

Replacement Systems: After the Armistice, it became necessary to release the 4th and 6th Depot Divisions, which were functioning as regional replacement depots, for return to the United States. On December 5 the Commanding General, First Army, was instructed to organize provisional replacement battalions at Revigny and Chelles and on December 20 the 40th Division (6th Depot) was released for return. The regional replacement depot at Saleux was abandoned. Similarly the Commanding General, Second Army, was instructed on December 9 to organize a provisional replacement battalion at Toul and on December 25 the 85th Division (4th Depot) was released for return.

Liberalization of Leave Policy: Early in December the Commander-in-Chief directed G-1, to make a thorough study of the subject of leaves with a view to adopting a more liberal policy, particularly in the matter of length of leave, permission to visit England and Italy and the granting of leaves to casuals ordered to the United States. The capacity of leave areas made an increase in the duration of duty-status impossible, but other classes of leaves were lengthened and the other two proposals were successfully carried out.

During the progress of work on the new order the Commander-in-Chief directed the consideration of a plan whereby all men in the A. E. F. should have a short leave to Paris, on account of the educational value of the experience. Opposition developed both from the French, on account of its economic effect, and from the Chief Surgeon, on account of the venereal danger, and it was not fully carried out, but a system of short individual leaves to Paris in special cases was developed which served much the same purpose. The new order was prepared in close cooperation with the Commanding General, S. O. S., the Provost Marshal General, the Judge Advocate, and G-4 and was published on January 13 as G. O. No. 14, A. E. F., 1919.

Disposition of Excess Casuals: After the Armistice the large number of Class A men evacuated from hospitals produced an excess of casuals for return to the Third Army. On January 12 the following disposition of this personnel was approved by the Chief of Staff:

(a) Hospital evacues to be returned to the armies to which they formerly belonged until all organizations were at maximum strength except rifle companies which were to be limited to 200.

(b) Excess enlisted personnel to be disposed of as follows: First, returned to their own organizations if they so elected; second, transferred to the Military Police Corps if they desired to do so and were qualified; or third, returned to the United States if no preference was expressed.

A report covering approximately 14,000 casuals available for evacuation to the Third Army showed that the choices were distributed as follows:

Transferred to Military Police Corps	600
Returned to divisions	1,400
Returned to United States	12,000
	14,000

Welfare Personnel: The shortage of welfare personnel became more acute than ever after the Armistice, because just at a time when the need of the army was for an increase in activity, many workers desired to go home. G-1 undertook to expedite the shipment of personnel from the United States by securing permission to use eastbound transports, but the War Department at first refused, giving permission instead to discharge officers and soldiers in France for the purpose of entering the service of the welfare societies. This authorization at first applied only to members of units scheduled for early return, but later was extended to cover the entire A. E. F. The efforts to secure additional personnel from the United States, particularly women, were not relaxed and on February 4 the War Department cabled that women welfare workers and entertainers representing any of the recognized welfare organizations and having the approval of the Commission on Training Camp Activities would be permitted to come to France on transports. Later, on March 4, similar permission was given for wives of Salvation Army workers.

Change of Deputy Assistant Chief of Staff, G-1: On December 17, 1918, Col. Bruce Palmer, G. S. Deputy Assistant Chief of Staff, G-1, who had been on duty in various capacities in the Section since December 14, 1917, was released from duty at his own request and returned to the United States on account of ill health. Col. Charles S. Lincoln, G. S., at that time chief of the Miscellaneous Division, was announced as Deputy Assistant Chief of Staff, G-1. At the same time the title of the Miscellaneous Division was changed to Administrative Division and the Tonnage Division, whose duties since the Armistice had almost entirely disappeared, was absorbed by it.

Replacement System: On December 18 when it was desired to release the 41st Division for return to the United States, the First Replacement Depot was organized at St-Aignan-des-Noyers (Loir-et-Cher) and took over all the functions of the 1st Depot Division. As other replacement depots were discontinued their remaining activities were transferred to the First Replacement Depot and it was also used as a reservoir for casuals ordered to the United States. Its establishment was announced in G. O. No. 242, A. E. F., December 30, 1918.

Military Police Matters: As already stated, military police activities increased greatly in importance on the cessation of hostilities. This was due to the removal of the incentive of active warfare to good discipline and the increase in opportunity for absence without leave due to the sudden release of a large amount of territory from enemy occupation. In order to provide for closer supervision of and greater assistance to the Provost Marshal General's Department, all subjects falling within its scope were on December 19, 1918, assigned to Col. M. A. Elliott, Jr., Infantry, who had recently been assigned to duty in the office of the Deputy.

One of the first subjects given special attention was the reduction of the offense of absence without leave. The matter was given thorough study in conjunction with the Provost Marshal General and a method of dealing with the situation was formulated and promulgated in G. O. No. 10, A. E. F., January 14, 1919 (amended by Par. 1, Sec. VI, G. O. No. 29, A. E. F., February 12, 1919). That order provided that soldiers who are convicted of absence without leave from the vicinity of their commands for more than twenty-four hours or who have been repeatedly absent with out leave will be transferred to provisional development battalions which it is the policy to retain in France as long as there is any need for labor troops. This order greatly reduced the offence of A. W. O. L. throughout the A. E. F.

Captured Material. G. O. No. 31, [A. E. F., 1918,] made it the duty of G-1 to supervise the disposal of captured material. After the conclusion of hostilities a number of conclusion of hostilities a number of considerations arose which rendered it advisable to transfer this subject to G-4. It was difficult at times to separate the supervision of the disposal of such material from that of material handed over under the Armistice; captured material was all in the hands of technical and supply services and its disposal was largely a problem of transportation. Accordingly, after consultation with G-4 transfer to them was recommended to the Chief of Staff and approved by him on February 12, 1919.

Arrival in France of Mr. Fosdick: Toward the end of December, Mr. Fosdick, Chairman of the War Department Commission on Training Camp Activities, who has already been spoken of in connection with the supervision of welfare activities, arrived in France and from then on close and cordial relations were maintained between him and G-1 in the effort to further welfare work. During the latter part of January an officer was sent from G-1 to make a detailed inspection of the welfare work in each corps area and at the same time the Commanding General, S. O. S., was instructed to make similar inspections. A little later the Assistant Chief of Staff, G-1, made an inspection of the welfare work in leave areas and, as a result of the reports of all these inspections, numerous recommendations, general and specific, were made to the societies as well as to the commanding officers concerned.

Entertainment: Prior to the Armistice, the matter of entertainment was left to the Y. M. C. A. and no special supervision was given the subject by G-1. Immediately upon the conclusion of operations the matter was taken up vigorously, and in collaboration with G-5 an athletic and entertainment program prepared, which was finally published in G. O. No. 242, A. E. F., December 29, 1918. This provided for the organization of soldier entertainment troupes in all units and the routing of these and professional troupes supplied by the Y. M. C. A. through division, corps, and army areas and, when justified, throughout the A. E. F. For this purpose the excellent entertainment department of the Y. M. C. A. was utilized, as were also the funds contributed by that organization and the other welfare societies. For the administration of this elaborate program an Assistant Entertainment Officer, A. E. F., was established in Paris and entertainment officers were appointed in all divisions, corps, and armies and S. O. S. units. It was the announced purpose of these headquarters to provide appropriate entertainment at every important point where American troops were located every night and this was substantially carried out.

Perferential Treatment of Alsatian-Lorrainers: In June, 1918, the French had requested the A. E. F. to transfer to them all Alsatian-Lorrainer prisoners of war in order that they might be accorded preferential treatment, but this proposal was declined on the ground that to surrender the custody of such prisoners to another belligerent would violate the treaty with Prussia of 1799. In October the French submitted the alternative proposal that these prisoners be given preferential treatment by the A. E. F. in accordance with their own practice. After extended negotiations this was acceded to in December. The Provost Marshal General was directed to segregate and orgainze into two or more companies all the Alsatian-Lorrainers in his custody and give them preferred treatment in accordance with detailed instructions. The question of nationality was to be determined in each instance by the French.

Sale by Y. M. C. A. of Quartermaster Supplies: The arrangement by which the Y. M. C. A. secured tobacco from the Quartermaster Department for resale at quartermaster prices has already been described. Subsequently the question came up of extending this practice to cover all quartermaster stores and so practically constitute the Y. M. C. A. a retail agency for the quartermsater. Negotiations extended throughout the fall of 1918 and culminated in an agreement between the Y. M. C. A. and the Quartermaster Corps under which the former surrendered the portion of its automatic tonnage devoted to post exchange supplies and the latter agreed to deliver a like amount of merchandise for sale at prices to be determined by it. The arrangement was announced in Bulletin No. 96, A. E. F., November 30, 1918, and went into effect January 1, 1919.

Horse Shows: Early in January the institution of horse shows in divisions, corps, and armies was proposed as an incentive to the proper care of animals and vehicles and received the hearty indorsement of the Commander-in-Chief. Accordingly a series of instructions for holding such shows, including regulations concerning the ribbons and prizes which should be awarded, was prepared by G-1 and published in Bulletin No. 3, A. E. F., January 17, 1919. Thereafter horse shows were held by all divisions, corps, and armies and proved to be of immense value not only as stimulating interest in the care of animals but also as promoting esprit and furnishing diversion and entertainment.

Sale of Gift Tobacco: In November, 1918, it was alleged in several instances that the Y. M. C. A. had sold cigarettes and tobacco which, according to cards found inside the cartons, had been donated by the New York Sun Tobacco Fund for the purpose of free distribution.   At the request of the Y. M. C. A. the matter was referred to the Inspector General for investigation.   He found that the gift tobacco had been sold to the Y. M. C. A. by various quartermaster depots, that the cases were either marked inconspicuously or not at all to indicate their special character, that nothing was placed inside them to indicate it except inside the cartons, so that when whole cartons were sold it was not known until after the sale that the tobacco was intended for donation.   Based on this report a cable was sent to the War Department recommending that in future cases of gift tobacco they be plainly marked on six sides and that labels be placed inside the top and bottom.

Venereal Rate: As was pointed out early in this chapter, G-1 has been called upon to handle important matters of an administrative character not expressly delegated to it by general orders.   This was increasingly so after the Armistice, when many novel problems were arising which demanded prompt and effective action.   One of the most important of these was the matter of the venereal rate.   On February 17 this was referred by the Commander-in-Chief personally to G-1 with directions that a general campaign be immediately instituted through the medium of the Medical Department, the welfare societies, the leave area commanders, and all other interested services for the purpose of bringing about a reduction. A conference was called by G-1 on February 27 at which the Chief Surgeon, the Judge Advocate, the Senior Chaplain, G-1, S. O. S., the Third Army, and the five welfare societies were represented.   The situation was thoroughly canvassed and a vigorous repressive campaign instituted which brought about a sharp reduction in the rate.

Transfer of Y. M. C. A. Exchanges to Quartermaster: The termination after the Armistice of the considerations which had instigated the request that the Y. M. C. A. undertake the operation of exchanges and so avoid depleting the personnel of combat organizations for that purpose and the concurrent need for an enlargement of the social and recreational work of the Y. M. C. A. prompted the Commander-in-Chief to direct that a study be made of the possibility of transferring this function back to the army.   At the same time the Y. M. C. A. made a formal request to be relieved of this work.   Early in February it was decided to make the change and after extensive conferences between representatives of the Quartermaster Corps and the Y. M. C. A. it was put into effect on April 1, 1919, in accordance with the plan announced in G. O. No. 50, A. E. F., March 17, 1919, that provides for the replacement of Y. M. C. A. canteens both by Quartermaster Sales Commissaries and co-operative camp exchanges in order that troops may be provided for so far as possible under all circumstances.
so far as possible under all circumstances.

Repatriation of Enemy Sanitary Personnel: In November the Provost Marshal General had first raised the question of repatriation of the enemy sanitary personnel among prisoners of war held by the A. E. F., but at that time the Judge Advocate ruled that it was not compatible with military exigencies within the meaning of the Geneva Convention.   The same view was taken in December when the question was raised again, but in January the Judge Advocate expressed the opinion that since the completion of the enemy withdrawal and the occupation of enemy territory it would be proper to repatriate such sanitary captives as were no longer needed.   The matter was laid befor the Chief of Staff in February, he approved repatriation on February 17 and instructions were immediately issued to the Provost Marshal General to carry it out.   These instructions provided for the following measures:

    (a)   Complete payment in accordance with the Geneva Convention.

    (b)   Return of personal effects and money in the custody of the Quartermaster.

    (c)   Complete outfits of clothing, in good condition, and also individual mess equipment.

    (d)   Baths and delousing, if necessary.

    (e)   Proper completion of statistical records and the preparation of a roster to be furnished the German authorities to whom the personnel would be turned over.

All arrangements were perfected and on March 23 the personnel in question was repatriated on two special trains.

Release of Alsatian-Lorrainers: In December the question of releasing Alsatian-Lorrainers
held by the A. E. F. as prisoners of war was raised by the French through the diplomatic
service and presented to G-1 by the Paris Embassy. This proposal did not involve the
surrendering of custody to the French but was accompanied by assurance that no attempt
would be made to control such persons, if liberated, for military purposes and that they
would be free to return to their homes or proceed to any other place they desired. The
Judge Advocate expressed the opinion that such a course would not be in violation of the
Prussian treaty or of international law and the President, who was then in France, expressed
his approval provided the War Department concurred. The matter was thereupon submitted
to the War Department by cable and on February 7 its approval secured, after which detailed arrangements were immediately made for the examination of all claimants by a
commission of French officers and the release of whose who succeeded in establishing their
nationality.

Welfare Officers: During the latter part of January instructions were issued by letter
inaugurating in divisions, corps, armies, and S. O. S. commands a system of joint control
and coordination of welfare work similar to that created in Paris for the entire A. E. F.
in November, and shortly thereafter directions were given to appoint in all such commands
an officer of field rank who should function under G-1 and devote his entire attention to
welfare matters. This action was followed by detailed instructions which designated the
officer referred to Welfare Officer and indicated the excat nature and extent of his duties,
and additional instructions were issued from time to time. One of the subjects specifically
committed to his care was morale, upon which he was directed to keep a close watch and make
detailed reports from time to time.

     The entire policy of G-1 with respect to welfare activities as de veloped from the
early fall of 1918, when a system of coordination was first undertaken to the extension of
this system which had just been described and the appointment of Welfare officer, was drawn
together and published in G. O. No. 46, A. E. F., March 10, 1919, which repealed all prior
orders and bulletins on the subject.

Dispostion of Animals: With the return of the A. E. F. to the United States the question
arose of the disposition to be made of animals. It was decided to sell them in Europe because of the great demand for reconstuction purposes, the danger of infection, the great
expense of converting ships for their return, and other reasons. The question was referred
to the Advisory Liquidation Commission and negotiations opened with the French. Pending
an agreement with them authority was given to dispose of surplus unserviceable animals in
Belgium and Luxembourg, but few were sold there on account of the shortage of forage in
those countries. About the middle of February an agreement was made with the French under
which they were to sell all surplus animals in good condition and retain 5% of the price
received to cover expenses. Subsequently authority was obtained to sell direct to private
French buyers and many horses were so disposed of.

Activities of Knights of Columbus: The number of K. of C. personnel which arrived during
the latter part of 1918 made that organization a potentially important factor in the relief
and recreation program. The principal problem was so to coordinate the activities of the
K. of C. and Y. M. C. A. that their efforts would not be duplicated and their resourses
wasted. In this behalf a certain measure of success was attained through the coordinating
machinery established in paris during October and November, which has already been described,
but it was plain that full benefit could not be derived from the activities of these two
organizations except by means of some sort of a territorial division between them. In
attempting to bring this about G-1 worked largely through Mr. Fosdick, who, by reason of
his connection with the United War Work Campaign in the United States, was in a strong
position to make suggestions concerning the work carried on with the money so raised.
Numerous conferences were held and the Y. M. C. A. offered to withdraw from any area designated by G-1 and surrender the field to the K. of C. This was approved in principle by

G-1 and after extended consideration of the area to be selected Base Section No. 2 was proposed on February 28.

At the same time consideration was given to participation by the K. of C. in the work in leave areas, which had grown to such proportions as to strain the resources of the Y. Y. M. C. A. the only agency then engaged in it. The Y. M. C. A. proposed that the K. of C. take over the Biarritz leave area, then about to be opened, and incidentally three small adjoining areas, and this opportunity was formerly offered to the K. Of C. by G-1 on February 27. Although the matter was understood to be settled, no move was ever made by the K. of C. to commence work and finally on March 15, after it had been necessary to ask the Y. M. C. A. to establish certain temporary facilities in the area, the offer to the K. of C. was withdrawn and the magter left to the Y. M. C. A.

After the request of February 28 that the K. of C. take over Base Section No. 2, the matter was discussed from time to time and finally, on March 12, the K. of C. advised that they were not in a position to undertake that work.

Dispostion of Hospital Evacues: By March 1, substantially all men sent to hospitals before the Armistice had been evacuated and continuation of the policy of giving hospital evacues of Class A the option of rejoining their organizations or returning to the United States would have placed a premium upon illness. Therefore on March 4, on the recommendation of the Commanding General, S. O. S., the following policy was approved.

(a) Class A hospital evacues whose organizations were still in France to be sent to them direct.

(b) Those whose organizations had sailed or were about to sail so soon that time would not permit them to rejoin, to be sent to the 1st Replacement Depot and assigned to returning divisions.

CHAPTER II

INTERNAL ORGANIZATION OF G-1

A. THE CHIEF OF SECTION

The chief of section, as its chief executive, is charged with the duty of organizing and directing all of the affairs of the Section and is directly responsible to the Chief of Staff for the efficiency of the Section. The first Chief of the 1st Section, General Staff, was Maj. (later Col., G. S.) James A. Logan, Q. M. C., who was appointed shortly after the publication of G. O. No. 8, A. E. F., July 5, 1917, and relieved from duty by G. O. No. 137, A. E. F., August 21, 1918.

An important change in the status of the chief of section took place during this period by G. O. No. 31, A. E. F., 1918, which order provided that each chief of section should, by virtue of his office, be an Assistant Chief of Staff to the Commander-in-Chief. As such Assistant Chief of Staff he was authorized to sign telegrams and correspondence and issue instructions, by order of the Commander-in-Chief, in his own name; and this system was followed continuously thereafter.

Col. (later Brig. Gen., G. S.) Avery D. Andrews, Corps of Engineers, reported for duty with the 1st Section, General Staff, G. H. Q., on July 23, 1918, and on August 21, 1918, was appointed Assistant Chief of Staff, 1st Section, G-1.

B. OFFICE OF THE DEPUTY

On November 18, 1917, Lt. Col. A. B. Barber, G. S., was designated Assistant Chief of the Administrative Section, General Staff, by an office memorandum which also distributed the duties of the Section among the several divisions. This memorandum stated that the assistant chief should in the absence of the chief perform his functions. It further charged him with the duty of distributing the work among the different divisions of the Section. In view of the increase of business transacted, it was later deemed impossible for one officer to be familiar with everything handled in the Section, and accordingly on January 31, 1918, Col. Barber was authorized to act and sign in behalf of the Chief.

[The next paragraphs list personnel changes in the office of the Deputy Assistant Chief of Staff, G-1.]

* * * * * *

The Deputy A. C. of S., G-1, has acted as assistant to the A. C. of S., G-1, in the supervision of the activities of all the divisions of G-1 and in the absence of the A. C. of S., G-1, has discharged his duties. In the ordinary course of business, all recommendations of chiefs of divisions and all outgoing communications prepared by divisions for the signature of the A. C. of S., G-1, passed through the hands of the Deputy who initialed them and passed them to the Chief of Section, or in his discretion recommitted them for further study or revision. He did not, ordinarily, take initial action on any class of business, but from time to time was charged by the Chief of the Section with the study of special questions not assigned to any division and with the initiation of action thereon. It has also been his duty to keep in close touch with the divisions in matters requiring prolonged study or a continued course of action, and to advise with them upon the progress of such matters. He has not infrequently taken an active part in the conduct of important negotiations and the determination or enforcement of important policies which in their subject matter were essentially within the sphere of particular divisions.

C. OFFICE OF THE SECRETARY

When the Administrative Section first took over its functions under G. O. No. 8, A. E. F., July 5, 1917, the volume of business and number of officers and clerks on duty was not sufficiently great to require the appointment of a secretary to supervise office routine. Purely clerical questions were at that time in charge of the Chief Clerk, while the detailed executive management of the Section was retained by the Chief. On September 1, 1917, when G. H. Q. removed from Paris to Chaumont, the Administrative Section numbered two officers, a civilian chief clerk, and two Army field clerks, and the number of communications received weekly was about thirty.

In October 1917, Maj. Charles H. Grant, Ordnance Department, attached to the Administrative Section in charge of matters relating to Ordnance, was also given the duties of Secretary of the Section. The position of Secretary of the Section existed continuously from that time, and for several months there was also an Assistant Secretary.

The Secretary has been generally responsible, under the supervision of the Chief of the Section, for all matters of office routine and management. This included the proper maintenance of records and files, proper systems of recording, distributing, following up, and dispatching business, procurement and general supervision of stenographic and clerical personnel, orderlies, etc., and procurement of necessary office equipment and supplies. He has been responsible for the form of correspondence, channels of communication, and proper methods of procedure, and had assisted the Deputy in supervising the substance of communications and proposed action prepared by the divisions.

[The report here enters into a detailed description of the office routine of the 1st Section.]

* * * * * *

D. PERSONNEL

[This section gives statistics on the changes in strength of the 1st Section.]

* * * * * *

E. DIVISIONS OF G-1

1. PERSONNEL DIVISION

a. Duties: The duties of the Personnel Division have remained practically unchanged during its existence, covering broadly the question of policies concerning personnel, the priority of overseas shipments of troops, and the replacement of losses in personnel.

For a time, from December 1, 1917 to January 23, 1918, it handled also the replacement of animals but this subject was transferred to the newly created Remounts and Billets Division on the latter date.

b. Organization and Personnel: [Lists personnel and their assignments to duty in the Personnel Division.]

* * * * * *

2. TONNAGE DIVISION

a. Duties: During 1917 and until August, 1918, the Tonnage Division balanced and coordinated all requisitions submitted by the several supply services for transmission to the United States and controlled the priority of shipments. It also supervised the operation of transports as to turn-around and detention in French ports and maintained a balance between tonnage of shipping available and tonnage of supplies requisitioned.

In August 1918, the detail work connected with the allotment of supplies, the checking of the cable and mail correspondence connected with these allotments and port and transport operations were transferred to the Headquarters, S. O. S. Being thus relieved of routine duties, the Tonnage Division since that time has handled only questions of policy in connection with problems of supply and ocean transportation.

b. Organization and Personnel: [Lists personnel and gives their assigments to duty in the Tonnage Division.]

* * * * * *

3. ORGANIZATION AND EQUIPMENT DIVISION

a. Duties: Under G. O. No. 8, A. E. F., July 5, 1917, as amended, the Administrative Section, General Staff, was charged with "Ratio of combat troops to Line of Communication troops" and "Details of organization and equipment of Line of Communication and Transportation Department troops and services." Memorandum No. 129, A. E. F., November 29, 1917, made no change in these duties, but G. O. No. 31, A. E. F., February 16, 1918, charged G-1 with "Organization and equipment of troops (in consultation with G-3)" and "Ratio of combat troops to S. O. S. troops." Since that time the Organization and Equipment Division of G-1 had prepared all tables of organization, all cables to the War Department relating to changes in existing tables, and all equipment manuals, collaborating with G-3 in the case of tables and manuals applying to combat troops.

b. Organization and Personnel: [Lists personnel and gives assignments to duty in the Organization and Equipment Division.]

* * * * * *

4. REMOUNTS DIVISION

a. Duties: Memorandum No. 129, H. A. E. F., November 19, 1917, included among the duties of the Administrative Section, General Staff, Remounts Service and Replacement of Men and Animals. The general problems which were handled under these headings were larger questions of policy regarding the procurement, distribution, care, and maintenance of animals and their disposition after the cessation of hostilities.

b. Organization and Personnel: [Lists personnel and gives assignments to duty in the Remounts Division.]

* * * * * *

There have been no subdivisions of the Remounts Division, but for purposes of liaison a representative of the Veterinary Corps has been detailed for duty in the Office of the Chief of the Remounts Division.

5. ADMINISTRATIVE DIVISION

The Administrative (formerly Miscellaneous) Division of G-1 has been the office to handle all matters not clearly the duty of one of the other divisions. As these duties have varied in number and importance, so the division has varied in strength of personnel. In the summer of 1918 all miscellaneous matters were handled by the Deputy A. C. of S., G-1, in addition to his other duties and there was no Miscellaneous Division as such. In the early part of 1919 the Administrative Division had grown to be the largest division of G-1 both in personnel and in volume of business handled. For these reasons a description of the duties of the division cannot be separated from the account of its organization and personnel.

On November 18, 1917, the duties of the Administrative Section, General Staff, were subdivided among several divisions, among them an Auxiliary Services Division, with Capt. C. Stewart Forbes, Inf., as its chief. The subjects assigned to it were Red Cross, Y.M.C.A., and other similar agencies, War Risk Bureau, Auditors, and Field Ambulance Service. A short time later Liaison with Other Nations was added. Capt. Forbes was relieved from duty with the Administrative Section, General Staff, on February 8, 1918.

Following the publication of G. O. No. 31, A. E. F., on February 16, 1918, the Miscellaneous Division of G-1 was created to handle the following subjects:

Disposition of captured men and material.

Provost Marshal questions.

Red Cross.

Y. M. C. A.

War Risk Section.

Auditors and similar agencies.

Leaves and leave areas.

Liaison Service.

[Here the report takes up personnel assignments and distribution of duties within the Administrative Division.]

* * * * * *

6. BILLETS DIVISION

a. Duties: The duties of the Billets Division have been the general supervision of questions of policy regarding the quartering of troops in France, a supervision of the activities of the Renting, Requsition and Claims Service and a maintenance of liaison on billeting work between G. H. Q., the Armies, the S. O. S., and the Allied government. This work was handled by the Operations Section until transferred to the Administrative Section by memorandum No. 129, H. A. E. F. Although that memorandum was dated November 19, 1917, the Operations Section carried forward to their conclusion certain questions then under consideration, and a complete transfer of the subject to the Administrative Section was not made until January 2, 1918.

b. Organization and Personnel: [Lists personnel and gives assignments to duty in the Billets Division.]

* * * * * *

7. STATISTICAL DIVISION

a. Duties: The Statistical Division of G-1 has been charged with the duty of compiling statistics of nearly every phase of the activities of the A. E. F., and presenting them in graphic form for the information of the Commander-in-Chief and members of the Staff. It has worked in close cooperation with the Statistical Section of the General Staff, S. S. O. S.

b. Organization and Personnel: [Lists personnel and gives assignments to duty in the Statistical Division.]

* * * * * *

8. ENTERTAINMENT DIVISION

Col. John R. Kelly, F. A., was assigned to G-1 on December 17, 1918, to take charege of the entertainment work of the A. E. F. He worked first under the Administrative Division, because of its supervision of the welfare societies, but on January 6, 1919, was assigned to the office of the Deputy A. C. of S., G-1. As the work grew in volume and importance the Entertainment Division was created on February 24, with Col. Kelly as its chief and 2d Lt. C. J. Martin, Inf., of the Administrative Division as his assistant.

On April 11, 1919, the Entertainment Division was abolished and the work again taken over by the Administrative Division. Co. Kelly was relieved from duty with G-1 a short time afterwards and Lt. Martin was assigned to the Administrative Division.

F. REPRESENTATIVE IN PARIS

[This section begins with a discussion of personnel assignments.]

* * * * * *

The G-1 Representative in Paris acts primarily as a channel of personal communication between G-1 and the various welfare societies, all of whose headquarters are located in Paris. His presence there had made it possible to adjust many matters much more expeditiously than could be done by correspondence. He has also represented G-1 at the meetings of the Central Joint Committee established under Bulletin No. 96, A. E. F., 1918 (G. O. No. 46, A. E. F., 1919). As Assistant Entertainment Officer, A. E. F., he has dealt as representative of G-1 with the Entertainment Department of the Y. M. C. A. and with the other societies participating in the entertainment program, and has been in charge of all officers and men detailed for general entertainment duty in the·A. E. F. He has also been responsible for effecting exchanges of entertainment troupes between S. O. S. and the several armies.

CHAPTER III

PRIORITY OF TROOP SHIPMENTS AND STATISTICS OF PERSONNEL

A. PRIORITY OF TROOPS SHIPMENTS FROM OVERSEAS

The General Organization Project of the A. E. F. was approved July 11, 917, and the Service of the Rear Project on September 18, 1917. The composition of the expedition having been definitely determined, the next step was the preparation of a program of troop shipments which should insure the gradual building up of a force in conformity with this project and at all times balanced and symmetrical. As the capacity and availability of transports was at that time undetermined this program took the form of a Priority Schedule which divided the initial force provided for by the two projects into six phases and allotted units to each. The original Priority Schedule was approved on October 7, 1917. Reorganizations and unforseen circumstances made it evident that from time to time the Priority Schedule would have to be altered, and a memorandum from the Chief of Staff dated October 16, 1917 prescribed the manner in which proposed changes in the program of troop shipments should be submitted for consideration. The troops already overseas were shown in their logical positions on the Priority Schedule and credit given to the phase to which each organization belonged. A general summary of the situation on January 5, 1918, is contained in cablegram P-454

Troop shipments under the Priority Schedule continued for several months without any important modification in the program although various groups of special personnel were requested from time to time in addition to the troops appearing on the Schedule. In the meantime, the division of staff functions in connection with the shipment of troops overseas was worked out and was defined in G. O. No. 31, A. E. F., 1918. G-1 was charged with "Priority of overseas shipments (troop shipments in consultation with G-3)"; G-3 was charged with "Schedule of troop shipments from the United States."

In order to regulate the priority of units of any phase it was necessary to keep acurate records of the arrival of units. These records were based, in the first instance, on reports of arrivals received from the various ports which reports were also used by G-4 in making the initial assignment to areas of troops arriving at the ports. Certain difficulties were encountered in accomplishing this before the completion of the organization of the ports and the issue of precise and comprehensive rules as to the manner in which reports of arrivals should be made. A system of item numbers for use in identifying units had been prescribed in the Priority Schedule but this was a highly confidential document an and many of the officers who were called upon to make early reports of arrivals were unfamiliar with these item numbers. In addition, many detachments arrived which were not included in the Priormty Schedule and consequently were not covered by the system of item numbers. In describing an organization that had arrived, frequently no mention was made of missing units. A regiment would be assumed from the reports to be complete in the A. E. F. until later reports showed the arrival of one or more of its companies. Many organizations were new and their designations were easily confused by officers making and handling reports. Special difficulty was found in keeping records of the arrivals of casuals who were for the most part not covered by the system of item numbers given in the Priority Schedule.

In order to correct these conditions the system of item numbers was extended to include all personnel to be shipped and the method of making reports was more clearly defined. Cablegram P-751, March 18, 1918, proposed to the War Department a system of item numbers for personnel not included in the Priority Schedule. The necessity of precise and accurate reports as to the arrival of units was brought to the attention of the Commanding General, S. O. S., by letter of April 13, 1918. Pursuant to the instructions contained in this letter detailed directions covering the preparation and form of these reports were issued to the Commanding Generals of all ports of debarkation on May 10, 1918.

The records showing the numerical arrival of personnel in France are closely related to those showing the arrival of units. A detailed discussion of this phase of the work is covered in the next Section of this chapter, B. Statistics of Troop Arrivals.

The first considerable departure from the program laid down in the original Priority Schedule was in consequence of the military situation in March, 1918, and was the direct result of an agreement with Great Britian following a meeting of the Supreme War Council in the latter part of the month. (See Cablegrams P-844, April 3, 1918; P-876, April 8, 1918; P-955, April 19, 1918; and P-961, April 24, 1918.) Under this agreement infantry and machine gun troops were to be brought to France in great numbers, by the use of British shipping, without reference to the Priority Schedule. The transports previously at the disposition of the United States were to continue work along the lines laid down in the original program, expediting the movement to the greatest possible extent. This agreement made necessary an extensive readjustment of the Priority Schedule, the recommendations for which were contained in Cable P-891, April 11, 1918. This cable was prepared by G-3 after a study of the G-1 records showing the status of shipments under the schedule in force up to that time.

Under the Abbeville agreement, May 2, 1918, the policy of giving absolute priority to infantry and machine-gun units was continued. (Cables P-1042, May 3, and P-1064, May 6). Based on this agreement a further revision of the Priority Schedule, to apply to shipments for May and June, was cabled in P-1099, May 12, 1918. A later agreement covering the transportation of American troops overseas in June and July was reported to the War Department by P-1236, June 3. The revision of priority made necessary by this was cabled June 8, in P-1267. Both P-1099 and P-1267 were prepared in the same manner as P-891.

On June 19, 1918, the outline of a program of troop shipments to be completed in May, 1919, was cabled to the United States. This program was designed to bring the American Expeditionary Forces to a strength of sixty-six divisions, supported by the proper number of Corps, Army, Services of Supply, and Replacement troops. This became a basis for the preparation of detailed programs of troop shipments for the months after July, 1918. The monthly distribution proposed in this cable provided for the completion of the original Priority Schedule, with slight modifications during August and the first part of September; this was the only priority of which the War Department was advised until the detailed program of troop shipments for August and September was cabled on August 7, 1918, in P-1569.

Following a conference of the Commander-in-Chief with Marshal Foch at Chaumont, June 23, 1918, Cable P-1369 was sent, on June 25, 1918, to the War Department. This proposed the placing in France of an army aggregating 46 divisions in October, 64 in the following January, 80 in April, and 100 in July, 1919. On June 28, 1918, a memorandum from the Deputy Chief of Staff to the Assistant Chiefs of Staff directed that a study be made of the possibility of carrying out a program such as that proposed in P-1369. These instructions were modified on July 9 by an additional memorandum which stated that the Commander-in-Chief desired that these studies be made on the basis of a force containing 80 combat divisions.

In the meantime, a letter, dated June 23, 1918, had requested a statement from the Commanding General, S. O. S., showing the troops that would be required by each of the Services of Supply under the program outlined in P-1342---the sixty-six-division program. This statement was received July 8, 1918. The aggregate of the estimates prepared by the various services was many times the allotment made to the S. O. S. in the sixty-six-division program, Par. 36, P-1342. The Department of Construction and Forestry estimated that its requirements alone would equal the allotment for all the services. In the consolidated statement prepared at Headquarters, S. O. S., which purported to give the absolutely minimum requirements, the allotment was still exceeded by many thousands.

A board of officers representing G-1, G-3, and G-4 was convened, pursuant to a memorandum from the Deputy Chief of Staff, dated July 21, 1918. This Board was directed to revise the estimates of the Services of Supply as to troops needed by them and to prepare a cable to the United States asking for the formation and shipment of the necessary troops. The first step taken by this board was to consider a study which had been made in G-1 of the status of troop shipments under the Priority Schedule. The various revisions and amendments of that schedule were considered in relation to the actual shipments of troops to date. It appeared desirable that a balance should be struck as of a certain date and these data cabled to the War Department in order that the War Department and the A. E. F. might have the same interpretation of the portion of P-1342 which related to August and the first part of September and which read: Complete general organization and priority project, less four brigades army tractor artillery for which material will not be available until late fall, total 255,000; 20,000 new Services of Supply troops, classes specified later and 50,000 replacements; grand total for August and first part of September 325,000. Additional revisions were made and the detailed program of troops for the balance of September was prepared. In view of the rate of troop arrivals, which had exceeded 310,000 in July, the total program for the months of August and September was increased to 600,000. The first recommendations of this board were approved and forwarded to the War Department in Cablegram P-1569, August 7, 1918. The same data in more complete form were also forwarded by courier.

The work of the board was continued by the representatives of G-1 and G-3. As a result cables were prepared proposing detailed programs for the months of October, November, December, and January; in each case the regular cables were supplemented by a courier cable giving the program in detail. The October program was stated in P-1655, September 3, and CP-172, September 7; the November program in P-1678, September 11, and CP-189 September 21; the December program in P-1701, September 18, and CP-198, September 28; the January program in P-1848, October 28, and CP-220, October 29. Such cablegrams as P-1563-1 C, P-1595-1, P-1618-4, P-1622-1, P-1626-2 B, P-1627-1 A, which were sent to cover special and urgent phases of the Priority of troop shipments were incorporated in the cablegrams giving the program by months.

In cablegram P-1713, September 21, 1918, a program covering the period from January to June, 1919, inclusive, was outlined and the monthly programs were defined as phases, each to be completed before beginning on the following phase. This program was designed to provide 80 divisions in the A. E. F. P-1717, September 23, 1918, sent by the Secretary of War, invited the attention of the War Department to the fact that this program was far in excess of what the War Department had considered as the eighty-division program. A-1982 insisted that it was impracticable to carry out the program outlined in P-1713. The reply was contained in P-1742, October 2, 1918. It recommended strongly the approval of the program contained in P-1713, especially as to the priority to be followed in the shipments. In accordance with this, a program for the January phase of 350,000 troops was cabled October 28, 1918, in P-1848. This was the last troop priority cable sent before the Armistice, after which all requests for the shipment of troops overseas were cancelled except a few covering a limited number of personnel required for special purposes.

Additional cablegrams which had a direct bearing on the Priority of troop shipments were P-1627, August 26, 1918, recommending the elimination of the replacement and school division of each corps and the constitution of corps of five line and one depot divisions each, and prescribing the changes in certain army and corps troops made necessary by this change; A-1896, August 30, 1918, in reply thereto which stated that the general proposal had been approved and asked further details relative to corps and army troops; P-1652, September 3, 1918, in reply which gave the information requested; A-1652, September 9, 1918, which stated that the program for shipping these troops would be carried out; and P-1691, September 15, 1918, which requested the organization of such units as would probably be required to meet the shipping schedule and permit modification and substitution without undue derangement of the system. These cablegrams related entirely to combat troops and were prepared by G-3. It should be noted that the word Corps as used in them referred to the units which should be shipped in order to provide for the organization of the average fighting corps. The number of divisions composing a corps in the field varied considerably.

To summarize this subject, the original Priority Schedule was the plan on which the A. E. F. was built. The surprisingly rapid developments of the summer of 1918 caused the shipments to exceed all expectations and to contain an excess of combat troops. In order to prepare the specialized units required for the Services of Supply, the War Department required from three to six months' notice. This much notice could not be given and as a result such troops as were already organized in the United States, principally combat troops, were shipped. The much needed Services of Supply troops lagged behind their proper place in the program and the campaign of 1918 was a series of crises for those services, which they met and overcame. It is believed that the shipments during the winter would have restored the balance and that the campaign of 1919 would have opened with a better proportioned as well as a more experienced force.

B. STATISTICS OF TROOP ARRIVALS

The need of accurate information regarding the arrivals of troops was recognized early in the existence of the A. E. F., and steps were taken to procure exact reports of all arrivals of personnel.

The earlier arrivals were tabulated by various agencies, but this arrangement was found not to give satisfactory results and a system was established which involved the collection of data from original sources and their compilation and tabulation in G-1. The establishing of such a system required a study of past arrivals as well as the devising of reliable methods for handling those occurring subsequently---neither procedure being a matter of easy accomplishment. This matter was first given a thorough study by the Administrative Section in November, 1917, and methods prescribed for the reporting of arrivals to G. H. Q. direct from the ports. Many circumstances, among which may be mentioned the lack of adjustment in the new administrative machinery of the ports of debarkation, the inexperience of the commanders of small detachments of troops shipped overseas, the absence of a clear general comprehension of the priority schedule and item number system, and especially the constantly increasing number of arrivals, operated to produce difficulties in the system. Results improved steadily, however, and in April, 1918, precise instructions as to the form and substance of arrival reports to be made were issued to the C. G., S. O. S. These instructions had been drawn up on a basis of past experience and after thorough study of what had been previously accomplished. The results obtained have been uniformly satisfactory and no further change or addition to these instructions has been found necessary.

The detailed instructions to which reference has been made were communicated to the Commanding General, S. O. S., in a letter from the V. in C., G-I, dated 13 April, 1918. The directions contained required a telegraphic report from the commanding general of the Port of Debarkation upon the arrival of any transport, showing the name of the ship, the port, the date of arrival, and the total number of officers, enlisted men, and other personnel on board. These telegraphic reports were also to give a complete description of all personnel on each transport, showing the designation of each organization, its item number, the number of officers and men attached (such as medical, ordnance and veterinary personnel), the arm of service of all casuals, and the item number of each. These instructions were accompanied by a model telegraphic report to illustrate the manner in which the length of the report could be cut down without its value being decreased. These reports were received as requested and the information contained in them formed the basis of G-1 arrival figures. Difficulties of the landing officers to obtain satisfactory reports from the officers in command of troops on the transport was the most frequent source of trouble.

Early reports of arrivals of replacement troops were frequently not clear owing to the fact that each detachment was composed of men of different arms of the Service and was reported merely as replacements. This prevented an accurate record of arrivals being kept and also resulted at times in the diversion of personnel to purposes for which it was not intended. The landing returns either did not contain the information or the landing officer failed to report it. If the landing return was not properly prepared it was impossible for the officer to secure the information after the troops left the transport and the delay that would have been caused by holding the troops on board until correct returns could be secured made this procedure out of the question. As troops arriving could not be identified in some cases, even as to arm of the service, it was inevitable that they could not be identified as to the particular request they were intended to fulfill. To remedy this latter condition it was decided to assign to each request for personnel an item number identifying it as automatic or exceptional replacements or for other explicit purpose. This item number was assigned to the individual or group upon sailing and reported to General Headquarters upon arrival at a port of debarkation. This system to a large extent remedied the difficulty of identification. The enforcement of orders to have landing returns with these item numbers thereon ready upon the arrival of the transport so that they were immediately available to the landing officer still further improved conditions. During the latter part of 1918 instances of personnel arriving without identification were rare.

A cablegram (P-454, Paragraph 1 J) dated January 5, 1918, was sent to the War Department requesting that monthly reports of all future sailings be furnished. This request was complied with, and records were thereafter received monthly giving in detail the troops on each transport and the date of sailing. As a check on reported arrivals this information has proven of great value. The figures in these reports were brought forward in cumulative totals, which have evidently been used as a basis for statistics of troop sailings from the United States. However, there are certain transports included in this total which returned to port, the personnel thereon embarking later on other transports, causing a duplication amounting to slightly more than 18,000. No deduction is made to offset this in the item Total Sailed in the embarkation report and as a result this item is higher than that of Total Arrivals in the A. E. F. arrival figures. Deaths and losses at sea also caused a difference between sailing and arrival totals.

It was necessary to secure a figure covering early arrivals which could be used as a basis for arrival totals and strength reports. This was done in the following manner:

The strength of all units according to the station list of November 22, 1917, was taken from field returns when available and from arrival figures in case no return had been made. This was carried up to date by means of adding all units arriving since the date of the station list, bringing figures up to date as of November 26. The figure thus arrived at was 118,289, which was used as a basis for future strength reports from G-1. The personnel represented was itemized as to arm of the service, and arrivals as they were reported were classified and added to those figures daily. In compiling strength returns, deductions for losses and returns were made as reported, but the total number of arrivals was carried throughout as a separate figure. On request of G-1 the War Department furnished copies of reports of troops sailing prior to the 1st of December, 1917, but the data concerning casuals were not complete in these early reports and consequently they were not of as much value as the later ones. * * *

C. GRAPHICS OF PERSONNEL

The preparation and issue of graphics of personnel were not provided for in the distribution or functions prescribed in G. O. No. 8, A. E. F., 1917, but the actual preparation of material of this character was initiated in November, 1917. The first graphics of personnel made were based on figures of strength taken from the Order of Battle issued by the Coordination Section (the greater part of whose functions are now performed by G-4) of the General Staff organized under G. O. No. 8, supplemented by subsequent arrival reports, the first phase of the Priority Schedule being used as a basis, all personnel therein being classified as to arm of service. All arrivals to date were divided into corresponding arms and the percentage of completion computed and charted by dates.

A summary was made on a separate graphic showing the percentage of each arm of the service in terms of the total of the first phase. These percentages could only be reduced to actual figures by means of an analysis of the first phase of the Priority Schedule, a copy of which accompanied the graphics. These graphics were of interest as showing the extent to which the Priority Schedule was adhered to, particularly as regarded engineer and quartermaster labor, but, in the interests of secrecy, gave no figures which would convey definite information without an analysis of the figures of the Priority Schedule.

The first series of curves was printed on white paper and the curves were carried on in ink on each set issued. Each set was issued in leather loose-leaf folders, holding 17 separate graphics and the abstract of the first phase of the Priority Schedule on which it was based and an explanation of the system used. The separate sheets were replaced from time to time as new data became available. These were first issued to the Commander in Chief, Chief of Staff, A. C. of S., G-1, A. C. of S., G-3, A. C. of S., G-4, and the War Department, Washington, D. C. Subsequently copies were furnished the A. C. of S., G-2, A. C. of S., G-5, Chief of Artillery, A. C. of S., G-1, S. of S., A. C. of S., G-1., First Army, and the American Representative at Marshal Foch's Headquarters.

Forms were made for strength reports of divisions and were included in the series as they became available. They were first made up from strength returns and arrival reports and later from the replacement requests, the percentage of each arm of the service being computed and shown in black against the total authorized strength, the balance in white representing shortage.

In February, 1918, G. O. No. 31, A. E. F., 1918, definitely charged the 1st Section of the General Staff with the duty of publishing graphics of personnel. The work was continued as before with minor changes and additions. The first complete regular weekly issue was made on August 14, 1918, since which date it has been continued in practically the same form. Since the cessation of hostilities the publication has been greatly reduced and at present contains only eight sheets. * * *

D. STRENGTH OF THE AMERICAN EXPEDITIONARY FORCES

From the entry of the United States into the war against Germany the success or failure of the American effort depended primarily on the ability to establish and maintain a powerful military force overseas. However large a force might be raised in the United States, however perfect a system of training devised, or however perfect a system of supply might be put into operation, the presence of an effective American force on the firing line was the one essential point of our participation in the war. If this were not dufficiently apparent without further evidence the fact that the enemy considered an effective understanding of this kind so far beyond possibility as to fell free to attack the most potentially powerful nation in the world is a final and decisive comment on the situation .

The accomplishment of this object constitutes in all probability the most extraordinary undertaking in the history of the world. An army of over 2,000,000 men, drawn from a territory whose center was more than 5,000 miles from the battle front, was transported across the sea, was there maintained, and took part in effective military operations.

The General Organization Project planned the organization and the proportion of troops of different classes to be sent overseas. The uncertainty as to the rapidity with which material could be obtained and troops transported made any definite time schedule out of the question. The project, however, indicated that it was expected to have in France in time for an offensive in 1918, one complete army and its auxiliary troops, amounting to an aggregate of about 1,000,000 men. The total arrivals in the American Expeditionary Forces (excluding civilians) to January 1, 1919, were 2,083,865, of which 84,020 were officers, 1,987,443 were enlisted men, 10,635 were nurses, and 1,767 were field clerks. In addition, 3,185 civilians were brought to Europe, principally for work with militarized aid societies.

The first contingent of American troops to arrive overseas consisted of 288 officers and men who left the United States on May 8 and landed at Liverpool on May 17, 1917. The first troops to come direct to France from the United States arrived on June 26, 1917. The largest number to arrive in any one month was 313,410, in July, 1918; the largest number arriving on any single day was 50,124, on September 21, 1918.

347 ships were used in the transporting of troops to Europe, making an aggregate of 1,228 voyages. Fourteen was the greatest number of voyages made by any one ship. The *Leviathan* carried the greatest aggregate number of troops overseas; in her 10 voyages a total of 94,095 was transported, the greatest number brought on any one trip being 10,867. The *Maurentania* which made seven trips carrying troops, the *Great Northern* which made ten trips, and the *Olympic* which made ten, all averaged 7 days to a trip, whicle the *Aquitania* on eight trips and the *Leviathan* on ten trips each averaged 8 days to a trip.

The eastward movement stopped abruptly upon the cessation of hostilities, the December arrivals being 1,728 as compared with 202,663 in October and 95,519 in November, the month in which the Armistice was signed.

* * * * * *

The duties of G-1 in connection with the priority of troop shipments required an exact knowledge of arrivals of personnel and in addition (also in connection with priority of shipments and the operation of the replacement system), a thorough understanding of the number of American troops in France. Information relative to the strength of the forces was therefore compiled primarily for use in the section, but the possession of re-liable data of this character soon caused G-1 to be looked to for this information and it was consequently required to prepare reports of strength.

During the early operations the accounts of arrivals gave very good indications as to the strength of the expedition as a whole and in detail and entire dependence was placed upon reports compiled directly from this source. Losses and accessions in Europe, transfers, and reorganizations operated to reduce the accuracy of results obtained by these methods and recourse was had to the Statistical Division, A. G. D., for information as to strength as soon as the causes mentioned began seriously to affect the work. The failure of organizations to render strength returns and the inaccuracy in the returns rendered during the trying conditions of actual warfare caused discrepancies which made it impossible at any time to compare the total of the forces as taken from the statis-tical records with the total obtained by substracting total losses from total arrivals unless a large number of personnel was accounted for as unidentified. With the stabili-zation of the forces and the perfecting of the methods of the Adjutant General's Depart-ment for gathering and compiling information, this discrepancy progressively decreased, until at the present time it is very nearly eliminated.

The reports and estimates of personnel prepared in G-1 consisted of numerical tables, prepared by coordinating the best available information from all sources, and graphics based upon these (described in detail in Chapter XIX, Miscellaneous Reports, Publications, Maps, and Tabulations, and the preceding section of this chapter (C. Graphics of Personnel), showing the strength of the Expeditionary Forces as a whole, classified in various cate-gories. A regular periodical production of this character has been a weekly estimate of the forces showing numbers by arms of the service, classified according to employment.

From the best information now available it appears that the A. E. F. attained their greatest strength on November 27, 1918, when they contained a total of 1,965,095 officers, field clerks, nurses, and soldiers. This is computed by subtracting the losses and returns reported to that date from the total arrivals and disregards accessions in Europe for which no figures are yet available.

As to future policy in this connection, it is obvious that an important feature of staff work is the preparation of strength reports, as practically every decision or plan is contingent upon the strength of the forces and of their component units. Accurate strength reports cannot be compiled by any section or department that has not full control over the agency by which the data are collected from original sources. In case of reorganization the entire work of gathering, compiling, and publishing statistics should be under one head.

The details of the reports mentioned and the sources from which the data therein were compiled are discussed in Chapter XIX.

E.   STATISTICS OF TROOP DEPARTURES

With the cessation of hostilities and the adoption of a program for the shipment of troops to the United States it became necessary to view the movement as the eastward movement had been viewed and consequently a system was established in G-1 for keeping accurate account of returning A. E. F. personnel.

However as the details of the westward movement were controlled entirely by the Commanding General, S. O. S., the proper utilization of camps, transportation, and shipping made it necessary for him to keep accounts even more detailed than those kept at G. H. Q., and embodying identical data. It was therefore decided to reply upon these accounts for such information of departure as might de desired at G. H. Q., and on February 15, 1919, all records pertaining to the former system were transferred to the 1st Section (G-1), General Staff, S. O. S.

It is necessary for that part of the general staff of an overseas expedition concerned with the control of troop shipments and the furnishing of replacements to have at hand accurate statistics of the arrival and departure of troops in several different forms. It is not a function of such a section to gather and compile these statistics; they should be furnished as and when desired by the agency which has the organization and machinery for, as well as the duty of, obtaining and arranging them. The most precise and detailed arrangements for procuring complete and accurate information of this character should be made prior to the formation of any future overseas expedition, whether large or small.

CHAPTER IV

REPLACEMENTS OF LOSSES OF PERSONNEL

A.   THE REPLACEMENT SYSTEM AS PROPOSED

The General Organization Project dated July 10, 1917, approved by the Commander-in-Chief on July 11, 1917, and transmitted to the United States by Colonel W. S. Graves provided for the organization of the American Forces to be sent to France, each army to consist of 5 corps and supplementary units designated as army troops.   Allowance was also made in the project for Line of Communication troops and services (later developed as the Service of the Rear Project which was approved by the Commander in Chief on September 18, 1917).

A corps was to have 6 divisions, four of which were to be combat divisions, one Replacement and School Division, one Base and Training Division, and supplementary units designated as corps troops. Provision was thus made for a replacement system of two echelons, each echelon to consist of a division from each corps.   From the divisions of the replacement system certain artillery and auxiliary units were to be withdrawn for use as a part of the army troops and corps troops, leaving the remainder to be engaged in the administration and training of replacement troops or available as replacements for army, corps, and combat divisional troops.   The forces so remaining on replacement duty would amount to the following percentages of the forces not so engaged:

> Infantry and machine gun and military police . . 42%
> Field Artillery 20%
> Engineers 23%
> Medical 19%
> Signal Corps 29%
> Supply and truck trains 28%

The function of the rear echelon (The Corps Base and Training Divisions) was to be the reception, classification, and preliminary training of replacement troops arriving from the United States.   The forward echelon (Corps Replacement and School Divisions) was to receive replacements from the base divisions, to continue their training, to forward them to the combat divisions and to supply the troops for the schools of the A. E. F. The operation of schools for the training of officers and soldiers was thus recognized as and important factor in the replacement of personnel.

It was stated in the General Organization Project that "after our forces are once engaged a minimum of 3,000 men per month for each army corps in France must be forwarded from the United States" and "in order to provide for reasonable training of officers and higher commanders in America before forwarding to France, it is believed that each corps should have a home division (7th) and in addition such recruit depot battalions as may be necessary."

In Cablegram P-171, par. 7, dated September 21, 1917, the following appears: "Have repeatedly requested without response information concerning War Department's final action on organization project transmitted by Colonel Graves . . . request information by cable . . . especially relative to . . . replacement troops and system. . ."   In reply to this, Cablegram A-216, par. 12, dated September 26, 1917, stated: "Your organization project for troops in France has been approved. Approval applies to . . . replacement divisions . . .   Your system of replacement approved excepting instead of seventh division in United States, for each corps, replacement battalions have been provided for here.   Replacement battalions are to be organized and given some training as infantry and are to be sent to your to feed into your replacement divisions as you see fit.   In case there be sufficient time training in this country of replacement troops will be extended to organizations and training in other arms before being sent to you."

On October 7, 1917, the Priority Schedule of troop shipments was approved and forwarded to the War Department. This schedule was prepared in accordance with the policy indicated in the General Organization Project. The third and sixth divisions to be shipped for each corps were to be the divisions for the replacement echelons and some army and corps troops were to be drawn from these divisions according to the recommendations contained in the General Organization Project.

The Priority Schedule provided for replacements by indicating the number which should be sent each month. Note B, opposite page 9 (and of 1st phase or corps) stated:

At this stage replacements required to maintain strength of the forces in France (Including Line of Communications troops) should be provided at the rate of 4,800 per month. Prior to this the necessary personnel should be sent to bring the 1st Division and other troops now in France to full strength and replacement drafts of proper strength based on above rate and number of troops in France each month should be sent monthly. Approximately 60 percent should be infantry and the remaining 40 percent should be apportioned among the other arms and services including L. of C.

These figures increase at the completion of each phase (corps of 6 divisions) approximately 4,500, until at the close of the 5th phase (30 divisions to be in France) replacements are requested at the rate of 22,400 per month.

The notes on the Priority Schedule thus provided for a percentage of the total forces in the A. E. F., including the Line of Communications (now the Services of Supply) to be shipped as replacements. The percentage to be used is not stated in the Priority Schedule but is stated as two percent in Cablegram P-212, par. 18, which cablegram to the War Department contained the important features of the Priority Schedule.

The replacement data studied in preparing the General Organization Project and the Priority Schedule were furnished by the British and the French, giving the losses of representative units for the various arms. The general conclusion drawn was that, in addition to establishing the two replacement echelons, two percent of the estimated strength of the entire A. E. F. at the end of each month should be shipped during the month as replacements. The plan provided for this number to be shipped by the War Department without further request from the A. E. F. These replacement troops were referred to as automatic replacements. It was contemplated that the percentages of the various branches of the service included in this draft should be varied to meet varying conditions, sixty percent being established as the initial rate for infantry. Replacements required in excess of the automatic replacements were to be made the subject of special requisitions on the War Department and to be known as exceptional replacements.

On December 20, 1917, in Cablegram P-399, par. 1, for the Chief of Staff, it was s stated:

In order to systematize the supply of personnel for replacement purposes each cable request for such purposes will begin with the words automatic replacements or exceptional replacements. Automatic replacements will refer to the monthly shipment of personnel in such ratio to the strength of troops in France and in such proportions among the various arms as may be established from time to time. Exceptional replacements will cover special replacement drafts necessary, in addition to the automatic shipments, in order to meet particular conditions such as an increase in the authorized strength of a unit or the arrival in France of a unit not up to authorized strength. All cables requesting replacements will be addressed to the Chief of Staff so as to enable you to see that any necessary portions of such cables are brought to the attention of the War Department bureaus concerned. It is obvious that the flow of replacements of all arms and services must be carefully watched by the War

Department General Staff and not decentralized among the various staff departments. The above was approved in Cablegram A-571, par. 1, dated December 27, 1917.

On January 28, 1918, Cablegram P-548, par. 2-E, stated:

Automatic Replacements. Beginning with month of March and continuing until further notice request monthly automatic replacements increased 50 percent, that is shipments to be based on 3 percent of total number of men to be in France during month affected.

In Cablegram A-728, par. 4, dated February 2, 1918, it was stated that the above was understood and would be carried out.

The requests for automatic and exceptional replacements were continued as indicated above until April, 1918. At this time the situation led to a departure which was to be of temporary duration, but under the emergency conditions of the closing months of the war, it was never possible to return to the original replacement scheme.

Under an agreement with the Allies a certain amount of shipping became available for transportation of troops overseas. This shipping was allotted, under the agreement, to infantry and machine gun units and such other units as were absolutely necessary. Under the plan as first drafted, 44,000 replzcements were to be shipped in May and June (Cable P-891, par. 1-G). Later the total of combat replacements to be sent for the months of May, June, and July was placed at 100,000 (Cable P-1267, par. 4).

From this time on the number of replacements to be shipped each month was determined by balancing the need against the need of the shipping space for other troops in preparing the schedule of troop shipments and request was made on the United States accordingly.

* * * * * *

The proposition was advanced to segregate replacement troops according to areas in the United States and to supply a unit which was organized in a certain part of the United States with replacements drawn from the same locality. * * *

B. THE SHORTAGE OF REPLACEMENTS

The shipment of replacements from the United States, from the very beginning, has been insufficient to bring all combat units to authorized strength, much less to provide for a reserve as was contemplated in the General Organization Project. There have been serious delays in the shipment of replacements requested and continued shipment of units below strength.

In addition to the need of personnel to replace losses in action, including killed, wounded, captured, stragglers, and other missing, replacements were necessary on account of:

Deaths due to disease, accident, or other causes.

Sickness or disability.

Desertion and unauthorized absences.

Transfers in the formation of new units and detachments.

Shortage in strength of units upon arrival.

Shortage due to increase in authorized strength.

Dropping of personnel for various causes.

Replacement and base divisions had been counted on to furnish the reserve of replacements, but instead of having two divisions out of every six available for use in the replacement system, only a single division could be sspared for such duty until the latter part of June, 1918.

Every time that a division which had been destined for use in the replacement system was utilized as a combat division there was not only a loss of personnel available for replacements but another division was added to those to which replacements must be furnished, requiring a proportionately increased flow of replacements not only to offset the loss of a division of replacements but also to provide for the increased number of combat divisions.

The number of replacements which could be furnished by the depot divisions was reduced by the detachment of some of their infantry units for duty in Russia, in England, and with the French, and in addition they were called upon to furnish personnel for corps replacement battalions and for school battalions, which organizations had to be formed for the performance of some of the functions intended for the replacement and school divisions.

It was thus very apparent that, if the divisions originally intended for replacement purposes had to be utilized as combat divisions and if a serious shortage of replacements was to be avoided, the necessary replacements must be shipped from the United States and requests were made to that effect.

Replacements were provided for by the General Organization Project and were requested from the United States in the Priority Schedule. Replacement requests for January, February, and March, 1918, were based on a percentage of the total number of troops expected to be in France at the end of the month for which the replacements were requested. The percentage of replacements for the various arms of the service was determined by the number of each arm expected in France the first of the following month. The above was the basis of the request for automatic replacements. Exceptional replacements were in addition to automatic replacements and were requested to bring organizations in France up to authorized strength add for other purposes. The system of requesting automatic and exceptional replacements proved unsatisfactory and the War Department requested in May that replacements be asked for by total numbers for each arm of the service. No cable was sent requesting replacements for April due to the fact that all available transportation was being used to send infantry and machine gun units of divisions to France. The request for May and June replacements was made in the general shipping program (Cable No. P-1089-S). Requests for replacements for following months were based on the existing shortages in the divisions and probable losses in the future.

[The report here quotes extracts from some of the many cables which were forwarded to the War Department between July 11, 1917, and July 7, 1918, referring to replacements to be furnished.]

* * * * * *

By the middle of August, 1918, the shortage of replacements had become serious. The arrival of replacements had not equalled the requests, there had been a great shortage in the arrival strenth of divisions and personnel had to be furnished to schools and corps replacement battalions. If immediate shipment had then been made of replacements to the number requested months in advance, the A. E. F. would have been relieved from the necessity of later adopting expedients which were far from satisfactory.

On August 14, 55,000 replacements were asked for, to be shipped during the month of September, and it was urgently requested that they be given precedence over other personnel shipments as early in September as practicable. The same cable stated:

It is understood where divisions are sent to France below authorized strength sufficient casuals or replacements will be forwarded immediately thereafter without requisition to bring organizations to authorized strength and that casuals and replacements thus sent will be in addition to replacements requested from here.

On August 16, cablegram sent to the War Department stated:

It is most urgent that S. O. S. auxiliary troops and replacements, sailing of which classes has been postponed in the past, should as far as possible have absolute priority over divisional troops. Attention is especially invited to the very great shortage in arrivals of replacements heretofore requested. Situation with reference to replacements is now very acute. Until sufficient replacements are available in France to keep our proven divisions at full strength, replacements should by all means be sent in preference to new divisions. The 105,000 replacements mentioned in Paragraph 1, my Cablegram 1569, should be increased rather than decreased.

On the same date a cablegram also stated: "There is at present a very heavy demand for officer replacements."

Due to the shortage of replacements it was necessary to make some transfers to divisions of the First Army in preparation for the St-Mihiel offensive and on August 16 and 19 instructions were issued transferring 2,000 men from each of the 7th, 36th, and 81st Divisions to the First Army.

On September 3, 1918, in cable requesting 55,000 replacements to be shipped in October, it was urgently requested that no divisions be shipped in October and the War Department was informed that replacements requested were in addition to replacements then due on former requests and that replacements were urgently needed. The cablegram further stated:

Due to units arriving under strength and failure of replacements to arrive, situation is now serious. After forwarding all available replacements from base divisions, combat divisions are now over 60,000 below strength and no reserve of replacements is available.

On September 11, 1918, in cable requesting 68,000 replacements to be shipped in November, it was stated:

It is understood that all replacements requested in previous cablegrams will be shipped and that organizations embarking under strength will be followed without request from here by enough casuals to fill them.

On September 14, 1918, cable stated: Current shortage in replacements requires men to be sent to first line divisions within five or six days after arrival in France.

On September 18, 1918, cable requested 106,000 replacements to be shipped in December with eight lieutenants included in each thousand replacements. It was stated: It is assumed that in addition to these replacements casuals are shipped after each unit in sufficient numbers to supply its shortage on the date of sailing.

* * * * * *

By the middle of September the number of men admitted to hospitals was rapidly increasing. In all estimations concerning replacements, consideration must be given to évacués from hospitals. About 85 percent of the sick and wounded are eventually discharged from the hospitals as of Class A, are potential replacements, and after a certain length of time there is a constant stream of men returning from hospitals to their organizations, which offsets in part the shortage caused by those who are wounded or who became sick. (Editor's Note---Under the provisions of General Orders No. 10, Hq. S. O. S., April 12, 1918, Class A included men who are physically fit for all duty; Class B, men who are temporarily unfit for combat service; Class C, men who are permanently unfit for combat service but able to perform other necessary work; Class D, men unfit for all duty with the A. E. F.) During the early period of large casualties, however, the wounded men enter hospitals which are more or less devoid of patients to be discharged and although the daily admissions are large, the daily discharges are small for a while. At the beginning of the AISNE-MARNE offensive on July 18, 1918, the number of sick and wounded in camp and base hospitals and convalescent camps was 29,013; by the time the St-MIHIEL offensive was begun on September 12, 1918, that number had been increased to 66,738, and in the two weeks which elapsed before the start of the MEUSE-ARGONNE offensive on September 26, 1918, the figures had mounted to 84,856. The peak was reached four days before the Armistice, there being 190,564 in the hospitals and convalescent camps on November 7, 1918, which number dropped to less than 100,000 within a period of shortly more than two months.

C. THE SKELETONIZING OF ORGANIZATIONS

The MEUSE-ARGONNE offensive started on September 26, 1918, and a report submitted to the Chief of Staff on September 28, 1918 indicated that conditions with respect to replacements were very unfavorable. It was apparent that the losses during this offensive were bound to be very heavy and it was vitally necessary that some prompt measures be taken to provide replacements for the divisions of the First Army. The 84th and 86th Divisions were in the vicinity of the base port near BORDEAUX, having recently arrived from the United United States. The first infantry elements of the 84th Division had landed on September 9. The first organizations of the 86th Division had reached France on September 21, and the division was complete in units by October 9.

Under date of October 2, 1918, a recommendation was submitted to the Chief of Staff to the effect that the entire personnel, both commissioned and enlisted, of the 84th and 86th Divisions be utilized at once for replacement purposes. It was stated that such action was necessary owing to the extremly seriousness of the replacement situation. This recommendation was approved with the proviso that a cadre was to remain with each division, rifle companies to consist of 25 men and each company to retain at least two officers. The divisions were to retain their identity as divisions and were to be reconstituted as soon as the necessary personnel was available. Only the infantry and machine-gun personnel of those divisions was made available for replacement purposes at that time as there were sufficient field artillery replacements available to meet the most imperative needs. Accordingly, on October 3, 1918, the Commanding General, Serviees of Supply, was directed to send 25,000 replacements to indicated divisions, of which 21,400 were to be infantry. 2,800 of those infantry replacements were furnished from the depots, 9,500 from the 84th Division, and 9,100 from the 86th Division.

It was most important that these 25,000 replacements reach the front at the earliest possible moment and instructions were given to expedite action in every possible way. There were numerous conditions which rendered this movement of replacements most difficult. The divisions were billeted near Bordeaux, a long distance from the front, and were heavily infected with influenza from which they had suffered quite severely. Some of the divisions for which the replacements were intended were armed with the Model 1903 rifle, while both the 84th and 86th Divisions were armed with the Model 1917 rifle. As it was also necessary to insure that these men were properly fitted with gas masks, it was decided that they must be passed through the 1st and 2d Depot Divisions on their way to the First Army. Many transportation difficulties had to be overcome.

The necessity for these replacements was so great that the Commander-in-Chief personally telegraphed to the Commanding General, Services of Supply, on October 5 stating that the speed with which they were delivered to their divisions had a vital bearing on the operations and that it would require extraordinary measures to deliver these 25,000 men to their divisions quickly as conditions required. All possible efforts were made to hurry the movement. Eighteen trainloads, carrying approximately 1,500 men to the train, left the stations in the vicinity of Bordeaux and were routed so that some of them would pass through the 1st Depot Division of St-Aignan and the others through the 2d Depot Division at Le Mans. Detailed arrangements were made to take care of each train upon arrival at the depot division. As soon as a train had stopped the men at once detrained, carrying their rifles, gas masks, and mess kits. Those who were destined for a division which was armed with the Model 1903 rifle turned in their rifles and passed through a storeroom where each man was issued a rifle of the necessary model. All men were passed through a gas chamber in order to test the gas masks, marched back to the railroad platform where a hot meal was served to them, after which they were loaded onto the train and were off for the front, only about an hour being lost at the depot division. All of the 18 trains arrived between October 9 and 12 at the regulating station at St-Dizier, where the First Army had a representative to assist in routing the trains to the divisions.

On October 3, 1918, cable to the War Department stated as follows:

Over 50,000 of the replacements requested for the months of July, August and September have not yet arrived. Due to extreme seriousness of the replacement situation, it is necessary to utilize personnel of the 84th and 86th Divisions for replacement purposes. Combat divisions are short over 80,000 men. Vitally important that all replacements due, including 55,000 requested for October, be shipped early in October. If necessary some divisions in the United States should be stripped of trained men and such men shipped as replacements at once.

On october 17, 1918, cable requested that in the different phases of troop shipment, every effort be made to give priority to replacements and stated that the supply of infantry and machine gun replacements was exhausted.

The necessity for replacements continued and on October 13, 1918, a report to the Chief of Staff stated that the First Army needed 27,000 additional replacements and recommended that the enlisted personnel of the 34th and 38th Divisions, which were beginning to arrive, be utilized as replacements. This recommendation was approved and instructions were issued on October 17 and October 23 to skeletonize all infantry and machine-gun units of the 34th and 38th Divisions as fast as they arrived on the same basis that the 84th and 86th Divisions had been skeletonized, the personnel thus secured to be passed through the depot divisions for training and utilized as replacements.

On October 16, 1918, a recommendation was made to the Chief of Staff that three regiments of white pioneer infantry, the 4th, 55th and 57th, be temporarily broken up and the personnel used as replacements. This recommendation was approved. These regiments had been scheduled to become infantry regiments of the 96th, 99th, and 100th Divisions, respectively, and were untrained, consequently it was necessary to pass the personnel through the 2d Depot Division at Le Mans for training and it was expected that they would be available as replacements by November 15. Instructions were issued that the cadre for each regiment would consist of one adjutant, one sergeant major, and a first sergeant from each company.

On October 17, 1918, a report to the Chief of Staff stated that the 31st Divisions, which had been designated on September 20 as a depot division, was arriving, and it was recommended in view of the fact that replacements were not being received rapidly and that there were in operation six depot divisions, and in view of the great shortage of replacements, that the personnel of the 31st Division, as fast as the units arrived, be passed through existing depot divisions and used as replacements. Upon approval of this memorandum, instructions were issued the same day to Commanding General, Services of Supply, to send the infantry and machine gun units of the 31st Division immediately upon arrival direct to one of the existing depots for necessary training as replacements, upon completion of which they were to be used to fill replacement priorities, and on October 23, 1918, he was instructed that all units of the 32st Div., which would normally function with it as a depot division, would be sent to the 2d Depot Division and the personnel used as replacements, each company or similar unit retaining one first sergeant, and each regiment or similar unit retaining one officer, this cadre to care for the records.

On October 22, 1918, in a report to the Chief of Staff, a recommendation was made in view of the fact that it was believed impossible to reconstitute the 34th, 38th, and 84th, and 86th Divisions for at least a number of months, that all of these divisions be reduced to the necessary personnel to care for the records, the balance being utilized as replacements. This matter was held in abeyance until October 28, when a memorandum to the Chief of Staff recommended that the companies of the 4th Depot Division (85th Division) and the 6th Depot Division (40th Division), which divisions had been ordered moved to forward areas to function as regional replacement units, be reduced to 2 officers and 25 enlisted men for each rifle company and each machine gun company, the personnel rendered surplus to be utilized as replacements; that the 3d Depot Division (76th Division) and the 5th Depot Division (39th Division) be abolished as depot divisions, their personnel to be utilized as replacements, with the exception of the force considered necessary to care for the records; that the 34th, 38th, 84th, and 86th Divisions, which had been reduced to 25 men per company, be further skeletonized and personnel utilized as replacements, with the exception of the necessary force to care for the records, and that the cadre to care for the records of the 31st, 34th, 38th, 39th, 76th, 84th, and 86th Divisions should consist of a first sergeant for each company which was skeletonized and an adjutant and sergeant major for each regiment, separate battalion, or other similar unit, the cadre for each division to be assembled in either the 1st or 2d Depot Division under the command of a field officer of the division; that the following units in a division be skeletonized: division headquarters, brigade headquarters, infantry regiments, machine gun battalions, train headquarters and military police, ammunition train, and supply train. These recommendations were approved and instructions to carry them into effect were issued October 29 to the Commanding General, Services of Supply.

In a communication dated October 22, 1918, to the Commanding General, First Army, the Chief of Staff stated:

> During the continuance of the present shortage of replacements, the authorized strength of divisions will be reduced by 4,000 men. This will require you to make certain readjustments within units so as to equalize infantry companies at about 174 men per company. Calls for replacements will be made on the basis of the full authorized strength as heretofore but only the requirements in excess of 4,000 men per division will be forwarded.

On October 24, 1918, a report to the Chief of Staff showed that based on requisitions of October 16, and 29 combat divisions needed 119,690 replacements, of which 95,303 were infantry, 8,210 machine gunners, and 9,475 field artillery, with only 66,490 infantry machine gunners who would be available as replacements within a reasonable time.

On November 2, 1918, a report was made to the Chief of Staff showing the situation as it existed on that date, and on the same day a cable to the War Department (No. P-1861-S) stated:

> It is evident that necessary preparations were not made to meet our replacement needs. It was reported to you that 50,000 of the replacements requested had not arrived up to the end of September. In addition 55,000 replacements were on were on priority for October. During October 33,000 replacements and casuals have been received. As a result we are short over 72,000 replacements which were requested and for which priority was given. Priority for November provides for 68,000 replacements. This makes a total of 140,000 replacements due by the end of November and conditions imperatively demand that they be shipped early in the month. Four combat divisions and three depot divisions have been skeletonized and four depot divisions have been reduced to training cadres in order to obtain replacements absolutely necessary for divisions in the line. It is again recommended that if necessary divisions in the United States be stripped of trained or even partially trained men and that they be shipped immediately. To send over entire divisions which must be broken up on their arrival in France so we may obtain replacements that have not been sent as called for is a wasteful method and one that makes for inefficiency but as replacements are not otherwise available there is no other course open to us. New and only partially trained divisions cannot take the place of older divisions that have had battle experience. The latter must be kept up numerically to the point of efficiency. Cannot this matter be given the consideration its importance deserves?

* * * * * *

The greatest impediment to military operations in the former wars of the United States has been primarily the weakness and inexperience of frontline organizations. In the Civil War original units were depleted practically to extinction by deaths, desertions, straggling, and the evacuation of hospital patients to points outside the control of the military authorities. The need for fighting strength was met by the organization of new regiments and to accomplish this successfully under the volunteer system, it was inevitable that each regiment should be new throughout - officers and men. The evils of this procedure are too obvious to require enumeration.

When at a critical stage of our operations in October, 1918, replacements were not available, due to the fact that shipments had been made of divisions instead of the replacements requested, there was but one course if action possible and that was to break up a few newly arrived divisions and utilize their personnel as reinforcements for the experienced divisions of the First Army.

Forty-two divisions arrived in France, including the 8th Division which was not complete, and not including the four colored regiments of the 93d Division. Of the forty-two divisions, twenty-nine were used as combat divisions, seven as depot divisions (of which three were skeletonized), four combat divisions were skeletonized, one (the 87th) was on S. O. S. duty, and one (the 8th) did not leave the ports. If the original replacement system had continued in operation fourteen divisions would have been assigned to replacement duty. As it was, only eleven were used in the replacement system, seven of which were skeletonized.

The skeletonizing in France of units of a division in order to provide replacements was a highly unsatisfactory but absolutely necessary measure to avoid a situation which had been foreseen and repeatedly called to the attention of the War Department. If replacements had arrived in the numbers requested, it would not have been necessary to break up divisions.

* * * * * *

D. DEPOT DIVISIONS

The provisions of the General Organization Project and the Priority Schedule contemplated that the third division in each corps (or group of six divisions) to arrive in France should be the replacement division and that the sixth division to arrive should be the base division. In this way schools for the corps could be established early in the training period of the corps, and the depot which would provide the replacements for the combat divisions would be well established before they entered the line. The depot for the reception of replacements from the United States would be established at the end of the shipment of the six divisions. Provision having been made in the Priority Schedule for an automatic shipment of replacements according to the estimated needs of the divisions as soon as they had arrived in the A. E. F., the training of these replacements would normally be well advanced by the time drafts on the replacement division made room for them to be forwarded to it.

The first four divisions to arrive in France were the 1st, 2d, 26th, and 42d, all having a considerable shortage in personnel upon arrival, this shortage being increased by changes made in tables of organization. Some of the units of the 2d Division arrived in France before any of the 26th Division arrived but the 26th Division was complete before the 2d. These two divisions were followed closely by the 42d Division.

In a memorandum to the Chief of Staff, dated November 21, 1917, the Chief of the Administrative Section stated that the 1st Division was short 8,514 soldiers, about half of whom might be expected to be supplied by replacements from the United States. He also referred to the fact that shortages existed in the other divisions in France. In this connection, the use of the 26th or the 42d Division as a replacement division was considered.

However, the first division to be designated for replacement purposes was the 41st, which was the fifth to arrive, the first units reaching France on December 11, 1917, and the last on February 6, 1918. It was at first intended that this division should become the replacement division of the I Corps but during the period of its assembly at La Courtine it was determined to utilize it as the base division instead. After a short time, its headquarters and certain other units were sent to St-Aignan-des-Noyers, Department Loir-et-Cher, where a depot for the handling of replacements was established. The division was formally designated as the Base and Training Division, I Corps, by G. O. No. 9, A. E. F., January 15, 1918, which designation was changed to Depot Division by telebram to the Commanding General, Service of the Rear, March 5, 1918.

The question as to the headquarters which should administer the base or depot division was raised, and on account of the geographical location of this division, well to the rear, and because of the fact that it must supply replacements for army troops as well as for the corps and divisional troops of the I Corps, it was placed under the command of the Commanding General, Line of Communications, by telegram dated January 8, 1918. He was not, however, permitted to order personnel from the base division except on authority from G. H. Q.

The need for personnel in all parts of the A. E. F. led to immediate drafts upon the first body of troops which was made available for replacement purposes. In order to prevent the wastage of these troops and to preserve them for the more important needs, it was necessary that all requisitions for them should be carefully scrutinized by one office. G. O. No. 64, A. E. F., November 21, 1917, required that pending the promulgation of formal orders relative to the routine to be followed in effecting replacements, all calls for replacements will be addressed to these headquarters, and by the approval of a memorandum to the Chief of Staff from the Administrative Section, General Staff, December 25, 1917, the releasing of troops from the replacement depots was centralized in the hands of the Chief, Administrative Section, General Staff.

The first instructions from the Chief of the Administrative Section to the Commanding General, 41st Division, relative to the furnishing of replacements were contained in letters of December 8, 1917, and January 1, 1918, and telegram of January 5, 1918, covering instructions concerning replacements to be furnished to the 1st and 2d Divisions.

The infantry brigades of the 41st Division furnished units for duty at schools and in the Line of Communications. Two of the regiments of the artillery were designated as corps artillery. Batteries of the other artillery regiment were ordered to schools for duty. The ammunition train was employed on remount work.

The division was also drawn on for replacements for the four combat divisions but notwithstanding the fact that there had been no serious losses in action, the arrivals of replacements up to this time had not been sufficient to make up for the deficiencies in the combat divisions or to provide a reserve for the 41st Division which had also arrived under strength.

On April 17, 1918, the Commanding General, Services of Supply, reported that after the requisitions now on file from the I Corps have been filled there will be nothing but the training cadres left in the depot division.

The necessity of providing the other echelon of the replacement system for the I Corps having been emphasized, on February 4, 1918, the 32d Divisions which was the sixth division to arrive, was announced as the replacement division of the I Corps in a memorandum from the Secretary of the General Staff. This division arrived between February 6 and March 26. On March 14, three infantry regiments of this division, the divisional machine gun battalion, and the engineer regiment were on duty with the Services of Supply and the artillery brigade and supply and sanitary trains were detached from the division. The portion of the division assembled in the 10th Area functioned as a replacement depot only until the threatening military situation caused by the great German offensive which began on March 21 led to the division being ordered into the line for training as a combat division. On April 10, 1918, telegrams were sent to Commanding General, Services of Supply, and to the

Commanding General, I Corps, stating that the 32d Division has ceased temporarily to function as a replacement division. The depot division (41st) will function both as a replacement both as a replacement and depot division.

About 4,000 men were withdrawn from the 32d Division during the short time it was a part of the replacement system.

G. O. No. 46, A. E. F., appeared March 26, 1918, during the great German drive, and formally put into operation the system which had been developed along the lines of the General Organization Project during the period that the six divisions of the I Corps had been arriving in France. In less than two weeks the 32d Division, the replacement division, had been ordered into the line for training as a combat division and had ceased to function as a replacement division. The military situation also led to the training of all divisions of the A. E. F., except the 41st, as combat divisions until the arrival of the 83d Division, which was designated as the 2d Depot Division in telegram of June 27, For three months the 41st Division had functioned as both replacement and depot divisions for the whole of the A. E. F., and at the time the 2d Depot Division was designated, there were nine divisions of the A. E. F. in line, seven others complete and in training, and six in process of arrival.

By the time that thirty divisions had arrived in France, only four of them had been designated as depot divisions. The 76th had been designated as the 3d Depot Division on July 14, 1918, and the 85th had been designated as the 4th Depot Division on July 28, 1918. The last-named division was the thirteenth division to arrive. The other twenty-six divisions were functioning as combat divisions. There were no replacement divisions but five corps replacement battalions had been organized and were functioning by that time.

Three other divisions were designaded as depot divisions: The 39th as the 5th Depot Division on August 14, 1918; the 40th as the 6th Depot Division on August 16; and the 31st as the 7th Depot Division on September 20, 1918. The latter division, however, never functioned as a depot division.

* * * * * *

A letter from the Commanding General, Services of Supply, dated September 9, 1918, reviewed the replacement situation and advised against establishing any more depot divisions. In the following month two of the depot divisions (4th and the 6th) were transferred to forward areas to operate as regional replacement depots, and two others (the 3d and the 5th) were broken up and their personnel used as replacements. The remaining two depot divisions continued in operation until after the Armistice was signed.

E. SPECIAL REPLACEMENTS DEPOTS AND BASE DEPOTS

In the replacement system of the American Expeditionary Forces, in addition to the depot division, regional replacement depot, corps replacement battalions, and advance replacement depots, there were a number of special replacement depots and base depots, which were authorized by the provisions of G. O. No. 46, A. E. F., March 26, 1918. These depots functioned along the same general lines as the depot divisions and handled replacements for special arms and services.

1. CASUAL OFFICERS' DEPOT AND BASE DEPOT FOR SERVICES OF SUPPLY THROOPS

This depot was established at Blois pursuant to telegraphic instructions sent to the Commanding General, Line of Communications, on January 8, 1918. At this depot replacements were handled for the Services of Supply and for the Medical Department organizations. It ceased to function for personnel of the Quartermaster Corps on May 15, 1918, when a special replacement depot was established at Gievres for that corps and it ceased to function for personnel of the Medical Department on July 15, 1918, after which time replacements for the Medical Department were handled in the First Depot Division. The depot also received and classified Class B and Class C men.

The activities at Blois were transferred to the First Replacement Depot at St-Aignan-des-Noyers at noon on February 15, 1919. During its existence there had been forwarded from the depot at Blois 52,679 officers and men.

2. THE FIELD ARTILLERY REPLACEMENT REGIMENT

On February 2, 1918, the Commanding General, Line of Communications, was directed to send the 147th Field Artillery of the 41st Division from Montrichard (Loir-et-Cher) to La Courtine (Cresuse) to receive and train all field artillery casuals and replacements and forward them to combat divisions. Upon the arrival of the training battalion of the 6th Field Artillery [6th F. A. Training Bn.], the Commanding Officer at La Courtine organized a provisional regiment which was designated as the Field Artillery Replacement Regiment. The last element of the 147th Field Artillery was withdrawn from La Courtine on June 29, 1918, and the training and forwarding of field artillery replacements was continued by the Field Artillery Replacement Regiment.

On July 16, 1918, the Commanding General, Services of Supply, was directed to move the Field Artillery Replacement Regiment from La Courtine to Le Courneau (Gironde), to which place field artillery casuals and replacements were sent for training and forwarding. The regiment was moved to Le Courneau on August 10, 1918. Replacements, both officers and enlisted men, were forwarded for field artillery regiments until February 2, 1919. Replacements for trench artillery were forwarded from the same units until September 20, 1918, after which time such replacements were handled by the trench artillery replacement battery. The activities at Le Courneau concerning replacements were transferred to the 1st Replacement Depot on February 2, 1919. Total replacements forwarded from La Courtine and Le Courneau, 48,740.

3. HEAVY ARTILLERY REPLACEMENT DEPOTS

On February 20, 1918, a cablegram to the War Department stated that it was most important that a replacement depot for heavy artillary should be established before April 1 and requested that one regiment of coast artillery troops be shipped to form the replacement depot troops for Army Artillery, A. E. F. On March 2, 1918, cable from the War Department stated that the 57th Artillery, C. A. C., would sail that month to form a depot regiment for the army artillery replacements. On April 5, 1918, cable from the War Department stated that the 60th Artillery was then at port of embarkation ready for shipment. Information was requested as to whether this regiment could be used as a replacement depot for heavy artillery in place of another regiment which had been scheduled but was not ready. On April 7, 1918, a cable to the War Department stated that the 60th Artillery could be used as a replacement depot in place of the 57th Artillery.

(a) Special Replacement Depot, C. A. C.: This depot was established at Mailly le Camp (Aube) near Haussimont on April 17, 1918, for the reception and distribution of Coast Artillery Corps casuals and replacements and other casuals and replacements for the heavy artillery. The depot was placed under the command of the Commanding General, Railway Artillery Reserve, First Army, and was not under the command of the Commanding General, Services of Supply. The 60th Regiment, C. A. C., was designated as the replacement regiment. It was prescribed that replacement requisitions from army artillery units (railway and heavy) would be sent to this depot through the Commanding General, Army Artillery. The Commanding General, Services of Supply, was directed to send all casuals and replacements for the Coast Artillery Corps and heavy artillery units from base ports direct to Camp Mailly. On April 25, 1918, the 54th Regiment, C. A. C., was designated to be the replacement regiment in place of the 60th Regiment, C. A. C. The Special Replacement

Depot, C. A. C., was ordered reorganized on August 31, 1918, and was divided into a heavy artillery training battalion, a tractor artillery replacement battalion, and a railway artillery replacement battalion. All these battalions functioned as such until November 23, 1918, when the 54th Regiment, C. A. C., was ordered to be concentrated at Angers, and on December 24, 1918, was ordered returned to the United States. Total replacements forwarded by the Special Replacement Depot, C. A. C., 4,475.

(b) The Heavy Artillery Training Battalion. On August 31, 1918, one battalion of the 54th Regiment, C. A. C., was designated as the Heavy Artillery Training Battalion. It was stationed at the Heavy Artillery School at Angers (Maine-et-Loire) under the command of the commanding officer of that school. Thereafter, all replacements of heavy artillery, trench artillery, and antiaircraft artillery were upon their arrival in France sent to the Heavy Artillery Training Battalion for classification and assignment, and instructions provided that with the exception of those selected for training as specialists and those required as replacements for units in training, the men would remain with the battalion only long enough to admit of their classification, when they were to be forwarded to the replacement battalions or batteries to which they were assigned. The specialists were forwarded as soon as their training was completed. No attempt was to be made at the station of the training battalion to train soldiers in their general duties as artillerymen, inasmuch as that training could best be given in the replacement battalions or batteries. Total replacements forwarded, 6,455, of which 4,132 were sent to other replacement battalions and batteries.

(c) The Tractor Artillery Replacement Battalion: This battalion was one of the battalions of the 54th Regiment, C. A. C., and was stationed at Doulevant-le-Chateau (Haute-Marne), under the command of the Commanding General, First Army, and furnished replacements for tractor-drawn artillery. Total replacements forwarded, 2,323.

(d) The Railway Artillery Replacement Battalion: This battalion was one of the battalions of the 54th Regiment, C. A. C., and was stationed at Mailly-le-Camp (Aube) and handled replacements for the Railway Artillery Reserve. It was under the command of the Commanding General, Railway Artillery Reserve. Total replacements forwarded, 1,116.

(e) The Trench Artillery Replacement Battery: Instructions issued on August 31, 1918, provided for the organization of a provisional trench artillery replacement battery, which was organized from the personnel at the Trench Artillery Center and stationed at Vitrey (Haute-Saone) under the command of the Commanding Officer of the Trench Artillery Center at that place. This battery trained and furnished replacements for trench artillery organizations. Total number of replacements forwarded, 1,171. Ordered to be returned to the United States February 10, 1919.

(f) The Antiaircraft Artillery Replacement Battery: A provisional antiaircraft artillery deplacement battery was organized from the personnel of the Antiaircraft Center under instructions issued on August 31, 1918, and was stationed at the Antiaircraft Artillery Center at Fort de Stains (Seine-et-Marne) under the command of the commanding officer of that center. This battery trained and furnished replacements to antiaircraft artillery organizations. Total replacements forwarded, 101. Ordered to be returned to the United States December 4, 1918.

4. ENGINEER REPLACEMENT DEPOT

On January 23, 1918, the Commanding General, Line of Communications was authorized to send the 116th Engineers and Train of the 41st Division from St-Aignan-des-Noyers to Angers (Maine-et-Loire) for the purposes of receiving, training, and forwarding engineer replacements. This regiment remained under the command of the Commanding General, 1st Depot Division, and replacements were forwarded direct from Angers to both combat and noncombat engineers. This depot functioned until February 6, 1919, when it was closed and the act-activities thereof were transferred to the 1st Replacement Depot. Total replacements forwarded from Angers, 29,126.

5. SIGNAL CORPS REPLACEMENT DEPOT

Replacements for Signal Corps troops were handled from the beginning by the 116th Field Signal Battalion, which was a part of the 41st Division, and under date of August 31, 1918, the Commanding General, Services of Supply was informed that it was desired there be only one depot in France for replacement of Signal Corps troops, namely the one then established at St-Aignan-des-Noyers as part of the 1st Depot Division, and he was instructed to send to that depot all Signal Corps personnel, both commissinned and enlisted, other than organizations arriving at base ports. He was further informed that the field signal battalion belonging to divisions which upon arrival were designated as depot divisions were to be detached from those divisions and sent to school areas for equipment and training and subsequent employment as corps troops or other special purposes. He was further informed that arrangements were to be made with each of the depot divisions from which Signal Corps troops had been taken for the conducting of a school for the training of infantry signalmen for the replacement of the personnel of signal platoons of infantry regiments. In order to accomodate the increasing number of Signal Corps replacements arriving in France, and owing to the limited accomodations for their training and forwarding at St-Aignan-des-Noyers, the depot was moved to Cour-Cheverny (Loir-et-Cher) and functioned at that place after October 9, 1918, until it was closed on December 21, 1918, and the activities transferred to the 1st Replacement Depot. Total replacements forwarded, 4,189.

6. QUARTERMASTER CORPS SPECIAL REPLACEMENT DEPOT

The replacements for the Quartermaster Corps were handled at Blois until May 15, 1918, upon which date the Quartermaster Corps Special Replacement Depot was established at Gievres (Loir-et-Cher) by the Commanding General, Services of Supply. At Gievres 10,895 replacements were forwarded.

The depot was moved from Gievres to Château-du-Loir (Sarthe) on November 5, 1918, by direction of the Commanding General, Services of Supply. Total replacements forwarded, 3,960. This depot was closed on February 25, 1919, and the activities thereat were transferred to the 1st Replacement Depot.

7. AIR SERVICE REPLACEMENT DEPOTS

The following depots were established for the handling of personnel of the Air Service:

(a) Air Service Replacement Squadron: This depot was established on December 4, 1917, at St-Maizent (Deux-Sevres) and was discontinued on March 7, 1919. Total replacements forwarded, 3,920.

(b) Air Service Replacement Squardon: This depot was established on April 18, 1918, at Colombey-les-Belles (Meurthe-et-Moselle) and has continued in existence up to the present time. Total replacements forwarded, 3,549.

(c) Ballon Replacement Company: This depot was established on June 5, 1918, at Camp de Souge (Gironde) where it remained until January 16, 1919, when it was moved to Romorantin (Loir-et-Cher) and is still in existence. Total replacements forwarded, 712.

8. TANK CORPS REPLACEMENT DEPOT

Replacements for the Tank Corps were handled by the Tank Center and Replacement Company, which was organized on February 14, 1918, and was stationed at Bourg (Haute-Marne). It was ordered to be returned to the United States on December 31, 1918. Total replacements forwarded, 138.

9. CHEMICAL WARFARE SERVICE REPLACEMENTS

For the purpose of handling replacements for this service, a provisional gas and flame company was organized under authority from General Headquarters American Expeditionary Forces, on March 26, 1918, with the same organization and equipment as a company of engineer gas and flame regiment Army troops. It was stationed at Ville-aux-Bois (Haute-Marne). On August 9, 1918, this company was designated as Company Q, 1st Gas Regiment. It was ordered to be returned to the United States on December 8, 1918. Total replacements forwarded, 498.

10. CHAPLAINS SCHOOL

Under date of June 7, 1918, the Commanding General, Services of Supply, was directed to send all chaplains arriving from the United States unassigned and those who were evacuated from hospitals as of Class A, B, or C, and all others who for any reason might be awaiting assignments, to Neuilly-sur-Suize, and he was informed that the Chaplains School at that place would constitute a special replacement depot for chaplains of the A. E. F. and that all requisitions for chaplains would be forwarded to General Headquarters for action. On September 12, 1918, Commanding General, Services of Supply, was directed to take the necessary action for the leasing of premises for the Chaplains School at Chateau-d'Aux, Loup-lande (Sarthe), and the Chaplains School was moved to that place.

11. DEPOT COMPANIES OF 369TH, 370TH, 371ST, AND 372D COLORED INFANTRY

On May 15, 1918, the provisional tables of organization for these four colored infantry regiments provided that one company of each regiment would serve as a depot or replacement company for the entire regiment. These companies were stationed in the rear of their respective regiments and changes station as the regiments moved from one part of the front to another. Casuals and replacements forwarded to these regiments were received by the depot companies, where they were trained and assigned to organizations according to necessity.

12. FLASH AND SOUND RANGING, SURVEYING, AND PRINTING REPLACEMENTS

Replacements and casuals for the above services, including men evacuated from hospitals, were handled by Company A, 29th Engineers, at Langres (Haute-Marne).

13. 1ST REPLACEMENT DEPOT

This depot was established at St-Aignan-des-Noyers (Loir-et-Cher) on December 18, 1918, and took over all the activities of the 1st Depot Division upon the relief of the 41st Division, which was ordered to the United States. It continued the functions of the 1st Depot Division under a different name, and as other replacement depots were discontinued their remaining activities were transferred to the First Replacement Depot, where casuals ordered to the United States were also sent. The establishment of this depot was announced in G. O. No. 242, A. E. F., December 30, 1918.

F. CORPS REPLACEMENT BATTALIONS

When the German offensive began on March 21, 1918, the replacement system in the A. E. F. was in operation as planned in the General Organization Project. In April the military situation was so threatening that it became necessary to use the 32d Division, which had been assigned as a replacement division, as a combat division, thus removing one echelon of the replacement system and shortly afterwards it became necessary to provide some sort of an organization to take over some of the functions which it had been intended that the replacement divisions would perform.

On February 22, 1918, in Cable P-635, authority had been requested to maintain replacement organizations at such strength as was necessary, and this request was approved on February 27, 1918, in Cable A-839. On April 6, 1918, in Cable P-965, authority was requested to organize such provisional replacement units as might be necessary from time to time and to maintain all replacement organizations at such strength as the military situation might demand. This authority was granted on April 12, 1918, in Cable A-1090.

On May 15th, the Commanding General of the III Corps was directed to organize within his corps a provisional replacement battalion and he was furnished a copy of the table of organization for that battalion. He had been previously advised that divisions which had been intended for duty as replacement and depot divisions of the III Corps were to be trained as combat divisions. It was realized that sick and wounded would be evacuated from the corps to the various hospitals of the Services of supply and it was desirable that these men, upon being discharged from such hospitals, should be returned to the units to which they belonged. To accomplish this efficiently it was necessary to have some organization located at a fixed point to which the hospitals could automatically evacuate officers and soldiers of the corps, who, upon their release from hospitals, were fit for duty with combat units. The selection of the place at which the corps replacement battalion was to be located was delegated to the corps commander.

Similar instructions were sent on the 30th of May to the Commanding General, II Corps, who was authorized to organize a corps replacement battalion, and his attention was particularly directed to the necessity for keeping on hand in that battalion a sufficient supply of clothing and equipment in order to insure that all soldiers passing through the battalion to their units would be properly clothed and equipped. On June 11th, instructions to organize a corps replacement battalion were sent to the Commanding General of the I Corps and he turned over the instructions to the Chief of Staff of the IV Corps, with a view to establishing a similar battalion for that corps.

When G. O. No. 111, A. E. F., was published on July 8, 1918, as a provisional order governing replacements of personnel, it was provided that in addition to the combat divisions assigned to each corps and the corps troops, a replacement battalion would be organized in each corps, the battalion to be under the command of the corps commander; such corps replacement battalion was to cease to exist when a corps replacement division was designated, as provided in the General Organization Project for the A. E. F.

The strength of a corps replacement battalion was not fixed. The table of organization provided for a small permanent personnel and in addition to this permanent personnel, there were to be such numbers of provisional replacement companies as might be attached to the battalion. The position of the battalion was fixed by the corps or army commander and was dependent upon the tactical situation and convenience of rail connection with the regulating station and the corps combat units. Its principal function was to receive and forward to their organizations officers and men evacuated from Army hospitals or S. O. S. hospitals who were fit for combat duty, and to keep on hand a small reserve of replacements for the corps. The casual personnel in the corps replacement battalion was at the disposal of the corps commander for replacements within the corps without reference or report to other authority. The general order referred to required a small reserve of equipment to be kept on hand so as to insure the complete equipment of officers and soldiers sent forward to combat units. Corps commanders were authorized to detach temporarily from divisions in the front line soldiers who were insufficiently trained and order them to the corps replacement battalion for the necessary instruction to bring them to a proper standard.

Corps replacement battalions for the V, VI, and VII Corps were established pursuant to the provisions of General Order No. 111, and all of the corps replacement battalions continued in existence until they were absorbed by the regional replacement depots.

1. I Corps Replacement Battalion: This battalion was established on June 27, 1918, at Vaires, Chelles, Torcy, and two other small towns a short distance east of Paris, where it remained until August 27, at which time it was moved to a French camp in the Bois

l'Eveque, with railhead at Maron, a short distance southeast of Toul. On October 25 it was moved to Eurville, not far from the regulating station at St-Dizier, and was absorbed by the First Army Advance Replacement Depot on November 7, 1918.

2. II Corps Replacement Battalion: The replacement battalion for the II Corps was authorized on May 30, and on June 23, the Commanding General of the corps reported that two companies had been formed for the purpose of receiving, equipping and distributing all casuals, replacements, personnel evacuated from hospitals, and other personnel belonging to or intended for United States troops, other than railroad engineer regiments and base hospitals serving on the British front under the administration of the II Corps, and stated that the replacement companies would also be used to receive officers and men believed to be physically unfit, for examination by disability board. Company A of the battalion was located at Eu (Seine-Inférieure) and Company B was located at Hesdigneul (Pas-de-Calais). Both of these places are northwest of Amiens. These companies continued to function until they were absorbed by the regional replacement depot which was established at Pont de Metz, with detraining station at Saleux (Somme).

3. III Corps Replacement Battalion: This battalion, which was the first corps replacement battalion authorized, was organized pursuant to instructions of May 15, and on June 11 report was received that it was located at Laignes (Côte-d'Or) and was then ready to receive replacements. It was moved to Bains-les-Bains (Vosges) on June 26, where it remained until July 24, on which date it was transferred to Pontoise (Seine-et-Oise) and occupied several small villages in the vicinity of that town. On August 29 it was moved to Chelles and occupied the towns which had just been vacated by the I Corps Replacement Battalion, where it functioned until absorbed by the regional replacement depot at Chelles on November 4.

4. IV Corps Replacement Battalion: This battalion was authorized on June 17. On June 30 the Commanding General of the IV Corps was granted authority to establish it in the town of Fréville (Vosges), a small town, not far from Neufchateau, where it was established on August 18. The personnel for this battalion was sent from the 1st Depot Division and on September 11 it was moved to Toul, where it remained until November 4, when it was moved to Bois l'Evêque and absorbed by the regional replacement depot established at that place.

5. V Corps Replacement Battalion: The replacement Battalion for the V Corps was organized from a part of the personnel of the former III Corps Replacement Battalion and was established at Bains-les-Bains (Vosges) on July 24, 1918, where it remained until August 31, when it was changed stations to Froidos (Meuse) and remained at the latter place until it was absorbed by the First Army Advance Replacement Depot on November 7, 1918.

6. VI Corps Replacement Battalion: On August 18, 1918, Commanding General, VI Corps, was authorized to arrange for the organization and location of a provisional replacement battalion for his corps and was informed that the necessary personnel would be obtained by replacement requisition or by transfer from troops which might be assigned to the corps. On August 30, he asked for the assignment of Chalindrey, Torcenay, and Culmont for the replacement battalion and these towns were assigned to him on the following day, the battalion being established with headquarters at Chalindrey (Haute-Marne) on September 8, where it remained until September 17, when it was moved to Toul and was absorbed by the regional replacement depot at Bois l'Evêque on November 4, 1918.

7. VII Corps Replacement Battalion: This battalion was established on September 28, 1918, and was located at Bains-les-Bains (Vosges), where it functioned for the 6th, 81st, and 88th Divisions. It was absorbed by the regional replacement depot at Bois l'Evêque on November 5, 1918.

G. REGIONAL REPLACEMENT DEPOTS

As the military situation developed during the summer and early fall of 1918, the corps replacement battalions proved to be impracticable. They were entirely too small and in many cases were unable to fulfill their purpose. The principle of the flexible corps having been adopted and the corps staffs being utilized as needed resulted in divisions being moved from corps to corps. Divisions fluctuated so much that it frequently occurred that some replacement battalions were filled with men intended for divisions which had been removed from the control of the corps to which the battalion belonged. Replacements, particularly casuals sent to the corps replacement battalions with a view to their being returned to their original organizations in many cases arrived in the replacement battalion after the transfer of the organization to another corps and area. The corps, presumably being a tactical unit only, must be kept mobile and should not be hampered with an organization which is actually regional in its activities and cannot be conveniently moved from place to place. If the corps moved to either flank, as it may, the replacement battalion is lost to the corps for a time at least, as the large amount of equipment on hand cannot be moved at once. An example of this was in the movement of the I Corps from the St-Mihiel Salient to the Argonne Forest wherein the well-organized and well-equipped replacement battalion of this corps had to be left for weeks at Bois l'Evêque, near Toul.

On September 8, 1918, orders were issued by the First Army requiring that in each corps replacement battalion a company would be designated as a replacement company for each division in the corps and that such companies would automatically follow their divisions when the latter were transferred from one corps to another. A change in divisions from one corps to another made it extremely difficult for the regulating station to distribute casuals and replacements to the proper corps battalion for forwarding to their divisions, and on September 23, the Commanding General of the First Army was instructed to keep the regulating officers advised of changes in composition of corps under the command of the First Army in addition to advising the regulating officers as to the locations of the corps replacement battalions.

Consideration was given to the form of an organization which could be substituted for the corps replacement battalion. It was realized that depot divisions must be well to the rear in order not to complicate the supply and training problem but that there must be other replacement units in the advance section to serve as reservoirs and rest camps, from which replacements would be promptly furnished, and it was decided that there should be one or more regional replacement depots for each Army, depending on the size of the Army and the amount of territory to be covered; that the regional replacement depots should be assigned to prescribed regions or areas and be prepared to furnish replacements to all combat troops that might be ordered to those regions and to take care of all stragglers and casuals, forwarding them to an advanced depot which is serving the divisions to which those men belong or direct to the divisions. A regional replacement depot under the control of the Army takes away from the corps an administrative function which can more easily be performed by the army, which is familiar with the replacement needs of all divisions within that army.

In the early part of October, the problem of returning men who had been admitted to hospitals to their units promptly upon discharge from such hospitals became a serious one. Divisional field hospitals should retain men who will be fit for duty in a few days but on account of the great influx of patients it was necessary to make bed space available at the field hospitals. As a result, men had to be sent from the field hospitals and the evacuation hospitals by hospital trains to the base hospitals in the rear. Occupying valuable space on the hospital trains and being lost to their commands for some time.

In order to obviate these unfavorable conditions, a recommendation was submitted to the Chief of Staff on October 21, 1918, to the effect that the 4th Depot Division (85th Division) and the 6th Depot Division (40th Division) be transferred from their locations to areas in the Advance Section for the purpose of constituting regional replacement depots in order to provide suitable facilities for the receipt, equipment, and prompt forwarding to combat divisions of large numbers of officers and men evacuated from hospitals, men who were absent without leave, casuals, and stragglers of all kinds.

At that time officers and men evacuated from hospitals were sent to either the nearest regulating station, to the replacement battalion of the corps to which they formerly belonged (if such replacement battalion was in the vicinity of the hospital), to a depot division, or direct to a combat division if it was operating in the vicinity of the hospital. Officers and men belonging to branches of the service for which there were special depots were evacuated to those special depots. Most of the personnel evacuated from the hospitals was sent to the regulating stations, from which a great many men were returned to the depot divisions in the rear, which resulted in a loss of time and unnecessary use of transportation. The officer or soldier who is evacuated from the hospital and who is to be returned to his organization should, when he leaves the hospital, begin his journey in the direction of his organization rather than start to a depot division in an opposite direction, only to double back at a later date.

In recommending the establishment of regional replacement depots, it was stated that all corps replacement battalions were to be absorbed by such depots.

The recommendation for the establishment of regional replacement depots was approved on October 23 and on the following day instructions were issued to the Commanding General, Services of Supply, to send the 4th Depot Division, less one regiment of infantry and a four-company machine gun battalion, to the vicinity of Toul, reporting to the Commanding General of the American Second Army. This division was located at first at BOIS l'EVEQUE, a short distance from Toule, but was later moved to Thouvenot Barracks near Toul. One regiment and a machine gun battalion were to establish another regional replacement depot at Bains-les-Bains, reporting to the commanding General, American VII Corps. The orders for the establishment of that depot, however, were revoke owing to a movement of the VII Corps. The 6th Depot Division, less two regiments of infantry and two machine gun battalions, was sent to Revigny, a short distance north of the regulating station at St-Dizier, reporting to the Commanding General, American First Army, and established a regional replacement depot at Revigny. One regiment and a machine gun battalion from the 6th Depot Division were sent to Chelles, near Paris, to establish a regional replacement depot there, and the other regiment of infantry and machine gun battalion from the 6th Depot Division was sent to Pont-de-Metz, near Amiens, establishing a regional replacement depot in that vicinity, with railhead at Saleux.

It was planned to operate a large rest camp at Revigny in connection with the regional replacement depot at that place, such rest camp to have a capacity of approximately 10,000 men. After the signing of the Armistice, however, all work was stopped on the construction plan for the classification camp at the regional replacement depot at Revigny and for the rest camp which sas being established near that place.

* * * * * *

After the signing of the Armistice the Commanding General, Second Army, was directed on December 9 to organize from the personnel of the 85th Division at Toul a provisional replacement battalion. Upon the organization of this unit to took over the functions of the 85th Division and that division was released on December 25 for return to the United States. Instructions were issued on December 5 to the Commanding General, First Army, for the organization of a provisional replacement battalion to take over the functions of that part of the 40th Division at Revigny and also one at Chelles for the same purpose. The 40th Division was released for return to the United States on December 20, the provisional battalions taking over the functions which it had performed at Revigny and Chelles and the regional replacement depot at Saleux being abandoned.

The regional replacement depot at Chelles was transferred to Clignancourt Barracks in Paris on January 24, 1919, and the regional replacement depot at Revigny was discontinued at noon on February 5, 1919.

H. ADVANCE REPLACEMENT DEPOT

The First Army established an advance replacement depot on November 7, 1918, by consolidating the corps replacement battalions of the I and V Corps, placing the advance depot under the command of the Commanding General of the regional replacement depot at Revigny.

This advance replacement depot was stationed at a French camp, with a capacity of 2,500 men, just southeast of Auzeville (Meuse) in the center of the evacuation hospital district. This advance replacement depot received hospital évacués who were fit for immediate assignment to combat duty, stragglers, and men going on leave, furnishing the necessary clothing and equipment.

I.   THIRD ARMY REPLACEMENT BATTALION

The Commanding General of the Third Army established a Third Army Replacement Battalion at TREVES, Germany, on December 5, 1918. This battalion received and equipped casuals and stragglers and forwarded them to their organizations.

J.   THE FUNCTIONS OF REPLACEMENT ORGANIZATIONS

The replacement system planned for the American Expeditionary Forces contemplated that in addition to the base divisions and the replacement divisions, which formed the two echelons of the system, there would be an automatic flow of replacement troops from the United States and that these replacements would receive a considerable part of their training before shipment to France. As it finally developed, the replacement system consisted of large replacement camps in the United States, where the drafted men were given some preliminary training, depot divisions in France to which the replacement drafts were sent immediately after arrival, the regional replacement depots in the Advance Section, and detachments at the divisional railheads for the reception and care of replacements and casuals.

The functions of any replacement organization, whether it be great or small, in the United States, in France, or anywhere else, must always include four lines of activity; 1st, the reception and preliminary care of replacements; 2d, their classification, the making of the necessary records, clothing, arming and equipping, 3d, training; and 4th, forwarding.

1. Reception of Replacements. [This section is a discussion of the details of reception, classification, training and forwarding of replacements.]

* * * * * *

K.   ORDERS COVERING REPLACEMENTS

[This section cites orders covering replacements.]

* * * * * *

L.   NUMBER OF REPLACEMENTS FORWARDED

The magnitude of the replacement problem in the American Expeditionary Forces is apparent when it is realized that in less than a year 710,033 replacements and casuals were forwarded from the depot divisions and other replacement organizations, of which number 435,285 were sent to the twenty-nine combat divisions in a period of eight months from May 1 to December 31, 1918. The 1st Depot Division alone sent forward 295,666 and of that number there were forwarded 31,754 in July; 31,632 in August; 43,197 in September; 43,231 in October and 33,839 in November.

[The remainder of this section lists sources of information regarding number of replacements forwarded to combat divisions.]

* * * * * *

M. REQUISITIONS FOR REPLACEMENTS

[This section discussed the routine and periodicity of requisitions for replacements and the establishment of priorities.]

* * * * * *

N. CIRCULATION OF REPLACEMENTS

Replacements arriving from the United States were sent by the Commanding General, Services of Supply, from the base ports to the particular depot at which there were training organizations of the same arm or service as that of the arriving replacements. Upon arrival at the depot the men were classified, properly equipped (see Sec. V, G. O. No. 111), and their training continued until such time as they were forwarded to combat or S. O. S. units. Casuals evacuated from hospitals to depot divisions as of Class A were handled in a similar manner, and when forwarded were returned to their former organizations. (See Par. 7-b, Sec. VII, G. O. No. 111.)

The original plan of the replacement of personnel of combat organizations provided that replacement divisions should forward replacements directly to combat units, and depot divisions should furnish replacements directly to the replacement divisions. The Replacement Division (32d) of the I Corps functions as such until April 10, 1918, when it was relieved from this duty and prepared for combat service. No additional replacement divisions were designated and their duties were performed by the depot divisions until the corps replacement battalions were established. After the 32d Division was discontinued as a replacement division, replacements were forwarded in large detachments via a regulating station direct to combat units. Casuals and small detachments of replacements were sent to a regulating station where they were grouped according to organizations to which assigned and then forwarded to the replacement battalion of the corps to which their division was assigned. The frequent changes in the composition of the corps made it extremely difficult for the regulating officer to forward casuals and small detachments of replacements to the proper corps battalion and in some instances the men had to be returned to the regulating station in order to be sent to the organization for which originally intended. The forwarding of replacements in large groups direct to combat divisions presented comparatively little difficulty, as they could generally be sent in trainload lots direct to the railhead of the division for which intended and thus obviate the necessity of re-sorting at the regulating station.

During the seven weeks from October 2, 1918, to November 20, 1918, the total number of replacements forwarded to combat divisions was 173,833. It was very essential that these replacements should reach the divisions for which requested in the shortest time possible. To facilitate the prompt delivery of these replacements to divisions of the First Army, for which most of them were intended, the army sent an officer to the regulating station at St-Dizier to which place an officer from Headquarters, Services of Supply had also been sent. The Commanding General, Services of Supply, notified the officers at the regulating station as to the point and hour of departure, name of train commander number of officers and men on the train, and the organization to which replacements were consigned, for each train of replacements. The officer of the First Army notified G-1 of the Army so that if necessary the replacements might be diverted to a division other than the one to which originally assigned. The divisions were in turn notified and made preparations to care for the men upon arrival at the railhead and forward them to the proper organizations. As divisions actually in the fighting line could not receive replacements, those for such divisions had to be held until the divisions came out of the line or diverted to another division.

In October, 1918, the railroad yard and regulating station at St-Dizier was so overtaxed that it was impracticable to split up trains at that point. Replacements were forwarded to divisions in trainload lots without alteration in the composition of trains or personnel on the train, even though original assignment lists contemplated replacements in specified numbers for certain divisions.

There were cases of improper routing of replacements owing to there being many towns of the same name, lack of information as to location of units, and movement of units while replacements were en route. The most frequent cases of wrong routing were those of casuals being returned to their former organizations. In order to reduce to a minimum the improper routing of replacements, arrangements were made on November 2, 1918, between G-1 and G-4 of the First Army that G-4 would furnish each railhead officer in the Army area with a complete list of railheads and units serving at these railheads. Similar lists were to be furnished to the regulating officer at Is-sur-Tille, the commanding General of the regional replacement depot at Revigny, and G-1 and G-4 of the Second Army.

O. REPLACEMENTS OF OFFICERS, NONCOMMISSIONED OFFICERS, AND SPECIALISTS

A most important feature of the replacement problem was the furnishing of officers, noncommissioned officers, and specialists of many kinds, the demand for all three classes far exceeding the supply.

As early as July 11, 1917, cablegram to the United States requested consideration of the large number of officers that would be needed for replacement purposes and numerous requests were made from time to time for officers to be utilized as replacements, many of which were not complied with.

Vacancies among officers were filled by promotion or replacement. Replacements were derived from three sources: (a) Commissioned personnel of depot and skeletonized divisions; (b) officers sent from the United States; (c) graduates of the Army Candidates School.

Par. 2, Sec. VIII, G. O. No. 46, A. E. F., 1918, directed that two-thirds of all vacancies due to casualties in all but the lowest commissioned grades would be filled by replacements and the remaining third might be filled by promotion. Par. 2, Sec. VIII, G. O. No. 111, A. E. F., 1918, did not require that two-thirds of the vacancies be filled by replacements but provided that requisition should be made for the necessary replacements to fill all vacancies existing in commissioned grades. However, if replacements who originally belonged to the division submitting the requisition, were not available in replacement depots, the commanding officer of such organization would be notified and would then make recommendations for promotion to fill the vacancies. A recommendation for promotion was to be considered as a vacancy filled in submitting subsequent requisitions.

Replacements required to fill vacancies in commissioned grades were furnished by the Commanding General, Services of Supply, from officers available in replacement organizations under his command. G. O. No. 94, A. E. F., June 12, 1918, included among the duties of the Personnel Bureau, "To make recommendations concerning the promotion of officers and the general subject of promotions."

After the signing of the Armistice, G. O. No. 221, A. E. F., was issued on December 1, 1918, and charged the Adjutant General, A. E. F., with the duties pertaining to the Personnel Bureau and later on, as there were no more officer replacements, G. O. No. 231, A. E. F., December 18, 1918, directed that replacement requisitions as required by Par. 2, Sec. III, G. O. No. 111, 1918, would no longer contain any reference to commissioned officers and that applications for the assignment of commissioned officers of any grade, needed to fill vacancies existing in organizations, would be made by telegram to the Adjutant General, A. E. F. * * *

Par. 2, Sec. VIII, G. O. No. 46, A. E. F., 1918, made the same provisions concerning the promotion and filling of vacancies in noncommissioned grades as in commissioned grades. G. O. No. 111 provided that if there were no men available in replacement depots who formerly belonged to the division submitting the requisition, necessary action would be taken to fill existing vacancies in noncommissioned grades. Par. 7, Sec. I, G. O. No. 41, A. E. F., March 14, 1918, directed that no noncommissioned officer or first class private would be reduced to a lower grade because of his being transferred to Class B, C, or D, unless the disability was the result of his own misconduct. Par. 3, Sec. VI, G. O. No. 111, stated that noncommissioned officers would not be reduced in rank by reason of a transfer incident to the operation of the replacement system. The action with reference to the disposition of surplus noncommissioned officers is shown in Sec. IV, G. O. No. 17, A. E. F., January 25, 1919.

Specialists in organizations were requested as vacancies occurred and as the services of especially trained men were required. Replacements arriving from the United States were classified when they reached the replacement depots and those who had had previous experience and training along special lines were sent to schools within the depot to continue their training preparatory to being sent forward on replacement requisitions.

P. CLASS A CASUALS

The term Class A Casuals as used herein refers to hospital évacués who were fit for combat service.

G. O. No. 46, A. E. F., March 26, 1918, provided that when officers and men of army troops, corps troops, or combat divisions were admitted to an S. O. S. hospital they would be dropped from the rolls of their organizations. G. O. No. 111, A. E. F., July 8, 1918, extended the provision to include army hospitals.

This provision was desirable in order that replacements might be furnished to fill vacancies caused by losses in battle without padding the organization rolls and was especially necessary in the case of noncommissioned officers and specialists as only the number of soldiers of those grades provided in the tables of organization can be carried on the rolls as members of an organization without a violation of the law and a resultant loss of pay.

1. Policy Concerning Return of Casuals to Their Former Organizations: From the very beginning it was the policy of the A. E. F. to return to their own organizations all men evacuated from hospitals as fit for combat duty. It was recognized that it is very necessary for the morale of a command to return to it its recovered casualties. Organizations are very glad to get back men who have formerly been with them and the men are likewise more contented when they rejoin their old units. The great importance of regimental and divisional spirit or pride was recognized. The enlisted man who has served some months in the line with his unit knows his own officers and has confidence in them and knows his comrades and is familiar with their plan of action under all circumstances. He becomes proud of the fact that his division, his battalion, or his company has never given up a foot of ground and he fights harder to maintain its reputation.

In order that this policy might be fully understood by all concerned, instructions on the subject were repeated many times in general orders, letters and telegrams.

Some of the instructions requiring that soldiers evacuated from hospitals would be returned to their former organizations were contained in the following [quotes parts of general orders, letters, and telegrams, of which the important ones will be printed in later volumes.]

* * * * * *

The orders to return évacués to their former organizations were generally observed but some men after being evacuated from hospitals were not returned to the units to which they belonged, due to the following:

(a) At times records did not accompany men and there was no way of determing the unit to which a man belonged. In such cases where the statement of the man himself had to be relied upon, many men did not know the designation of the organization of which they were members and others who did not desire to return to their former units gave incorrect information.

(b) Mistakes in assignments and orders made at hospitals, at regulating stations, and at replacement depots and other organizations.

(c) During the period of active operations some detachments of replacements (which included some casuals) forwarded for certain units were diverted by the armies to other organizations. This action was due to exigencies of the service.

2. Handling of Casuals after the Armistice: One of the first administrative questions taken up after the signing of the Armistice was that of returning hospital patients to the United States. It was decided to retain in Europe all Class A men then in hospitals who would be able to return to duty with their organizations within two months.

3. Delay in Returning Casuals. The change in the tactical situation after the Armistice, which brought about the forward movement of the Third Army and the withdrawal of the First and Second Armies to training areas, made it necessary as a matter of expediency to stop for the time being the forward flow of replacements and casuals. On November 17 instructions to this effect were given to the Commanding General, S. O. S. In order to prevent overcrowing of the depots, the Commanding General, S. O. S., ordered that all Class A personnel should be held in hospitals until further notice. This situation lasted for about six weeks during which time the number of men in hospitals waiting to be evacuated as Class A increased daily. The duration of the embargo was prolonged by the difficulty in securing railroad transportation from the French.

4. Excess of Casuals: The number of patients in hospitals decreased from 190,000 on November 14 to 99,000 on January 16. A large percentage of the men evacuated were Class A. On January 10, 1919, there were more casuals ready to go back to the Third Army than were needed to bring its units up to full authorized strength. On January 12 the Chief of Staff approved the following recommendations:

(a) That casuals evacuated from hospitals be returned to the armies to which they formerly belonged until enough had been sent to bring all organizations to maximum strength with the exception of infantry rifle companies, the maximum strength of which will be considered as two hundred.

(b) That excess enlisted personnel, when ready for evacuation from hospitals, be disposed of as follows: First, such men as desire to return to the organizations to which they formerly belonged shall be allowed to do so; second, such men as are qualified for the Military Police Corps, and volunteer for transfer to that corps, to be so transferred; third, all men who do not express a preference to return to the organizations to which they formerly belonged, or who are not transferred to the Military Police Corps, to be returned to the United States.

Complete figures are not available to show how many casuals were given the privilege of making the above-mentioned choice, but a report covering 13,960 Class A casuals available for evacuation to the Third Army can be taken as typical. Their choices were as follows:

To transfer to Military Police Corps	598
To return to their division	1,379
To return to the United States . . .	11,983
Total	13,960

Those who elected to return to the United States were, under orders of the Commanding General, S. O. S., sent to an embarkation center, where they were formed into casual companies.

5. Transfer of Casuals to their former Organizations: On February 11, 1919, a telegram was sent to the Commanding General, S. O. S., and to the Commanding General of each army, directing that an investigation be made to ascertain whether the orders on the subject of returning casuals to their divisions had been complied with. Similar directions were sent to the Provost Marshal General. The information received in reply to this message was submitted to the Chief of Staff in a memorandum dated February 27, 1919.

Instructions were issued for the transfer to their original divisions of all men who, as Class A casuals, had been sent elsewhere, providing the men desired to go back and, providing further, that they had not volunteered for the duty to which they were assigned.

6. Change in Policy in March, 1919: By March 1, 1919, practically all of the men who had been sent to the hospitals before the Armistice had been evacuated. The men then in hospitals were those who had become sick subsequent to the cessation of hostilities. To have allowed these men, upon evacuation, to have the option of rejoing their divisions or of going to the United States as casuals would have been to place a premium upon illness. The Commanding General, S. O. S., recommended that a change be made in the system. On March 4, the Chief of Staff approved the following recommendations.

(a) All soldiers in hospitals on being evacuated as of Class A, whose organizations are in the A. E. F., to be sent direct to their organizations from hospitals by section and district commanders. Those serving in Germany to be sent to regional replacement depot functioning for the Third Army.

(b) All soldiers in hospitals evacuated as of Class A, whose organizations have returned to the United States or are about to sail and time will not permit of soldiers rejoining before date of sailing, to be forwarded to the First Replacement Depot, there organized into detachments and forwarded to embarkation center to be assigned to divisions being prepared for return to the United States.

The instructions covering the carrying out of the new policy were given to the Commanding General, S. O. S., in telegram dated March 7, 1919.

Q. CLASS B AND C PERSONNEL

1. Definition: [The report quotes G. O. No. 41, A. E. F., March 14, 1918, which contains definitions of Classes A, B, C, and D personnel and outlines the plan for handling military members of the A. E. F.]

* * * * * *

2. Control by C. G., S. O. S: The fact that most of the hospitals from which pat patients were evacuated after reclassification were in the S. O. S. and that unit commanders in the forward areas were ordered to send all men presumed to be unfit for combat duty to the S. O. S. for examination placed the details of handling Class B and C personnel entirely under the direction of the Commanding General, S. O. S.

3. Policy in regard to Class B Enlisted Personnel: The policy of the Commanding General, S. O. S., in handling this personnel is reviewed in a report of a board of officers convened to investigate the subject of the utilization of wounded men in Headquarters Battalion, G. H. Q. and other places. [Qoutes from the report of the Board.]

* * * * * *

It was at all times the intention that Class B should serve only as a temporary classification and that the personnel so classified should in a reasonable time be reclassified either as Class A or Class C. The assignment of Class B men to duty in the S. O. S. interfered somewhat with the carrying out of this intention and it is probable that it to some extent tended to prevent men from becoming Class A as soon as they would have under different conditions. This phase of the question was the subject of study by the Chief Surgeon, A. E. F., and others. To remedy the condition the Medical Department established convalescent camps at hospital centers and convalescent training camps in the depot divisions where all potential Class A men were kept under control and given military training by line officers and athletic instructors. In November 1918, 10 convalescent camps were in operation with a capacity of 20,275.

In a memorandum to the above-mentioned Board of Officers, the Chief Surgeon, A. E. F., said:

The period now occupied by the changeable status of a Class B man will be taken up in the Convalescent Camp. By this plan, B Class men will invariably be held in groups, either at the Convalescent Camp, or subsequently at Training Battalion of Depot Divisions, and not scattered about in temporary assignments as is now the case. In other words, a Class B man is potentially a Class A man and every effort should be made to bring about his rehabilitation in training groups, either at the Convalescent Camp or the Training Battalion. The determination of Class C men can be made at Convalescent Camps in a manner more accurate and prompt than heretofore. Physical Classification Boards at Convalescent Camps will be chosen carefully, and will be composed of medical officers who will understand that they are charged with the high function of conducting sick and wounded back to a channel leading to the firing line, and they will be aware that the output from the hospital in the form of Class A men represents the highest military value among all classes of casuals or replacements.

4. Policy in regard to Class C Personnel: All men who were definitely classified as Class C were assigned to duty by the Commanding General, S. O. S., the nature of the duty depending upon the physical condition of the man. Wherever possible these men were used to replace Class A men held in the S. O. S. but the great demand for personnel for duty in the S. O. S. often prevented this.

At the time of the signing of the Armistice, arrangements were under way for the replacement of all Class A personnel on duty at G. H. Q. (except specialists) by Class B or C personnel. The same plan was to have been carried into effect at all other headquarters where possible.

5. Class B and C Officers: Under the plan adopted by the Commanding General S. O. S., Class B and C line officers were sent to Blois for assignment to duty. A study was made of the qualifications and physical condition of each officer and an effort made to assign him to the class of duty for which he was most fitted.

6. Chaplains: On the request of the Senior Chaplain, A. E. F., instructions were given the Commanding General, S. O. S., in October, 1918, to send all chaplains evacuated from hospitals as Class A, B, or C to the Chaplains School at Le Mans.

7. Re-examination of Class B Personnel: G. O. No. 41 provided for re-examination of Class B officers and soldiers once in every two months, but the need for personnel was so great in the S. O. S. that it often happened that these examinations were not made or that, if they were made and resulted in the restoration of the man to Class A, he was not released for combat duty. The specially pressing demand for combat replacements in the fall of 1918 resulted in the sending out of a telegram by the Commanding General, S. O. S., on September 30, 1918, directing an immediate re-examination of all Class B personnel and the sending of all officers and men restored to Class A to the 1st Depot Division for assignment to combat duty.

8. Effect of Armistice on Policy: The cessation of hostilities following the signing of the Armistice caused a marked change of policy in regard to Class B and C personnel. On November 15 a telegram from the Chief of Staff, A. E. F., to the Commanding General, S. O. S., authorized the latter to return to the United States all men evacuated from hospitals as Class C and such Class A and B men as would probably not be able to return to duty within a period of two months and on November 22 a telegram was sent to the Commanding General, S. O. S., embodying the same instructions in a slightly different form.

On November 19, the Commanding General, S. O. S., was authorized to replace B and C class men on duty in the S. O. S. by Class A men, utilizing not to exceed 10,000 men from the depot divisions for this purpose and to return to the United States the B and C class personnel so relieved.

9. Re-examination of Class B Men Abolished: See Sec. I, G. O. No. 216, A. E. F., November 26, 1918, read as follows:

The re-examination of Class B officers and soldiers with a view to their return to duty as of Class A under the provisions of Par. 5, G. O. No. 41, c. s., these headquarters, is no longer required.

As there was no longer a great demand for Class A men it was considered advisable to allow all Class B and C personnel to remain so classified and to be sent home as such as soon their services could be spared or Class A substitutes provided.

EXHIBIT 14d

GENERAL HEADQUARTERS AMERICAN EXPEDITIONARY FORCES

1st SECTION (G-1) GENERAL STAFF

Personnel Division

STATEMENT SHOWING NET ARRIVAL SHORTAGE IN ALL DIVISIONS WITH DATES OF ARRIVAL

	Net Arrival Shortage (Officers and enlisted) after crediting all casuals who arrived after the division and who could be identified.	Date of Arrival in France of the first and last units of the divisions.
1st Division – – – –	– 414 – – – –	June 26, 1917 to Dec. 22, 1917
2d Division – – – –	– 1,795 – – – –	Sept..20, 1917 to Mar. 12, 1918
3d Division – – – –	– 978 – – – –	Dec. 21, 1917 to June 19, 1918
4th Division – – – –	– 1,308 – – – –	May 13, 1918 to June 8, 1918
5th Division – – – –	– 2,796 – – – –	Mar. 12, 1918 to June 19, 1918
6th Division – – – –	– 2,353 – – – –	May 18, 1918 to July 26, 1918
7th Division – – – –	– 975 – – – –	Aug. 11, 1918 to Sept. 3, 1918
26th Division – – – –	– 1,382 – – – –	Sept. 20, 1917 to Jan. 12, 1918
27th Division – – – –	– 762 – – – –	May 23, 1918 to July 12, 1918
28th Division – – – –	– 1,295 – – – –	May 13, 1918 to May 31, 1918
29th Division – – – –	– 1,497 – – – –	June 26, 1918 to July 22, 1918
30th Division – – – –	– 695 – – – –	May 23, 1918 to June 25, 1918
31st Division – – – –	– 3,801 – – – –	Sept. 29, 1918 to Nov. 9, 1918
32d Division – – – –	– 3,533 – – – –	Feb. 6, 1918 to Mar. 26, 1918
33d Division – – – –	– 1,405 – – – –	May 18, 1918 to June 27, 1918
34th Division – – – –	– 3,292 – – – –	Sept. 29, 1918 to Oct. 24, 1918
35th Division – – – –	– 1,178 – – – –	May 7, 1918 to June 8, 1918
36th Division – – – –	– 976 – – – –	July 30 1918 to Aug. 12, 1918
37th Division – – – –	– 1,331 – – – –	June 22, 1918 to July 18, 1918
38th Division – – – –	– 1,876 – – – –	Sept. 28, 1918 to Oct. 25, 1918
39th Division – – – –	– 1,396 – – – –	Aug. 18, 1918 to Sept.12, 1918
40th Division – – – –	– 1,175 – – – –	Aug. 17, 1918 to Aug. 31, 1918
41st Division – – – –	– 1,156 – – – –	Dec. 11, 1917 to Feb. 6, 1918
42d Division – – – –	– 1,054 – – – –	Nov. 1, 1917 to Dec. 8, 1917
76th Division – – – –	– 932 – – – –	July 12, 1918 to Aug. 8, 1918
77th Division – – – –	– 890 – – – –	Apr. 12, 1918 to May 6, 1918
78th Division – – – –	– 698 – – – –	May 31, 1918 to June 12, 1918
79th Division – – – –	– 1,355 – – – –	July 15, 1918 to Aug. 3, 1918

	Net Arrival Shortage (Officers and enlisted) after crediting all casuals who arrived after the division and who could be identified.	Date of Arrival in France of the first and last units of the divisions.
80th Division – – – –	– 643 – – – –	May 30, 1918 to June 18, 1918
81st Division – – – –	– 1,402 – – – –	Aug. 11, 1918 to Aug. 25, 1918
82d Division – – – –	– 1,243 – – – –	May 7, 1918 to July 10, 1918
83d Division – – – –	– 2,589 – – – –	June 15, 1918 to Aug. 6, 1918
84th Division – – – –	– 1,043 – – – –	Sept. 9, 1918 to Oct. 25, 1918
85th Division – – – –	– 1,045 – – – –	Aug. 3, 1918 to Aug. 11, 1918
86th Division – – – –	– 2,057 – – – –	Sept. 21, 1918 to Oct. 9, 1918
87th Division – – – –	– 975 – – – –	Sept. 3, 1918 to Sept. 16, 1918
88th Division – – –	– 1,181 – – – –	Aug. 17, 1918 to Sept. 9, 1918
89th Division – – – –	– 3,125 – – – –	June 16, 1918 to July 10, 1918
90th Division – – – –	– 868 – – – –	June 21, 1918 to July 26, 1918
91st Division – – – –	– 2,069 – – – –	July 17, 1918 to July 26, 1918
92d Division – – – –	– 1,804 – – – –	June 19, 1918 to July 12, 1918
TOTAL	44,486	

The 8th Division is not included as only part of the division arrived in France.

CHAPTER V

OCEAN TONNAGE AND OVERSEAS SUPPLY SHIPMENTS

A. SHIPPING AND OCEAN TONNAGE

When the United States entered the war she had a small merchant marine and consequently only a very small number of available cargo ships. The Army Transport Service had certain transports, but the number was hopelessly inadequate for the new task. The Government faced a program of transporting overseas an army of a million or more men and the supplies necessary for its maintenance. It therefore became necessary to look to the world's shipping for such vessels as could be purchased or chartered to meet the immediate needs of the Expeditionary Forces. It was recognized that future needs could not be supplied from this source, and extensive plans were laid for the building of a large fleet. The Shipping Board came into existence to assume the task of making available the shipping immediately necessary and to plan for taking care of future needs. Some time necessarily elapsed before the work of the Board assumed substantial proportions, but eventually plans were perfected and shipping construction in the United States was begun on a scale never before known.

It was a function of the Shipping Board to requisition all shipping under the American flag, and allocate it for the use of the Army, the Navy, and the trades. Such tonnage as the Board thought necessary was put into service under the supervision of the Army authorities in so far as its actual operation was concerned. As the needs of the Army increased and were made known to the Board, additional tonnage, when available, was provided. A representative of the Board was sent to LONDON as a member of the Allied Maritime Transport Council, the function of which was to plan the distribution of the Allied and available neutral tonnage to the best interests of the Allied governments and the United States. Through the efforts of the United States representative, Mr. Stevens, [Mr. Raymond B. Stevens, member of Shipping Board] a considerable amount of neutral tonnage (Swedish) was allocated to the service of the American Army for the transportation of material from England to France.

The length of time required for the complete round trip of a troop or cargo ship or fleet is known as the turnaround and the efficiency of a fleet is largely dependent upon it. The important factors entering into the turn around are the speed of the vessels themselves and the port facilities. One of the first activities of the A. E. F. was the selection of base ports in Europe and the making of arrangements for the efficient and rapid reception and unloading of cargo and troop transports. It was recognized that an increase in the size of the fleet would work little advantage unless port facilities were sufficient to keep the average turnaround at a minimum figure. The activities of G-1 in this matter are described in detail in Section B of this chapter, Port Operations.

From the outset it was necessary to make frequent studies of the amount of supplies that would be necessary for the A. E. F. in view of the current troop shipment program. The computation was generally based on the number of pounds of supplies necessary for one man for one day. The amount necessary in the case of such articles as subsistence, clothing, ammunition, forage, and other supplies of an expendable nature, could readily be ascertained, but it was more difficult with supplies which were required for port improvements, construction transportation, and other general purposes. As a result, there was a wide variation in the basic figure used from time to time, depending on the method of computation, and this accounts in some degree for the differences in the results of various studies.

A study of the shipping necessary to transport and supply the A. E. F. was made by the French General Staff early in September, 1917, based on their experience with the armies of the Orient and the Salonica expedition. This was used as a guide in the preparation of a study by the General Staff of the A. E. F. during the latter part of September. Various transport turnarounds and pounds per man per day were used, and the computations were made both on the basis of 500,000 and 1,000,000 men in France by June 30, 1918. It was apparent from this study that the Shipping Board would have to put rapidly into service a large amount of both troop and cargo tonnage if the A. E. F. was to carry out its program. This information was submitted to the Commander-in-Chief for use at inter-allied conferences.

A board of officers was convened by S. O. No. 131, A. E. F., October 19, 1917, to report on the subject of troop movements via England. On November 3 it submitted its report, together with a study showing the anticipated traffice demands, including port and rail facilities, and the estimated shipping requirements of the A. E. F. The following recommendations were made:

That the War Department be informed that accommodations may be secured in England for 28,000 men, but that due to congestion on the British cross-channel boats and on the French railways leaving Le Havre, not more than 15,000 can be moved per month from England to our Camps in France. That, unless the British and French arrange to do more for us, the only way for us to improve the situation is to provide our own boats for the trip from Southampton to French channel ports, and our own naval convoys for these boats. Furthermore, that no heavy baggage or animal or mechanical transport should accompany troops coming via England.

That studies be made at once of Brest and the railways leading therefrom with a view to determining the number of troops that can be received there, and moved away daily by the railway; likewise the number of lighters, tugs and other facilities needed. That as soon as arrangements can be made to receive troops at Brest the War Department be notified of the fact, with statement of limitations as to coal, as to baggage and as to the number of troops which can be daily moved by the railways. The necessity of feeding troops on shipboard until railways can transport them, should should also be pointed out.

That similar studies be at once made of Cherbourg and any other available French channel ports with a view to determining their capacity to receive our troops coming from England, and to determine the capacity of railroad to move these troops.

That cable request be made for a shipping commissioner to come at once to France to explain the plans of the authorities at home, and to see for himself the needs of the situation in France so that he can at once provide the authorities at home with the information they lack.

That the War Department be advised of the estimate here made of our tonnage requirements as based on British experience, so that these figures may be used to check
those made in Washington.

That based upon exact information as to shipping and port capacities a program be
arranged with the Washington authorities as to the time and the order in which both
troops and stores will arrive, so that all necessary arrangements may be made.

That examination be made of the question of whether we are to receive supplies
and munitions for our fighting troops and labor, tools and material necessary for
receiving, forwarding and sheltering the same, at a rate equal to that of the arrival
of troops.

That consideration be given the idea of conferring with the British Government as
to the best way of allocating existing shipping and supplies. We may not want to pool
either shipping or supplies, but a conference with the highest members of the British
Government on this subject might serve to show each party how they could help the other
with advantage to the general cause. We are seeking many things from the British and
they from us. It would seem that there should be a clearing house where these claims
could be passed upon, with the requirements of the Allies as a whole in view.

As a result of these recommendations a combined tonnage study was prepared, based on the data
obtained from the French General Staff for the study of September 27 and that obtained from the
British for the study submitted with the board's report of November 3. It was made on the basis
of 1,000,000 men in France by June 30, 1918, and provided for a troop movement via England of
20,000 men a month as well as the movement of cross-channel cargo. On November 19 it was forwarded
to the United States and gave the War Department the best estimate possible at that time of the
necessary shipping, port facilities, and transportation required for a force of the size mentioned.

As a result also of the board's recommendations, troops coming by way of England were restricted in the matter of baggage to their necessary troop equipment. The question of using
American shipping for cross-channel transportation was left for determination by the Navy, and it
later developed that the more extensive use of the port of Brest was more desirable in view of the
greater safety of personnel and the saving of ocean tonnage.

On December 19, 1917, Colonel W. J. Wilgus, Railway Transportation Corps, was sent to the
United States to report to the Chief of Staff and inform him concerning (1) the requirements of the
transportation service in personnel and supplies; (2) the draft and berth facilities of French
ports, the necessity for increasing the present facilities, and the opportunities offered by further
dock and port projects; and (3) the general shipping situation as understood by the Allied Maritime
Transport Council.

On his return, Colonel Wilgus filed a report dated March 7, attached to which was a tonnage
study prepared by him on the requirements to transport and maintain 900,000 men in France by July 1,
1918. This was accepted by the General Staff, A. E. F., and the authorities in Washington as the
best basis upon which to calculate supply requisitions and the tonnage necessary to transport those
supplies overseas, as well as to indicate the necessary rolling stock to be put into service for
the movement of the supplies from base ports to the interior.

To promote the efficient use of cargo tonnage the Administrative Section, in December 1917,
made a study of all transport cargo manifests, copies of which were forwarded to G. H. Q. Statistics were compiled of the tonnage carried by various vessels on consecutive voyages, and data were
obtained which were valuable in checking tonnage figures on requisitions. For example, information
was secured concerning the nature and volume of bulky materials requisitioned, and steps taken to
avoid waste of cargo space, either by requiring better packing or by arranging to obtain such supplies in European markets. In a number of instances it was found that unnecessary supplies (e. g.,
sawdust for the Pigeon Service, baled wood shavings for meat and ice plants, caskets, and box shooks)
had been shipped, and arrangements were made to bring about the cancellation of additional requests
for such material.

Early in January, 1918, Washington was requested to furnish the A. E. F. with all available
information with respect to the shipping program adopted by the War Department and the Shipping
Board. In compliance with this request an outline of the ship tonnage situation as of January 1,

1918, a memorandum of the minimum import ship tonnage of the same date, a statement of necessary imports, a memorandum on French ports and a list of transports in Army service were furnished. In addition, periodic reports issued by the Bureau of Navigation and Shipping Board statistics covering the new ship construction program were sent from time to time. All of this information and data was necessary in order to enable the Administrative Section to restrict requisitions to the probable shipping available and for use as a basis of future tonnage studies.

On February 28 the Shipping Control Committee asked to be supplied with information concerning the tonnage discharge at French ports. Thereupon a weekly cable report was inaugurated showing:

(a) Tonnage discharged by ports.
(b) Tonnage evacuated by ports.
(c) Probable departure of vessels during the next week.
(d) Unusual delays to transports.
(e) Cargo and ballast on board vessels westbound.
(f) Repairs needed by ships on arrival U. S. ports.

The necessary information was furnished by the Director General of Transportation and transmitted to the U. S. This report was later changed to tri-monthly May 1) in order to conform to the periods of time adopted by the Embarkation Service.

On March 25, 1918 a tonnage study was made in G-1 for the transportation and maintenance of 2,000,000 men in 18 months, April 1, 1918, to September 30, 1919.

The shipment of horses from the United States had been practically stopped by cable of March 22, 1918, and animal transports had been stripped of their fittings and placed in cargo service. Thereafter, owing to the inability of the French to supply horses in France as intended, it became necessary to make up the existing shortages by calling on the United States for animals. To supply them would necessitate the withdrawal from cargo service of a large number of animal transports, and this reduction of cargo tonnage was thought to be un warranted by the War Department, in view of the increased troop movement. It was recommended by them on July 19, 1918, that in place of shipping animals, the shipment of motor transportation be expedited. However, owing to the serious shortage of animals (in spite of reductions in tables of organization and the replacement of horses as far as possible by bicycle and motor transportation), it was requested on July 26, that all animal transports be refitted for the transportation of animals and that the shipment of motor transportation be expedited as well.

On April 23, a copy of the report of the Allied Maritime Transport Council on military, naval, and commercial import tonnage was received at G. H. Q. The programs submitted by the several governments of their requirements for the year 1918 greatly exceeded the available tonnage and necessitated a reconsideration of tonnage requirements.

The Abbeville Agreement, adopted by the Supreme War Council about the first of May, provided for the transportation of American infantry and machine gun units in British shipping. These troops were to be brigaded with the British armies in France, and the British were to furnish troop ships to effect the movement.

During May, G-1 was called upon by the Commander-in-Chief to explain the differences between Colonel Wilgus' tonnage study of March 7 and the study made in G-1 under date of March 25, both of which have allready been referred to. It was pointed out in a memorandum of May 21 that the March 7 study was based on data obtained in December, 1917, while that of March 25 took into consideration later and more detailed information concerning the consumption of supplies and so arrived at smaller estimates of tonnage requirements. It appeared, however, that even these latter requirements would not be met by the proposed shipping program.

The Versailles Agreement concluded early in June between Marshal Foch, Lord Milner, and General Pershing, provided for the transportation of troops during June and July at the rate of 250,000 per month and gave absolute priority to combatant troops. This increased troop movement program called for a study of the possibility of obtaining additional ship tonnage, and the ability of the ports to discharge and evacuate the increased flow of supplies. A memorandum prepared in G-1 under date of June 12, 1918, showed that:

(a) The tonnage available according to the Shipping Board assignment chart dated April 30, plus all new construction, would amount to 1,680,000 short tons of cargo capacity by October 1,

1918, which, on the basis of 30 lbs. per man per day, would only provide for the maintenance of 1,200,000 men.

(b) The tonnage allotted to the Army by the Shipping Control Committee was only 388,000 tons, while the tonnage require for the troops in France, or en route thereto by July 1, was 592,000 tons.

The necessity for the rapid transportation of the American forces continued and led to a further change in the troop program to provide for the movement of 3,000,000 men by May, 1919, and later the so-called Foch agreement, June 25, called for the movement of 80 divisions by April, 1919 and 100 by July, 1919.

A tonnage study was made in G-1 under date of June 29 based on the troop movement program of 3,000,000 men by May 30, 1919, and a copy forwarded to the Commanding General, S. O. S., with the request that the several supply services carefully check the estimates. A copy was also sent to the American representative on the Allied Maritime Transport Council to be used by him as evidence of the needs of the A. E. F., with the result that shortly thereafter a number of Swedish boats obtained by charter were allotted to the army service to be used in the cross-channel coal traffic, and other concessions were made in the allocation of troop ships.

The Shipping Control Committee estimates of shipping available from August 1 to December 31, 1918, were received in a cable of July 10. A memorandum was prepared in G-1 under date of July 15 showing the tonnage requirements for maintenance based on 30 lbs per man per day as outlined in the tonnage study of June 29. From this it appeared that the estimate of available shipping just referred to was considerably below requirements, and furthermore that only about 50% of the new steel ship construction was being used for the A. E. F. An urgent request was thereupon sent to the U. S. (Cable P-1487) for the assignment of 500,000 dead-weight tons of vessels to be withdrawn from other trades and placed in army service to meet the existing urgent requirements. This request was not granted in its entirety, but more tonnage was allocated to the army from this time on. * * *

Later in July, two representatives of the Shipping Board came to France to examine the question of supply and shipping requirements of the A. E. F. and it was recommended that a thorough and detailed tonnage study be made of requirements from September, 1918, to June, 1919. This was to show the actual needs (by services) as closely as they could be forecast, so that the information could be presented to the Shipping Board and other Allied shipping interests as a concrete estimate of the necessities of the A. E. F. and an argument for obtaining the allocation of additional tonnage; and also for the purpose of providing the Supply Bureaus in the United States with a well defined outling of A. E. F. requirements on which to base their manufacturing programs.

This tonnage study was made under the direction of the Commanding General, S. O. S., by a board convened by S. O. No. 161, Par. 200, S. O. S., August 20, 1918. It was based on a troop program of 80 combat divisions and 16 depot divisions and a reduction of the reserve supply to be maintained in the A. E. F. from 90 to 45 days. The requirements of the several services were divided into the following classes:
August 20, 1918. It was based on a troop program of 80 combat divisions and 16 depot divisions and a reduction of the reserve supply to be maintained in the A. E. F. from 90 to 45 days. The requirements of the several services were divided into the foll,wing classes:

(a) Supplies from the United States involving transatlantic transportation.
(b) Supplies from Europe involving cross-channel transportation.
(c) Supplies from Europe not involving ocean transportation

The study was completed and forwarded to the United States, October 10, 1918, and was the most exhaustive and detailed compilation of the essential needs of the supply services yet prepared. Had the war continued it would have been of very great value both to the A. E. F. and to the War Department. However, the signing of the Armistice on November 11 so altered the requirements of the supply services that this study became of no further practical value.

The growing shortage of animals and motor transportation already referred to made the transportation problem increasingly serious, and the situation was again brought to the attention of the War Department by cable on October 9. As the available ship tonnage, including that obtained from the British, was insufficient to meet the requirements of the

November allotment, Washington asked for priority on the bulky materials. On October 19, possible reductions in the allotment were given to meet the situation. At the same time advice was received that additional tonnage had been secured and that as far as practicable future allotments would be met, but in spite of this the revised estimates of tonnage available for November necessitated still further reductions in the November priorities which were made on November 3.

B.   PORT OPERATIONS

Port facilities for supplying the American forces was one of the early problems presented to the General Staff for solution. The channel ports (Calais, Dieppe, Le Havre, and Cherbourg) had been taken over by the British and the A. E. F. was therefore restricted to ports situated on the Atlantic and Mediterranean coasts. The Mediterranean ports were deemed unsuitable on account of the additional submarine risks involved and the increased length of the voyage from the United States with its attendant problems of coaling stations and increased turnaround.

The first ports selected were St-Nazaire and Bordeaux, but before the Armistice was signed the A. E. F. was also using Nantes, Bayonne, Le Havre, Rouen, Brest, Cherbourg, Les Sables-d'Olonne, La Pallice, Granville, St-Malo, La Rochelle, Rochefort, Tonnay-Charente, and Marseille.

In order that the Administrative Section might be in a position to follow port operations accurately, the Commanding General, Line of Communications, was requested in December 1917, to forward daily telegraphic reports showing the total tonnage discharged and evacuated at each port. Based on this information graphic charts were kept showing the daily and cumulative tonnage receipts and evacuations at each port and served to keep both the Administrative Section and the Coordination Section fully informed.

On January 1, 1918 the Director General of Transportation instituted a system of daily reports of port operations on four forms designated as follows:

D. G. T. Form 8 - Report of Dock and Shed Operations.

D. G. T. Form 9 - Report of Car and Barge Operations.

D. G. T. Form 10 - Report of Boat Operations

D. G. T. Form 11 - Report of classified tonnage unloaded and evacuated from custody of Army Transport Service.

The information contained in these reports was compiled and forwarded daily by the Director General of Transportation to the Administrative Section where a system of charts was instituted to show graphically the daily tonnage discharged and evacuated from ports, classified by ports and services; the arrival and departure of transports; the detention of transports in French ports; and the turnaround of transports. These charts indicated;

1.   Average number of days turnaround of transports (per month).

2.   Number of days turnaround for each transport.

3.   Average detention of transports in French ports (per month).

4.   Number of days detention in French port for each transport.

5.   Transport position graphic.

6.   Comparison of actual tonnage discharged with dead-weight tonnage capacity of transports (per month).

7.   Actual versus estimated unloading capacity of ports.

8.   Tonnage discharged classified by services (per month).

9.   Total monthly port receipts, by ports.

10.   Total daily port receipts.

11.   Daily car situation, by ports.

An inspection of the base ports was made by an officer of the Administrative Section and a report submitted on February 17, 1918, covering the facilities of French ports and their ability to handle the increased tonnage which would result from an increase in the transport fleet, and indicating the possibilities of additional ports and further dock construction. His recommendations laid stress on the importance of providing adequate storage space near the ports and the construction of additional trackage. The existing low rate of discharge was found to be due to the lack of cars and adequate space on the docks, as well as the necessity for ships to change berths in order to utilize the few heavy duty cranes. The limiting factor in the transportation of supplies was the rate of discharge. In order to increase this it was recommended that:

(a) Additional storage space be obtained near ports to relieve existing congestion.

(b) Additional trackage be constructed to facilitate the movement of cars at terminals.

(c) All new dock construction projects be hastened to completion.

The development of ports to handle the cargo tonnage expected was also taken up by the Director General of Transportation and exhaustive studies made by his representatives, which studies were reviewed by G-1. Colonel Wilgus' report of March 7 (referred to in Section A) was analyzed and commented upon under date of March 23 as follows:

Attention was invited to the recommendations for (1) giving priority of shipment to cars, locomotive, and material for port and railway construction; (2) giving priority to personnel for port operation and construction; and (3) furnishing to the C-in-C reports of the Shipping Board, covering assignments of shipping and estimates of new ship construction The opinion was expressed that the possibility of improving and enlarging the facilities of French ports so as to transport to France and maintain a force of 900,000 men by July 1, 1918, was very much overestimated. Attention was also invited to the order issued February 16, 1918, by the Director of Storage and Traffic defining the duties of the Shipping Control Committee. It was recommended that similar order be issued defining the duties of the Army Transport Service, to make that organization responsible for the loading, operation, and control of docks and wharves and the construction of all facilities connected therewith.

The report of February 17 and the analysis of March 23 stimulated port construction and brought to the attention of the Commander-in-Chief the importance of the early completion of the S. O. S. organization so that it would be prepared to carry out its part of the military program.

Following these recommendations and in view of a cable received under date of April 16, 1918, regarding the ability of the A. E. F. to unload and handle promptly the tonnage required by the increased troop program, a board was convened by S. O. No. 20, S. O. S., April 2, 1918, to consider and report on the dock and port situation at that date and the future development to be undertaken to meet the increasing demands. The board was instructed to make recommendations that would provide facilities exclusive of the port of Marseille, for a daily discharge of 50,000 tons, but a difference of opinion developed as to the way in which this should be accomplished. The majority was of the opinion that the Talmont project was necessary to relieve the lighterage situation and provide adequate dock facilities and that the docks at American Bassens were not suitable for the heavy gantry cranes ordered. It recommended that the Talmont project be undertaken and that a lighter type of crane be obtained from England ,or use at Bassens and the gantry cranes disposed of to the French. The minority reported that the construction of the Talmont docks was unnecessary and that efforts should be directed to increasing the present facilities instead of embarking on the difficult Talmont project. On the question of gantry cranes the minority expressed the view that their rejection was unjustified at that time.

The question of the ability of available ports to handle the increased movement of supplies was the subject of a further study prepared in G-1 under date of June 26, 1918. This pointed out the low rate of discharge per ship discharging which was far below that estimated, and would have to be largely increased in order to meet the increasing requirements of the A. E. F.

As early as May, 1918, port conditions indicated that it would be impossible to handle the necessary tonnage of supplies for the maintainance of the force proposed, and it was strongly recommended by G-1 that the French be approached as to the use of 7 berths at

Marseille. This recommendation was favorably acted upon after consulation with Admiral Sims, even though it was clearly appreciated that the Navy would be called upon to provide a most difficult convoying system through the dangerous waters of the Mediterranean. Marseille was first used in July 1918, and up to January 1, 1919, there had been unloaded there approximately 430,000 tons of cargo, or about 13% of the transatlantic tonnage delivered to the A. E. F. during that period.

The views of the Embarkation Service regarding the A. E. F. port situation were expressed in a cable dated July 25, 1918. The position was there taken that owing to the detention of transports at French ports it would be useless to place additional tonnage in service, and it was pointed out that the vessels at that time in French ports, exclusive of cross-channel transports, equalled the number of berths available. It was apparent that port detention as figured by the Embarkation Service included the time waiting for convoy. Reply cables under date of August 14 were therefore sent, describing fully the existing port situation, giving the number of vessels in port and the number of idle berths, and demonstrating that French ports were not being worked to a maximum capacity owing to a lack of sufficient vessels. It was urgently requested by a subsequent cable dated August 16, 1918, that every effort be made to increase ship tonnage in order to keep the ports filled and working to maximum capacity.

A cable was received under date of September 6, 1918, estimating the tonnage to be moved in September at 792,000 tons. In view of this estimate an analysis of the port and berth situation was made in G-1 on September 12, setting forth the possibility of increasing facilities. It was recommended that the use of the ports of Marseille and Toulon be increased, and cablegrams were sent to the United States requesting the assignment of more cargo ships to Marseille, especially recommending that oil burners be so assigned. This was favorably acted upon by the embarkation authorities and vessels began to arrive at that port in numbers comparable to its facilities.

C. REQUISITION AND PRIORITY OF SUPPLIES

When the United States first began its shipment of troops to France the several organizations before sailing placed orders for certain equipment and supplies to follow overseas and took with them all those available for which space could be found. In many cases canteen equipment, company mess equipment, and other troop property was brought with the organizations at the expense of more essential supplies. The several supply bureaus in the United States placed orders for the manufacture and delivery of equipment and supplies, and as these were accepted by the government, they were rushed to seaboard. At the same time the heads of the supply services, A. E. F., began to cable instructions and orders to the United States for the shipment of such supplies and equipment as their best estimates indicated to be necessary.

This early lack of well organized machinery in the United States for the transportation and delivery of supplies to an embarkation port, and the fact that orders were being placed in the United States by the different supply services independently of one another, created at seaboard a condition which would have taxed to the limit a well established system, even if sufficient ocean tonnage had been available. Inasmuch as the tonnage was inadequate, the result was the discharge in France of a conglomerate cargo of supplies, insufficient to meet even the then existing demands. In other words, there was lack of coordination between requisition, purchase, delivery, and shipment in accordance with existing needs.

Under G. O. No. 8, A. E. F., July 5, 1917, the Administrative Section was charged with the supervision of the priority of supply shipments, and the locality of purchase of these supplies, as well as with the general weighing and balancing of demands and requirements in materials from the standpoint of the Operations Section. To enable it properly to carry out these functions, the several supply services were directed to furnish it with copies of all existing requisitions on order in the United States. When these were received it clearly appeared that, although they had been based upon the best estimates then available, the capacity for production of certain supplies in the United States, their delivery at seaboard, and the program of transatlantic transportation had not been carefully considered. It thereupon became the function of the Administrative Section to investigate carefully the shipping tonnage available for Army service, as well as to determine how much of this tonnage should be actually allocated to the Army by the Shipping Board.

As already stated, supplies for the original expedition were received by the individual supply departments on requisitions placed in the United States before sailing. Subsequently it became necessary to coordinate the entire matter of supply and adopt a general policy to govern this important phase of the operations of the A. E. F. Supplies were divided into two classes, automatic and exceptional. Under automatic supplies were included articles such as food, forage, clothing, ammunition, vehicles, etc., which are consumed each month in proportion to the number of troops in the A. E. F. Under exceptional supplies were included all articles not uniformly consumed, such as materials for construction and special supplies to make up existing shortages.

The unit adopted for automatic supply was 25,000 men; that is, all requisitions for automatic supplies were based on the supply of 25,000 men for one month, supplies being shipped from the United States in multiples of that unit depending on the strength of the A. E. F.

The reserve to be maintained in depots was fixed at 90 days' supply. This was to be built up by sending over a three months' supply with all troops sent to France, in addition to the one month's automatic supply for maintenance. The reserve supply was later referred to as initial supply.

On September 7, 1917, the foregoing classification was put into effect by instructing the chiefs of supply services to have their requisitions placed on a monthly automatic basis, providing for a reserve supply of 90 days as above outlined.

The imminent shortage of ocean tonnage made it necessary to provide some system of priority for essential supplies. On September 25, 1917, each supply service was requested to draft a statement showing the priority that it desired for the shipment of supplies on requisition. These statements were consolidated into a priority list and cabled the United States on October 6. In this connection, the Service of the Rear Project, dated September 6, 1917, and the Priority Schedule, giving the priority of shipments of personnel, dated September 22 were consulted in order to coordinate supply and personnel shipments.

The requisitions which were being forwarded to the United States at this time by the several supply services were apparently in excess of their requirements, and included duplications. In order to control this situation and obtain a complete record of all outstanding requisitions, a conference was held on December 26, 1917, with representatives of the supply services, at which a method of making out requisition and tonnage tables was outlined. These tables were divided into two classes, automatic supplies and exceptional supplies. The former showed a complete list of supplies requisitioned on an automatic basis, classified by items, and the latter a complete list of supplies requisitioned on an exceptional basis, classified by items, arranged according to the priority desired and divided into eight phases to correspond to the phases given in the priority schedule of troop movements. The requisition number, cable number, weight tons, and ship tons of each item were shown.

The purpose of these tables was to provide a list of all supplies on requisition either for shipment from the United States or for procurement in Europe through the General Purchasing Board. It was intended to add to them all future requisitions and check off all receipts in order to maintain a live record for the purpose of controlling and coordinating supply shipments. While furnishing an accurate list of all requisitions placed by the separate supply services and an indication of their requirements, these tables could not be maintained as intended, owing to the lack of sufficiently detailed information to check supplies received.

It became apparent in February, 1918, in spite of efforts that had been made to reduce tonnage requirements by purchase in Europe, that a more definite system for limiting shipments from the United States was necessary. A cable was sent to Washington on February 20 requesting information concerning any priority scheme that was being followed in the United States in forwarding supplies and the prospect of ocean tonnage movements for the next two months. The cable also requested a forecast of contemplated shipments, classified to show the supplies to be shipped by each supply bureau and the previous shipments of each. This information was to be used as the basis for allotments to each A. E. F. supply service for the following month. Subsequently the following cable was sent to Washington proposing a scheme of allotment which would provide priority for essential supplies and cause the supply departments to cut their existing requisitions to meet the tonnage situation:

681-S-1

March 5

For Chief of Staff. With reference to paragraph 1A our cablegram 628 in which we suggest that we make allotments of tonnage here following outlines our idea of handling this matter.

(A) On the 15th of each month you to cable us amount of tonnage dead weight of 2,000 pound tons and ship tons of 40 cubic feet which will probably sail from United States ports during the succeeding calendar month. This will not include tonnage for troop personnel or baggage and equipment of organizations which accompanies them. We will previously cable you what tonnage will probably sail from French ports in time to be counted in your estimate.

(B) We will set aside 10 per cent of tonnage you report to cover possible changes and allow for working margin in the United States. From remainder we will allot first, tonnage which should be devoted to the shipment of automatic supplies and initial Quartermaster supplies; second, allotments of remainder will be made to our different services according to their needs and calculated upon our whole military project.

(C) On notification of their allotments the different services will submit cables covering what they want shipped of known available exceptional supplies on their requisitions or of available supplies for which an emergency need has arisen. If they do not desire to cable for particular items, their respective services in the United States will be left to forward materials, within the limits of the allotments, as per existing requisitions.

* * * * * *

(E) If ten percent margin is available or unforeseen tonnage becomes available at time of loading utilization of such tonnage will be filled by you from requisitions as at present.

(F) Early reply on foregoing requested. Pershing.

This scheme was accepted by the War Department and the first allotment was cabled March 26, 1918, giving the priorities for April shipment. The allotments were exclusive of troop equipment, refrigerated tonnage, and oil in bulk shipped in tank steamers. They were calculated as follows:

(a) On receipt of the cable giving the estimates of the Supply Bureaus in the United States of freight available for April shipment, and the Shipping Board's estimate of the amount of shipping space that would be available, each service was allotted a certain amount of space, based upon its requirements, the general military program and the amount of supplies known to be available for shipment.

(b) In order to calculate the tonnage of automatic supplies, multipliers were used based on the estimated numbers of troops to be in France on April 1 and the program of troop shipments during April. To calculate the tonnage of initial supplies, multipliers were used based on the number of troops to be shipped to France during April.

(c) After deducting 5 percent of the Shipping Board's estimate of available tonnage, and certain essential requirements, such as automatic quartermaster supplies of food, forage and clothing, automatic medical supplies, etc., the remaining tonnage was divided among the several services in accordance with a summary of the supplies on requisition as given in the requisition and tonnage tables. (5% instead of 10% was deducted, as the estimate of the Shipping Board was below the tonnage required to meet the needs of the service.)

The allotments were balanced as far as possible with regard to weight tonnage (2000 pounds) and space tonnage (40 cubic feet) to provide cargoes for the maximum carrying capacity of all transports. Estimates covering the relation between weight tons and space tons for the different services were obtained from abstracts of manifests of cargo transports on previous voyages.

The allotments to the services thus determined were transmitted to the C. G., S. O. S. for the preparation by the chiefs of the supply departments of detailed priority cables giving the separate items in the order of their urgency. These several proposed cablegrams were submitted to G-1, S. O. S., whose duty it was to review them and consult G-4 on items that did not appear to be essential. When G-1, S. O. S., had approved the allotments they were sent to G-1, G. H. Q., for final approval, G-1, then reviewed the cables, made cuts or additions, consulted with G-3 on matters involving the supply of arms and ammunition to meet the operations program, and with G-4 on matters of general supply, transportation, etc., and forwarded the final approved priority cables to the embarkation authorities in the United States.

The proper distribution of tonnage under the allotment system was accomplished by the collection of all available information as to the needs of the several supply services as shown by their requisitions and by the military program, as well as by keeping closely informed of all the available ship tonnage which was to be put in the transatlantic cargo trade for the A. E. F. A careful study was prepared to show the relation of weight tons of 2,000 lbs. to ship tons of 40 cubic feet of all items on requisition by the several supply services, so the ship space consumed would not exceed the amount allotted.

In order to allow sufficient time for the supply bureaus in the United States to arrange the manufacture of supplies and control their movement to embarkation ports to conform to the priority schedules, the War Department requested by cable of April 21, 1918, that supplies be called for on a 90-day priority basis, and that at the time of submitting the monthly priority lists a tentative allotment be submitted for the two following months. A reply of April 22, 1918, outlined a tentative allotment scheme as follows:

At the time of cabling monthly allotments tentative priorities were to be cabled for the two succeeding months. In order to make an adjustment every 30 days, the practice of cabling specific allotments each month to supersede the tentative allotments theretofore made was to be continued. At the time the specific priority list was sent for the succeeding month a tentative allotment was to be sent for the third month in advance, thereby maintaining a 90-day priority.

The first tentative allotments were sent for the months of July and August at the time of cabling the June priority list. When the tentative allotments for July and August were cabled, it was stated that they were only to be used as a guide for the movement of supplies to ports. At the time of cabling the final July allotment it was further stated that the final allotment superseded and automatically cancelled the tentative allotment. However, it was apparent from a cable received under date of June 29, 1918, that confusion was caused by forwarding excess and tentative allotment cables and, on July 4, 1918, the A. E. F. was requested to hold supplemental tonnage and priority schedules in abeyance. By reason of this confusion the policy of forwarding tentative allotments was suspended.

However, owing to the difficulty experienced by the supply bureaus in identifying items on allotments and arranging shipments, the A. E. F. was requested by cable of August 10, 1918, to anticipate its needs three months in advance, and a reply cable of August 18, 1918, outlined a plan for the renewal of the tentative allotment system. The final allotments for each month were to be cabled to the United States by the middle of the preceding month, and at the same time the tentative allotments for the two following months were to be forwarded by courier, thereby maintaining the 90-day priority requested.

On May 2, a conference was held with representatives of G-4 and the Engineer Department for the purpose of making substantial cuts in the engineer requisitions then pending and so meeting the manufacturing conditions in the United States and the ship tonnage situation. Following this conference substantial reductions were effected. Cancellations were also made in the Transportation, Air Service, Motor Transport, Ordnance, and Quartermaster Corps requisitions of items such as steel buildings not absolutely necessary for the housing of heavy machinery, lumber, cranes, etc.

Following an agreement of the French to furnish horses, their shipment from the United States had been practically stopped by cable of March 22, 1918, and animal transports stripped of their fittings and placed in cargo service. An agreement of the French to supply the hay requirements of the A. E. F. to August 1, 1919, made it possible to reduce considerably the quartermaster allotment, to the benefit of the other supply services. The subsequent inability of the French government to meet fully the animal and hay requirements of the A. E. F. created a critical shortage of these two articles and it was necessary to ask that certain ships be withdrawn from general cargo service to be refitted for the transportation of animals from the United States. In addition, it was necessary to make an allotment of approximately 42,000 tons to meet the hay deficit. These reductions in available shipping tonnage curtailed the tonnage allotments to the supply services to such an extent that an urgent request was sent the United States on July 19, 1918, for additional shipping.

In order to avoid confusion on the part of the supply bureaus in the United States in connection with cables dealing with changes in priority and new requisitions, a new form of tonnage statement, to be used for all cables dealing with supplies, was adopted on May 11, 1918. These statements were to provide G-1 with the necessary information concerning dead-weight and space tonnage of the articles ordered and the date of delivery desired. The reverse side outlined the prescribed method of showing (a) changes in priority; (b) cancellations or additions to the allotment; and, (c) new requisitions to be placed, whether automatic or exceptional. The adoption of this form of requisition necessitated a careful preparation of supply cables and had a beneficial effect in that the service concerned was required to justify the order at the time it was placed and eliminate equivalent tonnage on its own allotment to provide space for new items.

[The report here discusses the allotments for April, May, June, and July, already mentioned, and quotes at length from Cable No. 1487, July 19, 1918, and G. O. No. 130, A. E. F., 1918. Of these, Cable No. 1487 is printed in Chap. I, this report.]

The Commanding General, S. O. S., was further authorized to send direct from his headquarters cables and other correspondence concerning supplies which did not involve large questions of policy. The adoption of this plan relieved G-1 of the duties of preparing tonnage allotments and priorities and of all correspondence and cables dealing with questions of supply except where policy was concerned.

It is not deemed practicable to annex to this report copies of the voluminous studies, estimates, and reports and the very large number of cables which dealt with the difficult question of tonnage from the inception of the A. E. F. to the signing of the Armistice. The more important of these exhibits have been referred to, and all are on record and are available for reference.

The insufficiency of adequate tonnage to meet the essential needs of the A. E. F. was a difficulty which continued with increasing acuteness from the beginning to the end. At no time was there sufficient tonnage, and consequently at no time were there sufficient supplies or equipment for the A. E. F. The general reasons for the world shortage of tonnage are well understood and need not be here discussed. In the face of such shortage, the immediate problem was that of allocation of available tonnage to best serve the purposes of the Allies and the United States. Every government, and every service of every government, needed and demanded additional tonnage, rendering the work of those whose duty it was to allocate tonnage a most difficult and complicated task.

Cables were exchanged with the War Department with great frequency upon this subject setting forth the vitally essential needs of the A. E. F. and urging increased allotments.

* * * * * *

The following is a brief summary of the tonnage cabled for from the United States in the critical months of July, August, September, and October; the amount assigned to the A. E. F. in the United States; the amount floated in the United States, and the amount actually received in France. All figures are exclusive of refrigeration, coal, animals, oil in bulk, and troop property.

TONS OF 2000 POUNDS

MONTH	CABLED FOR BY A. E. F.	SHIPPING BOARD'S ESTIMATE OF TONNAGE A-VAULABLE FOR A. E. F.	FLOATED IN U. S.	RECEIVED IN FRANCE FROM U. S.
July	480,891	475,000	519,304	438,047
August	700,527	700,000	599,840	511,261
September	869,438	750,000	643,450	530,018
October	1,022,135	850,000	722,222	623,689

Certain of the foregoing figures were adjusted after cable 1685 was sent on September 13, and therefore vary slightly from the figures there quoted.

Complete records of all tonnage and shipping matters were kept at all times in the Transportation Department of the Services of Supply; and after the issuance of G. O. No. 130, August 6, 1918, as already stated, all matters relating to supply and transportation, except matters of policy and certain specific reservations, were handled by the Commanding General, S. O. S. His report will give the full statistical and other detailed information concerning tonnage and transportation covering all the operations of the A. E. F. and should be referred to for that purpose.

Upon the signing of the Armistice steps were taken to cancel orders for supplies that were no longer essential due to the changed conditions. Suspensions and cancellations of requisitions were made by cable of November 15, and subsequent cancellations were made from time to time until the manufacturing and shipping programs at home were modified to meet the decreasing needs of the A. E. F.

D. SUPPLIES FROM EUROPEAN SOURCES

The inadequacy of available ocean tonnage to meet fully the supply needs of the A. E. F. made necessary the scientific utilization of European markets to the fullest extent possible.

To effect this end, and to prevent competitive bidding in Europe by various supply services, the General Purchasing Board was organized under G. O. No. 23, A. E. F., August 20, 1917. The General Purchasing Agent at the head of this Board was expressly designated the representative of the C. in C. to coordinate and supervise all purchasing agents in the A. E. F. Through representatives on the Board each Supply Service was kept in current touch with the resources of European markets, which were availed of in all possible cases in preference to the transportation overseas of supplies purchased in the United States.

To insure the utmost adherence to this policy the original requisitions of the supply services were examined in the Administrative Section and articles found to be purchasable in Europe removed. A memorandum of December 29, 1917, directed the supply services to furnish the Administrative Section and the General Purchasing Agent with a bi-monthly report of all purchases made in Europe showing outstanding orders, quantity of supplies delivered, pending orders, and an estimate of the tonnage involved. This information was supplemented by quarterly forecasts of requirements from European sources furnished in response to memorandum of January 25, 1918, and beginning with the second quarter of 1918 estimates of supplies procurable from European sources were furnished to the supply services by the General Purchasing Agent. This information was also furnished to the War Department by cable and appropriate cancellations were there made in outstanding requisitions.

All of these measures resulted in a great saving of ocean tonnage, particularly in bulky products like coal, lumber, and forage, and in animals. A marked saving was also effected in such manufactured products as aeroplanes and aviation supplies, artillery and ordnance supplies, and certain technical supplies for the Engineer and Signal Corps.

Under arrangements with the French for the supply of animals and hay, shipments of the former were suspended in April, 1918, and of the latter in May, 1918, although it proved necessary to resume them both in August.

The shipment of railroad ties was suspended in January, 1918, and all lumber in February.

French and British manufactured articles were in many instances made available for American purchase by the use of so-called replacement contracts under which the A. E. F. on purchasing undertook to replace in France and England the raw material involved. Such contracts effected a large immediate saving of tonnage, and the raw material to be shipped later to Europe required much less cargo space than the finished articles purchased. Steel billets, copper, picric acid, etc., are typical of the raw materials usually replaced.

In some cases independent replacement contracts were made by individual supply services. By memorandum of December 19, 1917, the supply services were required to submit to the Administrative Section for approval all requisitions in Europe involving replacement in kind or in raw material. The use of the specific replacement contract was abandoned in the spring of 1918 and the mutual needs of the Allied armies and the A. E. F. for finished products and raw material were coordinated by the Military Board of Allied Supply created under Section III, G. O. No. 100, A. E. F., June 20, 1918.

In the spring of 1918 the British agreed to supply the coal necessary to maintain the A. E. F. and, by agreement with the French, coal was to be delivered to the A. E. F. at any point in France where there was an available supply and replaced with English coal at French ports or other points agreed on. In order to carry out this arrangement a large amount of ship tonnage was assigned to the cross-channel coal service. Vessels of the *Lake* class and a fleet of chartered Swedish vessels were principally used for this purpose.

From June, 1917, to January, 1919, the A. E. F. received from England 1,390,000 tons of coal. Due to the advance of the enemy into the coal producing districts of France, the supply of French coal became so low that it was necessary to ship English coal into the interior to meet A. E. F. requirements, as well as to deliver to the French such coal as they needed to make up their own deficit.

A memorandum prepared in G-1 on October 5, 1918, summarized the coal situation as being more a question of the production and delivery of coal in England than of its cross-channel transportation, as the shipping necessary was by that time adequate to meet the demands.

CHAPTER VI

REMOUNTS

A. SUPPLY OF ANIMALS

On August 24, 1917, the problem of animal supply was summarized as follows in a memorandum from the Chief of the Operations Section to the Chief of Staff:

The most important aspect to the shipment of animals from America is the
amount of tonnage involved. It is estimated that the amount of tonnage space
required for the shipment of animals by sea is from 8 to 10 tons per head.
Estimating that 9,272 animals will be required for each division and adding
10% to cover animals in the hospital we find that on the ten-ton basis, the
total tonnage requirements of a division is 101,992 tons or for 10 divisions,
1,019,920 tons. The importance of this item is obvious.

During July, 1917, 2,821 animals were imported from the U. S. However, on July 1 a
letter had been received from the French Minister of War, stating that France would furnish
the American troops with a total of 7,000 animals per month, beginning September 1, 1917;
and animal shipments from the United States were therefore discontinued after July.

Scarcely had this change in plans been effected when the French advised, on August 24,
that it would be impossible to furnish the number of animals originally stated and that the
best they were able to do was to turn over 4,000 immediately on the understanding that these
would be replaced before November 1, 1917, by importations from the United States. It was
definitely stated that no promises for other deliveries to take place in the future could
be considered.

In view of the changed aspect given to the remount situation as a result of this information, a cablegram was immediately dispatched to the United States, requesting that
all troops being sent overseas be accompanied by authorized allowance of animals. On
September 15, 1917, the total requirements in animals were 11,470, the number on hand
6,123, and the shortage 5,347.

The preparation of horse transports was slow and shipments from the United States
were not resumed until November 10. Meanwhile the number of animals furnished by the
French was not restricted to the 4,000 referred to in their letter of August 24, but grave-
ly exceeded that amount, and all were delivered with the understanding that they would
later be replaced from America. Thus practically the entire animal transport of the 1st
Division and much of that of the 2d was furnished by the French.

On December 18 the French were approached with respect to the replacement of animals
previously furnished by them. It was pointed out that such replacements would immobilize
a considerable number of combat troops, that this would require the conversion of cargo
and passenger boats into horse transports, and that the result would but delay the movement
of American troops and French supplies from the United States. It was therefore requested
that the animals be sold outright to the Americans and this was subsequently done.

On December 25, 1917, 12,414 animals had been furnished by the French and 9,550 imported from the United States, making a total of 21,964 in the A. E. F.

A request was addressed to the French on January 29, 1918, with a view to purchasing
animals in the open market, a course that had not heretofore been resorted to. It was suggested that there was a vast number which could be made available for military service and
that aside from the tonnage problem it was highly desirable to obtain animals in France and
and thus eliminate the risk of sickness during the period of acclimatization. It was
stated that an attempt was being made to buy horses in Spain and other neutral countries
but that the possibility of obtaining any appreciable quantity in that manner was doubtful.

The letter closed as follows:

Would it be asking the French Government too much to request that the whole
question of our animal supply be given the most careful and complete governmental
consideration for the purpose of determining whether it will not be possible for

us to obtain in France the greater proportion of our immediate needs in animals. It is suggested that action on this request be expedited so that if it be determined that such a supply is available to us, immediate cable information may be transmitted to Washington to stop for the time being, the conversion of any more cargo carrying ships into animal transport ships.

The French authorities in reply asked that a statement be submitted showing the number of animals needed and the delivery dates desired. A statement was therefore prepared on the assumption that there would be in France by August 1, 1918, three full army corps, or 18 divisions, with the proper proportion of S. O. S. troops. The fire divisions already in France on February 6, 1918, were only 50% complete as far as animal strength was concerned. The estimated requirements by August 1 would be 187,608 animals. Against this current records showed that there were in France on February 1, 24,521, and 10,000 a month, or 50,000 by August 1, were expected to be received from the United States. The total expected resources for August 1, therefore, amounted to 74,521 animals, leaving 113,087 animals to be purchased in France to meet requirements.

Of this 113,087 it seemed unlikely that any material number could be delivered during February. It was therefore thought best to estimate the desired rate of delivery on a basis of five months (March, April, May, June, and July) with approximately equal numbers each month, or an average of 22,617 animals per month. The French authorities were requested to do the purchasing and subsequently to turn over the animals to us.

[The next paragraphs of the report trace the negotiations with France, Spain, and England and the resulting developments in the supply of animals during 1918, repeating, with some amplification, matter already given in Chapter I.]

* * * * * *

In the meantime the final success of the French requisition began to appear more dubious. On July 10, 1918, only 15,452 animals had been received against estimated receipts of 36,770 as of that date. M. Tardieu, Commissioner for Franco-American War Affairs, however, reiterated the intention of the French government to supply the A.E.F. 80,000 animals. They therefore, agreed that beginning July 20 all animals requisitioned would go to American Remount Service

Following this letter was received dated July 27, 1918, from the chief of the French Military Mission stating that if on August 1, 80,000 animals had not been delivered to the Americans, the deficit would be made up by turning over the necessary number from the French remount depots. The requisition proper netted 74,070 animals to which should be added 3,450 animals delivered from French remount depots and other sources. The grand total of the requisition was therefore 77,520 as compared with the 80,000 animals originally promised.

On September 4, Marshal Foch directed that 13,000 animals be immediately placed at the disposal of the A. E. F. to aid in the preparations for the Argonne offensive. This timely assistance rendered by the French did much to relieve the immediate situation and to allow the full effect of the American arms to be felt. About 8,000 animals were supplied in September and somewhat over 4,000 in October.

No animals were received from the United States in August; 1,839 in September, and 2,570 in October. The situation became so acute that on October 9 another cable was sent to Washington as follows:

On account of non-arrival of motor transportation and animals as hitherto requested our situation with respect to animal transportation is becoming increasingly and alarmingly serious.

P-1474, July 16, forecasted necessity of average shipment of at least 25,000 animals per month, to which A 1742 replied that not more than 11,000 could be shipped prior to September 1. P-1518, July 26 urged immediate transformation numerous vessels into horseboats and P-1684 estimated minimum requirements at 30,000 per month from October to June inclusively which was subsequently increased by C. G., S. O. S., to average of 31,700 per month.

A total of 1,839 animals were received in France in September which constitutes total receipts from U. S. since shipments were discontinued in April. We
are not advised of any further shipments.

The French at great inconvenience and sacrifice to themselves are continuing to furnish small numbers of animals and very few are coming from Spain and
Portugal. These receipts and an adequate supply of motor transportation were
fully considered and discounted in making up our minimum requirements of 31,700
per month which for reasons above given is now insufficient.

A continuing failure to receive animals as called for means immobilization
of our Armies. Please advise me what action will be taken on this request.

There were at this time with combat troops 139,511 animals, against requirements of
245,774, making a shortage of 106,263. The A. E. F. was therefore only about 57% complete
as far as animal strength was concerned.

[The supply of horses and mules from Spain, discussed in the next few paragraphs, is
repeated, in substance, from Chapter I.]

* * * * * *

The English also made some shipments during the early part of November, aggregating
approximately 2,500 animals, and agents were in Italy to examine the possibility of buying
animals in that country but no actual contracts were made for delivery.

17,000 animals had been shipped from the United States during October and 22,500 were
promised for November. 20,716 were received in France in November, and 12,250 in December,
when shipments were stopped. The total number of animals in the A. E. F. on November 11
when the Armistice was signed was 172,313, which represented 51% of the total requirements of approximately 334,000 animals.

Immediately following the signing of the Armistice an old difficulty presented itself
in an aggravated form, namely the shortage of rail facilities for animal trains. This
was caused by the necessity of moving the Third Army to the Rhine, the large number of
war prisoners returning to France, the repatriation of the civilian population of northern
France, and the necessity of at once sending supplies into the devastated regions. American remount depots which, on account of imports from the United States, England, and
Spain, were already crowded, were in danger of becoming hopelessly clogged. The situation was relieved by instructions issued on November 29 providing for an overland convoy
of 500 animals daily from Lux to Longuyon where they were to be taken over by the Third
Army. By this means and with the aid of an occasional train which was secured from the
French, the Third Army was supplied and the remount depots were relieved from the danger
of congestion.

On November 20, contracts for further purchases from Spain and Great Britain were
cancelled and shipments from the United States were ordered discontinued after November
30, 1918.

A final statement showing the total number of animals acquired from the various
sources is appended hereto:

SOURCE	HORSES CAVALRY	HORSES DRAFT	MULES DRAFT	MULES PACK	TOTAL SUPPLIED	
United States	5,937	32835	28,399	553	67,725	27.9
France	21,450	105,472	3,955	5,037	135,914	55.9
England	2,862	10,780	6,674	943	21,259	8.6
Spain	1,400	423	13,347	3,292	18,462	7.6
	31,650	149,510	52,375	9,825	243,360	100.0

B. DISTRIBUTION OF ANIMALS

The matter of distribution was influenced to a great extent by the question of supply. Had there been at all times a sufficient number of animals, distribution would of course have been made according to tables of organization.

The shortage in animals made itself evident with respect to distribution in two ways ---priority schedules and reduction in the allowance of animals in tables or organization.

1. PRIORITY SCHEDULES

A priority schedule as applied to the distribution of animals, was a schedule of the units of the A. E. F. arranged according to their relative importance and indicating the order in which they were to be supplied with animals. It provided a system for the distribution of animals whereby the active combat divisions would be assured of sufficient animals to maintain their mobility. These schedules were issued by G-3 after consultation with G-1. G-1 notified the Remount Service of the priorities established and animals were issued strictly in accordance with the schedule. On January 18, 1918, the priority was established in the following order:

1st Division

26th Division

42d Division

2d Division

A strict interpretation of the priority schedule proved to be a handicap for the newly arrived divisions due to the impossibility of their conducting field problems and training schedules, owing to the lack of the necessary draft animals. Orders were therefore issued that for instruction purposes each artillery brigade upon arrival would be furnished immediately with 200 animals. It was then expected that at the end of 3 weeks the number of animals would be increased to 400 and that the division would be completely equipped within 6 weeks. However, it was impossible to equip divisions six weeks after arrival due to the continuous shortage of animals.

Priority schedules varied of necessity from time to time depending on the expected activity of certain units. Thus, for example, on September 2 a list was issued giving priority to the First Army. This continued in effect until November 9 when certain selected divisions of the First Army were given priority in order to bring them up to strength. Just at the time of the Armistice the priority was shifted to the Second Army and again with the formation of the Third Army it was given priority even to the extent of drawing as many animals as needed from the First and Second Armies. While the priority schedules helped considerably in relieving the situation, it was evident, early in the operations of the A. E. F., that other additional measures would have to be taken in order to make the limited supply of animals cover a wider field of usefulness.

2. REDUCTION IN ALLOWANCES OF ANIMALS IN TABLES OF ORGANIZATION

[This section starts with a repitition of the initial allowance of animals and subsequent reductions given in Chapter I.]

* * * * * *

On August 25, 1918, a further reduction in the allowance of animals to 3,803 was authorized in the case of divisions to be motorized. These reductions were in general to be obtained by---

(a) Dismounting certain of the officers at division headquarters, in the engineer regiment, and in the military police.

(b) Motorizing a part of the baggage and ration wagons and a few other animal-drawn vehicles.

(c) Motorizing the regiment of 155's.

(d) Motorizing the trench mortar battery.

(e) Reducing the number of caissons per battery of 75's from 12 to 8.

(f) Motorizing one of the caisson companies of the horsed battalion of the ammunition train.

(g) Motorizing the remaining animal-drawn field hospital.

(h) Motorizing a part of the engineer train.

Since the reduction proposed was mainly contingent upon motorization, which could only be accomplished gradually, the new allowance was not published in the form of a general order, but was applied to each division after the motorization of its units had been completed. Copies of the new table were however furnished to the C. G., S. O. S., and to the First and Second Armies for guidance during the process of motorization.

In the case of dismounting certain officers and men, the saving in animals became immediately effective irrespective of motorization. Some immediate saving was also made in the case of those artillery brigades which had not yet joined their divisions by temporarily reducing the animal allowance for such brigades to 3,184 instead of 3,754 as provided in G. O. No. 92, a saving of 570 animals. This made a total allowance of 6,093 animals for the division.

It therefore appears that the reduction of August 25 did not relieve the situation to any great extent since the motorization necessary was not immediately available.

On November 22 instructions were issued by G-1 after consultation with G-3 under which the divisions in the Third Army had an authorized strength of 6,093 animals. The divisions in the First and Second Armies were allowed 5,562, the difference of 531 representing the animal allowance of the ammunition train which was not provided for in the smaller allowance.

In order to distribute the animals to better advantage a new table was issued December 5, 1918, from G-1 to the armies on the following basis:

Third Army

Army troops	6,000
Corps troops	4,000 each
Divisions	6,000 each

Second Army

Army troops	4,000
Corps troops	3,000 each
Divisions	3,000 each

First Army

Army troops	4,000
Corps troops	3,000 each
Divisions	3,000 each
Depot divisions	2,000 each

Instructions issued on December 13 kept the allowance of the armies at the same figure but permitted the distribution within the units of the armies under the direction of the commanding general. In other words, the greater part of the animals assigned to corps and army troops might at the direction of the commanding general of that army be divided among the divisions.

With the demobilization of the A. E. F. and the accrual of a surplus of animals left behind by organizations returning to the U. S., the allowance was again increased so that by February, 1919, each division that was not motorized had as nearly 6,093 animals as stable accommodations would permit.

C. CARE AND MAINTENANCE OF ANIMALS

1. CARE OF ANIMALS

During the period of hostilities, the condition of the animals in the A. E. F. had become unsatisfactory due to overwork, the strain of hard campaigns, and the lack of care inevitable in active warfare. In the effort to improve conditions and to give elementary instructions in the principles involved, the following publications were issued from these headquarters:

Bul. No. 8, A. E. F., February 5, 1918: Treatment of mange.
Sec. I, G. O. No. 65, A. E. F., April 30, 1918: General rules for care of animals.
Sec. I, Bul. No. 58, A. E. F., August 15, 1918: General rules for care of animals.
Bul. No. 104, A. E. F., December 19, 1918: General rules for care of animals.
Sec. II, Bul. No. 16, A. E. F., February 25, 1919: Standardized test 'or glanders.

Due to the limited number of animals available for issue and the consequent overworking of those on hand, the problem of keeping the animals with the Armies in serviceable condition was extremely difficult. At times the shortage of animals was so acute that organizations failed to evacuate their sick animals, knowing that they could not be replaced, and preferred to have the use of sick ones rather than none at all.

Mange was prevalent at times and accounted for more disability than any other disease. Mangy animals were sometimes kept with organizations after they should have been evacuated, with the result that a large percentage became permanently unfit for further service. A lack of medicine and necessary facilities for the treatment of this disease added to the gravity of the situation. As soon as these unsatisfactory conditions were discovered, instructions were issued on January 11, 1919, for the supply of the necessary medicines and for the construction of dipping vats, so that as soon as these facilities became available all animals could receive proper and effective treatment.

The remount depots and veterinary hospitals were operated under difficulties on account of the lack of trained personnel and proper equipment. The former made itself evident not only in the insufficient attention given to the animals, but also in the delay in completing construction work required for improving sanitary conditions.

Due to the lack of sufficient accommodations in the Advance Section, S. O. S., there was at first a continuous evacuation of large numbers of animals mostly affected with mange to hospitals in the Intermediate Sections, and even to hospitals at St-Nazaire and La Rochelle. The contamination of fresh clean horses from the United States was traced, in some instances, to the presence of these mangy animals. On December 4, 1918, these conditions were discovered and instructions were issued prohibiting the shipment of animals affected with contagious diseases, except when absolutely necessary, and requiring more strict segregation of diseased animals.

On February 1, 1918, steps were taken to formulate an agreement with the French for the mutual care of animals, whereby American animals left with the French or straying into French zones would be assured of proper care and treatment, whether left in French military establishments or with the French inhabitants. The substance of the agreements is published in Bul. No. 19, A. E. F., March 22, 1918. The rate of reimbursement allowed to civilians and to the French Army as there published was changed on October 1, 1918, by reason of the increase in the cost of forage and was published in Sec. 2, Bul. No. 106, A. E. F., 1918.

2. FORAGE

The question of forage has been the subject of considerable study, and it is believed that experience has proved that the present regulation ration is sufficient to keep animals in good condition while on active service. The scarcity of forage in Europe during the first half of the year 1918 forced a reduction in the ration, but this was increased as forage became available. The following table shows the daily allowance as given in army regulations and in general orders for 1918:

Daily allowance as authorized by	Classification	Forage Allowance, lbs. Oats	Hay
Army Regulations, Par. 1077	Horses, heavy draft	14	17
	Horses, light draft	12	14
	Mules	9	14
G. O. No. 14, A. E. F., Jan. 25, 1918	Horses	10	10
	Mules	8	10
G. O. No. 34, A. E. F., Feb. 25, 1918	Horses, heavy draft engaged in forestry operations	14	17
G. O. 79, A. E. F., May 27, 1918	Horses, heavy draft	12	14
	Horses, light draft	10	14
	Mules	8	12

Permission granted to increase forage ration to allowance given in army regulations, Par. 1077, when animals were engaged in heavy work and when in the opinion of division or separate organization commander such action was necessary to preserve the health and strength of the animals.

Daily Allowance as Authorized by	Classification	Forage Allowance, lbs. Oats	Hay
G. O. 174, A. E. F., Oct. 9, 1918	Horses, heavy artillery	14	14
	Horses, light artillery	10	10
	Horses, cavalry	9	9
	Mules, draft	9	10
	Mules, pack and riding	7	8
G. O. 208, A. E. F., No. 16, 1918	For animals employed continuously for ten hours or more per day on heavy forestry work or in hauling fuel wood from forest to roads.		
	Horses, heavy artillery	17	17
	Mules, draft	10	14

3. IMPROVEMENT OF CONDITIONS

It was obvious that any action toward improving the condition of animals in the A. E. F. must take into consideration two important factors: Instruction in the care of animals and personal interest of officers and men in their care.

On November 16, 1918, G-1 recommended to the Commander-in-Chief that schools for the care of animals be established in divisions, corps, and armies. This recommendation was approved and schools were started under the supervision of G-5. As a result of this measure a marked improvement took place in the condition of animals.

It is well recognized that the best way to stimulate interest in any subject is to create a spirit of competition. With this in mind, G-1 took up the question of holding horse shows in divisions, corps, and armies and on January 5, 1919, submitted a proposed bulletin to the Chief of Staff. The principle was approved, and with certain changes the bulletin was published as Bul. No. 3, A. E. F., January 17, 1919.

The results obtained from these horse shows have justified them from every point of view. The rewards offered for the best entries and penalties inflicted on organizations having animals showing a lack of proper care have brought into play a spirit of competition which has done more than any one thing to instill in the minds of both officers and men an interest in the proper care of animals.

D. DISPOSITION OF ANIMALS

1. DEAD AND CONDEMNED ANIMALS

The question of the disposition of dead and condemned animals came up early in the operations of the A. E. F. The problem with respect to dead animals was a particularly difficult one to deal with. There was without a doubt a demand for dead animals by salvage units, but there was difficulty experienced in getting the carcasses to the rendering plants, as the railroads refused to accept them for shipment. The only recourse was to dispose of caraasses in the most convenient manner on the spot. In some instances they were turned over to neighboring American or French salvage units; in other cases they were given to the local inhabitants who in turn for the hides agreed to remove and dispose of them.

The first action taken with regard to animals condemned as unfit for further military service was to dispose of them locally at auction. On June 15, 1918, a contract was entered into with a wholesale butcher in Paris for the taking over of condemned animals for butchery purposes. This contract, which expired on September 30, 1918, was made along lines similar to an agreement made by the English authorities for the sale of their condemned animals.

The French were of the opinion that many animals were being butchered which might be fit for agricultural purposes and finally after considerable discussion an agreement was consummated on October 5, 1918, whereby the French Government agreed to take over all condemned animals at a flat rate of 450 francs, each, regardless of conditions. This agreement was published in Sec. II, Bul. No. 84, A. E. F., October 28, 1918, and in Sec. I, Bul. No. 92, A. E. F., November 13, 1918.

In certain exceptional cases where an animal had been badly injured and had to be killed immediately, the French granted permission to turn over the animal in question to the local butcher.

2. AFTER THE ARMISTICE

[The sale of animals, discussed in this section, is also given in Chapter I.]

* * * * * *

Pending the execution of the agreement with the French, the number of surplus animals had been increasing, particularly in the Second and Third Armies, which were so situated that the French could not easily make arrangements for animal trains. As the divisions of these armies returned to the United States, the animals were left behind in the Army Areas and the best selected to replace animals in other divisions which were not in first class condition.

The majority of these surplus animals were not suitable for condemnation but the forage and cost of maintenance involved made it highly desirable that they should be disposed of at the earliest possible moment. To provide an outlet, authority was requested from the Liquidation Commission to dispose of the surplus animals by sale in Belgium and Luxemburg, inasmuch as there appeared to be a considerable demand for animals in both of these places. The request was approved on February 26, 1919, and the commanding generals of the Second and Third Armies were instructed to proceed on that basis. The shortage of forage in Belgium and Luxemburg was so acute that the civilian population could not purchase the much needed animals, and only a very small number of animals was actually sold.

Meanwhile the Third Army had been selling condemned animals, fit only for butchering, in the occupied German territory at prices which, in many instances, were higher than those obtained in France for sound animals.

On March 12, authority to sell surplus serviceable animals in occupied Germany was requested for the Liquidating Commission and was at first disapproved.

The sale of animals to the French was proceeding so slowly that the sale of animals in Germany appeared to be a necessity. Accordingly the matter was taken up again on March 31, and on April 5 the sale of animals in occupied Germany was approved as a military policy by the Commander-in-Chief, under conditions by which every animal was to be retained in that territory with a record of its location, so that all of them could easily be collected again in case of emergency.

On April 8 the Liquidation Commission was again consulted and permission was secured to sell 2,000 animals which were available at that time in occupied Germany; but with the provision that the sale of surplus animals in the future was to be undertaken after further consultation with the Commission.

The following is a statement of the disposition of animals as of April 9, 1919:

Total purchased for A. E. F.	243,360	
Total animal deaths in A. E. F.	56,603	
Balance	186,757	168,757
Total condemned animals turned over to French	4,569	
Total condemned animals sold to butchers	9,896	
Animals turned over to French Govt. for sale	14,954	
Animals sold by U. S. at private sale in France	4,066	
Animals sold by U. S. at public auction in France	6,680	
Animals sold by U. S. at public auction in Germany	3,307	
Animals in French veterinary hospitals	238	
	43,710	43,710
Grand total of animals in A. E. F., April 9, 1918		143,047

CHAPTER VII

BILLETS AND BILLETING

A. THE FRENCH BILLETING SYSTEM

The right of military requisition in France, including the right of billeting and quatering troops, is based upon the law of July 3, 1877, the decree of August 2, 1877, and subsequent laws, judgments, and ministerial decrees. These vest in the commanding generals of armies, army corps, and troops having special missions the full right of requisition. The right can be and in practice usually is delegated to chiefs of staff or to subordinate commanders.

The successful operation of the French billeting system demands that each town be prepared at all times to submit to the right of requisition and to accommodate as many troops as the spare capacity of the buildings will permit. Moreover, the billeting of troops must be accomplished in an orderly and rapid manner. It is obvious that these conditions cannot be complied with unless there has been a considerable amount of preparation, consisting mainly of billeting data which will indicate how the incoming troops may best be distributed. Therefore, in order to make the billeting system practicable and effective, the laws governing the procedure direct that the mayor of each town shall keep on file at all times a record of the location and number of available accommodations for officers, men, and animals, and, in addition, the amount of surplus space available for the storage of military supplies.

Whenever circumstances permit, the troops must be quartered in buildings belonging to the state, the department, the commune, or public establishments, but in the event that there are not sufficient accommodations in such buildings the troops may be billeted among the inhabitants.

The established rate of payment per night is as follows:

1 franc for each officer provided with a bed.

20 centimes for each noncommissioned officer or soldier provided with a bed.

5 centimes for each noncommissioned officer, soldier, or animal provided with shelter only.

After the commanding officer of the troops to be billeted has made his requisition, the mayor of the town consults his records and issues *billets de logement* or tickets bearing on their face the number and kind of accommodations to be furnished and the names of the inhabitants furnishing them. An acting town major is appointed from among the officers of the command whose duty it is to distribute the billets in such a way as to keep units together as far as possible and also to issue and enforce regulations relating to billets, water supply, washing, latrines, fire protection, refuse disposal, traffic regulations, and similar matters. In towns where French troops are habitually billeted or where their presence is a likely occurrence, there are permanent town majors. They take over the billeting duties from the mayor, keep the record of available quarters, make leases and requisitions, and, in general, look after the military interests in the town. In addition to the billeting duties of the mayor, they perform the duties outlined above for the acting town major, lay out the town so as to accommodate military units, and are responsible for enforcing suitable billeting instructions. The principal distinction between a town major and an acting town major is that the former is a permanent official having a fixed geographical position whereas the latter belongs to the organization billeting in the town and moves with it. Wherever there is a town major the commanding general of troops desiring billets makes his request directly to him and he makes all the necessary arrangements for compliance.

An improvement developed during the war was the formation of areas or districts comprising a number of adjacent towns with a total billeting capacity sufficient to accommo-

date a French division or artillery brigade. The advantage of this scheme was particularly evident in rest or training areas immediately in rear of the front lines, where a large
organization could be accommodated in an orderly manner with a minimum amount of confusion. These areas or, as they were often called zones, were placed under the administration of an officer known as a zone major or area commandant to whom the various town
majors reported.

B. ADOPTION OF BILLETING SYSTEM FOR THE A. E. F.

In the United States the billeting of troops on the civilian population, except in
time of war, is forbidden by the Federal Constitution and tentage has therefore always
been the main reliance as shelter for the military forces.

When the American Expeditionary Forces came to France the proper sheltering of troops
demanded an immediate decision between continuing to use tentage or barracks and using
the billeting facilities available in France. Some of the Advantages of the latter system follow:

Convenience. The headquarters for the soldiers are immediately available for occupancy and at the same time they can be evacuated on short notice.

Improved living conditions. The quarters are more roomy and weatherproof. The
soldier is to that extent more contented, sickness is reduced, and the morale maintained
at a higher standard.

Economy: The billeting system provides better shelter at a lower cost. A canvas
tent in use depreciates very rapidly, the average period of serviceability being from
6 to 9 months.

Saving in transportation: This includes not only the shipping space and tonnage involved in shipping tents overseas, but also the transportation in France.

Increased mobility of troops: Troops can evacuate billets rapidly and are not en-
cumbered with the transportation of thousands of tents.

For these reasons, and since the French offered their full assistance, the policy of
billeting troops in France was adopted by the A. E. F. The rate of payment per night
for American troops was the same as for the French.

Having adopted this policy, the next step was to arrange for the procedure to be
followed. On May 28, 1917, French General Headquarters submitted their recommendations
to the chief of the American Mission. It was thought advisable that the American divisions, immediately after their arrival in France, should be placed in camps or billets
at an intermediate point located in the central part of France where they would have an
opportunity to become acclimated and get their preliminary training before entering the
Zone of the Armies.

Following a stay in such a locality of from four to six weeks, the divisions were to
proceed to American training areas to be established near the front, in order that the
American soldiers might be in the atmosphere of war, be close to the French army schools
for instruction purposes, and be constantly in association with French troops recently
withdrawn from the front line, from whom they could acquire much valuable information as
to the latest methods employed at the front.

Four training areas were suggested for American use: Gondrecourt, Neufchâteau,
Saffais, Mirecourt. The first two were later accepted and became known as Areas No. 1
and 2.

In August, 1914, the British Expeditionary Forces had been granted the right to mili
tary requisition in France, and it was considered advisable that similar authority should
be obtained for the A. E. F., expecially in view of the prospect of conducting independent military operations. A letter from the French Under-Secretary of State for the General
Administration dated November 17, 1917, accorded to the commanding officers of American
troops the right of military requisition.

It was especially stipulated however that this right was not to be exercised except
in urgent cases and that the normal procedure should be to make requests through the

French Military Mission attached to G. H. Q. This procedure is further described in Section D of this chapter. As a matter of fact the right of requisition was exercised very little. The chief value of the right has been the effect which it had in inducing leases at reasonable rates. All cases of requisition were sent to a French appraisal board which was so burdened with work that often a year elapsed before the case was acted upon, and, in the end, the owner usually received less than we would have gotten under a lease.

C. LOCATION AND CLASSES OF BILLETING AREAS

The determining factors in the location of billeting areas were:
1. Military requirements demanding an area in a certain general vicinity.
2. Sufficient billeting accommodations.
3. Adequate railroad facilities.
4. Good health conditions, especially with relation to water supply.
5. A terrain well fitted for training purposes.

The first factor mentioned was by far the most important. It determined the general locality of the area and necessarily fixed it near the front, in the central part of France, or near the base ports. The remaining factors defined the exact position of the area within the general locality previously indicated, so that as far as possible the best of billeting accommodations, railroad facilities, and training conditions might provail.

Army Areas. Military requirements played a paramount part in the location of Army Areas. They were located in the Zone of the Armies not far distant from the front lines and were used mainly in connection with the movements of troops for military operations and also for rest areas when the troops were withdrawn from the front for a short time only. They were comparatively small, containing as a rule from 10 to 20 towns as against 30 to 60 towns in the Advance Section Areas next referred to. The maximum capacity of an Army Area was 15,000 troops. Although they were kept in an organized state at all times they were more or less elastic as to boundaries, and in general the accommodations were adapted to meet the requirements of the units ordered into them. * * *

Infantry Divisional Training Areas. Training areas for combat divisions were situated principally in the Advance Section immediately in rear of the Zone of the Armies and within a few days' march of the front. They were customarily known as Advance Section Areas and were the most important class used by the A. E. F. The principal use made of areas in such locations was for training newly arrived divisions. While military requirements made it necessary to establish training areas in the rear of the Army, considerable latitude was allowed in choosing tee exact situation so as to secure the greatest number of advantages. Unlike the Army Areas with their constantly changing boundaries, the Advance Section Areas were practically fixed, and although occasionally towns were added or taken away for some special purpose for the most part they were permanent establishments. By virtue of their position such areas could be used not only for training purposes but also as rest areas for divisions withdrawn from the front. They were likewise a great convenience in the case of massing troops for offensives. For example, prior to the St-MIHIEL offensive, the areas in rear of that particular sector were devoted entirely to the concentration of troops designated for participation in the attack. There were 24 Advance Section Areas, of which 20 were able to accommodate a full division, the remaining four being for the accommodation of army, corps, and special troops.

In March, 1918, an acute shortage of railroad transportation made it desirable that there should be areas located within easy marching distance of base ports. It was intended to use them for training newly arrived combat divisions when transportation could not be secured for moving troops to the Advance Section Areas where training was normally conducted. A glance at the map will show that many areas near the base ports were secured, but the railroad situation became less serious, and they were not used for combat divisions except in one instance. The principal use made of them during hostilities was to accommodate miscellaneous troops. During the return of troops to the United States, they were extremely valuable as concentration points for the base ports prior to embarkation.

Depot Division Areas: Military requirements played a less important part in the location of Depot Division Areas, which were used primarily for the accommodation of organizations training troops for replacements and occasionally for miscellaneous units and casuals. Full consideration was given to billeting accommodations, health conditions, and especially to training facilities. They were generally located in the central part of France, usually on the American lines of communication. Railroad considerations made it essential that divisions which were not intended for participation in combat should not be located in the Advance Section but should be held further to the rear, thus avoiding an unnecessarily long haul of supplies and the consequent danger of congestion.

Artillery Training Areas. Artillery Training Areas were located with the main consideration of providing a suitable terrain for training purposes. Training in artillery fire demands long ranges, and artillery areas were of necessity located in the more sparsely settled parts of France. Theoretically, it would have been better to have had the field artillery brigades in training located with their divisions in the Advance Section Areas, and such areas were usually equipped with a range prepared for artillery fire. But there was a considerable element of danger involved, and in order to allow the farmers to cultivate their fields, the ranges could only be used on certain days and then only between hours agreed upon in advance. Limitations of this nature tended constantly to interrupt the progress of training, and the policy was therefore adopted of detaching the artillery brigade from the remainder of the division on its arrival overseas and sending it to an Artillery Training Area where ample facilities for firing were provided. The Heavy Artillery Training Areas were located at points where the French had previously had artillery installations, which were turned over intact for the use of the A. E. F.

Miscellaneous Areas: In addition to the classes of areas enumerated above there were also established areas for the accommodation of special services such as Chemical Warfare Service, Tank Corps, Air Service, Medical Corps, Trench Mortar Artillery, and schools. These areas were small and, with the exception of the schools, not more than one was alloted to each special service.

There is one area which requires special mention, the Le MANS Embarkation Center. It was formed by combining several areas lying in the same general vicinity and occupied more territory than the State of Connecticut, having accommodations for 300,000 men. It served as a huge reservoir for troops preparatory to embarkation and many units returning to the United States remained there long enough to turn in the equipment no longer needed and perfect their records. This area was exceptionally well located, its situation being such that it had excellent railroad facilities over direct lines to all of the base ports.

D. ACQUISITION OF BILLETING AREAS

The area in the vicinity of GONDRECOURT was first to be developed for American occupancy and was subsequently used by the 1st Division. It had formerly been organized for a French division of 15,000 troops and it was therefore necessary to add many towns and undertake a considerable amount of construction before it could be made suitable for the larger American division. The Americans occupied the area in June, 1917, but the administration was for some time handled by the French, and all of the barracks and other temporary structures remained in French control.

Work on the second American area (Neufchâteau) started about July, 1917. This proved to be much more satisfactory than the Gondrecourt Area, mainly because it was formed along generous lines from the start and the facilities from every point of view were better.

G-1 endeavored at all times to have an adequate supply of billeting areas which would be available at such places as G-3 directed. As soon as the priority lists indicated that a unit was shortly expected to arrive overseas, G-3 was consulted as to its desired location. If there were no areas already available, a request was made through the French Mission at G. H. Q. that a preliminary reconnaissance be made by the French to determine the practicability of forming a billeting area near the place indicated by G-3.

Provided the French Military authorities had no objection to the establishment of such an area, a board of French officers was convened, an investigation made, and a detailed report submitted containing the following information:

1. Map of the proposed area.

2. List of the towns with statistics on the available shelter for officers, men and animals.

3. General scheme of distributing the units of the division throughout the towns of the area.

4. General description of the terrain, railroad facilities, sanitary conditions, water supply, hospitals, and health conditions.

5. Proposed outline of training facilities, rifle ranges, grenade fields, artillery ranges, and trench systems.

Upon receipt of the report by G-1, it was checked in order to ascertain whether the general requirements had been met, and if the result was satisfactory a letter of acceptance was sent to the French Military Mission.

Since the first fourteen Advance Section Areas were formed from French areas previously organized there was usually a considerable amount of construction work already completed. In such cases, the American zone major receipted for the barracks, mess halls, and other structures, and took over the leases of lands used for military purposes. The completion of these details and the letter of acceptance to the French Military Mission brought the area under American military jurisdiction.

The first four areas acquired were formed entirely under French supervision. This policy was not altogether satisfactory in meeting American requirements. Certain difficulties arose, due to the failure of the French to consider factors other than the mere housing of troops, as a result of which, training and administration were difficult. A change was therefore made early in February, 1918, by which a board of American officers with representatives from the Engineer and Medical Corps was formed at Hq., S. O. S., which investigated proposed areas and determined upon their suitability prior to acceptance.

Under the new arrangement a full report was made similar in form to the preliminary report received from the French. Due to the fact that American divisions were larger than French divisions, it was often necessary to make some alterations in the disposition of troops. The area was carefully studied from every point of view, and occasionally the investigation brought to light some fact which warranted its rejection. Thus, as a result of the investigations of the S. O. S. board, 39 of 130 billeting areas which the French recommedded for American use were rejected. The report of the American board was carefully reviewed and, if satisfactory, was accepted.

After an area had been completed in accordance with the original program, it frequently happened that towns lying immediately outside of the boundary were desired in order to provide additional space, better transportation facilities, or other similar advantage. In such cases a request to the French Mission usually received favorable action and permitted the addition sought.

On July 20, 1918, difficulties appeared in connection with certain areas due to the lack of satisfactory railheads. G-4 recommended that in fixing the limits of an area a satisfactory railhead should be first selected, and then the required billeting capacity located centrally about the railhead in order to reduce transportation difficulties. In order to meet this situation, the following billeting duties were transformed to Hq., S. O. S., on September 21:

1. To request from the French new areas, camps, sites, and barracks when located in rear of the Zone of the Armies.

2. To reconnoiter and accept from the French new areas and installations.

3. To distribute the billeting capacity thus obtained to units to be located there.

4. To keep suitable records showing the distribution of troops in American areas.

5. To furnish G. H. Q. with all information necessary to proper general supervision of billeting problems. G. H. Q. retained the duty of obtaining from the French additional areas of all kinds in the Zone of the Armies and also that of assigning troops to areas.

E. ADMINISTRATION OF BILLETING AREAS

From August 27, 1917, to November 15, 1917, the Advance Section Areas were under the command of the Commanding General of Divisional Areas, but on the latter date this office was discontinued and all areas in rear of the Zone of the Armies came under the command of the Commanding General, Line of Communications, where they continued thereafter.

[The report here quotes G. O. No. 18, A. E. F., 1918, which prescribed the system of administering billeting areas as finally developed.]

* * * * * *

The zone majors provided for in this order were permanently assigned. However there was not sufficient permanent personnel available to assign town majors at all points, and the duties of this office were largely performed by acting town majors who moved with their divisions. This situation gave rise to certain difficulties in the administration of billeting matters which would have been avoided if the requisite personnel had been available.

F. CONSTRUCTION PROJECTS

The French not only continued to maintain considerable administrative control of the first areas occupied by American troops through their zone majors, but they also performed much of the construction work. The structures in Areas 1 to 4 were erected wholly by the French. Thereafter, in Areas 5 to 13 the Americans took an increasingly large share in the work, and, commencing with area 14, performed all of the construction.

After the preliminary reconnaissance of an area and been completed a building project was formulated to supplement where necessary the existing billeting facilities. The construction planned included a sufficient number of barracks to meet the billeting requirements of officers, men, and usually in addition, one barrack per company for a mess hall, one barrack per battalion for a recreation room, one barrack per battalion for an infirmary, and one shower bath house for each village. Stables were also constructed where the shelters previously existed proved insufficient.

In general the amount of construction varied with the location of the areas. The Army Areas, with their devastated villages and the dense concentration of troops, required more construction work than any of the others. The Advance Section Areas also required a considerable amount of construction, especially Areas 1 to 14 which were formed from French areas already organized for French divisions of 15,000 men and were therefore unsuited for the larger American divisions. Due to the fact that the field artillery areas were located in sparsely settled territory, a great deal of construction was necessary not only for the proper housing of troops but also for providing shelter for the animals.

The building project after approval by G-1 was forwarded to G-4, and from there to the Commanding General, S. O. S., who was charged with the erection of the necessary structures.

G. RENTING, REQUISITION AND CLAIMS SERVICE

It has already been indicated that the lack of permanent personnel was a handicap in handling billeting matters. As early as August 25, 1917, the American town major at Gondrecourt called attention to the fact that there should be a service in the A. E. F. for handling all matters relating to claims, rentals, and billeting regulations.

The supervision which the S. O. S. exercised over all billeting areas in rear of the Zone of the Armies had further emphasized the necessity of placing all matters rel ting to billets and billeting under the control of a special service. Accordingly the Renting, Requisition, and Claims Service (R. R. & C.) was established by Section IV, G. O. No. 50, A. E. F., March 30, 1918.

The R. R. and C. Service was also handicapped from the start by a lack of personnel although this had been one of the essential reasons for its formation. This difficulty was of course due to the pressing need for officers for combat and other essential duties.

The American personnel engaged in R. R. and C. service in the field in general consisted of a zone major, an assistant, an enlisted man, and an interpreter. The services of French town majors were retained as far as possible, and acting town majors were appointed from among the American troops in the area. It was demonstrated, however, that acting town majors on account of their relation with troops, could not maintain the necessary interest in the R. R. and C. service.

In October, 1918, the French made a request that French personnel in American areas be relieved as rapidly as possible. To compensate for this loss it was decided to organize R. R. and C. companies, and a telegram authorizing this action was forwarded to the Commanding General, S. O. S. on October 22. It was planned to form companies at a strength of about 45 men each, and, on account of the pressing need for every able-bodied man at the front, Class C. personnel was to be utilized as far as possible.

These companies were intended for use as *Caserniers* or Billet Wardens, and as such to keep accurate inventories and records of the condition of all property occupied by troops, to report damages, and to maintain a general supervision over the billets in the particular locality.

The R. R. and C. companies were not a complete success, largely due to the quality of personnel and to the fact that as soon as the Armistice was signed, Class C men were sent to the replacement depots for return to the United States.

H. IMPROVEMENT IN BILLETING ACCOMMODATIONS DURING ARMISTICE

While it was always the policy of the A. E. F. to provide good billeting accommodations for troops, it was sometimes impossible under the stress of military circumstances to attain ideal conditions.

The Armistice, followed by the movement of the American lines forward to the Rhine, opened up a considerable territory, much of it undevastated, and the cessation of active military operations made unnecessary any large concentration of troops. This made possible a marked improvement in billeting conditions, but some organizations did not take full advantage of the situation, and on February 10, 1919, the Commander-in-Chief sent telegrams to all concerned directing that most earnest attention be given to the question of billets. A circular letter following on February 12, 1919, stated that it is intended to make the men of the A. E. F. as comfortable in their billets as circumstances will permit; also, that as billeting areas were vacated by troops, they would be allotted to neighboring units as far as possible.

In compliance with these instructions many American units were scattered more widely, and the billeting capacity of towns previously unoccupied was used, with the results that billeting conditions were greatly improved.

I. USE OF AMERICAN AREAS BY THE ALLIES

1. BY ALLIES ATTACHED TO THE A. E. F.

Many Allied officers and soldiers, principally from the British and French armies, were attached to American units mainly for the purpose of acting as instructors, interpreters, and liaison agents, and while acting in such capacity they were actually under the authority of the commanding officer of the American organization.

The question of the propriety of providing billets in such cases came up first on September 15, 1917, in relation to Allied liaison officers, but it remained unsettled until August 6, 1918, when it was presented for decision to the Judge Advocate. The reply of the same date stated that there was no existing authority for making expenditures in such cases. On September 7, 1918, the matter came up again in an inquiry received from the R. R. and C. Service, and on October 8, 1918, a memorandum was forwarded to the Chief of Staff recommending a new general order to provide for the payment of billets of Allied officers and soldiers attached to the American forces. This was approved and published as Sec. VII, G. O. No. 182, A. E. F., October 19, 1918.

The practice of paying for billets of Allied officers and soldiers attached to American units just referred to was never extended to officers and soldiers of the Allied armies present with the Americans for training purposes.

2. BY OTHER ALLIED UNITS

Since practically all of the American Advance Section Areas had been used to some extent by the French military forces previous to the time of American occupancy, there were many French depots and services left in isolated points in those areas. Arrangements were therefore made to permit such units to remain in the same location.

In addition to such cases, military activities were so closely coordinated that not infrequently detachments of Allied troops were serving with the Americans. For example, the French and British air services assisted the American forces during the period when the American Air forces were not fully developed. Bases of supplies, aviation grounds, and training centers were provided in American areas in such instances, but in general it was found advisable not to put Allied troops in the same town with American troops.

Occasionally small detachments of Allied forces moving from one part of the front to another were obliged to pass through American areas and they of course required billeting accommodations en route. The movement was always planned so as to permit temporary billeting accommodations for the night at stopping points previously determined.

Aside from the Zones of Passage which will be described later, the most serious disarrangement of areas due to Allied occupancy was caused by the change made in the eastern limit of the American zone on November 3, 1918. This change, which was made by direction of Marshal Foch in order to furnish billeting accommodations for the French in preparation for an attack in Lorraine, cut into portions of the 2d, 3d, 5th, and 6th areas. On December 5, 1918, after the emergency had passed a request was made that the original eastern boundary be restored, and this was approved by direction of Marshal Foch on December 12.

Permission for Allied forces to occupy towns or camps within the American billeting areas was obtained through the Military Mission of the proper Allied army at American G. H. Q. Since American forces had been frequently accommodated in Allied areas, arrangements were always made for Allied occupation of American areas as a matter of mutual concession.

3. BY CIVILIAN REFUGEES

During the months of April, May, June, and July, 1918, a large number of French civilian refugees from the recently invaded districts of France began to appear in the American Advance Section Areas. Zone majors reported that the influx was curtailing the billeting capacity of certain towns to such an extent that additional barrack construction would be necessary in order to accommodate divisional troops which might be ordered in.

The areas actually occupied by troops were not affected to any serious extent. The situation was felt principally in areas at that time unoccupied, but which nevertheless had to be kept in immediate readiness to receive troops. The capacity of many towns was reduced by 25 or 50% and in some cases as much as 90%. The French had made no regulations for taking in refugees except that the approval of the commanding general of the region in which the town was located had first to be obtained. In the case of areas that had never been occupied by the French for billeting purposes, refugees sometimes came and received permission from the French authorities, without due consideration to the needs of the American troops.

While it was highly desirable to accommodate these unfortunate civilians, it was at the same time necessary to take some action which would assure keeping areas available for use at all times without interference with military operations.

The matter was taken up with the French Military Mission on June 10th, and a proposal was made and later accepted to the effect that only blood relatives of the inhabitants of towns in American billeting areas would be permitted to remain and than in no case would refugees be taken in such numbers as to reduce by more than 15% the total billeting capacity of any particular town. It was thought that by a readjustment of units, and by a little crowding, a full division could still be accommodated in a divisional area in spite of a reduction of 15% billeting capacity in each town.

The difficulty in connection with the refugees was temporary. Many of them after a short stay left for the central part of France; others returned to their former dwellings after the German tide had been rolled back. Fy December, 1918, the situation with respect to refugees had become practically normal.

4. AS ZONES OF PASSAGE, DURING FRENCH DEMOBILIZATION

Shortly after the signing of the Armistice on November 11, 1918, the French government decided to demobilize a considerable number of French units, particularly those divisions formed from the older classes which had been in service in the inactive sectors near the Swiss border. This demobilization contemplated a movement of the units from the sector occupied at that time over to the general district from which they had originally come. The American Advance Section Areas and the Army Areas formed a practically solid block opposing such a movement. It was therefore necessary to establish two zones of Passage, each with an average width of about 12 kilometers. At the request of the Commander-in-Chief of the Allied Armies a conference was held at G. H. Q. on November 26, 1918, at which the establishment of the Zones was agreed to and the boundaries fixed.

By the terms of the agreement, twelve towns lying in the Zones were reserved for the Americans owing to large American establishment in these localities. The two largest towns reserved were Toul, Headquarters of the American Second Army, and Neufchâteau, Headquarters of the Advance Section, S. O. S. With these exceptions all towns in the Zones passed to the control of the French, and the entire billeting capacity was placed at the disposal of the French troops on the march.

It was further agreed that if it proved necessary to move large American units across the Zones in a northerly or southerly direction, staging areas providing halting points for the night would be temporarily reserved within them to permit such a movement.

J. RETURN OF AREAS TO THE FRENCH

Immediately following the Armistice the French expressed the desire that as many billeting areas, camps, and barracks as could be conveniently spared should be returned to their control. Several areas had been accepted in the central part of France and near the base ports which it was not intended to occupy except in case of emergency. It was therefore possible to comply with the French request on December 3 by releasing sixteen areas. The heavy artillery troops were among the first to be sent back to the United States, and the areas formerly used by them were, upon their evacuation, returned to French control.

All of the Advance Section areas, several Base Port areas, the necessary Depot Division areas and the Le Mans Embarkation Center were retained. Many of the Advance Section areas were not occupied, but it was deemed advisable to retain them in connection with possible troop movements and also to permit units to spread out and so improve billeting conditions.

On February 9, 1919, the Commander-in-Chief approved the policy of returning to French French control as rapidly as possible those areas which were not actually needed and which had been evacuated, and further reserving only the areas near the Base Ports, the Le Mans Embarkation Center and such towns and installations as were necessary for the accommodation of S. O. S. troops.

With regard to the details of returning an area to the French, G-3 indicated from time to time those areas which were no longer required. G-1 notified the Commanding

General, S. O. S., of the decision made and if the area in question had never been used by American troops the matter was concluded by a letter from the Commanding General, S. O. S., to the French Military Mission at Tours, announcing that the A. E. F. had no further use for it.

If, however, the area had been used by American troops a large amount of work had to be done before it could be turned back to the French. This consisted of the removal or disposition of barracks, stables, and other structures erected by the Americans, the repair of roads, the filling of trenches and ditches, and other work necessary to restore the area as nearly as possible to its original condition.

In view of the importance and extent of this work it was deemed advisable to turn over all areas not needed to the C. G., S. O. S. By such procedure the services of the troops themselves were utilized in the work of rehabilitation until their departure. After the departure of the troops the division engineers were retained long enough to finish the work in case it had not already been completed.

The necessary instructions were given to the C. G., S. O. S., relative to the removal of barracks, adjustment of rents and claims, and payment of damages, after which steps were taken to turn the area over to the French, thus closing the transaction.

K. BILLETING OUTSIDE OF ORGANIZED AREAS

When American troops were on the march they sometimes necessarily passed through territory not organized into areas. In such cases the commanding officer made a request for billeting accommodations through his French liaison officer. An acting town major was appointed for each town in which troops were billeted, and French practice was followed in all other particulars. The billeting records were kept by the acting town major and forwarded by him to the commanding general of the S. O. S. section in which the town was located.

A frequent cause of trouble in connection with billeting outside of organized areas was the settlement of claims for damages. The acting town major moved out with the troops. Therefore if claims were not reported promptly before the troops had left, there was no American official to investigate and pass on the claims. Troops on the march, under such conditions, were therefore likely to leave behind them unpaid claims which had to be investigated later by a special R. R. and C. officer who was personally unfamiliar with the details.

In the case of American divisions serving under British and French commands, the Americans were provided with billets by the Allied administration. Payment for billets occupied by Americans while serving with the British was included in an agreed per capita rate which covered all expenses. While serving with the French, the Americans made out billeting distribution lists and certificates as usual. The French paid the bills, marking the papers *Armée Américaine,* and later submitted a statement showing the amount due them for reimbursement.

L. BILLETING OUTSIDE OF FRANCE

1. LUXEMBURG

On November 20, 1918, Marshal Foch directed a letter to the Commander-in-Chief stating that the right of requisition would be exercised in Luxemburg, under the same conditions as in France, by means of orders and receipts given to the burgomaster of each Commune. Under a provisional agreement made on November 24, 1918, by the Commanding General of the Third Army with the Luxemburg government, it was arranged that all billeting expenses were to be paid in French money and in accordance with the terms of G. O. No. 18, A. E. F., 1918. This provisional agreement was later confirmed by an Allied agreement under date of March 1919, [agreement dated November 27, 1918; finally approved February 27, 1919].

G. O. No. 12, A. E. F., January 16, 1919, extended the functions of the R. R. and C. Service to include the Grand Duchy of Luxemburg.

2. BELGIUM

Billeting in Belgium was essentially the same as billeting in France, the only difference being with respect to the rates to be paid per night. Under the Belgian laws there was a sliding scale of rates depending on the period of occupancy. While perhaps more equitably figured than the French rates, the Belgian rates were troublesome for both billeting and disbursing officers in the amount of clerical labor involved. At the present time (April 15, 1919) negotiations have been undertaken with the view of making the billeting rates for American troops in Belgium the same as those in France.

CHAPTER VIII

EQUIPMENT OF TROOPS

When G. O. No. 31, was issued on February 16, 1918, there had been published no equipment manuals for service in Europe. As data for use in the preparation of such manuals there existed the old Quartermaster Department Tables of Fundamental Allowances and Unit Equipment Accountability Manuals published by the Adjutant General of the Army. Theretofore allowances of equipment had been determined by the various supply departments. It was decided as a basic principle on which to conduct the work of preparing new manuals, first, that G-1, after making a thorough study of conditions at the front both with American troops and with those of the Allies, should prescribe the requirements as to equipment of combat troops in the form of equipment manuals; second, that each manual should show all the equipment to be furnished the troops by all supply departments, and, third, that the manuals should serve both as a basis for requisition by troops and for supply by each supply department.

The Organization and Equipment Division of G-1, which was charged with the preparation of equipment manuals, was then so organized that at least half of its officers could be on duty with troops at the front at all times. During offensives, as many officers as could be spared visited some organization taking part and from knowledge gained from these studies and recommendations received from officers serving with front line troops all decisions as to equipment were made.

The determination of type, quantity per organization, and groups of equipment was an indispensable preliminary to the intelligent procurement of supplies for the armies. A knowledge of the requirements of organizations, both at the receiving and issuing end, was equally important. With this in view it was originally determined that the equipment of combat units should be divided into three general classes as follows: mobile equipment, trench equipment, and area equipment.

Mobile equipment comprised all government property issued to troops which is carried on the person or horse, or in combat, field, or divisional trains. This property, and only this property, is the permanent equipment of a division and moves whenever the division moves. Examples of this are clothing, arms, combat vehicles, escort wagons, and rolling kitchens.

Trench equipment comprised all additional equipment necessary for the maintenance of trench sector and was issued to troops on taking over a sector and turned over by them to the relieving organization. Examples of this are marmite cans, trench stoves, periscopes, pyrotechnics, engineer tools, timber, etc.

Area equipment comprised additional equipment for use while in training areas either on arrival in the A. E. F. or between tours of duty in the line. Examples of this are extra clothing, blankets, and other articles to provide additional comfort. This general plan was submitted to the Commander in Chief and was approved by him, with the exception of the provision for area equipment, of which none was to be prescribed. The issue of one bedsack and one or two extra blankets for each officer and enlisted man while in the training are was however authorized.

Equipment manuals for combat troops were divided into three series: A, B, and C, conforming to the latter designations of tables of organization for division, corps, and army troops, respectively. All efforts were at first concentrated on prescribing a list of equipment for the infantry division and for the infantry regiment in particular. The data for this list were secured from a study of British and French equipment and in a large measure from studies made by officers of G-1 with troops at the front. This method involved a mass of detailed work, the completion of which furnished a basis not only for the Infantry Regiment Manual but as well for those of all other units.

The first copies of the equipment manual for the infantry regiment were ready for distribution the later part of May, 1918. The manual was published with the title Equipment Manuals for Service in Europe, Series A, No. 1, Infantry Regiment. Manuals Nos. 2 to 14, Series A, which completed the units of the infantry division followed rapidly. Manual No. 15, Series A, Infantry Division Equipment, a summation of all the equipment of the infantry division, for the information division headquarters and division supply officers, was sent to the press August 24, 1918. This completed the Series A manuals.

As stated above, the framework for the first of the Series A equipment manuals served equally well for those of the other combat organizations and once it was determined upon the army and corps (Series B and C) lists of equipment were determined upon along with Series A manuals. They were published a little later, however, because there was a greater necessity for taking care of the infantry divisions, constituting as they did the major portion of the combat forces.

In working out the details of the form in which these manuals were to be published, it was decided, owing to the amount and variety of the articles of equipment to be included in them which were entirely new to the service, and particularly in view of the large proportion of inexperienced officers on duty with troops, that it would be advisable to indicate clearly just what would constitute a complete outfit for each individual officer and the proper distribution of property supplied for general use in an organization. To gain this end two tables, not theretofore used in the service, were prepared. The first, called "Sets of Individual Equipment for all Enlisted Men," grouped together the men who were identically armed and equipped and showed exactly what property of all kinds should be issued to them. The second, called "Article of Mobile Equipment Distributed as Directed," indicated to the company commander the men to whom special equipment should be given. While these tables would have been unnecessary under ordinary conditions or with experienced officers, they served as an invaluable guide to many officers recently commissioned, who were not only unfamiliar with the equipment itself, but were also at a loss to know how to dispose of it within their organization.

The most important table, and the one which was the real basis of the manuals, was called "Total Mobile Equipment." The form used in this table somewhat resemble that used by the Quartermaster Department in the preparation of G. O. No. 39, W. D. 1915. The new manuals, however, included in this one table all equipment authorized for an organization regardless of the source of supply. The articles were conveniently grouped under subheadings showing which department was to be called upon to provide them and the necessary number for each organization. Each supply department was consulted in preparing this table and the nomenclature of the various items coordinated so that no misunderstanding might come up after the publication of the manuals. This particular table of course was used much more extensively than any other as it served both as a basis for requisition and procurement. Two more tables were included, one showing "Trench Equipment," and the other showing "Over the Top Equipment." The first contained the articles really necessary for the proper functioning of combat units, but which problems of supply and transportation prohibited from accompanying the troops. The "Over the Top" table tabulated in detail the equipment of both the individual and the organization which should accompany troops in an offensive operation.

These four tables with the explanatory notes contained much valuable information. They informed the various supply departments what was expected of them and indicated to combat officers, as far down as platoon commanders, the correct disposition of individual equipment and of that supplied for general use, whether in a training area, on the march, in the trenches, or when engaged in war of movement. They covered a much more extensive field than had theretofore been attempted in equipment manuals for the American service.

After the detailed form of the various tables had been determined, a study was conducted of the articles to be included therein, and the first question made a subject of discussion was the clothing of the soldier. It was soon seen that for service in Europe certain changes were not only desirable but essential. These may be roughly divided into three classes: First, those necessitated by climated conditions; second, those growing out of the form of trench warfare which existed on the western front; and third, those in which the determining factors were supply and transportation. In all instances, however, the welfare and comfort of the soldier were given careful consideration.

Under the first class, the most important changes made were the discontinuance of cotton breeches and blouses as articles of issue and the authorization of two pairs of heavy field shoes for each soldier instead of one pair of marching shoes.

The most important changes falling under the second class were the elimination of the canvas legging the campaign hat. Early experience in the trenches proved conclusively that the canvas legging was entirely unsuited for that type of warfare. They were cold, very hard to clean and dry, and were known as mud catchers. The spiral wool puttee was substituted for them and immediately became popular with the men. They not only made a light flexible leg covering but were warm and easily cleaned and dried. The campaign hat was found to be an awkward article to care for in forward areas, where men were obliged to wear the steel helmet. It could not be carried in the pack and when attached to belt or pack carrier it presented a very unmilitary appearance. At the direction of the Commander-in-Chief a cap was developed which could either be work under the helmet or conveniently carried in a blouse pocket. These were known as oversea caps and as soon as available they superseded the campaign hat. It was also found to be necessary to add two pairs of socks to the equipment of each soldier, making a total of four. In most sectors the trenches were wet the greater part of the time and dry socks were valuable in helping combat trench feet.

Under the third class came such articles as horsehide gloves, fatigue suits, jerkins, rubber boots, and arctic overshoes. These articles while not absolutely necessary in the training areas were quite essential in the sectors. The demand for canvas, leather, rubber, etc., made upon the supply departments prohibited them from procuring these articles for each individual. Furthermore, it was not desirable to add any weight to the soldier's pack and the available transportation was not sufficient to carry them as company property. The question was solved by carrying all of these articles as sector property, thus placing these at the disposal of organizations when needed.

The question of personnal equipment other than clothing was next made a subject of study. This equipment was modified to a considerable extend, and practically all of the changes made were necessitated by actual combat conditions. An issue of dubbin was authorized for each soldier, to be used in waterproofing shoes, and the toilet kit was provided, the various components of it being renewed when destroyed or expended. The Medical Department was called upon to supply for each individual a box of foot powder or grease and for each twenty men a ten-yard roll of adhesive tape.

Soon after American troops had been in combat, it developed that the bacon can had no particular value in this war, as the emergency and reserve rations consisted almost entirely of cooked food, and it was discontinued as an article of issue. A number of officers also recommended that the condiment can be dropped, but alter an extended investigation it was decided that it should be retained principally on the ground that there might be many times when a soldier could make coffee, using for fuel the solidified alcohol which was being supplied.

In order to afford some protection to the magazine of the rifle when not actually in use and to provide a suitable instrument for cleaning the breach, the canvas breech cover and breech sticks were developed. These were especially beneficial in trench warfare.

In considering the mounted equipment it was observed that several articles usually considered essential for mounted men could be dispensed with and not seriously interfere with the functioning of mounted troops, so the watering bridle, lariat, and picket pin were dispensed with.

Perhaps the most far-reaching changes were the discontinuance of barrack bags and surplus kit bags. These two items were of so bulky a nature that it was an absolutely impossible task to have them accompany troops when changing stations. While the individual equipment now consisted only of what was either worn on the person or carried in the pack, the temptation existed, as long as these two articles were authorized, for soldiers to accumulate many useless souvenirs of no military value. After a brief experience in moving troops from one training area to another, both of these articles were dropped as an article of issue.

At this time it developed that owing to the large number of motor vehicles in use a standard list of chauffeurs' and motorcyclists' equipment was necessary. This subject was extensively studied and it was decided to authorize for each man operating an automobile, motor truck or motorcycle the following equipment: 1 pair hip rubber boots, 1 oilskin coat, 1 pair winter gauntlets, 1 pair heavy leather gloves, 1 pair goggles, 1 woolen toque or helmet, 1 mackinaw or jerkin, 1 pair arctic overshoes, 2 pairs extra heavy wool socks, and, for motorcyclists only, 1 pair of oilskin trousers

After the changes in clothing and personnl equipment had been settled and the complete list of individual equipment for soldiers of various arms had been decided upon, attention was directed toward the work of fixing the allowance of property to be issued for general use within an organization. This class of property of course differed considerably in the different branches of the service. It was determined, however, from the outset that no articles should be authorized in France that were not absolutely necessary to the efficient conduct of the organization. Practically no equipment of any kind not previously authorized in existing tables of allowances was included in this list, excepting that of a technical and special nature supplied for some particular propose by the Ordnance Department, Signal Corps, or Chemical Warfare Service. Substantially these articles were fire control instruments, special equipment for automatic arms and artillery, various kinds of equipment for communication, and anti-gas training sets. The Policy was adopted of providing at the outset a liberal allowance of equipment of this type, as it was to be used primarily in combat, and, if future experience should show any of it to be unnecessary, a suitable reduction could be made later.

It was obvious from the first that if the principle of high mobility was to be preserved much equipment usually issued would have to be eliminated, and just as the personal equipment authorized for the individual was limited to what could be conveniently carried in the pack, the allowance of property to be transported by an organization should in like manner be controlled largely by the transportation assigned to it for such purposes. On these grounds many articles were discontinued. They may be roughly classified as those rendered unnecessary by the institution of non-accountability, those which could be superseded by making use of the material at hand, and those the use of which was combined, either wholly or in part, with some other article. Under the first class, came all kinds of marking and stencil outfits, ordinarily used to identify the property of men, to brand animals, and to mark vehicles, excepting only the metal stamping outfit which was retained to letter identification tags. The second class consisted mainly of such equipment as folding chairs and tables, corn brooms, scrubbing brushes, handcuffs, mineral oil containers, field safes, tape measures, garbage cans, night urinal cans, etc. In the last class came field ranges, the cooking being done in rolling kitchens, drinking water containers and galvanized iron cans, which were not necessary when organizations were equipped with water carts, and the regimental and company small arms repair chests, which were turned in to the Mobile Ordnance Repair Shop.

After the completion of tables of individual and company property, the work of establishing the kind and allowance of various articles of trench equipment was undertaken. This presented difficulties not heretofore encountered, owing to the fact that the degree of activity in different sectors varied to a considerable extent. It was decided to authorize, however, a basic allowance for a quiet sector, commanding officers being empowered to make requisition for additional equipment when necessary.

One of the first questions to come up was that of providing some means of getting hot food to the men in the front line. The company kitchens were normally some distance behind the lines and it was usually found to be necessary to carry food by hand up to the forward trenches. The marmite cans and small milk cans were furnished for this purpose, the marmite cans being for solid food and the milk cans for coffee. The marmite kept the food hot for several hours and it generally reached the men in good condition. Solidified alcohol was supplied for reheating the coffee, if necessary, and this arrangement worked out successfully. Various articles of ordnance property were included, such as pyrotechnics, periscopes, etc., the amounts being determined largely upon the previous experience of Allies. The same is true of Chemical Warfare Service property, such as gas-proof blankets, wind vanes, etc., and engineer property used for repair and construction work.

[The report here inserts a table showing the comparison between Equipment A of the infantry soldier as prescribed in G. O. 39, W. D., June 24, 1915, and the individual mobile equipment of the infantry soldier as prescribed in Equipment Manuals for Service in Europe prepared and issued by G-1.]

* * * * * *

Due to the nesessity for limiting troop baggage to a minimum, the fact that a great many suggested lists of equipment were being published in the United States and the general lack of knowledge there was to the real requirements for overseas service, a study was made of the amount of baggage that could be fixed as a limit for both officers and soldiers. With this study as a basis, G-1 prepared a list of equipment to be brought to France by officers of all arms, corps, and auxiliary troops, and cabled it to Washington on June 25, 1918. * * *

* * * * * *

The matter of transportation received particular attention, resulting in the development of several vehicles which are superior to those formerly in use. The following are the most important.

Combat Wagon: The combat wagon originally supplied was a limbered caisson type vehicle, and was the first vehicle of this kind used in American service as an infantry combat wagon. It was objectionable for several reasons, and soon after it was put in use was subjected to much severe criticism. The fact that it was divided into compartments designed to carry only one size ammunition box, and its great weight were the principal grounds for complaint. Both of these were well founded. While there are some advantages in having a combat wagon that can be used only as such, they are more than offset by the disadvantages incurred, and a wagon suitable also for general purposes is much more desirable. The weight, approximately 2,900 pounds, was undoubtedly excessive. To overcome these objections as quickly as possible, a cable was sent to the United States to remove the partitions and flare boards, to put on a tail gate, and reduce the weight wherever possible. The wagons turned for salvage in France were similarly converted.

After this temporary expedient had been resorted to, the design of a new wagon for combat purposes was undertaken. It was decided after considerable discussion to adhere to the principles of supplying a vehicle of the limbered caisson type. This is much more flexible and mobile than one like the standard escort wagon and can be driven over roads not passable to a vehicle in which the wheels are rigidly connected. The question arose at the time as to whether it would not be advisable to make this new wagon postillion driven. There are many advantages to this method, especially when passing through congested roads at night, but in view of the shortage of leather, and the large number of extra men required, it was decided to have the wagon driven from the seat. The carrying capacity was based on the actual cubical volume of the authorized equipment, and the dimentions were such as would permit the equipment to be packed without loss of space. A wagon was built that was well balanced, comparatively noiseless, and weighed approximately 2,200 pounds. It also had the added advantage of being so constructed that it could quickly be knocked down for shipment.

Water Carts: The water cart was another vehicle, new to the American service, which gave rise to many complaints. The principal objections were the poor balance and weight. These carts weighed about 1,250 pounds empty, and had a tank of 150 gallons capacity, making a total weight when loaded of about 2,500 pounds. As only one animal was authorized for these carts and the extreme shortage of animals precluded any possibility for an increase in this allowance, it was obvious that some steps must be taken to lighten the cart as much as possible. Several investigations at the front showed that the pump, the extra faucets, and filtering apparatus were not essential. These were ordered stripped from the carts and helped materially in reducing the weight. In the meantime another water cart was constructed with a capacity of 100 gallons with the tank set much lower and with its long axis parallel to the axle of the cart. This reduced the total weight 748 pounds and gave it an excellent ballance.

Ration Cart: The American ration cart caused some complaint but nothing so universal as did the other two vehicles. Experiments showed, however, that by slight modifications the weight could be reduced 108 pounds and at the same time the carrying capacity increased by 7 cubic feet.

Medical Cart: The medical cart which was also very heavy had caused more or less trouble from the first time American troops participated in open warfare. It was found that one and in some cases two mules were unable to pull this cart fast enough to accompany the infantry battalions. After the St-Mihiel offensive, in which a number of the four-wheel German medical wagons were captured, the American cart was abandoned by several organizations and the German wagon used in its place. These seemed so much better that at the request of the Medical Department a new type wagon was constructed, designed along the general lines of the old horse-drawn ambulances. The body was built so that the medical combat equipment could be packed in such a way that it would not shift even on rough roads, thus greatly decreasing any liability of breakage.

In the combat wagon, water cart, and ration cart interchangeability of parts with the escort wagon was maintained. The parts of the medical spring wagon are interchangeable with the horse-drawn ambulance.

[Here the report inserts a list of equipment manuals published by G-1: Series A, Infantry Division, Equipment Manuals for Service in Europe.]

* * * * * *

CHAPTER IX

ORGANIZATION AND DESIGNATION OF UNITS IN THE A. E. F.

The preparation of tables of organization was a function of the Organization and Equipment Division of G-1. The organization of units was handled by the Personnel Division, G-1.

For several months after its adoption, the General Organization Project and the tables based upon it governed the organization of all units. For the most part, units arrived from the United States with their organization complete and requiring only replacement of such personnel as had been lacking at the time of embarkation or lost en route. However, a portion of the units which were in France before the adoption of the General Organization Project required reorganization in order to conform to it. The units of the 1st Division were notable examples of this. For instance, it was necessary to organize a motor supply train for that division. Truck Company 303, Motor Supply Train 401; Truck Company 12, 2d Motor Supply Train, 2d Division; and 6th Company, 101st Motor Supply Train, 26th Division, were transferred to the 1st Division as the nucleus of its supply train. The wagon supply train intended for the division under the 1917 Tables of Organization was assigned to the S. O. S. and became Wagon Companies 100 and 101. When a motor supply train which had been organized in the United States as the 1st Division Motor Supply Train arrived in May, 1918, it was redesignated as the First Army Motor Supply Train. Later it was redesignated as the 439th Motor Supply Train. The 1st Division Mobile Ordnance Repair Shop was also organized in the A. E. F.

Experience indicated the desirability of certain changes in organizations formed under the General Organization Project and of the creation of certain new types of units. After the approval of the tables of organization embodying such changes, in many cases units of the A. E. F. were reorganized and in others new organizations were formed here. For example, the 30th Engineers, a two-battalion regiment, was reorganized as the 1st Gas Regiment, with a table or organization providing for 6 battalions. Also the 2d Battalion, 29th Battalion, 29th Engineers (sound and flash-ranging troops) was organized from Companies B and C, 29th Engineers, Company F, 603d Engineers, Company F, 604th Engineers, and Company F, 605th Engineers. Later, by direction of the War Department, this battalion became a part of the 74th Engineers. The 56th Engineers (searchlight troops) was organized from four searchlight companies which had been known as Companies A, B, C, and D, 56th Engineers, and Companies D and E of each of the following engineer regiments: 603d, 604th, and 605th.

Many new units of varying types were organized in the Services of Supply. Certain services were entirely reorganized. For example, a number of sales commissary units, salvage companies, and camp hospitals, were organized. A great variety of units was organized in the Army Service Corps. The troops of the Department of Construction and Forestry, the Transportation Corps, and the Motor Transport Corps were reorganized.

Units of another type which were extensively organized in the A. E. F. were provisional replacement units. These included auxiliary organizations for depot divisions, corps replacement battalions, organizations for other replacement depots, such as the depot at Blois, and the Field Artillery Replacement Regiment and organizations for the various schools and training centers.

When it was considered advisable to form a new unit other than a replacement unit in the A. E. F., authority for the organization and a designation for the unit were requested from the War Department. If the request was approved, instructions for the organization of the unit were sent to the proper headquarters and the organization announced in general orders. If the unit was to be of a new type, a necessary preliminary to this action was the submission of a table of organization to the War Department for approval. This part of the process was a function of the Organization and Equipment Division, G-1.

In general, personnel for new units other than replacement units was drawn in part from older organizations of the same type, and the vacancies which were created in the old organization and which existed in the new were filled from replacement troops.

The procedure followed in the reorganization of a unit was identical with that described above except that a large nucleus for the organization already existed. The concurrence of G-3 was necessary in all steps taken to organize or reorganize a combat unit. In fact, such action was generally initiated by that section of the General Staff. G. O. No. 130, A. E. F., 1918, assigned these functions for troops, distinctively S. O. S., to the Headquarters, S. O. S. The organization of units in many of the services and in the Army Service Corps was completed without reference to General Headquarters.

Authority was requested from the War Department by cablegram dated April 6, 1918 (P-865, par 2) to organize such provisional replacement units as might be necessary. This request was granted by cablegram dated April 12, 1918 (A-1090, par 4). The procedure adopted was as follows: First, the preparation of a table of organization based upon data and recommendations submitted by the headquarters having need of the new organization. This table, when complete, was forwarded by the O. and E. Division, G-1, to the Personnel Division, G-1. Second, in the Personnel Division instructions were prepared authorizing the required number of organizations and assigning them suitable designations. As a rule, the organization was announced in general orders, although in some cases the authority for the organization was given only by a letter of instructions from G. H. Q. Third, action was completed, in so far as the work of the General Staff was concerned, by instructions covering the transfer of personnel to the new organization. Such personnel was drawn from replacement troops.

The following are some of the units organized in the A. E. F.: [List omitted].

The following are some of the changes in designation of units made in the A. E. F.: [List omitted].

CHAPTER X

THE ORDER OF BATTLE

The necessity for an Order of Battle for the A. E. F. was early recognized and responsibility for its preparation was assigned to the Coordination Section (the greater part of whose functions are now performed by G-4) of the General Staff organized under the provisions of G. O. No. 8, A. E. F., 1917. In accordance with this order the Coordination Section prepared and published the first Order of Battle as of the date September 29, 1917. The Order of Battle first appeared as a typewritten pamphlet containing a list of the American units which had arrived overseas and a brief statement of the strength of the forces and the ratio of different classes of troops. * * * In consequence of a redistribution of staff functions, the preparation of this document was removed from the jurisdiction of the Coordination Section and assigned to the Administrative Section in November, 1917. From that time, it was published at such intervals as circumstances demanded and allowed until, with the issue of March 15, 1918, its regular semi-monthly issue was begun. At this time the Order of Battle was put into a definite form, modeled on the British Order of Battle, and the statistical features were discontinued. This form, with minor changes made from time to time, continued in use until December 1, 1918. * * *

The entire scheme of arrangement of the data in the Order of Battle and the method of presentation was given a thorough study during October and November, 1918, with the result that a new form of publication was adopted, to be issued monthly. The new form was an extension of that formerly used, rather than a change, and was devised with a view to giving the Order of Battle the greatest possible usefulness for administrative and historical purposes and also with the view to facilitating the matter of keeping the information up-to-date by means of change sheets issued periodically. A weekly change sheet was issued. A cross reference and index was added for the purpose of making it easier to identify any organization and quickly determine its assignment. * * *

As the new monthly Order of Battle was somewhat voluminous and was brought up-to-date once a week only, a necessity was believed to exist for a compact statement of the assignments of the units contained in the armies in the field, brought up to date daily. In consequence of this a weekly abstract, giving this information and corrected by a daily change sheet, was issued each Wednesday from November 6, 1918, to January 22, 1919. It was discontinued with the issue of the latter date on account of the decrease in its practical usefulness due to the cessation of hostilities. * * * When the weekly abstract was discontinued a daily change sheet was adopted for the monthly Order of Battle.

In order to carry on the work it was found necessary to establish a card file of organizations early in 1918; this file was kept constantly in use and showed the complete history of each unit that at any time formed a part of the A. E. F., so far as arrival, assignment, and departure for the United States are concerned.

The greatest problem involved in the work of preparing the Order of Battle was the obtaining of accurate information for this card file, from which the publication was compiled. * * * Inspection will indicate that these sources are so numerous, some of the data so intermittent in character, and the responsibility of transmitting information to the Order of Battle so light as compared to other responsibilities of the agencies concerned as to require a great amount of ingenuity and study on the part of those responsible for the publication. The frequent and complex reorganizations of many units and services made even more difficult the problem of periodically showing the status of the forces, and their rapid growth added to its complications.

The distribution of the Order of Battle varied between wide limits, depending upon practical requirements and upon the current military situation. After October 23, 1918, its distribution was regulated by the Chief of Staff. * * *

The distribution of the Order of Battle of any expedition depends, with certain exceptions, on local conditions. It is clear that the Commander-in-Chief and all agencies which in their functions must consider the force as a whole should be kept informed as to the administrative relationship existing between the parts. All agencies which supervise the distribution of men, animals, supplies, and materiel to units rather than to localities must also have this information. Further distribution of an Order of Battle depends upon the composition of the forces and the circumstances under which they are operating and will vary between wide limits. A subordinate and not entirely legitimate function of the publication is the identification of units by their correct designations. In a force, parts of which are reorganized and where units are given new designations, the usefulness in this respect is in correcting any tendency on the part of organizations to cling to obsolete designations or to adopt unauthorized ones.

It is believed that the use and value of the Order of Battle should be discussed in the Field Service Regulations or other official publication, and that its form, scope, and arrangement, manner of preparation and production, and the general rules covering its distribution should be prescribed in sufficient detail to insure that a standard publication shall in future be issued under this name beginning with the first formation of any expedition or other concentration of forces.

The force necessary for the production of an Order of Battle will vary with the size of the forces concerned and with the complexity of the organization. A minimum would include one officer of experience in administrative work, one field clerk, one file clerk, and one typist. Files for papers vouching for the correctness of all entries and a card file showing the history of each organization while a part of the force are essential. The necessary equipment and personnel for producing the requisite number of copies will be in addition to the above.

A clearly-arranged, complete, and correct Order of Battle is indispensable for both administrative and historical purposes.

The considerations just mentioned concern the production and distribution of the Order of Battle. With its necessity recognized and its form prescribed the vital problem of obtaining the necessary data is to be considered. An accurate and clear cut tabulation of the units of any army can be made only under the two conditions that each unit and service have a definite and fully authorized organization and that the fullest information as to the administrative relationships of each unit are required to be periodically reported to the agency which prepares the Order of Battle.

* * * * * *

CHAPTER XI

SUPERVISION OF PROVOST MARSHAL SERVICE

A. EARLY ORGANIZATION

At the outset the Provost Marshal General's Department was not expressly subject to supervision by a designated General Staff Section. Under G. O. No. 8, A. E. F., 1918, the department was organized as an administrative service with the Provost Marshal General at its head and functioning directly under the Chief of Staff. Thus G. O. No. 30, A. E. F., September 1, 1917, which charged the Provost Marshal General with supervision of military police in the Zone of the Armies and on the Lines of Communication expressly announced that subject to the approval of the Commander-in-Chief, and by his authority, the Provost Marshal General will issue such instructions and regulations for the use and government of military police as may be necessary.

It was not until the issuance on February 16, 1918, of G. O. No. 31, A. E. F., 1918, that the Provost Marshal Service was placed under the supervision of G-1. This order like-wise placed the Provost Marshal Service, with the other technical and administrative services, under the C. G., S. O. S., through whom the supervision of the General Staff was exercised.

Prior to the spring of 1918, no comprehensive organization of the Provost Marshal Service had been provided. The general duties of the service had been outlined in G. O. No. 8, A. E. F., 1917, and G. O. No. 29 and G. O. No. 63, A. E. F., 1917, defined them more in detail. On December 10, 1917, G. O. No. 71 placed the technical control of the service in the Provost Marshal General, the Provost Marshal, Lines of Communication, and Assistant Provost Marshals in the various sections of the S. O. S. The only provision of this order for furnishing personnel for the Provost Marshal Service was as follows:

The necessary personnel for military police, traffic control, examining posts and other duties of the Provost Marshal Department will, as far as practicable, be assigned from troops specially provided for these purposes. Such additional personnel as may be necessary will, however, be assigned by the responsible commanders.

The rapid increase in the size and activities of the A. E. F. which commenced in the spring of 1918 soon made apparent the necessity for a substantial extension and strengthening of the Provost Marshal Service.

B. FORMATION OF MILITARY POLICE CORPS

To meet this situation G. O. No. 111, A. E. F., July 8, 1918, was issued directing the organization in the A. E. F. of a special force to be known as the Military Police Corps. The basic unit of this corps was the military police company and the total strength of the corps was limited to 7/10 of 1% of the total strength of the A. E. F., or approximately 125 military police (one company) to every 20,000 men.

The order made general provision for personnel for the new corps as follows:

(a) Traffic police and headquarters guards to be absorbed in the Military Police Corps.

(b)   One military police company to be assigned to each division, corps, and army.

(c)   Establishment of a training depot to receive, train, and forward to military police units suitable personnel.

It should be remarked that under this new order military police companies assigned to tactical units or sections of the S. O. S. remained as they had been in the past under the military command of the tactical or section commander, the Provost Marshal General exercising technical and administrative control through such commanders.

The Military Police Training Depot provided for in this order was established at Autun on September 9, 1918, and continued in operation until April 15, 1919.

C.   REORGANIZATION OF MILITARY POLICE CORPS

By G. O. No. 180, October 15, 1918, a substantial reorganization of the Military Police Corps and a new definition of its duties and functions was announced. This order not only prescribed the personnel for the overhead organization of the Provost Marshal General's office but likewise made effective a new table of organization for military police companies increasing the enlisted strength from 125 to 200. The total strength of the corps was similarly increased from 7/10th of 1% to 1% of the strength of the A. E. F. Definite provision was also made for commissioned Military Police Corps personnel of appropriate rank and for provost marshals of armies, corps, and divisions.

The physical standards for soldiers of the Military Police Corps were announced in this order and provision made for the transfer of enlisted men thereto. G. O. No. 180, A. E. F., 1918, wholly superseded the Section of G. O. No. 111, A. E. F., 1918, under which the original organization of the corps was authorized.

Shortly after the publication of this order, and as a result of recommendations based on provost marshal experience in the A. E. F., a detailed letter of instructions relating to the organization of the Military Police Corps was sent under date of October 31, 1918, by the Adjutant General of the Army to commanding generals of divisional camps, bureau chiefs, and the C. in C., A. E. F.

The provisions of G. O. No. 180, A. E. F., 1918, were supplemented on November 9, 1918, by G. O. No. 200, A. E. F., 1918, which announced in detail the Military Police Corps organization for the various sections of the S. O. S. The order also authorized the Provost Marshal General to call on the Adjutant General, A. E. F., for the necessary officers and soldiers for the formation of Military Police Corps units and made further provision for transfer into the Military Police Corps.

It should be noticed that while these two orders last discussed gave the Provost Marshal General full technical supervision of Military Police Corps units, each unit remained under the military command of the tactical or section commander to whose organization it was assigned.

D.   TRANSFER OF PROVOST MARSHAL GENERAL TO G. H. Q.

Under both of the general orders last discussed the Provost Marshal General was continued as a member of the staff of the C. in C. but the Department still functioned under the C. G., S. O. S., like the other technical and administrative services. A radical change in this regard was effected by G. O. No. 217, A. E. F., November 27, 1918, which transferred the headquarters of the Military Police Corps to G. H. Q., thus bringing the functions of the corps directly under the First Section of the General Staff at General Headquarters. This order also provided for the organization of a Criminal Investigation Department with enlisted and commissioned personnel and civilian employees.

E.   THE ARMISTICE

Although under the provisions of G. O. No. 200, A. E. F., November 9, 1918, the Military Police Corps units there authorized for the S. O. S. were if possible to be organized by November 20, the plan was far from completion by the end of the month. To meet this situation the Provost Marshal General recommended that one additional company of military police be organized in each division for assignment to duty in the S. O. S. While this plan would have provided without delay thoroughly disciplined personnel for military police duty, it was believed at that time inadvisable to withdraw men from combat units and after consultation with G-3 the plan was disapproved.

However, the Provost Marshal General was given authority to recruit personnel at the Le Mans Embarkation Center and among Class A men evacuated from hospitals, but was limited in each case to soldiers volunteering for military police duty. Voluntary enlistment however failed to produce soldiers in the numbers needed and on December 4 the recommendation was again made for the formation of extra companies in combat divisions. As a result the organization of nine military police companies in the First Army and seven in the Second Army was authorized. These companies were promptly organized and placed on duty in the S. O. S. where they were urgently needed.

With the cessation of active operations on November 11, 1918, there occurred a psychological reaction in the personnel of the A. E. F. natural to a great body of men suddenly released from the high tension and stimulation of war. This situation called for increased activity and vigilance on the part of military police as well as the devising of new methods to meet special features of the situation as they arose. On December 19, 1919, Colonel Milton A. Elliott, Jr., Infantry, was assigned to duty in G-1 for the purpose of studying this situation and, in cooperation with the Provost Marshal General, formulating appropriate measures to meet it.

One of the most apparent manifestations of the condition referred to was the increase in the number of men absent from their commands without leave. Ordinary means of discipline failed to meet the situation or to lessen the commission of this grave military offense. As early as November 27, 1918, the Provost Marshal of the Advance Section, S. O. S., had submitted a memorandum to the P. M. G. on the subject, in which he recommended the establishment of stockades where all deserters and men A. W. O. L. when apprehended should be assembled, and investigations there conducted to determine necessary action in each case. The matter was discussed extensively in conference between G-1 and the Provost Marshal General, and in the latter part of December, 1918, a decision was reached, which took form in G. O. No. 10, A. E. F., January 14, 1919. Before being published the order was submitted to the Judge Advocate's Department for legal consideration, and certain amendments recommended by that department were adopted. The order, while intended to be drastic in its action, left it to the soldier to determine for himself whether he would remain with his organization and return with it to the United States or suffer the penalty consequent on extended unauthorized absence and be among the last returned.

From the reports of the Provost Marshal General and his assistants and from those received from individual officers throughout the A. E. F. it is believed that no order ever issued in the A. E. F. has accomplished more prompt and effective results than did this.

By Par. 1, Sec. 6, G. O. No. 29, A. E. F., February 10, 1919, G. O. No. 10 was amended by substituting Provisional Development Battalion for Labor Battalion.

Colonel Elliott's work on military police matters continued under the supervision of the A. C. of S., G-1, in cooperation with the other staff sections and the Provost Marshal General. In the early months of 1919, Par. 1 and 2, Sec. II, G. O. No. 19, A. E. F., 1919, regarding commutation of rations and quarters for members of the Criminal Investigation Department and Pars. 1 to 8, G. O. No. 22, A. E. F., 1919, relative to the attachment of line troops to the Military Police Corps and the detail of provost marshals of divisions were published.

The revision and final approval of a proposed Military Police Manual (prepared by the Provost Marshal General) was also accomplished with the advice and concurrence of other staff sections.

CHAPTER XII

SUPERVISION OF LIAISON SERVICE

A. SCOPE OF SERVICE

The word liaison has been used so broadly that it is considered advisable to preface this report with the statement that it covers only the Liaison Service operating as a separate organization under the supervision of G-1, G. H. Q., and charged with facilitating the transaction of business between the allies and the A. E. F. It does not include tactical liaison or the various liaisons maintained directly by the other staff sections and by the technical and administrative services.

* * * * * *

B. ORIGIN AND DEVELOPMENT

1. UP TO THE PUBLICATION OF G. O. No. 2?

As early as July 16, 1917, the Commander in Chief wrote to the Commander in Chief of the French Armies of the North and Northeast requesting permission to send Messrs. H. H. Harjes and Ralph Preston to his headquarters as liaison agents. This permission was granted and on July 30, 1917, Mr. Harjes and Mr. Preston were ordered to report to the chief of the American Military Mission at French General Headquarters. From this time until the early part of December no constructive work was done to establish an American Liaison Service, due undoubtedly to the fact that the size of our forces did not warrant such action and because there existed a very efficient French Mission at G. H. Q.

On December 3, 1917, the General Purchasing Agent took the first step in constructive liaison work and instructed Major H. H. Harjes to proceed with the establishment of a proper liaison with the French War Office and the Ministries, as well as the French General Headquarters, in order to:

(a) Further facilitate and accelerate the execution of the requisitions which the A. E. F. might make on the French government.

(b) Obtain more accurate information concerning the exact status of French resources in the way of raw material and manufactured products.

In carrying out the instructions of the General Purchasing Agent, Major Harjes consulted with the French authorities, who were in favor of placing American liaison officers with the various services, but suggested that for the present their efforts be confined to obtaining advance information. It was also suggested that they be authorized to represent the Commanding General, L. of C., the Director General of Transportation, and the General Purchasing Agent in negotiations, and Major Harjes submitted his report to this effect to the General Purchasing Agent. The liaison proposed by the French authorities included more services than the General Purchasing Board, and the question was referred to these headquarters with the recommendation that Major Harjes be designated to discuss the question of inter-ministerial liaison with the French authorities. As the Administrative Section was charged under the provisions of G. O. No. 8, A. E. F., 1917, with questions of general policy and with liaison with technical and administrative services on questions of policy, the matter was referred to this section.

The recommendations of the General Purchasing Agent were concurred in and on December 11, 1917, with the approval of the Chief of Staff, Major Harjes was designated, together with representatives of the Commanding General and the Director General of Transportation, to discuss the question of inter-ministerial liaison. However, the proposed conference was not held inasmuch as the principle of assigning American liaison officers to French services had already been approved by the French authorities and on December 19 this official recognition was confirmed in Article II of "General Instructions for the organization and working of the Franco-American Service of Liaison, Decree of the Presidency of the Council of December 19, " which stated that permanent liaison agents chosen preferably from among the American officers attached to the Franco-American sections or services assure the rapid transmission and ascertain the status of questions under consideration each day. They report both to the French and American authorities.

On January 14, 1918, Major Harjes was appointed Chief Liaison Officer in addition to his other duties and as such was to report directly to the Administrative Section, General Staff, G. H. Q. With this appointment immediate steps were taken to further develop the liaison service and accordingly the French authorities were requested to submit in respective order of urgence the points at which liaison officer should be placed. In reply the French authorities submitted a list of 36 stations, and based on this the Administrative Section, in cooperation with Chief Liaison Officer, started the preparation of a general order.

On February 13, Sec. I, G. O. No. 28, A. E. F., 1918, was issued establishing the liaison service. The order was made broad in its scope in order to permit an aggressive development along experimental lines. Liaison officers were authorized with the various French governmental administrations and with the regions. They were to transmit all orders, all requests for information, and all demands of any kind formulated by Allied authority to the competent and interested American authority, and vice versa. Tactical liaison being handled by combatant commanders was not included in the duties.

2. AFTER THE PUBLICATION OF G. O. No. 28, 1918

With the approval of the French authorities on the placing of American liaison officers with the French services (on December 31, 1917), three officers had been placed with the 1st, 3d, and 4th Bureaus, respectively, and three other officers with the 4th and 5th Bureaus and *Service de Santé*, under those first named. Three officers were also assigned to the Ministry of Armament. No further action was taken until the publication of G. O. No. 28, when liaison officers were placed with such regions and administrative services in Paris as were authorized in the order.

As already stated no provisions were made in the order for placing officers of the Liaison Service with combat units, but on February 15, General Maud'huy, commanding the French XI Corps, requested the assignment of such an officer to his corps. In connection with this request the Chief Liaison Officer proceeded to French General Headquarters to ascertain the views of the military authorities regarding the placing of officers of the Liaison Service in the Zone of the Armies. As a result he was authorized to place such officers with a few combat units. At first there was some confusion between their functions and those of the tactical liaison officers but this was soon eliminated by directing the officers of the Liaison Service not to participate in tactical liaison, merely reporting items of general interest regarding troop movements to these headquarters.

On May 15 the *Sous-Secrétariat d'Etat de la Présidence du Conseil* wrote a letter to the Chief Liaison Officer giving a report on the Liaison Service, in which he expressed for the heads of the French Department their great satisfaction with the valuable help which it had rendered. He particularly called attention to the importance of having all requests to the French submitted through liaison officers and requested that more such officers be assigned to the regions.

The work of the liaison service as finally developed can be divided into the following three classes, all of them distinct, but having certain features in common:
    (1) Liaison with the French bureaus and administrations in Paris.
    (2) Liaison with the regions.
    (3) Liaison with the armies.

Of these, G. O. No. 38 had authorized the placing of liaison officers with the bureaus in Paris and with certain regions. It had also provided for the further expansion of the service by providing that additional liaisons would be effected as needed.

By August, 1918, the Liaison Service had developed beyond the provisions of G. O. No. 28, and a reconsideration of the situation became necessary with a view to determining:

(a) The scope and routine of the work.

(b) Its use by the services of the A. E. F. in the past.

(c) The future development of the service.

It was found that wherever the service has been used it had been of real value, and it was decided to prepare a new general order expanding the service and making its functions more definite. To assist in the preparation of this order the Chief Liaison Officer was directed to send to these headquarters an officer from the Liaison Service. Major J. L. Coolidge was designated and came here on temporary duty. The new order as drafted extended the service to include more French combat units and established liaison officers with the five British armies. Provision also was made for the placing of liaison officers with the Belgian and Italian armies as necessity arose, subject to arrangements to be made with the Belgian and Italian authorities. The proposed general order was submitted to the French and British authorities for approval and on November 6, G. O. No. 197, A. E. F., 1918, was published, revoking the provisions of G. O. No. 28.

The new liaisons authorized by the order were never put into effect as the signing of the Armistice rendered them unnecessary and in fact permitted the recall of many other liaison officers. At the same time, however, the Peace Conference and the Food Commission requested liaison officers and some officers recalled from other stations were stationed with them. Later, on March 6, 1919, it was decided to recall all liaison officers with French combat troops as their services were no longer necessary.

C. ORGANIZATION AND DUTIES

1. PERSONNEL

a. Selection: With the final decision on the establishment of a liaison service, the first questions considered were the personnel and where to obtain it. The duties which they would be required to perform necessitated carefully selected officers, having a knowledge of French customs and language, a certain amount of military experience, an adaptability to circumstances, and a great amount of tact and good judgment. At first, efforts were made to obtain the personnel from the divisions, but out of a list of 40 names submitted, the Chief Liaison Officer was able to select on personal interview only two with the proper qualifications. Attempts to obtain personnel from the Casual Officers Depot at Blois were also of no avail. It was found however that the War Risk Bureau had some officers qualified and from these a few officers were selected. Also on March 18, 1918, cable P-745-1 was sent, requesting that certain officers with proper qualifications be ordered here for liaison duty. The men requested were sent. With the exception of one or two officers who were commissioned from the ranks, these were the sources from which the personnel was originally obtained.

b. Training: Under G. O. No. 28, no provisions had been made for the training of officers assigned to the liaison service, but in the consideration of G. O. No. 197, it was considered advisable to provide some training. Accordingly, all officers entering the service were required to report to the Chief Liaison Officer to receive instructions as to the general scope and nature of the work and were then assigned to duty as subordinates to officers of experience before being assigned to independent posts.

c. Transportation and Travel Orders: The functions of the officers, particularly in the regions and with the armies, required constant travel. In so far as it was possible, automobile transportation was furnished. Furthermore, the Chief Liaison Officer was authorized to issue general instructions permitting the travel of officers in his service and reporting the travel to G. H. Q., where the necessary order of confirmation was approved by G-1 and issued by the Adjutant General.

2. LIAISON WITH FRENCH BUREAUS AND ADMINISTRATIONS IN PARIS

It has been shown in the above how the liaison service developed out of the need of the General Purchasing Board for representatives with the various French services and how this liaison developed to include not only representation of the General Purchasing Board but also of the Commanding General, L. of C., and the Director General of Transportation. When officers were placed with these bureaus it was decided not to limit their functions, except that they were not to replace the proper authority in deciding principles or executing measures. When developed, their functions were very broad and included the handling of such subjects as supplies, labor, land requisitions, settlements of accounts between the A. E. F. and Allied governments, transportation, and general matters of police and intelligence. The most important of these was the settlement of accounts, as all payments of invoices from and to the French and Allied governments were made through the liaison officer with the *Direction du Contrôle, Ministère de la Guerre.*

3. LIAISON WITH FRENCH REGIONS

Under G. O. No. 28, officers were placed with the Headquarters of French regional commanders, but as their duties were unknown no restrictions were placed on them. On the publication of G. O. No. 197, it was still considered inadvisable to limit their functions as experience had shown that they handled such matters as troop movements, billeting, interchange of perishable supplies, concessions of buildings and barracks, and in particular the straightening out of small difficulties arising from misunderstandings between the troops in their regions and the local French authorities. However, the value of their service was so evident that it was provided that before an American demand was definitely formulated for presentation to regional authorities it should be presented to the local liaison officer for advice as to the form in which it should be presented and for opinion as to the ability and inclination of the French to comply with the demand.

4. LIAISON WITH COMBAT UNITS

a. With French Armies: As has been shown above, no provisions were made in G. O. No. 28 for the placing of liaison officers with combat units, but on the request of the French authorities such officers were afterwards placed. The functions of these officers were stated in G. O. No. 197, which provided that they were placed with Allied staffs for the purpose of maintaining a close liaison: First, between such staffs and American units operating in the same or adjacent territory; second, between such staffs and the General Staff at G. H. Q. In the exercise of these functions they were to keep the Allied staffs informed concerning matters of interest pertaining to the activities of the A. E. F., to report to G-2 and G-3, G. H. Q., matters of interest such as movement of enemy troops, and to submit periodical reports on operations, organization, tactics, and equipment.

b. With Other Allied Armies: It was decided, with the publication of G. O. No. 197, to increase the liaisons with combat units to include the other Allied armies, their functions to be the same as those of officers serving with French units. However, these liaisons were never placed as the signing of the Armistice made them unnecessary.

CHAPTER XIII

LEAVE

A. THE LEAVE PROBLEM

1. NEED FOR LEAVE

The liberal provisions of Army Regulations for leaves to officers and furloughs to soldiers were, like many other peacetime privileges, necessarily curtailed for the duration of the war. In the United States, however, it was comparatively easy for the majority of troops to get permission from time to time to visit either their families or large cities in the vicinity of the training camps.

The need of relaxation was much greater in the A. E. F. than in the United States, because of the constant physical and mental strain under which men worked, as well as their isolation from their homes. Early in the history of the A. E. F. it was recognized that, in order to protect the morale as well as the health of officers and soldiers, some system of leaves and furloughs was necessary.

2. SITUATION IN THE A. E. F.

For the armies of our allies the leave problem was a comparatively simple one. The French could and did permit their soldiers to visit their homes at regular intervals. The British, too, arranged for a regular cross-channel service which enabled their men to get from trench to home in a comparatively few hours.

With the A. E. F. the situation was radically different and, as in the case of so many important matters, there were no precedents to serve as a guide. It was obviously impossible for men to return to their homes on leave because of the shortage of those two vital elements in the war, time and transportation. Nor could soldiers, many of them without adequate funds, be given liberty to travel where they pleased in a strange country whose transportation system was already overburdened by the needs of the war.

3. EARLY REGULATIONS

On the arrival of the first American forces in France no special regulations were made as to the amount of leaves or furloughs, but week-end passes were allowed to men to visit the towns in the vicinity of their units. Unfortunately, the desire of the soldier for a good time and the fact that he usually had more money than his fellow French soldier, combined with his lack of knowledge of French customs, in some cases caused disturbances of a more or less serious character. These facts and the shortage of railroad transportation made it necessary first to limit such leaves and later to suspend them entirely until the publication of a general order on the subject.

However, commanding officers of the engineer units serving with the British were authorized to grant leaves under the same conditions as the British, and subject to the approval of the British commander under whom they were serving. Such leaves were not to exceed seven days every four months, the first to begin no earlier than four months after arrival in France.

B. THE LEAVE SYSTEM

I. DURING HOSTILITIES

1. Preparation of a General Order: The development of an A. E. F. leave policy was inaugurated on August 25, 1917, when the Chief of Staff requested the recommendations of the Chief Surgeon as to the advisability of granting leaves at regular periods. The Chief

Surgeon expressed the opinion that a leave system was essential to the health of officers and soldiers and recommended the adoption of the French and British systems of leaves of from seven to fourteen days every four months. During September the question was studied in greater detail, the Commanding General, 1st Division, the Provost Marshal General, and the head of the Y. M. C. A. being consulted.

On October 10 there was submitted to the Chief of Staff the first draft of a general order on the subject, which was based on the following general principles:

(a) The granting of leaves as a matter of policy.

(b) Leaves to be granted where required and withheld when not required.

(c) Leaves to be limited by the necessities of the service.

(d) Leaves to be limited to transportation facilities.

(e) The exercise of necessary control over men on leave and the allowance of as much freedom as was consistent with such control.

Estimates based on one ten-day leave every four months indicated that a maximum of 8.3% of all personnel would be absent on leave at one time. In actual experience the percentage was lower, due to casualties, withdrawal of privileges, lack of sufficient funds, and similar causes.

As the cooperation of the French was necessary to the success of any leave system, the French Mission was consulted and, at their recommendation, a conference of French and American officers was held at the French Ministry of War on November 8. At this conference the following propositions were made by the French:

(a) A leave of seven days, time of travel not included, to be granted to officers and soldiers every four months, the first period to begin on February 15, 1918.

(b) Leave centers to be chosen by the American authorities with the concurrence of the French, as very few members of the A. E. F. had families in France.

(c) Officers and soldiers having near relatives to be permitted to visit such relatives on producing a certificate of relationship. In case the locality was in the Zone of the Armies, the approval of the French G. H. Q. was to be secured.

(d) The development of leave areas progressively in accordance with the needs of the A. E. F., such development to be subject to the approval of the French authorities.

(e) The organization of special trains for men on leave.

(f) Discipline to be maintained by the military police on trains, particular emphasis being placed on the fact that men should not carry arms.

(g) The same rules to apply to units in the interior as to units in the line.

(h) Leaves of twenty-four hours not to be granted in the armies, as they were not given to French soldiers, although such leaves could be granted in the interior.

(i) The details of the application of the above principles to be arranged by American and French representatives of the services interested.

With some minor modifications these suggestions were embodied in the proposed order, which was revised during December and published on January 8th, as G. O. No. 6, A. E. F., 1918. Under the provisions of this order the term "leave" was used to designate both leaves of absence and furloughs. The administration of the order was made the duty of the C. G., L. of C., to be carried out through his P. M. G. Department in cooperation with the Y. M. C. A. (accommodations and entertainment) and the D. G. T. (transportation.) The principal features of the leave system established by this order and modified by later orders, are described below.

2. Leave Privileges: a. Prescribed in Orders. G. O. No. 6 prescribed that officers and men might be granted one leave of seven days every four months, time of travel to and from destination in France not included. The leave began at 12:01 a. m. (night) following arrival at destination, and expired at midnight after the lapse of the number of days authorized, after which the first available trains had to be taken back. In the case of leaves in exceptional cases to points outside of France, the time of leave was counted as beginning on departure from France and terminating on arrival back in France. Special exception to the above regulations was made in the case of the personnel of higher

headquarters who might be granted authorized leaves each four months in the form of several short leaves, if in the interest of the service.

b. Suspension for Tactical Reasons: In accordance with the suggestion of the French, the first leaves began on February 15, 1918. Unfortunately the military situation soon necessitated the cancellation of leaves and on March 3 the C. G., L. of C., was told that no more leaves would be granted. These instructions remained in effect until May 24, when they were modified to apply only to troops actually on the part of the front from Rheims to the North Sea, or actually under orders to go to the front. On June 29 this was changed to read from Verdun to the North Sea.

Because of the impending offensive leaves were discontinued for all units of the First Army on September 1 and not resumed until October 13.

3. Leave Areas: a. The Leave Area Principle: When the question of leaves was first considered in August, 1917, the Y. M. C. A. proposed a scheme for taking men on leave first to Paris, where they would be taken to visit the points of interest, and then to some place in the Alps where opportunities for athletics and entertainment would be furnished. The plan was not adopted because it would tie the men down with too many restrictions and it was desired to give them as much liberty as possible while on leave.

In October the *Office National du Tourisme* suggested that men who could afford it be allowed to travel anywhere they wished on leave, while those without funds would be taken in large groups to some of the resorts of France. This proposal was considered at the November conference with the French officials who objected to any soldiers being allowed to travel wherever they wished but approved the idea of special leave centers for everyone. The leave area principle was thus definitely adopted at this conference and was incorporated in G. O. No. 6, A. E. F., 1918.

b. Selection of Leave Areas: Leave areas were selected by the C. G., L. of C., in cooperation with the Y. M. C. A. Aix-les-Bains, the first one chosen, was opened on February 16, 1918, and was the only one in operation until the opening of the Auvergne area on September 21. Certain of the attractive resorts near the Swiss or Spanish borders which would have made suitable leave areas were objected to at first by the French or by G-2, G. H. Q., because of the danger of enemy espionage activities. The opening of a leave area in the Principality of Monaco was disapproved for the same reason. Some of these restrictions, however, were removed in August and September.

At a conference with the French on October 2 at which a representative of G-1, G. H. Q., was present, the question of new leave areas was discussed. Thirteen areas with a total capacity of 40,000 beds were considered in detail, and it was decided to make a reconnaissance of other areas to bring the total up to 70,000 beds. This capacity was never reached, however, even during the Armistice, because of the limiting factor of transportation.

c. Duty Status: The original plan for leaves contemplated that soldiers would pay their own expenses for board and lodging. On arriving at a leave area they could make their own choice of hotel or *pension*, registering their addresses with the A. P. M. Several French organizations offered their assistance in preparing lists of suitable accommodations and the Association of French Homes proposed to furnish the names of private families who would be glad to entertain American soldiers on leave. This plan, however, proved impracticable on further examination.

Immediately after the first leave area was opened it was found that the system of having men go on leave at their own expense would not work out satisfactorily, because of their lack of sufficient funds. As there was no provision for paying commutation of quarters for men on leave, it was decided to establish the leave areas as military posts and order men to them on a duty status so that quarters could be furnished in kind, in the same manner as at any other station. The usual rate of commutation of rations being insufficient to meet the cost of board commutation at the rate of $1.00 per day was authorized at the same time, the two measures being combined in Section I, G. O. No. 38, A. E. F.,

1918, which was published on March 9. Men who went on leave to places other than regular leave areas could not, however, be considered as on a duty status and only commutation of rations at 60 cents per day, with no commutation of quarters, was given them.

Arrangements were made later whereby rations were furnished in kind on contracts between the army and the leave area hotels.

d. Protection against Venereal Disease: The experience of the French and British Armies was that from 60% to 70% of the cases of venereal disease among their men had been contracted while on leave. Every precaution, therefore, was taken to safeguard our own men in this respect. G. O. No. 6 provided that each man be examined before departure on leave, to establish his freedom from venereal disease, and be instructed in the prophylactic regulations. The other also prescribed that all A. P. M. stations be provided with suitable prophylactic facilities.

e. Discipline: After a study of the French and British systems of handling men on leave, a leave paper suited to our own needs was prepared. * * * This form and G. O. No. 6 give in detail the regulations for visé and registry.

Arrangements were made for men going on leave to turn in their rifles, bayonets, and pistols, and no liquor, firearms, or explosives of any kind were allowed to be carried. Misconduct while on leave was reported by A. P. M.'s to the offenders' commanding officers for disciplinary action and men guilty of serious breaches of discipline were promptly returned to their organizations.

4. Transportation: The greatest difficulty in establishing a comprehensive and satisfactory system of leaves was the shortage of transportation. The French authorities desired that all men going on leave travel on special trains in order to avoid congestion on the regular trains. This was provided for in G. O. No. 6, transportation on special leave trains being furnished by the Government. Where special trains were not available, travel on regular trains was at the expense of the soldier. The order also specified the class of accommodations to be used by officers, nurses, field clerks, N. C. O.'s and others.

On August 24, Sec. V, G. O. No. 139, A. E. F., 1918, was published, providing for transportation at government expense of soldiers going to regular leave areas and traveling by commercial trains in the event of special leave trains not being available.

5. Exceptional Destinations: In addition to the leave area system outlined above, the following provisions were made for leaves to exceptional destinations.

a. Paris: Leaves to Paris were limited for several reasons, primarily because of the serious veneral situation in the city. The shortage of accommodations was another difficulty which the Y. M. C. A. offered to help overcome by building barracks. This offer was not accepted because of the bad effect that the presence of a large number of American soldiers on the stredts of Paris would have on the morale of the French people at a time when the military situation demanded the greatest possible effort at the front.

A limited number of leaves to Paris were allowed, however, these being allotted to units of the A. E. F. by the P. M. G.

b. Other destinations: Soldiers were not permitted to go on leave to places other than regular leave areas or Paris, except to visit immediate relatives or for other very exceptional reasons. Even in such cases the approval of the French Military Mission was necessary before leaves could be granted to certain localities specified in G. O. No. 6.

6. Officers: The frequency and duration of leaves which might be granted to officers were the same as for soldiers. There was no limitation as to the points to be visited on leave, other than Paris, except that for points in the French Zone of the Armies the concurrence of the French Military Mission was required.

In August, 1918, there was established in Paris an Officers' Leave Bureau. Its functions, as described in Section II, Bulletin No. 62, A. E. F., 1918, were to collect and distribute data concerning accommodations available in all localities where officers were permitted to spend their leave. It was also instrumental in establishing the American Officers' Hotel at Paris for the use of officers on leave or passing through the city which is described in Bulletin No. 103, A. E. F., 1918.

1. More Liberal Policy: On December 9, 1918, the C. in C. directed that a most liberal policy be adopted with reference to leaves and that a thorough study of the subject be made. He wished special attention to be given to the following points: (a) The extension of the duration of leave periods; (b) the extension of leave areas; including Great Britain and Italy; and (c) the granting of leaves to men ordered to the United States, before embarkation.

G-1 immediately undertook a study of the question and the preparation of a new order to supersede G. O. No. 6, A. E. F., 1918. The controlling factor in the situation was then, as always, that of transportation. The C. G., S. O. S., was able to increase the number and capacity of leave areas but could not secure sufficient train equipment to keep these areas filled at all times. With the restricted transportation available it was likewise impossible to give every man in the A. E. F. a leave every four months. The other two measures mentioned by the C. in C. were, however, successfully developed.

The new order was carefully worked out in consultation with the C. G., S. O. S., the P. M. G., the Judge Advocate, and G-4. Several drafts were prepared and the final one was published on January 13 as G. O. No. 14, A. E. F., 1919. The order was so drawn that its provisions were elastic and could be expanded as the increase of transportation and lodging facilities permitted. Its new features and their development are described below.

2. Classes of Leaves: G. O. No. 14 provided for five classes of leaves as follows:
Class A for soldiers to regular leave areas.
Class B for officers, and for soldiers to points other than regular leave areas.
Class C for officers and soldiers to Paris.
Class D for casual officers and soldiers ordered to the United States.
Class E for officers and soldiers in exceptional cases.

Soldiers on Class A leave were considered to be on duty status and their necessary expenses were paid. In all other classes of leave, soldiers were not on a duty status and their expenses, therefore, could not legally be paid by the Government, although they received commutation of rations.

3. Leave Areas: On December 1, 1918, there were in operation five leave areas with a capacity of 15,000 beds. By March 1, 1919, this had been increased to 18 areas with a capacity of approximately 33,000 beds. The number of men sent to leave areas from the time the first one was established in February, 1918, until December 1, 1918, a period of 9 1/2 months, was 74,000. In the three months following, December 1, 1918 to March 1, 1919, 199,000 men visited these areas on a duty status. The organization and administration of leave areas and their allotments to units under the new order were handled by the C. G., S. O. S., as before.

At the request of the C. G., S. O. S., bands were detailed in January from the regiments of the First and Second Armies to visit a number of leave areas. Each band remained two weeks when it was replaced by another from the same army.

4. Transportation: a. Special Leave Trains: As mentioned above, all necessary expenses of soldiers on Class A leaves were paid by the Government, special leave trains being provided whenever possible. There was considerable difficulty in getting suitable equipment from the French to operate special leave trains, but the situation gradually improved during the Armistice. By March 1 there were in operation 39 special leave trains in each direction, requiring 24 complete sets of train equipment, as compared with three sets of equipment operating December 1, 1918. By this time the use of box cars had also been almost entirely eliminated, the French having been persuaded to furnish passenger coaches.

b. Discipline: All special leave trains were furnished by division and separate organization commanders with a guard of officers and soldiers who were responsible for the maintenance of order both on the train and at the stations. G. O. No. 14 provided that men involved in any violations of orders or breach of discipline would be turned over by the guard to the A. P. M. at the nearest station for return to their organizations under guard for suitable disciplinary action. In case of serious disturbance en route to a leave area the guard was to report to the A. P. M. at the nearest station, who would arrange with the railroad authorities to sidetrack the train at the first convenient place and return it to the point of departure. Any such cases were to be reported by the P. M. G. to G. H. Q. in order that the leave privileges for all units involved might be suspended. This action, fortunately, was never necessary.

5. Exceptional Destinations: a. Paris: While the new leave order was in course of preparation the C-in-C on December 22 directed a study of some plan whereby all men of the A. E. F. might have an opportunity to visit Paris before leaving France. He wished our men to have, if possible, the educational advantage of a trip to Paris and further believed that the announcement of this privilege would decrease the number of men then going to Paris A. W. O. L. His suggestion was that men might be taken to Paris by battalions or regiments, perhaps half a division at a time, for a three or four days' stay.

Strong opposition to any plan for granting leaves to Paris developed from several sources. The Chief Surgeon reported on the serious venereal situation in the city and urged that no leaves be granted. Marshal Foch wrote personally to the C-in-C and urged that large numbers of American soldiers be not allowed to visit Paris because of the already overcrowded conditions of the city and because from the very fact of their extreme popularity, their easy going ways, and their unfailing generosity, they would find themselves exposed in this city, more than ever, to exploitations which the French authorities, ambitious for the good reputation of Paris, wish to avoid.

Because of this opposition a scheme for sending large detachments to be quartered in barracks outside of Paris and convoyed each day through the city in motor trucks to the points of interest, was abandoned and replaced by the plan incorporated in G. O. No. 14, which provided for a special three-day leave to Paris to a smaller number of men.

b. England: In reply to an inquiry made on December 9, the British Mission stated on January 4 that 150 officers and men a day could be handled by channel transportation to visit the British Isles on leave and that there would be no limitation on their free circulation after arrival. In this case, as in all the others, transportation was the factor which determined the number of men who could be given leaves.

c. Italy: For men going to Italy, forty places were reserved on a train operated by the French and leaving Dijon every other day. This provided for an average of 140 men a week which was much less than the applications from Italian-born members of the A. E. F. to visit their relatives. In March it was possible to increase this allowance to 100 men a day, improved transportation facilities having been arranged for.

d. Belgium: The Belgian Mission was consulted with reference to the number of American soldiers who might be permitted to travel in Belgium on leave and replied on January 8 that there would be no restrictions. In view of the lack of military police control, however, 500 was arbitrarily fixed as the maximum number of officers and soldiers who might be on leave in Belgium at any one time.

e. Alsace-Lorraine: At the request of the French Mission, leaves to Alsace-Lorraine were granted to officers and soldiers only with the approval of the French authorities.

f. Greece: Applications for leaves to Greece were considered only in very exceptional cases. When granted they were deducted from the allotment to Italy and did not exceed 14 days. As nearly all of this time would be consumed in travel these restrictions were practically a bar to any leaves to that country for men serving in France.

The Commanding Officer of the 332d Infantry, which was then in Italy, was authorized on March 15 to grant leaves to 30 men of Greek birth to visit Greece.

g. Neutral Countries: Many requests were received for the granting of leaves to neutral countries. Through diplomatic channels the Scandinavian countries asked that men of Scandinavian origin be permitted to visit their relatives before returning to the United States, while the Hotelkeepers Association and other interests in Switzerland made strong representations on the subject of establishing leave areas and arranging for itineraries to the points of interest in their country.

On January 9 the Judge Advocate expressed the opinion that, under the rules of International Law, there were no objections to members of the A. E. F. visiting neutral countries, either in or out of uniform. He stated that if a soldier were traveling individually, without arms or equipment and for his own pleasure or business, the fact that he was a member of the military force of a belligerent nation did not jeopardize the neutrality of the country he visited.

In March the military attaché at Berne brought the subject up again, stating that the Swiss government was very anxious to have members of the A. E. F. visit their country and would permit their entry with no more formalities than their identification cards and leave orders.

However, because of the difficulty of controlling men on leave in a neutral country and the prevalence of Bolshevistic propaganda in Switzerland, no plan for granting such leaves was adopted.

h. Allotments: The administration of the new leave system was made the duty of the C. G., S. O. S., except that G. H. Q. reserved to itself the determination of the number of leaves to exceptional destinations and their allotment among the A. E. F. This was done because of the necessary negotiations with other governments.

In a letter of January 19 to the commanding generals of the three armies and of the S. O. S., allotments were made as follows:

	First Army	Second Army	Third Army	S. O. S.	G. H. Q.	TOTAL
England (officers and soldiers per day)	30	30	30	55	5	150
Belgium (total officers and soldiers absent at one time)	80	80	80	240	20	500
Italy (officers and soldiers every other day)	7	7	7	17	2	40
Paris (officers daily)	58	58	58	151	8	333
Paris (soldiers daily)	145	145	145	388	10	833

On February 16 the allotments to Paris were increased to 175 for each of the three armies, 465 for the S. O. S., and 10 for G. H. Q., a total of 1,000. On February 18 those to Italy were increased to 18 for each of the armies, 44 for the S. O. S. and 2 for G. H. Q., a total of 100 daily in place of the previous allowance of 40 every other day.

6. Leaves for the Army of Occupation: Because of the difficulty in getting transportation from occupied territory to the regularly established leave areas in France, the Third Army in the latter part of December established Corps Recreation Centers at Neuwied, Andernach, Coblenz, and Ehrenbreitstein, where 12,000 men could be handled at one time. Arrangements were also made for steamer trips on the Rhine for men on leave.

In February the transportation situation improved and a regular system of special trains to the leave areas in France was established for the Third Army.

7.   Troops Serving With Allied Forces or Outside of France: Commanders of troops serving with allied forces were authorized to grant leaves in accordance with the principles of G. O. No. 14 and subject to such regulations of the allied army as were applicable. During the Armistice the United States Army Ambulance Service, with approximately 4,500 officers and men serving with the French, was the most important unit concerned. Those in France or occupied territory were placed on the same basis as troops in the S. O. S.

In the case of all troops outside of France or occupied territory, leaves to visit France were first approved by G. H. Q.

CHAPTER XIV

SUPERVISION OF WELFARE SOCIETIES

[Omissions are matters of detail]

INTRODUCTION

The following is submitted as a report of the supervision exercised by the General Staff, especially by the Administrative Section, subsequently the First Section, of the General Staff, over the activities of the welfare societies associated with the A. E. F. from the commencement of their work in France to April 15, 1919.   It does not purport to be an account of the activities of the societies themselves or a critical study of the work performed by them.

* * * * * *

A.   TO DECEMBER 31, 1917

1.   Y. M. C. A.

The official recognition of the Y. M. C. A. as an agency of the A. E. F. and the determination as to the status of its personnel were based upon the order of the President issued April 26, 1917 and published in G. O. No. 57, W. D., May 9, 1917.   This order, in accepting the Association's tender of its services for the benefit of the enlisted men, determined that it should continue as a voluntary civilian organization, enjoined officers to render it the fullest practicable assistance and cooperation in its work, and called attention to the precedent and policy already established by certain Acts of Congress and general orders in the matters of providing facilities, assigning sites for buildings, supplying transportation, caring for tents and grounds, according secretaries the privilege of purchasing supplies from the Q. M. Dept., and furnishing tentage when practicable.

The practical beginning of the Y. M. C. A.'s work for American troops in France is recorded in a letter from the Association's representative in Paris to the Adjutant General, A. E. F. June 22, 1917, announcing the opening of an American Army and Navy Y. M. C. A. building at 31 Ave. Montaigne, Paris. * * *.

On July 9, 1917 Mr. E. C. Carter, Chief Secretary in Europe, submitted to the Commander-in-Chief a statement of the field of activity of the American Army and Navy Y. M. C. A. in Europe, covering in a broad way the providing of recreation for officers and men all the way from the ports to the front, including the establishment of clubs, cafes, hotels, lectures, educational classes, entertainments, athletics, religious activities, and direct and indirect attack upon the menace of prostitution.   The intention to undertake recreative work on a large scale for the French Army was also stated.   This program was heartily approved by the Commander-in-Chief in a letter to Mr. Carter dated July 16, 1917.

The extension of the activities of the Y. M. C. A. into the training area is signalized by the granting of authority in July, 1917, to certain of its representatives to proceed into the Gondrecourt area to take up their work with the 1st Division. The carrying of the work into the field, first into the training areas and subsequently into combat areas, was attended by certain fundamental difficulties which were apparent in the early stages and which persisted to a greater or less extent throughout the period of hostilities, which should not be overlooked in any effort to make a just appraisal of the aggregate service rendered by the Y. M. C. A. and other welfare societies. Though not strictly a part of the army, they were dependent on the assistance and cooperation of the army to a far greater extent than in their work at home, and this assistance and cooperation the army was frequently unable, for military reasons, to accord them as fully as it would have wished. * * *

Difficulties also arose with respect to the purchase and transportation of material and supplies. On August 4, 1917, the Quartermaster Department was directed to furnish transportation to the Y. M. C. A. when available. In the matter of purchases it was found essential to stop the civilian agencies from purchasing in the open market in competition with the Army. Early in August arrangements were made for the purchase of lumber by the Y. M. C. A. through the office of the Chief Engineer. Soon afterwards, by G. O. No. 23, A. E. F., August 20, 1917, a General Purchasing Board was established to coordinate and supervise all purchases made by the A. E. F., and representatives of the Red Cross and the Y. M. C. A. were appointed on the board as well as those of the various supply departments (G. O. No. 28, A. E. F., August 30, 1917). The societies were required to submit to the board full information as to proposed purchases and negotiations as well as immediate transactions.

The necessity of coordinating the work of civilian agencies and preventing duplication of effort became apparent as their activities began to develop and resulted in the publication of Sec. II, G. O. No. 26, A. E. F., August 28, 1917, prescribing a broad division of activities between the Red Cross and the Y. M. C. A., the Red Cross to provide for relief work and the Y. M. C. A. for amusement and recreation by means of its usual program of social, educational, physical, and religious activities. This guiding rule, though departed from in many instances by reason of the exigencies of particular situations, has been adhered to as a policy throughout the history of the A. E. F. It was amplified by Sec. II, G. O. No. 48, A. E. F., October 20, 1917, approving an arrangement between the two societies for the joint provision of recreation facilities in army hospitals, an arrangement which continued until September, 1918, when the Red Cross took over this phase of the work entirely.

The status of the personnel of the Y. M. C. A. and other welfare societies (exclusive of the Red Cross, whose position in this respect has been somewhat different) as militarized civilians has been a matter of considerable perplexity to all concerned. On July 22 and July 28, 1917, the War Department cabled for recommendations with respect to the claim of Y. M. C. A. officials that they could not do their work properly without assimilated military rank. The Commander-in-Chief reported adversely on this proposition but recommended that he be authorized to give a limited number of honorary commissions not above major, without pay or emolument, to enable the principal Y. M. C. A. officials to wear uniforms of their grades with Y. M. C. A. brassards, to assist them in their intercourse with the French. This authority was granted the Commander-in-Chief by War Department cable August 1, 1917, but never exercised. The question of status was of importance particularly in the matter of circulation privileges, as to which very strict rules had been laid down by the French government. * * *

Closely connected with the question of military status was that of uniforms, an important consideration especially from the point of view of the Provost Marshal General's Department, charged with supervising the circulation of all classes of personnel connected with the A. E. F. The uniform established by the Y. M. C. A. for its male workers, the regular U. S. Army uniform with bronze letters U. S. on the right and Y. M. C. A. on the left of the collar, and a red triangle with the letters Y. M. C. A. across it on the right sleeve was approved by the Chief of Staff, A. E. F., October 23, 1917. Subsequently specifications of uniforms for women workers were filed and furnished to the Provost Marshal General.

Post Exchanges: In response to a verbal request from the Chief of the Coordination Section, Mr. Carter,* Chief of the Y. M. C. A., wrote the Adjutant General, A. E. F., on June 21, 1917, intimating the willingness of his society to undertake the operation of canteens for the A. E. F. similar to the post exchanges in the American Army and the Expeditionary Force canteens in the British Army. * * *

* * * * * *

Leaves: In November, 1917, the subject of making provision for the granting of leaves to officers and soldiers of the A. E. F. was taken up in conference with the French military authorities. As a result of this conference and a study submitted by the French, a G. O. was drafted and the cooperation of the Y. M. C. A. was enlisted. * * * The providing of entertainment and recreation, essential to the success of the plan, was left entirely to the Y. M. C. A., which has admirably fulfilled its part of the work.

* * * * * *

A report submitted by the Y. M. C. A. as of December 15, 1917, shows approximately the following distribution of its personnel:

Headquarters staff, 150; Paris area workers (including recreation hut at 31 Ave. Montaigne, Hotel Richmond for officers, Hotel Pavillon for enlisted men) 25; workers in the field at 75 different stations, 300.

2. AMERICAN RED CROSS

On June 20, 1917, the Chief of Staff, A. E. F., directed the Adjutant General to convene a board consisting of certain army officers and certain officials of the Red Cross to consider in detail the best method of coordinating in Europe the American Red Cross and the other relief activities, their relations to one another and to the military service, and to submit a working plan. The board submitted a report recommending that the Commander-in-Chief establish a Red Cross department on his staff and attach to his staff Major G. M. P. Murphy, Red Cross Commissioner for Europe, to insure conformity between the operations of the American Red Cross and the policies of the Commander-in-Chief. It further recommended a line of demarcation between the functions of the Medical Corps and the Red Cross, the former to have exclusive charge of all sanitary operations both in the zone of the advance and the zone of the line of communications, within which field the Red Cross should furnish only such luxuries, supplies, and additional service as the Medical Corps might request; auxiliary services such as convalescent homes, etc., to be maintained by the Red Cross, subject to inspection and control by the Chief Surgeon, A. E. F. These recommendations were substantially adopted. * * *

* * * * * *

On August 29, 1917, a statement purporting to represent the views of practically all the American relief workers in Paris, many of whom had been engaged in such work long prior to our entrance into the war, was cabled by the Red Cross Commission in France to the War Council in America, acknowledging the value of the work theretofore performed by

* Mr. E. C. Carter, Chief Secretary of the A. E. F., Y. M. C. A.

Americans in that field and pointing out the new situation brought about by the coming of the American Army, especially in the matter of transportation, both ocean and inland, making essential the creation of new machinery and a complete pooling of interests. The recommendations made were that the Red Cross organization in France classify, standardize, and requisition in the order of their importance the relief supplies which were needed and determine what might be purchased in Europe or dispensed with altogether, and that the Red Cross organization at home, aided by other experienced organizations there, provide in a systematic way for furnishing the relief supplies so indicated as needed in Europe and for their shipment in the order of their urgency.

* * * * * *

The status of Red Cross personnel was at the outset quite as puzzling as that of the Y. M. C. A. The Board heretofore mentioned recommended complete militarization of the active personnel, involving the granting of commissions either in the Reserve Corps or in the Red Cross (if authorized by Congress) and the enlistment or enrollment of all other personnel under contract, for the period of the war or some definite period, as camp followers of the American Army. The Judge Advocate, being consulted on this point, ruled (August 21, 1917) that all persons accompanying or serving with our armies in France became subject to the disciplinary provisions of the Articles of War and to trial by courts-martial for infractions thereof, irrespective of contract, and that the desirability of a contract of employment was therefore wholly a matter for the determination of the Red Cross itself. The question of commissions for Red Cross officers was the subject of cable correspondence between the Commander-in-Chief and the War Department commencing in July. The Commander-in-Chief was at first opposed, as in the case of the Y. M. C. A., to the granting of commissions except of an honorary character to a few of the higher officials, but later, after further conference with the Red Cross authorities, expressed the opinion that some sort of militarization was probably desirable. This matter was settled by the publication of G. O. No. 82, W. D., 1917. * * *

* * * * * *

On August 2, 1917, the Red Cross wrote the Chief of Staff offering the services of its Bureau of Information of Casualties as a medium of communication between the American soldiers and their relatives at home. The plan was further developed in a letter to the Commander-in-Chief dated September 15, 1917, proposing that Red Cross searchers be stationed with all regiments and at all hospitals, convalescent camps, and rest stations. Inasmuch as the Adjutant General's Department was at this time organizing a statistical section, whose functions it would be to compile and keep all data relating to the personnel of the A. E. F., advantage was taken of the opportunity to establish close cooperation between these services, and the Red Cross was authorized (Sec. II, G. O. No. 81, A. E. F., December 24, 1917) to attach a searcher to each statistical section of the Adjutant General's Department and to hospital subsections, to whom information as to casualties, etc., would be freely furnished for transmission through Red Cross headquarters to the Central Bureau of Information of the Red Cross, by which bureau alone such information might be given out.

Prior to this time, arrangements had been made for the Red Cross to send food from Switzerland to American prisoners in Germany. The Secretary of War in November, 1917, authorized the Quartermaster Department to turn over supplies to the Red Cross for this purpose and arrangements were perfected (January 3, 1918) for obtaining the same as needed for shipment to Switzerland through the Chief Quartermaster, A. E. F. This work was efficiently and successfully carried on in spite of the obvious difficulties and was the means of saving the lives and alleviating the hardships of countless American prisoners.

* * * * * *

A report submitted by the American Red Cross as of December 17, 1917, shows a total personnel of 1,627, subdivided substantially as follows: Headquarters and similar activities, 174; Medical and surgical division, 358; U. S. Army division (including such activities as recreation and welfare work, information of casualties, chaplain's supplies, rest stations, etc.), 43; French Army division, 98; Civil affairs, 405; Transportation and supplies, 549.

3. OTHER SOCIETIES

(a) Salvation Army: On July 30, 1917, Lieutenant Colonel William S. Barker, representative of the Salvation Army in France, after a visit to the Gondrecourt Area and consultation with commanding officers and chaplains, submitted to the Commander-in-Chief a plan of activity for his society, outlining an administrative organization and suggesting an immediate program of recreational and religious work in the Gondrecourt Area, not essentially different in character from the scheme of the Y. M. C. A. The plan was personally considered by the Commander-in-Chief, who instructed the Adjutant General to go into the situation further, especially cautioning against admitting another society to the field unless it was in a position to do a necessary work not done by others. No formal recognition was given to the Salvation Army at this time, but early in August authority was given to its representatives to proceed into the Gondrecourt and the Nevers and Valdahon Areas for the purpose of carrying on the work of the society with the American troops, and approval was given to an arrangement with the Quartermaster Department for furnishing the Salvation Army with motor and other supplies and transportation. On August 18, 1917, the uniform specifications submitted by the Salvation Army, consisting of a khaki uniform with the letters U. S. and S. A. on the collar and the words Salvation Army on shoulder straps and cap, were officially approved.

* * * * * *

A report submitted by the Salvation Army as of January 3, 1918, shows that it had then in operation huts at eight different stations in the area of the 1st Division, with general headquarters in Paris and divisional headquarters at Ligny-en-Barrois, the number of workers employed being 37, 20 of them men and 17 women.

(b) Knights of Columbus: On November 10, 1917, Mr. Walter N. Kernan, representative of the Knights of Columbus, presented a letter to the Commander-in-Chief setting forth in a general way the desire of that society to participate in the religious and recreational work among our troops. He was invited to confer with Major Murphy of the Red Cross and Mr. Carter of the Y. M. C. A. with a view to developing a plan for directing the energies of the K. of C. into channels which would not conflict with the work being done by the other societies. Thus at the end of 1917, the K. of C. was recognized by the War Department and the A. E. F. as an official agency for welfare work in France, along with the other three organizations, but the K. of C. had not up to that time actually entered the field of practical work.

The subsequent history of welfare work in the A. E. F. is the history of the activities of the four major societies above named, supplemented later by several subsidiary societies which are required to work through the medium of one or more of the major societies, so far as official relations with the army were concerned, and of the efforts of the General Staff to direct, assist, and coordinate these activities.

B. JANUARY 1, 1918 TO JUNE 30, 1918

1. IN GENERAL

The period recorded under Part A, may be termed the formative period, in which the

general scheme of activity of the welfare societies as a whole, the status of their personnel and their relations to the Army, and particularly to the General Staff, were evolved
along lines which were thereafter pretty consistently adhered to. The period now under
consideration was a period of development and growth, coincident with the development and
growth of the A. E. F. The supervision of the activities of the welfare societies was a
function of the Administrative Section (after publication of G. O. No. 31, A. E. F.,
February 16, 1918, the 1st Section, G-1) of the General Staff. In the exercise of this
function the General Staff pursued a policy of noninterference in the internal affairs of
the societies, nor did it attempt to direct their administration in the same sense as it
directed the administration of the various military services. Thus the supervision
actually exercised by G-1 during this period may be summarized somewhat as follows:
Passing upon a large variety of questions submitted by the societies themselves and by
chiefs of services or commanding officers; enlisting the cooperation of the societies in
new projects and approving or disapproving their proposals to enter upon others; adjusting
their relations from time to time with the French and British authorities; considering the
requests for assistance from the army and granting the same when compatible with the exigencies of the military situation. Whenever the need of new or improved service at any
point or with any unit came to the knowledge of G. H. Q. it was promptly brought to the
attention of the appropriate welfare agency, which was always found eager to respond to
the extent of its facilities. The weakness of the General Staff supervision during this
period lay in the lack of machinery to seek out the opportunities and needs for welfare
service and to take positive steps to insure the furnishing of such service by the agency
best fitted to furnish it. Scarcity of available personnel and constant pressure of more
essential duties upon staff officers offer ample explanation for the failure to develop
such machinery in the early months of 1918, but in looking back upon the work accomplished
it is indisputable that, had it been possible to build up and pursue a policy of more
active direction by the army itself during the early days of development and growth, the
welfare agencies would have been enabled to direct their energies more intelligently and
with less waste of effort and to accomplish even more than they did in fact accomplish
for the comfort and well being of the Army.

2. YOUNG MEN'S CHRISTIAN ASSOCIATION

* * * * * *

3. AMERICAN RED CROSS

* * * * * *

4. OTHER SOCIETIES

* * * * * *

C. JULY 1, 1918 TO NOV. 11, 1918

1. IN GENERAL

During this period, covering the closing months and from the American standpoint the
most active months of hostilities, the history of the welfare activities, and especially
of the staff work with respect to them, tends to become a joint history rather than a
collection of several. The rapid growth of the A. E. F. produced a corresponding increase
in the magnitude of the service required of the welfare societies which brought more

clearly to light the need of increased supervision. At the same time the lesser organizations were beginning to assume proportions which rendered imperative a closer coordination
of their activities with those of the major societies. Thus from a viewpoint of a staff
report, the growth of a general policy of supervision, especially during the last two
months of hostilities, overshadows the problems of the individual agencies. * * *

* * * * * *

2. YOUNG MEN'S CHRISTIAN ASSOCIATION

* * * * * *

3. AMERICAN RED CROSS

* * * * * *

4. OTHER SOCIETIES

* * * * * *

D. NOVEMBER 12, 1918 TO APRIL 22, 1919

1. IN GENERAL

The period following the signing of the Armistice has been one of greatly increased
supervision by the army over the activities of the welfare societies. The reasons for this
may be summarized as follows: First, the necessity for more thorough supervision and
coordination of these activities was already recognized before the Armistice, and steps
were actually being taken, as pointed out above, to create the machinery required to render
them effective; Second, the changed conditions which immediately arose upon cessation of
hostilities enlarged both the need and the opportunities for recreational and other welfare
work, as opposed to strictly relief work, and gave rise to many new problems which could
only be solved by cooperation on a large scale between the army and the welfare societies;
Third, the let-up in the purely military demands upon personnel and material resources made
it possible for the higher staff officers to give more attention to the work of the auxiliary agencies, made available the officers required to carry out a systematic policy of
supervision as well as personnel of all ranks for direct assistance to the societies and
participation in their activities, and made it possible to furnish transportation and
supplies to an extent which was previously out of the question.

During this period even more than in the preceding period the record of staff work
performed must be written in reference to the welfare activities as a whole, and those
matters which can be segregated under the headings of the individual societies will be
found to be relatively few.

* * * * * *

2. YOUNG MEN'S CHRISTIAN ASSOCIATION

* * * * * *

3. AMERICAN RED CROSS

* * * * * *

4. OTHER SOCIETIES

* * * * * *

E. CONCLUSIONS

As stated at the outset, this is a report of staff work and does not purport to be a history of welfare work performed in the American Expeditionary Forces. Therefore, any attempt to summarize the results attained by the welfare societies would be out of place. Moreover the Inspector General is conducting an investigation of the activities of all the societies with special reference to the justice or injustice of criticisms which have been advanced against some of them, and it would obviously be inappropriate to record any general conclusions as to those activities in advance of the receipt of the Inspector General's report. However, it is deemed appropriate to venture some conclusions with respect to the general scheme of organization and control of welfare work in the Army based on the experience of the First Section of the General Staff, A. E. F.

Any discussions of this subject must start with a full recognition of the splendid service rendered by the welfare societies as a whole and their men and women workers, in order that criticism of the scheme of organization may not be miscontrued as   of appreciation of the great amount of good work done.

The first and almost irresistible conclusion to be drawn from this experience is that the welfare work, exclusive of what may be termed strictly relief work, would have been better performed by a single agency than by the several independent agencies which have conducted it in the A. E. F. This includes the entire work of the Y. M. C. A. (exclusive of the *Foyer du Soldat)*, K. of C., S. A., J. W. B., and Y. M. C. A. (except its work among French women) and those branches of the Red Cross work which were carried on for the benefit of the American Army other than the activities directly associated with the work of the Army Medical Corps.

Relief work for the benefit of the civil population seems essentially within the scope of the Red Cross as the recognized international relief agency. Work of various kinds for the benefit of the soldiers of allied or friendly armies might well be centralized, but is somewhat outside the scope of this report. Whether the activities carried on in this war by the Red Cross as auxiliary to the Medical Department of the A. E. F. would better have been absorbed by the Army, handled by a distinct department of a single Army welfare organization or retained by the Red Cross is a question upon which the Medical Department itself and the section of the general staff charged with supervision of hospitalization (G-4) are better qualified to pass judgment. The work of the A. L. A. may also be excepted as it undoubtedly possessed unique opportunities for providing books, and its distribution could have been carried on just as well or better through a single welfare agency as through the several existing agencies.

Excluding from consideration the activities specifically mentioned in the last paragraph the opinion is expressed without qualification that all the welfare work within our own Army should be conducted by a single agency, and it is believed that that agency should be a distinct organization created for the purposes of the Army and wholly independent of existing civilian associations.

Should this supposed agency be a civilian organization auxiliary to the Army or should it be an integral part of the Army? As to this question there is more room for difference of opinion. There is no doubt that the civilian societies associated with the A. E. F. suffered in efficiency from the detached viewpoint of many army officers with respect to their work, from the absence of that feeling of responsibility on the part of the Army to make their work a success which it had for those services which were part and parcel of the Army itself. The Army was also handicapped in its efforts to direct these activities by the fact that it could not enforce compliance with its orders to the same extent that it could in the case of other services. Moreover the status of their personnel as militarized civilians was never fully understood and was unsatisfactory to the Army and to the societies and individuals concerned, both from the point of view of morale and from that of practical convenience in such matters as circulation, rights and privileges of numerous sorts, and enforcement of discipline. It is also believed that the absence of ranks or grades among their personnel (except in the case of the Red Cross), though having some advantages, gravitated against efficiency in what were necessarily semi-military organizations. On the other hand, the freedom of the directing heads of the societies from the restrictions of legislation and Army Regulations gave to their work an elasticity which no department of the government could ever have, and countless instances might be enumerated in which the resources of the welfare societies were promptly made available for emergency needs with which no army officer had the authority to cope. Nor should we completely overlook the stimulating effect upon patriotism and public support of the Army which voluntary giving undoubtedly has upon the people at home.

From a balancing of the considerations briefly outlined above the conclusion is drawn that the active personnel of the proposed welfare organization should be enlisted and commissioned in a distinct service or corps of the Army and completely under army command, but that the funds by which the work is supported should be derived from voluntary contributions and should be appropriated and disbursed by trustees clothed with a broad discretion and accountable only to the public, but acting in close cooperation with the section of the general staff directly responsible for supervision and direction of the actual conduct of the work.

It is improbable that any such organization as is outlined above could have been evolved in the present war had hostilities continued, because the existing agencies had developed too far to make so radical a change possible. Even such approximation to a single organization as exists today in the system of coordination and supervision built up during the Armistice could hardly have been brought about under continuing combat conditions, for though officers might have been made available for central supervision and inspection, they could never have been spared within combat units or, if designated, would never in practice have found it possible to devote their entire time to this work. If at the very outset all welfare personnel could have been incorporated in a distinct army service this difficulty would have been obviated because such a service would provide its own supervising and directing officers and they would not have to be drawn from combatant personnel.

CHAPTER XV

ENTERTAINMENT

A. ORGANIZATION AND ADMINISTRATION

From the arrival of the first American troops in France until the signing of the Armistice practically all entertainment activities were conducted by the Y. M. C. A., which was the only society having an organized system with professional entertainers. Only general supervision over this work was exercised by the Army.

With the cessation of hostilities, however, the need for entertainment on a much larger scale was foreseen and steps were taken for the organization and utilization of the actors and performers, both amateur and professional, in the A. E. F. An officer of G-1 was detailed to take general charge of entertainment work and coordinate military activities with those of the welfare societies in this direction. At the same time a comprehensive system was devised for administering the subject and was finally perfected and published in Section II, G. O. No. 241, A. E. F., December 29, 1918.

Under this order, officers were detailed in each army, corps, division, and S. O. S. unit to be responsible for all entertainment activities within organizations, and all

commanders were directed to give every encouragement, consistent with military requirements, to the development of soldier talent. Provision was also made for the detail of
officers and soldiers for entertainment purposes, in which case they were to report to the
entertainment officer of their organization for assignment. Subsequently, on January 13,
1919, provision was made for releasing personnel for entertainment purposes from organizations scheduled for return to the United States and attaching it for administrative purposes to the 1st Replacement Depot.

The Y. M. C. A., with the approval of the Commander-in-Chief, had organized a Department of Entertainment for supervising the routing of professional and amateur entertainers, assisting in the development and training of soldier talent, and assisting and managing qualified groups of entertainers who might be developed in the Army. An officer was
appointed Assistant Entertainment Officer, A. E. F., with station in Paris, to work in
liaison between the Y. M. C. A. Entertainment Department and G. H. Q., and soldiers detailed for general entertainment duty, not in connection with division, corps, armies, or
S. O. S units, were ordered to report to him. They were then combined into small groups
and sent out by the Y. M. C. A. booking system. However, this method of forming entertainment groups was only an expedient. As fast as possible the Y. M. C. A. decentralized
their activities in this line and organized branch Soldier Actor Sections at various
centers where they assisted the local entertainment officer in organizing groups of
soldier entertainers.

On January 28, 1919, Entertainment Bulletin No. 1, was published for the purpose of
enlarging upon and defining in detail the procedure to be followed in carrying into effect
the general policy announced in G. O. No. 241. It was prepared after numerous conferences
between the officer in G-1 charged with entertainment and various unit entertainment officers. Subsequently it was republished as Sec. 1, Bul. No. 15, A. E. F., February 21, 1919.

From time to time circular letters and telegrams were sent to the commanding generals
of armies, corps, divisions, and the S. O. S. for the purpose of securing greater uniform-
ity in the handling of various matters, such as transportation, expense accounts, messing
and quartering of personnel, etc., and promoting cooperation with the welfare societies.
* * *

By the procedure outlined above a strong organization was built up and tremendous
impetus given to entertainment throughout the A. E. F. Excellent material was found to be
available for almost every class of entertainment, including minstrels, vaudeville,
musical comedy, short plays, and stock companies.

It was planned that not only should nightly performances be given in all important
centers but that frequent and suitable shows should be provided which would be accessible
to every member of the A. E. F., and this program was substantially carried out.

Particular attention was given to the display of moving pictures and, in addition to
the establishment of many permanent installations, portable machines were mounted on converted ambulances and sent on tour for the benefit of units billeted in isolated sections.

A most effective form of outdoor entertainment was the horse show. The first of
these was held by the 82d Division and proved so successful that the Commander in Chief
directed that, as far as practicable, similar shows be held in all divisions, to be
followed in turn by corps and army shows. This was provided for in Bul. No. 3, A. E. F.,
January 17, 1919, and will be found further referred to in Chapter VI, Remounts.

A report on entertainment activities was made to the War Department by cable under
date of March 10. * * *

On January 1, 1919, 150 soldier units had already been organized and were playing.
On March 31, 640 soldier units, either organized and in operation or in the process of
organization, were reported.

During January, February, and March the number of entertainment stations increased in
spite of the reduction of the A. E. F. as shown by the following table:

1919	No. of Stations
January 31	337
February 28	1,377
March 31	1,491

During January and February an average of 2.45 theatrical and motion picture shows per week per station were given. This average was increased to 4.05 during the month of March. It should be emphasized that the above figures do not include athletics (boxing and wrestling), band concerts, lectures, educational features, etc., which, although not considered part of the entertainment program and therefore not summarized in this report, nevertheless proved of great value in furnishing recreation and diversion.

On March 31, 7,883 military persons were engaged in entertainment duty as follows:

Officers detailed under G. O. No. 241	362	
Soldiers detailed under G. O. No. 241	4,644	5,006
Officers on entertainment duty not detailed under G. O. No. 241	128	
Soldiers on entertainment duty not detailed under G. O. No. 241	2,749	2,877
		7,883

B. HOUSING, CONSTRUCTION, AND LIGHTING

Prior to the signing of the Armistice practically all indoor entertainment was conducted in Y. M. C. A. huts and auditoriums or in other buildings designated for the purpose. After the cessation of hostilities the increasing activity in all branches of entertainment endeavor made it necessary to provide additional accommodations, particularly in view of the approach of winter. The Air Service had a large number of hangars which eventually proved very suitable for this purpose. The large size measured 110' x 100!. The need of these hangars by the Air Service declined rapidly after the Armistice and negotiations were entered into for taking over a number of them for entertainment purposes.

All hangars in the First and Second Army Area not in use were placed at the disposal of army commanders. In addition, the Commanding General, S. O. S., was requested to ship available hangars to the First and Second Armies, with the result that 67 were sent to the First Army and 33 to the Second.

The lighting of these hangars was accomplished by means of Delco sets and electricity obtained from local plants. Arrangements to supply Delco sets were made through G-4 and on February 26 seventy-five were assigned to the First Army and the same number to the Second. In addition, the Second Army salvaged a number of generator plants, mounted them on trailers, and assigned them to corps and divisions.

In compliance with a request from the Y. M. C. A. dated February 3, G-4 authorized the Commanding General, S. O. S., to issue 75 double-walled tents as a loan to the Y. M. C. A. These tents were sent to the Third Army but did not prove particularly suitable for entertainment purposes and were therefore used chiefly as reading rooms and in a few instances for moving pictures.

C. TRANSPORTATION

The transportation of entertainment units was accomplished partly through the agency of the Y. M. C. A. and partly at government expense. The question was covered in a communication from G-1 to the Commanding General, 77th Division, dated January 9, 1919, as follows:

> Officers and men detailed for entertainment duty may be transported on such duty at government expense, on orders issued by competent authority. Travel within the division will be on orders of the division commanders, within the corps or army on orders issued by or pursuant to authority of the corps or army commanders, as the case may be. The Y. M. C. A., however, has agreed that when an entertainment unit is traveling on tour, arranged through its booking system, it will transport such unit by rail and defray the expenses of the unit to the extent that same are not covered by government allowance.

According to Par. 1, Sec. II, G. O. No. 64, A. E. F., 1917, privates traveling on entertainment duty were confined to the use of 3d class accommodations. This caused considerable hardship and confusion as it frequently happened that the only trains which would enable entertainment units to meet their schedules were not equipped with third class coaches and instances occurred of the forced cancellation of performances while the troupe spent the night at some way station because only trains with first and second class coaches had passed through. Furthermore, the fact that Y. M. C. A. entertainers traveled first class had a discouraging effect upon the enlisted personnel who were forced to travel 3d. After the congestion of railroad transportation brought about by the French demobilization program had been relieved, Sec. V., G. O. No. 62, A. E. F., 1919, was published amending G. O. No. 64, A. E. F., 1917, and directing that all soldiers on entertainment duty travel 2d class.

Transportation within divisional and similar areas was difficult to secure in numerous instances. Entertainment officers were handicapped in their work by lack of means of getting about and the efficiency of many units was reduced on account of sickness resulting from exposure, due to inability to secure suitable closed transportation. To meet this situation it was recommended to G-4 that if the necessary cars were available, each division and corps be assigned one and each army three closed automobiles to be used for entertainment purposes. In compliance with this recommendation G-4, after communicating with the armies, gave instructions on March 10, 1919, for the issue of closed cars as follows:

First Army	9
Second Army	7
Third Army	30

On January 11, 1919, the Commanding General, First Army, requested 60 motor ambulances for distribution to corps and divisions to be used for the transportation of entertainment groups and portable motion picture equipment. This project was strongly approved by G-1 with the result that on January 21 authority was granted by G-4 for the use of ambulances by the First Army as requested. To take the place of these, 60 G. M. C. ambulances were ordered to the First Army from the stock of crated machines on hand at base ports and 50 were ordered to the Second Army for the same purpose. In this way the transportation situation was greatly relieved.

Towards the end of March and during April as the First and Second Armies were reduced, these ambulances were redistributed, some going to the Third Army and some to the Advance Section, S. O. S.

D. FINANCIAL

The greater part of the expense of entertainment was borne by the Y. M. C. A. * * * showing a total proposed expenditure of 6,988,500.00 francs. This included all expenses to be borne by the Y. M. C. A. and was distributed so as to cover the cost of salaries of the Y. M. C. A. field entertainment staff and traveling entertainers, the expenses of soldier units and professional shows, the purchase of properties, costumes, and musical instruments (excepting pianos), and the rent of local theaters.

The other societies were willing to contribute their proportionate share of the expense but lacked the machinery for effectively disbursing the money. Mr. Raymond B. Fosdick and his associate, Dr. Joseph E. Haycroft, of the War Department Commission on Training Camp Activities, undertook to effect a distribution in proportion to the shares of the several societies in the joint fund subscribed by the public, which was as follows:

Y. M. C. A.	70 percent
K. of C.	24 percent
S. A.	3 percent
J. W. B.	3 percent

Numerous conferences were held to consider this matter and an arrangement finally adopted under which, in addition to the Y. M. C. A. appropriation, three other welfare societies agreed to furnish sums as follows:

Knights of Columbus up to $75,000 per month.
Salvation Army up to $50,000 per month, if needed.
Jewish Welfare Board 3% of the total entertainment budget.

It was contemplated that these additional funds would be available for such purposes as the entertainment officers of the army might designate. Whenever special entertainment needs arose, not provided for in the Y. M. C. A. budget, entertainment officers might call upon any one of the other three organizations for the necessary expenditure, and in this way it was hoped to adjust the expenditures roughly to the desired proportions. G-1 undertook no responsibility for effecting this adjustment but agreed to cooperate in pointing out desirable opportunities for expending the money appropriated. To this end, a letter was written to army and S. O. S. entertainment officers, March 25, calling attention to the existence of these funds and instructing them to communicate requests for appropriations for special purposes to the Assistant Entertainment Officer, A. E. F., in Paris. This officer kept in touch with the various societies and suggested to them from time to time expenditures for entertainment needs brought to his attention by unit entertainment officers or otherwise.

Soldier entertainment units were quartered and rationed by the government whenever practicable. According to Par. 17, Sec. I, Bul. No. 15, the Y. M. C. A. agreed to furnish funds to cover the expenses of such units to the extent that they were not covered by government allowances. In a circular letter to the commanding general of armies, corps, divisions, and the S. O. S., dated March 1, 1919 this as well as the keeping of Y. M. C. A. expense accounts was enlarged upon and fully explained.

CHAPTER XVI

BANDS OF THE A. E. F.

A. AUTHORITY FOR REORGANIZATION OF BANDS

The first important step towards the general development of all bands in the A. E. F. in order to provide an abundance of musicians at all times was taken March 3, 1918. On that date a cablegram, P-675, was sent to the War Department stating "excellent bands capable of rendering stirring material music would be valuable adjunct in instilling and maintaining martial spirit in our troops. Our bands now deficient in this respect and greatly inferior to French bands." This cablegram contained recommendations for:
   (a) The increase in size of all authorized bands.
   (b) The assignment of a commissioned band leader to each authorized band.
   (c) The organization of a bugle and drum corps in each regiment of infantry.
   (d) The procurement in France of necessary instruments to complete the equipment of all bands there or en route.
The War Department replied in cablegram A-1359, dated May 31, 1918, authorizing the increase in size of bands for the period of emergency and providing for commissioning of band leaders. The instructions contained in the above-mentioned cablegram were published in Section II, G. O. No. 183, A. E. F., October 21, 1918. This general order set forth the instrumentation of a properly authorized band and called attention to an increase in the allowance for the purchase of music. (This increase in allowances for purchase of music had previously been announced in Section I, Bulletin No. 73, A. E. F., September 25, 1918.) Further instructions relative to band music were published in Bulletin No. 23, A. E. F., March 24, 1919.

B. BAND REPLACEMENTS FROM UNITED STATES

In order to have on hand bandsmen to be used as replacements, a cablegram, P-1588, par. 1-A, was sent to the War Department August 12, 1918, requesting that thereafter with each 1,000 combatant replacements there be included 8 bandsmen distributed in proportion to instrumentation of authorized bands. Cablegram A-1844, par. 9, dated August 14, 1918, referred to this request and stated that the replacements which included the bandsmen would be shipped as early as possible in September. The records of arrivals of personnel in the A. E. F. do not show that these band replacements were received.

C. BANDMASTERS AND MUSICIANS SCHOOL

To carry out properly the provisions of G. O. No. 183, it was found necessary to establish a school for:
   (a) The training of band masters.
   (b) The training of musicians in the study of certain instruments. Bulletin No. 84, A. E. F., October 28, 1918, announced the establishment of this school at Chaumont and set forth in detail information concerning the courses of instruction and the procedure which would be followed in regard to applications for commissions as band leaders. This school was operated under the direction of the 5th Section, General Staff.

D. BAND MUSICIANS SCHOOL AND DEPOT AT GONDRECOURT

On December 2, 1918, the Commander-in-Chief approved the recommendations contained in a memorandum to the Chief of Staff from the Assistant Chief of Staff, G-1, which included:

   (a) The establishment at Gondrecourt of a school for band musicians, the present band leaders and musicians school at Chaumont to be continued.

(b) The school for band musicians also to function as a replacement unit for band musicians.

(c) The school for band musicians to be under the supervision of G-5. Replacements to be furnished on requisitions approved by G-1, and in accordance with priority furnished by G-1.

(d) The bands of the seven divisions and three regiments of pioneer infantry which had been skeletonized for replacement purposes, to be ordered to the school for band musicians and their personnel to be examined, trained, and utilized as replacements.

(e) All band replacements now in depot divisions or other replacement organizations to be ordered to the school for band musicians at Gondrecourt, for the necessary examination, training, and assignment.

(f) Musicians to be supplied as replacements to bands in accordance with priority to be determined as follows: Each division commander to fix the priority for the bands in his division. Priority among divisions to be fixed by G-1, G. H. Q.

(g) All organizations in France whose authorized strength includes bands to utilize any qualified personnel for band musicians and to submit replacement requisitions to G-1, G. H. Q., for necessary personnel to complete the bands.

(h) As soon as possible, selected bands to be designated for concert tours in hospital centers, leave areas, etc.

Telegraphic instructions were immediately given to the Commanding General, S. O. S., covering the sending of the bands of the skeletonized units (except the band of the 303d Infantry, which was on duty in Paris and was allowed to remain there) and all band replacements to Gondrecourt and the return of all casual bandsmen to their organizations.

The commanding generals of the First, Second, and Third Armies were informed by telegram dated December 3, 1918, that the Commander-in-Chief had personally directed that all bands be increased as soon as possible to the strength authorized in G. O. No. 183 and that every possible effort should be made to improve all bands. It was directed that division commanders be ordered to comb all units for competent band musicians and to assign them to bands of the division. If any excess musicians were found in any division, they were to be transferred by the army commander to other divisions where their services could be utilized. As soon as a division had transferred all its competent musicians to its bands, requisitions were to be submitted by each division commander for replacements needed to bring each band to the authorized strength. These requisitions and weekly reports of the requirements of each band were to be submitted by the division commander to G-1, G. H. Q. Army commanders were directed to indicate the priority in which it was desired that band replacements be furnished to the divisions within the army, and division commanders were directed to fix the priority of bands within the divisions.

The school for band musicians at Gondrecourt began to function as a replacement depot on December 5, 1918. Between that time and March 1, 1919, it handled 1,457 bandsmen and 32 band leaders, most of whom were sent out as replacements to organized bands. These men came from 32 bands which were sent to the depot to be broken up and from various divisions which reported surplus band musicians. The examination, classification, and training of the musicians at the depot were under the supervision of the 5th Section, General Staff. Their utilization as replacements was directed by the 1st Section, General Staff. The depot was first under the administration of the Commandant I Corps Schools, but on the closing of the schools the control passed, on January 19, 1919, to the Commanding General, Combat Officers Depot. The executive officer was furnished with copies of the requisitions submitted to G-1 by various bands and was instructed, as musicians became available, to send them out to the lowest priority numbered band needing their services. The priority was established by G-1 in accordance with the instructions of the Commander-in-Chief to the effect that the bands of the Third Army should be filled first, and in accordance with the wishes of the army and division commanders. (The only bands which were given precedence over those of the Third Army were the G. H. Q. band, the Bandmasters and Musicians School band, and the 303d Infantry band on duty at Headquarters, District of Paris.)

Nearly every authorized band received some of the musicians it needed and those with low numbered priorities were practically filled up. There was a surplus of cornetists, trombone players, and drummers, and a shortage of players of more difficult instruments. On March 1, 1919, there were unfilled requisitions from the authorized bands of the three armies for 1,885 replacements. At that time there were 187 musicians in the depot available for use as replacements but very few of them played instruments needed by the bands.

Replacements sent out from the depot took their instruments with them. Difficulty in obtaining a supply of instruments caused a considerable delay in filling requisitions, but as fast as the instruments were secured, the men were sent out. A bugle and drum corps of 26 pieces was organized in the depot and, under instructions from G-1, was sent to Paris for duty with the band stationed there.

E. BANDS FOR HOSPITAL CENTERS AND LEAVE AREAS

The breaking up for replacement purposes of the 31st, 34th, 38th, 39th, 76th, 84th, and 86th Divisions, and the 4th, 55th, and 57th Regiments of pioneer infantry, in October, 1918, made 31 bands available for other duty. These bands were temporarily under the control for the Commanding General, S. O. S., and were used by him in hospital centers, leave areas, and other places where music was most needed.

On December 3, 1918, these bands were sent to Gondrecourt to be broken up for replacement purposes. The necessity was felt for an abundance of good music in the hospital centers and leave areas but no bands were available for permanent assignment to this duty and there was no material from which to organize new bands for this purpose. Under the approval of the Chief of Staff, on the recommendation of the A. C. of S., G-1, the commanding general of the First Army was instructed on December 31, 1918, to assign 10 designated leave areas to the 10 divisions of his army and to direct division commanders to send to the leave area assigned to them the bands of their divisions in turn for a period of about two weeks. At the same time the commanding general of the Second Army was instructed to send the bands of the 88th Division, in turn, to an area assigned to it. The cutting down of the number of divisions in the First Army made it necessary later to call upon the Second Army to take care of three additional leave areas, one of which was the portion of the Savoie Area set apart for colored troops (a colored band was sent to this area). On March 1, 1919, the Commanding General, S. O. S., was authorized by telegram to send to six leave areas bands from divisions in the Le Mans area preparing for return to the United States. It was stipulated that not more than one band should be taken from a division at one time and that all bands would rejoin their organizations before the departure of the latter for the United States. This system of rotation of bands in the leave areas made it possible for the men on leave to have the benefit of music at all times without depriving units of their bands for any great length of time. It also resulted in giving many bands the benefit of a visit to the leave areas.

F. BANDS OF HOME-GOING UNITS

Many requests were received at G. H. Q. from division and other commanders that bands or bandsmen of home-going units be detached and held in France for service with other units. Such requests were disapproved as a matter of policy on the theory that every authorized band should be permitted to accompany its own organization to the United States.

CHAPTER XVII

WAR RISK INSURANCE

A. THE WAR RISK INSURANCE ACT

The Act of Congress of October 6, 1917, entitled the War Risk Insurance Act, provided for:

(1) Compulsory allotment of pay for the support of families and other dependents,
(2) Voluntary allotment of pay,
(3) Insurance at fixed rates for men enrolled in the military service of the U. S.

The period of time allowed for taking out insurance was 120 days from date of enlistment, or, for men already in the service prior to October 15, 1917, up to and including February 12, 1918. The Act superseded all former laws providing for payments in the event of death in the service of the U. S.

On February 14, a cable was received (War Risk No. 5) advising that the President had approved a joint resolution of Congress for the extension of the time limit from February 12, 1918 to April 12, 1918.

The Act of Congress approved March 8, 1918, entitled The Soldiers and Sailors' Civil Relief Act, provided for the protection of persons in the active military service of the U. S. against the lapsing or forfeiture of certain life insurance contracts with commercial life insurance companies.

B. ORGANIZATION IN THE A. E. F.

Captain S. H. Wolfe, Q. M. C., was designated by the Treasury Department (Cable 314-A, paragraph 1, dated October 25, 1917), as their representative in the A. E. F. to handle questions arising under the War Risk Insurance Act. He was assigned to duty by Sec. I, G. O. No. 50, A. E. F., October 27, 1917, as chief of the European office, War Risk Insurance, with headquarters in Paris, and was instructed to proceed with the organization of the Paris office under the direction of G. H. Q. for the purpose of bringing to the attention of all those entitled to insurance under the act, the benefits to be derived therefrom.

The original organization of the Paris office consisted of a detail of enlisted men for the purpose of handling insurance applications and six lieutenants temporarily assigned for training as insurance officers.

Captain Wolfe was notified November 10, 1917, by two Treasury Department cables (2767 and 2772) that Major Willard Straight, A. G., had been appointed to take charge of the European office and would sail shortly. A later cable (2782) further advised that Major Straight would bring an organization with him and directed that no civilian help be employed by Captain Wolfe. On this account it was not possible to proceed with the organization of a permanent office in Paris and an additional detail of enlisted men was requested by Captain Wolfe on November 16 to carry on the work pending the arrival of Major Straight.

The proposed organization of the European office was stated in War Department cable 483-A, December 7, 1917, as follows:

To perform additional work required of Army administration in connection with War Risk Insurance Act, officers and enlisted personnel will be assigned to headquarters of organizations under your command as follows:

At General Army Headquarters, [sic] 15 officers and 37 enlisted men.

At headquarters each tactical division, 2 officers and 8 enlisted men.

At headquarters and lines [of] communication in France, 2 officers and 5 enlisted men.

Attached to your headquarters to deal (a) with special troops on detached service in France, 4 officers and 20 enlisted men (b) with train service and casual camps in England, 2 officers and 8 enlisted men.

This proposed organization was submitted to the Chief of Staff December 12, 1917. On account of the crowded condition and lack of accommodations at G. H. Q. as well as the specialized nature of the work it was recommended that the personnel provided for G. H. Q. be assigned to Headquarters, L. of C. On account of the necessity of restricting to the minimum the personnel attached to the headquarters of combat divisions and the inadvisability of maintaining important record with the divisions during periods of active operations, it was also recommended that the 2 officers and 8 enlisted men provided as assistants to division adjutants be assigned instead to the Advance Section, L. of C., and that the extra personnel for division headquarters be authorized for base and replacement divisions only.

G. O. No. 5, A. E. F., 1918, was published on January 7 establishing the War Risk Section at Headquarters, L. of C., under the direction of the C. G., L. of C.; a field force known as the Advance Group, War Risk Section, consisting of 2 officers and 8 enlisted men at Headquarters, Advance Section, L. of C., for the purpose of covering the zone of advance; and branch offices at the headquarters of each replacement and depot division and at Headquarters, Base Section No. 3, L. of C. (England). The personnel of these branch offices was not to exceed 2 officers and 8 enlistec men for each office. The War Risk Section at Headquarters, L. of C., in addition to its supervisory duties was charged with the War Risk operations in the L. of C. and among all troops on detached service and those not otherwise provided for. Major Straight was assigned to duty as chief of the War Risk Section, and Captain Wolfe relieved.

In order to carry out the organization outlined in Cable 483-A, G. O. No. 149, W. D., 1917, was published authorizing 3 officers and 8 enlisted men for division headquarters as assistants to the division adjutant. However, in cable 492-P, January 14, 1918, the attention of the War Department was invited to the necessity of restricting personnel at division headquarters to a minimum and they were advised that for this reason it would not be possible to adopt the organization proposed. At the same time Sec. II, G. O. No. 25, A. E. F., February 9, 1918, was published announcing that, in view of the organization of the War Risk Section at Headquarters, L. of C., in accordance with G. O. No. 5, the personnel authorized by G. O. No. 149, W. D., would not be organized and that all war risk personnel arriving with combat divisions would be detached on arrival and assigned to duty with the War Risk Section, Headquarters, L. of C. War Risk personnel arriving with depot or replacement divisions was to be retained at division headquarters and their names only reported to the War Risk Section. At the close of the period originally allowed for taking out war risk insurance, February 12, 1918, Major Straight was relieved from duty as chief of the Section and Major H. D. Lindsley, A. G., was appointed in his stead.

Final tables of organization adopted for the War Risk Section, submitted September 13. 1918, and approved September 17, 1918, provided for a main office at Headquarters, S. O. S., branch offices in each of the base sections, and a department of traveling adjusters. The total organization at that time consisted of 38 officers and 176 enlisted men.

C. CHANNELS OF COMMUNICATION

1. Distribution of Information: The European office, War Risk Insurance, as authorized by Sec. I, G. O. No. 50, A. E. F., 1917, was under the direction of General Headquarters and all information relating to war risk insurance was published to the command through the Adjutant General, A. E. F., in circulars, bulletins, or general orders.

Following the organization of the War Risk Section by G. O. No. 5, A. E. F., 1918, the Commanding General, L. of C., was empowered by Sec. III, Bul. No. 6, A. E. F., January 29, 1918, to publish "by authority of the Commander-in-Chief" all war risk bulletins and circulars for distribution throughout the A. E. F. However, this procedure led to confusion, as commanding officers in some cases did not consider authority contained in circulars and bulletins so issued sufficient to warrant deductions on pay rolls. It was necessary to issue telegraphic instructions from G. H. Q. in certain cases and it was also necessary to issue instructions to all paying quartermasters supplied with copies of war risk circulars and bulletins. To avoid these difficulties the authority referred to was revoked by Sec. III, G. O. No. 185, A. E. F., October 25, 1918.

2. Correspondence within the A. E. F: Direct correspondence with the European office, War Risk Insurance, on all questions involving allotments and insurance was authorized by G. O. No. 56, A. E. F., 1917, for both officers and enlisted men. After the creation of the War Risk Section and the establishment of branch offices in the Advance Section, L. of C. and at headquarters of base and replacement divisions, communications with the War Risk Section were handled through those offices. Under Sec. 2, Bul. No. 16, A. E. F., December 17, 1917, reports of death, discharge, desertion, or other separation from the service of men having allotments of war risk insurance were made to the A. G., A. E. F., who in turn furnished a copy for the information of the War Risk Section.

3. Correspondence with the U. S.: Applications for war risk insurance and allotments were made out in triplicate, one copy for file with service records to be used in making out pay rolls and 2 copies for the War Risk Section, Headquarters, L. of C. Of the latter, one copy was forwarded to the War Risk Bureau in the United States.

In order to provide complete records of all allotments and insurance policies it was requested in cables 549-P and 562-P to have copies of all applications made by troops in the United States forwarded to the War Risk Section here prior to their embarkation. This was disapproved in War Department cable 725-A. Thereupon it was requested (cable 585-P) in lieu thereof that organization commanders proceeding overseas prepare lists of all the personnel who had executed allotments and war risk insurance applications prior to their embarkation, and this arrangement was adopted.

D. ACTIVITIES IN THE A. E. F.

The function of the overseas organization was to interpret to the A. E. F. their rights under the War Risk Insurance Act of October 6, 1917, and the subsequent rulings of the Treasury Department. Information concerning insurance, compulsory and voluntary allotments, and the necessary deductions to be made on pay rolls was published from time to time in bulletins and general orders issued from G. H. Q.

Early in December, 1917, instructions were given by the Administrative Section to the Chief of the European office to visit each division and explain the benefits to be derived from the War Risk Insurance Act and answer questions and clear up doubtful points of procedure in making out the necessary insurance applications. A report was required from each division as of December 15 of the number of men who had availed themselves of the opportunity to take out government insurance.

On February 8, 1918, a report was requested from all war risk officers in the field, showing the organizations covered, the number of men who had had war risk insurance explained to them and had failed to avail themselves of it, and the number of men who had submitted applications in the United States prior to embarkation, up to and including February 12, 1918. This information was cabled to the War Department on February 15, 1918 (Cable P-605).

A joint resolution of Congress announced in war risk cable No. 5, dated February 14, 1918, extended the time allowed for taking out insurance from February 12 to April 12, 1918, and permitted the continuation of the campaign. A report of the operations of the War Risk Section during this period, showing number of men insured, amount of insurance taken out, and other pertinent data, was submitted to the Commander-in-Chief on May 14, 1918.

After the period of writing insurance the activities of the War Risk Section were largely reduced. Thereafter it was principally an office of record and bureau of information.

On account of the numerous complaints received concerning nonpayment of allotments, instructions were issued in Sec. III, G. O. No. 137, A. E. F., August 21, 1918, to all commanding officers to interview the personnel of their commands and render a report through division headquarters direct to the War Risk Section, as of September 10, 1918, giving a list of the men whose dependents had complained of nonpayment or delayed payment of allotments and at the same time to have these men execute duplicate copies of Form I-B and submit there with a statement of the facts constituting the complaint and any additional information relating thereto.

Following the signing of the Armistice, November 11, 1918, a number of bulletins were published calling attention to the advisability of continuing war risk insurance on account of the opportunity offered by the government to convert it into some form of standard government insurance.

CHAPTER XVIII

CAPTURED ENEMY MATERIAL

In describing the duties of the Salvage Service, Sec. III, G. O. No. 10, A. E. F., January 16, 1918, mentioned that captured enemy property is the property of the U. S. and will be collected.

The distribution of staff duties in G. O. No. 31, A. E. F., February 16, 1918, gave to G-1 the supervision of the disposal of captured material. In June, Sec. V, G. O. No. 105, A. E. F., 1918, was prepared by G-1. This order directed attention to the 79th and 80th Articles of War and pointed out that no individual had any private right in captured enemy public property. Instructions were given that all captured material, except aircraft, be turned over to the Salvage Service to be disposed of by them in the same manner if it were unserviceable material of like character belonging to the A. E. F.; hostile aircraft were to be reported to the nearest United States aircraft unit and guarded until such unit took it over.

A week after the Armistice was signed, the War Department directed that all captured material suitable for trophies be returned to the United States as fast as transportation became available, these instructions being forwarded to the Commanding General, S. O. S., for compliance. There were numerous requests from division and other units for the shipment of individual guns and other trophies captured by them to certain cities in the United States. In view of the instructions from the War Department mentioned above, reply was made in all cases that such applications should be addressed to The Adjutant General of the Army.

The disposition of all enemy material acquired during the Armistice, whether turned over under the terms of the Armistice or abandoned in the enemy's withdrawal, was handled by G-4, and on February 13, 1919, the Chief of Staff approved a recommendation that G-4 supervise the future disposition of all enemy material, captured, or otherwise acquired.

CHAPTER XIX

MISCELLANEOUS REPORTS, PUBLICATIONS, MAPS, AND TABULATIONS

A. REPORTS

G-1 has prepared a great number of regular and special reports on personnel, most of which were issued to the staff sections and to the allied missions attached to General Headquarters.

Practically all of the regular reports on personnel covered arrivals, departures, returns, and replacements and estimates of strength of the A. E. F. As the need for reports furnishing certain information became apparent, new reports were prepared and issued regularly. Some reports were discontinued or the information contained in them was incorporated in others.

Numerous reports were also prepared from time to time to comply with requests for information or statistics of a special nature.

* * * * * *

B. GRAPHICS AND CHARTS

In March, 1918, a chart showing the organization of the First Army, as called for in the Priority Schedule, was prepared and issued. Following that, charts which showed graphically the organization of the different services of the A. E. F. were prepared and issued. As changes in organizations were made, new charts were drawn and replaced those rendered obsolete by the changes. While most of these charts were used at General Headquarters and at Headquarters, S. O. S., the chart of the First Army was given a much wider distribution.

Miscellaneous diagrams and graphics were prepared, which covered such subjects as the operation of the replacement system, statements of replacements furnished, etc. * * *

C. MAPS AND PUBLICATIONS

In addition to the reports and graphics which were prepared by the Personnel Division of G-1, considerable work was done on maps, map indices, and various publications.

As the need for a properly coordinated map of France with map index became apparent, work was started on such a map. All towns in Alsace-Lorraine and Belgium were also indexed and later a publication was issued covering the work. The Map Index of France, a publication of 244 pages with the coordinated map, which accompanies it, was printed and has been widely distributed. Large roller maps of France were arranged for use in the different offices of G-1.

A great deal of study was given to the General Organization Project, Service of the Rear Project, Priority Schedule, and Troop Shipment Programs. Revising, copying, and considerable original work was done on all of these publications.

* * * * * *

D. SOURCES OF INFORMATION

The personnel reports were largely prepared from records and data which were tabulated in G-1, the information being obtained from various weekly, bi-weekly, and monthly strength reports, and daily telegraphic reports.

The sources from which much of the information was obtained were, at time, more or less unreliable, but every effort was made to eliminate errors and furnish the best reports possible. * * *

GENERAL HEADQUARTERS, A. E. F.,

May 19, 1919.

COMMISSIONED PERSONNEL IN THE AMERICAN EXPEDITIONARY FORCES 1917-1919

PART I

The Personnel Bureau

Although the Personnel Bureau came formally into existence with the publication of General Orders No. 94, General Headquarters, American Expeditionary Forces, June 12, 1918, it had been operative since the late autumn of 1917. On November 15, 1917, Paragraph 32, Special Orders No. 158, G. H. Q., American Expeditionary Forces, relieved Major James A. Shannon, Infantry, from duty with the 42d Division upon the arrival of his unit in the divisional area, and directed him to report to the Chief of Staff at these headquarters for duty with the General Staff, American Expeditionary Forces. Lieutenant Colonel Shannon reported and was assigned to station at Chaumont, Haute-Marne, in accordance with Paragraph 60, Special Orders No. 166, G. H. Q., American E. F., November 23, 1918. Although Lieutenant Colonel Shannon's work in the office of the Chief of Staff was at first more varied than it later became, nevertheless even by 22 December 1917, he had already founded the activities which later were to develop into the Personnel Bureau.

It should be noted that the handling of personnel in the American Expeditionary Forces falls historically into two main periods. Of these, the first which concerns the Personnel Bureau proper, extends from shortly before 7 January 1918, until 23 November 1918; the second concerns the later history of the Personnel Bureau after it had become the Personnel Division of the Adjutant General's Office and is treated in Parts II, III, and IV of the present monograph. The first period which concerns the Personnel Bureau proper, most naturally falls into four parts:

1. From 23 November 1917, the date on which Lieutenant Colonel Shannon took up his duties in the Office of the Chief of Staff, until 15 January 1918, when the Commander-in-Chief gave explicit and definitive instructions as to the activities of his Personnel Officer.

2. From 15 January 1918, to 12 June 1918, the date of the publication of General Orders No. 94, G. H. Q., American E. F.

3. From 12 June 1918, until 25 September 1918, the date of the Tables of Organization for the Personnel Bureau.

4. From 25 September 1918, to 23 November 1918, the date of which the Personnel Bureau finally became the Personnel Division of the Adjutant General's Office.

On 22 December 1917, approximately one month after Lieutenant Colonel Shannon had reported for duty, the Secretary of the General Staff addressed to the Chief of Staff, American E. F., a memorandum on the "Method of handling such personnel matters as are assigned to the Office of the Chief of Staff." Colonel (now Brigadier General) Frank McCoy divided the activities of the Personnel Branch of the Chief of Staff's Office, which was then functioning satisfactorily under Lieutenant Colonel Shannon, into four headings: Promotions; Reduction in Temporary Rank, Retirements, and Eliminations; Rewards, Commendations, and Recommendations; Waiting and Suggestive Lists. At that time, he stated, recommendations for promotions were being handled under the provisions of General Orders No. 132, War Department, 10 October 1917; General Orders No. 62, G. H. Q., American E. F., 16 November 1917; and General Orders No. 76, G. H. Q., American E. F., 15 December 1917. The Personnel Branch was keeping in close liaison with the Replacement Branch of the Administrative Section of the General Staff (G-1), and in addition it made use of the machinery of The Adjutant General's Office and its Personnel Branch (i. e., Officers Division), for all routine. Recommendations for promotion from other headquarters were prepared for submission to the Commander-in-Chief for his personal approval in the light of all available information. Under existing orders there were two possible channels to the grade of second lieutenant: The first through what later became the Army Candidate School at Langres, the second through gallantry in action on recommendation of intermediate and other commanders. Promotions from first lieutenant to colonel were accomplished in the regular manner upon the usual and necessary recommendations. Such promotions were made for demonstrated efficiency. Promotions to the rank of general officer would, it was stated by the Secretary of the General Staff, be made by the War Department upon recommendation of the Commander-in-Chief.

Hand in hand with such promotion went promotions in temporary rank, retirements and eliminations. Though it would seem that at this time these matters were merely under study and that no definite rules of procedure had as yet been worked out, upon the recommendation of the Judge Advocate of the American E. F., an advisory committee had been formed, composed of the Personnel Officer, an officer from the Operations Section (G-3), and an officer from the Intelligence Section (G-2), which was at that time preparing a number of cases for action. Such action would, it is inferred, be subject to the conditions laid down in General Orders No. 62, G. H. Q., American E. F., 1917, and Paragraph 11 of General Orders No. 132, War Department, 1917.

On 1 October 1917, a memorandum had been forwarded from General Headquarters, American Expeditionary Forces, to the War Department, recommending that Medals of Honor and Distinguished Service Medals be awarded for officers and men of the American E. F., and a file of officers and enlisted men recommended for medals and decorations had, by the date of this memorandum, been begun. It was the belief of General Headquarters that General Orders No. 134, War Department, 1917, prescribing the Wound Ribbon and method of award, would delay action and really defeat the purpose of the award. To quicken action, therefore, a cablegram had already been prepared recommending to the War Department that the conferring of such decorations should be delegated to the Commander-in-Chief in his descretion. Already a policy governing graded citations, the fourragere, and other decorations had been taken under consideration.

Waiting and suggestive lists for detail as acting general staff officer, and other important duty, had been compiled upon the general principles recommended by the Operations Section (G-3) and the Training Section (G-5), of the General Staff. It was purposed to keep such lists ready at all times for the inspection or information of the Commander-in-Chief. They were maintained up to date and frequently formed the subject of conference between the Chiefs of the Sections of the General Staff.

The relations of the Personnel Branch of the Office of the Chief of Staff to The Adjutant General's Office, American E. F., concerned, in the main, orders and records. Requests for orders were forwarded by the Personnel Officer to The Adjutant General who issued and signed necessary orders. Most of the records of the Personnel Officer were kept in the files of The Adjutant General's Office. So long as Lieutenant Colonel Shannon was in the Personnel Bureau, he maintained that his should not be an office of record.

The relation of the Personnel Officer to the Secretary of the General Staff and to the other members of the General Staff was one of close coordination, and cooperation. "Recommendations are now being worked up by the Personnel Officer," wrote General McCoy on 22 December 1917, "from the suggestions and experience of all Chiefs of Staff Departments here as to the considerations which should govern those making recommendations for promotion, and the particulars desirable to be covered in the various classes of promotions * * * The general effect on the command is so important and the responsibility resting on this office for the most discriminating recommendations so fully realized, that every effort will be made to avail ourselves of the experience of the French and British services, as well as frequent conferences with Chiefs of the General Staff

Sections and Chiefs of Staff Department, on both policy and individual cases, so that the recommendations will not only be discriminately, but sympathetically handled."

The relation of the Personnel Officer to the Commander-in-Chief is discussed in the memorandum from Lieutenant Colonel Shannon for the Chief of Staff, dated 9 January 1918, quoted below.

It may be well to record at this point that the qualifications of Lieutenant Colonel Shannon to perform the duties of Personnel Officer were widely recognized. Of acute and discerning judgement, he had, in spite of his own statement that he knew only approximately three per cent of the officers in the American Expeditionary Forces in January 1918, a wide acquaintanceship in the Army, both permanent and temporary. His energy and activity were indefatigable. Lieutenant Colonel Shannon died of wounds received in action 8 October 1918, at Bravegeny, Aisne, while leading the 112th Infantry Regiment, which he had been assigned to command.

On 7 January 1918, the Commander-in-Chief transmitted the following memorandum:

MEMORANDUM FOR the Chief of Staff:

Please establish a Personnel Bureau under The Adjutant General and place Colonel Shannon in charge of it. The idea is that this will develop into a bureau which will handle confidentially all matter relating to the personnel of officers as far as it is necessarily of record at these headquarters. As such it will be a special section of the A. G. O., not connected with the Statistical Bureau nor with the ordinary routine of The Adjutant General's Office, but under it for convenience and good administration. The A. G. O. will provide the necessary clerical assistance. Its duties will be -

1. To collect all official information regarding officers, such as reports and recommendations from superiors, etc.

2. To prepare efficiency blanks for distribution, upon which the efficiency of officers is to be recorded.

3. To keep lists of officers available for various classes of duty in the several staff departments and their qualifications for command.

4. To keep track of personnel of divisions and other units, and to see that they are correctly balanced according to organization tables and with officers of proper rank.

The most stringent rules will be put in force by The Adjutant General, confining the information of the Personnel Bureau to the officer in charge and selected subordinates and clerks, all of whom will be charged with the necessity of absolute secrecy in guarding these records.

Accordingly, the Personnel Bureau was established with Lieutenant Colonel Shannon in charge, and with a force of two clerks.

On the same date, General Harbord addressed to the Chief, Operations Section (G-3), a memorandum:

The Commander-in-Chief has sent me the accompanying memorandum (quoted above) which represents his wishes with regard to the handling of the personnel of officers as far as it is necessarily of record at these headquarters. He has not definitely decided, however, that this office should be under The Adjutant General.

As all our various agencies exist in order that operations may succeed, opinion is requested:

1. Is the keeping of this class of records preferably a General Staff or an Adjutant General's function?...

2. As against this office being either part of The Adjutant General's Office or of any existing agency in the General Staff, would you favor a separate bureau for it?

3. If a General Staff matter, should it be a part of any existing section of our General Staff, or of the Office of the Secretary?

Before concluding his memorandum, General Harbord remarked that: "This class of personnel has thus far been handled in the Office of the Secretary of the General Staff and is of frequent reference by me during the course of each day. Any agency that looks after this must be of the most convenient access to the Commander-in-Chief and the Chief of Staff."

On 8 January 1918, General (then Colonel) Fox Conner, Chief of the Operations Section (G-3), submitted to the Chief of Staff, in reply to the memorandum 7 January 1918, his opinion on the Personnel Bureau. He writes:

For the first time in our history, these forces are developing a General Staff which is becoming a real agency of the several Commanders in all that pertains to planning, coordinating, supervising and executing.

There can be no doubt but that these are the proper functions of the General Staff. ...

Instructors at schools are in a sense officers of the General Staff and should be selected as are General Staff Officers.

The exercise of control over promotions and details to the General Staff does not necessarily imply that the agency exercising such control must be the office of record. At the same time...each office must have records of some sort... It is perfectly possible that an office may make extracts and abstracts from original records and return such records to a central office for file. ...

A separate bureau for considering promotions would be advisable only if such bureau depended directly on the Chief of Staff.

The Commander-in-Chief is unusually vigorous, both physically and mentally, but it is believed that he is already carrying too great a load and to attempt to regulate promotions, etc., by a bureau reporting directly to him would be a vicious solution. ...

With reference to Item 4 of the Commander-in-Chief's memorandum (quoted above), it is believed that the Administrative Section is the proper agency for the performance of the duties named.

General Conner's recommendations were, in part, as follows:

(a) That promotions and General Staff and school details be handled by the General Staff; at these headquarters by the Secretary's office, or by a bureau directly under the Chief of Staff.

(b) That replacements, including balancing of rank, etc., be handled by the Administrative Section, General Staff (G-1).

(c) That all other personnel matters be handled by The Adjutant General.

General Conner further recommended almost complete decentralization of the control of personnel; that is, he would make commanders of units as low as divisions, the Chief of army artillery, the Commanding General, Line of Communications (Advance Section, Service of Supply), and the Director General of Transportation responsible for promotions and assignment of officers within their units.

At this point it may be stated that on 10 January 1918, General McCoy, Secretary of the General Staff, in a memorandum to the Chief of Staff on the subject of personnel, concurred in the recommendations of the Chief, Operations Section (G-3). Among the reasons which he gives, stands the following:

It (personnel) is under the direct supervision of the Chief of Staff and by officers of his personal choice. The waiting lists (suggestive eligibility and available waiting lists) are subject to his immediate call and are based on information which is only known to himself and the officers in his own office.

The following memorandum from the Personnel Officer to the Chief of Staff on the subject of the Personnel Bureau bears the date of 9 January 1918. It is so important that fuller quotation is given than might at first be considered essential.

I. My conception of what the Commander-in-Chief wants from the personnel officer at these headquarters is as follows:

1. Accurate information concerning the military ability of senior officers not below the grade of major, and probably not below the grade of colonel. This information to be carefully prepared and catalogued so as to be easy of access. This information would come from several sources: (a) From personal knowledge of the personnel officer; (b) from efficiency reports; (c) from commendatory or critical letters; (d) from reports from schools; (e) by application to the Chiefs of General Staff Sections. ...

III. I have considered the question of the location of the Personnel Bureau. The points that have impressed me so far are the following:

(a) A large part of the information about officers which will be desired by the Commander-in-Chief will necessarily come from official papers, efficiency reports or other papers. I have gone over a list of the officers of the Expeditionary Forces and I am personally acquainted with only about three per cent of them.

(b) This being the case, all papers referring to that class of officers about whom the Commander-in-Chief will want information (majors and above) should be automatically checked to the personnel officer and should not be filed unless they show that they have been to the personnel officer. It is quite probable that this could be done with more ease and certainty if the Personnel Bureau was in the Adjutant General's Department. I do not at the present time see any other reason for putting the Personnel Bureau under the Adjutant General's Department.

(c) Neither do I see any special reason why it should be a part of any General Staff Section, nor in the Office of the Secretary of the General Staff, except that the records should be at all times convenient of access for the Commander-in-Chief and the Chief of Staff. The personnel officer should have the confidence of the Commander-in-Chief and the Chief of Staff to the extent that they will know that he is putting before them in any case the best and most accurate recommendations he is able to give. And whatever department or section the Personnel Bureau may be assigned to, it is respectfully submitted that no officer should be able to dictate to the personnel officer what his recommendations to the Commander-in-Chief and the Chief of Staff shall be. In that sense, at least, he should be directly under the Chief of Staff. A personnel officer who does not have this confidence of the Commander-in-Chief and the Chief of Staff should be relieved and replaced by another officer.

IV. Recommended:

1. That the Personnel Bureau stay where it is, in the Office of the Secretary of the General Staff, for convenience of access of the Commander-in-Chief and the Chief of Staff.

2. That The Adjutant General check to the personnel officer all papers referring to officers of field rank and above, and take steps to see that no such paper goes to file without showing on its face that it has been seen by the personnel officer.

On January 13, 1918, General Harbord submitted to the Commander-in-Chief the above quoted memorandums with certain other papers; he concurred in the memorandum from the Operations Section (G-3).

The action of the Commander-in-Chief upon these papers is found in a pencil note to his Chief of Staff, dated January 15, 1918. Extracts from this important document are as follows:

I have not now nor have I had any idea of personally handling the Personnel Bureau. It would be under the General Staff in the sense that all departments or bureaus of service, supply, etc., are under the General Staff.

If in The Adjutant General's Office, controlled as I have indicated in my memorandum, the General Staff would be freed from a lot of detailed work that is not naturally a part of its role.

Naturally the General Staff would be called on for recommendations from time to time, but this does not make it necessary that the records in question be kept in whole or in part by the General Staff (nor does the above preclude consultation with any other department chief of office regarding promotions).

The instructions contained in my original memorandum will be carried out except as to replacement control which as now will be with the Administrative Section.

The general plan laid down by the O. S. (Operations Section) will be followed with the understanding that it shall be the duty of the personnel division to keep a close scrutiny over all promotions made by subordinate commanders.

The Chief of the Personnel Division will handle these matters there under The Adjutant General instead of under the Secretary of the General Staff and will furnish the Chief of Staff data or recommendations of records when called for, and follow generally the line of action in handling personnel that may be indicated by the C-in-C or the C. of S.

This memorandum marks the close of the initial period in the history of the Personnel Bureau. The Commander-in-Chief placed in charge of officer personnel in the American Expeditionary Forces an officer of wide acquaintance and independent judgment, whose duties are defined in various memorandums of instruction. At the same time, it was not the intention of the Commander-in-Chief to handle the bureau in person. On the other hand, the Personnel Officer was to be responsible directly to the Commander-in-Chief or his Chief of Staff, without intermediaries. Thus the decisions and policies of the Personnel Bureau, as expressed in its action, might be expected to represent as accurately as possible the desire of the Commander-in-Chief.

The second period, which may be classed historically as another phase of the formative development, began at this time and extended to the publication of General Orders No. 94, G. H. Q., American E. F., 1918.

Further instructions to the Personnel Officer exist in the form of a fragment of a typewritten memorandum evidently dated about this time, which was probably dictated by the Commander-in-Chief or the Chief of Staff:

3. Please give direction to Colonel Shannon to keep himself sufficiently posted on organization of brigades, divisions, and corps to assure us at all times that they have sufficient well-trained staff officers to conduct efficiently these various offices.

It is believed that in these directions lie the beginnings of the Information Section of the Personnel Bureau and the reason for Lieutenant Colonel Shannon's visits to various organizations of the American E. F. For instance, Paragraph 15, Special Orders No. 140, G. H. Q., American E. F., May 20, 1918, directs travel to Paris, British General Headquarters at Montreuil, and other points; Paragraph 10, Special Orders No. 148, G. H. Q., American E. F., May 28, 1918, confirms travel between March 5 and March 11, 1918, from General Headquarters to Neufchateau, Luneville, Baccarat, and return, and from May 11 to May 12, 1918, from these headquarters to Bar-le-Duc and return. This travel represents only a small proportion of the personal visits undertaken by Lieutenant Colonel Shannon to carry out the instructions of the Commander-in-Chief. Other chiefs of the Personnel Bureau have made similar trips from time to time.

On April 5, 1918, Lieutenant Colonel Shannon wrote the following memorandum:

MEMORANDUM: FOR COLONEL COLLINS, A. D. C.

SUBJECT: Personnel Bureau.

1. The Personnel Bureau was established by memo from the Commander-in-Chief dated January 7 and 15 (copies attached) which define its duties.

2. At present this bureau is handling, in addition to duties prescribed therein, questions of eliminations of unfit officers, awards and decorations, and many questions of transfers of officers.

3. METHOD: The method of handling the personnel question at present is as follows:

(a) All official information such as reports, recommendations, etc., regarding officers are kept in special files.

(b) A record is kept of all recommendations for promotions whether the promotions were made or not.

(c) A record is kept of all officers eliminated for inefficiency.

(d) Efficiency blanks are now coming in and they are filed in such a way as to make information easily accessible.

(e) Lists showing the organization of all staffs, from Brigade to General Headquarters, are also on file.

(f) A file is also kept showing all officers and enlisted men who have been decorated by an American decoration.

It is believed that the above method is working fairly well as far as keeping all records, etc., is concerned; but it is not believed that it (the Personnel Bureau) is a force of any great value. To make it such a force the following recommendations are made:

(a) The entire commissioned personnel of the A. E. F. should be classified so as to show accurately the qualifications and capacity of each officer. There are in the A. E. F. experts in every walk of life. There are also in the A. E. F. positions requiring an expert in every walk of life. A broad system which will succeed in placing the expert in the position where he can use his knowledge will be of great value to the whole force. The first step in that system has been taken. A committee on classification is now here from the War Department.

They have a system whereby every officer is being classified according to his military and civil capacity. They also have an excellent cataloging system whereby the information thus gained can be easily gotten at. Practically all officers in the United States have already been classified. A beginning is now being made in France with the students at the School at Langres. It is believed that this system will soon have developed to the point where we can begin gradually to place officers in the positions for which they are best fitted, without, in any way interfering with the work of the A. E. F., and that it will gradually result in getting the right man for the right place. This system will have its main application in the S. O. S., but it should have a bearing on the combat units by releasing regular officers of long experience with troops from purely administrative duties. It is also believed that it can prove as an aid to the correct placing of officers in combat units.

(b) In order to keep the Commander-in-Chief constantly informed of the manner of performance of duty and relative efficiency of officers with the combat units it is believed that reports and records cannot be relied on solely; but that there should be constant inspection going on by an officer of the Personnel Bureau. To do this however it will be necessary to have another officer in the Personnel Bureau, so that one officer can handle the work of the office demanding prompt attention, while the other is out inspecting. A list of names is now being prepared to be submitted to the Chief of Staff for selection of another officer for this work.

SCOPE: The above remarks give the present scope of the work of the Personnel Bureau. The matter of awards and decorations although not mentioned in the memo of the Commander-in-Chief seems to fall naturally to this department of The Adjutant General's Office along with other matters of commendatory nature.

It is also believed that the policy with regard to promotions has become well enough established and understood so that all promotions to the grades of 1st lieutenant and captain might now be made by corps headquarters.

PERSONNEL: The present personnel of this bureau consists of one officer and three clerks which is ample to take care of all the office work at the present time. If it is intended that the inspections referred to above should be made; a matter· which is of great importance, it will be necessary to have one other officer for duty.

Major (then Captain) Walter Ullrich, Adjutant General's Department, National Army, reported at General Headquarters, American E. F., on 27 April 1918, and soon after was assigned to duty in the Personnel Bureau. He was placed in charge of eliminations and demotions. This department, together with promotions, the list of eligible officers, including various phases of qualifications, civil and military, the keeping of efficiency reports, and Lieutenant Colonel Shannon's more or less frequent personal visits to organizations represent the activities of the Personnel Bureau before they were formally defined by General Orders No. 94, G. H. Q., American E. F., 1918. It should be noted, however, that Lieutenant Colonel Shannon had meanwhile been directed to report, as Personnel Officer, at conferences of Chiefs of General Staff sections in the Office of the Chief of Staff.

Mention has been made in the preceding paragraph of a measure to ascertain and keep available the civil and military qualifications of officers, so that they might be utilized to the best advantage in the American Expeditionary Forces. This subject in relation to an organization engaged with the enemy, is not intimately connected to the work of the Committee on Classification of Personnel in the Army, operating under direction of The Adjutant General of the Army, but a short discussion of various phases of this matter is necessary at this point in order to explain the later independent development of the Personnel Bureau. It should be borne in mind that most of the activity of this committee as directly affecting the American E. F. falls within this second period. As early as 19 December 1917, The Adjutant General of the Army had sent to the Commander-in-Chief of the American E. F. a cablegram (Paragraph 1, Cable No. A-537), commanding the work of this committee and recommending that it be studied with a view to possible utilization in France. This was in line with a memorandum, dated 29 November 1917, written by Lieutenant Colonel Shannon for the signature of General McCoy as Secretary of the General Staff, which reads as follows:

MEMORANDUM FOR Chiefs of all Staff Sections and Heads of Administrative and Technical Staff Sections.

1. It is proposed to start a personnel record which will give all possible information about officers in the Expeditionary Forces which might be of any value to any part of the Command.

2. It is believed that among the new officers, especially, are many men with qualifications which would be invaluable in some part of the force, which are not being utilized because information about these officers is not available. ...

3. In order to get this information with the least possible inconvenience to officers engaged on other work, it is proposed to make a list, as complete as possible, of the various qualifications which would be of value in an officer for any position in the army except straight line duty. ...

4. You are requested to submit as soon as practicable a partial list of this kind, making same as complete as possible to cover every qualification which you would desire to have in an assistant in your department.

Replies to this memorandum fall within two classes: Those of which the memorandum of the Director General of Transportation, Brigadier General W. W. Atterbury, in typical, and which define in detail technical qualifications, and those without great detail, typefied by memorandum signed by General (then Major) Robert C. Davis, Adjutant General, which stresses administrative experience and executive ability. A direct result of this canvass of opinion is stated in Lieutenant Colonel Shannon's memorandum of 4 December 1917, for the Chief of Staff on the development of the personnel office:

> (3) ADAPTABILITY FILES: Under this a request was made ... (for) ... list of qualifications desired ... in officers serving in various departments. ... Replies will be recorded in catalogue and information sent to the various departments. After this file is in operation, it is hoped that the information about officers can be obtained before they reach France so that men especially adapted to any position in the force can be promptly assigned thereto.

The fact that a distinction was implied between civil occupations and military occupations is important because it is believed that later the distinction became the reason why the work of the Committee on the Classification of Personnel in the Army was placed finally under the Statistical Division of the Adjutant General's Department, and not under the Personnel Bureau.

A reply to the cablegram of The Adjutant General of the Army was sent, after due consideration, on 27 December 1917 (Paragraph 2, Cablegram No. P-418). It was implied that the system at present could be of little value to a combatant organization. In addition, headquarters of combat organizations must be kept small and mobile. It was stated, on the other hand, that the system might ultimately be put in operation for Base Replacement Divisions.

To consider this matter more fully, a board was informally detailed, consisting of Lieutenant Colonel J. A. Logan, General Staff, president, Lieutenant Colonel James A. Shannon, Infantry, and Lieutenant Colonel (then Major) T. Edward Hambleton, Adjutant General's Department. The result of the deliberations of this board may be found in a letter from the Commander-in-Chief to The Adjutant General of the Army, dated 2 January 1918, in reply to a communication of 12 November 1917, giving further reasons and explaining more fully the conditions in the American Expeditionary Forces which led to the

About 1 March 1918, Mr. Robert C. Clothier, member of the civilian Committee on Classification of Personnel, came from Washington for the purpose of studying the situation as regards personnel work in France. During this visit Mr. Clothier frequently consulted Lieutenant Colonel Shannon. His conclusions are set forth with enthusiasm in his letter of 14 June 1918, to the Commander-in-Chief, on Maximum Utilization of Manpower. Two days previously, Mr. Clothier had addressed to the Adjutant General of the American E. F. a letter on the system as installed by the committee in camps and at mobilization points in the United States. He inclined to the opinion that the whole matter should be placed under the control of the Assistant Chief of Staff (G-1). General Davis in turn addressed a memorandum to G-1 which set forth the plan practically as it was later adopted. The development of this work is more properly considered in the history of the Statistical Division of The Adjutant General's Office, under which it was finally placed.

Among the first problems of the Personnel Officer stood promotions. Though the subsequent history of promotions must be considered in the history of the Promotions Section of the Personnel Bureau, nevertheless, it is advisable at this time to review the development of policy as regards promotions between 10 August 1917, and 12 June 1918, or a short time thereafter, in order that a sufficient perspective may be established for a consideration of the more liberal policy made operative by General Orders No. 124, General Headquarters, American E. F., 29 July 1918. It should be recalled that strictly speaking the problem of promotion in the American Expeditionary Forces was never solved; the cessation of hostilities 11 November 1918, and consequent cable instructions from the War Department to discontinue promotions on that date really cut the knot, did not untie it. Furthermore, the shaping of a policy as regards promotions, and especially the study and investigation of the problem between November and July, lay mainly upon the shoulders of the Personnel Officer.

The whole subject of promotions in the American Expeditionary Forces is complicated by its interrelation with such problems as concern the Tables of Organization, vacancies caused by transfer within or out of the Forces, by casualty and by promotion itself, the effectual utilization of officer material, reward for gallantry in action, replacement of officer personnel, the return of officers to the United States as instructors, the most advantageous proportion of Regular Army Officers in various units, and the acute shortage which later developed in both line and staff owing in part to the rapid formation of new divisions and higher organizations. In addition, the adjustment of promotions concerns the general relation of the American Expeditionary Forces to the War Department and particularly to the Army of the United States as a whole. After the appearance of War Department General Orders No. 78, 22 August 1918, which rescinded War Department General Orders No. 132, 1917, the difficulties in adjusting promotions became immeasurably less.

It is believed that the activities of the Personnel Bureau in an endeavor to establish a policy of promotion were governed by two main demands. Of these, the first was proved efficiency and consequent promotion by selection. This principle was first enunciated by the Commander-in-Chief, and later adopted by the War Department. The second demand was justice to all. However devious may seem the attempt to establish parity in promotion and at the same time to reward conspicuous efficiency in the performance of duty, it must be recalled that a promotion to be valid must be sanctioned by the then-existing military laws of the United States as operative in the American Expeditionary Forces, both with and without reference to other parts and branches of the Army of the United States. General Orders No. 132, War Department, 1917, cannot be considered an entire success. The phrase "Justice to all" implies under that order "Justice to the Regular Army, the Officers Reserve Corps, the National Guard and the National Army." Furthermore, it implies justice to units of the Marine Corps serving under the Commander-in-Chief. Even before Belleau Wood, General Orders No. 132, War Department, 1917, was out-worn; if it had continued in operation until the Argonne, it would have prevented much of the military achievment of that campaign. Fortunately the tension was relieved shortly after the Vesle.

In point of time one of the first questions raised by the Commander-in-Chief was that of increased rank and allowances for certain services. In response to a memorandum from the Chief of Staff dated 31 July 1917, the Judge Advocate General considered the question and rendered opinion in a memorandum dated 10 August 1917. The subject was discussed pro and con and a study was made of both the French and the British methods of promotions. On 9 March 1918, the Commander-in-Chief was addressed on this subject by his Chief of Staff. It appears that the Commander-in-Chief had made known a desire for such authority that his assignment of an officer of any grade to a certain command or staff position should thereby confer upon that officer a rank which, if higher than that which he already held, should be temporary, and should continue only while he held the command or staff position to which he had been assigned. In other words, the Commander-in-Chief appears to have favored a policy of attaching rank to a position instead of to an individual. This is in accordance with the policy of the British Army. It would likewise constitute, as the Chief of Staff remarked in his memorandum 9 March 1918, "what was well recognized in the late Confederate States but has never otherwise been recognized by law in our country, that rank should be commensurate with command. It will at the same time put a premium on efficiency by awarding a rank that continues only during the satisfactory performance of duty." Such a policy would have been in accordance with the desire of the Commander-in-Chief to inaugurate promotion for efficiency. The Chief of Staff at the conclusion of his memorandum suggested that the Commander-in-Chief consult the Secretary of War upon the matter.

Accordingly on 18 March 1918, cablegram (No. P-747, confidential), was sent to The Adjutant General of the Army, attention of the Chief of Staff. The most salient features of this cablegram are shown by the following quotations:

Our experience has already shown that many officers of high rank, line and staff, will have to be replaced by better qualified juniors who might later have to yield to others more competent. In order to utilize practical selection without being confined to a limited few officers where seniority and efficiency are united in same individual and to avoid surplus of incompetent officers in high grades recommend adoption of British system which attaches rank to position filled rather than to the individual. British system gives rank always commensurate with command and is logical extension to other duties of our law under which Commander-in-Chief Amexforce and Chief of Staff U. S. Army held their present grades. British Armies, corps, and divisions are commanded by officers of permanent or temporary grades which are fixed in their organizations. Following legislation recommended: An officer assigned to command troops or to a staff position in the American Expeditionary Forces by orders issued by competent authority shall, during such assignment, have the rank and be entitled to the pay and allowances appropriate to the command so exercised or the staff position so occupied as shown in approved organization tables. An officer so assigned to command shall take rank over all officers in the command to which he is assigned. The Secretary of War approves this plan in principle. ...

Indeed from a previous cablegram (Subparagraph 2-D, Cablegram No. P-693, 7 March 1918), it appears that studies had already been begun "regarding question of appropriate rank for various positions in the American Expeditionary Forces organization so that officers detailed to these duties may have necessary rank which should be carried by the office and not by the individual." The question was finally settled by a reply to the recommendation of the Commander-in-Chief dated 13 May 1918 (Paragraph 3, Cablegram No. A-1306):

The provisions of Section 7 of Act of April 26, 1898, Paragraph 639 Military Laws of the United States, and the delegation to you of power to assign officers under the provision of 119th Article of War provide sufficient means for the accomplishment of object desired and Secretary of War has decided it is inexpedient and inadvisable for the War Department to recommend at this time as a war measure legislation relating to the subject of promotion.

Meanwhile the Personnel Officer had requested from the Judge Advocate, 29 March 1918, in the name of the Chief of Staff, an answer to the question whether, "those Chiefs of Staff of divisions who are at the present time lieutenant colonels become automatically colonels in conformity with the provisions of the Tables of Organizations, or whether it is necessary that they be recommended for promotion to the grade thus authorized." By first indorsement dated 1 April 1918, the Judge Advocate, Brigadier General Bethel, replied, "In the absence of a law conferring rank on these lieutenant colonels other than that which they received in their appointment as such, I am of the opinion that they did not become colonels automatically upon approval of Organization Tables, and that they will remain lieutenant colonels until they receive appointment to a higher grade."

The Table of Organization, though already provided for combatant units as high as divisions, had not been developed for the Services of Supply, schools, centers of instruction and the various new and special services brought into existence by the War. The spring of 1918 was the period during which such tables were in process of development. Though their proper devising was the duty of the Assistant Chief of Staff (G-1) and hence not properly a function of the Personnel Bureau, nevertheless, it has been necessary to touch upon this matter since a Table of Organization is the basis upon which vacancies for promotion must be computed.

The conditions under which promotions could be made throughout the second period of the history of the Personnel Bureau are set forth in a memorandum of the Personnel Officer dated 29 December 1917. This memorandum is considered now rather than previously in this discussion because increase of pay and allowances and the question of rank attaching to office rather than to an individual are really antecedent to the present question.

In this memorandum Lieutenant Colonel Shannon states that the question of promotions may be considered under two heads: First, the authority to make promotions; secondly, the policies that should govern promotions. The authority for making promotions is found in various laws, acts, orders, and regulations, as follows:

The Act of 1 October 1890, vests in the President the authority to promote in the Regular Army, with confirmation by the Senate. The substance of the act, which is contained in Army Regulations 21 to 26, may be characterized 'Promotion by Seniority.'

Appointment and promotion of officers in the National Army and National Guard in Federal Service are covered in the Act of Congress dated 18 May 1917, published to the Army in Bulletin No. 32, War Department 24 May 1917.

Authority for appointment and promotion in the Officers Reserve Corps is contained in the Act of 3 June 1917, published to the Army in Special Regulations No. 43, War Department, 1917.

Hence all authority for appointment or promotion of officers is vested in the President who is the Commander-in-Chief of the Armies of the United States in certain cases by and with the advice and consent of the Senate, but in General Orders No. 132, War Department, 10 October 1917, the President delegated certain of his appointive and promotive powers to the Commanding Generals of National Guard and National Army Divisions, Corps Commanders and Commanding Generals of Expeditionary Forces. It will be seen in the course of this discussion that General Orders No. 132, War Department, 1917, really discriminates against officers of the regular establishment.

"The general policy governing promotions in the American Expeditionary Forces," wrote Lieutenant Colonel Shannon, "has been emphatically stated by the Commander-in-Chief in General Orders No. 66, H. A. E. F., 1917, and may be briefly stated as promotion by selection for demonstrated efficiency." Lieutenant Colonel Shannon further recommended that an officer should not be promoted simply because of the fact that he has been an expert in civil life in the line in which he is now working in the military service. The reason for this recommendation will be seen when the questionaire of the Chief of Staff, dated 18 September, 1918, is discussed. His further recommendations are that promotions in special cases be given to assure seniority in the position of the officer. "For the present", he wrote, "the policy should be to hold back our promotions, especially in the senior grades in the Staff Corps and Departments. Line troops should be kept filled up with officers for the sake of efficiency and training." This principle carried to its logical conclusions found expression in the letter prepared in the Personnel Bureau for the signature of The Adjutant General under date of 15 October 1918, which will be considered below. Lieutenant Colonel Shannon urged further that promotion be adjusted between troops serving in France and troops serving in the United States. The reason for this contention and some of the difficulties involved may be apparent shortly. Such were the difficulties as seen and forseen by the Personnel Officer before the beginning of 1918.

Reference has been made to the questionaire prepared by the Secretary of the General Staff, dated 18 December 1917, and addressed to the Chiefs of General Staff Sections and Chiefs of the Technical Departments. Therein he asks four questions, the last of which is of importance only as it reflects the consideration of the American Expeditionary Forces:

(a) Should an officer with very brief military service be promoted because he is known to have been an expert in civil life in the same line in which he is now working? For example, take the case of a doctor or engineer who has been eminently successful in civil life in the same branch of his profession as he is now working. Should he be promoted simply on that account alone?

(b) Do you believe that troops nearest the front should be favored in the matter of promotions? If so, have you any suggestions to make with reference to adjusting promotions between such troops and troops of the rear?

(c) Have you any suggestions with regard to the matter of adjusting promotions between the line and the staff?

(d) Does the attached cablegram meet with your approval? Please add to it or make any corrections that you think would assist in adjusting the matter of promotions in the United States as compared with promotions here. "

On the whole the answers to these questions submitted by the Chiefs of General Staff Sections and of Technical Departments indicate a surprising unanimity of opinion. The question whether success in civil life should be made the basis of promotion in the military service was answered in the negative. Brigadier General Williams, Chief Ordnance Officer at this time, wrote as follows:

When the Government has need of the services of an expert and gives him a commission for the purpose of being able to utilize his services as it may see fit, the fact that the man is an expert and in consequence thereof be of extraordinary service to the Government should be taken into consideration in determining the rank of the commission originally given to him. Once having been commissioned in the proper rank, the expert should be promoted in the ordinary way. If there be at present cases where experts have not been given a sufficiently high rank when originally commissioned this error should be corrected and promotion thereafter taken the normal course.

To the second question replies were divided, but the concensus of opinion seems to have been that, "it is in the interest of contentment that troops nearest the front should receive their full allowance of promotion and be favored, if it is possible to do so, " as the Chief Surgeon expressed it. The Chief of the Operations Section (G-3) to this question replied in the affirmative, adding, "this should be regulated by giving everyone a chance at the front. "

The third question also reflects some difference of opinion, but the answer of the Adjutant General sums up the matter as follows:

I believe staff officers should be given equal promotion with their brothers of the line, and especially the permanent staff officers of the Regulars. I do not believe that senior regular line officers, detailed in the Staff Departments, should be given promotion in the Staff Departments. ... This suggestion is made, believing that in the course of time most of the staff work can be done by qualified reserve officers or junior line officers, and senior regular line officers who are

The practical application of this opinion came during August, 1918.

The third question of the Secretary of the General Staff raised the point of parity in promotion between staff and line. A still greater difficulty was continually presenting itself in the fact that under the law a Regular Army officer who accepted a commission in the National Army was thereby deprived of his right to temporary promotion in the Regular Army to a grade higher than that which he held in the National Army. The whole question is discussed in a series of cablegrams from which the following quotations are taken:

Cablegram No. A-704, 28 January 1918
From: The Adjutant General of the Army
To : The Commander-in-Chief

(Par. 6) Subparagraph A. ... Policy has consistently been followed that when an officer goes into National Army, he is obliged to remain unless interests of service demand his transfer. He has taken his chances for promotion and should be required to stand by them. ... This has been the policy always followed. Any other policy would not be equitable. According to law temporary promotions in Regular Army cannot be given to officers in National Army.

Cablegram No. P-576, 6 February 1918
From: The Commander-in-Chief
To : The Adjutant General of the Army

Subparagraph 1-C. ... When an officer becomes entitled according to Regular Army list to temporary promotion in Regular Army is he automatically relieved from commission he holds in same grade in National Army? Can an officer resign his National Army commission to accept temporary commission in Regular Army same grade when his turn comes? Request full explanation of this matter which so seriously affects many officers of the Regular Army.

Cablegram No. A-789, 14 February 1918
From: The Adjutant General of the Army
To : The Commander-in-Chief

Paragraph 1-D. ... Your questions both answered in the negative. In order to avoid unnecessary changes in commissioned personnel of divisions, opinion of the Judge Advocate General was approved to the effect that any officer accepting commission in National Army was removed from list of Regular Army officers as far as right to temporary promotion in Regular Army were concerned. Any officer who had become entitled to temporary promotion in Regular Army prior to time appointed to same grade in National Army was not by this opinion deprived of right to temporary promotion in Regular Army. ...

Cablegram No. P-629, 21 February 1918
From: The Commander-in-Chief
To : The Adjutant General of the Army

Paragraph 5, Subparagraph B. ... Request reconsideration of ruling that an officer accepting commission in National Army is deprived of right to temporary promotion in Regular Army to higher grade than that held in National Army. The inconvenience of changes in personnel is small in comparison with the inevitable conclusion by the line of Army that ruling is unjust. The officers of infantry and cavalry appointed to majorities and lieutenant colonelcies in National Army after many of their juniors in the artillery had been promoted under ruling to confine appointments in the artillery to that army comprise some of the best in those arms. To further overslaugh such officers now holding National Army commissions by promoting over them men of their own permanent army is routine manner in Regular Army seems unfair.

Cablegram No. P-537, 29 January 1918
From: Commander-in-Chief
To : The Adjutant General of the Army

Paragraph 1, Subparagraph A. ... Effort has been made here to preserve an approximate parity between promotions in staff and line. There are several line officers performing at these headquarters as important duties as those performed by officers referred to and in some cases with additional claims of longer service. ... I believe it contrary to the best interests of the service to promote reserve officers to field rank, or to promote to higher grades those already holding field rank, except in special cases, until they have had further opportunity to demonstrate their efficiency in the military service. ...

Cablegram No. P-629, 21 February 1918
From: The Commander-in-Chief
To : The Adjutant General of the Army

Paragraph 5, Subparagraph C. ... The attempt to maintain parity between promotions in staff and line when both classes are employed side by side in war would appear only plain justice. Instances have occurred where high rank of officers offered us from America has prevented their employment under satisfactory chiefs their juniors here. It is a difficult problem to adjust duty to existing rank of officers from generals down particularly in case of officers permanent staff departments offered for designated positions without regard to tables of organization or question of duties commensurate with rank. We must obtain results without regard to individual interests, and high rank conferred in advance of tryout here may be a positive disadvantage to officers in limited field in which they may be employed. Practical effect some cases will be that unusual promotion there will deprive them of service here. ...

Cablegram No. A-839, 27 February 1918
From: The Adjutant General of the Army
To : The Commander-in-Chief

Paragraph 1. With reference to Paragraph 5-B your 629 situation appreciated and satisfactory solution being studied. Promotion will be coordinated with you as far as possible. Necessary organization here requires staff rank at time higher than you recommend but this is for officers remaining here except in cases when you will be notified. Recommendations for staff promotions in France have been made in order to coordinate with those necessary here. Promotions abroad will be made on your recommendations.

Subparagraph A. With reference to your 640 Paragraph 2. Agree to your principle and endeavoring to carry it out and also to give good regular officers opportunity abroad. All foreign possessions and other sources are being drained for regular officers. ...

With the question of parity in promotions may be considered also the maintenance of lineal lists. This matter is discussed in a memorandum from the Acting Assistant Chief of Staff (G-4) to the Chief of Staff under date of 2 April 1918:

With reference to Par. 4, Cablegram 1014-R, it is desired to submit the following:

1. The War Department states that it has adopted the following policy with regard to promotion of Regular Army officers: 'A line officer detailed on staff duty will be promoted only when promotion becomes normally due him according to his place on lineal list of his arm.' This is a manifest injustice to certain officers.

2. Regular Army officers were detailed on staff duty with the National Guard and National Army Divisions presumably on account of particular fitness and efficiency. They find themselves associated with officers of these services and should enjoy all the same privileges as regards promotion which these officers have. The present scheme for promotion of officers of the National Guard and National Army contemplates the advancement of the best suited and most efficient. However, the present ruling quoted in Par. 1 debars a Regular Army officer from advancement even though he be the logical candidate for promotion it also permits of National Guard and National Army staff officers, serving on the same Staff with Regular Army officers, to receive their promotion which cannot be given to the latter.

3. The War Department has not been consistent in its announced policy as recently it has promoted officers to grades which they have not reached in the permanent establishment.

4. The Army has undergone a great expansion since the beginning of the present war and the call for officers has been enormous. The National Guard was called into the Federal Service and the National Army has been created. Regular Army officers have been detached from their proper commands to fill in gaps in both of these services and when they have made good it seems only just to them that they should reap the benefits of their labors, instead of being branded as a Regular and made to stand aside to let those he brought into the service, as it were, pass over him. It can

only be by placing the right man in the right place, regardless of his status, that we can expect to build up our military establishment.

A similar protest is contained in a personal letter dated 18 May 1918, from General Johnson Hagood to Lieutenant Colonel Shannon. Meantime the War Department clung steadfastly to its policy of lineal promotion:

Cablegram No. A-1073, 9 April 1918
From: The Adjutant General of the Army
To : The Commander-in-Chief

Paragraph 2, Subparagraph A. ... Policy is to make promotion lineally unless special reasons for other procedure exists.

As early as 14 December 1917 (Cablegram No. P-380, Subparagraph 1-A), the Commander-in-Chief had gone on record as follows:

With reference to General Orders Number 132, your office, system of promotion therein enunciated while satisfactory for National Army and National Guard, seems inapplicable to Regular Army in commands wholly or partially regular. Also system of lineal promotion in Regular Army involving units as widely separated as America, Europe, and Philippines cannot be applied in present emergency and should give way for time being at least to promotion by selection. Conditions of active service will in short time force interchange of officers between Regular, National Guard, and National Army Divisions. To promote officers to National Army and carry them in new grades attached to the Regular Army or National Guard and likewise with officers of National Army or National Guard attached to Regular would involve endless paper work and would probably in the end substantially result in transfer regular commissioned list to National Army. Believe better consolidate all forces on one list for period of war according to date of present commissions securing rights of regular officers as to retirement, and proper place in reorganization at close of war. ...

From what has previously been written it is evident that by the middle of August 1918, practically no course was open to the War Department except an abolition of the distinction between the National Army, National Guard, Reserve Corps, and Regular Army.

The memorandum of the Personnel Officer dated 29 December 1917, discussed also the subject of elimination for inefficiency. He was of the opinion that to the Commander-in-Chief should be delegated the right of elimination. The matter increased in importance until it was deemed advisable to send the following cablegram (No. P-578, Paragraph 1) on 6 February 1918:

... For the Chief of Staff: ... in the case of incompetency of National Guard or National Army ... such incompetency has been followed up by discharge from the service. It is not believed that there should be difference in treatment for similar conditions of inefficiency (in the regular service). ... The paramount consideration as far as the war is concerned is present fitness rather than past history. The 118th Article of War and Section 1230 of the Revised Statutes contemplates discharge or dismissal from service of regular officers during war by order of the President. I recommend that this authority be delegated to me during the present emergency. My policy in such event would be to take no action looking to depriving a regular officer of his commission without a hearing to such officer and in case of long and honorable service and physical condition justifying it to order such officer before a retiring board instead of resorting to discharge. ...

Reply to this request is contained in Subparagraph 1-C, Cablegram No. A-789, dated 14 February 1918:

As to authority for you to discharge regular officers ... this is not believed advisable. In special cases, authority will be requested from here. It would be better to send these officers to United States with a statement as to reasons for relief. On account of great shortage regular officers it is believed that they may be utilized to release other officers who can be placed on duty with troops. ...

A general statement of the attitude of the Commander-in-Chief as regards efficiency and promotion on that basis is to be found in the following cablegram (No. P-680, 4 March 1918):

> For Secretary of War and Chief of Staff. With reference to Paragraph 5 your Cablegram 846, the question is so vital to proper organization and future efficiency of our armies in the field, that attention is again invited to the extreme advisability of reasonable parity of promotion between line and staff and of special care and restraint at this time in the matter of giving high rank in either line or staff. Appointive promotions should be made only when absolutely necessary for the proper performance of duty or as a just reward for duty already especially well performed. Our experience here and that of our allies shows that it is very unwise to bestow rank wholly on basis of peacetime achievement. There is almost invariably a letting down when an officer reaches the highes grade to which he may reasonably aspire if for good service. The General Staff is the directing head of our military organization and efficiency requires that the technical, supply, and administrative officers of permanent staff departments with whom the General Staff is associated should not overshadow the latter in rank. The same principle applies to our line officers who bear the heavy burdens and hardships at the front in the trenches under adverse and trying conditions where their lives are constantly imperiled. These line officers some of whom are on detailed staff duty should not be lightly passed over by officers of the permanent staff department whose chiefs happen to be in Washington urging greater promotion for their particular departments. There are here many most excellent medical officers as deserving of promotion as any in America but there are none whose performance of present duty would be facilitated by and advance to the grade of brigadier general and none to whom it is now due if this grade is to be earned as a reward. The same remark applies to other permanent staff departments here but it applies with much greater force to those departments at home. I do not consider it timely to take up the matter of promotions to high rank for the present, and strongly recommend that promotions to the grade of brigadier general in the medical, ordnance and other permanent staff departments be deferred until we have a larger army in France that will warrant it. The duties to which such high officers would be assigned can be very well performed with their present rank during which their services should be the subject of efficiency tests that may or may not warrant their selection later. In the meantime we are gradually weeding out the unfit here and I assume the same process is being carried out at home, so that within a reasonably short time we shall have sufficient data for selection in both line and staff based on efficient service and not upon seniority, which must at present be the principal basis of promotion especially among officers of the permanent staff at home. To follow the course in making high promotions as indicated by recent cables from War Department is to invite ridicule from our Allies, in whose armies promotions have been made for efficient service during the war.

At this point a word should be said with respect to promotion in special arms of the service, such as the Corps of Engineers and the Medical Officers' Reserve Corps, a subject which received a good deal of attention during the second period of the history of the Personnel Bureau. The chief difficulty in the situation, aside from the line of demarkation drawn between the Regular Army and the Reserve Corps, seems to have lain in the question of percentage of officers in various grades. During February, 1918, the Personnel Officer was at work upon the problem of promotion in the Medical Reserve Corps. By May, when 3,585 Medical Officers had arrived in Europe, a definite policy had been promulgated.

It was the contention of the Chief Surgeon, American Expeditionary Forces, that, "Promotions in the Medical Reserve Corps have no connection or relation with any Tables or Organization and therefore should not be held up awaiting the preparation of such lists." During the latter part of March and April, several cablegrams were exchanged with The Adjutant General of the Army and the Surgeon General upon this subject. On 28 June 1918, the Personnel Officer, over the signature of The Adjutant General, American Expeditionary Forces, had determined upon the following policy as governing promotions of Medical Reserve officers:

(a) All officers of the Medical Reserve Corps in Europe will be placed on a roster according to age in each grade. An officer's age will be determined by his actual age plus four months for each month of service.

(b) All lieutenants whose actual age is above thirty-one and who have completed one years service shall be eligible for recommendation for promotion to captain.

(c) Promotion in general will be according to seniority as determined by these rosters.

(d) Taking the number of first lieutenants of the Medical Reserve Corps in the American E. F. at any time as a basis, the number of officers in grades of captain and major shall not be greater than that authorized by the proportion of one lieutenant to three and nine-tenths captains to one and seven-tenths majors (approximately the proportion between the same grades in the Regular Medical Corps at the time of the passage of the Medical Reserve Law).

(e) Recommendation upon the part of the military superior of each officer with statement that his services have been satisfactory, will be required in each case of recommendation for promotion.

The same policy was adopted for officers of the Dental Reserve Corps. At this time an attempt was also made by the Personnel Officer to coordinate the matter of promotion in Administrative Services by requests for similar action addressed to the Chief Quartermaster and Chief Signal Officer. Under these provisions recommendations for promotion received by the Personnel Officer in accordance with later General Orders were referred to the respective Chiefs of Services for recommendation.

The complexity of the situation as regards promotion perhaps can now be more readily seen. One of the chief results of the publication of General Orders No. 94, G. H. Q., American E. F., 1918, was the sectionalization of the Personnel Bureau. Directly after it appeared, the Promotion Section was organized. The later development of policy as regards promotion and particularly as affecting the filling of vacancies occasioned by casualties and its relation to replacement will be discussed later.

The third period in the history of the Personnel Bureau, which begins with the publication of General Orders No. 94, General Headquarters, American E. F., 12 June 1918, saw the Bureau in its most acutely formative stage. It is true that a policy concerning promotion had already been formulated, but the exigencies of more active and costly service on the part of the American Expeditionary Forces made necessary certain modifications and revisions, although the general outlines remained practically the same. On 7 August 1918, the War Department, in General Orders No. 73, considerably simplified the problem of promotions by its abolition of distinctive appelations such as the Regular Army, Reserve Corps, National Guard, and National Army, and its substitution of the single term The United States Army. Further problems constantly presented themselves in questions of vacancies, the difficulty of proper interpretation and application of principles, especially as affecting promotion in the Corps of Engineers, parity between line and staff, the Medical Corps - owing largely to the lateness in shaping a final policy with respect to Medical officers - the Motor Transport Corps, the Army Service Corps, and finally the larger problem of replacements.

Eliminations progressed more smoothly after the appearance of certain telegrams and letters of instructions and especially the publication of General Orders No. 131, G. H. Q.,

American E. F., 7 August 1918. Decorations were conferred and the record system for awards was further developed.

It was occasionally the duty of the Personnel Officer or his assistants to prepare for the signature of other officers' letters commending the action or service of officers in the field. In addition, incoming letters respecting the efficiency of officers and their personal qualifications were filed and kept available as necessary.

It is impossible to write a connected history of the Transfers and Assignments Sections of the Personnel Bureau. In the beginning the activities of this section were intimately bound up with the more personal phases of the Bureau. Generals commanding divisions often came to the Personnel Officer, or wrote to him, with requests that certain officers whose efficiency and qualifications were known to them should be transferred to their organizations. In general, the policy of the Bureau was that no such transfer should be consumated unless the commanding officer under whom the officer requested was then serving, gave consent. Accordingly the procedure developed was as follows: First, the request was received; secondly, a telegram was sent to the commanding officer to ascertain if the services of the officer requested could be spared; thirdly, the transfer was made or not made in accordance with the reply received. In many cases it was found necessary to issue orders for transfers when it was stated that officers could not be spared, but in all such cases the Personnel officer assured himself that the new duty was of sufficient importance to warrant the reassignment in the light of the best interests of the service.

To handle the increasing volume of business it was necessary to augment the number of officers, field clerks, and enlisted men on duty in the Bureau. Though the records of the Bureau at all times were kept at the minimum consistent with efficient operation, a pending file for cases under action was installed which, though seemingly extensive, was always kept subordinate to the records of The Adjutant General and independent of them. All these matters will be more adequately discussed in the history of the various sections of the Bureau.

On 28 August 1918, Brigadier General Julius A. Penn reported at these Headquarters. Paragraph 43, Special Orders No. 255, G. H. Q., American E. F., 12 September 1918, assigned him to station at Chaumont, Haute-Marne, and announced him as Chief of the Personnel Bureau. It was realized that the activities of the Bureau demanded an officer of high rank properly to administer the work.

The further development of the Personnel Bureau entailed the constant establishment of new policies and the more or less constant revision of old to meet the changing conditions of combat. It should be borne in mind that the Personnel Bureau was concerned primarily with combat troops. Most of its work was of necessity performed at top speed; there could be no temporizing and little delay. Indeed, it would be difficult to find a section or bureau at General Headquarters the activities of which depended more directly upon combat conditions. Hence, it should be stated, with the cessation of hostilities the activities of the Personnel Bureau were considerably reduced both in volume and in pressure.

Among the most serious problems presented to the Personnel Bureau by conditions at the front stood shortage of officers and the equitable adjustment of supply to the constantly increasing demand. This problem became more acute as the proportion of trained and tried officers in combat units decreased. Thus a division freshly arrived from the United States, however excellent its material, had before going into action to be supplied with a leaven of officers in both field and company grades who should have seen previous combat service under the trying conditions of modern warfare. Casualties were inevitable; the more extensive the action the greater the proportion of losses. From 18 July 1918, until 11 November 1918, there was no day that did not take its toll of officer personnel. Other causes of evacuation had to be reckoned with. Furthermore, it was necessary to provide for schools and new units a proper proportion of seasoned officers. In July a policy was adopted with respect to colored organizations which entailed the transfer of from five to twenty-five officers from a number of other divisions to command them. Nor was the origin of such demands confined directly to the American Expeditionary Forces.

The formation of new units in the United States made necessary, under cable instructions from the War Department, the return of a large proportion for training and command in mobilization and instruction camps. The beginnings of such returns to the United States is to be found in Paragraph 2, Cable No. A-1425 under date of 31 May 1918, which called for the return of 4 colonels, 8 majors, 121 captains, 160 first lieutenants, and 100 second lieutenants of the Corps of Engineers, effective August 1. In all, no fewer than twenty-eight such cables were received up to 31 August 1918, covering all branches of service, both staff and line, and ranging from a call for one colonel of Cavalry (Paragraph 12, Cablegram No. A-1718, 15 July 1918) and one major, Quartermaster Corps (Paragraph 6, Cablegram No. A-1827, 11 August 1918), to 45 lieutenant colonels, 40 majors, 151 captains, 508 first lieutenants, and 572 second lieutenants, in addition to 6 officers for general staff duty with new divisions, rank not specified, called for on 12 July 1918 (Cablegram No. A-1706), a total of 1,322 officers. When it is recalled that these demands covered every branch of the service and touched nearly every division which had seen active combat duty, the seriousness of the problem will perhaps be appreciated.

On 29 August 1918, the Deputy Chief of Staff made provision, by memorandum, for a board of officers consisting of representatives from G-1, G-3, G-5, and the Personnel Bureau to meet and consider the problem with respect to shortage of officers. The findings of this board, set forth in its proceedings dated 3 September 1918, were that the situation with respect to shortage of officers was not so serious as had been supposed. It recommended, however, that steps be taken to secure a suspension of the return of officers to the United States and to make available many officers now in England and France assigned to duty inconsistent with their rank and position as officers of the Army. The board further concluded: A supreme difficulty in improvising a great army (the phrase is significant) is the production of officers with some idea of tactics. Intelligence and civil education are not alone sufficient. Though this board did not at this time recommend that the supply of officers to the United States be made automatic, an attempt was later inaugurated to place such return upon this basis. In November the Personnel Officer, then Colonel Walter H. Johnson, General Staff, initiated by cablegram to The Adjutant General of the Army a plan which would have provided, had it been accepted, an adequate supply of officers in all grades for new units under organization in the United States.

At this point it may be stated that although combat divisions generally acted with promptness and dispatch upon demands for officers to be returned to the United States, there was a more or less extended feeling that such demands seriously decreased the efficiency of organizations at the front. This feeling was not without foundation. To some division commanders it seemed that no sooner had an officer been adequately and efficiently trained in either line or staff duty, than it became necessary to return him to the United States. The British and French High Command had learned by costly experience that the staff of a division, to be truely efficient, must function as a unit for a sufficient time to enable all staff officers to become familiar with the personal qualities and characteristics of their associates both at headquarters and in the line. Thus, the constant drain upon a command could not but be a source of uneasiness to any general officer in a combat organization. Too often, it seemed, an officer had just become useful when he was recalled to form or train new units in the United States. Of this feeling the Personnel Officer was cognizant and it is safe to say that, so far as his orders permitted, he and his assistants endeavored to distribute the demands fairly and equitably.

It should be noted that the shortage of officers in the American Expeditionary Forces is a general term with two aspects. The first concerns the supply of officers with some idea of tactics and the qualities of leadership, mainly for combat duty. The second aspect involves the finished officer. Whatever may have been the achievements of the Army of the United States in the present war, or in previous wars, no formula has been devised for the production of experienced officers except service. It has been more or less seriously estimated that three years is the minimum time required to make a finished officer of even the lowest grade. However willing the candidate, however intelligent the material, and however intensive the training, it is self-evident that an officer of broad experience cannot be manufactured to order in a training camp. Furthermore it follows that more or less extended service with troops is the only course for the adequate development of fully trained officers. Such service could have been secured only in the Regular Army. No reflection is intended upon training camps or the various other devices, which all students of military art must consider mere make-shifts for the filling of vacancies of officer personnel. The system of training as developed in the present war in both the United States and Europe has been emphatically a success considering the end in view and the means to attain it; yet the indubitable fact remains that extensive service in the Regular Army is the only means for developing a completely trained officer.

In view of this fact, during July it became evident that certain positions on Division Staffs such as Quartermaster, Inspector and Commander of Trains, and others in the Services of Supply could be filled under combat conditions by officers not of the regular establishment. Accordingly, as the result of the deliberations of a committee on the selection of officers instituted by memorandum of the Deputy Chief of Staff dated 23 July 1918, Commanding Generals of Divisions and the Commanding General, Service of Supply, were instructed to make available certain trained regular officers for combat or technical staff duty. Commanding Generals of Divisions were informed on 13 August 1918, that all regular officers serving as Division Quartermasters would be considered as available for other duty on and after 1 October 1918. The statement of the policy and the initiation of this movement fall within the history of the Personnel Bureau but its execution concerned other bureaus and other agencies.

Some difficulty had been further experienced in cases where Division and Corps Commanders had relieved officers of General Staff and Administrative Staff from duty to which they had been assigned by these headquarters and had assigned them to other duty without authority from a higher commander. Although strictly speaking such action is within the province of the Division Commander under the provisions of Section 1, War Department General Orders No. 52, May 25, 1918, nevertheless it was found necessary to institute a direct control of General Staff officers at these headquarters. The quotation above is from the letter of the Deputy Chief of Staff, dated August 9, 1918, to the Commanding Generals of Corps, American Expeditionary Forces. Paragraph 2 of this letter is as follows follows:

2. General Staff officers are appointed by these headquarters and assigned to General Staff duties. They are not to be relieved from such duties without authority of these headquarters.

These instructions were later confirmed by general order.

The problem of shortage of officers is further represented in the activities and report of a committee convened under verbal instructions of the Chief of Staff to study personnel, dated July 22, 1918, consisting of Lieutenant Colonel Jens Bugge, General Staff, Lieutenant Colonel James A. Shannon, Infantry, Colonel (then Major) T. Edward Hambleton, A. G. R. C. This committee after visiting General Headquarters of the French forces, Headquarters of the 1st, 2d, 4th, 26th, 28th, 42d, and 89th Divisions, Headquarters Services of Supply, and the Replacement Depots at St-Aignan, Angers, Blois, and Gievres submitted an extensive report. The essential feature of this report lies in the fact that no change in the then present organization was recommended. A policy of rotation of officers and noncommissioned officers between training depots and combat units was however advanced; this later found expression in a letter of instructions from The Adjutant General, dated September 6, 1918, on rotation of training cadres. It was further recommended that closer liaison be established between the Personnel Bureau and the Reclassification Board at Blois and that upon the Bureau be placed the responsibility for the replacement of battalion and higher commanders: This Bureau should be responsible that divisions have at all time their full complement of commissioned personnel above the grade of captain. That is, if for any reason the regular replacement system fails to provide the officers authorized by Tables of Organization, it should be the duty of the Personnel Bureau to discover this fact and provide the necessary personnel, maintaining charts for this purpose. The approval of The Adjutant General to this report is dated 15 August 1918. The significance of this addition of responsibility with respect to the Personnel Bureau can be appreciated when the fact is pointed out that although the Bureau was charged with replacement, no reservoir upon which to draw for such replacement was provided. No control was established over the return of officers from the Services of Supply, hospitals, or depot divisions to their former organizations and no source of supply to meet the ever-increasing demand was instituted except the make-shift of transfer from one division to another, robbing Peter to pay Paul.

As Personnel Officer, Lieutenant Colonel Shannon made constant attempts to keep in contact with the needs of the organizations, by correspondence and by personal visits. Indeed, he realized fully the necessity of the personal element in all effective work, staff or line. This relation may have led to abuse by certain officers who considered themselves misplaced or ill used, and who wrote directly to the Personnel Officer for relief from such conditions. In other words, such officers mistook the Personnel Officer for an agent in classification. At one time so acute did this volume of business become that Lieutenant Colonel Shannon was driven to the necessity of devising a form-letter for the return of unauthorized applications for transfer to division commanders. It should be noted that Personnel Officer considered himself a kind of stabilizer between supply and demand and thus endeavored to carry out the provisions of General Orders No. 94, G. H. Q., American E. F., 1918, "to establish ... a system for the gradual assignment of officers to those positions where they can be of greatest value to the whole force."

Paragraph 2, War Department General Orders No. 78, 1918, provided that a personnel board will be organized in each separate unit and regiment or higher unit. The board will be appointed by the unit commander to recommend to him details, assignments, and appointments of officers. The board will be permanent but the members thereof will be changed so that no member will serve continuously more than three months, and having served three months he will not serve again until the expiration of three months. Paragraph 20, Special Orders No. 256, G. H. Q., American E. F., 13 September 1918, announces the following members of the Personnel Board:

Lieutenant Colonel James A. Shannon, Cavalry
Major Basil D. Edwards, Infantry
Major Robert E. Carmody, Cavalry

This order continued in operation until 30 October 1918, when it was revoked and the following board was appointed under provisions of Paragraph 69, Special Orders No. 303, G. H. Q., American E. F.:

Lieutenant Colonel R. A. Jones, Infantry
Major R. E. Carmody, Cavalry
Major Howard J. Savage, A. G. D.
Major W. H. Kobbe, Engineers

The second board considered the question of fairness and parity in promotion between officers of the American Expeditionary Forces and those still in the United States, but by 11 November 1918, had reached no decision.

Mention has been made above of the details to schools for purposes of instruction. In cooperation with G-5 it was within the province of the Personnel Bureau to detail instructors as required by the General Staff for duty in the Candidates' School, Corps Schools, the School of the Line, and the Army General Staff College. Effort was made to distribute the detail of such instructors as equitably as possible and when practicable to spare the combat divisions the necessity of yielding up officers in a greater proportion than circumstances required. Upon recommendation also of G-5 relief of student officers from the Army Schools, Langres, was accomplished through the Personnel Bureau. Furthermore the Bureau was the clearing house for graduates of the Army General Staff College. It was not, however, until Major (then Captain) Arthur M. Scully, 47th Infantry, was given the responsibility of nomination for the staffs of armies, army corps, and divisions that a complete and practicable system was devised.

As the program of training laid down by 5th Section of the General Staff developed, the relation of schools to the problems of replacement and promotion became more evident. The board of officers which met pursuant to the instructions of the Deputy Chief of Staff, dated 29 August 1918, and which submitted its report on 3 September 1918, was unanimously opposed to wholesale commissioning from the ranks in the American Expeditionary Forces. Among its reasons may be noted the superior quality of officers obtained by organized training in schools, the superior knowledge of tactics to be gained through such training, and finally the unprejudiced quality of such selection. Said the board, "The greatest single influence against efficiency in the Militia Divisions lies in the politics and local home affiliations with which all are infected. To further their political ambitions and their personal friendships militia officers generally wish to have their men commissioned directly and retained in their original organizations. Maximum efficiency can only be obtained by destroying the last remnant of such politics, and this can most promptly be done by subjecting all candidates to the unbiased and uniform standards of the Candidates' School and then being able to use the successful ones wherever their services are most needed." In other words, the policy of G-1 in conjunction with G-5 was to feed at the bottom a constant supply of junior company officers who, upon demonstrated efficiency for promotion, should be advanced in grade. Thus the policy in connection with schools was coordinated with the matter of promotion and replacement.

During this third period of the history of the Personnel Bureau there seems to have been a growing belief in the minds of various officers that replacement in general and field grades should be handled in the Personnel Bureau. "I agree," wrote Lieutenant Colonel Shannon in a memorandum for Colonel Bowman, "with the idea that the entire subject of replacement of commissioned officers should be handled by one organization." On the other hand, the provisions of General Orders No. 111, G. H. Q., American E. F., 8 July 1918, the provisional order governing replacements of personnel, made no junction with the activities of the Personnel Bureau. In addition to this, instructions sent out during the summer by telegram later confirmed by Section 1, Paragraph 1 (e), General Orders No. 144, G. H. Q., American E. F., 29 August 1918, considerably complicated matters of promotion as affected by replacement. The provisions, though later annulled by General Orders No. 162, G. H. Q., American E. F., 24 September 1918, were long considered by some organization commanders to be in force. The Personnel Bureau occupied the anomalous position of being responsible for the replacement or substitution of certain officer personnel but of being powerless to provide replacements except by taking them from one division and giving them to another. The culmination of this difficulty was reached during October and will be considered chronologically under the fourth period of the history of the bureau.

On 7 September 1918, a memorandum from the Deputy Chief of Staff to the Personnel Officer contains the following sentence: The Commander-in-Chief desires that the organization of the Personnel Bureau on a sound basis be pushed to early completion. After considerable discussion and consultation, Lieutenant Colonel Shannon devised for the Personnel Bureau a table or organization which, though never approved and put in force, is nevertheless of the utmost significance as showing what personnel Lieutenant Colonel Shannon considered necessary for the operation of the Bureau:

TABLES OF ORGANIZATION

For the

PERSONNEL BUREAU

Chief of Bureau: Major General or
                    Brigadier General

- - - - - - - - - - - - - - - - - -

                        :
                        :

- - - - - - - - - - - - - - - - - -

Executive Officer: Colonel or
                      Lieutenant Colonel

- - - - - - - - - - - - - - - - - -

                        :
                        :

- -

Promotions Section	(Chief of Section: Colonel or Lieutenant Colonel
	(Chief of Line Subsection: Lieutenant Colonel or Major
	(Chief of Staff Subsection: Lieutenant Colonel or Major
	(Two Assistants: Captains or Lieutenants
Efficiency Section	(Chief of Section: Colonel or Lieutenant Colonel
	(Two Assistants: 1 Lieutenant Colonel or Major
	(1 Captain or Lieutenant
Decorations Section	(Chief of Section: Colonel, Lieutenant Colonel or Major
	(Two Assistants: Captains or Lieutenants
Transfers and As-signments Section	(Chief of Section: Colonel or Lieutenant Colonel
	(Chief of Line Subsection: Lieutenant Colonel or Major
	(Chief of Staff Subsection: Lieutenant Colonel or Major
	(Chief of Miscellaneous Subsection: Lieutenant Colonel or Major
	(Three Assistants: Captains or Lieutenants
Infantry and	(Chief of Section: Colonel or Lieutenant Colonel
	(Two Assistants: 1 Lieutenant Colonel or Major
	(1 Captain or Lieutenant
Information, Lists Rosters, etc.	(1 Captain
	(2 Lieutenants

if these tables had been approved, it is safe to say that however heavy the burden of work placed upon the Bureau, the Bureau would have sustained it. The third period did not close with a definite organization for the Bureau.

    Before entering upon a discussion of the fourth period a word should perhaps be said of the relation of the Personnel Officer to the General Staff. In the spring of 1918 the Personnel Officer occupied an office adjacent to that of the Commander-in-Chief. Until the Bureau passed under the control of The Adjutant General, the Personnel Officer reported directly to the Chief of Staff or Deputy Chief of Staff; he thus became essentially a mouthpiece of the Commander-in-Chief in matters affecting personnel. This policy continued during the incumbency of Colonel Walter H. Johnson, General Staff, who became

Personnel Officer on 23 October 1918, when General Penn left the Bureau for line duty.

Early in the fourth period of the history of the Bureau Colonel Johnson, working upon the Tables of Organization as devised by Lieutenant Colonel Shannon, developed a tentative organization chart (see appendix). Although efficiency of operation demanded certain changes in this chart almost as soon as it was issued, it nevertheless was followed in a greater or less degree throughout the whole of the fourth period.

Before the Meuse-Argonne offensive had been a week under way, it was evident that a serious shortage of personnel would result in field grades in combat divisions. Matters at least reached the state where no replacements of field officers were available. Accordingly it was determined that, since all sources of supply had been exhausted, recourse for filling vacancies must be had to a policy of promotion much more rapid than had been adopted in the past. A letter was therefore drafted in the Personnel Bureau to go to the commanding generals of all divisions, corps, and armies, as follows:

GENERAL HEADQUARTERS, AMERICAN EXPEDITIONARY FORCES

France, October 15, 1918

From: Adjutant General, A. E. F.

To: Commanding General

Subject: Promotion of Officers

1. You will submit at once, by courier, direct to The Adjutant General, these headquarters (attention Personnel Bureau), recommendations for promotions to fill all vacancies existing in your division in the grades from colonel to first lieutenant, inclusive. Recommendations must be made from officers holding the next lower grade, and, if none suitable for promotion are in the division, report of the fact will be made. All officers of each grade in the division will be considered for the promotion recommended. In order to avoid duplication, if recommendations include any heretofore submitted, that fact will be stated, with date of previous recommendation.

2. The recommendations will be accompanied by a report which will give a summary by grades and arms of service of the number of vacancies existing in the division if, and after, the promotions recommended are made.

3. Report of physical examination on Form 395 will accompany each recommendation. If it be not practicable to obtain full physical examination, a statement from a medical officer that the officer recommended for promotion is physically fit to perform the duties of the next higher grade will be accepted in lieu thereof.

4. Each recommendation for promotion will take the form of the attached letter.

5. The provisions of G. O. No. 162, c. s., these headquarters, and G. O. No. 78, War Department, copy enclosed, govern. Section III, G. O. No. 179, October 14, 1918, now being issued, amends Section VII, G. O. No. 111, c. s., these headquarters, to provide that officers ordered to the Army General Staff College as instructors or students will be dropped from the rolls of their organizations.

Not long after this the Chief of the Personnel Bureau, Colonel Johnson, came to the conclusion that, "From a careful study of this matter it is apparent that if the divisions are permitted to continue indefinitely the filling of all vacancies by promotion, there will come a time when no replacements above the grade of second lieutenant will be possible, assuming that casualties cease to occur to any great extent in the near future, as is possible. The result will be that in a short time there will be a large number of field officers for whom there will be no possible assignment." It was recognized that the letter of 15 October 1918, was "to cover an emergency that existed due to the shortage of officers in many divisions." With the signing of the Armistice and the cessation of hostilities 11 November 1918, such a condition would soon have existed, had it not been that promotions ceased upon War Department order. On the other hand, it should be borne in mind that casualties in officer personnel were extremely heavy during the Meuse-Argonne offensive and it is doubtful if, without the most liberal application of promotion, the supply of officers and the morale of combat units would have been fully sustained.

Under the provisions of General Orders No. 94, G. H. Q., American E. F., 1918, the Personnel Bureau was made the repository of efficiency reports of officers of field grade. These reports, due 1 October 1918, were late in arriving because of delay in supply of forms. Furthermore, combatant organizations found it difficult to submit reports on officers while they were engaged with the enemy. The system of reports, however, on General Officers begun earlier in the history of the Bureau, continued to function and become a valuable portion of the office records.

Mention has been made in a previous paragraph of the interrelation of replacement and promotion. The following quotations from a memorandum for the Assistant Chief of Staff (G-1), submitted 8 November 1918, by the Chief of the Personnel Bureau (from which quotation has already been made) discuss the matter:

4. The present system of replacement of field officers is unsatisfactory. For example, a regiment in a front line division is in need of a colonel. An officer of that grade is supplied by the S. O. S. on requisition. Of that fact the Personnel Bureau has no knowledge. A telephone message is received by the Personnel Bureau from that division asking for a colonel. The Personnel Bureau knows of a replacement and such replacement is sent. In the meantime, due to the fact that the division has not complied with Sec. III, Par. 1, G. O. 162, but has complied with the letter of October 15, a recommendation has been received by the Personnel Bureau for the promotion of a lieutenant colonel which has been promptly acted upon and the lieutenant colonel has been promoted. The result: Two colonels arrive; one is promoted; three on hand but only one can be used. The other two must return to a replacement depot unless the Personnel Bureau can find a vacancy. Under the present system it is impossible for the Bureau to determine whether or not a vacancy exists in a combat division at any time. In this connection attention is invited to the fact that front line divisions do not desire to use replacements in field grades, but the fact remains that they must be used somewhere.

5. Assuming that the present procedure is allowed to continue, the result will be that every line regiment in every division will fill all vacancies in field grades by promotion and that all field officers who have been wounded, or have been returned to a replacement depot, or who for any other reason are available as replacements, will be surplus with no possible vacancy to which the S. O. S. or the Personnel Bureau can assign them. The following is therefore recommended:

(a) That the Personnel Bureau be charged with the duty of handling all promotions and replacements of field officers of the line. That there be no assignment of field officers of the line (or staff of an army, corps, of division), except by the Personnel Bureau.

(b) That prior to promotion in a line regiment the division commander comply with Sec. III, Par. 1, G. O. 162, c. s., and ascertain by telegraph to Personnel Bureau whether or not a replacement is available.

(c) That S. O. S. furnish the Personnel Bureau daily with a list of all field officers of infantry, cavalry, and artillery available for use as replacements. In connection with such list the information from S. O. S. to the Personnel Bureau should include name, rank, branch of service, physical condition (Class A), and if possible a statement as to whether or not the officer has had previous combat experience. (This data can be arranged by code if necessary.)

(d) The Personnel Bureau is to notify all division commanders of the procedure to be followed; G-1 to notify S. O. S. as to the procedure to be followed. The Personnel Bureau, in case of replacements in the artillery, to maintain direct liaison with the Chief of Artillery.

6. If the Personnel Bureau is to function it must have knowledge of, and control of, the supply as well as knowledge of the demand. The two are so intimately connected that any other system is bound to be a failure.

The direct result of this memorandum is seen in the following telegram from the Assistant Chief of Staff (G-1), dated 9 November 1918:

TO: Commanding General S. O. S.

Number 3752 G-1. In order to coordinate replacement of general and field officers with promotions, hereafter all assignments of general officers and field officers of infantry, cavalry, and artillery to combat units will be made by the Personnel Bureau, these headquarters. Commanding General S. O. S. G-1 will notify the Personnel Bureau daily by telegraph the name, rank, branch of service, physical class, suitability for combat duty, and such other information as will insure proper assignment of all officers becoming available for assignment. (Signed) ANDREWS

At the same time the following courier letter was dispatched:

COURIER LETTER No. P. B. 1.

From: The Adjutant General, A. E. F.

To: All Army, Corps, and Division Commanders

Subject: Replacement in General and Field Grades and Promotion.

1. In order to coordinate replacement of general and field officers with promotion, hereafter all assignments of general officers and field officers of infantry, cavalry, and artillery to combat units and to independent units will be made by the Personnel Bureau, these headquarters.

2. Request or requisition for the assignment of general and field officers of the line in infantry, cavalry, and artillery will be forwarded by telegraph or by courier letter to the Personnel Bureau direct, as necessity arises.

3. Vacancies which it is contemplated to fill by promotion will, before recommendations are submitted, be reported to the Personnel Bureau, as provided in Sec. III, Par. 1, G. O. 162, c. s., these headquarters in order to prevent confusion between promotion and replacement.

4. Surplus in field grades will be reported as heretofore. Replacement requisitions other than those specified in Paragraph 1 of this letter will be submitted as heretofore.

5. Receipt of this letter will be acknowledged by telegraph to the Personnel Bureau, these headquarters.

By Command of General Pershing:

N. W. Larimore,
Adjutant General.

Although it was evident that hostilities would cease within three months, it was not believed at this time that the end would come so quickly. The policy of the Personnel Bureau was to push forward replacements to the utmost and be constantly prepared for any emergency or any development as regards shortage of personnel. It has been said that the United States Army waged war as if the struggle were to last forever. This might have been said with equal truth of the Personnel Bureau.

On account of the increased volume of work in the bureau, a policy of decentralization had been developed since the middle of the summer, with the purpose of reducing to the minimum the number of papers which passed over the Personnel Officer's desk. For instance, memorandums on the transferring and assigning in line and staff were prepared under the supervision and with the initials of Lieutenant Colonel Ralph A. Jones or Major Scully. Officers on duty in the Personnel Bureau were instructed to advise the Personnel Officer of all matters concerning which questions might be put to him, but to decide routine questions so far as possible for themselves. Memorandums addressed from the Personnel Officer to higher authority were of course signed by the Personnel Officer, and most of the communication with sections of the General Staff passed over his desk. The success of such a system largely depended upon the type of officer on duty in the bureau. This procedure was necessary under the stress of operations. After the cessation of hostilities matters took a different turn. The volume of business handled by the Personnel Bureau decreased materially in volume and pressure.

On 3 September 1918, the Deputy Chief of Staff issued the following memorandum:

Memorandum for .... A. C. of S. G-1
G-5
Personnel
Chief of Artillery
Judge Advocate
A. G.

Subject: Officers.

1. It is desired that a Board be appointed to consist of one officer from G-1, one from G-5, and one from the Personnel Bureau (Adjutant General, Chief of Artillery, and Judge Advocate also to be consulted), to study and make recommendations to the Chief of Staff regarding the following matters:

(a) As to who should be responsible for the supply of officers of the line, various staff departments, and special services.

(b) To what extent should division, corps, and army commanders be authorized to assign and transfer within their units officers of the line and staff.

(c) To draw up an order covering the above points.

(d) What should be the source of supply for assistants to the G's of divisions and higher units.

(e) What should be the relative availability of staff officers as between divisions, corps, and higher units.

(f) In what way should the Reclassification system for officers at Blois be connected with the general system of replacements of officers.

(g) To draw up an order coordinating the system of replacements of commissioned officers with the system of promotion.

(h) To make a definite recommendation as to whether or not the entire matter of replacement of officers shall be handled in the Personnel Bureau.

2. G-1 will be responsible for initiating the meetings of this Board, and reporting result of same promptly.

3. Conference with S. O. S. suggested.

Eltinge
D. C. S.

The Board consisted of Colonel George T. Bowman, General Staff, for G-1; Lieutenant Colonel L. W. Cass, General Staff, for G-5; and Lieutenant Colonel James A. Shannon, Cavalry, for the Personnel Bureau. Conference was had with the Commanding General, Services of Supply, and the Adjutant General, Chief of Artillery, and the Judge Advocate General, who were requested to express their opinions. The Board submitted on 23 September 1918, a tentative report, which may be digested under the eight topics proposed by the Deputy Chief of Staff.

To the question who should be responsible for the supply of officers of the line and various staff departments and special services, the answer is in part as follows:

The Chiefs of Infantry, Artillery, and Cavalry, and the Chiefs of each Staff Department and Special Service, hereinafter referred to as the Chiefs of Services, should be charged with the immediate responsibility for the supply and replacement of officers of their respective services, under the general supervision of and coordination by the General Staff.

The Board recommended that Army and Division Commanders should have authority to transfer officers of the line up to and including the grade of major, and that Corps Commanders should not have this authority except when their Corps were operating independently. An order covering these points was drafted by the Board. The question of supply of assistants to the G's of divisions and higher units was answered by the proposed formation of a divisional training class at each division headquarters in addition to the functions of the General Staff College.

As for the reclassification system for officers at Blois -

A board of carefully selected officers representing different services, and to be known as the General Classification Board, with broad powers and presided over by a general officer, should sit in continuous session at Blois under the supervision of the General Staff, General Headquarters. Officers reclassified by this board should be assigned to duty as directed by the General Staff. The board should have power to classify and reclassify, and to recommend promotions, demotions, and eliminations.

A draft of an order coordinating the system of replacements in commissioned officers with a system of promotion was presented.

As to Paragraph (h) of the memorandum of the Deputy Chief of Staff -

the immediate responsibility for the replacement of officers should be placed upon the Chiefs of Service, the whole system of replacements, assignments, reclassification, promotions and rewards for distinguished service, to be supervised and coordinated by the General Staff. Good administration does not require the General Staff to undertake the detail work and large organization necessary to do this work itself. On the contrary, better results, with less overhead organization, will be secured by placing this work in the hands of those who are most directly concerned, viz: The Chiefs of Services, including the new Chiefs of Infantry and Cavalry, under the general supervision and control of the General Staff.

This would reduce the work of the Personnel Bureau by transferring much of the present detail to the Chiefs of Services, and particularly to the new Chiefs, Chief of Infantry and Chief of Cavalry. This would leave the Personnel Bureau, as now organized, the direct responsibility for supply of General Staff Officers, and partial supervision over commissioned replacements, assignments, reclassification, elimination, promotions, and awards for distinguished service.

The replacement of all enlisted personnel, and that of commissioned personnel insofar as the operation of the various depots is concerned, is under G-1. This dual system with respect to commissioned personnel leads to confusion, delay and inefficiency. The supervision and coordination of all matters relating to commissioned personnel is a General Staff function; and it therefore follows that the work of the Personnel Bureau, as herein limited and defined, should be consolidated with a section of the General Staff.

While it is not desirable to discuss details in this report, it may be briefly suggested that the proper organization would be the consolidation of all matters relating to commissioned personnel into a separate division of G-1, to be known as the Officers' Division. This would leave all matters of enlisted personnel and priority of troop movements in the present Personnel Division of G-1, to be known hereafter as the Enlisted Division.

It is further suggested that, in view of the great importance of the subject, a new and separate Division of G-1 be established whose special function it would be to study and act upon all matters connected with awards, decorations, citations, and reports of meritorious service, with a view of making liberal use of all proper means of rewarding good service and of improving and maintaining the morale of the Army upon the highest possible plane.

A note at the end of these proceedings runs as follows:

Lieutenant Colonel James A. Shannon, who is the third member of the Board, has agreed to the above, with exception of reply under (h); a copy of his statement is hereto attached.

Lieutenant Colonel Shannon's memorandum, of 24 September 1918, addressed to Colonel Bowman upon this subject, runs as follows:

Reference question H of the memorandum of the Deputy Chief of Staff, September 3, 1918.

I agree with the idea that the entire subject of the replacement of commissioned officers should be handled by one organization, but I consider the work of the Personnel Bureau as now organized too large and too important to be put under one of the present General Staff sections as a subordinate department. Also the work of the Personnel Bureau is growing rapidly larger. I believe it should remain, as at present, a separate organization. It might be made a separate section of the General Staff and called G-6 and be charged with the whole matter of replacement of officers and enlisted men.

As an alternative to the above those sections of the Personnel Bureau which are intimately connected with the replacement system, namely, Transfer and Assignment Section, Promotion Section, Elimination Section, might be transferred to G-1, and the Personnel Bureau be left to consist of the Decoration Section, and an Efficiency Section to handle efficiency reports of senior officers only.

The second paragraph of the above memorandum was approved by Lieutenant Colonel Hammond.

Of the views submitted by Chiefs of Administrative Service, that of the Adjutant General is quoted almost in full:

2. An examination of these proceedings shows that two members of the Board favor the absorption of the present Personnel Bureau by G-1, G. H. Q., while one member recommends that the Personnel Bureau continue to function as an independent office, or offers, as an alternative, the transfer to G-1, of certain sections of the present Personnel Bureau, leaving to that bureau only such sections as consider the questions of decorations and the efficiency of higher officers.

3. I am of the opinion that the question of replacement of officers is so closely connected with the question of promotion, elimination, and assignment that all of these subjects should be handled by the same office; but I do not see the advantage of breaking up the established Personnel Bureau and the assignment of its present duties to a section of G-1, G. H. Q. G. O. No. 31, c. s., charges G-1, G. H. Q., with the general question of replacements of men and animals, but all the details of receiving and filling requisitions for replacements have been delegated to G-1, S. O. S., while G-1, G. H. Q., establishes the priority in which these replacements will be furnished from the United States and depots.

4. It is not believed that the office for furnishing commissioned replacements, especially those of field and higher rank, to combat troops should be transferred from G. H. Q. to the Headquarters, S. O. S., and the advantages to be gained by the creation of a new commissioned replacement Section in G-1, G. H. Q., are not clear, while there are certain objections to this proposed action.

5. The present Personnel Bureau is intended primarily to attend to the important questions of the promotion and elimination of officers, and to the awarding of

decorations. The officer in charge of this Bureau is personally selected by the Commander-in-Chief; is one in whose judgment the Commander-in-Chief has personal confidence; he reports directly to him on questions submitted for decision, and his decisions, recommendations for promotion, demotion or decoration, necessarily are almost always accepted. It is evident that were the work performed by the Personnel Bureau transferred to a section of General Staff it would be one of the many duties with which the Chief of that section would be charged, and the Chief would be unable to give the many questions connected with this particular work the personal atten- tion that they now receive. A subordinate officer in any of the sections of the General Staff, who might be charged with making these decisions, would not have the direct responsibility to, or enjoy the direct communication with, the Commander-in-Chief that seems desirable. The necessity for making this Personnel Bureau an additional section of the General Staff is not evident, for it is not believed that the General Staff should be burdened with the administrative details which comprise so great a part of the work of this office.

6. At present all communications for the Personnel Bureau are received in the Adjutant General's Office and recorded, routine ones, handled there, others relating to promotions, demotions, decorations, etc., checked to the Personnel Bureau for decision, and when it has been made the Adjutant General's Office executes it, publishing the orders, forwarding them to the War Department for confirmation, making the assignments, notifying the divisions of all decorations conferred, etc. This system seems to be satisfactory, and notwithstanding the close relationship between the Personnel Bureau and the Adjutant General's Office for the same reasons given in Paragraph 5, it would not seem to be desirable to necessarily place this bureau under the Adjutant General.

7. For the reasons stated, it is not believed that the office charged with promotions and eliminations should be a subsection of one of the sections of the General Staff or that it should be an additional section; hence, it is recommended that responsibility for supplying commissioned replacements be vested in the Personnel Bureau.

8. It is believed that it is in the interests of efficient administration to place the classification plant at Blois directly under G. H. Q., and the recommenda- tion for the formation of a permanent Board of Classification to sit at Blois is con- curred in.

9. With reference to the recommendations of the Board under Paragraph (b), see G. O. 52, W. D., 1918.

It will be noted that the findings of the Board were not unanimous. A second board was constituted, consisting of Colonel Bowman, Colonel Johnson, Personnel Officer, and Lieutenant Colonel Cass, which submitted a second report dated 24 October 1918. In general the recommendations of this Board were identical with those of the previous Board except under (b) in which recommendation was made that "transfers and assignments should be effected as prescribed by General Orders No. 52, War Department, May 25, 1918". Under (f) the recommendations previously made concerning the Reclassification Board at Blois were somewhat extended. Under (h) the last two paragraphs run as follows:

It is recommended that all matters relating to commissioned personnel be con- solidated into a separate division of G-1, to be known as the Officers' Division. This would leave all matters of enlisted personnel and priority of troop movements in the present Personnel Division of G-1, to be known hereafter as the Enlisted Division, G-1.

It is further recommended that, in view of the great importance of the subject, a new and separate Division of G-1 be established whose special function it would be to study and act upon all matters connected with awards, decorations, citations, and reports of meritorious service, with a view of making liberal use of all proper means of rewarding good service and of improving and maintaining the morale of the Army upon the highest possible plane.

The recommendation, which received the approval of the Commander-in-Chief, was prepared by the Deputy Chief of Staff on 25 October 1918:

Memorandum.

There is question whether there should be a Personnel Bureau or whether that subject should be handled by G-1.

Board to consider the subject recommends whole matter be transferred to G-1.

Reasons for:

As promotion and demotion are intimately connected with replacements, the whole subject should be handled by one agency. The reports on which bulk replacements of officers are based go to G-1, which then directs S. O. S. to forward the required replacement.

A reclassification section at Blois would naturally work best under G-1, these headquarters.

Reasons against:

Much of Personnel Bureau's work is detailed rather than a matter of policy, it is not proper General Staff work and would require a large plant.

Present system can readily be modified so as to work.

Personnel Bureau has more direct connection with Adjutant General than with G-1.

RECOMMENDATION: That proceedings of this Board be disapproved and referred to new Chief of Personnel Bureau for his information.
- I think the Classification Board idea sound, but it can be organized independent of the remainder of this project.

Eltinge, D. C. S.

On 7 November 1918, the new Chief of the Personnel Bureau, referred to in the approved recommendation just quoted, addressed to the Deputy Chief of Staff a memorandum on the present status of the Personnel Bureau. An extract from this memorandum follows:

III. The following recommendations are made to serve as general guides to the improvement of the present situation:

1. The scope of the Personnel Bureau should be broadened by centralizing in it as much of the control of the officer personnel of the A. E. F. as practicable. That its functions should be curtailed to deal solely with promotion and demotion and with the transfer and assignment of officers upon request by name from commanding officers of combat and other organizations is impracticable.

2. It is further recommended that G. O. 94, G. O. 111, Sec. IV of G. O. 131, and G. O. 162 be rescinded and that one order be issued discussing the following points:

(A) Replacements of (a) General Officers; (b) Field Officers; (c) Company officers; (d) enlisted personnel - whether or not this function remain under the control of the Commanding General, S. O. S.

(B) The supply of officers for schools to be ordered from units arriving from United States under terms of the proposed cablegram recently sent The Adjutant General of the Army.

(C) The question of requests from organizations and officers by name.

(D) Replacement requests.

(E) Efficiency reports.

(F) Eliminations and demotions.

(G) Promotions, particularly as affected by vacancy and replacement.

(H) Return to the United States upon call and automatic supply, and especially the establishment of priority for officers returned in the event of the conclusion of hostilities.

(I) Transfers and assignments, with or without promotion, of all officers no matter what organization, arm or branch of the service. In this connection, G. O. 54, W. D., 1918, should be either rescinded or so amended as to be applicable to conditions in the A. E. F.

(J) Upon the establishment of the offices of Chief of Infantry and Chief of Cavalry, coordination of all of the Chiefs of the various arms of service in the A. E. F. with respect to personnel.

(K) Coordination of depot divisions, reclassification camp at Blois and base ports by a system of reports which shall show officers available as follows:

    (a) For instruction
    (b) For assignment to combat organizations
    (c) For assignment to non-combat duty
    (d) For return to United States as Class D.

3. It is further recommended that provisions be made to carry out the intent of Sec. H, G. O. 94. It is thought that the proper interpretation of this section will place control of all commissioned personnel for assignment and transfer, promotion, elimination and return to United States, whether in Zone of the Advance or Services of Supply, under direct control of the Personnel Bureau.

Up to the signing of the Armistice, the Personnel Bureau continued to function according to the recommendations contained in the memorandum of The Adjutant General quoted above. On 23 November 1918, the Bureau passed under the control of The Adjutant General and its offices were moved from A-prime Building to the top floor of A Building. Section I, General Orders No. 221, G. H. Q., American E. F., 1 December 1918, provides that, "the Adjutant General, A. E. F., is charged with the duties pertaining to the Personnel Bureau established under the provisions of General Orders No. 94, c. s., these headquarters". Thereupon the Bureau became the Personnel Division of The Adjutant General's Office. Its activity is discussed in Part II of the present monograph.

So much for the general history of the policies and activities of the Personnel Bureau. It is necessary now to discuss the activities of its various sections: Decorations, Promotions, Eliminations, Efficiency, Information, Cables and Records.

The Decorations Section: By an Act of Congress, approved 9 July 1918, the law relating to the award of medals of honor was amended to authorize the President to present decorations in the name of Congress to any officer or enlisted man of the United States Army who, in actual conflict with the enemy, distinguished himself conspicuously by gallantry and intrepidity at the risk of his life, above and beyond the call of duty. The same Act authorizes the President to present a Distinguished Service Cross to any person who, while serving in any capacity with the Army of the United States since 6 April 1917, has distinguished himself or herself by extraordinary heroism in connection with military operations against an armed enemy; and also the Distinguished Service Medal to any person who, while serving in any capacity with the Army of the United States since 6 April 1917, has distinguished, or who hereafter shall distinguish himself or herself by especially meritorious service to the Government in a duty of great responsibility. The Distinguished Service Cross and the Distinguished Service Medal are authorized by General Orders No. 6, War Department, 12 January 1918, which was republished in General Orders No. 26, G. H. Q., American E. F., 11 February 1918.

The first awards of the Distinguished Service Cross were made on 18 March 1918, to Second Lieutenant J. M. Green, 6th Field Artillery, Sergeant William Norton, 18th Infantry, and Private Patrick Walsh, 18th Infantry, by the Personnel Officer with the approval of the Chief of Staff. Such procedure for the award of decorations continued in effect until the publication of General Orders No. 94, G. H. Q., American E. F., 12 June 1918. After the appearance of this order the Decorations Section of the Personnel Bureau was established under the supervision of Lieutenant Colonel Shannon, with First Lieutenant William D. Meyering, Infantry, as chief of section.

The Decorations Section of the Personnel Bureau was later divided into two subsections. The American Decoration Section dealt with recommendations for the Medal of Honor, Distinguished Service Cross, and Distinguished Service Medal; the Foreign Decoration Section handled all matters pertaining to decorations by Governments of the Associated Powers.

Under the provisions of General Orders, recommendations for American decorations were forwarded by Commanding Officers through division headquarters. When a recommendation for a Medal of Honor was received, it was passed to the Board of Awards for consideration. If, in the opinion of the Board, the case was worthy of the award, it went through the hands of the Chief of the Decoration Section to the Chief of the Personnel Bureau. He presented the case to the Commander-in-Chief, who either disapproved it or directed that the nomination be cabled to the War Department, where final decision as to the award was made.

Upon the receipt of a recommendation for the Distinguished Service Cross, it was passed upon by the Board of Awards and either approved or disapproved. Such action was reviewed by the Chief of the Decorations Section. It should be added that officers serving on the Board of Awards were chosen with a view to former service with combat organizations in some of the heaviest fighting done by the American Expeditionary Forces. The majority of them had previously themselves been decorated and many had been wounded in action.

With the growth of the American Expeditionary Forces, the work and consequently the personnel of the Decorations Section was greatly increased. Up to 23 November 1918, the following figures summarize its activities:

MEDAL OF HONOR

Recommendations received		24
Approved	4	
Disapproved	20	

DISTINGUISHED SERVICE CROSS

Recommendations received		2,688
Approved	1,416	
Disapproved	1,272	

DISTINGUISHED SERVICE MEDAL

Recommendations received		98
Approved	6	
Disapproved	92	

PENDING, 23 NOVEMBER 1918

Medals of Honor	9
Distinguished Service Crosses	775
Distinguished Service Medals	332

Practically from the beginning of the section, recommendations have been passed upon by a board of three officers, all of whom have been engaged against the enemy. The following officers have been successively in charge of the Decorations Section:

First Lieutenant William D. Meyering, Infantry
Major Oliver P. Newman, Field Artillery
Colonel W. W. Taylor, Jr., General Staff
Major W. S. Biddle, Adjutant General's Department
Lieutenant Colonel J. A. Ulio, Adjutant General

Authority for officers and men of the United States Army to accept decorations conferred by other Governments is authorized in the Act of Congress of 9 July 1918, which was published to the American Expeditionary Forces in Bulletin No. 50, G. H. Q., American E. F., 26 July 1918.

When a proposition to decorate American officers was received from representatives of an Associated Power, it was handled by the Foreign Decorations Subsection. Propositions were either with or without citations. The Chief of the Subsection was responsible for the preparation of all papers relating to such matters for submission to the Commander-in-Chief, in whom rests decision. The proposition returned by the Commander-in-Chief was then forwarded to the respective mission at General Headquarters, and in from five to eight weeks the decoration arrived.

Records of the Decorations Section were maintained on cards complete for every recommendation, whether approved or disapproved, together with an entry of the citation. The Foreign Decoration Subsection maintained a record of propositions received showing when and by whom recommendations were made, and a copy and translation of citations, if any. Most citations have been for recipients of the Croix de Guerre. The section has also been instrumental in delivering a large number of decorations awarded by the Allied Forces which for various reasons could not be presented personally to the officers and enlisted men so honored.

The Promotions Section: The Promotions Section was established at about the same time as the Decorations Section, to handle recommendations for such promotions of officers in the American Expeditionary Forces as the Commander-in-Chief was permitted to make under the provisions of General Orders No. 162, War Department 1917. Such recommendations were submitted by unit commanders to fill vacancies, either original under the Tables of Organization, or the result of transfer, promotion, or casualty in the commissioned personnel. General Orders No. 124, G. H. Q., American E. F., 29 July 1918, further established the procedure. It was superseded in part by General Orders No. 144, G. H. Q., American E. F., 29 August 1918, which further simplified the process of promotion, under the provisions of War Department General Orders No. 78, 1918. The conditions of promotion and the information to be given in each case were as follows: (1) The name, rank, organization, and arm of service of the person recommended for promotion; (2) grade to which recommended; (3) definite statement as to whether a vacancy existed and how such vacancy was caused; (4) physical examination. General Orders No. 78, War Department, 1918, further provided for promotion in all grades by selection.

The Promotion Section was divided into three heads, as follows:

1. Chief of Section: General supervision and construction of policies governing promotions.

2. Chief of Line Promotions: Supervision and review of promotions of all officers of line units.

3. Chief of Staff Promotions: Supervision and review of all promotions of officers in Staffs, and Staff Corps and Departments.

There was instituted a card system by which record was kept of all recommendations for promotion whether approved or disapproved, together with a summary of all action on each case. Upon receipt, a recommendation was entered on a card and checked as to whether it was an original recommendation or a recommendation subsequent to one or more previously submitted. The papers were then checked to make certain that they contained all necessary information under the provisions of existing orders. They were then forwarded to the officer in charge of either the line or the staff subsection for decision as to possibility of promotion. After a final approval by the Chief of Section, recommendations were forwarded to The Adjutant General's Office where the necessary special orders were prepared and the officer notified of his promotion. Recommendations for promotion of officers in cases not within the authority of the Commander-in-Chief were forwarded by courier letter to The Adjutant General's Office, War Department. Washington.

The Commander-in-Chief possesses authority to commission for demonstrated ability, leadership and gallantry in action an enlisted man from the ranks without attendance at the Army Candidates' School. In such cases the Promotions Section based its decision largely upon the data submitted by the commanding officer who originated the recommendation. When an enlisted man was commissioned for extraordinary heroism a telegram bearing the signature of the Commander-in-Chief was sent, as follows:

> The Commander-in-Chief takes pleasure in appointing . . . . . .
> . . . . . a Second Lieutenant . . . . in the United States Army in recognition of his gallantry in action and demonstrated fitness. Direct him to accept this commission.

The matter of commissioning from the ranks is discussed in Paragraph 7, General Orders No. 162, G. H. Q., American E. F., 24 September 1918, and Section II, Paragraph 1, Belletin No. 53, G. H. Q., American E. F., 1918.

It is estimated that the Promotions Section of the Personnel Bureau handled 18,000 recommendations, of which approximately 12,000 were approved and promotions made. Unless a recommendation had to be submitted to the Chief of a Staff Corps for remark and approval or disapproval, promotions were made on the date recommendation was received. For instance, on one day, of a total of 499 cases handled, 487 officers were promoted. During the week ending 1 November 1918, 2,637 cases were handled with a total of 1,985 promotions.

The Eliminations Section: Though the Eliminations Section of the Personnel Bureau was incorporated in that organization, and though its activities were under the control of the Personnel Officer and later of the Chief of the Bureau, it was for all practical purposes an independent unit.

The authorities for procedure in cases of officers found unfitted for one reason or another to hold their commissions are, first, general, applying to the United States Army as a whole and secondly, special, operative only in the American Expeditionary Forces. Of the general authorities Section 9 of an Act of Congress "to authorize the President to increase temporarily the military establishment of the United States," 24 May 1917, provides:

> That the appointments authorized and made as provided by the second, third, fourth, fifth, sixth, and seventh paragraphs of section one and by section eight of this act, and the temporary appointments in the Regular Army authorized by the first paragraph of section one of this act, shall be for the period of the emergency, unless sooner terminated by discharge or otherwise. The President is hereby authorized to discharge any officer from the office held by him under such appointment for any cause which, in the judgement of the President, would promote the public service; and the general commanding any division and higher tactical organization or territorial department is authorized to appoint from time to time military boards of not less than three nor more than five officers of the forces herein provided for to examine into and report upon the capacity, qualification, conduct, and efficiency of any commissioned officer within his command other than officers of the Regular Army holding permanent or provisional commissions therein. Each member of such board shall be superior in rank to the officer whose qualifications are to be inquired into, and if the report of such board be adverse to the continuance of any such officer and be approved by the President such officer shall be discharged from the service at the discretion of the President with one month's pay and allowances.

In addition, War Department General Orders No. 76, 1917, sets forth the means of eliminating officers from the service.

In the matter of the discharge in the American Expeditionary Forces of officers for inefficiency, the following citations may be made:

Cablegram No. P-288, 16 November 1917
From: The Commander-in-Chief
To : The Adjutant General of the Army

Paragraph 9. With reference to paragraph 1 your Cablegram 362 authorizing me to discharge inefficient Coast Artillery Officers under orders cited, request same authority as to officers of all branches of the service.

Cablegram No. A-426, 23 November 1917
From: The Adjutant General of the Army
To : The Commander-in-Chief

Paragraph 1. Paragraph 9 your 288. Authority granted you to discharge by order of the President inefficient officers of all branches of the service without citing statute or General Orders. This includes all officers excepting those holding permanent commissions in Regular Army or officers given temporary promotion in Regular Army. It includes discharge or regular officers from their National Army commissions also officers holding temporary appointments in Regular Army as distinguished from officers who have been given temporary promotion. This replaces instructions in our Number 362, Paragraph 1. Cable this office action in each case.

It should be noted that this cablegram authorized the discharge of officers without citing statutes or General Orders, but it did not give authority to disregard the provisions of War Department General Orders No. 76, 1917. Now General Orders No. 76, 1917, are found in part upon statute. There was therefore uncertainty whether the President meant to delegate the power which he holds independently of statute or merely that power which he possesses under statute. The following interchange of cablegrams decides the point:

Cablegram No. P-338, 3 December 1917
From: The Commander-in-Chief
To : The Adjutant General of the Army

Paragraph B. Does paragraph 1 your cablegram 426 authorize me to discharge officers without the action of board under General Orders 76, and where report of board is not adverse.

Cablegram No. A-489, 8 December 1917
From: The Adjutant General of the Army
To : The Commander-in-Chief

Paragraph B your 338 answered in the affirmative and applies to all officers excepting those holding permanent or provisional commissions in the Regular Army or officers given temporary promotion in the Regular Army.

From the quotations given above it will be seen that the Commander-in-Chief may, with or without the action of the board, discharge for inefficiency officers of the National Army, National Guard, and Officers Reserve Corps, and temporary officers of the Regular Army as distinguished from permanent regular officers temporarily promoted to higher grade. He may likewise discharge officers of the Regular Army from National Army appointments and provisional officers of the Regular Army after action by a board, which may recommend the discontinuance of the officer in the service under his commission.

The gist of this matter was published to the American Expeditionary Forces in General Orders No. 62, G. H. Q., American E. F., 10 November 1917. This order which is dependent upon War Departmen General Orders No. 76, 1917, and it provides for the elimination of provisional officers who have not the suitability and fitness for permanent appointment. On 25 March 1918, General Orders No. 45, G. H. Q., American E. F. Under its provisions officers not holding permanent commissions in the Regular Army might be examined in regard to efficiency, suitability and fitness. The order provides for a board of not less than three officers and not more than five to be appointed by commanders of separate brigades, divisions, and higher organizations, each member to be superior in rank to the officer under investigation. Witnesses are sworn, testimony is, if practicable, recorded in full and where not practicable, by summary. The officer under investigation has the privelege of objecting to any member of the board; in addition he has the right to submit a written statement to be considered by the board and incorporated in its report, and he may make any statement, oral or written, sworn or unsworn, to be incorporated in the records; under oath, he is asked whether he desires counsel. In this the procedure is like the procedure of a retiring board. It protects the Army against incapacity, misconduct and inefficiency on the part of officers, and it guarantees to each officer investigated an opportunity to defend his commission before a regularly constituted and impartial tribunal. There is one more authority for the action of the Commander-in-Chief in the case of inefficient officers, found in Paragraph 3, General Orders No. 46, War Department, 9 May 1918, as follows:

In the American Expeditionary Forces the Commanding General will continue under the authority heretofore granted him, to discharge, by order of the President, inefficient officers of all branches of the service below the grade of brigadier general other than officers of the Regular Army. Officers of the Regular Army holding temporary appointments therein, or commissions in force other than the Regular Army, may be discharged from such appointments and commissions by the authority herein granted. In all cases where, in the opinion of the Commanding General, American Expeditionary Forces, an officer of the Regular Army, who has been given temporary promotion therein, is considered as unfit to exercise the duties of such temporary increased rank, the commanding general will report such fact to the War Department for the action of the President. In all cases in the American Expeditionary Forces where an officer of the Regular Army has been discharged from temporary commission with increased rank in the National Army or from commission to which temporarily promoted in the Regular Service, the conditions indicated in Paragraph 2 hereof shall apply.

In addition, at General Headquarters there was constituted upon the advice of the Judge Advocate General of the American Expeditionary Forces an advisory board consisting of three officers designated by the Chief of Staff, whose duty it is to review the action of the boards forwarded for approval and to recommend to the Commander-in-Chief such final action as appears to be just and fair. Such recommendations fall within four classes: First, that the officer should be discharged as recommended by the board; secondly, that he be transferred to other duty; thirdly, that he be subject to further trial and disciplinary measures; and, fourthly, that the proceedings be disapproved. Later the advisory board was instructed by the Commander-in-Chief to submit for his personal action only those cases in which discharge was believed to be the only action in justice to the interests of the Government and the officer concerned. Where possible, the board was instructed to recommend the officers for duty in organizations where it appeared from testimony that their services could be utilized. In cases of officers recommended for further trial and disciplinary measures, the advisory board was directed to notify the officer concerned that under instructions from the Commander-in-Chief the immediate execution of the sentence of dismissal was suspended and that he would be given further trial, with a view to demonstration of fitness. Appropriate letters of reprimand were forwarded when necessary, and a copy was made a part of the officers' records.

The work of the Eliminations Section was closely related to the Office of the Inspector General and the Office of the Judge Advocate General. Numerous cases required investigation by the Inspector General and upon his finding that an officer had violated military law his case naturally involved action by the Judge Advocate General's Department for trial by general courts-martial. The elimination of officers is also related to the matter of reclassification, and the work of reclassification at the Casual Officers' Depot is reviewed and made of record in this section.

Under date of 31 July 1918, a circular letter was sent by the Adjutant General, American E. F., to Commanding Generals of Armies, Corps, and Divisions, upon the reclassification of officers. The instructions are as follows:

1. In connection with Paragraph 2, G. O. No. 117, G. H. Q., A. E. F., July 16, 1918, and letter from these headquarters to the Corps Commanders, dated July 17, 1918, it is directed that when officers are sent to the Casual Officers' Depot, Blois, for reclassification, the following information will be immediately furnished direct to the Commanding General, Services of Supply, in order that proper disposition be made of the officers in connection with their classification:

    (a) Name of officer concerned.
    (b) Rank and Branch of service commissioned in.
    (c) Complete military history.
    (d) Full statement as to education, languages, etc.
    (e) Business in civil life.
    (f) Accurate estimate of his qualifications or disqualifications, good or bad.
    (g) Statement of what led to his being relieved from duty with troops.
    (h) Statement of any duty which he has ever performed in the military service which he has performed well, and for which he is recommended.

These instructions were further supplemented by the provisions of the following circular letter to Commanding Generals of Armies, Corps, and Divisions, and the Commanding General, Services of Supply, under date of 2 August 1918:

1. Division Commanders are authorized to relieve officers from duty with their commands who are considered unfit for combat duty. If the division is serving in a corps such officer will be ordered to corps headquarters. If the division is not serving in a corps such officer will be ordered direct to Blois. At the time he issues the order relieving an officer from duty with his division, the Division Commander will submit a full and complete report to the Corps Commander (if the division is not serving in a corps, to the Commander-in-Chief, A. E. F.), giving in detail why the officer is considered unfit for combatant duty. In this report the Division Commander will express an opinion of the capacity, qualifications, and efficiency of the officer reported on.

2. Corps Commanders are authorized to relieve officers from duty with their commands who are considered unfit for duty in the corps. Such officers will be ordered direct to Blois. At the time he issues the order relieving an officer from duty with his corps, the Corps Commander will submit a full and complete report (or forward the report of the Division Commander), to the Commander-in-Chief, A. E. F., giving in detail the reasons why the officer is considered unfit for duty in the corps. In this report the Corps Commander will express an opinion of the capacity, qualifications and efficiency of the officer reported upon.

3. The Commanding General of an Army is authorized to relieve officers from duty with his command who are considered unfit for duty in the Army. Such officers will be ordered direct to Blois. At the time he issues the order relieving an officer from duty with his command, the Army Commander will submit a full and complete report to the Commander-in-Chief, A. E. F., giving in detail the reasons why the officer is considered unfit for duty in the Army. In this report the Army Commander will express an opinion of the capacity, qualifications, and efficiency of the officer reported on.

4. Whenever an officer is sent to Blois under the authority of this order, the Commanding General of the S. O. S. will be informed by telegraph. Officers received at Blois will be reclassified and assigned to duty by the Commanding General, S. O. S.

5. Every officer relieved under the provisions of this order will be informed personally by the Division, Corps, or Army Commander, or by his Chief of Staff, of the reasons why he is so relieved. Where a Division, Corps, or Army Commander considers that an officer is so inefficient that he should be discharged from the service (or if a Regular officer, that he should be discharged from his National Army commission), he will convene a Board of Officers, as prescribed in G. O. No. 45, H. A. E. F., 1918.

Under all such provisions, Division Commanders were empowered to order officers whose services were in their opinion unsatisfactory to report to Commanding Generals of Army Corps. With such officers were sent papers showing their service, deficiencies and qualifications. If the Army Corps Commander could utilize the services of these officers he assigned them to duty with organizations under his control; if he found it impossible so to utilize them, the officers were ordered to report to the Commanding General of the Army for duty, or to the Commanding General of the depot at Blois for reclassification. At this depot sat a board before whom the officer appeared for examination to determine his suitability and fitness for service. Officers undergoing reclassification were permitted to summon witnesses and secure depositions under oath. The board, having heard testimony and considered each case in all its phases, found the officer either fit or unfit to hold a commission, and recommended disposition according to the evidence presented. Such recommendations were of three classes: First, that the officer, having been found unfit for any duty, forfeit his commission, if a temporary officer, or revert to his rank in the permanent establishment, if a Regular officer, or that, if his offense was subject to disciplinary action, he be returned to his organization for trial by General Courts Martial or other suitable disciplinary action; secondly, that he, having been found fit to hold a commission, be transferred for duty to the Services of Supply, in case his deficiencies lay in his handling of men during combat or training; and thirdly, that the officer, if found efficient, be ordered to report to the commander of a combat organization for duty, generally with a different unit from that with which he had previously served. Proceedings of all such boards for efficiency are carefully reviewed by the Advisory Board of three field officers sitting at General Headquarters in the Personnel Bureau, who approved or disapproved the proceedings and recommended action by the Commander-in-Chief. Records of cases were filed in a confidential file in the Personnel Bureau, and, after 23 November 1918, became part of a confidential file in the Adjutant General's Office.

The following extract of an indorsement dated 2 October 1918, illustrates the policy in force at General Headquarters to discover some duty for all officers of the American Expeditionary Forces in whose cases no moral turpitude or physical incapacity is involved:

In connection with the attached memorandum from your headquarters, and the correspondence from the 29th Division, relative to relieving officers from duty with their organizations and sending them to the Casual Officers' Depot, Blois, for reclassification, and your proposed indorsement in the case of officers referred to therein, has the full and firm approval of these headquarters.

The policy has received careful consideration at these headquarters in connection with a letter from the Commanding General, Services of Supply, wherein he states that it appears, in practice, that no boards are being convened by Division and Corps Commanders under Paragraph 2, Section 4, G. O. 131, G. H. Q., A. E. F., August 7, 1918, but that the practice appears to be to avoid the necessity of convening these boards by simply relieving the officers from duty with their organization and sending them to Blois for reclassification.

Paragraph 1 of the order referred to directs that in the case of officers who are considered unfit for combat duty and where the division in which such officers are serving is in a corps, these officers will be sent to the Corps Headquarters. In view of the policy that some duty be found for all officers of the American Expeditionary Forces now in France, who are not incapacitated and in whose cases no moral turpitude is involved, it seems an excellent practice that whenever possible these officers be given further duty and thorough try-out at the Corps Headquarters as to their professional fitness and qualifications, even going so far as to give them full opportunity for further training in order that they may demonstrate their worth; providing, of course, that the facilities for such training are available at the Corps Corps Headquarters.

There is sufficient machinery in existence for the elimination of officers who have fully demonstrated their inefficiency and whose conduct is reprehensible. Such officers should not be saddled upon the Services of Supply, but their cases should be acted on at the Divisional or Corps Headquarters.

The view expressed in your memorandum in Paragraph 1 in connection with the sending of officers to Blois, with reference to the future usefulness of these officers and the recommendation that they be sent there only when the ordinary processes of obtaining efficiency have proven to be useless, are concurred in.

The method of affecting an officer's discharge for inefficiency was as follows: After the proceedings of the board and of the advisory board had been approved by the Commander-in-Chief, orders were issued at General Headquarters for the officer to proceed to the Casual Officers' Depot for discharge. The actual orders for his discharge were published at General Headquarters and were delivered to the officer at the depot:

By order of the President and pursuant to authority contained in Cablegrams, War Department, Numbers 995 and 426, the following named officers are honorably discharged from the service of the United States, effective upon date of receipt of order at their present station: . . .

The date of actual notification of discharge was, by instruction, cabled to the War Department and all papers were transmitted to The Adjutant General of the Army upon application of the order of discharge. Only in extreme and meritorious cases has the War Department authorized the return of officers to the United States for discharge or resignation, and even then authority had to be obtained by cablegram in each case. The following cable instructions govern:

Cablegram No. A-1550, 17 June 1918
From: The Adjutant General of the Army
To : The Commander-in-Chief

Paragraph 6. With reference to your Paragraph 1, your 1297. Secretary of War considers it undesirable to grant authority to you to accept resignations of officers on duty with American Expeditionary Forces for the good of the service. All such cases have to be reviewed by him anyway and as a general thing resignation of officers at the front in the presence of the enemy should not be accepted. The machinery for the discharge of officers who are incompetent or immoral is at present sufficient to deal with all cases.

The following extract from a memorandum for the Commander-in-Chief submitted by The Adjutant General, 5 December 1918, though drafter after the Personnel Bureau had ceased to function independently, bears upon the subject of resignations:

Resignations for the good of the service in order to avoid consequences of misconduct were not cabled or forwarded to the War Department, as a general rule, but recourse was had to Efficiency Boards, Courts Martial or Summary Discharge under the 118th Article of War. A few cases have arisen wherein, in the interest of public morals, or on account of moral degredation and other abnormal circumstances connected, it became necessary to call for immediate unconditional resignation of the officer concerned, and a short resume of such facts was cabled to Washington, and authority was then granted to accept such resignations here. As stated, these cases have been but very few in number, and in no way alter the general rule that there is no authority at these headquarters for the acceptance of resignations of officers of the American Expeditionary Forces now in France.

The moral value or benefit to any officer of separation from the Army, by resignation as compared with separation by honorable discharge or musterout, is not apparent. Now that war conditions have changed, and that the emergency military establishment is being dissolved and reduced as fast as circumstances will permit, the same object sought by resignation, i. e., honorable separation from the service, may be speedily obtained by returning an officer to the United States with the class whose services are no longer required.

In addition, the Eliminations Section of the Personnel Bureau acted upon the cases of officers recommended for discharge by the Inspector General or the Judge Advocate General, or directed discharge by The Adjutant General of the Army. Such cases were of a kind which could not be brought before an efficiency or an elimination board. Summary discharges under the 118th Article of War also reached the section for review and disposition. Inability to stand the strain of active field service owing to old age, tempermental disposition, inadequate physical development and similar conditions, which hardly were of a nature to warrant the action of a medical board, were disposed of in other ways. The section has also acted upon recommendations for demotion of Regular Army officers from their temporary rank. Such recommendations in all cases required cabled authority from the War Department for action which involved General Officers, but direct action was taken under the authority delegated by the President to the Commander-in-Chief in cases of colonels and other officers. A number of Regular Army officers have thus reverted to their rank in the permanent establishment. The proceedings, reports and papers upon which these and all other action in the Eliminations Section were based are confidential.

The relation of this section to reclassification boards sitting at Combat Officers' Replacement Depot, Gondrecourt, is discussed in Parts II and III of the present monograph.

Confidential Files and Efficiency Reports: In addition to the efficiency reports rendered upon field officers of the American Expeditionary Forces every three months, the Personnel Officer was the custodian of a set of confidential files which contain data respecting promotions to and within the grades of general officer. Such records consist of various consolidated reports, cards and books of record showing promotions and recommendations for promotion to these grades. Favorable and unfavorable comment upon general officers and candidates recommended for promotion to the grade of general officer is kept in a looseleaf binder. The various files are cross indexed. In addition, a board was kept showing assignment of all general officers in the American Expeditionary Forces. From the Personnel Bureau issued all telegraph orders concerning the assignment of general officers.

The Information Section: The Information Section was begun in August 1918, by First Lieutenant (then Second Lieutenant) William Richards, Infantry. During October the section was supervised and developed by First Lieutenant Walker L. Martin, Quartermaster Corps, and during November by Second Lieutenant George T. Curry, Infantry. The section maintained a series of charts showing the field officers, line and staff, on duty with each corps and division, a pending file and an alphabetical card file of staff and field officers with corps and divisions, and brigade and battalion commanders. The pending file was a list of officers ordered to duty with corps and divisions who had not yet reported in compliance with orders. Upon their arrival, their names were entered on the charts and the cards removed from the pending file.

All records of this section were changed daily to agree with information secured from telegrams leaving the bureau, extracts of daily telegrams, on changes in status of field officers furnished by the Statistical Division, and extracts of special orders from the Orders Department of the Adjutant General's Office. The section issued a daily report to the chief of the division showing the transfers and assignments made during the previous twenty-four hours, compiled from telegrams sent out from the bureau and extracts of various special orders. A file was further maintained of field officers of Pioneer Infantry Regiments.

The Cable Section: The Cable Section of the Personnel Bureau was organized during the first of July 1918, by Second Lieutenant (then Private) N. A. Francis, Infantry, in order to give a complete history of all matters taken up in cablegrams. The system consists of an incorporate file together with a series of cross-references. From 23 July 1918, to 26 August 1918, Sergeant Garrett S. Wilson was in charge of the system. On 26 August 1918, First Lieutenant Clinton I. Stillman, Marine Corps, became chief of the section. The work of the Cables Section reached its maximum during the week previous to the signing of the Armistice.

The Records Section: The Records Section of the Personnel Bureau was established because of the need of immediate access to correspondence or documents originating in the bureau. No correspondence or documents were filed in the Personnel Bureau until the information had been duplicated in the Records Division of the Adjutant General's Office. The records of the Bureau thus contained memorandum copies of correspondence, but they considerably accelerated business because they eliminated the necessity of waiting for records from the Adjutant General's Office many times each day.

The records Section was established and perfected by Army Field Clerk M. W. Knarr during July 1918. At that time the bureau was rapidly expanding and the need for a systematic record for handling its correspondence was evident. Accordingly the personnel file, with an accurate system of cross reference indices and filing jacket for each name, was installed. The section expanded until one field clerk and seven enlisted men were employed in keeping the records, but the rapidity with which cases could be handled was extraordinary; retained copies of memorandums were filed within five minutes after a piece of correspondence had left the bureau. October was the section's heaviest month; as many as 2,000 cases a day were sometimes handled. A large proportion of the business of the bureau was done by telegraph.

The Records Section functioned also as a distribution section and a follow up section. When original correspondence came into the office, all previous papers in the case were assembled. Often this entailed the gathering of from five to twenty previous items but when all the supplemental papers had been brought together the case was absolutely ready for action. The file of papers was then sent to the officer of the bureau who should handle it. After final action, the case was returned to the Records Section where the office file was detached and out-going correspondence released. Army Field Clerk George L. Callahan, as chief clerk of the Personnel Bureau, was in charge of the section.

After 23 November 1918, the Records Section was incorporated in the Records Division of the Adjutant General's Office.

Part II

THE PERSONNEL DIVISION
Adjutant General's Office.

On 23 November 1918, in accordance with verbal instructions of the Commander-in-Chief, the Personnel Bureau became a part of the Adjutant General's Office, thereafter known as the Personnel Divisionl The division was moved from the second floor of A-prime Building to the fourth floor of A Building; it thus became an integral part of the Adjutant General's Office. The organization remained intact except as regards personnel and records.

Colonel Walter H. Johnson, General Staff, was relieved from his duties as Chief of the Personnel Division by Lieutenant Colonel J. S. Jones, A. G. D., Major Arthur M. Scully, Infantry, formerly in charge of Staff Personnel was transferred to Advance General Headquarters. His duties were taken over by his assistant, Second Lieutenant Arthur S. Booth, Infantry. The executive officer ceased to function as such. Major Carmody, upon the departure of Lieutenant Booth for the United States, was charged with supervision of staff personnel.

Certain alterations were also made in the method of keeping the records. The personnel file was absorbed by the Adjutant General's Record Division. The only records retained in the Personnel Division were copies of telegrams sent and certain files of important cases pending. Since the division was now a part of the Adjutant General's Office, the practice of requesting the issuance of orders by the Officers' Division was discontinued and the Personnel Division wrote and issued all orders with which it was concerned.

The work of the Personnel Division includes transfers, replacements, decorations, demotion and eliminations, adjustments of personnel for discharge or appointment in the Regular Army, promotion, and since March 1919, original appointments.

The Transfers and Assignments Section of the division, concerned with replacements in staff, infantry, field artillery, and other services, underwent a decided alteration. It should be recalled that after the signing of the Armistice the work of this section had greatly decreased in both pressure and volume. Hence it became possible to charge the section with control of replacements not only in field grades but of all officer personnel. The class graduating from the Army Staff College at Langres was distributed and assigned through the Personnel Division. Instructing staffs of various schools, upon completion of their duties, were broken up and reassigned. Infantry officer replacements were sent out on orders issued by the Personnel Division. Officers of field artillery were assigned or relieved nominally upon recommendation of the Chief of Artillery; but actually, in most cases, the Chief of Artillery wrote his own orders and sent them to the Personnel Division for record and issue. The Chief of Artillery about the middle of December, practically relinquished control of officers in the Coast Artillery Corps but with the understanding that the general policy should be to retain in France all Regular officers of the corps and to return to the United States for discharge all temporary officers whose services were not required by the Commanding General, Services of Supply. Replacements for other services were assigned directly or indirectly upon recommendation of representatives of Chiefs of Services in the Fourth Section of the General Staff.

Before discussing further the internal organization of the Personnel Division, it is necessary to turn to the provisions of General Orders No. 231, G. H. Q., American E. F., 18 December 1918, which established at Gondrecourt (Meuse), a depot for the reassignment of surplus combat officers and for the reclassification of officers. The most salient provisions of this order were as follows: The Casual Officers' Depot at Blois continued to function only as a replacement depot and reclassification camp for the Services of Supply. Replacement of officer personnel passed from the control of the First Section, General Staff, to the Adjutant General. Replacement requisitions for officers, instead of being required periodically from combat organizations were required whenever a vacancy occurred. This provision made it possible to utilize to the full the officer personnel remaining in the American Expeditionary Forces. In addition army commanders were directed by this order to send to Gondrecourt all surplus officers in their commands. Requests for officers to be ordered from the depot to combat organizations were to be submitted to the Personnel Division which controlled the flow of officers from Gondrecourt to organizations. In this connection it may be stated that when the depot was first organized it became necessary to coordinate the flow of replacements from the rear to the Third Army in Germany by suspending temporarily replacements from Gondrecourt and permitting the Commanding General, Services of Supply, to send forward *in toto* the officer replacements which he then had available. The reclassification of officers proceeded at Gondrecourt through the agency of two boards, senior and junior, appointed by General Headquarters special orders. The system of reclassification was further amended and stabilized by the provisions of General Orders No. 231, G. H. Q., American E. F., 1918. The great advantage gained by the establishment of the Combat Officers' Replacement Depot lay in the exercise of the functions of replacement, demotion, and supply of officer personnel through one agency, the Personnel Division, which coordinated and controlled the situation. It should be stated that this advantage was partially modified by the provisions of Section II, General Orders No. 23, G. H. Q., American E. F., 2 February 1919, which provided that officers evacuated from Services of Supply hospitals should return directly to their old organizations. Thus one branch of replacements passed from under the control of the Adjutant General. The Combat Officers' Depot ceased operations on 30 April 1919, and thereafter its functions as a replacement center were assumed by the First Replacement Depot, St-Aignan---Noyers, under the Commanding General, Services of Supply.

On December 13, 1918, the memorandums given below were issued to define the relation of the Officers Division and the Personnel Division:

The Officers Division will handle:

All officer personnel except generals, general staff officers and colonels.

Colonels will be a matter of discussion between the Officers Division and the Personnel Division.

All transfers of officers by name.

Return of casual officers to the United States for discharge.

Discharges in France, other than for inefficiency.

The Personnel Division will handle:

Generals, general staff officers, colonels.

All replacements of field officers, including army, corps, and division staffs.

Colonels will be a subject of discussion between the Personnel Division and the Officers Division.

When divisions are ordered back to the United States, the transfer to those divisions of officers desirable to send back to the United States, and the transfer from those divisions of officers desirable to be retained in France in other divisions.

Eliminations.

Promotions.

It should be recalled that though promotions were suspended in accordance with cable instructions from the War Department, there still was more or less correspondence upon the subject.

The function of the chief of the division and exercise of supervision by him is, in a measure, defined in the following memorandum dated December 13, 1918, from Lieutenant Colonel Jones to Lieutenant Colonel Coope, Chief of the Transfers and Assignments Section (later known as the Personnel Section of the Personnel Division).

1. I wish to sign all telegrams and orders referring to General Officers and all orders referring to General Staff officers. Any papers where a question of policy is involved, I also desire to pass on, and either sign or present to General Davis for signature.

2. Anything else that is out of the ordinary, I would like to be kept in touch with.

Under Lieutenant Colonel Coope the functions of the officers of the Personnel Division had developed by December 23, 1918, as shown in the following memorandum:

MEMORANDUM.

The following division of work in the Personnel Division will be effective at once:

Officers personnel to be handled as follows:

Generals,	(Major Carmody.
All Staff officers,	(
Witnesses at Gondrecourt,	(Lieutenant Richards.
All Infantry officers,	(Major Holmes,
	(Captain Kraus.
All Artillery officers, including Ammunition Trains,	(Major Savage. (
All remaining classes of officers, Lists of officers at Gondrecourt,	(Lieutenant Woods. (

Means were provided to notify the Commanding Generals of Armies and Army Corps of changes in status of field officers. Lieutenant Colonel Coope's instructions on 16 December 1918, were, "Whenever a telegram is sent direct to a Division Commander, which affects the status of a field officer, a copy of this telegram should be sent by wire to the Corps and Army Commanders under which the division comes."

The Decorations Section, under direct supervision of Lieutenant Colonel Jones, continued to function as it had operated in the Personnel Bureau. One exception, however, may be noted. Foreign decorations were separated from American decorations and were left in C Building under Major Biddle. Later the Foreign Decorations Subsection removed to B Building.

The section is divided into two subsections. The American Decoration Section deals with recommendations for the Medal of Honor, Distinguished Service Cross and Distinguished Service Medal; the Foreign Decoration Section handles all matters pertaining to decorations by Governments of the Associated Powers.

Under the provisions of general orders, recommendations for American decorations are forwarded by commanding officers through division headquarters. When a recommendation for a Medal of Honor is received, it is passed to the Board of Awards for consideration. If, in the opinion of the Board, the case is worthy of the award, it goes through the hands of the Chief of the Decoration Section to the head of the Personnel Division. The Adjutant General presents the case to the Commander-in-Chief, who either disapproves it or directs that the nomination be cabled to the War Department, where final decision as to the award is made. Upon the receipt of a recommendation for the Distinguished Service Cross, it is passed upon by the Board of Awards and either approved or disapproved. Such action is reviewed by the Chief of the Decorations Section. Recommendations for the Distinguished Service Medal are passed upon by the Board for Decorations, which consists of four general officers and is entirely separate and distinct in personnel and function from the Board of Awards. The action of the Board for Decorations is reviewed in all cases by the Commander-in-Chief. It should be added that officers serving on the Board of Awards have been chosen with a view to former service with combat organizations in the American Expeditionary Forces. Both during the time when decorations were administered by the Personnel Bureau, and after they came under the administration of the Adjutant General, the officers selected for the Board of Awards had served with combat organizations in some of the heaviest fighting done by the American Expeditionary Forces. The majority of them had previously themselves been decorated and many had been wounded in action.

A summary of awards of American decorations up to and including 30 April 1919, is as follows:

	Medal of Honor	D. S. C.	D. S. M.
United States Army	76	4,629	307
Other Armies:			
French		94	187
British		3	82
Italian			17
Belgian			17
Totals	76	4,726	610

When a proposition to decorate American officers is received from representatives of an Associated Power, it is handled by the Foreign Decorations Subsection. Propositions may be with or without citations. The chief of the subsection is responsible for the preparation of all papers relating to such matters for submission to the Commander-in-Chief, in whom rests decision. The proposition returned by the Commander-in-Chief is then forwarded to the respective Mission at General Headquarters. In from five to eight weeks the decoration arrives or word is received that the proposed recipients should report at a certain place at a certain time, to receive their decorations.

Awards by governments of the Associated Powers, through both the Personnel Bureau and the Personnel Division, to 30 April 1919, may be summarized as follows:

FRENCH

Legion of Honor	719	
Medaille Militaire	285	
Croix de Guerre	10,424	
Medaille d'Honneur des Epidemies	246	
Medaille de la Reconnaissance	11	
Medaille de Sauvetage, en Bronze	1	
Medaille Merito Agricole	1	11,687

BRITISH

Companion of the Bath	38	
Knight Commander of the Bath	5	
Military Cross	282	
Military Medal	222	
Distinguished Conduct Medal	67	
Distinguished Service Order	61	
Distinguished Flying Cross	19	
Meritorious Service Medal	22	
Bar to Military Cross	5	
Most Distinguished Order of St-Michael and St-George	3	
Knight Commander of St-Michael and St-George	15	
Companion of St-Michael and St-George	39	
Order of British Empire	8	
Companion of British Empire	2	
Knight of British Empire	1	
Member of British Empire	13	802

Belgian Croix de Guerre	407	
Chevalier de l'Ordre de Leopold II	25	
Decoration Militaire	20	
Grand Officier de l'Ordre de Leopold	6	
Commandeur de L'Ordre de Leopold	21	
Officier de l'Ordre de Leopold	22	
Chevalier de l'Ordre de Leopold	17	
Commandeur de l'Ordre de la Couronne	17	
Officer de l'Ordre de la Couronne	23	
Chevalier de l'Ordre de la Couronne	48	
Medaille de la Reine (with cross)	1	
Medaille de la Reine (without cross)	4	
Medaille de la Maison du Roi	3	
Medaille de la Maison de la Reine	1	615

ITALIAN

Merito Diguerre	2	
Cross of War	1	
Bronze Medal for Valor	1	
Service Bar (ribbon)	363	
Italian Decoration	8	375

GREEK

Gold Cross of Officer of the Redeemer	1	1

MONTENEGRO

Fifth Degree of Order of St-Danile	1	1

Grand Total	13,481

Records of the American Decorations Section are maintained on cards complete for every recommendation, whether approved or disapproved, together with an entry of the citation. The Foreign Decoration Subsection maintains a record of propositions received showing when and by whom recommendations were made, and a copy and translation of citations, if any. Most citations have been for recipients of the Croix de Guerre.

In addition, an engraved citation is sent by the Commander-in-Chief to recipients and non-recipients who have been recommended for decoration.

The provisions of General Orders No. 231, G. H. Q., American E. F., 1918, amended in part General Orders No. 131, G. H. Q., American E. F., 1918, respecting the reclassification of officers, but the essential features of the former continued. The following memorandum under date of 21 December 1918, further clarified the procedure with respect to officers ordered before efficiency boards. Paragraph 5 indicates the method followed at the time with respect to replacements whether reclassified, original, or evacuated from Services of Supply hospitals:

MEMORANDUM:

1. At Gondrecourt efficiency boards will be called, from time to time, for officers located at various parts of the American E. F., as witnesses in cases before these efficiency boards.

2. Judgement will have to be exercised in the matter of ordering these officers to Gondrecourt in such cases. If the officer wanted as a witness is in the First or Second Armies it will usually be found that he can be sent to Gondrecourt for temporary duty as a witness, in which case he will be ordered there by telegraph, and telegraphic notification sent to General Nuttman of action taken.

3. If the officer is in the Third Army or is attending one of the schools, his testimony will have to be taken by deposition.

4. It will be necessary for Gondrecourt to submit periodically lists by name, grade, and arm of service of officers available as replacements.

5. Under proposed General Orders No. 231, replacements of captains and lieutenants will be placed by this division. It is proposed to do away with the weekly replacement requisition; the commanding general of a division telegraphing the Adjutant General whenever a vacancy exists. For vacancies in captains and lieutenants, so many will be sent by number. Vacancies in the field and staff will be filled as heretofore by name.

The process of reclassification of officers at the Combat Officers' Depot, Gondrecourt, was an extension and improvement over the system in operation at the Casual Officers' Depot, Blois, when the Personnel Bureau became a part of the Adjutant General's Office. Under orders and letters of instruction issued previously to General Orders No. 231, 1918, division commanders were empowered to order officers whose services were considered by them unsatisfactory to report to Commanding Generals of Army Corps. With such officers were sent papers showing their service, deficiencies, and qualifications. If the Army Corps Commander could utilize the services of these officers he assigned them to duty with organizations under his control; if he found it impossible so to utilize them, the officers were ordered to report to the Commanding General of the Army for duty, or to the Commanding General of the depot at Blois for reclassification. With the establishment of the Combat Officers' Depot at Gondrecourt, the procedure up to this point remained unchanged, but officers were sent there instead of to Blois. At both depots sat boards before whom the officer appeared for examination to determine his suitability and fitness for service. Officers undergoing reclassification were permitted to summon witnesses and secure depositions under oath. The board, having heard testimony and considered each case in all its phases, found the officer either fit or unfit to hold a commission, and recommended disposition according to the evidence presented. Such recommendations were of three classes: First, that the officer, having been found unfit for any duty, forfeit his commission, if a temporary officer, or revert to his rank in the permanent establishment, if a Regular officer, or that, if his offense was subject to disciplinary action, he be returned to his organization for trial by General Courts Martial; secondly, that he, having been found fit to hold a commission, be transferred for duty to the Services of Supply, in case his deficiencies lay in his handling of men during combat or training; and thirdly, that the officer, if found efficient, be ordered to report to the commander of a combat organization for duty, generally with a different unit from that with which he had previously served. Proceedings of all such boards for efficiency are carefully reviewed by an Advisory Board of three officers sitting at General Headquarters, at first in the Personnel Bureau, and later in the Personnel Division, who approve or disapprove the proceedings and recommend action by the Commander-in-Chief. At Gondrecourt the accommodations for officers were exceptionally well arranged and cared for. Every effort was made to provide the officers with ordinary comforts, to maintain their self-respect and to enable them to prepare and present their cases, with or without counsel, fully and convincingly. Records of cases are filed in a confidential file in the Personnel Division, and when it has become necessary to return certain of such cases to the War Department, copies of all papers involved have been retained. The total number of cases for reclassification handled to 30 April 1919, is 1,024.

On 27 November 1918, the following cable instructions were received from the War Department (Paragraph 1, Cablegram No. A-2257, 26 November 1918):

PERSHING   AMEXFORCE.

Paragraph 1. Instructions issued to all commanders in the United States require officers to be discharged in the following order when not longer needed: First, officers desiring full and immediate separation from the service; second, officers desiring prompt separation from the service and subsequent appointment or reappointment in the Officers' Reserve Corps and whom commanding officers recommend for such appointment; third, officers desiring appointment, if opportunity permits, in the Regular Army, and whom commanding officers recommend for such appointment. It is desired that so far as practicable you readjust assignments and duties of officers in such manner as to retain in Europe as many as possible of the officers desiring appointment in the permanent establishment and believed qualified for same.

HARRIS.

Accordingly the following letter was promptly dispatched by the Adjutant General:

From: Adjutant General

To: (Commanding Generals of Divisions not under S. O. S., and
            Commanding Generals of Armies and Corps.)

Subject: Reports on Officers.

1. To comply with cabled instructions from the War Department, the following reports will be submitted to this office:

(a) By Commanding Generals of Armies - For Corps Commanders and all officers belonging to their respective Armies that are not assigned to corps or divisions. In the case of units or army troops larger than a battalion, the unit commanders will submit the desired report, through the Army Commander, as regards officers belonging to their several units.

(b) By Commanding Generals of Corps - For Division Commanders and all officers belonging to their respective Corps that are not assigned to divisions. In the case of units of corps troops larger than a battalion, the unit commanders will submit the desired report, through the Corps Commander, as regards the officers of their several units.

(c) By Commanding Generals of Divisions - For Brigade and Regimental Commanders and all officers belonging to their respective Divisions that are not assigned to regiments.

(d) By Regimental Commanders - For all officers belonging to their respective regiments.

2. In each case the report desired will include:

(1) Names of Regular Army officers, with regular and temporary rank; and duty to which each is at present assigned.

(2) Names of temporary officers who desire appointment, if opportunity permits, in the Regular Army. In the case of each officer recommended for appointment in the Regular Army, there will be given his present rank and arm of service, together with rank and arm of service for which he is recommended. If appointment in the Regular Army is recommended, same will be stated.

(3) Names of temporary officers who desire prompt separation from the service, and subsequent appointment or reappointment in the Officers' Reserve Corps. In the case of each officer recommended for appointment in the Officers' Reserve Corps,

there will be given his present rank and arm of service together with rank and arm of service for which he is recommended. If appointment to the Officers' Reserve Corps is not recommended, same will be stated.

(4) Names of officers desiring full and immediate separation from the service.

3. Division Commanders are charged with the communication of the instructions contained in this letter to commanding officers of regiments belonging to their several divisions, while Army and Corps Commanders are charged with the same responsibility, insofar as army and corps troops are concerned.

4. The reports from all units will be forwarded to this office through military channels, and it is desired that higher commanders, through whose headquarters said reports may be transmitted, make any suitable remark, or recommendation, thereon. It is requested that the submission of this report be expedited.

By command of General Pershing:

Robert C. Davis,
Adjutant General.

A similar report was requested from the commandant of each school and the chief of each section of the General Staff and each administrative service at these Headquarters. Furthermore, a similar request was made to the Commanding General, Services of Supply, for a report concerning officers serving under him, but by indorsement dated 2 December 1918, the Commanding General, Services of Supply, expressed the opinion that owing to conditions in his Service it would not be practicable to supply the information desired, and also that such information if supplied would have no practical value at General Headquarters with respect to personnel in the Services of Supply; the Commanding General, Services of Supply, he added, is charged with full responsibility with regard to the evacuation and detention of all officers under his command. These recommendations were approved.

Under Second Lieutenant T. D. Jenkins, Quartermaster Corps, who took charge of this work 5 December 1918, the reports as received were digested on various colored cards and filed by organizations. As divisions or other units were ordered to the United States, those officers who had signified their desire for appointment in the Regular Army were transferred to divisions selected to remain in France, and officers who desired full and immediate separation from the service were transferred to home-going divisions. By 1 May 1919, approximately 1,334 officers desiring appointment in the permanent establishment and 1,478 desiring discharge had been so transferred. Some difficulty was experienced because certain officers who had expressed their desire for service in the Regular Army later changed their minds and indicated their wish to remain with their divisions and to return to the United States. In most cases orders previously issued were revoked and the officers were thus accommodated. It has been the belief of those officers who have administered such transfers that, so far as practicable, the personal desires of these officers would be followed, with the two limitations of the possible renewal of hostilities and the good of the service.

When the Personnel Bureau became the Personnel Division of the Adjutant General's Office, the records of promotions remained intact. Under instructions from the War Department, promotions and original appointments had closed on 14 November 1918. Previously to that date decisions were made in the Personnel Bureau, while orders were issued in the Officers' Division, but with the transfer of the Personnel Bureau, it was possible to make preparation for handling both branches of the work in the Promotions Section of the Personnel Division, under Major William H. Stayton, Jr., A. G., should the restriction upon promotions be at any time removed.

Authority again to commence promotion in temporary rank was received 27 January 1919 (Paragraph 1, Cablegram A-2557). The general provisions were made that the object of all such temporary promotions was to treat the American Expeditionary Forces as a living organization and not to reward past meritorious services. Already under instructions issued from these headquarters, boards of officers convened at headquarters of divisions and similar organizations had selected a cadre of officers who would be promoted if instructions to the contrary had not been received from Washington, and the recommendations of these boards were first considered when promotion was resumed. On 11 February one promotion was made, and on the following day promotion was well under way. Later, under the provisions of General Orders No. 67, 18 April 1919, promotions were in full force under the provisions made by the War Department.

In order to correct real apparent injustices Brigadier General Wilson B. Burtt visited various headquarters with authority to promote on the spot any officers whose just deserts made such action advisable, and his work was coordinated with that at General Headquarters.

Authority to resume original appointments was received on 10 March 1919 (Paragraph 8, Cablegram A-2905), and the first appointments were made two days later. Except in the Quartermaster Corps, where examinations were required, appointees were graduates of the Army Candidates' School. Such appointments were made properly to officer combat and other organizations, whose ranks had been depleted by casualty, details to schools and educational institutions, transfers to the United States for discharge, etc.

A summary of promotions and original appointments between 11 February and 30 April 1919, is as follows:

PROMOTIONS

Infantry	1,490
Field Artillery	510
Engineers	561
Cavalry	31
Coast Artillery Corps	37
Quartermaster Corps	607
Ordnance	325
Signal Corps	172
Air Service	285
Tank Corps	34
Army Service Corps	82
Transportation Corps	227
Motor Transport Corps	142
Postal Express Service	10
Adjutant General's Department	80
Judge Advocate General's Department	16
Inspector General's Department	2
Medical Corps	3,328
Dental Corps	604
Sanitary Corps	171
Veterinary Corps	42
American Ambulance Service	8
Chemical Warfare Service	42
Corps of Interpreters	8
Chaplains	60
Military Police Corps	54
Total	8,928

— — —

Original appointments as second lieutenants:

Infantry	2,169
Field Artillery	401
Corps of Engineers	417
Signal Corps	32
Motor Transport Corps	48
Band Leaders	60
Coast Artillery Corps	33
Corps of Interpreters	2
Quartermaster Corps (on examination)	3
Total	3,165

Part III
THE COMBAT OFFICERS' REPLACEMENT DEPOT
Gondrecourt

By provision of General Orders No. 231, General Headquarters, American Expeditionary Forces, 18 December 1918, the Combat Officers' Depot was under the control and direction of the Adjutant General. The Personnel Division issued to the Combat Officers' Depot telegraphic instructions as to the forwarding of commissioned replacements to combat organizations and to such other units as stood in need of officers.

On 20 November 1918, Brigadier General Louis M. Nuttman was directed to organize the Combat Officers' Depot. The town of Gondrecourt (Meuse), was chosen as the site because it was expected that the I Corps Schools, which were located there would cease to operate about 20 December. Thus, the plant and equipment of the schools would be available for use by the new depot. After an inspection of the Casual Officers' Camp at Blois, organized under the Commanding General, Services of Supply, General Nuttman proceeded to Gondrecourt, accompanied by Captain Jeremiah Quinn newly appointed executive officer. They arrived 5 December and at once made plans for the development of the depot.

General Nuttman's instructions were to provide accommodations for any number of officers under 1,500. Part of the plant of the I Corps Schools was available upon his arrival. The use of a group of Swiss huts was obtained from the Chief Engineer of the Advance Section, Services of Supply, and several barracks were also secured. The barracks were divided by partitions into three large rooms. Personnel, including cooks and the mess attendants, and a certain amount of equipment, including dishes, were loaned by the I Corps Schools. Other equipment, such as bunks, mattresses, and some tableware, was obtained from hospitals which were about to cease operation. Transportation and other supplies were furnished by Fourth Section, General Staff, General Headquarters. Upon the arrival of the first casual officers, 11 December 1918, the depot was ready to care for them. Gradually the entire plant of the I Corps Schools, including most of the personnel, was turned over to the depot although this was not accomplished until after the beginning of the new year.

The personnel on duty at the depot beside the commanding general and his personal staff included an executive officer, the adjutant and one assistant, the personnel adjutant and his assistants who supervised arrivals and departures, the quartermaster and his assistants, including a disbursing officer, a billeting officer with assistants, a surgeon and assistant surgeons, and company officers on duty with the organizations into which the enlisted personnel was divided. During December 282 enlisted men were sent by the Commanding General, Services of Supply, for duty with the depot. With few exceptions these were laborers. This personnel was sufficient to operate the depot during December when only a few officers arrived.

The personnel office at the Combat Officers' Depot represented an adaptation of the statistical classification system in the Adjutant General Department. Error had been reduced to a minimum. A system was devised which was capable of expansion to care for some 1,200 officers per day, including daily arrivals and departures of 400. Up to 30 April 1919, a total of 3,486 officers had been received at the depot and 158 had been reclassified (29 of the Regular Army, 34 of the National Guard, and 95 of the National Army and the Officers' Reserve Corps).

One of the chief functions of the depot was classification and reclassification. This work was done by four boards. The Senior Reclassification Board, with membership of four Colonels, including one surgeon, considered all cases of field officers ordered to the depot for reclassification. The Junior Reclassification Board, consisting of four officers of field rank, including one surgeon, performed similar duties with reference to company officers. For such officers counsel was provided whenever desired, and every opportunity was afforded to prepare cases. The Physical Reclassification Board, consisting of three medical officers, considered those officers who claimed physical defects. To this board also were referred a number of cases considered by the two Reclassification Boards; in such event the reference had been requested by the Senior or the Junior Board. It was the duty of the Qualification Board to examine all officers arriving at the depot, and to ascertain from them and from official reports their past experience and education, with a view to their reassignment to duties for which they were best suited. The Reclassification Boards were provided in the order creating the depot and were organized by the Adjutant General. The Qualification Board, however, was organized at the depot as soon as its necessity became apparent. The work of these four boards was thorough, sympathetic, just, and satisfactory.

When an officer arrived at Gondrecourt en route to the depot, he was met by an officer especially assigned to that duty. Transportation was waiting, and baggage was given into the charge of a second officer. The new arrival was then conducted to the Records Office where he presented his orders and filled out certain forms devised to give complete information about prior experience or service. The Billeting Officer conducted such arrivals to billets in which fires were already lighted. When trains arrived as late as 11 p. m., officers were taken to the mess hall for a hot meal for the preparation of which cooks were held on duty.

Officers in the Records Office had special instructions as to courtesy, and the assistance to be given the new arrivals. It was the duty of the Billeting Officer to visit billets each day, and especially to ask if anything was desired. For field officers Swiss huts were reserved, accommodating two, three, and four each. Captains and lieutenants were billeted in comfortable barracks. Mess charges were reasonable. Each day two hours of instructions were given concerning various features of war, tactical questions, and other problems. Occasionally moot courts and debates were held.

Besides such personal comforts, shower baths with hot and cold water always available were provided. Entertainment included moving pictures, boxing matches, music, especially at mess, and occasionally a play. At least one hour of physical exercise was required each day. Club facilities were available to officers in the form of two huts operated by the Y. M. C. A.

The attempt was made in each case to make the officer feel that he was welcome in the depot, and that he was receiving personal attention. Though it was recognized that the first impression is of great importance in establishing the reputation of such a depot, the Commanding General made personal and special efforts to continue the initial impression however long officers might remain. Officers assigned left expeditiously with the same attention to personal comfort as they received when they arrived. In short, particular attention was paid, in cases where special need existed, to maintain not only self-respect, but also initiative and a feeling of personal responsibility. From letters written by officers, and from personal comment, it is evident that such treatment has been fully appreciated. The depot ceased to function 30 April 1919, and thereafter replacement was conducted through the First Replacement Depot, Saint Aignan-Noyer, which is under the Commanding General, Services of Supply.

Part IV

The Suspension and Resumption

of Promotions after the

Armistice

On November 15, the following cablegram was received from the War Department:

No. 2191-R, November 14, Pershing - Amexforces, HAEF (Confidential). War Department has adopted as a policy not to appoint or promote any further officers in the United States Army for the period of the emergency. This policy to be effective November 11, 1918. March.

Immediately upon the receipt of this cablegram, no further consideration was given to such recommendations for promotion as had been received at these headquarters; and the contents of this cablegram were communicated by telegram to all inferior headquarters in the American Expeditionary Forces.

On November 17, however, the following cablegram was sent to the War Department:

No. 1903-P, November 17, AGWAR - Washington, Paragraph 1. For Chief of Staff. No promotions or appointments of officers have been made since receipt of A-2191 on November 15. Some promotions had been made between November 11 and November 14 which could not be recalled.

Subparagraph 1-B. Reference A-2191. There are a large number of enlisted band leaders in the A. E. F. who, had they passed the necessary examination, would have been entitled to be commissioned before now. Due to unavoidable delays their examination was not started until November 15. Request information if these men can be commissioned, assuming they pass the necessary examination. Pershing.

In reply to the question asked in the second paragraph, the following reply was received on November 22:

No. 2231-R, November 21. Pershing - Amexforce, H. A. E. F. Paragraph 5. Reference P 1903 Paragraph 1-B. No change in policy of not issuing further commissions can be made. Harris.

The decision of the War Department that there would be no further appointments, or promotions produced great dissatisfaction throughout the entire American Expeditionary Forces. During the weeks immediately preceding the signing of the Armistice, most of the combat organizations had been so busily engaged with the enemy that time had not been available for recommendations for promotions to be made, and many officers whose rank was not commensurate with the positions they had been filling with credit felt aggrieved that they had been denied this recognition of their meritorious services. Many enlisted candidates for commissions had been detailed to the several Candidates' Schools with a promise of being commissioned should they successfully complete the course of instruction at those institutions. All these enlisted men had been selected from their organizations on account of the efficiency they had displayed, and the War Department orders denied them the just reward of their labors. Certain of the staff corps of the American Expeditionary Forces were in process of organization at the time of the signing of the Armistice. Many selected officers and enlisted men had been detailed for duty with these departments with a promise of promotion, to ranks commensurate with the duties they were expected to perform, as soon as the Tables of Organization of these Staff Departments had been approved, and the promised promotions could legally be made. Approval of these tables had just been given a few days before November 11, and the recommendations for promotion of the officers authorized by these tables were either in course of preparation, or enroute to these headquarters when the War Department notice of suspension was published. Information received from every part of the American Expeditionary Forces indicated the widespread dissatisfaction as a result of the prohibition of further appointments and promotions, and several letters of protest against this action were received of which the following are good examples:

HEADQUARTERS I ARMY CORPS

American E. F.

24 November 1918

From: Commanding General, I Army Corps

To: Commanding General, First Army

Subject: Promotions.

 1. In connection with the recent decision of the War Department to make no further promotions, it is believed that certain facts should not be lost sight of.

 2. During the recent operations in which the army has been engaged, the casualties among officers have been considerable. Many junior officers have been called on to assume the duties of the higher grades and, in many cases, they have performed these duties in such a creditable manner as to warrant their promotion. Many others have won recommendations for promotion because of the efficiency shown in their own grade.

 3. It would seem only just to give to these officers the promotions which they have won. The officers would be satisfied, would feel that their work had received recognition, and they would finally leave the service in a more contented frame of mind than they will do if, in the hour of victory when the great result has been accomplished, they are made to feel that they are to receive no reward, and that the Government, having finished with them, takes no further interest in their personal aspirations.

 4. Aside from the question of justice there is a broader question of policy to be considered. Our entire military policy will depend after this war upon the good will and the interest of the American people. If, from the present army, there are turned back into civil life many men who feel that they have not been justly treated, not only will the military establishment suffer because of having made enemies rather than friends, but any broad military policy looking to the training of the youth of America, fathered by the War Department, will not have the support that it would have if the splendid work of these citizen officers were given the recognition which is due it.

 5. While it is recognized that in the interests of economy the vacancies in divisions can be filled by breaking up other divisions, it is believed that the small outlay involved in additional pay to the officers that would be promoted, especially in view of the short period during which they would receive this pay before being finally mustered out, would be more than compensated for by the satisfaction that it would give to these men upon their release and in after life.

 6. These young men will look upon this war as the greatest event of their lives, and they will take the keenest interest in the army and in being able to tell their children that during the war their services had merited promotion which was accorded them.

W. M. Wright,
Major General, U. S. A.

1st Ind.

Hq. First Army, Am. E. F., France, Nov. 28, 1918 -
To C-in-C, G. H. Q., American E. F., forwarded approved.

1. It is earnestly requested that recognition of the decision of the War Department by urged.

2. The operations of this army from November 1 to November 11 remain unrewarded. Many officers are deprived of well earned promotions to vacancies incident to action. This is believed to be unjust.

H. Liggett,
Lieutenant General,
U. S. Army.

EBH.

American Expeditionary Forces
Office of the Chief Engineer.

21 November 1918

From: The Chief Engineer, A. E. F.

To: Commander-in-Chief, A. E. F. (through C. G., S. O. S.)

Subject: Suspension of Promotions.

1. Telegram from G. H. Q., dated November 17, 1918, addressed to Commanding General, S. O. S., announces that the War Department has adopted a policy of not appointing or promoting any further officers in the Army of the United States for the period of the emergency, effective November 11, 1918.

2. It is appreciated that this policy has been adopted due to the fact that by the demobilization of organizations, many officers of appropriate rank will be made available for transfer to fill vacancies in organizations retained in the service.

3. Up to the present time, the principle of promotion within divisions and regiments, at least to include the grade of lieutenant colonel, has been adopted. I am of the opinion that this policy should be continued during the period of occupation, between the date of the signing of the Armistice and the date of the signing of the Treaty of Peace, as the wholesale introduction into an organization of officers unacquainted with local conditions, or with the personnel of the organization, which should absolutely block all promotions, will tend to destroy esprit-de-corps and ambition.

4. In the Engineer Department the adoption of this policy will cause particular hardship, as much important engineer work still remains to be done, both in the S. O. S., and forward areas. As a result there will be a smaller proportional reduction in engineer troops than in other branches of the service. Moreover, the greater number of engineer officers who will be released by demobilization of other organizations, or by reduction or suspension of construction work, are of the non-combatant types, and are not fitted for service with sapper regiments, in which the greater number of vacancies now exist, and will occur in the future.

5. Under existing orders sapper regiments have been and are still compelled to return a certain number of officers to the States, aggregating in all total of 489. The policy adopted will prevent the replacement of these officers or the promotion of men who are entitled to promotion as a reward for faithful and meritorious service.

6. It is a military necessity that the vacancies in the engineer regiments with

our Army of Occupation be filled, and it is also of the utmost importance that these vacancies be filled, not only by men qualified, but by men who have gained the confidence and respect of their superior officers and subordinates, and who are familiar with local conditions. At present there are in this department many recommendations for promotions pending which were initiated prior to November 11, 1918. These at least should be forwarded, and should receive favorable consideration.

7. In this connection I am in receipt of a telegram from the Chief Engineer, First Army, dated November 21, 1918, which in substance is as follows:

As the war has progressed it has been possible to determine from first-hand knowledge the suitability of officers and men for promotion. Many promotions are now pending and other recommendations are about to go in. If no further promotions are to be made many men will go home under the command of officers not worthy of command. Special dispensation is requested in the case of the 25th, 26th, and 27th Regiments of Engineers, which have never had battalion organizations, but which have been recently authorized. Officers to fill the vacancies now created by the change in table of organizations whould be filled by promotions from their respective regiments.

8. In view of the foregoing facts it is recommended that steps be taken to have the policy enunciated in the cablegram of the War Department modified or revoked.

W. C. Langfitt,
Major General, U. S. A.

1st Ind.

210.2/311
Hq. S. O. S., France, November 23, 1918 - To the C-in-C, A. E. F.

1. Forwarded with recommendation that the matter referred to be given careful consideration; and, unless it is known that further action is contemplated by the War Department with respect to promotions in the A. E. F., that the matter be taken up with the War Department with a view to a modification of the policy announced in War Department Cable 2191-R, November 15, 1918, so as to meet the conditions which will necessarily arise in the organizations which are not to be immediately returned to the United States.

2. Since the receipt of your Telegram No. O-4428, November 17, 1918, all recommendations for promotion have been returned with information that no more promotions or appointments of officers would be made.

J. G. Harbord,
Major General, U. S. A.,
Commanding.

2d Ind.

G. H. Q., A. E. F., France, 27 November 1918 - To Hq. S. O. S., A. E. F. Returned.

1. War Department will make no exception to rule already established and it is not considered advisable to request further consideration.

By command of General Pershing:

J. S. Jones,
Adjutant General.

On December 8, by direction of the Commander-in-Chief, the following cablegram was prepared, and sent to the War Department:

No. 1962-P Dec. 7, AGWAR - Washington (Confidential). Paragraph 1. For the Secretary of War. Reference A-2191, it is urgently recommended that the decision of the War Department to discontinue further appointments or promotions, of officers, be reconsidered, insofar as the American Expeditionary Forces is concerned.

Subparagraph A. On account of the activity of operations that continued to the date of the signing of the Armistice, it was impossible, in many cases, for commanding officers to learn the facts before November 11 upon which to base recommendations to these headquarters of officers and soldiers, whose gallantry or conduct, during the period from November 1 on, had entitled them to this reward.

Subparagraph B. Due to the casualties among officers, during the recent operations, many junior officers had been called on to assume the duties of higher grades; and, performed these duties in such creditable manner as to warrant their promotion.

Subparagraph C. At the date of signing of the Armistice, different staff corps and auxiliary services were in the process of organization. Officers had been attached for duty with these services, and were occupying positions of increased responsibility but, as the details of organization and tables had only recently been approved, these officers had not received the promotion to which they were entitled by the character of their duties, and the positions they have occupied.

Subparagraph D. At the different candidate schools, many selected soldiers had been assured of commissions should they successfully complete the course prescribed. Some of the soldiers in question were graduated after the date of prohibition of further appointments, while others are now about to graduate.

Subparagraph E. The failure of all these officers and soldiers to receive the recognition, to which they are entitled, has produced very great dissatisfaction, as it is felt, now the war is won, the government has not given them the consideration they deserve, and that it takes no further interest in regarding their efficient and loyal efforts. This attitude is general and it is of course natural.

Subparagraph F. The duty of all connected with the military establishment to exercise the greatest economy, and to inaugurate every measure calculated to reduce the expense of maintaining our army is fully appreciated, but it is believed that the small outlay involved in giving these officers their promotions, especially in view of the short period during which they would receive this pay before being finally mustered out, would be more than compensated by the satisfaction that it would give to these men to receive well merited reward from a government they have so faithfully served.

Subparagraph G. Beyond the question of justice there is a question of policy to be considered. The entire military policy will depend after this war upon the good will and the interest of the American people. If, from the present army, there are turned back into civil life many men who feel that they have not been justly treated, not only will the military establishment suffer because of having made enemies rather than friends, but any broad military policy looking to the training of America, fathered by the War Department, would not receive the support that it would have if the splendid work of these citizen officers were given just recognition. Moreover, action taken now may avoid criticism and probable action by Congress.

Subparagraph H. In view of the above statements, it is earnestly requested that I be authorized to make such appointments and promotions in the American Expeditionary Forces as have been merited, and as the continued efficiency of these forces may require; and, if the Secretary of War does not personally desire to modify the rule prescribed by A-2191, I request his approval of my taking it up with the President upon his arrival in France. Pershing.

And, in reply to this, there was received the following cable:

No. 2300-R, Dec. 10th. Pershing - Amexforce, HAEF (Confidential). Paragraph 1.
Reference P 1962, the policy of the War Department about the appointment or promotion of officers in the United States Army for the emergency was very carefully considered. There were a very large number of candidates for commissions who were about completing their courses in Training Schools in America as well as officers who had been recommended for promotion by selection in all branches of the army in addition to those officers in the American Expeditionary Forces on a similar status whose cases had to be considered. The policy of the War Department with reference to such cases is to offer all officers who have been recommended for promotion by selection a commission in the Reserve Corps on discharge in the grade to which they would have been promoted had the Armistice not been concluded. In the same manner candidates who successfully graduated from the Training Schools for officers are offered commission in the Reserve Corps in the grade to which they were ranking on their qualifying in the schools. This gives them an opportunity to show to their people at home the fact of qualifications and at the same time does not place us in an indefensible position before Congress which is now engaged in engaged in investigating every phase of expenditure which the War Department has embarked upon during the entire period of the war. The policy enunciated in the foregoing has met with unanimous approval on the part of members of the House and Senators but they state openly that if any waiver of this policy is made by the War Department they then desire to have men advanced who are known to them and they put tremendous pressure upon the War Department to advance such men anyway.
Paragraph 2. The recognition of extraordinary gallantry in action is met by the bestowal by you of the Distinguished Service Cross and the recognition of distinguished service in positions of responsibility not involving valor is met by the bestowal of Distinguished Service Medal and this it is believed will be more appreciated by the recipients and their friends than advancement of a grade carrying with it a commission which will not bear a statement of the fact that it is given for gallantry in action. The department does not see its way clear to modify its policy although the points advanced by you are deserving of the utmost consideration and had received such consideration before the policy was determined upon.
Paragraph 3. The matter of having enough officers for the diminished American Expeditionary Forces was considered and you have authority as you know to transfer to divisions which are left behind whatever officers are necessary from divisions scheduled to be sent home, to keep up the personnel throughout the Army of Occupation which it is the hope and belief of the department will be speedily reduced to a very small force. It is the policy of the department to return to the United States all the American Expeditionary Force to the extent permissible by the shipping at our disposal at earliest practicable date.
Paragraph 4. The Secretary of War asks me to say to you that he has no objections to your speaking to the President on this or any other subject. March.

Upon receipt of this cablegram, the Commander-in-Chief is understood to have discussed this question with the President; and, subsequent to this conversation, he directed the sending of the following letter to all subordinate commanders of the American Expeditionary Forces:

December 25, 1918.

From: Adjutant General

To: All Division Commanders

Subject: Recommendations for promotion

1. For his personal information in order that it may be of record and not because of a probability that there will be a resumption of promotions, the Commander-in-Chief is desirous of obtaining a list of such officers of the American Expeditionary Forces as, on November 11, 1918, merited promotion from the character of the services they had performed; and would have been recommended for such promotions as a recognition of their merit, had not the Armistice, and the consequent War Department prohibition of further promotions intervened.

2. With a view of securing the desired information, it is directed that you convene a Board consisting of yourself, your Chief of Staff and the Brigade commanders of your division, which will examine into the services of all commissioned officers who were members of the division on November 11, 1918, and report the names of such of these as merited, and would have been recommended for promotion had hostilities continued.

3. The Board will be instructed in making its report.

(a) That recommendation of any officer will only be made when a strict examination of the record of his services shows that he undoubtedly earned this recognition of his merit.

(b) The fact that any officer has previously been recommended for promotion to fill an existing vacancy does not in itself justify the inclusion of his name on the list submitted.

(c) It must not feel obliged to recommend for promotion any officers for vacancies in any grade that may have existed in the division on November 11, 1918, and the fact that no such vacancies existed does not prohibit recommendations.

(d) It must make no recommendations simply as a compliment for past services rendered, but in case it will assure itself that the officer recommended is physically and mentally qualified to perform the duties that would have been required of him had hostilities continued.

(e) The submission of a list that from its size indicates a noncomprehension of the searching inquiry and strict test that is desired applied in each case, will result in the entire list in question receiving no consideration.

4. The inquiry conducted by the Board will be expedited and its report will be secret and will be submitted to this office by special courier with the least possible delay. Acknowledgment of these instructions will be made by telegraph.

By command of General Pershing:

Adjutant General.

As rapidly as replys were received to this letter, they were examined and tabulated; and the complete statement thereof was submitted, upon completion, to the Commander-in-Chief. On January 28 the following cablegram was received from the War Department:

No. 2557-R, Jan. 27th. Pershing - Amexforce, HAEF (Confidential).
Paragraph 1.

You are authorized to make such promotions among officers of the line up to and including the grade of colonel as will give the officers who in your judgment deserve it, rank equal to the command exercised by them. Under this authority you will make these promotions which are appropriate in an organized army to fill vacancies existing or arising. Surplus officers in the various grades will be returned to the United States. It is not intended hereby to authorize promotions merely as a reward for past service, the policy of the department being that recommendations for such promotions should be carefully noted in order that reserve commissions at the recommended grade may be issued on discharge, in accordance with the policy previously announced. The authority here granted will authorize you to fill vacancies in organizations by promotion rather than by transfer where in your judgment that course is wise. You are also authorized to make such promotions in the Medical, Chaplain and other Corps of the army as are within the Tables of Organization and are necessary to confer rank commensurate with authority exercised or work to be done under such tables.

Paragraph 2. The Secretary of War especially desires it to be understood by you as to the American Expeditionary Forces that this relaxation of the rule with regard to promotion does not invite a departure from the principles hitherto established that promotion cannot be made merely as a reward for past service however meritorious. The rule is relaxed only to permit the army which must remain undemobilized to be treated as a living organization with such promotions as would be normal in times of peace to fill vacancies existing or as they may arise. March.

When this was received the Commander-in-Chief decided, after advising with the Chief of Staff, the Adjutant General, and the Judge Advocate, to proceed at once with the promotion of such temporary officers as had been recommended for promotion by the Boards of Officers, convened pursuant to his letter of December 28, and to have investigated further the records of the regular officers recommended by the same boards, to conduct this investigation, to arrange for the transfers necessary to provide vacancies for certain of the promotions and to examine cases of alleged injustice that had not been corrected by the recommendations of the various promotion boards. Brigadier General Wilson B. Burtt, U. S. Army, was ordered to report to the Chief of Staff, and, with a party of officers and clerks, was sent to visit the different organizations of the American Expeditionary Forces.

As the War Department cable of January 28 only covered the question of promotions, and did not refer to appointments, there was sent to the War Department, on February 26, the following cable:

No. 2172-P. Feb. 26th. AGWAR - Washington (Confidential). Paragraph 1.

For Chief of Staff. It is requested that the authority to make certain promotions in these forces, granted by A 2557 Paragraph 1, be extended to authorize the appointment of second lieutenants to fill vacancies that exist or may arise, in both the line and the staff.

Subparagraph A. The appointment of second lieutenants is necessary in order to fill existing vacancies, those that may be caused by the promotions already authorized, and to permit the army which must remain undemobilized to be treated as a living organization.

Subparagraph B. The requirements of the Army Educational Commission for instructors and their approved plan of sending temporary officers and soldiers to European universities, have necessarily detached many officers from combat units. In addition, the demands of the Commission to Negotiate Peace and the Hoover Commission have created many vacancies in the commissioned personnel of these forces that cannot be entirely filled by the retention in France of officers belonging to home-going divisions, who desire to remain in the service.

Subparagraph C. There are many enlisted men in the American Expeditionary Forces, who are graduates of candidates schools and whose appointments as second lieutenants were prevented by the Armistice, who have demonstrated their qualifications for commission; and it is urgently recommended that I be authorized to make such appointments as second lieutenants, as are necessary to fill vacancies provided for by tables of organization and are required to maintain the continued efficiency of these forces. Pershing.
No reply being received to this, the following was cabled on March 10:

No. 2217-P. Mar. 10th. AGWAR - Washington (Confidential). Paragraph 1.

For Chief of Staff. It is earnestly requested that an early and favorable decision be made on my request to make a limited number of appointments as second lieutenants, contained in Cablegram P 2172. Pershing.

Subparagraph A. There are numerous vacancies in the grade of second lieutenant in the American Expeditionary Forces for which no replacements are available; and it is believed that approval of the request, made in Cablegram P 2172, is necessary to maintain the continued efficiency of these forces. Pershing.

And, on March 11, this reply was received:

No. 2905-R. Mar. 10th. Pershing - HAEF. Paragraph 8.

No. 2905-R. Mar. 10th. Pershing - HAEF. Paragraph 8.
Reference P 2172. Your request approved. Harris.

It was decided, in making appointments of second lieutenants, to limit action at first to enlisted graduates of candidates' schools, and to such enlisted men as were recommended for commission for gallantry in action. As far as possible, all men commissioned were returned to their original organizations, and any surplus was assigned to necessary duties in the Army of Occupation and the S. O. S.

Upon completion of the promotions recommended by the boards, convened pursuant to our letter of December 28, a normal flow of promotion in the American Expeditionary Forces was authorized by the publication of General Orders Nos. 64 and 67, which are herewith quoted:

G. H. Q.

American Expeditionary Forces

General Orders)   France, April 11, 1919
   No. 64   )

Promotion of Officers

1. Pursuant to authority granted by Par. 1, War Department Cablegram No. 2557, January 27, 1919, the following rules governing the recommendation of officers of this command for promotion to the grade of colonel, inclusive, are published for the information and guidance of all concerned:

1. Vacancies: Within the meaning of this order, the term "vacancy" means that there is a position authorized by the War Department and that this position is either unoccupied or is occupied by an officer of a grade lower than the grade authorized by the War Department. This position is authorized by the War Department in one of two ways:

First, by the approval of a table of organization.

Second, by a statement that certain classes of officers may consist of a definite number in each of several grades, or that authority is granted for the officers in those classes to occupy the several grades according to a prescribed proportion or percentage.

There is, then, a vacancy when a position in the table of organization is not occupied by carrying on the rolls of the organization an officer of a grade as high as that authorized, or when a grade is not occupied by the entire number authorized under an allowance which authorized a definite number in the various grades or, in lieu thereof, a certain proportion or percentage.

2. Recommendation for Promotion in Tactical Units:

(a) When vacancies exist in a division, the division commander will ascertain from these headquarters if replacements are available. If he receives a negative reply, he will then, by courier, send direct to these headquarters recommendations for promotion to fill said vacancies, stating in each case that he has been informed by G. H. Q. that no replacements are available therefore. The division commander will sign the statement regarding vacancies required by Par. 5 (c), Sec. I, of this order.

(b) The corps commander will do likewise in the case of officers serving with the corps who are not part of the divisions comprising corps.

(c) An army commander will do likewise in the case of officers serving with the army who are not part of the corps or divisions comprising the army.

(d) The commanding officers of separate tactical units and of organizations detached from their proper commands will do likewise in the case of officers of their commands.

3. Recommendations for Promotions in the S. O. S.:

(a) When a vacancy exists in a staff corps, department or service in the S. O. S., the chief of staff corps, department or service concerned will, through the Commanding General, S. O. S., make recommendations for filling the vacancy by promotion. The chief of said staff corps, department or service will sign the statement regarding vacancies, required by Par. 5 (c), Sec. I, of this order.

(b) In the case of all other officers in the S. O. S., the Commanding General, S. O. S., will make recommendations for their promotion. The Commanding General, S. O. S., will sign the statement regarding vacancies required by Par. 5 (c), Sec. I, of this order.

4. Officers not Covered by the Above Paragraphs: The Chiefs of their respective staff corps, departments or services, and their commanding officers or the officers to whom they report, will make recommendations for the promotions of officers not covered by the preceding paragraphs of this order.

5. Data to Accompany Recommendation: Officers making recommendation for promotion will furnish the following data:

(a) Full name, rank, organization, and arm of the service of the person recommended for promotion.

(b) Grade for which recommended.

(c) A definite statement that there is or is not a vacancy, within the meaning of Par. 1, Sec. I, of this order, and if there is one, how the vacancy was caused, and a citation of the tables of organization authorizing the position, or of the War Department order prescribing the specified number, or proportion, or percentage of officers for the various grades.

(d) A certificate that the officer has been examined by a medical officer and found physically fit to perform the duties of the grade to which he is recommended for promotion will be forwarded with the recommendation.

G. H. Q.

American Expeditionary Forces

General Orders)   France, April 18, 1919.
    No. 67   )

G. O. No. 64, c. s., These Headquarters - Promotion of Officers - Amended

I. Paragraphs 3 and 4, Sec. I, G. O. No. 64, c. s., these headquarters, are revoked and the following substituted therefore:

3. Recommendations for promotions in the S. O. S.:

(a) When a vacancy exists in a staff corps, department or service in the S. O. S., for which no replacement is available, the chief of the staff corps, department or service concerned may, through the Commanding General, S. O. S., make recommendation for filling the vacancy by promotion. The chief of said staff corps, department or service will sign the statement regarding vacancies, required by Par. 5 (c), Sec. I, of this order, and will state either that the particular vacancy can not be filled by replacement, or that, in his opinion, the promotion of the officer recommended is required for the best interests of the service.

(b) In the case of all other officers in the S. O. S., the Commanding General, S. O. S., may make recommendations for their promotion, if no replacements are available or if he considers that the promotions recommended are necessary for the continued efficiency of those forces. The Commanding General, S. O. S., will sign the statement regarding vacancies required by Par. 5 (c), Sec. I, of this order.

4. Officers not covered by the above paragraphs: The chiefs of their respective staff corps, departments or services and their commanding officers or the officers to whom they report, may make recommendations for the promotions of officers not covered by the preceding paragraphs of this order, and for whom vacancies exist, which cannot be filled by replacement; or in cases where it is considered that the continued efficiency of the corps, department or service in question requires the promotions of the officers recommended. In each case, the recommending officer will sign the statement regarding vacancies required by Par. 5 (c), Sec. I, of this order; and will state either that the particular vacancy cannot be filled by replacement, or that, in his opinion, the promotion of the officer recommended is required for the best interests of the service.

Since the resumption of promotions in the American Expeditionary Forces the following had been made to 19 May 1919, inclusive:

Promotions Recommended by Boards.	7, 146
Promotions made by General Burtt.	1, 587
Promotions made under Provisions of G. O. No. 64, as Amended by G. O. No. 67.	
Total	4, 142
	12,875
Promotion of Temporary Officers.	12, 505
Promotion of Regular Army Officers.	370
Total	12,875

- - - - - - - - -

STATISTICS

- - -

GHQ, AEF: C-in-C Rept. File: Fldr. 55, Part 6: Summaries

Status of the American Expeditionary Forces at Critical Periods

[Extract]

The tables which make up this report, were prepared by G-1 and show the numerical status of the American Expeditionary Forces on the following critical dates during the year 1918, selected by G-3.

(a) March 21, 1918 - Initiation of German SOMME offensive.
Status of entire A. E. F.

(b) May 27, 1918 - Initiation of German CHEMIN-des-DAMES
offensive towards PARIS.
Status of A. E. F. combat troops.

(c) August 10, 1918- Date of formation of First Army.
Status of A. E. F. combat troops.

(d) September 12, - St-MIHIEL attack.
1918   Status of A. E. F. combat troops.

(e) October 12, - Date of formation of Second Army,
1918   during progress of MEUSE-ARGONNE offensive.
Status of A. E. F. combat troops.

(f) November 11, - Date of Armistice.
1918   Status of entire A. E. F.

* * * * * *

The strength shown for each class of personnel is the sum of the strengths of units assigned to that duty. The assignment of units is as shown by the Order of Battle nearest the date in each case. The strengths, in most cases, were furnished by the Statistical Division, A. G. O. In some cases they represent permanent records made at the time, and in others figures specially prepared for this purpose. Many of the smaller units rendered incomplete returns, in some cases no returns at all. Where no figures were available, certain aero squadrons, aero service squadrons, aviation instruction centers, observation wings, pursuit groups, provisional ordnance depots, and companies, mobile ordnance repair shops, automatic arms repair detachments, camp hospitals, hospital trains, sanitary squads, field hospitals, engineer wagon companies, engineer regiments, engineer truck companies, chauffeur companies, machine shop truck companies, motor truck companies, and pack trains, are assumed to have been at full strength as shown by tables of organization, and in the cases of those provisional units for which there are no tables of organization, estimates have been made. In case of consolidated returns covering units of the same class average unit strengths were used. In most cases the strengths given are those reported on the Wednesday nearest the critical date.

The foregoing remarks upon the method of preparation of this report are made in order that it may be understood that the present tabulation is simply an exposition of the facts as known, and as obtained from the best sources available at the present time, in such a form as to show the disposition of the A. E. F. on the dates in question.

STATUS OF A. E. F. 21 MARCH 1918

TOTAL A. E. F.

Table 1

	DIV.	INF. & MG.	ARTY.	ENGRS.	SIG. C.	MED.	OTHERS	TOTAL
Divisions, Complete and Assembled:	1st	16239	5511	1815	472	527	2760	27324
	2nd	15941	4940	1420	487	340	2821	25949
	26th	16442	5068	1616	442	648	2888	27104
	42nd	16483	4832	1562	370	457	2821	26525
	Subtotal	65105	20351	6413	1771	1972	11290	106902
Divisions Complete, not Assembled:	32nd	13430	4250	1973	400	97	1384	21534
Incomplete Divisions	3rd	1203	319	1769	482	14	0	3787
	5th	110	409	670	0	0	0	1189
	93rd	2653	0	0	0	0	0	2653
	Subtotal	3966	728	2439	482	14	0	7629
Total for all Divisional Troops:		82501	25329	10825	2653	2083	12674	136065

Table 2

	INF. & MG.	ARTY.	ENGRS.	SIG. C.	MED.	A. S.	C.W.S.	TANK C.	OTHERS	TOTAL
G. H. Q. Troops	0	4829	0	0	0	0	0	0	0	4829
Army Troops, Unassigned	0	0	5384	0	0	0	0	0	0	5384
Corps Troops, Unassigned	0	4335	0	240	403	0	0	0	0	4978
S. O. S. Troops	0	0	31096	2239	9630	39191	0	0	4566	86722
Replacements	Replacement figures not available by arms of the service								11226	11226
Troops in other establishments (a)									54907*	54907
SUBTOTAL	0	9164	36480	2479	10033	39191	0	0	70699	168046

GRAND TOTAL A. E. F. 304111

* Figures not available by arms of service.

(a) Headquarters, schools, hospitals, liaison service and other special services.

EXHIBIT 1

STATUS OF A. E. F. IN FRANCE 27 MAY 1918
COMBAT ONLY

FIRST CORPS
Corps Troops

	CORPS TROOPS AUTHORIZED	CORPS TROOPS ASSIGNED	AMERICAN SUBSTITUTES ATTACHED	FRENCH TROOPS ATTACHED	TOTAL AMERICANS ON DUTY	PERCENT OF AUTHORIZED STRENGTH
Military Police	0	0	0	0	0	
Pioneer Infantry	3551	0	0	0	0	
Cavalry	3158	0	0	0	0	
Engineers	2655	0	0	0	0	
Artillery	6924	5952	0	0	5952	86
Signal Corps	2556	697	0	0	697	82.6
Air Service	Incl. in S. C.	810	605	0	1415	Incl. in S. C.
Remount Service Q. M. C.	200	0	0	0	0	
Trains	1924	430	0	0	430	21.3
Other Corps Troops	465	275	0	0	275	59.1
TOTAL	21433	8164	605	0	8769	40.8

DIVISIONS IN FIRST CORPS

	DIV.	INF. & M. G.	ARTY.	ENGRS.	SIG. C.	MED.	OTHERS	TOTAL
	1st	16325	5163	1734	470	543	3032	27267
	2nd	16805	4973	1611	484	467	3148	27488
Divisions, Complete and	26th	16834	5149	1718	457	502	3240	27900
Assembled	32nd	15902	1556	1744	474	399	1862	21937
	42nd	16964	4778	1650	463	1205	2274	27339
	Subtotal	82830	21619	8457	2353	3116	13566	131931

EXHIBIT 2.

Sheet 1 of 3 sheets.

STATUS OF A. E. F. IN FRANCE 27 MAY 1918
COMBAT ONLY

DIVISIONS UNASSIGNED

	DIV.	INF. & M. G.	ARTY.	ENGRS.	SIG. C.	MED.	OTHERS	TOTAL
Divisions Complete, not Assembled	3rd	15687	4375	1702	448	315	1400	23927
	77th	16714	5156	1897	633	2174	2081	28655
	Subtotal	32401	9531	3599	1081	2489	3481	52582
Incomplete Divisions	4th	4492	4784	1581	502	146	283	11788
	5th	15080	0	1647	435	417	442	18021
	27th	14904	0	1742	444	0	324	17414
	28th	16925	61	0	0	294	238	17518
	30th	12711	0	0	0	92	162	12965
	33rd	14973	0	1729	472	362	543	18079
	35th	16803	4746	1638	0	206	673	24066
	78th	0	0	0	0	0	293	293
	80th	10101	0	0	0	0	28	10129
	82nd	15868	1323	0	488	181	242	18102
	93rd	10400	0	0	0	0	0	10400
	Subtotal	132257	10914	8337	2341	1698	3228	158775
Total for all Divisional Troops		247488	42064	20393	5775	7303	20265	343288

	INF. & M. G.	ARTY.	ENGRS.	SIG. C.	MED.	A. S.	C. W. S.	TANK C.	OTHERS	TOTAL
G. H. Q. Troops	0	4572	0	0	0	0	0	573	0	5145
Army Troops Unassigned	0	16925	11838	471	614	0	0	0	5354	35202
Corps Troops Unassigned	0	0	0	449	0	0	0	0	2956	3405
Replacements									11035*	11035*
Subtotal	0		11838	920	614	0	0	573	19345	54787

* *Figures for Replacements not available by arms of service.*

EXHIBIT 2.

Sheet 2 of 3 sheets.

STATUS OF A. E. F. IN FRANCE 27 MAY 1918
COMBAT ONLY

RECAPITULATION

	INF. & M. G.	ARTILLERY	ENGINEERS	SIGNAL	MEDICAL	AIR SERVICE	OTHERS	REPLACEMENTS	TOTAL
A. E. F. Combat Troops (a)	247488	69513	32231	7392	8347	1415	29423	11035	406844

(a) *Figures do not include combat troops in schools, on S. O. S. duty, liaison service, and other special services.*

EXHIBIT 2.

Sheet 3 of 3 sheets.

STATUS OF A. E. F. IN FRANCE ON 10 AUGUST 1918

FIRST ARMY TROOPS

	AUTHORIZED	ASSIGNED	AMERICAN SUBSTITUTES ATTACHED	FRENCH TROOPS ATTACHED	TOTAL AMERICANS ON DUTY	PERCENT OF AUTHORIZED STRENGTH
Military Police	512	0	0	0	0	
Pioneer Infantry	42612	0	0	0	0	
Chemical Warfare Service	5107	530	0	0	530	10.4
Engineers	18899	887	0	0	887	4.7
Artillery	62820	6543	0	0	6543	10.4
Signal Corps	1665	801	0	0	801	48.0
Air Service	10329	2671	149	0	2820	27.2
Medical Corps	2604	700	222	0	922	35.5
Truck Trains	2792	0	0	0	0	
Others	1795	395	0	0	395	22.0
TOTAL	149135	12527	371	0	12898	8.6

EXHIBIT 3.

Sheet 1 of 7 sheets.

STATUS OF A. E. F. IN FRANCE ON 10 AUGUST 1918

FIRST CORPS
Corps Troops

	CORPS TROOPS AUTHORIZED	CORPS TROOPS ASSIGNED	AMERICAN SUBSTITUTES ATTACHED	FRENCH TROOPS ATTACHED	TOTAL AMERICANS ON DUTY	PERCENT OF AUTHORIZED STRENGTH
Military Police	128	0	0	0	0	
Pioneer Infantry	3551	0	0	0	0	
Cavalry	3158	452	0	0	452	14.2
Engineers	2007	528	0	0	528	26.5
Artillery	6924	6214	54	300	6268	96.5
Signal Corps	713	660	0	0	660	92.5
Air Service	1843	795	0	150	795	43.1
Remount Service Q. M. C.	200	0	0	0	0	
Truck Trains	1924	0	0	0	0	
Others	465	404	460	150	864	186.0
TOTAL	20913	9053	514	600	9567	45.8

FOURTH CORPS
Corps Troops

	CORPS TROOPS AUTHORIZED	CORPS TROOPS ASSIGNED	AMERICAN SUBSTITUTES ATTACHED	FRENCH TROOPS ATTACHED	TOTAL AMERICANS ON DUTY	PERCENT OF AUTHORIZED STRENGTH
Military Police	128	0	0	0	0	
Pioneer Infantry	3551	2981	0	0	2981	84.0
Cavalry	3158	416	0	0	416	13.1
Engineers	2007	0	0	0	0	
Artillery	6924	1710	0	0	1710	24.6
Signal Corps	713	187	0	0	187	26.2
Air Service	1843	1649	640	0	2289	124.0
Remount Service Q. M. C.	200	0	0	0	0	
Truck Trains	1924	0	0	0	0	
Others	465	356	761	0	1117	240.0
TOTAL	20913	7299	1401	0	8700	41.6

EXHIBIT 3.

Sheet 2 of 7 sheets.

STATUS OF A. E. F. IN FRANCE ON 10 AUGUST 1918

DIVISIONS IN FIRST ARMY BUT NOT ASSIGNED TO CORPS

Divisions Complete and Assembled:

DIV.	INF. & M. G.	ARTY.	ENGRS.	SIG. C.	MED.	OTHERS	TOTAL
1st	12668	5234	1808	467	535	3079	23791
2nd	13207	4910	1795	477	528	3230	24147
3rd	17675	4889	1621	464	459	3374	28482
4th	14233	1609	1600	464	1274	1886	21066
26th	16611	6108	1632	438	1403	2262	28454
35th	16674	4891	1662	482	351	2338	26398
42nd	16408	5303	1585	460	1316	3262	28334
82nd	16067	5004	1596	472	355	2339	25833
Subtotal	123543	37948	13299	3724	6221	21770	206505

Divisions Complete, not Assembled:

DIV.	INF. & M. G.	ARTY.	ENGRS.	SIG. C.	MED.	OTHERS	TOTAL
5th	14789	4626	1644	500	1575	2049	25183
33rd	15494	4549	1551	467	859	582	23502
78th	15761	4685	1601	466	808	604	23925
79th	16980	4825	1641	485	354	1619	25904
80th	16018	4760	1602	435	590	502	23907
89th	11876	4300	1674	471	1182	1331	20834
90th	16498	4630	1554	465	534	2023	25704
91st	15785	4631	1619	442	455	1088	24020
Subtotal	123201	37006	12886	3731	6357	9798	192979
Total of Div. Troops in First Army	246744	74954	26185	7455	12578	31568	399484

GRAND TOTAL FOR FIRST ARMY

PION. INF.	INF. & M. G.	ARTILLERY	ENGINEERS	SIGNAL	AIR SERVICE	OTHERS	TOTAL
2981	246744	89475	27600	9103	5904	48842	430649

EXHIBIT 3.

Sheet 3 of 7 sheets.

STATUS OF A. E. F. IN FRANCE ON 10 AUGUST 1918

CORPS NOT IN FIRST ARMY

SECOND CORPS
Corps Troops

	CORPS TROOPS AUTHORIZED	CORPS TROOPS ASSIGNED	AMERICAN SUBSTITUTES ATTACHED	FRENCH TROOPS ATTACHED	TOTAL AMERICANS ON DUTY	PERCENT OF AUTHORIZED STRENGTH
Military Police	128	0	0	0	0	
Pioneer Infantry	3551	0	0	0	0	
Cavalry	3158	0	0	0	0	
Engineers	2007	0	0	0	0	
Artillery	6924	0	0	0	0	
Signal Corps	713	213	0	0	213	29.7
Air Service	1843	0	0	0	0	
Remount Service Q. M. C.	200	0	0	0	0	
Trains	1924	0	0	0	0	
Others	465	404	560	0	964	207.0
TOTAL	20913	617	560	0	1177	

DIVISIONS IN SECOND CORPS

	DIV.	INF. & M. G.	ARTY.	ENGRS.	SIG. C.	MED.	OTHERS	TOTAL
Divisions Complete and Assembled:	30th	16023	4888	1658	445	980	625	24619
Divisions Complete, not Assembled:	27th	15004	4667	1735	433	379	927	23145
Total Div. Troops in Second Corps		31027	9555	3393	878	1359	1552	47764

EXHIBIT 3.

Sheet 4 of 7 sheets.

STATUS OF A. E. F. IN FRANCE ON 10 AUGUST 1918

CORPS NOT IN FIRST ARMY

THIRD CORPS
Corps Troops

	CORPS TROOPS AUTHORIZED	CORPS TROOPS ASSIGNED	AMERICAN SUBSTITUTES ATTACHED	FRENCH TROOPS ATTACHED	TOTAL AMERICANS ON DUTY	PERCENT OF AUTHORIZED STRENGTH
Military Police	128	0	0	0	0	
Pioneer Infantry	3551	3304	0	0	3304	93.0
Cavalry	3158	201	0	350	201	6.3
Engineers	2007	1471	2210	350	3681	183.5
Artillery	6924	1155	2528	4330	3683	53.0
Signal Corps	713	654	0	50	654	91.5
Air Service	1843	213	0	520	213	11.4
Remount Service Q. M. C.	200	0	0	0	0	
Trains	1924	225	0	120	225	11.7
Others	465	450	789	0	1239	267.0
TOTAL	20913	7673	5527	5720	13200	63.0

DIVISIONS IN THIRD CORPS

	DIV.	INF. & M. G.	ARTY.	ENGRS.	SIG. C.	MED.	OTHERS	TOTAL
Divisions Complete	28th	15964	4853	1701	457	336	2444	25755
	32nd	11679	5910	1370	462	472	2956	22849
	77th	15561	4956	1662	455	483	3362	26479
Total of Div. Troops in Third Corps		43204	15719	4733	1374	1291	8762	75083

EXHIBIT 3.

Sheet 5 of 7 sheets.

STATUS OF A. E. F. IN FRANCE ON IO AUGUST 1918

CORPS NOT IN FIRST ARMY

FIFTH CORPS
Corps Troops

	CORPS TROOPS AUTHORIZED	CORPS TROOPS ASSIGNED	AMERICAN SUBSTITUTES ATTACHED	FRENCH TROOPS ATTACHED	TOTAL AMERICANS ON DUTY	PERCENT OF AUTHORIZED STRENGTH
Military Police	128	0	0	0	0	
Pioneer Infantry	3551	0	0	0	0	
Cavalry	3158	0	0	0	0	
Engineers	2007	0	0	0	0	
Artillery	6924	477	0	0	477	6.8
Signal Corps	713	203	0	0	203	28.0
Air Service	1843	367	0	0	367	19.9
Remount Service Q. M. C.	200	0	0	0	0	
Trains	1924	0	0	0	0	
Others	465	474	415	0	889	191.5
TOTAL	20913	1521	415	0	1936	9.2

DIVISIONS IN FIFTH CORPS

DIV.	INF. & M. G.	ARTY.	ENGRS.	SIG. C.	MED.	OTHERS	TOTAL
29th	15639	4599	1667	474	1322	1065	24766

Divisions Complete, not Assembled:

EXHIBIT 3.

Sheet 6 of 7 sheets.

STATUS OF A. E. F. IN FRANCE ON 10 AUGUST 1918.

DIVISIONS NOT IN CORPS AND NOT IN FIRST ARMY

DIVISIONS UNASSIGNED

	DIV.	INF. & M. G.	ARTY.	ENGRS.	SIG. C.	MED.	OTHERS	TOTAL
Divisions Complete, not Assembled:	6th	14792	4595	2809	463	1326	1293	25278
	36th	14500	3370	1549	461	392	1121	21393
	37th	15593	4771	1617	466	379	2347	25173
	92nd	16272	4445	1345	438	379	2066	24945
	Subtotal	61157	17181	7320	1828	2476	6827	96789
Incomplete Divisions:	7th	8264	0	1719	0	0	0	9983
	81st	11814	1803	1577	0	0	807	16001
	93rd	12791	0	0	0	0	0	12791
	Subtotal	32869	1803	3296	0	0	807	38775
TOTAL		94026	18984	10616	1828	2476	7634	135564

	PION. INF.	ARTY.	ENGRS.	SIG. C.	MED.	ORD.	A. S.	C.W.S.	TANKS	OTHERS	TOTAL
G. H. Q. Troops	0	3087	0	0	0	0	0	0	2819	5358	11264
Army Troops Unassigned	8877	30934	13358	665	0	350	0	0	0	2178	56362
Corps Troops Unassigned	0	1473	2592	475	0	123	0	0	0	2218	6881
S. O. S. Troops	0	0	87563	5100	23578	3590	53170	1002	0	38820	212823
Replacements										17709*	17709
Troops in other establishments (a)										263943	263943
SUBTOTAL	8877	35494	103513	6240	23578	4063	53170	1002	2819	330226	568982

GRAND TOTAL A. E. F.	1299124

TOTAL FRENCH TROOPS ATTACHED	6320

(a) Headquarters, schools, hospitals, liaison service and other special services.
* Replacement figures not available by arms of service.

Exhibit 3.

STATUS OF A. E. F. IN FRANCE ON 12 SEPTEMBER 1918

FIRST ARMY

ARMY TROOPS

	ARMY TROOPS AUTHORIZED	ARMY TROOPS ASSIGNED	AMERICAN SUBSTITITES ATTACHED	FRENCH TROOPS ATTACHED	TOTAL AMERICANS ON DUTY	PERCENT OF AUTHORIZED STRENGTH
Military Police	512	0	0	0	0	
Pioneer Infantry	42612	20818	0	0	20818	48.8
Chemical Warfare Service	5107	0	0	0	0	
Engineers	22852	18261	277	350	18538	81.0
Artillery	62820	14911	1257	5190	16168	25.7
Signal Corps	1665	1519	20	0	1539	92.5
Air Service	10329	4458	1369	900	5827	56.4
Medical Corps	2604	4827	2927	0	7754	298.0
Truck Trains	2792	558	915	0	1473	55.0
Others	1795	511	421	0	932	51.6
TOTAL	513088	65863	7186	6440	73049	47.7

EXHIBIT 4.

Sheet 1 of 10 sheets.

STATUS OF A. E. F. IN FRANCE ON 12 SEPTEMBER 1918

FIRST CORPS
Corps Troops

	CORPS TROOPS AUTHORIZED	CORPS TROOPS ASSIGNED	AMERICAN SUBSTITUTES ATTACHED	FRENCH TROOPS ATTACHED	TOTAL AMERICANS ON DUTY	PERCENT OF AUTHORIZED STRENGTH
Military Police	128	0	0	0	0	
Pioneer Infantry	3551	3335	0	0	3335	94.0
Cavalry	3158	215	0	0	215	6.8
Engineers	2007	1690	401	0	2091	100.4
Artillery	6924	0	4035	6620	4035	58.2
Signal Corps	713	655	330	0	985	138.0
Air Service	1843	1367	84	200	1451	78.6
Remount Service Q. M. C.	200	70	0	0	70	35.0
Trains	1924	429	0	0	429	22.3
Others	465	417	562	600	979	210.0
TOTAL	20913	8178	5412	7420	13590	65.0

DIVISIONS IN FIRST CORPS

	DIV.	INF. & M. G.	ARTY.	ENGRS.	SIG. C.	MED.	OTHERS	TOTAL
Divisions complete and assembled	2nd	18708	5107	1848	524	656	3386	30229
	5th	14514	4828	1649	467	1454	2310	25222
	35th	16494	5187	1635	474	396	3249	27435
	82nd	15522	4953	1573	480	532	3479	26539
	Subtotal	65238	20075	6705	1945	3038	12424	109425
Divisions complete not assembled	78th	15663	4688	1623	462	413	1565	24414
	90th	16546	4686	1560	453	668	3658	27571
	Subtotal	32209	9374	3183	915	1081	5223	51985
Total of Divisional Troops in First Corps		97447	29449	9888	2860	4119	17647	161410

EXHIBIT 4

Sheet 2 of 10 sheets.

STATUS OF A. E. F. IN FRANCE ON 12 SEPTEMBER 1918

FOURTH CORPS
Corps Troops

	CORPS TROOPS AUTHORIZED	CORPS TROOPS ASSIGNED	AMERICAN SUBSTITUTES ATTACHED	FRENCH TROOPS ATTACHED	TOTAL AMERICANS ON DUTY	PERCENT OF AUTHORIZED STRENGTH
Military Police	128	0	0	0	0	
Pioneer Infantry	3551	3171	0	0	3171	89.5
Cavalry	3158	631	0	0	631	20.0
Engineers	2007	1611	0	0	1611	80.5
Artillery	6924	2535	1376	4980	3911	56.3
Signal Corps	713	687	0	0	687	97.0
Air Service	1843	1387	85	0	1472	80.0
Remount Service Q. M. C.	200	292	0	0	292	146.0
Trains	1924	477	0	0	477	24.8
Others	465	456	572	0	1028	221.5
TOTAL	20913	11247	2033	4980	13280	63.4

DIVISIONS IN FOURTH CORPS

	DIV.	INF. & M. G.	ARTY.	ENGRS.	SIG. C.	MED.	OTHERS	TOTAL
Divisions complete and assembled	1st	17470	5062	1778	465	924	3185	28884
	3rd	17774	4988	1723	494	366	3451	28796
	42nd	16776	5231	1625	474	477	3220	27803
	Subtotal	52020	15281	5126	1433	1767	9856	85483

	DIV.	INF. & M. G.	ARTY.	ENGRS.	SIG. C.	MED.	OTHERS	TOTAL
Divisions complete not assembled	89th	14841	4857	1649	465	559	3479	25850
Total of Divisional Troops in Fourth Corps		66861	20138	6775	1898	2326	13335	111333

EXHIBIT 4

Sheet 3 of 10 sheets.

STATUS OF A. E. F. IN FRANCE ON 12 SEPTEMBER 1918

FIFTH CORPS
Corps Troops

	CORPS TROOPS AUTHORIZED	CORPS TROOPS ASSIGNED	AMERICAN SUBSTITUTES ATTACHED	FRENCH TROOPS ATTACHED	TOTAL AMERICANS ON DUTY	PERCENT OF AUTHORIZED STRENGTH
Military Police	128	0	0	0	0	
Pioneer Infantry	3551	2352	2245	0	4597	129.5
Cavalry	3158	0	0	0	0	
Engineers	2007	1311	0	0	1311	65.4
Artillery	6924	2863	0	14330	2863	41.4
Signal Corps	713	683	0	0	683	96.0
Air Service	1843	1284	24	0	1308	71.0
Remount Service Q. M. C.	200	0	0	0	0	
Trains	1924	474	26	70	500	26.0
Others	465	474	133	2630	607	129.5
TOTAL	20913	9441	2428	17030	11869	57.2

DIVISIONS IN FIFTH CORPS

	DIV.	INF. & M. G.	ARTY.	ENGRS.	SIG. C.	MED.	OTHERS	TOTAL
Divisions complete and assembled	4th	16763	1390	1527	478	1347	2372	23877
	26th	18165	1589	1750	482	526	3200	29212
	80th	15968	4719	1641	451	1052	1000	24831
Total of Divisional Troops in Fifth Corps		50896	11198	4918	1411	2925	6572	77920

EXHIBIT 4

Sheet 4 of 10 sheets.

STATUS OF A. E. F. IN FRANCE ON 12 SEPTEMBER 1918

SIXTH CORPS
Corps Troops

	CORPS TROOPS AUTHORIZED	CORPS TROOPS ASSIGNED	AMERICAN SUBSTITUTES ATTACHED	FRENCH TROOPS ATTACHED	TOTAL AMERICANS ON DUTY	PERCENT OF AUTHORIZED STRENGTH
Military Police	128	0	0	0	0	
Pioneer Infantry	3551	0	0	0	0	
Cavalry	3158	0	0	0	0	
Engineers	2007	0	0	0	0	
Artillery	6924	0	0	0	0	
Signal Corps	713	686	0	0	686	96.0
Air Service	1843	0	0	0	0	
Remount Service Q. M. C.	200	36	0	0	36	18.0
Trains	1924	0	0	0	0	
Others	465	445	19	0	464	99.9
TOTAL	20913	1167	19	0	1186	5.6

DIVISIONS IN SIXTH CORPS

DIV.	INF. & M. G.	ARTY.	ENGRS.	SIG. C.	MED.	OTHERS	TOTAL
36th	14267	4552	1633	457	403	2272	23584
91st	14761	4410	1635	428	390	2027	23651
	29028	8962	3268	885	793	4299	47235

Divisions complete not assembled

Total of Divisional Troops in Sixth Corps

GRAND TOTAL FOR FIRST ARMY

PION INF.	INF. & M. G.	ARTILLERY	ENGINEERS	SIGNAL	AIR SERVICE	OTHERS	TOTAL
31921	244232	96724	48400	11634	10058	67903	510872

EXHIBIT 4

Sheet 5 of 10 sheets.

STATUS OF A. E. F. IN FRANCE ON 12 SEPTEMBER 1918

CORPS NOT IN FIRST ARMY

SECOND CORPS
Corps Troops

	CORPS TROOPS AUTHORIZED	CORPS TROOPS ASSIGNED	AMERICAN SUBSTITUTES ATTACHED	FRENCH TROOPS ATTACHED	TOTAL AMERICANS ON DUTY	PERCENT OF AUTHORIZED STRENGTH
Military Police	128	0	0	0	0	
Pioneer Infantry	3551	0	0	0	0	
Cavalry	3158	0	0	0	0	
Engineers	2007	0	0	0	0	
Artillery	6924	0	0	0	0	
Signal Corps	713	218	0	0	218	31.1
Air Service	1843	419	0	0	419	22.8
Remount Service Q. M. C.	200	36	0	0	36	18.0
Trains	1924	0	0	0	0	
Others	465	404	610	0	1014	220.0
TOTAL	20913	1077	610	0	1687	8.1

DIVISIONS IN SECOND CORPS

DIV.	INF. & M. G.	ARTY.	ENGRS.	SIG. C.	MED.	OTHERS	TOTAL
27th	14766	4675	1625	468	384	1014	22932
30th	16360	4857	1684	457	973	601	24932
Total of Divisional Troops in Second Corps	31126	9532	3309	925	1357	1615	47864

Divisions complete not assembled

EXHIBIT 4

Sheet 6 of 10 sheets.

- 328 -

STATUS OF A. E. F. IN FRANCE ON 12 SEPTEMBER 1918

CORPS NOT IN FIRST ARMY

THIRD CORPS
Corps Troops

	CORPS TROOPS AUTHORIZED	CORPS TROOPS ASSIGNED	AMERICAN SUBSTITUTES ATTACHED	FRENCH TROOPS ATTACHED	TOTAL AMERICANS ON DUTY	PERCENT OF AUTHORIZED STRENGTH
Military Police	128	0	0	0	0	
Pioneer Infantry	3551	3307	0	0	3307	93.0
Cavalry	3158	211	0	0	211	6.6
Engineers	2007	1428	1134	0	2562	128.0
Artillery	6924	1105	4117	0	5222	75.4
Signal Corps	713	669	0	0	669	94.0
Air Service	1843	413	0	0	413	22.4
Remount Service Q. M. C.	200	22	462	0	484	242.0
Trains	1924	0	0	0	0	
Others	465	510	550	0	1060	212.7
TOTAL	20913	7665	6263	0	13928	65.8

DIVISIONS IN THIRD CORPS

	DIV.	INF. & M. G.	ARTY.	ENGRS.	SIG. C.	MED.	OTHERS	TOTAL
Divisions complete not assembled	33rd	14832	4907	1634	461	1032	1090	23956
	79th	16677	4678	1654	466	393	2136	26004
Total of Divisional Troops in Third Corps		31509	9585	3288	927	1425	3226	49960

EXHIBIT 4

Sheet 7 of 10 sheets.

STATUS OF A. E. F. IN FRANCE ON 12 SEPTEMBER 1918

CORPS NOT IN FIRST ARMY

SEVENTH CORPS
Corps Troops

	CORPS TROOPS AUTHORIZED	CORPS TROOPS ASSIGNED	AMERICAN SUBSTITUTES ATTACHED	FRENCH TROOPS ATTACHED	TOTAL AMERICANS ON DUTY	PERCENT OF AUTHORIZED STRENGTH
Military Police	128	0	0	0	0	
Pioneer Infantry	3551	0	0	0	0	
Cavalry	3158	0	0	0	0	
Engineers	2007	0	0	0	0	
Artillery	6924	0	625	0	625	9.0
Signal Corps	713	678	0	0	678	95.5
Air Service	1843	168	0	0	168	9.2
Remount Service Q. M. C.	200	0	0	0	0	
Trains	1924	0	0	0	0	
Others	465	151	459	0	610	130.0
TOTAL	20913	997	1084	0	2081	10.0

DIVISIONS IN SEVENTH CORPS

DIV.	INF. & M. G.	ARTY.	ENGRS.	SIG. C.	MED.	OTHERS	TOTAL
6th	14136	0	1625	454	1325	1340	18880
29th	15363	0	1639	471	1330	1363	20166
92nd	16885	4767	1360	451	400	2355	26218
Total of Divisional Troops in Seventh Corps	46384	4767	4624	1376	3055	5058	65264

Divisions complete not assembled

EXHIBIT 4

Sheet 8 of 10 sheets.

- 330 -

STATUS OF A. E. F. IN FRANCE ON 12 SEPTEMBER 1918

DIVISIONS NOT IN CORPS

	DIV.	INF. & M. G.	ARTY.	ENGRS.	SIGNAL	MEDICAL	OTHERS	TOTAL
Divisions complete and assembled	28th	12849	4747	1721	470	441	3299	23527
	32nd	10713	4639	1699	476	436	997	18960
	77th	13636	4833	1635	442	495	3306	24347
	Subtotal	37198	14219	5055	1388	1372	7602	66834
Divisions complete not assembled	7th	14706	4799	1596	470	1437	1128	24136
	37th	15697	4750	1628	464	388	2353	25280
	81st	13975	4709	1491	463	1324	1142	23102
	88th	15856	4800	1656	463	1334	550	24659
	Subtotal	60234	19058	6371	1860	4483	5173	97177
Incomplete Divisions	87th	13484	3305	1756	451	902	1545	21443
	93rd	12537	0	0	0	0	0	12537
	Subtotal	26021	3305	1756	451	902	1545	33980
Total for all Divisional Troops not in Corps		123453	36582	13182	3699	6757	14320	197991

	PION. INF.	ARTY.	ENGRS.	SIG.	MED.	ORD.	A. S.	C.W.S.	TANKS	OTHERS	TOTAL
G. H. Q. Troops	0	4131	0	0	0	0	0	0	6586	0	10717
Army Troops Unassigned	13579	24211	9424	679	0	917	0	0	0	1865	50675
Corps Troops Unassigned	0	3073	2738	0	0	96	0	0	0	4300	10207
Replacements										38356	38356(a)
TOTAL	13579	31415	12162	679	0	1013	0	0	6586	44521	109955

(a) Replacement figures not available by arms of service.

EXHIBIT 4

Sheet 9 of 10 sheets.

STATUS OF A. E. F. IN FRANCE ON 12 SEPTEMBER 1918

RECAPITULATION

	PION. INF.	INF AND M. G.	ARTILLERY	ENGINEERS	SIGNAL	AIR SERVICE	OTHERS	REPLACE-MENTS	TOTAL
First Army	31921	244232	96724	48400	11634	10058	67903	(b)	510872
Combat Troops not in First Army	16886	232470	97728	39127	1416	1000	53992	38356	488730
A. E. F. Combat Troops (a)	48807	476702	194452	87527	20805	11058	121895	38356	999602

(a) Figures do not include combat troops in schools, on S. O. S. duty, liaison service, and other special services.

(b) Replacements included in figures for "OTHERS".

TOTAL FRENCH TROOPS ATTACHED 35670

EXHIBIT 4

Sheet 10 of 10 sheets.

STATUS OF A. E. F. IN FRANCE ON 12 OCTOBER 1918
COMBAT TROOPS ONLY

FIRST ARMY

ARMY TROOPS

	ARMY TROOPS AUTHORIZED	ARMY TROOPS ASSIGNED	AMERICAN SUBSTITUTES ATTACHED	FRENCH TROOPS ATTACHED	TOTAL AMERICANS ON DUTY	PERCENT OF AUTHORIZED STRENGTH
Military Police	512	101	0	0	101	19.6
Pioneer Infantry	42612	20687	0	0	20687	48.5
Chemical Warfare Service	5107	0	0	0		
Engineers	25046	2051	0	230	2051	80.0
Artillery	62820	20808	1488	8260	22296	35.3
Signal Corps	1665	1315	0	0	1315	79.0
Air Service	10329	5142	1844	700	6986	67.5
Medical Corps	2604	3269	5456	0	8725	335.0
Truck Trains	2792	426	934	0	1360	48.6
Others	1795	1243	1580	540	2823	157.0
TOTAL	155282	73042	11302	9730	84344	54.2

EXHIBIT 5

Sheet 1 of 12 sheets.

STATUS OF A. E. F. IN FRANCE ON 12 OCTOBER 1918

FIRST CORPS
Corps Troops

	CORPS TROOPS AUTHORIZED	CORPS TROOPS ASSIGNED	AMERICAN SUBSTITUTE ATTACHED	FRENCH TROOPS ATTACHED	TOTAL AMERICANS ON DUTY	PERCENT OF AUTHORIZED STRENGTH
Military Police	128	92	153	0	245	191.0
Pioneer Infantry	3551	2775	0	0	2775	78.0
Cavalry	3804	0	0	0	0	
Engineers	2007	1710	1537	0	3247	162.0
Artillery	6374	1377	0	4820	1377	21.6
Signal Corps	713	697	0	0	697	98.0
Air Service	1843	1313	52	100	1365	74.0
Remount Service Q. M. C.	200	0	303	0	303	150.0
Trains	1924	1002	92	70	1094	56.8
Others	465	417	2163	0	2580	554.0
TOTAL	21009	9383	4300	4990	13683	65.0

DIVISIONS IN FIRST CORPS

	DIV.	INF. & M. G.	ARTY.	FNGRS.	SIG. C.	MED.	OTHERS	TOTAL
Divisions complete and assembled	1st	17028	4798	1712	485	505	3170	27698
	77th	15289	4874	1480	440	515	3266	25864
	82nd	15261	4882	1584	486	536	3348	26097
	Subtotal	47578	14554	4776	1411	1556	9784	79659
Divisions complete not assembled	78th	14645	4545	1542	445	572	2737	24486
	91st	13600	4808	1412	414	504	3219	23957
	Subtotal	28245	9353	2954	859	1076	5956	48443
Total of Divisional Troops in First Corps		75823	23907	7730	2270	2632	15740	128102

EXHIBIT 5

Sheet 2 of 12 sheets.

STATUS OF A. E. F. IN FRANCE ON 12 OCTOBER 1918

THIRD CORPS
Corps Troops

	CORPS TROOPS AUTHORIZED	CORPS TROOPS ASSIGNED	AMERICAN SUBSTITUTES ATTACHED	FRENCH TROOPS ATTACHED	TOTAL AMERICANS ON DUTY	PERCENT OF AUTHORIZED STRENGTH
Military Police	128	96	96	0	192	150.0
Pioneer Infantry	3551	3240	0	0	3240	91.2
Cavalry	3804	210	0	0	210	5.5
Engineers	2007	1672	0	0	1672	83.5
Artillery	6374	1407	1172	3250	2579	40.4
Signal Corps	713	661	5	60	666	93.5
Air Service	1843	1396	0	300	1396	75.8
Remount Service Q. M. C.	200	36	0	0	36	18.0
Trains	1924	211	95	0	306	15.8
Others	465	510	2241	0	2751	59.2
TOTAL	21009	9439	3609	3610	13048	61.8

DIVISIONS IN THIRD CORPS

	DIV.	INF. & M. G.	ARTY.	ENGRS.	SIG. C.	MED.	OTHERS	TOTAL
Divisions Complete and Assembled:	3rd	17527	4885	1572	457	571	3307	28319
	4th	14060	4986	1658	469	1344	2512	25029
	80th	15168	4681	1706	444	1374	2298	25671
	90th	15713	4752	1564	441	551	2718	25739
	Subtotal	62468	19304	6500	1811	3840	10835	104758
Divisions Complete, not Assembled:	5th	15687	4729	1691	466	1257	2162	25992
	6th	15075	4910	1660	502	1397	1357	24901
	Subtotal	30762	9639	3351	968	2654	3519	50893
Total of Divisional Troops in Third Corps		93230	28943	9851	2779	6494	14354	155651

EXHIBIT 5

Sheet 3 of 12 sheets.

STATUS OF A. E. F. ON 12 OCTOBER 1918

FIFTH CORPS
Corps Troops

	CORPS TROOPS AUTHORIZED	CORPS TROOPS ASSIGNED	AMERICAN SUBSTITUTES ATTACHED	FRENCH TROOPS ATTACHED	TOTAL AMERICANS ON DUTY	PERCENT OF AUTHORIZED STRENGTH
Military Police	128	127	348	0	475	370.0
Pioneer Infantry	3551	3226	0	0	3226	91.0
Cavalry	3804	0	0	0	0	
Engineers	2007	1410	0	0	1410	70.4
Artillery	6374	1077	1768	4110	2845	44.5
Signal Corps	713	622	0	0	622	87.2
Air Service	1843	1257	151	200	1408	76.0
Remount Service Q.M.C.	200	0	0	0	0	
Trains	1924	0	89	100	89	4.6
Others	465	474	919	930	1393	300.0
TOTAL	21009	8193	3275	5340	11468	54.6

DIVISIONS IN FIFTH CORPS

	DIV.	INF. & M. G.	ARTY.	ENGRS.	SIG. C.	MED.	OTHERS	TOTAL
Divisions Complete and Assembled:	32nd	15010	6438	1675	467	527	3074	27191
	42nd	18469	5178	1596	494	534	3209	29480
	Subtotal	33479	11616	3271	961	1061	6283	56671
Divisions Complete, not Assembled:	89th	15760	4681	1507	444	446	3396	26234
Total of Divisional Troops in Fifth Corps		49239	16297	4778	1405	1507	9679	82905

EXHIBIT 5

Sheet 4 of 12 sheets.

STATUS OF A. E. F. ON 12 OCTOBER 1918

DIVISIONS IN FIRST ARMY BUT NOT ASSIGNED TO CORPS

DIVISIONS UNASSIGNED

	DIV.	INF. & M. G.	ARTY.	ENGRS.	SIG. C.	MED.	OTHERS	TOTAL
Divisions Complete and Assembled:	26th	16825	4936	1753	459	463	3400	27836
	35th	15730	5151	1609	459	435	3155	26539
	Subtotal	32555	10087	3362	918	898	6555	54375
Divisions Complete, not Assembled:	29th	15363	4635	1629	469	1363	1144	24603
	33rd	15309	4650	1619	467	1274	2312	25631
	Subtotal	30672	9285	3248	936	2637	3456	50234
	TOTAL	63227	19372	6610	1854	3535	10011	104609

GRAND TOTALS FOR FIRST ARMY

PION. INF.	INF. & M. G.	ARTILLERY	ENGINEERS	SIGNAL	AIR SERVICE	OTHERS	TOTAL
29928	281519	117616	55349	11608	11155	86635	593810

EXHIBIT 5

Sheet 5 of 12 sheets.

STATUS OF A. E. F. IN FRANCE ON 12 OCTOBER 1918

SECOND ARMY
ARMY TROOPS

	ARMY TROOPS AUTHORIZED	ARMY TROOPS ASSIGNED	AMERICAN SUBSTITUTES ATTACHED	FRENCH TROOPS ATTACHED	TOTAL AMERICANS ON DUTY	PERCENT OF AUTHORIZED STRENGTH
Military Police	512	0	0	0		
Pioneer Infantry	42612	4242	0	0	4242	10.0
Chemical Warfare Service	5107	0	0	0	0	
Engineers	25046	8137	425	0	8562	34.0
Artillery	62820	8704	400	6040	9104	14.5
Signal Corps	1665	865	0	0	865	52.0
Air Service	10329	0	0	100	0	
Medical Corps	2604	1703	1752	0	3455	132.5
Truck Trains	2792	75	0	0	78	2.8
Others	1795	192	1655	150	1847	102.5
TOTAL	155282	23921	4232	6290	28153	18.1

EXHIBIT 5

Sheet 6 of 12 sheets.

- 338 -

STATUS OF A. E. F. IN FRANCE ON OCTOBER 12, 1918

FOURTH CORPS
Corps Troops

	CORPS TROOPS AUTHORIZED	CORPS TROOPS ASSIGNED	AMERICAN SUBSTITUTES ATTACHED	FRENCH TROOPS ATTACHED	TOTAL AMERICANS ON DUTY	PERCENT OF AUTHORIZED STRENGTH
Military Police	128	102	259	0	361	280.0
Pioneer Infantry	3551	2192	0	0	2192	61.8
Cavalry	3804	194	0	0	194	5.1
Engineers	2007	918	0	0	918	45.6
Artillery	6374	1570	1824	840	3394	53.2
Signal Corps	713	667	0	0	667	92.8
Air Service	1843	1287	44	0	1331	72.2
Remount Service Q. M. C.	200	92	153	0	245	122.5
Trains	1924	1405	484	0	1889	98.3
Others	465	456	1020	100	1476	317.0
Total	21009	8883	3784	940	12667	60.0

DIVISIONS IN FOURTH CORPS

	DIV.	INF. & M.G.	ARTY.	ENGRS.	SIG. C.	MED.	OTHERS	TOTAL
Divisions Complete and Assembled:	28th	12432	4663	1631	423	440	3103	22692
Divisions Complete, not Assembled:	7th	14127	4769	1578	463	1351	1195	23483
	37th	13538	0	1656	465	352	1982	17993
	92nd	16338	5061	1572	450	407	2416	26244
	Subtotal	44003	9830	4806	1378	2110	5593	67720
Total of Divisional Troops in Fourth Corps		56435	14493	6437	1801	2550	8696	90412

EXHIBIT 5

Sheet 7 of 12 sheets.

STATUS OF A. E. F. IN FRANCE ON 12 OCTOBER 1918

SIXTH CORPS
Corps Troops

	CORPS TROOPS AUTHORIZED	CORPS TROOPS ASSIGNED	AMERICAN SUBSTITUTES ATTACHED	FRENCH TROOPS ATTACHED	TOTAL AMERICANS ON DUTY	PERCENT OF AUTHORIZED STRENGTH
Military Police	128	126	0	0	126	97.4
Pioneer Infantry	3551	3229	994	0	4223	119.0
Cavalry	3804	0	0	0	0	
Engineers	2007	1674	742	0	2419	120.0
Artillery	6374	0	0	0	0	
Signal Corps	713	404	0	0	404	55.8
Air Service	1843	0	0	0	0	
Remount Service Q. M. C.	200	27	0	0	27	13.5
Trains	1924	893	0	0	893	46.4
Others	465	445	249	0	694	149.0
TOTAL	21009	6801	1985	0	8786	41.8

EXHIBIT 5

Sheet 8 of 12 sheets.

STATUS OF A. E. F. IN FRANCE ON 12 OCTOBER 1918

SEVENTH CORPS
Corps Troops

	CORPS TROOPS AUTHORIZED	CORPS TROOPS ASSIGNED	AMERICAN SUBSTITUTES ATTACHED	FRENCH TROOPS ATTACHED	TOTAL AMERICANS ON DUTY	PERCENT OF AUTHORIZED STRENGTH
Military Police	128	96	0	0	96	75.0
Pioneer Infantry	3551	0	0	0	0	
Cavalry	3804	108	0	0	108	2.8
Engineers	2007	0	0	0	0	
Artillery	6374	0	0	0	0	
Signal Corps	713	676	0	0	676	95.0
Air Service	1843	254	0	0	254	13.8
Remount Service Q. M. C.	200	28	0	0	28	14.0
Trains	1924	1148	0	0	1148	59.5
Others	465	151	460	0	611	130.0
TOTAL	21009	2461	460	0	2921	13.9

DIVISIONS IN SEVENTH CORPS

DIV.	INF. & M. G.	ARTY.	ENGRS.	SIG. C.	MED.	OTHERS	TOTAL
81st	14536	4694	1502	456	1316	1111	23615
88th	15704	4847	1634	474	1392	1553	25604
Total of Divisional Troops in Seventh Corps	30240	9541	3136	930	2708	2664	49219

Divisions Complete, not Assembled:

DIVISIONS IN SECOND ARMY BUT NOT ASSIGNED TO CORPS

	INF. & M. G.	ARTILLERY	ENGINEERS	SIGNAL	AIR SERVICE	OTHERS	TOTAL
Divisions Complete, not Assembled: 79th	13310	5992	1481	391	467	2297	23938

GRAND TOTALS FOR SECOND ARMY

PION. INF.	INF. & M. G.	ARTILLERY	ENGINNERS	SIGNAL	AIR SERVICE	OTHERS	TOTAL
10657	99985	42524	22953	5734	1585	32658	216096

EXHIBIT 5.

Sheet 9 of 12 sheets.

STATUS OF A. E. F. IN FRANCE ON 12 OCTOBER 1918

CORPS NOT IN ARMIES

SECOND CORPS
Corps Troops

	CORPS TROOPS AUTHORIZED	CORPS TROOPS ASSIGNED	AMERICAN SUBSTITUTES ATTACHED	FRENCH TROOPS ATTACHED	TOTAL AMERICANS ON DUTY	PERCENT OF AUTHORIZED STRENGTH
Military Police	128	0	0	0	0	
Pioneer Infantry	3551	0	0	0	0	
Cavalry	3804	0	0	0	0	
Engineers	2007	0	0	0	0	
Artillery	6374	0	0	0	0	
Signal Corps	713	630	0	0	630	88.4
Air Service	1843	431	0	0	431	23.4
Remount Service Q. M. C.	200	30	0	0	30	15.0
Trains	1924	0	0	0	0	
Others	465	404	263	0	667	14.2
TOTAL	21009	1495	263	0	1758	8.4

DIVISIONS IN SECOND CORPS

	DIV.	INF. & M. G.	ARTY.	ENGRS.	SIG. C.	MED.	OTHERS	TOTAL
Divisions Complete and Assembled:	30th	15561	4824	1587	442	963	587	23964
Divisions Complete, not Assembled:	27th	13739	4630	1590	453	383	1016	21811
Total of Divisional Troops in Second Corps		29300	9454	3177	895	1346	1603	45775

EXHIBIT 5

Sheet 10 of 12 sheets.

- 342 -

STATUS OF A. E. F. IN FRANCE ON 12 OCTOBER 1918

DIVISIONS NOT IN CORPS

	DIV.	INF. & M. G.	ARTY.	ENGRS.	SIG. C.	MED.	OTHERS	TOTAL
Divisions complete and Assembled: 2nd		15210	4820	1726	475	553	3277	26061
Divisions complete, not Assembled: 36th		13237	4678	1537	467	407	2275	22601
87th		15326	4755	1751	504	917	1976	25229
Subtotal		28563	9433	3288	971	1324	4251	47830
Incomplete Divisions 8th		0	0	1715	0	0	0	1715
93rd		12505	0	0	0	0	0	12505
Subtotal		12505	0	1715	0	0	0	14220
Total Div. Troops not in Corps		56278	14253	6729	1446	1877	7528	88111

	PION. INF.	ARTY.	ENGRS.	SIG. C.	MED.	ORD.	A.S.	C.W.S.	TANKS	OTHERS	TOTAL
G. H. Q. Troops	0	4378	0	0	0	0	0	0	5179	0	9557
Army Troops Unassigned	32154	24365	4186	924	0	909	0	0	0	2072	64610
Corps Troops Unassigned	0	5378	3985	0	0	217	0	0	0	5276	14856
Replacements										43617*	43617*
TOTAL	32154	34121	8171	924	0	1126	0	0	5179	50965	132640

*Replacement figures not available by arms of service.

EXHIBIT 5

STATUS OF A. E. F. IN FRANCE ON 12 OCTOBER 1918

RECAPITULATION

	PION. INF.	INF. & M. G.	ARTILLERY	ENGINEERS	SIGNAL	AIR SERVICE	OTHERS	REPLACEMENTS	TOTAL
First Army	29928	281519	117616	55349	11608	11155	86635	(b)	593810
Second Army	10657	99985	42524	22953	5734	1585	32658	(c)	216096
Combat Troops not in 1st or 2nd Armies	32154	85578	57828	18077	3895	431	26704	43617	268284
Total A. E. F. Combat Troops (a)	72739	467082	217968	96379	21237	13171	145997	43617	1078190

(a) Figures do not include combat troops in schools, on S. O. S. duty, Laison service, and other special services.
(b) Replacements included in figures for "OTHERS".
(c) Replacements included in figures for "OTHERS".

TOTAL FRENCH TROOPS ATTACHED 30900

EXHIBIT 5

Sheet 12 of 12 sheets.

- 344 -

STATUS OF A. E. F. IN FRANCE ON 11 NOVEMBER 1918

FIRST ARMY
Army Troops

	ARMY TROOPS AUTHORIZED	ARMY TROOPS ASSIGNED	AMERICAN SUBSTITUTES ATTACHED	FRENCH TROOPS ATTACHED	TOTAL AMERICANS ON DUTY	PERCENT OF AUTHORIZED STRENGTH
Military Police	820	660	0	0	660	80.6
Pioneer Infantry	42612	25474	0	0	25474	60.0
Chemical Warfare Service	5107	0	0	0	0	
Engineers	55342	21109	0	200	21109	38.0
Artillery	62711	25619	0	4630	25619	40.8
Signal Corps	1624	1656	0	0	1656	101.6
Air Service	11274	7205	0	900	7205	63.8
Medical Corps	2659	4264	3880	0	8144	312.0
Truck Trains	3340	1382	0	0	1382	41.3
Others	1850	1626	2349	620	3975	215.0
TOTAL	187339	88995	6229	6350	95224	50.8

FIRST CORPS TROOPS

	CORPS TROOPS AUTHORIZED	CORPS TROOPS ASSIGNED	AMERICAN SUBSTITUTES ATTACHED	FRENCH TROOPS ATTACHED	TOTAL AMERICANS ON DUTY	PERCENT OF AUTHORIZED STRENGTH
Military Police	205	0	0	0	0	
Pioneer Infantry	3551	2637	0	0	2637	74.4
Cavalry	3804	729	0	0	729	19.2
Engineers	2007	1675	0	0	1675	84.0
Artillery	6510	4385	0	100	4385	67.4
Signal Corps	726	684	0	0	684	94.2
Air Service	1715	1256	155	100	1411	82.1
Remount Service Q. M. C.	200	36	153	0	189	95.0
Trains	1898	1003	105	0	1108	58.3
Others	537	417	1274	40	1691	314.5
TOTAL	21153	12822	1687	240	14509	68.5

DIVISIONS IN FIRST CORPS

	DIV.	INF. & M. G.	ARTY.	ENGRS.	SIG. C.	MED.	OTHERS	TOTAL
Divisions Complete, not Assembled:	36th	11951	4599	1675	471	333	2180	21209

EXHIBIT 6

Sheet 1 of 9 sheets.

STATUS OF A. E. F. IN FRANCE ON 11 NOVEMBER 1918

THIRD CORPS
Corps Troops

	CORPS TROOPS AUTHORIZED	CORPS TROOPS ASSIGNED	AMERICAN SUBSTITUTES ATTACHED	FRENCH TROOPS ATTACHED	TOTAL AMERICANS ON DUTY	PERCENT OF AUTHORIZED STRENGTH
Military Police	205	107	0	0	107	52.0
Pioneer Infantry	3551	2821	0	0	2821	79.5
Cavalry	3804	201	0	0	201	5.2
Engineers	2007	1714	0	300	1714	85.6
Artillery	6510	1234	0	100	1234	19.0
Signal Corps	726	760	44	80	804	110.0
Air Service	1715	1412	0	200	1412	82.4
Remount Service Q. M. C.	200	36	163	0	199	99.5
Trains	1898	656	63	0	719	37.8
Others	537	433	2422	40	2855	532.0
TOTAL	21153	9374	2692	720	12066	56.7

DIVISIONS IN THIRD CORPS

DIV.	INF. & M. G.	ARTY.	ENGRS.	SIG. C.	MED.	OTHERS	TOTAL
Divisions Complete and Assembled:							
1st	17015	5007	1387	365	433	2973	27180
3rd	14719	5554	1478	387	410	2519	25067
32nd	15083	4571	1661	405	501	2984	25205
90th	11330	4141	1474	382	510	2955	20792
Subtotal	58147	19273	6000	1539	1854	11431	98244

	INF. & M. G.	ARTY.	ENGRS.	SIG. C.	MED.	OTHERS	TOTAL
Divisions Complete, not Assembled: 5th	12877	5373	1479	468	1176	2139	23512
Total of Divisional Troops in Third Corps	71024	24646	7479	2007	3030	13570	121756

EXHIBIT 6

Sheet 2 of 9 sheets.

STATUS OF A. E. F. IN FRANCE ON 11 NOVEMBER 1918

FIFTH CORPS
Corps Troops

	CORPS TROOPS AUTHORIZED	CORPS TROOPS ASSIGNED	AMERICAN SUBSTITUTES ATTACHED	FRENCH TROOPS ATTACHED	TOTAL AMERICANS ON DUTY	PERCENT OF AUTHORIZED STRENGTH
Military Police	205	351	0	0	351	175.0
Pioneer Infantry	3551	3141	0	0	3141	88.3
Cavalry	3804	0	0	0	0	
Engineers	2007	1709	0	0	1709	85.0
Artillery	6510	4216	0	700	4216	64.8
Signal Corps	726	719	0	0	719	99.0
Air Service	1715	1436	0	200	1436	83.6
Remount Service Q. M. C.	200	153	0	0	153	76.5
Trains	1898	680	35	170	715	37.6
Others	537	605	639	0	1244	232.5
TOTAL	21153	13010	674	1070	13684	64.6

DIVISIONS IN FIFTH CORPS

	DIV.	INF. & M. G.	ARTY.	ENGRS.	SIG. C.	MED.	OTHERS	TOTAL
Divisions Complete and Assembled:	2nd	16385	5010	1651	424	540	3161	27171
	42nd	13819	5055	1538	484	464	3115	24475
	77th	12450	4969	1465	430	519	3172	23005
	Subtotal	42654	15034	4654	1338	1523	9448	74651
Divisions Complete, not Assembled:	6th	14161	5455	1647	495	1346	2242	25346
	29th	11902	4607	1495	489	1240	1258	20991
	78th	11581	4022	1436	399	253	1795	19486
	80th	12985	4778	1652	482	1435	2259	23591
	89th	13901	4589	1498	455	541	3689	24673
	Subtotal	64530	23451	7728	2320	4815	11243	114087
Total of Divisional Troops in Fifth Corps		107184	38485	12382	3658	6338	20691	188738

EXHIBIT 6

Sheet 3 of 9 sheets.

STATUS OF A. E. F. IN FRANCE ON 11 NOVEMBER 1918

SEVENTH CORPS
Corps Troops

	CORPS TROOPS AUTHORIZED	CORPS TROOPS ASSIGNED	AMERICAN SUBSTITUTES ATTACHED	FRENCH TROOPS ATTACHED	TOTAL AMERICANS ON DUTY	PERCENT OF AUTHORIZED STRENGTH
Military Police	205	189	0	0	189	95.0
Pioneer Infantry	3551	0	0	0	0	
Cavalry	3804	107	0	0	107	2.6
Engineers	2007	0	0	0	0	
Artillery	6510	0	0	0	0	
Signal Corps	726	647	0	0	647	89.0
Air Service	1715	255	0	0	255	14.9
Remount Service Q. M. C.	200	35	0	0	35	17.5
Trains	1898	742	0	0	742	39.0
Others	537	151	460	0	611	112.6
TOTAL	21153	2126	460	0	2586	12.2

DIVISIONS IN FIRST ARMY BUT NOT ASSIGNED TO CORPS

DIV.	INF. & M. G.	ARTY.	ENGRS.	SIG. C.	MED.	OTHERS	TOTAL
Divisions Complete and Assembled:							
26th	13264	4898	1715	373	391	3151	23792
Divisions Complete, not Assembled:							
79th	9563	4619	1475	452	453	4374	20936
81st	14261	3841	1640	466	1451	2196	23855
Subtotal	23824	8460	3115	918	1904	6570	44791
Total of Divisional Troops	37088	13358	4830	1291	2295	9721	68583

GRAND TOTAL FOR FIRST ARMY

PION. INF.	INF. & M. G.	ARTILLERY	ENGINEERS	SIGNAL	AIR SERVICE	OTHERS	TOTAL
34073	227247	116542	52573	11937	11719	84264	538355

EXHIBIT 6

Sh 4 of 9 sheets.

STATUS OF A. E. F. IN FRANCE ON 11 NOVEMBER 1918

SECOND ARMY
Army Troops

	ARMY TROOPS AUTHORIZED	ARMY TROOPS ASSIGNED	AMERICAN SUBSTITUTES ATTACHED	FRENCH TROOPS ATTACHED	TOTAL AMERICANS ON DUTY	PERCENT OF AUTHORIZED STRENGTH
Military Police	820	1034	0	0	1034	126.0
Pioneer Infantry	42612	13396	0	0	13396	31.4
Chemical Warfare Service	5107	0	0	0	0	
Engineers	55342	18725	0	0	18725	33.8
Artillery	62711	7652	0	2650	7652	12.2
Signal Corps	1624	992	0	0	992	61.0
Air Service	11274	2135	0	100	2135	19.0
Medical Corps	2659	2007	646	0	2653	99.9
Truck Trains	3340	838	0	0	838	25.1
Others	1850	469	1576	150	2045	110.1
TOTAL	187339	47248	2222	2900	49470	26.4

EXHIBIT 6

Sheet 5 of 9 sheets.

STATISTICS OF A. E. F. IN FRANCE ON II NOVEMBER 1918.

FOURTH CORPS
Corps Troops

	CORPS TROOPS AUTHORIZED	CORPS TROOPS ASSIGNED	AMERICAN SUBSTITUTES ATTACHED	FRENCH TROOPS ATTACHED	TOTAL AMERICANS ON DUTY	PERCENT OF AUTHORIZED STRENGTH
Military Police	205	205	0	0	205	100.0
Pioneer Infantry	3551	3037	0	0	3037	85.6
Cavalry	3804	0	0	0	0	
Engineers	2007	1632	0	0	1632	81.5
Artillery	6510	5246	0	0	5246	80.6
Signal Corps	726	643	0	0	643	88.5
Air Service	1715	1251	0	0	1251	72.8
Remount Service Q. M. C.	200	97	108	0	205	102.5
Trains	1898	1018	23	0	1041	54.8
Others	537	1028	0	100	1028	192.0
TOTAL	21153	14157	131	100	14288	67.5

DIVISIONS IN FOURTH CORPS

	DIV.	INF. & M. G.	ARTY.	ENGRS.	SIG. C.	MED.	OTHERS	TOTAL
Divisions Complete and Assembled:	4th	11069	5078	1603	501	996	1048	20295
Divisions Complete, not Assembled:	7th	14404	4918	1625	475	532	2983	24937
	28th	13581	4657	1586	402	531	3863	24620
	Subtotal	27985	9575	3211	877	1063	6846	49557
Total of Divisional Troops in Fourth Corps		39054	14653	4814	1378	2059	7894	69852

EXHIBIT 6

Sheet 6 of 9 sheets.

STATUS OF A. E. F. IN FRANCE ON 11 NOVEMBER 1918

SIXTH CORPS
Corps Troops

	CORPS TROOPS AUTHORIZED	CORPS TROOPS ASSIGNED	AMERICAN SUBSTITUTES ATTACHED	FRENCH TROOPS ATTACHED	TOTAL AMERICANS ON DUTY	PERCENT OF AUTHORIZED STRENGTH
Military Police	205	138	0	0	138	69.5
Pioneer Infantry	3551	2956	0	0	2956	83.0
Cavalry	3804	0	0	0	0	
Engineers	2007	1624	0	0	1624	81.2
Artillery	6510	1723	0	0	1723	26.4
Signal Corps	726	687	0	0	687	94.5
Air Service	1715	504	0	0	504	29.1
Remount Service Q. M. C.	200	52	27	0	79	39.5
Trains	1898	620	0	0	620	32.7
Others	537	668	30	0	698	130.5
TOTAL	21153	8972	57	0	9029	42.0

DIVISIONS IN SIXTH CORPS

	DIV.	INF. & M. G.	ARTY.	ENGRS.	SIG. C.	MED.	OTHERS	TOTAL
Divisions Complete and Assembled:	92nd	15914	5060	234	437	477	3280	25402

DIVISIONS IN SECOND ARMY BUT NOT ASSIGNED TO CORPS

	DIV.	INF. & M. G.	ARTY.	ENGRS.	SIG. C.	MED.	OTHERS	TOTAL
Divisions Complete and Assembled:	35th	15372	4697	1482	393	297	2424	24665
Divisions Complete, not Assembled:	33rd	11817	4704	1576	448	1534	2218	22297
	88th	4967	4586	1528	458	1366	1653	14558
	Subtotal	16784	9290	3104	906	2900	3871	36855
Total of Divisional Troops in Sixth Corps		48070	19047	4820	1736	3674	9575	86922

GRAND TOTAL FOR SECOND ARMY

PION. INF.	INF. & M. G.	ARTILLERY	ENGRS.	AIR SERVICE	SIGNAL	OTHERS	TOTAL
19389	87124	48321	31615	3890	5436	33786	229561

EXHIBIT 6

Sheet 7 of 9 sheets.

STATUS OF A. E. F. IN FRANCE ON 11 NOVEMBER 1918

CORPS NOT IN ARMIES

SECOND CORPS
Corps Troops

	CORPS TROOPS AUTHORIZED	CORPS TROOPS ASSIGNED	AMERICAN SUBSTITUTES ATTACHED	FRENCH TROOPS ATTACHED	TOTAL AMERICANS ON DUTY	PERCENT OF AUTHORIZED STRENGTH
Military Police	205	0	0	0	0	
Pioneer Infantry	3551	0	0	0	0	
Cavalry	3804	0	0	0	0	
Engineers	2007	0	0	0	0	
Artillery	6510	0	0	0	0	
Signal Corps	726	555	0	0	555	76.4
Air Service	1715	0	0	0	0	
Remount Service Q. M. C.	200	0	0	0	0	
Trains	1898	0	36	0	36	1.9
Others	537	404	163	0	567	105.5
TOTAL	21153	959	199	0	1158	53.8

EXHIBIT 6

STATUS OF A. E. F. IN FRANCE ON 11 NOVEMBER 1918

CORPS NOT IN ARMIES
SECOND CORPS (Continued)

DIVISIONS IN SECOND CORPS

	DIV.	INF. & M.C.	ARTY.	ENGRS.	SIG. C.	MED.	OTHERS	TOTAL
Divisions Complete, not Assembled:	27th	9721	4618	1219	569	370	1676	18173
	30th	9931	4704	1436	508	1114	339	18032
Total of Divisional Troops in Second Corps		19652	9322	2655	1077	1484	2015	36205

DIVISIONS NOT IN CORPS

	DIV.	INF. & M.C.	ARTY.	ENGRS.	SIG. C.	MED.	OTHERS	TOTAL
Divisions Complete, not Assembled:	37th	11628	4748	1509	443	326	2323	20977
	82nd	13109	4796	1435	399	287	2003	22029
	87th	15881	4785	1691	489	1701	1642	26189
	91st	12222	4499	1410	410	464	2517	21522
	Subtotal	52840	18828	6045	1741	2778	8485	90717
Incomplete Divisions	8th	3184	4636	1217	0	0	0	9037
	93rd	12318	0	0	0	0	0	12318
	Subtotal	15502	4636	1217	0	0	0	21355
TOTAL		68342	23464	7262	1741	2778	8485	112072

	INF. & M.G.	ARTY.	ENGRS.	SIG. C.	MED.	ORD.	A. S.	C.W.S.	TANKS	OTHERS	TOTAL
G. H. Q. Troops	255	4677	245	0	0	0	0	0	5377	2957	13511
Army Troops Unassigned	2637	34918	4348	1009	0	906	562	0	0	3261	47661
Corps Troops Unassigned	16623	5134	599	0	0	154	0	0	0	5009	27519
S. O. S. Troops	6498	0	79861	6093	51026	6949	61621	390	0	132191	344629
Replacements										72180*	72180
Troops in other establishments (a)										455863	455863
SUBTOTAL	26013	44729	85053	7102	51026	8009	62203	390	5377	671461	961363

GRAND TOTAL A. E. F. 1878714

TOTAL FRENCH TROOPS ATTACHED 11308

*Replacement figures not available by arms of service.
(a) Headquarters, schools, hospitals, liaison service and other special services.

EXHIBIT 6

Sheet 9 of 9 sheets.

STRENGTH OF 29 COMBAT DIVISIONS IN AMERICAN EXPEDITIONARY FORCES

On the Last Day of Each Month From Nov., 1917 to Dec., 1918, Inc.
Where Blanks Occur No Returns Available.
Figures Taken From Original Returns of Organizations, but Should be Considered as Approximate Only.
Source of Information: Demobilized Records Branch, Rolls and Rosters Subsection, A. G. O.

DIV.	1917		1918											
	NOV.	DEC.	JAN.	FEB.	MAR.	APRIL	MAY	JUNE	JULY	AUG.	SEPT.	OCT.	NOV.	DEC.
1	21,239	23,016	26,230	29,582	28705	28,222	27,639	25,952	24,208	29,433	28,249	26,257	24,686	22,857
2	10,636	12,339	18,037	19,895	24,863	27,056	26,512	26,103	21,384	28,136	28,981	28,321	27,746	27,933
3	6,401	13,464	13,474	12,561	21,567	22,226	26,614	27,009	29,562	28,673	29,708	25,573	26,616	26,301
4	Org.-12/10	12,169	15,158	16,868	27,693	26,108	25,203	26,510	26,775	28,272	27,028	22,057	25,441	25,575
5		2,210	2,254	2,312	14,210	17,414	16,088	20,654	26,052	26,072	25,385	25,472	20,884	20,937
6	No Complete Returns Prior to June, 1918.							20,462	25,793	24,611	25,291	22,875	23,899	24,690
7	Org. 12/6		1,213	1,286	1,290	4,776	16,878	19,845	21,340	19,394	25,072	25,540	23,930	23,534
26	18,507	25,597	26,748	25,780	25,777	26,077	27,160	27,244	26,734	27,654	28,504	24,683	21,401	27,581
27	25,545	26,222	25,103	24,489	24,345	25,589	25,368	26,514	25,618	25,710	24,345	19,493	19,570	25,766
28	No Complete Returns Prior to May, 1918.						16,869	19,906	20,244	22,362	24,678	24,402	22,084	27,920
29	26,798	25,987	23,646	23,142	21,917	20,819	25,991	18,483	26,083	26,224	25,857	21,267	23,573	25,693
30				23,838	24,907	26,918	27,887	26,992	26,772	27,297	26,768	20,540	21,313	25,668
32	25,647	27,541		19,682	18,501	20,422	20,355	28,527	28,306	22,685	25,587	26,115	23,839	24,002
33	24,572	23,989	23,932	21,881	21,526	23,839	26,188	25,524	25,695	25,373	20,827	23,366	23,248	24,715
35	24,638	24,168	24,174	23,734	23,815	20,405*	27,252	26,691	27,392	27,695	26,909	25,039	25,884	27,568
36	24,738	24,377	23,576	23,537	23,201	22,468	21,673	24,789	25,630	24,140	17,445	14,328	24,360	26,691
37	24,022	23,506	22,252	20,902	20,174	20,135		19,756	19,846	25,584	18,811*	18,226*	23,395	21,097
42	24,013	24,331	25,235	27,904	27,631	30,208	28,927	26,165	26,951	29,344	29,857	24,335	24,196	23,591
77	18,500	24,004	20,507	25,814	23,262	21,182*	21,380*	22,419*	27,076	25,175	26,228	23,627	25,516	27,779
78	12,692	14,365	11,577	17,508	10,218	21,962	20,190	19,810	19,111	19,838	19,404	22,186	13,783	25,689
79	22,123	18,635	18,143	14,721	14,855	13,793	13,112	25,775	27,550	27,809	25,493	23,189	20,777	20,450
80	23,186	18,318	16,303	17,709	17,339	26,665		25,679	25,268	26,211	26,164	24,331	24,559	26,330
81	12,470	11,693	13,197	10,985	10,709	10,086	12,565	26,485	26,973	24,438	24,310	26,223	23,908	24,002
82	27,076	26,326	25,983	24,722	25,060	26,788	25,382°	26,087	27,537	27,136	26,723	20,132	19,549	27,548
88	9,647	8,401	9,085	22,264	16,762	17,916	23,368	25,531	21,057*	20,509*	26,590	20,869	19,390	26,368
89	20,365	22,787	21,937	18,996	18,120	17,156		26,293	25,003	24,966	24,646	25,790	22,203	22,313
90	22,412	21,551	20,770	19,665	16,340	16,474	25,621	26,897	27,203	27,140	26,811	24,173	20,144	20,358
91	27,448#	25,668#	27,363#	24,651#	23,364#	23,439#	28,369	18,777	21,835	20,642	17,168	22,379	22,186	21,457
92	16,792	20,667	20,076	20,573	23,039	24,205	27,306	26,250	26,053	26,305	25,449	27,098	24,587	26,294

*F. A. Brigade Detached From Division.
#19th Inf. Brigade Attached to Division.
°Less Supply Train and Mobile Ordnance Repair Shop.

RECORDS OF COMBAT DIVISIONS COMPARED

Source of Information: Special Report No. 135 Prepared by
Statistics Branch, General Staff, March 10, 1919

DIVISION	PRISONERS CAPTURED			ARTILLERY AND MACHINE GUNS CAPTURED			DAYS IN FRONT LINE	KILOMETERS ADVANCED ON FRONT LINE
	OFFICERS	MEN	TOTAL	GUNS	TRENCH MORTAR	MACHINE GUNS		
1st	165	6,304	6,469	119	62	413	221	51
2d	288	11,738	12,026	343	58	1,350	137	60
3rd	31	2,209	2,240	51	103	1,501	86	41
4th	72	2,684	2,756	44	2	28	42	24 1/2
5th	48	2,308	2,356	93	74	802	103	29
6th	0	12	12	0	0	3	40	0
7th	1	68	69	0	5	28	33	1
26th	61	3,087	3,148	16	15	132	193	37
27th	65	2,292	2,357	3	25	307	57	11
28th	10	911	921	16	0	63	80	10
29th	52	2,135	2,187	21	5	250	82	7
30th	98	3,750	3,848	81	26	426	57	29 1/2
32d	40	2,113	2,153	21	66	190	95	36
33d	65	3,922	3,987	93	24	414	59	36
35th	13	768	781	24	3	85	97	12 1/2
36th	18	531	549	9	17	277	23	21
37th	26	1,469	1,495	29	2	261	62	30
42d	14	1,303	1,317	25	25	470	162	55
77th	13	737	750	44	46	277	113	71 1/2
78th	6	426	432	4	0	43	38	21
79th	1	1,076	1,077	35	6	266	45	19 1/2
80th	103	1,710	1,813	88	35	606	18	38
81st	5	96	101	0	4	44	31	5 1/2
82d	18	827	845	11	32	279	97	17
88th	0	3	3	0	0	0	28	0
89th	192	4,869	5,061	133	32	455	83	48
90th	32	1,844	1,876	42	36	204	68	28 1/2
91st	12	2,400	2,412	33	5	466	29	34
92d	0	38	38	0	0	10	53	8
Total	1,449	61,630	63,079	1,378	708	9,650	2,232	782 1/2

U. S. GOVERNMENT PRINTING OFFICE : O—1950